Daniel Hutt

THE LECTIONARY COMMENTARY

THE LECTIONARY COMMENTARY

Edited by

Roger E. Van Harn

Consulting Editors

Richard Burridge
Thomas Gillespie
Colin Gunton
Robert Jenson
James F. Kay
Hughes Oliphant Old
Fleming Rutledge
Marguerite Shuster

THE LECTIONARY COMMENTARY

Theological Exegesis for Sunday's Texts

THE FIRST READINGS

The Old Testament and Acts

Edited by

Roger E. Van Harn

WILLIAM B. EERDMANS PUBLISHING COMPANY
GRAND RAPIDS, MICHIGAN / CAMBRIDGE, U.K.

CONTINUUM
LONDON · NEW YORK

Published 2001 in the United States of America by
Wm. B. Eerdmans Publishing Co.
255 Jefferson Ave. S.E., Grand Rapids, Michigan 49503 /
P.O. Box 163, Cambridge CB3 9PU U.K.
www.eerdmans.com
and in Great Britain by
Continuum
The Tower Building, 11 York Road,
London SE1 7NX
www.continuumbooks.com

Printed in the United States of America

06 05 04 03 02 01   7 6 5 4 3 2 1

Library of Congress Cataloging-in-Publication Data

The lectionary commentary: theological exegesis for Sunday's texts /
edited by Roger Van Harn.
p.   cm.
Contents: v. 1. The Old Testament and Acts (the first readings) —
v. 2. Acts and the Epistles (the second readings) —
v. 3. The Gospels (the third readings).
ISBN 0-8028-4751-X (v. 1: cloth: alk. paper);
ISBN 0-8028-4752-8 (v. 2: cloth: alk. paper);
ISBN 0-8028-4753-6 (v. 3: cloth: alk. paper)
1. Bible — Homiletical use. 2. Bible — Criticism, interpretation, etc.
3. Common lectionary (1992) 4. Lectionary preaching.
I. Van Harn, Roger, 1932- II. Common lectionary (1992)

BS534.5.L43 2001
251'.6 — dc21

2001040531

British Library Cataloguing-in-Publication Data

A catalogue for this book is available from the British Library.
ISBN 0-8264-5681-2 (Vol. 1)   ISBN 0-8264-5751-7 (Vol. 2)
ISBN 0-8264-5752-5 (Vol. 3)   ISBN 0-8264-5867-X (Set of 3)

Contents

Preface   xviii

Genesis 1:1–2:4a   1
    YEAR A   *First Sunday after Pentecost (Trinity Sunday)*

Genesis 1:1-5   4
    YEAR B   *First Sunday after the Epiphany*

Genesis 2:15-17; 3:1-7   7
    YEAR A   *First Sunday in Lent*

Genesis 6:9-22; 7:24; 8:14-19   11
    YEAR A   *Second Sunday after Pentecost*

Genesis 9:8-17   17
    YEAR B   *First Sunday in Lent*

Genesis 12:1-4a   20
    YEAR A   *Second Sunday in Lent*

Genesis 12:1-9   23
    YEAR A   *Third Sunday after Pentecost*

Genesis 15:1-12, 17-18   27
    YEAR C   *Second Sunday in Lent*

CONTENTS

Genesis 17:1-7, 15-16   30

    YEAR B   *Second Sunday in Lent*

Genesis 18:1-15; (21:1-17)   32

    YEAR A   *Fourth Sunday after Pentecost*

Genesis 21:8-21   36

    YEAR A   *Fifth Sunday after Pentecost*

Genesis 22:1-14   39

    YEAR A   *Sixth Sunday after Pentecost*

Genesis 24:34-38, 42-49, 58-67   43

    YEAR A   *Seventh Sunday after Pentecost*

Genesis 25:19-34   48

    YEAR A   *Eighth Sunday after Pentecost*

Genesis 28:10-19a   52

    YEAR A   *Ninth Sunday after Pentecost*

Genesis 29:15-28   56

    YEAR A   *Tenth Sunday after Pentecost*

Genesis 32:22-31   61

    YEAR A   *Eleventh Sunday after Pentecost*

Genesis 37:1-4, 12-28   64

    YEAR A   *Twelfth Sunday after Pentecost*

Genesis 45:1-15   69

    YEAR A   *Thirteenth Sunday after Pentecost*

Genesis 45:3-11, 15   72

    YEAR C   *Seventh Sunday after the Epiphany*

Exodus 1:8–2:10   76

    YEAR A   *Fourteenth Sunday after Pentecost*

Exodus 3:1-15   79

    YEAR A   *Fifteenth Sunday after Pentecost*

Exodus 12:1-14   85
    YEAR A   *Sixteenth Sunday after Pentecost*

Exodus 14:19-31   88
    YEAR A   *Seventeenth Sunday after Pentecost*

Exodus 16:2-15   92
    YEAR A   *Eighteenth Sunday after Pentecost*

Exodus 17:1-7   95
    YEAR A   *Third Sunday in Lent*

Exodus 17:1-7   95
    YEAR A   *Ninteenth Sunday after Pentecost*

Exodus 20:1-4, 7-9, 12-20   99
    YEAR A   *Twentieth Sunday after Pentecost*

Exodus 20:1-17   99
    YEAR B   *Third Sunday in Lent*

Exodus 24:12-18   102
    YEAR A   *Last Sunday after the Epiphany (Transfiguration)*

Exodus 32:1-14   105
    YEAR A   *Twenty-first Sunday after Pentecost*

Exodus 33:12-23   108
    YEAR A   *Twenty-second Sunday after Pentecost*

Exodus 34:29-35   111
    YEAR C   *Last Sunday after the Epiphany (Transfiguration)*

Leviticus 19:1-2, 9-18   115
    YEAR A   *Seventh Sunday after the Epiphany*

Numbers 21:4-9   120
    YEAR B   *Fourth Sunday in Lent*

Deuteronomy 5:12-15   124
    YEAR B   *Ninth Sunday after the Epiphany*

Deuteronomy 11:18-21, 26-28   128
    YEAR A   *Ninth Sunday after the Epiphany*

Deuteronomy 18:15-20   132
    YEAR B   *Fourth Sunday after the Epiphany*

Deuteronomy 26:1-11   135
    YEAR C   *First Sunday in Lent*

Deuteronomy 30:15-20   139
    YEAR A   *Sixth Sunday after the Epiphany*

Deuteronomy 34:1-12   143
    YEAR A   *Twenty-third Sunday after Pentecost*

Joshua 3:7-17   146
    YEAR A   *Twenty-fourth Sunday after Pentecost*

Joshua 5:9-12   150
    YEAR C   *Fourth Sunday in Lent*

Joshua 24:1-3a, 14-25   153
    YEAR A   *Twenty-fifth Sunday after Pentecost*

Judges 4:1-7   156
    YEAR A   *Twenty-sixth Sunday after Pentecost*

Ruth 1:1-18   160
    YEAR B   *Twenty-fourth Sunday after Pentecost*

Ruth 3:1-5; 4:13-17   163
    YEAR B   *Twenty-fifth Sunday after Pentecost*

1 Samuel 1:4-20   166
    YEAR B   *Twenty-sixth Sunday after Pentecost*

1 Samuel 2:18-20, 26   169
    YEAR C   *First Sunday after Christmas*

1 Samuel 3:1-10, (11-20)   172
    YEAR B   *Second Sunday after the Epiphany*

1 Samuel 3:1-10, (11-20)   172
YEAR B   *Second Sunday after Pentecost*

1 Samuel 8:4-11, (12-15), 16-20; (11:14-15)   176
YEAR B   *Third Sunday after Pentecost*

1 Samuel 15:34–16:13   179
YEAR B   *Fourth Sunday after Pentecost*

1 Samuel 16:1-13   182
YEAR A   *Fourth Sunday in Lent*

1 Samuel 17:(1a, 4-11, 19-23), 32-49   185
YEAR B   *Fifth Sunday after Pentecost*

2 Samuel 1:1, 17-27   189
YEAR B   *Sixth Sunday after Pentecost*

2 Samuel 5:1-5, 9-10   192
YEAR B   *Seventh Sunday after Pentecost*

2 Samuel 6:1-5, 12b-19   196
YEAR B   *Eighth Sunday after Pentecost*

2 Samuel 7:1-11, 16   199
YEAR B   *Fourth Sunday of Advent*

2 Samuel 7:1-14a   203
YEAR B   *Ninth Sunday after Pentecost*

2 Samuel 11:1-15   206
YEAR B   *Tenth Sunday after Pentecost*

2 Samuel 11:26–12:13a   210
YEAR B   *Eleventh Sunday after Pentecost*

2 Samuel 18:5-9, 15, 31-33   214
YEAR B   *Twelfth Sunday after Pentecost*

2 Samuel 23:1-7   217
YEAR B   *Christ the King*

CONTENTS

1 Kings 2:10-12; 3:3-14   222
YEAR B   *Thirteenth Sunday after Pentecost*

1 Kings 8:(1, 6, 10-11), 22-30, 41-43   225
YEAR B   *Fourteenth Sunday after Pentecost*

1 Kings 8:22-23, 41-43   225
YEAR C   *Ninth Sunday after the Epiphany*

1 Kings 17:8-16, (17-24)   230
YEAR C   *Third Sunday after Pentecost*

1 Kings 18:20-21, (22-29), 30-39   233
YEAR C   *Second Sunday after Pentecost*

1 Kings 19:1-4, (5-7), 8-15a   236
YEAR C   *Fifth Sunday after Pentecost*

1 Kings 21:1-10, (11-14), 15-21a   239
YEAR C   *Fourth Sunday after Pentecost*

2 Kings 2:1-12   243
YEAR B   *Last Sunday after the Epiphany (Transfiguration)*

2 Kings 2:1-2, 6-14   246
YEAR C   *Sixth Sunday after Pentecost*

2 Kings 5:1-14   249
YEAR B   *Sixth Sunday after the Epiphany*

2 Kings 5:1-14   249
YEAR C   *Seventh Sunday after Pentecost*

Nehemiah 8:1-10   253
YEAR C   *Third Sunday after the Epiphany*

Esther 7:1-6, 9-10; 9:20-22   257
YEAR B   *Nineteenth Sunday after Pentecost*

Job 1:1; 2:1-10   260
YEAR B   *Twentieth Sunday after Pentecost*

Job 23: 1-9, 16-17   265
  YEAR B   *Twenty-first Sunday after Pentecost*

Job 38:1-7, (34-41)   267
  YEAR B   *Twenty-second Sunday after Pentecost*

Job 42:1-6, 10-17   271
  YEAR B   *Twenty-third Sunday after Pentecost*

Proverbs 1:20-33   274
  YEAR B   *Seventeenth Sunday after Pentecost*

Proverbs 8:1-4, 22-31   278
  YEAR C   *First Sunday after Pentecost (Trinity Sunday)*

Proverbs 22:1-2, 8-9, 22-23   281
  YEAR B   *Sixteenth Sunday after Pentecost*

Proverbs 31:10-31   285
  YEAR B   *Eighteenth Sunday after Pentecost*

Song of Solomon 2:8-13   288
  YEAR B   *Fifteenth Sunday after Pentecost*

Isaiah 1:1, 10-20   291
  YEAR C   *Twelfth Sunday after Pentecost*

Isaiah 2:1-5   295
  YEAR A   *First Sunday of Advent*

Isaiah 5:1-7   298
  YEAR C   *Thirteenth Sunday after Pentecost*

Isaiah 6:1-8   302
  YEAR B   *First Sunday after Pentecost (Trinity Sunday)*

Isaiah 6:1-8, (9-13)   305
  YEAR C   *Fifth Sunday after the Epiphany*

Isaiah 7:10-16   310
  YEAR A   *Fourth Sunday of Advent*

CONTENTS

Isaiah 9:1-4   **314**
　　YEAR A　　　　　*Third Sunday after the Epiphany*

Isaiah 9:2-7   **316**
　　YEARS A, B, C　*Nativity of the Lord (Christmas Day)*

Isaiah 11:1-10   **320**
　　YEAR A　　　　　*Second Sunday of Advent*

Isaiah 35:1-10   **324**
　　YEAR A　　　　　*Third Sunday of Advent*

Isaiah 40:1-11   **327**
　　YEAR B　　　　　*Second Sunday of Advent*

Isaiah 40:21-31   **330**
　　YEAR B　　　　　*Fifth Sunday after the Epiphany*

Isaiah 42:1-9   **336**
　　YEAR A　　　　　*First Sunday after the Epiphany (Baptism of the Lord)*

Isaiah 43:1-7   **339**
　　YEAR C　　　　　*First Sunday after the Epiphany (Baptism of the Lord)*

Isaiah 43:16-21   **343**
　　YEAR C　　　　　*Fifth Sunday in Lent*

Isaiah 43:18-25   **347**
　　YEAR B　　　　　*Seventh Sunday after the Epiphany*

Isaiah 49:1-7   **350**
　　YEAR A　　　　　*Second Sunday after the Epiphany*

Isaiah 49:8-16a   **353**
　　YEAR A　　　　　*Eighth Sunday after the Epiphany*

Isaiah 50:4-9a   **356**
　　YEARS A, B, C　*Palm/Passion Sunday*

Isaiah 52:7-10   **360**
　　YEARS A, B, C　*Nativity of the Lord (Christmas Day)*

Isaiah 55:1-9   363
YEAR C   *Third Sunday in Lent*

Isaiah 55:10-13   367
YEAR C   *Eighth Sunday after the Epiphany*

Isaiah 58:1-9a, (9b-12)   371
YEAR A   *Fifth Sunday after the Epiphany*

Isaiah 60:1-6   375
YEARS A, B, C   *Epiphany of the Lord*

Isaiah 61:1-4, 8-11   378
YEAR B   *Third Sunday of Advent*

Isaiah 61:10–62:3   381
YEAR B   *First Sunday after Christmas*

Isaiah 62:1-5   384
YEAR C   *Second Sunday after the Epiphany*

Isaiah 62:6-12   388
YEARS A, B, C   *Nativity of the Lord (Christmas Day)*

Isaiah 63:7-9   392
YEAR A   *First Sunday after Christmas*

Isaiah 64:1-9   396
YEAR B   *First Sunday of Advent*

Isaiah 65:17-25   400
YEAR C   *Twenty-sixth Sunday after Pentecost*

Jeremiah 1:4-10   402
YEAR C   *Fourth Sunday after the Epiphany*

Jeremiah 1:4-10   402
YEAR C   *Fourteenth Sunday after Pentecost*

Jeremiah 2:4-13   407
YEAR C   *Fifteenth Sunday after Pentecost*

CONTENTS

Jeremiah 4:11-12, 22-28   411
    YEAR C   *Seventeenth Sunday after Pentecost*

Jeremiah 8:18–9:1   415
    YEAR C   *Eighteenth Sunday after Pentecost*

Jeremiah 17:5-10   419
    YEAR C   *Sixth Sunday after the Epiphany*

Jeremiah 18:1-11   422
    YEAR C   *Sixteenth Sunday after Pentecost*

Jeremiah 23: 1-6   426
    YEAR C   *Christ the King*

Jeremiah 29:1, 4-7   430
    YEAR C   *Twenty-first Sunday after Pentecost*

Jeremiah 31:7-14   434
    YEARS A, B, C   *Second Sunday after Christmas*

Jeremiah 31:27-34   437
    YEAR C   *Twenty-second Sunday after Pentecost*

Jeremiah 31:31-34   441
    YEAR B   *Fifth Sunday in Lent*

Jeremiah 32:1-3a, 6-15   444
    YEAR C   *Nineteenth Sunday after Pentecost*

Jeremiah 33:14-16   448
    YEAR C   *First Sunday of Advent*

Lamentations 1:1-6   451
    YEAR C   *Twentieth Sunday after Pentecost*

Ezekiel 34:11-16, 20-24   455
    YEAR A   *Christ the King*

Ezekiel 37:1-14   460
    YEAR A   *Fifth Sunday in Lent*

Hosea 1:2-10   463
    YEAR C   *Tenth Sunday after Pentecost*

Hosea 2:14-20   467
    YEAR B   *Eighth Sunday after the Epiphany*

Hosea 11:1-11   470
    YEAR C   *Eleventh Sunday after Pentecost*

Joel 2:23-32   473
    YEAR C   *Twenty-third Sunday after Pentecost*

Amos 7:7-17   477
    YEAR C   *Eighth Sunday after Pentecost*

Amos 8:1-12   481
    YEAR C   *Ninth Sunday after Pentecost*

Jonah 3:1-5, 10   484
    YEAR B   *Third Sunday after the Epiphany*

Micah 5:2-5a   488
    YEAR C   *Fourth Sunday of Advent*

Micah 6:1-8   491
    YEAR A   *Fourth Sunday after the Epiphany*

Habakkuk 1:1-4; 2:1-4   497
    YEAR C   *Twenty-fourth Sunday after Pentecost*

Zephaniah 3:14-20   500
    YEAR C   *Third Sunday of Advent*

Haggai 1:15b–2:9   505
    YEAR C   *Twenty-fifth Sunday after Pentecost*

Malachi 3:1-4   509
    YEAR C   *Second Sunday of Advent*

Acts 1:1-11   512
    YEARS A, B, C   *Ascension of the Lord*

CONTENTS

Acts 1:6-14   516
    YEAR A   *Seventh Sunday of Easter*

Acts 1:15-17, 21-26   519
    YEAR B   *Seventh Sunday of Easter*

Acts 2:1-21   524
    YEARS A, B, C   *Day of Pentecost*

Acts 2:14a, 22-32   528
    YEAR A   *Second Sunday of Easter*

Acts 2:14a, 36-41   532
    YEAR A   *Third Sunday of Easter*

Acts 2:42-47   535
    YEAR A   *Fourth Sunday of Easter*

Acts 3:12-19   539
    YEAR B   *Third Sunday of Easter*

Acts 4:5-12   543
    YEAR B   *Fourth Sunday of Easter*

Acts 4:32-35   547
    YEAR B   *Second Sunday of Easter*

Acts 5:27-32   550
    YEAR C   *Second Sunday of Easter*

Acts 7:55-60   553
    YEAR A   *Fifth Sunday of Easter*

Acts 8:26-40   556
    YEAR B   *Fifth Sunday of Easter*

Acts 9:1-6, (7-20)   559
    YEAR C   *Third Sunday of Easter*

Acts 9:36-43   563
    YEAR C   *Fourth Sunday of Easter*

Acts 10:34-43   566
    YEARS A, B, C   *Resurrection of the Lord*

Acts 10:44-48   569
    YEAR B   *Sixth Sunday of Easter*

Acts 11:1-18   573
    YEAR C   *Fifth Sunday of Easter*

Acts 16:9-15   576
    YEAR C   *Sixth Sunday of Easter*

Acts 16:16-34   580
    YEAR C   *Seventh Sunday of Easter*

Acts 17:22-31   583
    YEAR A   *Sixth Sunday of Easter*

Preaching as Worship   587
    HUGHES OLIPHANT OLD

Contributors   603

Index of Authors   607

Index of Readings for Years A, B, and C   610

Preface

Preaching pastors, ministers, and priests know how rapidly Sundays come and go in the pressures of parish life. Protecting time for study and theological reflection is an art not easily mastered once and for all. Flyby Sundays tend to collide with that steady resolve harbored since theological college and seminary to ground preaching in careful exegesis and extensive dialogue with biblical texts. The result is that sermon preparation suffers.

These volumes will not slow the pace of the weekly calendar, but they will provide tastes of theological exegesis for Sunday's texts that will stimulate reflection. These are not books of sermons. They leave homiletical work to the preachers, who are called to contextualize the gospel from biblical texts. Exegetes who have contributed to these volumes have come to name their work affectionately as exegetical "jump starts" for preaching. As such, they provide a place to stand in the text for starting a sermon.

The lections are all derived from the Revised Common Lectionary, Years A, B, and C. All the Sundays of the three-year cycle are included, as well as the texts for the Nativity of the Lord (Christmas Day), the Epiphany of the Lord, and the Ascension of the Lord. The pericope for each entry is identified in bold type in the heading and is accompanied by a listing of the other lections for the day. Although the responsorial psalm is not exegeted, it is listed following the first lesson and may be read or sung for liturgical purposes or used as a preaching resource. The applicable day(s) for each lection is indicated with each heading. Worded titles such as "Water into Wine," "Blind from Birth," or "The Prodigal Son" have been intentionally omitted. Such identifications may get ahead of the exegesis and may block the preacher's dialogue with and exploration of the text. When these happen, the preacher is prevented from seeing and hearing fresh possibilities for the sermon.

With seventy-eight exegetes representing a variety of traditions contributing to these volumes, the reader can expect a wide variety of styles and insights. No attempt has been made on the part of the editors to homogenize these styles. Exegetes have been asked to answer this question concerning their assignments: What does the preacher need to know about this lesson in order to preach a faithful sermon from it? The resulting literary and theological variety, therefore, is similar to the variety in the biblical genres themselves. The resulting unity derives from the story of what God has done for the salvation of the world in the history of Israel and in the person of Jesus Christ. Faithful preaching is not about Bible texts; rather, it proclaims the good news of God to which the texts witness.

Each exegetical essay includes some combination of three elements: engagement with the biblical text, theological reflection, and awareness of the context in which the sermon will be spoken and heard. While the reader will find these elements present in differing degrees, they suggest and stimulate the concerns the preacher brings to sermon preparation. The preacher will also bring the specific congregational context into dialogue with the text in order to discover and express the pastoral and evangelical purposes of the gospel. Wherever the exegesis illumines events of our history, features of our culture, or characteristics of the church that call for celebration or judgment, these may be indicated by the exegete or discovered by the preacher for possible inclusion in the sermon.

The three volumes are organized according to the first, second, and Gospel lections for each day. The lections are arranged in their canonical order in each volume. Each volume appends an essay for preaching: "Preaching as Worship," by Hughes Oliphant Old (vol. 1); "Preaching from the Letters," by Colin Gunton (vol. 2); and "Augustinian Preaching and the Nurture of Christians," by C. Clifton Black (vol. 3). Two indexes provide a ready reference for the lections of the three-year cycle and the contributors to the three volumes.

Through the long months of preparation, the publishers are indebted to the consultants whose guidance gave shape and direction to the project: Richard Burridge, Thomas Gillespie, Colin Gunton, Robert Jenson, James F. Kay, Hughes Oliphant Old, Fleming Rutledge, and Marguerite Shuster. Their wisdom contributed to whatever value these volumes offer; lapses of good judgment and faithful insight are solely the responsibility of the editor.

Preachers who follow the Revised Common Lectionary will find these volumes useful. The organization and content will also serve other preaching patterns and possibilities such as a modified *lectio continua* or a thematically arranged series. However they are used, they are hereby offered as an aid to those commissioned to preach the gospel from biblical texts for the congregations they serve.

Roger E. Van Harn,
Editor

Trinity Sunday, Year A

First Lesson: Genesis 1:1–2:4a
(Psalm 8)
Second Lesson: 2 Corinthians 13:11-13
Gospel Lesson: Matthew 28:16-20

"In the beginning God." Although it is perhaps a bit unnatural to stop the Bible's opening sentence before getting to that verse's verb, looking at just the first four words of the English translation is striking. In some ways this says it all: "In the beginning, *God!*" God is where we begin. God is the one who lies behind and beyond the limits of science.

As instruments like the Hubble Space Telescope become more and more powerful, we are able to peer deeper and deeper into the far reaches of space. Because of the way light travels, the farther out we look, the farther *back* we look as well. Indeed, whenever we gaze into the night sky, we witness the past. If tonight while looking at the sky you witnessed a star suddenly exploding in some kind of supernova cataclysm, what would be new information to your eyes would actually be old news, cosmically speaking. If the star were thirty light-years distant from the earth, then the explosion you saw would actually have happened thirty years ago — it just took the light beams that long to travel from the explosion out in space to your eyeballs in Missouri.

So the farther into space the Hubble telescope looks, the deeper into history it looks. Scientists now say it could be possible to look so far "back" in time as to get close to the moment of the Big Bang and the beginning of all we know. But even if such a form of virtual time travel is possible, what we will never see when peering into only the physical sphere is the God who was and is this universe's beginning. "In the beginning God." As science reminds us, this statement remains singularly and solidly an article of faith alone.

On Trinity Sunday it is this most basic of all faith tenets on which we focus our attention. More than that, it is the Christian belief in the *triune* God that is of particular importance for this Sunday's preaching and teaching. However, taken all by itself, Genesis 1 is not an obviously trinitarian text. Although in history Christian commentators have been tantalized by the plural exhortations of "Let *us* make man in *our* own image . . . ," Hebrew scholarship long ago dispensed with the notion that this refers to any actual plurality within God — this was not in the minds of those who composed Genesis and so ought not be understood that way by later readers either.

So to use Genesis 1 in a trinitarian way requires the honest admission

1

that we are reading this passage within the larger circle of the entire biblical context. If, as Erich Auerbach famously asserted, all biblical texts are "fraught with background," then the broader background Christian preachers bring to Genesis 1 is the notion that behind the apparent simplicity of the text is a rich dance of three persons — a dance whose choreography includes specific creation roles assigned to each of the three divine persons as the fullness of God is in service to the grand goal of fashioning a fitting home for God's creatures.

The Word of God active in executing the creation in Genesis 1 is, according to John 1:1-5 and now the Christian tradition generally, the Son of God. This second person of the Trinity would one day be made flesh and named Jesus, the light of the world shining in a darkness that cannot compromise this light. (Again, Genesis 1 itself does not contain a whisper of such trinitarian thought. However, some Bible translations try to hint at the Trinity anyway, as when the New International Version not only translates the Hebrew *ruach* in verse 2 as "spirit," but also capitalizes "Spirit," thus invoking the third person of later trinitarian doctrine. Other translations like the New Revised Standard Version avoid such a doctrinal import into Genesis 1 by presenting the more literal translation of "a wind from God" hovering over the void.)

A legitimate question for preachers to face is how helpful it is to "spin" Genesis 1 in a trinitarian direction. Is the sheer import and drama of Genesis 1 enhanced by parsing this account into trinitarian components? If the opening of John's Gospel is taken to be a divinely authorized exegesis of Genesis 1, then Christian preachers are surely correct to see creation as the work of a triune God (even if the specifics of how that work was parceled out are nowhere detailed for us). Still, does a triune picture of the God who speaks creation into being change Genesis 1?

In some ways the answer to that question is no. The theological and pastoral grandeur of Genesis 1 can shine through without casting it into trinitarian terms. However, if the later redemption of all that exists (everything from tadpoles to aspen trees) was, as the New Testament presents it, a united work by the three persons of the Godhead, then there is a lovely parallel to be appreciated in recognizing that these same three divine persons lovingly, thoughtfully, and personally created in the beginning the very "stuff" they later reclaimed through the death and resurrection of the Son.

Thomas Aquinas once noted that any mistake about creation leads finally to a mistake about God. One of the most common mistakes people make at the intersection of God and creation has nothing to do with the debates surrounding evolution but rather with the relationships that exist among God, creation, and redemption. Too often redemption in Christ becomes "spiritualized." Jesus died to save the human soul only, and, what's more, Jesus will one day by and by transport this redeemed humanity into a heavenly realm that is frequently depicted as a place profoundly *un*like our present earthly home. The picture of white-robed (if not winged) saints flitting among clouds as they strum golden harps is not only a Hallmark-like way by which the afterlife is envisioned, but too often such ethereal depictions can be found among Christians as well.

This tendency to separate the physical creation from the work of Jesus lies, at least partially, behind the church's historical slowness to recognize the spiritual significance of the environmental movement. (Indeed, in some places there is still resistance to connecting salvation in Christ to things like preserving wetlands and coral reefs.) If this cosmos of bubbling creeks and snarling bobcats is destined to disappear in the flash of God's consuming judgment one day (to be replaced by our eternal home in the clouds), then why should Christians be much bothered with the ecological movement now? If God is not going to keep it, why should we?

A slogan of my first theology professor was, "Where you begin in theology determines where you end up." Many Christians clearly want to begin with the cross and the incarnate Christ who became a human being in order to save human beings. But the Bible begins with God not on a cross but in the act of creation. In the beginning *God*. In the beginning God *created*. Creation is where we begin, and for that reason creation needs to be where we end up in theology, too.

The concept of the Trinity is tightly bound up in most people's minds with only the New Testament and its centerpiece event in the death and resurrection of Christ. This lection should remind us that the first trinitarian act of which we know was the creation. This triune God will not abandon his premier work of fashioning the height, breadth, and depth of this universe. Seen within the light of Genesis 1, the cross itself becomes a logical *continuation* of the grand work begun in creation, not an abandonment of it.

Trinity Sunday may, at first blush, seem like a strange time to present what could be called an "ecological sermon." Yet one of the Bible's dearest revelations is that human beings were created in the image of God. The notion of God as Trinity vastly deepens the concept of what it means to bear this God's image — seeing God as a zestful, loving community opens up whole new vistas as to what being like this God may entail. So for the Trinity Sunday on which Genesis 1 is in view, it may be well to note that a big part of what it means to worship this threefold God is to see, appreciate, celebrate, and preserve the physical cosmos. Throughout Genesis 1, beginning with verse 4, God is said to step back from creation to see and declare it

3

"good." Contemporary Christians who sometimes spend vast amounts of their lives in windowless offices staring at artificial computer displays could well be challenged on Trinity Sunday to wonder when they last delighted in creation, doing the God-like thing of seeing how good it is and so, in this way, giving glory to Father, Son, and Holy Spirit.

Scott Hoezee

First Sunday after the Epiphany, Year B

First Lesson: Genesis 1:1-5
(Psalm 29)
Second Lesson: Acts 19:1-7
Gospel Lesson: Mark 1:4-11

Our text contains the first verses of the sixth-century-B.C. Priestly account of creation, Genesis 1:1–2:4a, which was perhaps used as a liturgy for New Year's Day. It has been called the most consciously theological chapter in the Bible, rivaling John 1, which echoes it. Every word is carefully thought through, and it represents centuries of theological reflection on Israel's experience with God.

The whole chapter is intended not as a scientific account of how God created the heavens and the earth, but as a confession of faith. "In the beginning God." That is the foundational statement. In answer to the age-old question "Why is there something, why not nothing?" our text confesses, "In the beginning God." Without God there would be nothing. Our modern scientists may think they can create life in the laboratory, using DNA. But from whose hand came the DNA? "In the beginning God." From his activity all things and persons came forth, and human beings can only work with the results of God's creative labor.

With the beginning of all things, time is also created. God who dwells in eternity begins the history of nature and human beings. He is the Alpha and the Omega. Time originates with God's creation, and it flows forward until God brings it to an end. So history is linear in the Bible. It does not go

4

around in a circle, in the endless round of birth, life, and death. Indeed, the cycle of nature's life itself is subject to God's linear time, and human life is to be understood not in the context of the natural world's recurring repetition, but in the context of the ongoing flow of God's purpose. Our times are in God's hand, and we are subject to him.

We are told in verse 2 of our text that the earth was without form and void *(tohu wabohu)* and darkness was upon the face of the deep *(tehom)*. One of the basic beliefs of the Christian faith is that God created the universe *ex nihilo,* out of nothing. But does that accord with what we have here in verse 2? Certainly Genesis is not interested in speculative questions, but our text is talking about void, darkness, nothingness. And how do you talk about "nothing"? Verse 2 does so by portraying it in terms of a watery chaos. In the beginning everything is chaos, having no form, and God's act of creation consists in bringing order into that formless void (cf. Isa. 45:18-19).

We are told that the Spirit *(ruaḥ)* of God was moving over the face of the great deep. Thus it has been thought — and indeed incorporated into some baptismal liturgies of the church — that God's Spirit is brooding over the waters and will bring forth light and life. The pairing of our text with the account of the Holy Spirit in both Acts and Mark would seem to confirm that thought. In addition, feminist theology has laid great emphasis on a female Spirit "hatching" the egg of creation. But all of that clearly contradicts what follows in our chapter. God does not create by his Spirit. He creates heaven and earth and all that is in them by his Word. "He spoke and it came to be" (Ps. 33:9). "He commanded and they were created" (Ps. 148:5). The *"ruaḥ"* of God in verse 2 is therefore to be read as "wind," as it often is, and what we have in our text is a picture of stormy, chaotic, dark waters, which God will now order by his creating Word.

God's first creating command is "Let there be light." Over against the darkness, chaos, void, and nothingness that is like the nothingness of death, God sets his creative Word that brings forth the life-giving light, separating the day from the night. That is the Bible's first instruction in the nature of the Word of God. When God speaks, he does not simply impart new information. Rather, he brings forth a new situation. The Word of God is active, effective force that does that of which it speaks. As the Lord proclaims in Second Isaiah, "my word . . . shall not return to me empty, / but it shall accomplish that which I purpose" (Isa. 55:11). God works through his Word, bringing forth always a new situation. And so the New Testament assures us that if any person is in Christ, that person is a new creation; the old has passed away and the new has come (2 Cor. 5:17). God's active Word incarnated in Jesus Christ transforms us and makes us new.

Further, our Genesis text tells us that God's only connection with his world is through his Word (and later, through his Spirit). The Fourth Gospel can declare, therefore, that all things were made through Jesus Christ, the eternal Word, and that "without him was not anything made that was made" (John 1:3). So the Lord is not bound up in his creation or limited by it, but stands outside of it and speaks to it. Many persons in our society have erroneously thought to worship God as identical with the life forces in the natural world. But no. God is the transcendent Lord who has created all life forces through his Word and who is not contained in them but remains as Sovereign over them.

The fact that God's first act of creation is to bring forth the light is startling if we read further in our chapter, in verses 14-19, and find that it is only on the fourth day that God creates the sun, moon, and stars "to give light upon the earth," "to rule over the day and over the night, and to separate the light from the darkness." In other words, we have two kinds of light here — that given by the Word of God, in verse 3, and that given by the heavenly bodies, in verse 17. That is a fact that continues throughout the Scriptures.

If we pursue the subject, we find that the light given by the heavenly bodies is light that is given, in the grace of God, to all persons. "He makes his sun rise on the evil and on the good," Jesus teaches (Matt. 5:45). But the light given by the Word of God, as in verse 3 of our text, is given only to the faithful or to those who are favored by the Lord. Thus, in the story of the plagues in Exodus, there is darkness for three days over the land of the Egyptian oppressors, "but all the people of Israel had light where they dwelt" (Exod. 10:23). Or in Job, that sufferer mourns for the days when God watched over him, and "by his light I walked through darkness" (Job 29:3). "Let us walk by the light of the LORD," calls Isaiah (2:5), that is, by the light given by God's word. And when that Word is incarnate in Jesus Christ, he becomes "the light of the world" so that whoever follows him "will not walk in darkness, but will have the light of life" (John 8:12). Christ is the "true light" who can enlighten every person (John 1:9), the light shining in the darkness that the darkness cannot overcome (John 1:5).

Those are powerful figures to which our Genesis text introduces us, for they symbolize the fact that over against the darkness, chaos, and nothingness of the void of death God has created his light, which cannot be extinguished and which is given to every soul who will walk by God's word. In the New Testament, therefore, the followers of Christ, the Word, are urged to be "the light of the world," reflecting the light of their Lord. "Let us then cast off the works of darkness and put on the armor of light," writes Paul (Rom. 13:12), for from the beginning God has conquered the void of darkness and throughout the Scriptures the faithful testify to that victory. "The wicked shall be cut off in darkness," affirms Hannah (1 Sam. 2:9). But "light rises in the darkness for the upright," sings the psalmist (Ps. 112:4). The darkness cannot hide us from God (Ps. 139:12), who is Master over its terrible night. Surely in a world such as ours that lives in the shadow of that gloom, the fact that the Lord is victor over all our death-dealing darkness is cause for hope and rejoicing!

It has long been noted by scholars that this priestly confession in Genesis 1 has some affinities with the mythical Babylonian account of creation, the Enuma Elish. The deep or *tehom* in Genesis 1:2 may be the linguistic equivalent of the name of Tiamat in that Babylonian myth. And the portrayal of the world that is drawn bears many similarities to those found throughout the ancient Near East. But Genesis has left the world of myth far behind, and has totally demythologized its borrowings. In the myth there are many gods; in Genesis there is only one. In the myth the creating god Marduk must battle with the forces of dark chaos; in Genesis God simply speaks and creation is accomplished. The myth takes place in timelessness; God's creation begins history's time. Genesis deals not with mythical speculations, but with the truth of God and his creating word that is finally confirmed and made sure in the incarnation of our Lord Jesus Christ.

Elizabeth Achtemeier

First Sunday in Lent, Year A

First Lesson: Genesis 2:15-17; 3:1-7
(Psalm 32)
Second Lesson: Romans 5:12-19
Gospel Lesson: Matthew 4:1-11

The Yahwist writer (who writes the Genesis stories that frequently refer to God with the proper name Yahweh, "LORD" in most English translations) can tell a good story. It is believed that the story before us could be as old as the tenth century B.C.E., among the oldest parts of the Bible. Unlike the later creation account in Genesis 1:1–2:4a, this one is concerned not so much with the ordering of creation as with the nature of the humanity that the Lord has created. The story is old, very old, going back deep into human consciousness. The story is new, contemporary, giving explanation for why we are in the fix we are in today.

Our text begins well enough, in a garden. This first part of our text concerns the world and humanity as God intends them to be. Life itself is a divine gift (2:7). Humanity is God's idea and creation, therefore God has the right to demand what God intends for life. The man is given a task, to "till it and keep it" (2:15). God gives the earthling permission to "freely eat of every tree of the garden" (2:16). There is one exception, "the tree of the knowledge of good and evil" (2:17). Why not this tree? We are not told in the text. Perhaps the thing that separates creatures from Creator is that creatures know not the difference between good and evil. We do not always know the right path to take, the right decision to make. We are not gods. The garden is good and lush, but there are still limits, limits having to do with the nature of human life.

The story jumps ahead to introduce a creature who, unlike the man and the woman, is "crafty" (3:1). The man and the woman in the story are not presented as sinless, just innocent. As we shall find, when they get their first opportunity to rebel against the divinely imposed limits, rebel they do. The serpent is no semidivine creature, no Satan, at this point. It is simply a crafty, subtle, smooth-talking creature, whereas the man and the woman are not.

The serpent wants to talk about God with the two creatures (making the serpent, say some, the world's first theologian!). The crafty, savvy serpent is good with words, particularly questions. He asks, "Did God say, 'You shall not eat from any tree in the garden?'" (3:1), in direct contradiction to what God actually said. God prohibited only one tree. The woman replies to the serpent, repeating what God has told her. Still, the question has been planted in the immature brains of the woman and the man.

Then the serpent moves from questions to outright defiance: "You will not die . . ." (3:4). The woman then notices that the fruit is "a delight to the eyes, and that the tree was to be desired to make one wise, [so] she took of its fruit and ate" (3:6), and the man, without questions or reasons, joins her in her defiance. The man and the woman are equal in their rebellion. This is not a story about how a woman led the man into sin, but how the first humans, when given half a chance to rebel, rebel together, seeking to be as wise as God.

"Then the eyes of both were opened" (3:7), but how little they see! They had desired to be as wise as God, to know good from evil, to know everything, and now that they have eaten of the forbidden fruit, they know only one new thing — they are naked. Surely the ancient writer means for us to smile. The once innocent woman and man have now had their eyes opened. They can now know and see. And what do they see? Genitals. The story ends as the woman and man are busily fashioning fig leaves together in a vain attempt to protect them from their nakedness (3:7).

It is a story, a true story, about the truth of us. Each human being, in our own intellectual growth and development, tends to recapitulate this ancient tale in our own growing awareness of ourselves and the world. We begin in an uncomplicated way, unself-conscious, the two-year-old romping naked through the living room after a bath. Then we grow up. Our eyes are opened. We see not just our nakedness, but also our vulnerability. We are frail, fragile, naked creatures who need to cover ourselves, to protect ourselves against the awesome knowledge that "you shall die" (2:17; 3:3).

The philosopher Ernest Becker claimed that all human creativity, all art, architecture, clothing, literature, and philosophy arise out of our vain, futile, human attempt to find some means of protecting ourselves from our finitude. Death is not so much our punishment from God for our disobedience as a consequence of being animals and not gods. All our attempts to deny or overcome death, to make a name for ourselves, to go on forever are little more than a few pitiful fig leaves stitched together in a rather pitiful attempt to cover our nakedness.

Thus our text may be read as a story of emerging human self-consciousness, a story of the limits under which we humans live, as a primordial tale about how we move from innocence to knowledge, wiser but also sadder. We want to know, need to know, are full of burgeoning curiosity. Our eyes get opened, we go around the block once or twice, grow up, get smart, but see now only one thing, that we surely will die.

The contrast between the promising beginning of our story, with the man and the woman well situated in a good garden, sharing in the creativity of God in their stewardship of the garden, and the ending of the story, with the frail man and woman anxiously fashioning fig-leaf garments for themselves, is a rather dramatic move. Early Christian theologians called this a "fall," and some sort of downward fall it is, but nothing in the story suggests that God planned things this way or that it took some external, angelic-like being to cause it. Rather, the man and the woman, endowed with natural curiosity and wonder, find that those noble human traits, when used in disobedience, bring them to grief. The trouble all began when the humans desired that which would "make one wise" (v. 6). Is not wisdom a good thing?

9

Even a good think like knowledge, in our rebellious hands, brings with it much sadness.

It is an appropriate move for the Christian season of Lent; thus we read this text on the very first Sunday of that somber, self-reflective, penitential season. It is now that the church will force us to look in the mirror of truth at ourselves, to be honest about our sins, and our limits. We were created for the idyllic pleasures of a lush garden, but look at the mess we made of it. We shall move from a lush garden to a wild desert where there shall again be temptation, not by a crafty serpent, but by Satan. There the tempter shall not succeed, even when bread is offered after forty days of hunger. The story will then seem to be rewritten, as if beginning again. As for us now, at this point in the story, we show that we are not content to be God's beloved creatures; we want to be gods unto ourselves. And the rest is history.

In contemporary debates about what is wrong with the world, we tend to focus on what the theologians spoke of as "natural evil," the earthquakes, hurricanes, and natural calamities that mysteriously come our way. Evil is something that happens to basically good people like us, innocent and undeserving.

Our text from Genesis seems to plant the source of human misery and pain squarely at our feet. Our greatest sadness has to do with our sin, our relentless human determination to be gods unto ourselves. Our problem is not one of out-of-control forces of nature; our problem is moral, a matter of out-of-control us. Once G. K. Chesterton was asked to contribute an essay to an English journal on the theme "What Is Wrong with the World?" He sent back to the editors a two-word essay. "What Is Wrong with the World?" Chesterton's answer: *I am.*

The story does not really have an ending, at least not a happy ending. The story is the first story, a prelude, to all the other stories that Scripture has to tell us. Now we have been honest about who we are and the fix we are in. Now, what is to become of these rather silly, sad, frail, and forlorn creatures, crouching in the bushes, sewing fig leaves together for themselves? We expect that the future, if they are to have one, will not be up to them. They have taken the initiative, launched forth, taken matters into their own hands. And look where it got them.

If anything is to be done, it will surely be the doing of the one who initiates this story, the one who begins the action in our text, the Lord God (2:15). These creatures arose from the creativity and purposes of God. God gave them a lush garden and limits. Will God now cease the conversation, turn away, give up, break the mold, and start over with new sorts of creatures? We must wait until the next story to find out. Church is a place of stories, a place that stands in acknowledged vulnerability for the need for God to continue the conversation. If God does not speak, does not continue to work with the creatures, then there is no world, no future, no us.

Thus we may take this text not only as a story that begins the season of Lent, but also as one that begins the whole Bible. The creatures, male and female, have shown that they are not content to live within divinely ordained limits. They have also shown that they will rebel if given half a chance. What shall become of the relationship between creatures and the Creator? We shall have to wait until the next installments of the story to find out.

William H. Willimon

Second Sunday after Pentecost, Year A

First Lesson: Genesis 6:9-22; 7:24; 8:14-19
(Psalm 46)
Second Lesson: Romans 1:16-17; 3:22b-28, (29-31)
Gospel Lesson: Matthew 7:21-29

In assigning readings from this long narrative, the lectionary suggests reading 6:9-22; 7:24; and 8:14-19. If one is going to preach this particular narrative, however, it is better to read the entire narrative, or at least 6:9-22; 7:11–8:3a; and 8:13-22.

For an overall view of the structure of this narrative, it is well to consider a possible chiastic structure, first proposed by B. W. Anderson (*JBL* 97 [1978]: 38; see Wenham's commentary on Genesis 1–15):

Transitional introduction (6:9-10)
  1. Violence in creation (6:11-12)
    2. First divine speech: resolve to destroy (6:13-22)
      3. Second divine speech: "enter ark" (7:1-10)
        4. Beginning of flood (7:11-16)
          5. The rising flood (7:17-24)
            God remembers Noah

6. The receding flood (8:1-5)
7. Drying of the earth (8:6-14)
8. Third divine speech: "leave ark" (8:15-19)
9. God's resolve to preserve order (8:20-22)
10. Fourth divine speech: covenant (9:1-17)
Transitional conclusion (9:18-19)

The value of this literary structure is that it makes us aware that this narrative is carefully crafted; it gives us an overall view showing parallels between various parts, and it clearly exposes the central point of the narrative: "God remembers Noah."

For exegetical and preaching purposes, however, it is more valuable to be clear about the plotline, the story line: What is the narrative conflict? Where does it begin? Where is the climax? How is the conflict resolved? Sketching the plotline not only helps one determine the tension in and the point of the narrative, but also helps in retelling the story in a narrative sermon form.

Genesis 6:9 begins a new *toledot* ("account," "family history"): "These are the descendants of Noah." This is the third of ten such "accounts" in Genesis (cf. 2:4; 5:1). The narrator immediately provides some rare (for Hebrew narrative) but significant character description: "Noah was a righteous man, blameless in his generation; Noah walked with God." The words characterize Noah in ascending order: he was "righteous" *(ṣaddiq),* living in the right relationship with God, his neighbors, and all God's creatures; he was "blameless" (cf. 17:1), walking "with integrity of heart" (see syn. par. Ps. 101:2); and "he walked with God," as only Enoch did before him (5:22, 24). This character description of Noah stands in sharp contrast to the violence, lawlessness, and godlessness of his contemporaries: "The earth was corrupt in God's sight, and the earth was filled with violence. And God saw that the earth was corrupt; for all flesh had corrupted its ways upon the earth" (6:11-12; cf. 6:5).

"God *saw* that the earth was corrupt." In the beginning, when God created his kingdom on earth, "God saw everything that he had made, and, indeed, it was very good" (1:31). But now "God saw that the earth was corrupt" — ruined like a spoiled potter's vessel (Jer. 18:4). "The earth was filled with violence" — such violence as to make the ordered development of society impossible (cf. Lamech's boast, 4:23-24). The earth no longer honored its Creator King; it was no longer a manifestation of the kingdom of God. It grieved God to see this corruption of his beautiful creation; "it grieved him to his heart" (6:6). What will God do to his ruined handiwork? Will he smash it like a potter smashes a spoiled clay pot?

The narrative conflict is generated when God says to Noah, "I have determined to make an end of all flesh, for the earth is filled with violence because of them; now I am going to destroy them along with the earth" (6:13). The heavenly Judge has seen the evidence of diabolical evil and pronounces sentence. But God's judgment is infused with redeeming grace. God intends to save a remnant: Noah, his family, and a selection of animals, for God instructs Noah to build an ark: a huge wooden box, as Wenham writes, "about 450′ (135 m) long, 75′ (22 m) broad, and 45′ (13 m) deep." And Noah obeys God without question (6:22; cf. 7:5; 7:9; 8:18).

God repeats: "For my part, I am going to bring a flood of waters on the earth, to destroy from under heaven all flesh in which is the breath of life; everything that is on the earth shall die" (6:17). The flood is no accident. It is a deliberate act of God to destroy that which has turned intrinsically evil. But again, God's judgment is infused with redeeming grace. God says to Noah, "But I will establish my covenant with you . . ." (6:18). This is the first time the Bible uses the significant word "covenant" *(berit)*. God will establish a special relationship with Noah, and not only with Noah but also with his family and all the creatures that will enter the ark (see 9:9-17). Then God gives a detailed listing of all the creatures that are to enter the ark (the slowing of the pace underscores the importance): ". . . you shall come into the ark, you, your sons, your wife, and your sons' wives with you. And of every living thing, of all flesh, you shall bring two of every kind into the ark, to keep them alive with you. . . . Of the birds according to their kinds, and of the animals according to their kinds, of every creeping thing of the ground according to its kind, two of every kind shall come in to you, to keep them alive" (6:18-20). The ark is to function as a rescue capsule that will keep alive human beings as well as representatives of all the kinds of birds and land animals God created in the beginning (see 1:21-25). If the ark survives, it will mark a new beginning for God's kingdom on earth. But if it doesn't?

The conflict intensifies when God orders Noah and his family and all the animals into the ark and states, "In seven days I will send rain on the earth for forty days and forty nights" (7:4). Forty days and forty nights indicates a full period of time (cf. 7:12; 8:6; Exod. 24:18; 34:28; Matt. 4:2). For a full period of time the corrupted earth will be subjected to God's judgment. God's judgment will be severe and complete.

Again the narrator provides a listing of all the creatures that enter the ark to escape God's judgment, "to escape the waters of the flood" (7:7-9, 13-16). And then it happened: "In the six hundredth year of Noah's life, in the second month, on the seventeenth day of the month, on that day all the fountains of the great deep burst forth, and the windows of the heavens were opened" (7:11). In the beginning God had separated the waters below from the waters above by a dome, and set boundaries for the waters so that dry land could appear (1:6-10). Now God withdraws his upholding hand; he reverses his acts of creation, and chaos returns to the earth as in the beginning (1:2; cf. 2 Pet. 3:5-7). But there is a glimmer of hope that this is not the end of God's kingdom on earth: there is that ark with all these creatures inside. Will it survive the flood? There is a hopeful sign: in contrast to the Babylonian flood story, Gilgamesh, where, as Wenham writes, "the gods were frightened by the deluge" and the hero "battened up the entrance," in the Genesis account the Lord is sovereign over the waters and it is the Lord who shuts the door of the ark (7:16).

The conflict reaches a climax in 7:17-24. The narrator again slows the pace, relating first that "the waters increased and bore up the ark" (7:17). Though bobbing in the dangerous flood like a cork in the ocean, the ark rises above God's judgment. Still, the waters keep swelling (repeated in 7:18, 19, 20, 24), reaching higher and higher until the highest mountains are covered. "And all flesh died that moved on the earth . . . ; everything on dry land in whose nostrils was the breath of life died" (7:21-22). The One who gave his creatures "the breath of life" (1:30; 2:7) has seen fit to take it away. God's judgment is complete. "He blotted out every living thing that was on the face of the earth. . . . Only Noah was left, and those that were with him in the ark. And the waters swelled on the earth for one hundred fifty days" (7:23-24). Will the inhabitants of the ark survive this awesome judgment?

The narrator moves to the resolution: "But God remembered Noah . . ." (8:1). That's the turn in the narrative: "God remembered Noah." Not that God had forgotten Noah; when God "remembers" someone, he remembers in order to save (cf. 19:29; 30:22). And God remembers not only Noah, but "all the wild animals and all the domestic animals that were with him in the ark. And God made a wind (*ruah*, see 1:2) blow over the earth, and the waters subsided . . ." (8:1). As in Genesis 1, God reins in the destructive waters by closing "the fountains of the deep and the windows of the heavens" (8:2; cf. 7:11 and 1:6-9). Gradually the waters subside.

The conflict is fully resolved when dry land appears (8:13-14, repeated three times), and God says to Noah, "Go out of the ark, you and your wife, and your sons and your sons' wives with you. Bring out with you every living thing that is with you of all flesh — birds and animals and every creeping thing that creeps on the earth — so that they may abound on the earth, and be fruitful and multiply on the earth" (8:16-17; cf. 1:28). Noah is the new Adam in a renewed creation.

The narrative concludes with Noah dedicating the cleansed earth to

God by building an altar to the Lord and God's promise, "I will never again curse the ground because of humankind, for the inclination of the human heart is evil from youth; nor will I ever again destroy every living creature as I have done.

> As long as the earth endures,
>> seedtime and harvest, cold and heat,
> summer and winter, day and night,
>> shall not cease."   (8:20-22)

The conflict has been resolved: God has judged and cleansed the world of corruption, but in his grace God will still seek to build his kingdom on earth through Noah, the new Adam, and his descendants (Gen. 9).

This narrative, therefore, has to do with new beginnings (compare 9:1 with 1:28). We can formulate its theme somewhat as follows: even as God judges the earth for its corruption, in his grace he continues his kingdom on earth by making a new start with Noah, his family, and the animals with him.

And how was Israel to hear and respond to this message of new beginnings? Suppose Israel heard this story while living in peace and prosperity in the Promised Land. The narrative would teach them that their God is a God of justice as well as grace. It would teach them that God sees what happens on earth, and it would warn Israel against corruption and violence in the Promised Land. The Promised Land was to be a showcase of the peace and justice of the kingdom of God. If Israel failed to live up to God's expectations, it also would fall under God's judgment, albeit "never again" with a flood (8:21).

Or suppose Israel heard this story while undergoing God's judgment in exile. The narrative would teach Israel about God's covenant faithfulness in building his kingdom on earth. It would comfort them with the thought that God could still accomplish his purposes, even through a remnant. It would encourage them to rely on God's saving grace and "compassion" (see Isa. 54:9-10).

Depending on its circumstances, the church today may apply the message of this narrative in similar ways. For the theme of this narrative is but a part of a "longitudinal theme" that runs through Scripture from this point to the last day. We meet the theme of God's judgment and God's grace again at the tower of Babel, where God "sees" and judges by confusing "the language of all the earth" (11:5, 9) and makes a new start with Abram (12:1-3). We meet this theme again in God's judgment of Israel with the deportation to Assyria (722 B.C.) and the exile to Babylon (587 B.C.) and God's new start with the remnant (538 B.C.). These are all precursors of God's judgment on "the day of God" when "the heavens will be set ablaze and dissolved, and the elements will melt with fire," and of God's grace in establishing "new heavens and a new earth, where righteousness is at home" (2 Pet. 3:12-13).

And not only does the flood foreshadow the final day of judgment (cf. Matt. 24:37-44), 2 Peter uses it also to assure his beleaguered readers of the reality of God's judgment and grace in *their* day: "If he [God] did not spare the ancient world, even though he saved Noah, a herald of righteousness, with seven others, when he brought a flood on a world of the ungodly . . . , then the Lord knows how to rescue the godly from trial, and to keep the unrighteous under punishment until the day of judgment . . ." (2 Pet. 2:5, 9).

Noah is clearly a type of Jesus Christ: a new Adam representing the human race (cf. Rom. 5:14); "a righteous man, blameless in his generation . . . , who walked with God" (Gen. 6:9); a person who obeyed God without question (Gen. 6:22; 7:5, 9; 8:18); a person through whom God would save the world. But the contrast between Noah and Christ is even more striking: Noah escaped God's judgment while Christ took the full brunt of God's judgment. Paul writes, "For our sake he [God] made him to be sin who knew no sin, so that in him we might become the righteousness of God" (2 Cor. 5:21). In this statement Paul shows that God's judgment of his only Son, Jesus, was also infused with God's grace. God's judgment and God's grace — both come together in the cross of Christ. But God's grace wins out. "Noah found favor in the sight of the LORD" (Gen. 6:8). So did Abraham. So did Israel. So did Jesus Christ ("This Jesus God raised up," Acts 2:32). So did and does the church. And so does every Christian (cf. 1 Pet. 3:20-21). Even in the final judgment God's grace will win out, for God's final judgment will purge this world once for all of all corruption and issue in God's glorious new creation. So the church can live in good hope. In Christ, we also can count on God's new beginnings both now and on the last day.

Sidney Greidanus

16

First Sunday in Lent, Year B

First Lesson: Genesis 9:8-17
(Psalm 25:1-10)
Second Lesson: 1 Peter 3:18-22
Gospel Lesson: Mark 1:9-15

Lent begins, at least so far as the first lessons on the first two Sundays of Lent are concerned, with covenant. This Sunday a promise is made to Noah and to his descendants. Next Sunday a promise will be made to Abraham and his. Next Sunday God shall make a promise to make a nation, Israel, out of nothing but a couple of old people. This Sunday God promises to make a relationship with all of the human race out of the mud and death-dealing waters of the flood.

We read Genesis 9:8-17 in the context of a culture that leads us to believe that the world is mostly the result of our decisions, our actions, and our choices. We have the world and its future in our hands. It is up to us to make human history come out right, or right will not be done. God help us if this is our situation, for we have proved time and again that our hands are bloody and we cannot do the right, no matter how hard we try. God help us.

This is typically Lenten talk, for Lent is a season for honesty about our sin and the human condition. We begin the practice of honesty the First Sunday of Lent against the backdrop of covenant. It is only the gracious promise of God not to give up on us that enables us to be honest about ourselves.

Now, after the flood, the next move is up to God. Genesis has told a story of the first human parents who were the first to be disobedient, and the first human progeny who became the first fratricide. A world was given unto us, and look what we did with what we got. Now it is up to God to make something out of the mud and mess after the flood. What will God do with us and our sin?

Genesis 9 renders a God who acts, speaks, inserts, intrudes, makes promises. The future is not solely of our devising. God makes promises. Any promise, when you think about it, is an act of creation, a means of contributing something fresh and new to the world, a way to make a difference in the future. When, for instance, a man and a woman stand before the altar of God and make promises to one another in marriage, they are projecting themselves into the future, adding something new to the world — their marriage.

In Genesis 9:8-17, God comes on the scene to make a promise to Noah and his descendants. After so much water, and so much destruction and death, it is as if there will not be a future for humanity unless God makes it so. A future is made possible with the opening words, "Then God said to Noah and to his sons with him, 'As for me, I am establishing my covenant with you and your descendants . . .'" (9:8). As for us, the stories in Genesis show that we will lie, rebel, kill, and crush our way into the future. As for God, "I am establishing my covenant with you and your descendants. . . ."

We are reading the work of the Priestly writer, the one who earlier depicted creation as a separation of the waters and the establishment of an ordered world (Gen. 1). In the flood, the Creator becomes the Destroyer as were opened the "fountains of the great deep . . . and the windows of the heavens" (7:11). Now, in chapter 9, it is as if the Creator returns to the story, once again making order out of chaos, bringing life out of death, this time with a promise. The earlier command to be fruitful (1:28) is repeated, along with the promise that human beings are to be over the other creatures. But the humans who in the earlier covenant were permitted to eat the plants are now given permission to take the lives and to eat the animals, though murder is prohibited. In this new promise, we are in a considerably more violent world. Perhaps the Creator has realized that God's human creations have an unrestrained propensity to sin and death and merely acknowledges this tendency, setting upon it a few boundaries rather than attempting to stop humanity completely from killing.

All of this is the speech of God in sovereign, solemn pronouncement. The repetitive clauses serve to emphasize the importance, the finality, the sovereignty of what is being promised here. All this is a work of God, with humanity as the recipient of God's sovereign promise. We who are taught by our culture to think of the world as our creation, the result of our choices, will find this language challenging. Humanity has made a mess of things, in only nine chapters of Genesis. Now God steps in, again, and attempts to promise a new future, a fresh start into being. "As for me, I am establishing my covenant with you and your descendants. . . ."

The covenant is not just with Noah but with all future generations, Jew and Gentile alike, all people. It is a covenant not just with humanity but with the animals as well. It says only what God will do, demands, and expects. God gives humanity that which humanity had not the wisdom even to ask for, much less the right to expect. Thus the covenant to Noah is rightly conceived of as an early act of sovereign, undeserved grace. A gift.

"Never again," repeats God (vv. 11, 15), never again will humanity be the recipient of God's judgment in this way. Not that humanity will never again deserve punishment in this bloody, violent world in which we make our way after the flood. The story is about the goodness of God, not the potential goodness of humanity. The covenant is a promise to us that we make our way not alone. From Genesis 9 the rest of the story follows, an evangelical story in which God keeps coming back to humanity even after humanity has turned away from God, in which God continues to make and keep promises to people even when people have not kept our promises to God.

And just to make sure that the promise of "never again" is kept, God puts a great rainbow in the sky as a heavenly reminder of the covenant (vv. 9, 11). There may be those who wonder why on earth God needs a rainbow in the heaven to remind God of God's promise not to give up on the human race. Yet consider the information given in a freshman course in world history, or think of the death and destruction that marked the just-passed twentieth century, and well, we can be grateful that God has a rainbow to remind God not to give us what we deserve. Lord, keep your eye on that rainbow!

Thus surely we Christians are justified in hearing in this primal story a kind of echo of another story that we shall again enact at the end of the forty days of Lent. After a particularly bloody and horrible weekend of death at a place called Calvary, when the earth shook and chaos reigned supreme, there was Sunday. What we thought was the end of the story turned out to be the beginning. What we well assumed to be the last chapter in God's gracious dealings with humanity turned out to be the first chapter in a whole new story of promise. God came back, this time as the risen Christ, saying, "Brothers and sisters — and all you hurting, bloody, violent members of the human race — I love you yet."

William H. Willimon

19

Second Sunday in Lent, Year A

First Lesson: Genesis 12:1-4a
(Psalm 121)
Second Lesson: Romans 4:1-5, 13-17
Gospel Lesson: John 3:1-17

Strictly speaking, the story of Abram and Sarai — eventually to be Abraham and Sarah (Gen. 17:5, 15) — begins in Genesis 11. There we learn (vv. 27-32) that Terah had taken Abram, his son, Lot, his grandson (and Abram's nephew, Lot's father Haran having already died [v. 28]), and Sarai, his daughter-in-law, from *'ur Kaśdim* (Ur of the Chaldeans) and embarked for the land of Canaan. No motive for this journey is provided. Nor is there any explanation why the group stopped short of Canaan and settled in Haran. However, whatever the motivations, so far only human initiative plays a role.

That changes abruptly when the Lord (YHWH) speaks to Abram (12:1). Suddenly, God generates the action. With a crisp command ("you get going"), God tells Abram to break completely with his past. His land, place of birth, and father's house are all to be left behind as he heads toward a land whose location God will subsequently reveal. No longer is the journey ordinary. It has become a function of divine command. Ironically, while Terah's reasons for traveling toward Canaan are never disclosed, God's command transforms that particular land into a divine destination. Human designs are no longer in view; Abram and Sarai now travel by the Lord's directives.

The initiative, instructions, and motivations all come from God. There is no mention whatsoever of the couple's state of mind, religious stance, or prior knowledge of the Lord. Nor has there been any hint that Abram or Sarai were somehow worthy of God's call. Considering how much Christianity (and Judaism) stresses Abram's (and Sarai's) faith, openness to God, and impressive willingness to obey, the absence of these themes in the text is remarkable. The accent falls completely on God. Thus God, not Abram (or Sarai), is the main "character" in the unfolding story. At this juncture, neither Abram nor Sarai even knows where they are going — God will have to make that clear.

Divine purposes continue to be highlighted as the Lord outlines the reasons for this epochal journey (v. 2). The Lord plans to make Abram a "great nation" *(goy gadol),* to bless him, to make his name great, and to make him a blessing. It begins to dawn on us that what God is doing with and

20

through Abram transcends him as an individual. Such a litany makes us realize that we cannot comprehend "the Abram and Sarai story" unless we are aware of broader issues. Abram's (and Sarai's) divine election is cosmic in scope. This becomes clearer when we notice the connections between this initial episode and Genesis 1–11.

For example, the Lord's setting out to "make [Abram's] name great" has an echo in the Babel episode when the folk decide to build a city and a tower in order to "make a name for ourselves" (11:4). Here is an instance of "name building" counter to divine purposes that ends in divine judgment (11:7-8); in contrast, the "name building" that God has in mind when calling Abram eventuates in divine blessing. The "name" motif is further underscored by the fact that the Babel story and the Abram story are connected by a genealogy that runs from Shem — whose name *means* "name"! — to Abram. The Babel incident illustrates one way of getting a name; the Abram story illustrates another.

Also, the call of Abram represents God's attempt to "re-bless" the world through a particular couple and a special people after the failure of earlier blessings. In the primeval story, God's purposes for humanity were rooted in blessing (1:22, 28; 5:2; 9:1; cf. 2:3). However, bad human choices translated blessings into curses (['rr] 3:14, 17; 4:11; 9:25). Even before the Abram episode, God had used Noah to remove or at least lessen the curse on the ground (5:29; 8:21). In Genesis 1–11, two different words for curse are used: 'rr and qll (8:21). Both terms are combined when God announces to Abram that "I will bless any who bless you, and I will curse ('rr) any one who curses (qll) you" (12:3). Henceforth, God's response to the world will depend on its response to the divine mission being played out in Abram and Sarai.

Equally, the Lord's references to a "great nation" and "families" (12:2-3) allude to previous material. Genesis 10 narrates the establishment of "nations" and "families" from the descendants of those who were aboard the ark (vv. 5, 20, 31, 32; cf. 8:19). Since this is the postdiluvial period, it represents a time *after* God's universal judgment when God begins to restore the created order. In that sense, the "nations" and "families" that are founded in the so-called Table of Nations (Gen. 10) are to be seen as consonant with God's plans for the future. At the same time, there is no explicit divine affirmation of the "spreading abroad" of these families and nations (*nipredu;* [v. 32]). Furthermore, the subsequent Babel story, with its account of "city building" *against* the grain of divine purposes, may be an implicit caution against regarding the spread of families and nations as an unmitigated good (11:1-9). In this episode, God "scatters" (*wayyapes;* [v. 8]) the people as an act of judgment and foreclosure. In the final analysis, what God has in

21

mind for the world's families and nations is to be understood in the context of the divine blessing that will come through Abram (and Sarai). God is proposing "a more excellent way" for human families and nations.

There is perhaps one more way to view the relationship between Genesis 1–11 and the start of this first ancestral story. As the primeval narrative proceeds, it calls attention to the progression of human disobedience. The first couple eats the forbidden fruit (Gen. 3), Cain kills Abel (Gen. 4), the "sons of God" cohabit with the "daughters of men" (6:1-4), and then we are told that the human capacity for evil cannot be exaggerated (6:5ff.). Even after the devastation of the flood and God's attempt to start all over again with the descendants of Noah (9:1ff.), evil continues, most notably in the actions of Ham (9:20-22) and the builders of Babel.

Each of these sinful acts is followed by a corresponding act of judgment. In the garden God curses the ground, the woman is to experience painful childbirth and be ruled by her husband, and the serpent is condemned to crawl on its belly and be in constant conflict with humanity (3:14-19). Cain's punishment involves an increased curse on the ground and banishment (4:11-14). The great flood follows the illicit union of the "sons of God" and "daughters of men" (6:5–8:19). Finally, Noah curses Ham's son (9:25-27) and God scatters the people of Babel and confuses their tongues (11:8-9).

But that is not all there is to the pattern. After each act of divine judgment there are corresponding acts of grace. In the garden Adam and Eve do not immediately die as God warned; furthermore, God clothed them with animal skins before expelling them from the garden (2:17; 3:21). Though Cain's brutal murder was deserving of capital punishment, God precluded this ultimate penalty by marking Cain (4:15). Even with the great flood, grace was manifest in that God preserved Noah, his family, and representatives of the animal world (6:8, 18-19). Likewise, Noah's cursing of Canaan did not prevent God from repopulating the whole earth through Noah's progeny (9:26-27; 10:1).

However, the pattern breaks down with the Babel story. There is no corresponding act of grace in that episode. In fact, this account draws Genesis 1–11 to a close with a haunting question: "Is humanity doomed always to be a victim of the 'Babel syndrome'?" That is, from now on will human beings be condemned to be scattered (i.e., unable to live in community) and confused (i.e., unable to communicate)? If ever a story cried out for a corresponding act of divine grace, this one does.

It turns out that there is such a corresponding act of divine grace, even though it does not immediately follow the Babel account. It needs to be kept in mind that the Babel story and the Abram/Sarai story are connected by the reference to a "great name." Also, the two stories are connected by a genealogy that runs from Shem to Abram. Thus the Abram/Sarai story is the corresponding act of grace to the Babel story. Since the Abram/Sarai story is the beginning of the "history of salvation," it turns out that the entire remainder of the biblical story is an "answer" to the questions posed by the Babel episode. God's people Israel are the "answer" to Genesis 1–11. Apart from Abram and Sarai, Israel as God's people would have been impossible. Moreover, in light of the Christian Bible, the story that begins with Abram and Sarai and continues with Israel culminates dramatically and conclusively in the story of the death, resurrection, and exaltation of Jesus the Christ.

Accenting the theme of grace in this episode is the notation that Abram may not have been completely obedient to God. To be sure, upon reception of the command, "Abram went, as God told him" (v. 4). But in the next breath we learn that "Lot went with him." Were not Abram's kin to have been left at home? While the text is subtle at this point, it should not be lost on us that every single episode featuring Lot in the subsequent story is negative (Gen. 13; 14; 19). This underscores the fact that the unfolding story is much more about divine grace than human obedience. God desires the latter, but is sufficiently gracious to work in spite of it if that becomes necessary.

Frank Anthony Spina

Third Sunday after Pentecost, Year A

First Lesson: Genesis 12:1-9
(Psalm 33:1-12)
Second Lesson: Romans 4:13-25
Gospel Lesson: Matthew 9:9-13, 18-26

The context of our passage is exceedingly important, because Genesis 12:1-9 serves as God's reaction to what happened before the call to Abraham. According to the primeval history in Genesis 1–11, God created the universe "very good." But still today our human attempts to slip the bonds of our creaturehood and be our own gods and goddesses, determining our own right and wrong and our own destinies, have corrupted every area of God's creation. Human community has become impossible — between husband and wife, sibling and sibling, society and society, nation and nation. The fecundity of nature has been corrupted. The birth of offspring has become life threatening. The battle of the sexes has broken out. The way to paradise has been lost. And over all hangs the curse of futility, of pain, of loneliness, and finally of death. As our text begins, therefore, the Lord God speaks his word into human life and begins that history of salvation which will finally reverse the effects of human sin and bring his blessing to all humankind.

We know from archaeology that there was a migration of Semitic peoples from upper Mesopotamia into Canaan sometime between 2000 and 1700 B.C. Apparently Abram, his wife Sarai, and his nephew Lot were among those Semites. Abram's father, Terah, took them from their original home in Ur of the Chaldees to journey to Canaan, but when they reached Haran in upper Mesopotamia, the clan settled there, and there Terah died (Gen. 11:31-32). Significantly, Abram had no son, because his wife Sarai was barren (11:30). Such is the background of our text.

Sometime in the eighteenth century B.C. (say, 1750), God speaks his powerful word of promise to Abram (12:1-3), and from that time on human history is never the same. God takes that Semite into his service and gives him a command. Abram is to leave behind everything he has known — his accustomed life in his country, his residence among his clan kin, his father's house full of close relatives — and is commanded to journey toward an unnamed land that God will show to him.

Amazingly, says our text, Abram packs up and goes. Now why? Because God gives him a threefold promise. First is the promise of a land for his descendants to call their own, although the Lord does not state that explicitly until verse 7. Second, God promises he will make of Abram and his descendants "a great nation." That, of course, seems preposterous because Abram's wife Sarai is barren, and Abram himself is seventy-five years old. Nevertheless, Abram believes that God will make good on his word. Third, the Lord promises that through Abram and his descendants he will bring blessing on all the families of the earth, thus reversing the effects of humankind's sinful rebellion of which we heard in Genesis 3–11. We lost our paradise, according to Genesis 3; God therefore promises a new land flowing with milk and honey. Our sin has made all harmonious community impossible; God answers with a promise of a new people. We live under the curse of death; the Lord replies that the curse will be turned into blessing.

Although there is no specific mention in these first three verses of Abram's trust, it is clear from Abram's actions that his faith consists in his belief in the promises of the Lord. God has promised a glorious future to this ancient patriarch and his descendants. Abram therefore reaches out for that future and obeys the Lord's command to travel toward it.

That this threefold promise concerns Abram's future is a telltale sign that the effects of God's promise are not to be understood as confined to Abram's life. This is a promise that concerns the whole of humankind and its destiny. Indeed, verse 3 tells us that God will bless whoever blesses Abram and will curse whoever curses him. Our whole destiny as a human race is wrapped up in this promise, and the outcome of our lives will be determined by whether or not we too believe God was working through Abram and his people.

It is not surprising, therefore, that much of the salvation history that follows in the Old Testament and in the New can be understood as the story of God's working to keep this word to our father in the faith. Israel is given its land and then loses it, but is promised it once again in the form of a new Jerusalem in a new heaven and a new earth. Israel multiplies but then loses her population and her nationhood, until the bounds of her nationality are burst by the One who becomes the cornerstone of a universal people. Israel is blessed, but is then cursed with her sin, until there comes the Descendant of Abraham who dies for the sin of all and who defeats forever the curse of everlasting death. This promise to father Abraham runs like a golden thread through the whole history of God's salvation, so that the apostle Paul can finally write that "all the promises of God find their Yes" in Jesus Christ (2 Cor. 1:20). We are introduced here in these three little verses to the universal purpose of God for all people, and Abraham is called to leave his home in Mesopotamia not because he is especially privileged, but because the Lord God wishes to bring his blessing on every one of us. It is a long and complex story, this story of God's working for us. It has its heights and depths, and it seems as if it will never come out right. But God has spoken his word to Abram, and God always keeps his promises.

As our text continues in verse 6, Abram journeys southward to "the place at Shechem," which was located in the central hill country of Canaan and was actually an important urban center on the route of trade during the patriarchal period. Significantly, however, our text tells us that "at that time the Canaanites were in the land" (v. 6). This is followed immediately by the promise in verse 7: "To your descendants I will give this land." In other words, Abram himself is not given the land, according to this text. The Canaanites possess it, and the land is only promised as a gift in the future to

Abram's descendants. In fact, as Genesis's story continues, Abram never owns the land, but he is given a little foretaste of the gift, in Genesis 23, when he buys the field at Machpelah as a burial ground. There not only Abraham but also Isaac, Rebekah, Leah, and Jacob are buried (49:31; 50:13). God's promise to the patriarchs themselves and to two of their wives is fulfilled only in death, and the fulfillment of the promise is postponed until all of Israel can participate in it.

Subsequently, after the gift of the Promised Land to Israel under the leadership of Joshua, Shechem became the first site of the central sanctuary of the twelve-tribe federation in the time of the judges. It was destroyed by the armies of Assyria in 722 B.C., but was then rebuilt about 350 B.C. and became the religious center of the Samaritans, who erected their temple there on Mount Gerizim (cf. John 4:21).

The fact that the patriarchs have only a little foretaste of the gift of the Promised Land is typical in God's relations with his covenant people. Always his promise stretches out toward the future. For example, Moses is allowed only to glimpse the Promised Land, spread out before him, from the top of Pisgah on the eastern side of the Jordan (Deut. 34:1-4). And similarly, we too have only a foretaste in the Lord's Supper of the heavenly banquet, of eternal life in the kingdom of God. In our worship we are given some feeling, some glimpse of the eternal glory that lies before us. But the final gift of that kingdom lies in the future in the resurrection. God is working on toward his goal, working on to restore the goodness to his creation that he intended for it in the beginning, working on toward the establishment of his kingdom come on earth, even as it is in heaven. So Paul can write, "Not that I have already obtained . . . but I press on to make it my own" (Phil. 3:12).

Like Paul and like Abram in our text, we journey on, calling on the name of the Lord, following the destiny of servanthood to which the Lord has called us. Sometimes, like Abram, we do not know where we are going. But we do know that there is One who has gone before us, even through the valley of death, "the pioneer of our faith" (Heb. 12:2), Jesus Christ, who has given us his Spirit as the "guarantee," the foretaste that the goal is certain (2 Cor. 5:5; Eph. 1:14). God has promised eternal life in his everlasting kingdom, and God always keeps his promises, as he kept them to Israel and in Jesus Christ. Our task therefore is that of trust in his word, like Abram's trust. "Abram went as the LORD had told him." Let us get on with it.

Elizabeth Achtemeier

Second Sunday in Lent, Year C

First Lesson: Genesis 15:1-12, 17-18
(Psalm 27)
Second Lesson: Philippians 3:17–4:1
Gospel Lesson: Luke 13:31-35

According to Genesis 12:2, when God called Abram out of Mesopotamia, he promised that he would make Abram a "great nation" with many descendants. We now are given an account in which the Lord begins to fulfill that promise. He promises that Abram will have a son.

We have three differing accounts in Genesis of the promise of a son to the patriarch and his wife. This text contains the first. The second is found in 17:15-18, the third in 18:9-15. Though each account is interwoven with other traditions and reflects the concern of its particular author, the three share a common motif. In none of the stories does Abram or his wife Sarai initially believe the promise of a child. In short, the promise is not given as a reward of faith or goodness. Faith and evident piety are initially lacking, and the promise comes simply as a free gift of God's grace in his ongoing work of fulfilling his purpose.

Customarily, on the basis of their styles, their use of divine names, and their theology, the account in Genesis 17 has been assigned to Priestly tradition, the account in Genesis 18 to the Yahwist. Our text is said to come from the Elohist (E) source of the ninth or eighth century B.C. Whether E was actually a unified source or not, this is the first occurrence of the promise to Abram of a son, and characteristic of E, that promise is given to Abram in a vision.

The text begins with a prophetic formula, "the word of the LORD came to Abram," a usage that is strange to Genesis but frequent in the prophetic writings. We moderns have to admit that we have no notion of what that means. But God speaks his word to Abram at night, in a vision, and Abram is fully awake. As is true of most confrontations of God with human beings, the word startles Abram and he is afraid. But as is also frequently the case, the divine assurance is given, "Fear not" (cf. Matt. 14:25-27; Luke 2:10). Then the promise is immediately proclaimed. God is Abram's shield or defense in life, and his "reward," that is, his progeny, will be very great or numerous.

Abram recovers quickly from his fright and, in fact, replies in an almost blasphemous manner. God has told him, "You will have many heirs."

Abram's reply is, "No, I won't." Following a custom which we know from the Nuzi tablets of fifteenth-century-B.C. Mesopotamia, Abram explains that because his wife is barren, his only heir will be Eliezer, the son of his slave woman. But Abram quickly learns that he is dealing not with human custom but with divine purpose. God takes him out of his tent into the night and tells him to look at the stars and number them if he is able. "So shall your descendants be," as many as the stars of heaven (cf. Deut. 1:10; Rom. 4:18; Heb. 11:12). And, we are told, "Abram believed the LORD, and he reckoned it to him as righteousness."

Here we find the first instance of justification by faith in the Bible, that justification to which the apostle Paul later refers in Romans 4:3 and Galatians 3:6. That is not a doctrine deduced only from the New Testament, but is contained here in Genesis from the beginning of salvation history. "Righteousness" throughout the Scriptures signifies the fulfillment of the demands of a relationship, and basic to that righteousness in our relationship with God is trust in the plan and working of the Lord. Abram here accepts God's promise and believes that God will fulfill it. That is his faith, his trust, and that trust makes him acceptable in the eyes of his God. Faith here, therefore, is not belief in some doctrine or the performance of some good work — although both may flow out of faith. Rather, faith is trusting God's promise and acting as if it will be fulfilled. Throughout the Bible, God makes many promises — specifically in the New Testament, for example, "Lo, I am with you always" or "whoever lives and believes in me shall never die" or "I will not leave you desolate; I will come to you." Genuine biblical faith clings to those promises of our Lord Jesus and acts as if they are true.

Our text deals not only with the promise of many descendants to Abram, but also with the promise of a land. Verse 7, in a very old tradition harking back to Abram's origin in Ur of the Chaldees (Gen. 11:31), goes behind the promise of 12:7 and 15:18 to give the land to Abram himself, rather than to his descendants only. That is a hint of the fact that, lying behind these stories, we have an old patriarchal tradition of the divine gift of land and progeny given to Abram personally in the cult of "the God of the Fathers." When that old tradition was incorporated into Genesis's present sources, however, it became subject to the salvation history in which the promise to Abram is postponed until all his descendants can share in its fulfillment. None of that is pertinent to preaching from this text, but it exhibits the hoary antiquity of parts of these stories. The preacher will want to stick with the promise to Abram's *descendants* of a land to call their own, as in 12:7 and 15:18. And the subsequent guarantee of that promise by the making of a covenant with Abram should also be seen from the perspective of 15:18.

In verses 7-12, 17-18 we find the covenant making with the patriarch. This is the second covenant ceremony recorded in the Old Testament, following that with Noah in 9:8-17. Like that Noachic covenant, this one too follows the pattern of a "royal covenant," in which a king simply grants favor to a subject, without any action on the subject's part. Abram has asked how he will know that he (and his descendants) are given the land to possess (v. 7). The Lord therefore bids Abram to prepare a covenant sacrifice.

Abram fetches a three-year-old heifer, she-goat, and ram, along with a turtledove and a young pigeon. He cuts the heifer, goat, and ram in two, but, as in the law of Leviticus 1:14-17, he does not cut the birds in half. The rationale behind the division of the animals is that the covenant partners who pass between the pieces will be cursed with the same fate if they do not fulfill the covenant promise. The strange mention of the birds of prey in verse 11 perhaps harkens back to ancient traditions of evil spirits which may distort the covenant making. Or perhaps they signify the difficulties lying ahead in the fulfillment of the covenant. We frankly do not know.

Then our text enters the realm of mystery. The sun is going down, and darkness begins to fall on the land. Abram lapses into a deep sleep, like that in Genesis 2:21 when the Lord made woman from the rib of the man, or in Job 4:13-14 or 33:15 when God communicated and terrified. The normal activities of Abram's mind and spirit are extinguished, and he is totally passive, the recipient of only that which the Lord does.

Verses 13-16 are an obvious later insertion into the narrative, dealing with Israel's later captivity and slavery in Egypt.

The covenant ceremony continues in verse 17. Total darkness falls. And between the pieces of the sacrifice pass a smoking firepot and a flaming torch, symbolizing the presence of God. God's appearance frequently is associated in the Bible with fire (cf. Exod. 3:2-4; 19:18; Heb. 12:29; et al.), although God's own appearance is never described, any more than Jesus Christ's is ever described. No one can see God and live (Exod. 33:20; Deut. 5:26), and in the few instances where a human being says he has seen God, the gaze immediately shifts to describe only God's surroundings (Exod. 24:10; Isa. 6:1-2). We should therefore not speculate or push the symbolism of the firepot and flaming torch too far. Obviously they designate God's participation in the covenant ceremony, but they leave any description of God's divine person shrouded in mystery. The text can leave us filled with awe and the hairs of our skin standing up, but we human beings still "see through a mirror darkly" and cannot fully define God's being.

Instead, as in all of the Bible, we are presented with God's word. In verses 18-21 Abram's descendants are promised a land stretching from the eastern limit of the Nile Valley to the Euphrates River in Mesopotamia. The boundaries that are set forth are those of the empires of David and Solomon, and the text looks toward those future possessions of the land. In the meantime, the peoples listed are in possession of the promised territory. The Lord God, however, has made a promise, and he will keep it.

Elizabeth Achtemeier

Second Sunday in Lent, Year B

First Lesson: Genesis 17:1-7, 15-16
(Psalm 22:23-31)
Second Lesson: Romans 4:13-25
Gospel Lesson: Mark 8:31-38

Our text begins with God coming to a very old man, a man without much of a future, a geriatric with few prospects. On the Sunday before this text is read, in Year B of the Revised Common Lectionary, God comes to another older man named Noah and makes a covenant (Gen. 9:8-17), promising not to desert him or his descendants, promising to make out of him and his family many families.

That theme of God-initiated covenant continues in Genesis 17. The Priestly writer organizes the story of God as a series of promises, each promise becoming progressively more focused than the previous one, covenants that culminate in the great covenant of Sinai in Exodus 19. When God began making promises, God made covenant even with the birds and animals (Gen. 9:10). On Sinai, God's great covenant in two tablets of stone included only Israel. This Sunday's covenant promises that Abraham will be the father of "a multitude of nations" (17:4).

In all the early covenants, two themes emerge. God promises both land and progeny. We therefore do well to think of Genesis 17 as a family story, a promise of children and place, a promise coming first to an old man who had neither. Genesis 12–50 is a saga of a family. In other parts of the Old Testament, we read of kings and kingdoms. In these chapters of Genesis all is very domestic, familial.

We believe that the earliest parts of Genesis are the work of the Yahwist, who probably wrote during the time of Solomon, when Israel enjoyed great power and prosperity, having occupied the Promised Land, with the family secure and serene, at rest in the security of a promise fulfilled. Genesis 17 is, we suppose, from the hand of the Priestly writer, who attempts to give hope in the time of devastating Babylonian exile.

What do a people do when they are strangers in a strange land, up-rooted, aliens? One thing they do is remember, recall time past, lovingly reiterate the promises of God. All present evidence to the contrary, the Priestly writer insists that the covenant of God still holds. Israel, now persecuted and laid waste by the nations, is destined to be the family above all families, the nation before all nations.

Many would name the present situation of the North American church as exile. Here, at the beginning of the twenty-first century, we Christians are feeling like strangers in the very culture that we thought we had made safe for Christianity, missionaries within the world we thought we owned. Pushed to the margins, uprooted, disestablished, what ought we to do?

We can remember the promises of God, God's relentless determination to make us into a holy people, a light to the nations. Genesis 17 embodies the great originating promise — God is determined to have a family, and have a family God will.

What to remember? We are told, in verse 1 of chapter 17, that (1) Abraham is old and that (2) God appeared to Abraham. Note that everything that follows in the text, with the exception of the first part of verse 3, consists of God's speeches to Abraham. God is clearly the main character here, the initiator and the content of the covenant. Without the intrusive speech of God, there is no future, no possibility, no progeny, no land.

Abraham's response to God's gracious promise is singularly impressive. "Abraham fell on his face and laughed" (v. 17).

Surely we are meant to enjoy the patriarch's reaction. The humor is undeniable. On the one hand we have the sovereign, solemn promises of God to make something out of this old man and woman. On the other hand we have the unrestrained, geriatric laughter of Abraham and Sarah.

For an unfutured, weak, bleak-prospect people, the promises of God are sure to seem laughable. Sarah and Abraham, old and childless, are called "barren." They are — without progeny, without a future, barren, desolate. A people in exile, powerless, homeless, landless, are barren, desolate. Into this

31

desert intrude the powerful promises of God. And we laugh. Is it mocking, derisive laughter at the preposterousness of the promise? Or is it the joyful, playful, surprised laughter of those who once had, in their desolation, nothing but tears but who now, because of the promises, have laughter?

Later, a child of Abraham and Sarah would promise his people, "Blessed are you who weep now, for you will laugh" (Luke 6:21b). The evangelical promises of this God transform tears to laughter. Because of the promise, the future is considerably more open than we, in our desolation, first imagined. In exile, there is a promise of home. In decline and infertility, there is a promise of family.

Many of us read this covenant story in situations of church decline and deep concern over the future. Will we have a future as the church in North America? Is it possible for there to be a family of God, gathered not the way the world gathers (by class, race, status, etc.) but rather by the promises of God?

Such questions move us back to the way this story began: with the words and acts of a God who intrudes, promises, declares, makes a way when there is no way. Our existence, our family of God, our church, our future — everything hinges upon the promises of God and God's faithfulness in keeping the promise.

William H. Willimon

Fourth Sunday after Pentecost, Year A

First Lesson: Genesis 18:1-15; (21:1-7)
(Psalm 116:1-2, 12-19)
Second Lesson: Romans 5:1-8
Gospel Lesson: Matthew 9:35–10:8, (9-23)

The mystery of God's presence and work. The fulfillment of God's promises. The crucial importance of hospitality in the life of faith. All these themes and more are found in this rich and familiar narrative. Since the conclusion of the episode does not come until the optional portion of the lection, it should surely be included lest the hearers be left asking, "And what happened? Did the baby arrive?" The initial portion begins a much larger unit of material that includes all of chapter 19 and serves to contrast in a most dramatic way the contours of the faithful life (Abraham's) with those of the unfaithful life (Lot's). A helpful way to sense the movement of the narrative is to imagine it being told around a campfire by a skilled storyteller who is seeking to convey God's power, mystery, and faithfulness to later generations.

The narrator announces to the reader what Abraham does not know, that the strangers passing by his tent, where he sits like any nomad in the heat of the day, are divine beings. The ensuing episode is indeed a theophany, although God will remain incognito until verse 14. That knowledge does not deflate the story, but heightens the drama by encouraging the reader to engage in searching out God's presence in the story just as is done in the reader's own life. In a movement reminiscent of the father in Jesus' parable of the prodigal son, Abraham rushes out to greet the potential visitors. Steeped in the hospitality of the desert, he offers the strangers water with which to wash, a tree's shade in which to rest, and a "little" food to refresh them before they continue their journey. Respectful of their persons and privacy, Abraham does not pry into their identity or destination with questions. He is far too gracious to do so.

A "little" turns out to mean a lot of fine food — cakes of choicest flour, a fine veal calf ("tender and good") from his herd, curds and milk (this is a prelaw meal and not kosher). The food preparation must take some considerable time, so the strangers' stay is leisurely. The drama unfolds slowly, and the reader's anticipation builds with Abraham's. The first hint that these three "men" are more than they appear is given when they ask about Sarah, knowing her name without her having made an appearance or been introduced. She, in accordance with her subordinate position of wife in that culture, has stayed in the background, out of sight, away from the men. That will soon change.

The story switches from third-person plural to third-person singular in verse 9, and the mystery is thereby heightened concerning who this "he" is. "He" announces Sarah will bear a child upon his return in the spring, the season of rebirth and new beginnings. There is a brief interlude during which the narrator explains that Sarah, in what was no doubt common practice, had been listening to the men's conversation concealed by the tent flap, and that Sarah and Abraham were well past their childbearing years. To underscore the latter point, to make sure there is no doubt about the miraculous nature of what is coming, the narrator comments that Sarah is postmenstrual.

The flow of the story resumes with Sarah laughing at "his" announcement. Perhaps she thinks this "man" knows precious little about where babies come from; perhaps she finds the idea of being a mother while old enough to be a great-grandmother amusing; perhaps she is simply delighted with the news. It may well be that others will find a woman pregnant at Sarah's age quite humorous, as when aged politicians father children with young women. Sarah's laughter parallels that of Abraham earlier when he fell on his face, astonishingly not in worship but in mirth, when God made the same announcement (17:17). Nevertheless, "the LORD" reveals his identity in response to Sarah's honest laughter, and asks the question the reader wishes to ask, "Why did Sarah laugh?"

No definitive answer is given. The Lord goes on to ask if "anything is too wonderful for the LORD" (compare Jesus' words in Mark 10:27 and Matt. 19:26), and then repeats the promise made previously (v. 10), that the child will be born in spite of Sarah's doubts. Seemingly embarrassed and afraid, Sarah denies laughing at God. But God, graciously and with complementary divine good humor, says, "Oh yes, you did laugh." In the additional verses from chapter 21, the child Laughter (the meaning of the name Isaac) is born as Sarah and many others join in laughter over the gift God has at last given the old couple in fulfillment of the covenant.

The slow pace at which this story unfolds accords well with the slow pace with which God fulfills the covenant with Abraham and Sarah. In the Hagar episode, they have already witnessed and known the pain born of their impatience. Perhaps they have at last learned to "wait upon the LORD" (Isa. 40:31), to linger until the laughter-bestowing blessing is extended in God's good time. Taking matters under our own control or trying to force God's hand simply does not work. The discipline of waiting to see the new thing God will do does not come easily, neither to Sarah and Abraham nor to contemporary hearers, but it is essential at many points in the Christian journey.

In the midst of their waiting for God, Sarah and Abraham have continued in faithfulness to the calling of hospitality. By not neglecting "to show hospitality to strangers, [they] have entertained angels" (Heb. 13:2). Sarah's laughter may be born of some understandable and honest doubt, but she and her husband have not drifted into apathy or despair that would lead them away from welcoming strangers and treating others well. Theirs is an active waiting, full of treating others as they would like to be treated, of searching strangers' eyes and words to see what gift of truth they might bring. Sarah and Abraham do not live in fear or despondency. Their hospitality is generous and respectful and, on this occasion, bears fruit almost beyond imagining.

Sarah is not very severely admonished by God for her laughter. God was more emphatic, even stern, with Abraham when he fell down in laughter at God's preposterous promise. God understands her disbelief (see Ps. 103:14: "he knows how we were made, he remembers we are dust") and deals gently, even humorously with it. The gracious gift of a child in fulfillment of the covenant is matched by God's gracious interaction with Sarah. And the divine sense of humor is sealed in the child's name.

This story begins saying "the LORD appeared to Abraham," but as it unfolds, it is Sarah who moves more and more to center stage, particularly in the closing section in chapter 21. But is God not in the business of drawing people in from the margins? Sarah, marginalized by gender and barrenness, finds herself drawn into the center of God's faithful work. Is not God in the business of bringing new life where none seems possible? God is the Giver of life and of new life again and again to barren women (compare 1 Sam. 1), and even to the dead (1 Kings 17:17; John 11:38ff.). The ways in which God works are often mysterious, hidden, slow to unfold. But this story, in its repetition of God's promise, is clear that God's way will not be thwarted, even when it runs against utterly human expectation and experience. Who, after all, believed the Republic of South Africa would end apartheid without a race war? Who foresaw the coming down of the Berlin Wall? God is faithful to promises made even when God's people see no possible means for their fulfillment. Is this not the message of the resurrection?

A final note. It may be tempting to see the strange, traveling trio as in some way prefiguring the Trinity. Indeed, the Trinity is sometimes so represented in Orthodox iconography. This temptation should be resisted, as it is certainly a more likely contextual understanding of the story that God speaks as one accompanied by members of the heavenly host (see Gen. 1:26 and 6:7). "Christianizing" the story by unfounded allusions to the doctrine of the Trinity will lead the hearer away from its main and potent themes.

Lawrence W. Farris

Fifth Sunday after Pentecost, Year A

First Lesson: Genesis 21:8-21
(Psalm 86:1-10, 16-17)
Second Lesson: Romans 6:1b-11
Gospel Lesson: Matthew 10:24-39

God had promised Abraham numerous offspring, but Sarah, his wife, could not have children. She had therefore suggested that Hagar act as a surrogate mother and bear Abraham's child (see Gen. 16). That resulted in a breakdown in the relationship between the two women. Sarah's affliction of Hagar then made Hagar run away, but God's aide appeared to her and told her to go back. That tough requirement was also an act of grace: membership in Abraham's family meant membership in the people promised God's blessing. That is underlined by the promise that Hagar will indeed become mother of a vast people. Initially she will be mother of a boy called Ishmael, *yishma'el,* God hears. It will be an appropriate name. Hagar has proved God as one who hears and gives heed to her affliction. In turn, Hagar herself has given God a new name, *'el ro'i.* The name looks as if it means something like "God sees me," which makes a similar point, though the story has Hagar taking up the idea that she is someone who has seen God.

Abraham thus acquired his son. Through him he will indeed become a great nation, as God promised. But God also made clear that Sarah herself would have a son with whom God would have a special covenant relationship (chap. 17). Sarah understandably laughed at this idea (18:9-15). But in due course she had her son, and Abraham called him Isaac, *yishaq,* "he laughs" or "he plays." God has indeed given Sarah reason to laugh (21:1-7).

So the laughing/playing baby begins to grow into a laughing/playing boy. But he is not the only person laughing and playing. Ishmael is also doing so, and gets into trouble with Sarah for it, though there is more than one understanding of why this happens. The Septuagint and the Vulgate have him playing *with* Isaac at Isaac's weaning party. This perhaps implies that his weaning took place rather later than we might expect. But the Hebrew text simply says he was laughing/playing. He was behaving like his half brother. This was what offended Sarah. (If he was indeed playing *with* Isaac, the point is not really affected.) She knows Ishmael is the eldest son, the one through whom she had suggested God's promise could be fulfilled. She has changed her mind about that, but she cannot be sure that (e.g.) Abraham,

Hagar, and Ishmael himself will cooperate with her new desire, even though God backs it. If Ishmael is behaving as if Isaac's name applies to him, will he soon be behaving as if Isaac's promise applies to him?

She therefore determines that Hagar and her son must go, as once she had determined when he was still in Hagar's womb. This time she seeks to get Abraham to do her dirty work. Abraham again behaves like a wimp, caught in the rivalry between his two women. We might also have preferred God to have acted with more apparent awareness that Hagar and Ishmael were again being treated rather toughly. But God declines to stand up to Sarah, too. For Sarah is right. It is through Isaac's line that God's main promise is to be fulfilled. But Hagar and Ishmael do have a promise of their own. Ishmael will become the beginning of a nation.

"So Abraham rose early in the morning." Old Testament stories are generally sparing in the information they give us on people's feelings and motives. They tell us about people's actions more than about their inner workings, and leave us to work out what was going on inside people. In this respect they are more like movies than novels. So we must pay attention to what we are told about people's actions if we are to determine what was going on in their hearts. When we get up early to do something, it is a sign that we are committed to it and want to set about doing it. Abraham is evidently so committed.

He gives Hagar some basic provisions and sends her away to wander in the waterless and resourceless wilderness of this foreign land. When their water is gone, she puts her child under one of the spiny bushes that grow there in the desert and sits a distance away, not wanting actually to watch her child die. Presumably she wrestles with some agonized questions about the supposed promise of God concerning her child, as well as with the pain of a mother forced to wait for her child to die. She weeps and howls.

The story does not say she prays. Once more she anticipates the experience of Israel in her homeland. They will cry out in their pain. The story does not tell us that they cry out to God, and neither does Hagar. She simply cries out.

But this does not stop God from hearing and responding. Except that the cry to which God responds is actually the boy's. For God knows it is impossible to allow this child to die. A promise attaches to him. God's aide reaffirms the promise and points Hagar to a well she had not seen before. Was it there all the time, or is this a miraculous provision? From now on, God is "with" Ishmael. It is a key expression to describe God's relationship with Abraham (21:22), Isaac (26:24), Jacob (28:15), Joseph (39:21), and later with Israel as a people (e.g., Isa. 41:10; 43:5). It signifies not merely an inner sense of God's presence but an objective reality that issues in visible experience of God acting. The expression also applies to Ishmael, and has the same implications for him (Gen. 21:20).

There is a broader significance to the sentence about Abraham rising early in the morning. The expression recurs in 22:3, when Abraham gets up early to set out to offer his other son as a sacrifice. They are two parallel but strange ventures that God sets him on. It is also noteworthy that so much space is given to the story of Ishmael. It is Isaac, after all, who is the one through whom God's most far-reaching promise is to be fulfilled.

The stories in Genesis 12–22 come in pairs. There are two stories when Abraham is charged by God to go off and do something and is promised God's blessings. There are two about his adventures in a foreign land that involve passing off his wife as his sister; two about Lot in danger and about Sodom; two about covenant making; and two about Hagar and Ishmael. They are arranged thus:

12 The call; blessing promised
   12 Abram in a foreign land; wife-sister story
      13–14 Lot in danger; Sodom
         15 Covenant
            16 Hagar and Ishmael
         17 Covenant
      18–19 Lot in danger; Sodom
   20 Abraham in a foreign land; wife-sister story
      21 Hagar and Ishmael
22 The call; blessing confirmed

God's promise regarding Isaac is theologically central to the story of Abraham, yet oddly, Ishmael occupies the structural center of the chapters. Then just before the end we get another story about Ishmael to accompany the first, disturbing the neatness of the overall arrangement. It is as if there have to be a pair of stories about Ishmael to balance the other pairs. It was by Sarah's initiative that Ishmael came to be part of this story, and she can wish he was not part of it, but she cannot now eliminate Hagar and her son.

This is good news for Gentiles who listen to sermons on this text. God's promise to Abraham did itself put the Gentile world into the frame of the story of Abraham. In Abraham all the peoples of the world were to find blessing. But Sarah's action also brought an actual Gentile and her son into the center of the story. In one sense Sarah is our mother, but in another Hagar is thus our mother. It is further noteworthy that Hagar is an African, a woman, and a slave. It is such a woman who stands at the heart of the story of Abraham. The story thus also brings good news to women. It brings good news to people who are enslaved or oppressed, or have slavery or oppression in the history that has shaped them. It brings good news to people of African descent, or of other descent than that of the Asia in which the gospel was born and the Europe in which it long found its best-known home.

It is then noteworthy that Ishmael himself is the ancestor of the nomadic Arab peoples who live around Israel. The story is a reminder that God stands in covenant relationship with them as well as with Israel. This might imply that God is committed to the Palestinians and the other Arab peoples around Israel as well as to Israel, and to the Islamic community as well as to the Jewish and Christian communities. That would be an extra basis for prayer for the gospel to reach them and for them to be treated fairly in Middle Eastern politics.

John Goldingay

Sixth Sunday after Pentecost, Year A

First Lesson: Genesis 22:1-14
(Psalm 13)
Second Lesson: Romans 6:12-23
Gospel Lesson: Matthew 10:40-42

Abraham asked no questions in Genesis 22. We ask a bevy of questions *about* Genesis 22. Abraham walked resolutely and without stumbling on his way to Mount Moriah. We walk hesitantly, tripping again and again over the multiple theological scandals we encounter as we try to follow Abraham. The language of Genesis 22 is crisp and unwaveringly direct. We cry out for caveats, for escape hatches, for insertions into the text that will explain God's request.

Apparently ours is a different world than the one from which this story emerged. Indeed, after traveling to the Holy Land, many people return home to report how much closer they now feel to the Bible, its stories, and its characters. But some time back I read a report from someone who had the opposite reaction: "walking where Jesus walked" drove home for this person the vast gulf that yawns open between the biblical culture and our own. Too often people like Abraham and Sarah become such familiar inhabitants on the landscape of our imaginations that we come to think of them as being pretty much like our next-door neighbors. The truth, however, is that Abraham and Sarah's world was so different from our own that they and we may as well come from different planets.

What is striking about the text of Genesis 22 is how wholly unconcerned it appears to be with the kinds of questions we want to raise. The author is not unaware of how difficult this test is for Abraham, but far from trying to nuance God's command, the author has crafted the text so as to *heighten* the very difficulties we find nearly unacceptable. The hammering phrase "your son, your *only* son, whom you *love*" makes this story heartbreaking to read. Similarly, the oft-repeated verbal picture of Abraham and Isaac trotting along "together" (vv. 6 and 8) presents a Norman Rockwell–like portrait of father and son. This is Sheriff Taylor and his boy Opie walking together in the opening sequence to the old *Andy Griffith Show*: a classic portrait of father-son togetherness. But this time the father bears the knowledge that he will return from this outing *alone*.

Curiously, the text of Genesis 22 is not principally concerned with the emotional side of Abraham's losing a son. Instead its focus seems to be that *this particular* sacrifice would jeopardize the future of the covenant. Isaac was the "laughter" of Abraham and Sarah's old age, but he was also to be the cosmic laughter of all nations because from him sprang the promise of redemption. If Laughter died, then what would become of the covenant?

These questions of covenant and salvation appear to loom much larger for the author of Genesis 22 than they typically do for modern readers. But perhaps that is because what lies behind this hard text is the equally difficult notion that salvation is going to be a costly enterprise purchased in blood. The binding and near-death of Laughter — and the foreshadowing phrase that "God himself will provide" for the sacrifice — give early biblical clues that eliminating evil is going to require enormous effort and sacrifice.

Indeed, as Old Testament scholar Ellen Davis has noted (in a lecture delivered at the Center of Theological Inquiry, Princeton, New Jersey, July 1999), the Bible takes a great risk putting a story like this one so near the beginning of Scripture. If, naturally enough, you were to begin reading Scripture in Genesis 1, you would go a scant twenty-one chapters before encountering this story, replete with its potentially off-putting portrait of a God who commands so horrid a thing as child sacrifice. So why would the canonical form of Scripture as it has come down to us run the risk of so offending readers with this dire test in Genesis 22 — a story so grim as to tempt a reader to close this book and never open it again? Perhaps because we *need* to learn early on something about the nature of God, sin, and the cost of redemption.

This story is "fraught with background," as Erich Auerbach put it (*Mimesis: The Representation of Reality in Western Literature,* trans. Willard R. Trask [Princeton, N.J.: Princeton University Press, 1953], p. 12). Genesis 22 does not drop out of a clear blue sky. Instead verse 1 tells us that God's command to Abraham comes "some time later" (NIV); a better translation would be "after these things" (NRSV). After *what* things? Presumably all that had gone on earlier in the Abraham cycle of stories in Genesis, chief among which are a bevy of stories detailing Abraham's failures of trust. Twice Abraham passed Sarah off as his sister because he feared for their lives despite God's promise that nothing would happen to them until they had a son. Then there were those occasions when both Abraham and Sarah laughed at God's promise of a son being born to senior citizens like themselves. (Recall Frederick Buechner's fanciful retelling of the story where Abraham asks Yahweh's angel, "Shall a child be born in the geriatric ward? Shall Medicare pick up the bill?") Because of this doubt, Abraham and Sarah sought a way around God's promise of the *two* of them producing a child by having Abraham rush God's plan through his liaison with Hagar.

"After these things" God now tests to see where Abraham — and so, where the harbinger of the covenant — was at. But not just after "these things" in the life of Abraham, but this story also follows the first twelve chapters of Genesis, which detail humanity's steady moving away from God the Creator. God and humanity had become alienated. But with Abraham the world was to begin again. This had to go just right because on this man's faithfulness all depended.

In short, this was a unique test for a unique figure in salvation history. It was also an event that foreshadowed the death of the beloved son as the way to seal the covenant. Yet we tend to resist the notion of an evil so deeply entrenched that it requires even God to go to dangerous and shocking lengths of sacrifice to root it out. Too often we want our God to be tame and predictable, quietly resisting a God who is utterly surprising, a God whose grace always comes with blood on it. (It is reminiscent of that classic moment in C. S. Lewis's Narnia chronicles where one of the children asks Mr. Beaver about Aslan the Lion. "Is he quite safe?" "Safe? 'Course he isn't safe. But he's good. He's the King, I tell you.")

41

We don't want Laughter to die — as a matter of fact, we want the laughter without the tears. If so, then the question the church needs to face vis-à-vis Genesis 22 is whether and to what extent we are willing to be *shaped* by such a text. Genesis 22 is a notoriously difficult story, and preachers should not pretend otherwise. The narrative has jagged edges that cut into our flesh when we handle it. Yet this story stubbornly stands in Genesis, refusing our attempts to explain it away. It won't go away, and in the larger scheme of Scripture it *must not* go away in that it calls readers to conform their thinking to God's view of sin and salvation — a point of view that is uncompromising both on how vital the process of eradicating sin from the world is and on how dearly it will end up costing God and all of us.

The lectionary oddly cuts off this reading at verse 14, though this story is by no means finished at that juncture. What follows in verses 15-18 is God's joyful eruption in response to Abraham's faithfulness (although oddly no emotional reaction is recorded about Abraham). The covenant is reaffirmed, and one has the sense that with Abraham the cosmos has turned a corner. The tale then concludes in verse 19 when, in a reprise of the image we received in verses 6 and 8, Abraham and Isaac leave the mountain "together" after all.

In a sense it's a "happy ending," but not unalloyedly so. Laughter is returned to Abraham and Sarah, but now it's a hard laughter — a laughter tempered by suffering and sacrifice. It's a hard laughter because now Abraham knows what God seems to have known all along: namely, the fulfillment of the covenant cannot come painlessly. "Blessed are you who weep now, for you will laugh," Jesus famously said. Among the multiple questions posed to us by a text like Genesis 22 is the meta-issue of whether we are willing to go through the weeping along with God, because the path to the joy of salvation will wend its way through many veils of tears, climaxing on another hill far away where God's provided lamb bawls out his forsakenness. Resurrection comes, of course, and with it all the laughter Jesus ever promised. But as Genesis 22 makes clear early on in the biblical witness, there are no shortcuts to that joy.

Scott Hoezee

Seventh Sunday after Pentecost, Year A

First Lesson: Genesis 24:34-38, 42-49, 58-67
(Psalm 45:10-17)
Second Lesson: Romans 7:15-25a
Gospel Lesson: Matthew 11:16-19, 25-30

B ecause this is a rather long narrative, the lectionary suggests reading verses 34-38, 42-49, and 58-67, parts of Abraham's servant's report to Rebekah's family as well as Rebekah's decision and meeting with Isaac. But in preaching on this narrative, it is better to read either the whole narrative or the narrator's description of the servant's journey, verses 1-33, and the outcome, verses 50-67.

God had promised Abraham the land of Canaan, many offspring, and that through him all the families of the earth would be blessed (Gen. 12:1-7; 22:17-18). Abraham and Sarah saw the initial fulfillment of this promise in their old age with the birth of the miracle child Isaac. But now God's promises seem to run into a dead end. The narrator informs us that Abraham is old — for emphasis he adds, "well advanced in years" (24:1) — and Sarah, the matriarch, has died (Gen. 23). Thus there is no mother in Israel. Unless Abraham can find a wife for Isaac, there will not be any more offspring, no Israel, and ultimately no Messiah through whom "all the families of the earth shall be blessed" (12:3). That's the issue addressed by this narrative: How will God fulfill his promises to Abraham?

We overhear Abraham's last recorded words. Abraham says to his trusted servant, "Put your hand under my thigh and I will make you swear by the LORD, the God of heaven and earth, that you will not get a wife for my son from the daughters of the Canaanites, among whom I live, but will go to my country and to my kindred and get a wife for my son Isaac" (vv. 2-4). Not marrying a Canaanite was important, for God had separated Abraham from the nations (12:1). Later, Isaac will send Jacob back to Rebekah's family to marry one of his cousins (28:1-2). Still later, the law will expressly forbid marriage to Gentiles: "Do not intermarry with them . . ." (Deut. 7:3; cf. Ezra 10; Neh. 13:23-27; cf. the NT, 2 Cor. 6:14-18 and 1 Cor. 7:39).

But the servant immediately spots a problem in Abraham's request: "Perhaps the woman may not be willing to follow me to this land; must I then take your son back to the land from which you came?" (v. 5). This is a good question. Which young woman would wish to leave her father and mother, her family and friends, and follow a stranger to some distant land to marry an unknown man? But Abraham is adamant that the servant not take Isaac back to Mesopotamia. The promise of the *land* is at stake. Isaac is to raise his family in the Promised Land. "See to it that you do not take my son back there" (v. 6, repeated in v. 8).

What an impossible assignment the servant faces: to travel over four hundred miles to find a woman who is related to Abraham and who is willing to go back to Canaan with the servant in order to marry a stranger. But Abraham assures the servant, "The LORD . . . will send his angel before you, and you shall take a wife for my son from there" (v. 7).

With the assurance of the Lord's guidance, the servant prepares a caravan of ten camels, loads them down with provisions and gifts, and sets out for the distant country. After a long journey, he arrives at the city of Nahor and stops by the well of water. It is evening, and soon the women, as is customary, will come out to draw water. But how will the servant know which is the right woman?

The servant is a man of prayer. He puts out a fleece, as it were, asking the Lord to give him a clear sign of his guidance. He prays fervently: "O LORD, God of my master Abraham, please grant me success today and show steadfast love to my master Abraham. . . . Let the girl to whom I shall say, 'Please offer your jar that I may drink,' and who shall say, 'Drink, and I will water your camels' — let her be the one whom you have appointed for your servant Isaac" (vv. 12-14). It is quite a test. Which young woman will offer to go down the steps to the spring and haul up enough water for ten thirsty camels? This is a major chore! But it will also reveal something about the woman: she will have to be kind, hospitable, and not afraid of hard work.

"Before he had finished speaking, there was Rebekah" (v. 15). The narrator raises our hopes that she may be the Lord's "appointed" woman by informing us that she is related to Abraham, is very beautiful, and is a virgin (v. 16). But will she offer to water ten thirsty camels? Rebekah goes down the steps to the spring, fills her jar, and comes up again. The servant runs over and applies his test: "Please let me sip a little water from your jar" (v. 17). She gives him a drink and then volunteers, "I will draw for your camels also, until they have finished drinking" (v. 19). Ten thirsty camels! "The man gazed at her in silence to learn whether or not the LORD had made his journey successful" (v. 21). That is the key question in this narrative, "whether or not the LORD had made his journey successful."

The servant does not yet know whether she is related to Abraham. So after giving her a gold nose ring and even costlier bracelets, he asks her straight out, "Tell me whose daughter you are" (v. 23). She answers, "I am the daughter of Bethuel son of Milcah, whom she bore to Nahor" (v. 24).

44

When Abraham's servant hears that she is a niece of Abraham, he worships the Lord and says, "Blessed be the Lord, the God of my master Abraham, who has not forsaken his steadfast love and his faithfulness toward my master. As for me, the Lord has led me on the way to the house of my master's kin" (vv. 26-27).

"The Lord has led me." The narrator clearly highlights the Lord's providence in this search for a wife for Isaac. Rebekah is literally a Godsend. Abraham testified that the Lord would send his angel to guide the servant. The servant himself prayed at the well for the Lord's guidance. And now the servant testifies openly, "The Lord has led me on the way to the house of my master's kin" (v. 27). But there are still more hurdles to overcome. Will Rebekah be willing to leave her family and go with a stranger on a long journey in order to marry an unknown man? And will Rebekah's family be willing to let her go?

Rebekah runs off to let her family know about the stranger she met by the well. When her brother Laban sees the gold nose ring and bracelets (v. 30), he is very interested. Since Laban has an eye for wealth (cf. 31:7), he can hardly wait for his sister to finish her story. He rushes out to the well and finds the servant "standing by the camels" (v. 30). Only superrich people had camels. Laban welcomes the stranger with open arms, takes him home, even unloads the camels for him (v. 32), and offers a fine meal.

But before the servant will eat, he insists on telling Rebekah's family about his errand. He is now going to have to convince them to let their beautiful daughter Rebekah go with him to a distant, foreign land to marry a total stranger. Astutely, he begins by telling them about the riches of Abraham: "The Lord has greatly blessed my master [cf. v. 1], and he has become wealthy; he has given him flocks and herds, silver and gold, male and female slaves, camels and donkeys. And Sarah my master's wife bore a son to my master when she was old; and he has given him all that he has" (vv. 35-36). There it is: by marrying Isaac, Rebekah will not be marrying a pauper. Then the servant repeats the whole story of the Lord's divine guidance: from Abraham's assurance that "the Lord . . . will send his angel with you and make your way successful" (v. 40), to his prayer at the well that the Lord would make his way "successful" (v. 42) and the test he devised to discover which woman the Lord had "appointed" (v. 44), to Rebekah's passing the test with flying colors, to his final prayer acknowledging the Lord's guidance (vv. 45-48).

In response, even Laban and Bethuel must testify, "The thing comes from the Lord. . . . Look, Rebekah is before you, take her and go, and let her be the wife of your master's son, as the Lord has spoken" (vv. 50-51). Hearing this, the servant bows to the ground before the Lord and then lavishes more costly gifts on Rebekah and presents a bride-price to her family. Business having been taken care of, it is time to eat.

The next morning the servant wishes to return with Rebekah to his master. But another problem crops up. Rebekah's brother and mother ask for a delay of at least ten days. But the servant insists on leaving right away, again appealing to the Lord's guidance: "Do not delay me, since the LORD has made my journey successful . . ." (v. 56). Rebekah is called in to decide the issue: either leave right away for a foreign land and an unknown husband or stay with her family at least another ten days. How will she respond? The relatives ask her, "Will you go with this man?" And much like Abram went when God called him to go (12:1, 4), she says, "I will go" (v. 58, see the Hebrew).

Rebekah's relatives honor her decision and send her away with the blessing,

> May you, our sister, become thousands of myriads;
> may your offspring gain possession of the gates of their foes.
>
> (v. 60; cf. 22:17)

After a long journey Rebekah and the servant arrive in Canaan. When Rebekah sees a man walking toward them, she quickly dismounts, and hearing that this is Isaac, her future husband, she covers herself with her veil. The servant tells Isaac all that has happened. And Isaac also acknowledges that this is from the Lord, for he brings her "into his mother Sarah's tent. He took Rebekah, and she became his wife; and he loved her. So Isaac was comforted after his mother's death" (v. 67). Sarah's tent is occupied again. There is again a mother for Israel.

In preaching this story, we must be careful to avoid the moralizing of character-imitation preaching. Avoid applications such as: like Abraham, believing parents today must warn their children against marrying unbelievers; or, like the servant, we must be people of prayer, set up a test, and follow the Lord's leading; or, like Rebekah, we must be friendly, help strangers, work hard, and respond positively to the Lord's call to go; or, like Isaac, a groom must love his bride. These applications are not unbiblical, but they have nothing to do with the point of this text; in fact, these applications will obscure the point of this text in the sermon.

We should ask, how did the narrator intend Israel to hear this story? He has clearly laid out the track: Sarah's tent is empty; Abraham sends the servant on an impossible mission; in answer to prayer the Lord leads him straight to Rebekah; the Lord inclines Rebekah's heart to say, "I will go"; he inclines her relatives' hearts to let her go with their blessing; he brings another ancestress into Sarah's tent; and he unites Isaac and Rebekah in love. In case we missed the theme of God's providence, the narrator manages to repeat four times the phrase "the LORD made his journey successful" (vv. 21, 40, 42, 56). The Lord led the servant and gently molded the hearts of Rebekah and her family so that his plan was accomplished. The Lord's providence!

But this is not a sermon about the doctrine of providence in general. The story begins with Sarah's tent being empty, and it ends with Sarah's tent being occupied. We might phrase the theme of this narrative somewhat as follows: In his inscrutable providence, the Lord provides another mother for Israel. As Israel later heard this story, it must have reminded them of the greatness of the Lord, "the God of heaven and earth" (v. 3; cf. v. 7), who accomplishes his plan not only through mighty miracles as in Egypt, but who also gently molds and shapes the hearts and wills of people to accomplish his plan (see Gerhard von Rad's Genesis commentary). And his plan was, in this instance, to provide another ancestress for Israel. It is only due to the Lord's mysterious providence in the distant past that the nation of Israel exists. What gratitude to the all-wise, faithful covenant God Israel must have felt.

In the fullness of time, in his inscrutable providence, the Lord provides more than an ancestress to accomplish his plan of salvation: "God so loved the world that he gave his only *Son,* so that everyone who believes in him may not perish but have eternal life" (John 3:16). As Israel saw its existence as the fruit of God's providence in the distant past, so the church sees its existence as the fruit of God's providence in the distant past — going back all the way to the time of Abraham and Sarah (Gal. 3:29) and Isaac and Rebekah, but more immediately to God's sending of his Son Jesus Christ. If God had not sent his Son into the world, there would not have been a New Testament church and you and I would not have been Christians. But because God sent his Son, the gate of salvation has opened wide not just to Israel but to all nations of the world. Today we are seeing the fulfillment of God's promise to Abraham that "in him all the families of the earth will be blessed" (Gen. 12:3).

How grateful we must be to God that in his grace he called his people into being, that he provided for their continued existence throughout the ages, and that we may now be members of this "holy catholic church" (Apostles' Creed). How thankful we must be that in his providence God not only provided a mother for Israel but that "he gave his only Son, so that *ev-*

eryone who believes in him may not perish but have eternal life" (John 3:16). In his inscrutable providence, the Lord guides his church and provides for its continued existence until Christ comes again to bring his kingdom in perfection. At that time, according to Revelation 11:15,

> The kingdom of the world has become the kingdom of our Lord
>   and of his Messiah,
> and he will reign forever and ever.

Sidney Greidanus

Eighth Sunday after Pentecost, Year A

First Lesson: Genesis 25:19-34
(Psalm 119:105-12)
Second Lesson: Romans 8:1-11
Gospel Lesson: Matthew 13:1-9, 18-23

This lection begins with one of the formulae on which the book of Genesis is structured (2:4; 5:1; 6:9; 10:1; 11:10, 27; 25:12, 19; 36:1[9]; 37:2; see also 10:32; 25:13). The formula — "This is the *story/genealogy* of" — introduces either a narrative which recounts the exploits of a main character (or characters) or a "vertical" or "horizontal" genealogy. Vertical genealogies list those through whom God is working to implement the divine plan. Horizontal genealogies enumerate all others who are being affected by the divine plan. In this instance, the formula introduces the story of Isaac and Rebekah, from whom will come the one who will provide the name for God's elect people: Jacob = Israel.

As the story commences, the forty-year-old Isaac has married Rebekah, whom his father Abraham procured for him in their ancestral land (v. 19; see 24:1-67). The daughter of Bethuel and brother of Laban, Rebekah was an Aramaean. Nevertheless, this is "family" (see 24:3-4).

As was the case with Sarah (11:30; 15:2; 16:1-2; 17:17; 18:11-15),

48

Rebekah was barren. But unlike Abraham, Isaac prayed in his wife's behalf, a prayer which the Lord answered. Three other times this same verbal form *(wayy'etar)* is used in the Old Testament, each time with the same positive result (Exod. 8:26-27 [Eng. 8:30-31]; 10:18-19; Judg. 13:8-9). Thus Rebekah's pregnancy was the result of divine intervention.

Still, the pregnancy was problematic. We are told that "the sons" *(habbanim)* were "struggling" in her womb (v. 22). Already we are informed that Rebekah is carrying at least two male babies. The "struggling" in which the womb denizens are engaged appears to be a vying for position; that is, each is trying to ensure that he will be the firstborn. How the occupants of Rebekah's womb can know the importance of being delivered first involves prolepsis: a situation in which characters can know something before it is logically possible. In any case, as we shall see, this same struggle continues till the day of birth (v. 26).

Before the birth, however, Rebekah is so distraught she seeks the Lord. Her distress renders her all but incoherent (v. 22: "If thus . . . why this . . . I . . . !"). At this point the Lord reveals the future. Rebekah is told that in her womb are two nations/peoples who will be divided from each other. But the division will be unequal, for one people will be stronger than the other. More surprising, the elder will serve the younger (v. 23), thus upsetting social conventions. This underscores a highly ironic feature of the story, namely, that it actually was advantageous in this instance to have been born second! Vying for position ends up being a disadvantage, since the Lord had other arrangements in mind.

At the same time, the Lord gives Rebekah no instruction. Is she to help implement this "prophecy"? Should she inform Isaac or the twins what God said? None of these questions is answered. As the story unfolds, Rebekah is the only one who knows the outcome. While she subsequently acts to insure that her younger son is ascendant, she does so with duplicity, deceit, and betrayal (27:1-17, 41-46).

Just as the divisions of which God spoke had been adumbrated in the twins' struggling, further division soon emerges. One child was born covered with red hair (v. 25; later we discover that his sibling was "smooth" [27:11]). The second child grabbed his brother's heel during the birth process (v. 26). The names of the respective children are related to these details (Edom means "red"; Jacob means "he grabs [the heel]" [the meaning of Esau is obscure]). When the children are grown, other divisions become apparent. Esau was a man who knew hunting — a man of the field (v. 27). Jacob's occupation is not mentioned. Instead, we learn that he was *tam*, a word often translated "quiet" or "mild." But the word usually means "blameless" or "upright" (see Pss. 37:37; 64:4; Job 1:1, 8; 2:3; 8:20; 9:20, 21, 22; Prov. 29:10; cf. Gen. 6:9; 17:1; 25:5-6). Presumably, translators have selected words like "quiet" or "mild" because in the unfolding story Jacob is hardly "blameless" (but he is not exactly "quiet" or "mild" either!). But *tam* is what Jacob is *supposed* to be as the child of promise and the one whose name will one day be synonymous with God's people. For now, he is *tam* only potentially (see Gen. 35).

Besides having the designation *tam,* Jacob is said to inhabit tents. Does this refer simply to Jacob's mundane lifestyle? Should we view the reference as a contrast to Esau — one brother spent time in the field, the other stayed around home? Or are we to see in these references a subtle connection to his father and grandfather, previous "sons of the promise" whose involvement with tents seems to transcend common living arrangements? Both Abraham and Isaac responded to the Lord's promise of land or progeny by *pitching a tent,* building an altar, and calling on the name of the Lord (Gen. 12:7-8; 26:24-25; cf. 13:3-4). Furthermore, it was specifically in a tent where the Lord appeared to Abraham as three men (Gen. 18:1, 2, 6, 9, 10). Later, in the account where Jacob acts as a religious reformer (Gen. 35) — and implicitly as *tam?* — he also *pitches a tent* and builds an altar when God reaffirmed the ancestral promise to him at the site where he had his first divine encounter (vv. 3, 7, 21; cf. vv. 14-15). Curiously, Esau is never associated with tents even though he was a man of the field.

A final division between the brothers is a function of family dynamics. Isaac loved Esau because "game was in his mouth" (i.e., Isaac enjoyed eating the game Esau caught and prepared [see 27:3-4]). But Rebekah loved Jacob. No reasons are given for her maternal affection. Was it because of what the Lord had told her? Was it because Jacob stayed closer to home? Was it to balance Isaac's partiality? Or was it some combination of these reasons? The text remains silent, though in chapter 27 Rebekah pulls out all the stops to make sure her son ends up with the best blessing. In any case, in the space of a few verses the picture is crystal clear that Esau and Jacob have been "divided" from the beginning.

In that light, the final episode in this lection is virtually predictable. The first time either of the twins speaks is when Esau returns from the field and finds Jacob cooking. He asks crudely to "let me feed myself with some of that red stuff." The verb is used only here in the Old Testament, but in later Hebrew is used of feeding animals! In any case, Esau, who is hungry (v. 29) but imagines himself to be starving to death (v. 32), is all "inarticulate appetite" (Alter) at this point. Being utterly victimized by his appetite, he foolishly agrees to sign over his birthright — his rightful familial hold on the future — to obtain food from his brother. Having made a pledge and sold his birthright, Esau eats hurriedly and in silence, and then abruptly leaves (see the succession of uninterrupted verbs: "he ate, drank, got up, and left" [v. 34]). In the narrator's judgment, these actions meant that Esau "despised his birthright," that is, treated it as a mere trifle. This "man of the field" is not a compelling figure.

But neither is Jacob, even though his ability to transfer his brother's birthright to himself puts him in position to be the bearer of the family's future. Granted, Jacob is smarter than Esau, quicker on his feet, more able to discern an opportune moment, but he is not the least bit fraternal. Why would he need *anything* from Esau in exchange for a bowl of food? Plus, Jacob seems almost to have been waiting to seize on just such an opportunity — asking a brother to swear over his birthright is scarcely a natural reaction to a sibling's request for a bite of lunch! In moral terms, neither brother inspires confidence.

Still, the difference between the two men is telling. Esau was utterly consumed by appetite and therefore could see no further than a single meal. For him there was no future, only a hungry present. By contrast Jacob, though not moral in any sense, was looking out for his future. Given these circumstances, Jacob's ability to exploit Esau was almost a given.

It turns out that the Lord's prediction (v. 23) about the fate of the twins came about in part by Jacob's selfishness and Esau's rash stupidity. Later, Rebekah and Jacob will conspire together to take Esau's primary blessing as well, even though this will require the betrayal of husband, son, father, and brother (chap. 27). Thus this episode cannot be read moralistically ("Cheat, exploit, steal, and God will reward you for it!"). It has to be read theologically. That is, attention must be paid to God's ability to work through circumstances that are ambiguous at best and utterly immoral at worst. Yet, in light of God's unfathomable grace, the divine ability to effect salvation through such unsavory means is not and cannot be diminished. Jacob will become Israel. Israel will eventually be the name of God's people.

Frank Anthony Spina

Ninth Sunday after Pentecost, Year A

First Lesson: Genesis 28:10-19a
(Psalm 139:1-12, 23-24)
Second Lesson: Romans 8:12-25
Gospel Lesson: Matthew 13:24-30, 36-43

Although the lectionary calls for the reading of Genesis 28:10-19a, the narrative unit includes Jacob's response to God's promises and thus extends to verse 22.

Jacob is on the run. He is running for his life. Jacob, "the deceiver," has gone too far this time. It was not enough for him to swindle his older twin, Esau, out of his birthright. When his father Isaac became old and blind and wished to pass on God's blessing to Esau, Jacob deceived his father by dressing in Esau's clothes and pretending to be the hairy hunter. Jacob received the blessing, but Esau was so angry he said he would kill his brother Jacob (27:41). When Jacob's mother, Rebekah, heard of this threat, she feared for the life of her favorite son and urged him to flee to her brother Laban's place in Haran. She also convinced Isaac that Jacob should leave Canaan lest he marry a local woman. So Isaac sent Jacob off with instructions to take as wife "one of the daughters of Laban, your mother's brother" (27:46–28:5).

"Jacob left Beer-sheba and went toward Haran" (v. 10) — a distance of over four hundred miles. Haran is the place where the Lord appeared to his grandfather Abram and told him to go to a land he would show him (12:4). The Lord promised to make of him a great nation and to bless all the families of the earth through him (12:2-3). Abram obediently undertook the long journey from Haran to the Promised Land and settled finally in Beersheba (22:19). Now Jacob undertakes the reverse journey, from Beersheba to Haran. Jacob flees for his life from the Promised Land.

Fear that Esau may catch him drives him on that entire day. Finally he must stop because the sun has set and it is rapidly becoming too dark to travel safely. Jacob quickly finds a level place and uses one of the stones as a pillow. He has traveled some fifty miles. Without knowing it, he has arrived at the place where his grandfather Abram, upon reaching the Promised Land, had built an altar to the Lord (12:8). But Jacob has never met this God. He had heard his grandparents and parents talk about the Lord, but Jacob has never met him. He has learned to take care of himself. Yet he must have been worried about the long, dangerous journey ahead: strange places and people, ferocious animals, and foreign gods.

Exhausted, Jacob lies down and falls asleep. Sometime during the night he has an awesome dream. God sometimes revealed himself and his plans in dreams — think of Joseph's dreams of his brothers bowing down to him (37:5-11); think of the dreams of the chief cupbearer, the chief baker, and Pharaoh (40:1–41:36). So God reveals himself to Jacob in a dream. In his dream Jacob sees "a ladder set up on the earth, the top of it reaching to heaven; and the angels of God were ascending and descending on it" (v. 12). It is not clear whether the "ladder" (Heb. *sullam*) indicates a ladder with rungs or a stairway up a temple tower (ziggurat, see 11:4). Whatever the case, the important point is that Jacob sees in his dream that heaven and earth are not two separated, independent worlds: a ladder links heaven and earth and God's angels are "ascending and descending on it."

Verse 13 is ambiguous in the Hebrew. The NRSV translates the Hebrew word *'alayw* as "And the LORD stood *beside him*" (with a footnote, "stood above it"), while the NIV translates, "There *above it* [the ladder] stood the LORD" (with a footnote, "There beside him"). Although good arguments can be made either way, the translation "above it" is to be preferred for two main reasons. First, the suffixes of verse 12, "the top of it" and "on it," both refer to the ladder. One would expect that the next suffix (v. 13) would refer to the same ladder: "above it [the ladder] stood the LORD." Wenham, in his commentary on Genesis 16–50, also points out that "the vision is described through Jacob's eyes, so 'over me' might be expected, if Jacob was the referent (cf. 40:9, 'before me')." Second, the context (v. 12) speaks of a ladder with its top "reaching to *heaven*," that is, the dwelling place of God. This tilts the translation of verse 13 to "there *above it* [the ladder] stood the LORD." The sovereign Lord speaks to Jacob from his heavenly throne.

Much more important, however, than the place from which the Lord speaks is the content of what is spoken. This is the heart of this narrative. The Lord says to Jacob, "I am the LORD, the God of Abraham your father and the God of Isaac; the land on which you lie I will give to you and to your offspring" (v. 13). The God of his fathers is speaking to Jacob and gives him the same promise he gave to Abram, "To your offspring I will give this land" (12:7). But Abram received this promise when he first *came* to this land; Jacob receives it when he is about to *leave* the land.

The Lord continues by extending to Jacob all the covenant promises he had given to Abram at various times: "Your offspring shall be like the dust of the earth, and you shall spread abroad to the west and to the east and to the north and to the south; and all the families of the earth shall be blessed in you and in your offspring" (v. 14). Amazing! Almighty God seeks out this fleeing scoundrel Jacob and tells him that all these rich promises given to

Abraham and Isaac are now for him. He has indeed received God's special blessing. And it is completely God's initiative. Jacob has done absolutely nothing to deserve God's covenant promises. It is all God's grace!

But God is not finished speaking. He has a special promise for Jacob: "Know that I am with you and will keep you wherever you go, and will bring you back to this land; for I will not leave you until I have done what I have promised you" (v. 15). As Jacob is about to leave the Promised Land and enter countries where other gods appear to rule, the Lord, the God of his fathers, promises to go with him and keep him safe. This is the specific message of this particular narrative: The Lord promises to be with Jacob, keeping him wherever he goes and returning him safely to the Promised Land.

Jacob wakes up and is astonished. He exclaims (v. 16), "Surely the LORD is in this place — and I did not know it!" Jacob is afraid, for he has received a glimpse of the sovereign God who rules the nations from his heavenly throne. Heaven and earth are not separated realms; they are linked. And the sovereign Lord rules both. Jacob exclaims, "How awesome is this place! This is none other than the house of God, and this is the gate of heaven" (v. 17).

At first daylight, Jacob gets up and takes the stone he had used for a pillow and places it upright as a pillar. He consecrates this pillar with oil as a shrine to the Lord. And he calls the place Beth-el, that is, House of God. Then Jacob makes a vow: "If God will be with me, and will keep me in this way that I go, and will give me bread to eat and clothing to wear, so that I come again to my father's house in peace, then the LORD shall be my God, and this stone, which I have set up for a pillar, shall be God's house; and of all that you give me I will surely give one tenth to you" (vv. 20-22). Is Jacob, the deceiver, trying to strike a deal with God with a conditional "If . . . , then . . ."? This is certainly possible, given his natural tendencies to strike a bargain both before this incident and afterward with Uncle Laban. It is not until Jacob has a second encounter with God at Peniel that he becomes a changed man and his name is changed from Jacob, "the one who deceives," to Israel, "the one who struggles with God" (32:28). One must also realize, however, that the "if . . . , then . . ." form may be a standard construction for vows (see, e.g., Judg. 11:30-31 and 2 Sam. 15:8): If God will do certain things, then the person who makes the vows will do certain things. In this case Jacob may be saying, "If God will be with me . . . and return me safely to the Promised Land, then the LORD will be my God, and Bethel (and the whole Promised Land) shall be God's house, and of all that you give me I will give one tenth to you."

In any case, the important point for this narrative is that in Jacob's vow the central message of this narrative about God's presence and protection is repeated: "If God will be with me, and will keep me. . . ." That was God's promise. It is a promise God will later repeat to Jacob as he instructs him to return to the Promised Land: "Return to the land of your ancestors and to your kindred, and *I will be with you*" (31:3; cf. 31:13). And again, when Jacob is old and has decided to bring his whole family to Egypt, God promises, "*I myself will go down with you* to Egypt, and I will also bring you up again" (46:4). The Lord promises to be with Jacob wherever he goes!

How did Israel later hear this story about father Jacob and the Lord's promise to be with him wherever he goes? Imagine Israel in the land of Canaan hearing this story. Hostile enemies are invading the country: perhaps Moabites, or Philistines, or Assyrians; all certainties are gone. Imagine the comfort: the Lord promises to be with Jacob/Israel. In fact, this theme of God's presence became part of the priestly blessing pronounced on the Israelites: "The LORD bless you and keep you" (Num. 6:24). Later, when the nation of Judah was fearful of being annihilated, God gave them a sign: "Look, the young woman is with child and shall bear a son, and shall name him Immanuel" (Isa. 7:14). The sign is, God is with us!

Imagine Israel in exile in Babylon hearing this story about the Lord promising Jacob to be with him wherever he goes and fulfilling this promise. The Babylonian armies had destroyed God's temple and violently removed God's people from the Promised Land and dragged them to a land ruled by the powerful Babylonian gods Bel and Nebo. Imagine the comfort: the Lord promises to be with Israel wherever they go. Even in Babylon, God is with us (cf. Isa. 41:10; 43:2).

In the New Testament, Matthew reveals the significance of the birth of Jesus by quoting from Isaiah 7: "'Look, the virgin shall conceive and bear a son, / and they shall name him Emmanuel,' which means, 'God is with us'" (Matt. 1:23). As nothing else, Jesus' birth shows that God is with us. Later, Jesus himself will refer to this Old Testament passage. When Nathanael meets Jesus and exclaims, "Rabbi, you are the Son of God! You are the King of Israel!" Jesus says, "Very truly, I tell you, you will see heaven opened and the angels of God ascending and descending upon the Son of Man" (John 1:49, 51). This is a clear allusion to Jacob's ladder, but notice that the reference to the ladder is missing. Jesus himself is the ladder. He is the link between heaven and earth, the mediator between God and humanity. As Jesus will say later, "I am the way, and the truth, and the life. No one comes to the Father except through me" (John 14:6). Through Jesus' death and resurrection the connection between heaven and earth, between the holy God and sinful humanity, is restored. Jesus is Jacob's offspring (seed) through whom all families of the earth will be blessed.

The church today may live in this confidence that through Jesus the connection between heaven and earth, between God and humanity, has been restored. We are not on our own in an evil world. God is with us on our journey. Even when the way leads through dark valleys of disease and death and down treacherous paths of opposition and persecution, God has promised to be present with us, to protect us, and to lead us safely to the "new earth, where righteousness is at home" (2 Pet. 3:13). Jesus promised his church even as he sent her on a dangerous mission to all nations: "I am with you always, to the end of the age" (Matt. 28:20; cf. Heb. 13:5-6).

Sidney Greidanus

Tenth Sunday after Pentecost, Year A

First Lesson: Genesis 29:15-28
(Psalm 128)
Second Lesson: Romans 8:26-39
Gospel Lesson: Matthew 13:31-33, 44-52

Although the lectionary assigns Genesis 29:15-28, the narrative is not completed until verse 30, possibly even verse 36.

This wedding narrative of Jacob has much in common with the wedding narrative of Isaac (Gen. 24). There the Lord had promised Abraham and Isaac numerous offspring (22:17); here the Lord has promised Jacob numerous offspring (28:14). There the narrative conflict was that Sarah had died and her only son Isaac was still single; here the narrative conflict is that Jacob is still single — unless he finds a wife and begets children, there will not be offspring "like the dust of the earth"; there will be no Israel. There Abraham told his servant, "You will not get a wife for my son from the daughters of the Canaanites, among whom I live, but will go to my country and my kindred and get a wife for my son Isaac" (24:3-4); here Isaac tells Jacob, "Do not marry a Canaanite woman. Go at once to Paddan Aram, to the house of your mother's father Bethuel. Take a wife for yourself there, from among the daughters of Laban, your mother's brother" (28:1-2). There the servant came to the well at the city of Nahor (24:10); here Jacob comes to a well where he finds shepherds from Haran who know "Laban, son of Nahor" (29:4-5). There the servant meets Rebekah, sister of Laban; here Jacob meets Rachel, daughter of Laban.

But the *contrast* between Abraham's servant acquiring a wife for Isaac and Jacob acquiring a wife for himself is even more telling. Abraham's servant was clearly dependent on and guided by the Lord: Abraham said to him, "The LORD . . . will send his angel before you" (24:7); arriving at the well, the servant prayed fervently to the Lord and set up a test to make sure he would bring back the wife "appointed" by the Lord (24:12-14); meeting Rebekah, "the man gazed at her in silence to learn whether or not the LORD had made his journey successful" (24:21); when he found out that she was a relative of Abraham, he "bowed his head and worshiped the LORD and said, '. . . the LORD has led me on the way to the house of my master's kin'" (24:26-27); even such unlikely characters as Rebekah's brother Laban and her father Bethuel confirmed, "The thing comes from the LORD" (24:50). The narrator's emphasis cannot be missed: in his providence, the Lord provides a wife for Isaac. But where is the Lord in the wedding narrative of Jacob? He is not mentioned, not even once. The Lord seems to be absent. Jacob, the deceiver, seeks to fulfill the Lord's promise of numerous offspring with his own ingenuity and scheming.

When Jacob comes to the well, he does not pray to the Lord for guidance but right away takes matters into his own hands. Jacob appears downright insolent. As soon as the shepherds tell him that Rachel, the daughter of Laban, is coming with the sheep, he tries to send the shepherds on their way: "Look, it is still broad daylight; it is not time for the animals to be gathered together. Water the sheep, and go, pasture them" (29:7). Is he the perfect shepherd or does he want time alone with Rachel? When the shepherds protest that they cannot water the sheep until all the sheep are gathered together, Jacob ignores their custom. As soon as he sees Rachel, he displays enormous strength by single-handedly rolling the stone from the well's mouth and then waters "the flock of his mother's brother Laban" (29:10). Then he kisses Rachel and explains to her that he is her cousin. Like Rebekah before her, Rachel runs home to tell her father Laban about the stranger, and, probably remembering the costly gifts from Abraham's servant, Laban again runs to the well to welcome this stranger to his home. But this stranger has no camels and is not loaded down with gifts. Still, Laban invites him to his home and hears Jacob's story (v. 13): deceiving his brother Esau and his father Isaac for the blessing, fleeing for his life, looking for a wife. Laban says, "Surely you are my bone and my flesh!" (v. 14). With these first words of Laban the narrator probably intends to reveal more of Laban's character than mere kinship (see Robert Alter's *Art of Biblical Narrative* on the importance of "the initial words spoken by a personage"); he probably signals that Laban and Jacob are cut from the same cloth (cf. 2:23): both greedy deceivers. In any event, Laban invites Jacob to stay and, having heard about his strength from Rachel, puts him to work.

After a month of observing Jacob, Laban knows that Jacob is a hard worker and that he is in love with his younger daughter Rachel. Craftily, Laban says to Jacob, "Because you are my kinsman, should you therefore serve me for nothing? Tell me, what shall your wages be?" (v. 15). As J. P. Fokkelman writes in *Narrative Art in Genesis*, "Wages and service — those are the two key-words which dominate the Haran phase [of Jacob], especially in regard to Laban. . . . Whenever a lord would like to take on a servant (and Laban would like to have Jacob very much) and with mealy mouth invites him to make the first proposal as to the wages . . . , there exploitation lies in wait." Before Jacob states his wages, the narrator informs us that Laban has two daughters, "the name of the elder was Leah," probably the unflattering meaning of "cow," "and the name of the younger was Rachel" (v. 16), which is Hebrew for "ewe." The narrator also provides some (for Hebrew narrative) unusual and significant character description: "Leah had weak eyes, but Rachel was lovely in form, and beautiful" (v. 17 NIV). Although the NRSV translates "Leah's eyes were lovely," since Leah is contrasted with the beautiful Rachel, it is more likely that *rakot* (soft) must be some negative quality. Wenham, in his commentary on Genesis 16–50, writes, "What makes eyes 'soft' . . . is unclear; most commentators think it means they had no fire or sparkle, a quality much prized in the East." But most importantly, "Jacob loved Rachel" (v. 18). So Jacob makes a surprisingly high offer (see Gerhard von Rad's Genesis commentary), which Laban cannot possibly turn down: "I will serve you seven years for your younger daughter Rachel" (v. 18). Crafty Laban readily agrees: he keeps the services of his daughter for seven more years, plus he gains the services of Jacob for seven years. Though Jacob pays a high bride-price, these seven years seem but a few days to Jacob because he is madly in love with the beautiful Rachel (v. 20).

When the seven years are up, Jacob demands that Laban give him Rachel as his wife. "Normally, a wedding involved processions to and from the bride's house, a reading of the marriage contract, and a large meal attended by both families and neighbors," Wenham writes in his commentary. "The first day's celebration ended with the groom wrapping his cloak around the bride, who was veiled throughout the ceremony (24:65), and taking her to the nuptial chamber where the marriage was consummated." But Laban fools Jacob by substituting the plain Leah for Rachel. Jacob never notices: the bride is veiled, the night is dark, and the groom is probably slightly intoxicated. "When morning came, it was Leah!" (v. 25). We can imagine Jacob's shock. The deceiver was deceived, and by the same trick he had used on his blind father. Jacob had pretended to be his older brother Esau; now Leah has pretended to be her younger sister Rachel. But Laban is behind it all.

Jacob immediately confronts Laban: "What is this you have done to me? Did I not serve you for Rachel? Why then have you deceived me?" (v. 25). But Laban does not bat an eye; he simply asserts, "This is not done in our country — giving the younger before the firstborn" (v. 26). You, Jacob, may have put yourself in front of the firstborn Esau, but in our country this (deception) is not done! In Uncle Laban, Jacob has met his match. Jacob had tricked his father Isaac into giving him the blessing of the firstborn. Now Laban has tricked Jacob into marrying the firstborn, Leah. But Laban agrees to have Jacob marry his beloved Rachel as well: wait one week till the honeymoon with Leah is over, marry Rachel, and then serve me another seven years (v. 27). Jacob has no choice. He has been outmaneuvered. Having agreed originally to work seven years for Rachel, he can hardly haggle about the bride-price at this point, though it is very steep. Jacob agrees and after one week with Leah also marries her younger sister Rachel. "So Jacob went in to Rachel also, and he loved Rachel more than Leah. He served Laban for another seven years" (v. 30). The words "he loved Rachel more than Leah" do not bode well for the tranquility of this family, as the sequel will show. And "he served Laban for another seven years." But these years do not fly by like a few days for Jacob. They are long, difficult years. His father-in-law Laban has become his adversary, and with two wives and their maids, there is constant tension in his household (see 30:8). Jacob has made a mess of his life. And still no word about the Lord.

But the Lord is not absent. We see this in the sequel. "When the LORD saw that Leah was unloved, he opened her womb; but Rachel was barren" (v. 31). The Lord has a habit of lifting up "the lowly" (see Luke 1:52). And Leah testifies to the Lord's faithfulness: "Leah conceived and bore a son, and she named him Reuben; for she said, 'Because the LORD has looked on my affliction; surely now my husband will love me'" (v. 32). Leah conceives a second son, and again acknowledges the Lord as the giver, naming the son Simeon (v. 33). Leah conceives a third son, naming him Levi. Then she conceives a fourth son and says, "This time I will praise the LORD" — and she names him Judah (v. 35). Leah, the unloved wife, gives birth to the forebears of four important tribes in Israel — one of these, the tribe of Levi, will serve the Lord in his temple; another, the tribe of Judah, will bring forth the royal line of kings like David and Solomon and finally the Messiah. As Leah gives birth to these future patriarchs, she testifies to the Lord's leading even through human deception.

How would Israel later hear this story? There are twelve tribes, and all twelve can trace their origin to the marriages of Jacob to Leah and Rachel and their two maids. They would clearly hear the message that the faithful covenant God works even through human deception and scheming to fulfill his promise to Jacob of numerous offspring. The narrator wishes to assure later Israel that the Lord's plan for salvation is not derailed by human failings; the amazing fact is that the sovereign Lord fulfills his promises even using human deception.

In the fullness of time, the Messiah would be born of the tribe of Judah, the son of the unloved Leah. In writing his Gospel, Matthew begins with Jesus' genealogy: "Abraham was the father of Isaac, and Isaac the father of Jacob, and Jacob the father of Judah and his brothers, and Judah the father of Perez and Zerah by Tamar, and Perez the father of . . . Joseph the husband of Mary, of whom Jesus was born, who is called the Messiah" (Matt. 1:2-16). Through this long list of names, Matthew reminds us of human sin and deception, particularly with names like Judah and Tamar (Gen. 38), and David and "the wife of Uriah" (2 Sam. 11). But through it all, God accomplishes his plan and the Savior of the world is born. Jesus, too, will be deceived by people: his own disciple, Judas, will sell him for thirty pieces of silver and betray him with a kiss. But God uses that betrayal to accomplish his plan of salvation (see Matt. 26:24).

Today we often wonder where God is when people deceive each other. Nations go to war and kill the innocents; Christians are persecuted and killed; children are abused. Is God absent? Is he not aware of what is going on? The wedding narrative of Jacob tells us that God is not absent and that he is aware of what is going on. But God has also given humans the freedom and responsibility to plan and to act. Because we are sinful creatures, we often mess up. But even then, we can be sure that somehow the sovereign Lord will fulfill his purposes also through our failings. Because Jesus Christ has come, "we know that all things work together for good for those who love God, who are called according to his purpose" (Rom. 8:28).

Sidney Greidanus

Eleventh Sunday after Pentecost, Year A

First Lesson: Genesis 32:22-31
(Psalm 17:1-7, 15)
Second Lesson: Romans 9:1-5
Gospel Lesson: Matthew 14:13-21

Jacob, the conniving trickster and ancestor of Israel, encounters God in two separate instances, once when he is fleeing from Canaan in Genesis 28:10-17 and a second time when he is returning home to Canaan in Genesis 32. These two scenes of divine encounter form the pivotal transition points within the story of Jacob, which runs from Genesis 25 to 36. The occasion for Jacob's fleeing from Canaan in Genesis 28 is a threat against his life by his twin brother, Esau. Jacob had tricked his brother Esau out of his birthright (25:29-34) and out of their father's "blessing" (Heb. *berakah*), which rightfully belonged to Esau as the eldest son (Gen. 27). The text reports that "Esau hated Jacob," and Esau resolves within himself that "I will kill my brother Jacob" (27:41).

Because of the threat to his life from Esau, Jacob leaves his home and family in Canaan and makes a new life with the family of his uncle Laban in Haran in Mesopotamia, the native birthplace of Abraham and Sarah. While Jacob is in Haran, God is with Jacob and blesses him richly with wives and children and much livestock. After many years, Jacob finally resolves to return home to Canaan. As Jacob crosses the Jordan River into Canaan, he prays the longest prayer in all of Genesis (32:9-12). He begs God, "Deliver me from the hand of my brother Esau, for I am afraid of him; he may come and kill us all" (32:11). The day before the brothers' reunion, Jacob sends his servants with several herds of livestock as a present for Esau, offering him a total of 580 goats, sheep, donkeys, cows, and camels. Then we come to the mysterious scene in this Sunday's text, Jacob's wrestling match with God.

The narrative begins in 32:22-23 with Jacob sending all his wives and children and everything he owned across the ford at the Jabbok. Jacob is left alone, solitary and stripped of everything dear to him. With Jacob alone on the other side of the river, suddenly out of the nighttime darkness, "a man wrestled with him until daybreak" (v. 24). Amazingly, Jacob holds his own; "the man saw that he did not prevail" (v. 25). But suddenly, all is reversed. "The man" touches the hollow of Jacob's thigh, and in a moment Jacob is lying there helpless and crippled. Now with the desperate grip of one who has been defeated, Jacob will not let "the man" go "unless you bless me." But this blessing will come not through the wit or strength of Jacob. It will come to Jacob as a gift given to one who has used up all his own strength and resources and been defeated. Jacob's name is changed to Israel, which in Hebrew means "the one who wrestles with God." Jacob asks "the man" for his name, but the man deflects the question with another question, "Why do you ask my name?" And then "the man" blesses Jacob and disappears.

Now that Jacob has been named Israel, he does some naming of his own. He names the place Peniel, which means "Face of God," for, he says, "I have seen God face to face, and yet my life is preserved" (v. 30). For the first time, we now know the true identity of "the man" who wrestled Jacob — it is God. And Jacob arises from this divine encounter with a blessing, a new name, and the sun rising on a new day. But he walks away also with a limp — a reminder of the cost of wrestling with God. God is here the beloved enemy, the one who blesses us and wrestles with us at the same time.

This mysterious narrative has generated a wide variety of interpretations in the history of its reception over the centuries. Hosea 12:2-4 interprets the story of Jacob's wrestling with God as part of Jacob's punishment for his misdeeds. The earliest Christian interpretations suggested that the story is really about how an angel was trying to bring Jacob back to faith. Form critics reconstructed the earliest oral version of the story as a tale of a hero named Jacob who wrestled and overcame a river demon, which made it safe for him and his ancestors to cross the river at the ford.

More recently, some have offered a psychological interpretation which views "the man" that Jacob was wrestling as actually Jacob's own inner ego. Jacob is a narcissistic individual who is struggling within himself toward psychological wholeness.

However, a better starting point for interpretation may be the three etiologies or explanations for the origins of things within the story. The first is that Israelites are not to eat the sinew of the hip or the sciatic nerve of any animal because this part of the body was touched by the divine hand of the one who wrestled Jacob (v. 32). The second is the name of the place called Peniel or Penuel, meaning "Face of God." The place became a holy site, and the story explained the significance of its name. The third etiology or explanation is the change of Jacob's name to Israel, which means "the one who wrestles or strives with God." While the first two etiologies reflect earlier stages in the development of the story which were preserved into the final form, it is the third etiology within the larger story of the people of Israel in the Old Testament that takes precedence. With the change from the individual name Jacob to the name that came to be used for the whole people of God, Israel, the story renders the figure of Jacob as a metaphor for the experience of the people of Israel with God throughout their history. Jacob does not get away free and unchanged from his encounter with God. He has gotten away with stealing the blessing from his father Isaac, his brother Esau, and his uncle and father-in-law Laban. But not from God! Jacob's limping becomes a metaphor or paradigm of Israel's life with God. Israel, like Jacob, will struggle and wrestle with God for the blessing. God will promise and give blessing to Israel, but God will also struggle to tame and break the unruly and often disobedient Israel.

The story's meanings expand further in light of the narrative that follows. After the dramatic wrestling match and after crossing the river Jordan, Jacob looks up and sees his brother Esau coming along with an army of 400 men (33:1). The last words we have heard out of Esau's mouth were these: "I will kill my brother Jacob" (27:41). But in a scene that responds to Cain's earlier murder of Abel, Jacob and Esau come together and Esau "embraced him, and fell on his neck and kissed him, and they wept" (33:4). Forgiveness breaks the cycle of revenge, and reconciliation substitutes for murder. Just as Jacob is a metaphor for the nation of Israel, so Esau is a representative of the nation of Edom, which bordered Israel to the east. The twin brothers had fought already in their mother's womb like two nations at war (25:23), and Edom and Israel were at times enemies, especially because of Edom's aid to the Babylonians when they conquered Judah (Obad. 1-21; Ps. 137:7). Two notable themes emerge from this reconciliation between Jacob/Israel and Esau/Edom. One is that Jacob offers herds of livestock as a "present" or "blessing" (Heb. *berakah*) to Esau (Gen. 33:11). This word *berakah* (blessing, gift) is the same word used for what Jacob originally stole from Esau in the incident with their old blind father Isaac (27:41). The second remarkable note in this reconciliation story is that Jacob says to Esau, his enemy and his brother, "Truly to see your face is like seeing the face of God" (33:10). Both themes link up with the earlier story of the wrestling match with God in Genesis 32. There Jacob had for the first time received a blessing as a pure gift when all his strength and resources were spent. Now with Esau, Jacob is eager for the first time not to steal but to give a gift, a blessing to another human being, his estranged brother. Moreover, the motif of seeing the face of God links the two stories as well. As Jacob had seen the face of God in the struggle and reconciliation with the wrestler, so Jacob sees the face of God in the face of his reconciled enemy/brother who had sought to kill him. In both cases Jacob encounters the beloved enemy, one divine and one human, and emerges from the struggle with greater blessings and a more abundant life.

Dennis T. Olson

Twelfth Sunday after Pentecost, Year A

First Lesson: Genesis 37:1-4, 12-28
(Psalm 105:1-6, 16-22, 45b)
Second Lesson: Romans 10:5-15
Gospel Lesson: Matthew 14:22-33

A lthough the lectionary, because of time constraints, selects for reading only verses 1-4 and 12-28, when preaching on this narrative it will be better to read the entire narrative, that is, the whole of chapter 37.

The author of Genesis begins his tenth and final *toledot* ("account," "family history") with verse 2: "This is the story of the family of Jacob." This "account" runs through chapter 50 to the death of Joseph. Joseph, being the main character of this account, is immediately introduced as a young lad, "being seventeen years old," who was a "helper" to his older brothers in shepherding the flock (v. 2).

The narrator immediately zeroes in on the problem in this particular narrative: Joseph's brothers hated Joseph. It began when "Joseph brought a bad report of them [his brothers] to their father [Jacob]" (v. 2). Joseph was a tattletale who cast his brothers in a bad light. As if that were not enough, the narrator next relates that "Israel [Jacob] loved Joseph more than any other of his children" and "had made him a long robe with sleeves" (v. 3). The robe was a special dress coat — distinguished from a normal robe by its extra length and long sleeves. The robe was a symbol of Jacob's special love for Joseph. As Walter Brueggemann writes in his *Genesis,* "Jacob thereby designated his son as his special heir." But this favoritism increased his brothers' hatred of him: "They hated him, and could not speak peaceably to him" (v. 4).

The hatred of the brothers increased even more when Joseph shared with them his dream. The narrator emphasizes their increasing hatred with the inclusion "they hated him even more" framing Joseph's retelling of the dream (vv. 5, 8). Joseph said to them, "Listen to this dream that I dreamed. There we were, binding sheaves in the field. Suddenly my sheaf rose and stood upright; then your sheaves gathered around it, and bowed down to my sheaf" (vv. 6-7). The brothers immediately understood the meaning of the dream. Joseph was implying that his brothers would bow down to him; the "helper" would "reign over" them; the younger brother would "have dominion over" the older ones (v. 8). But this was completely contrary to custom. The brothers probably felt that their status in the family was threatened by this brash, spoiled dreamer, and they hated him even more.

64

But Joseph would not let up. He had a second dream, similar to the first. He eagerly told it to his father and brothers: "Look, I have had another dream: the sun, the moon, and eleven stars were bowing down to me" (v. 9). Again the meaning is clear to the hearers: the sun is father Jacob, the moon is Joseph's stepmother Leah (Rachel having died earlier [35:19]), and the eleven stars are the eleven brothers. All will bow down to Joseph. This time even Jacob rebukes Joseph: "Shall we indeed come, I and your mother and your brothers, and bow to the ground before you?" (v. 10). Ridiculous! And yet . . . ? "His father kept the matter in mind" (v. 11). You never know with these dreams. Jacob himself had met the Lord in a dream (28:12-17). Just wait and see what happens. But Joseph's brothers' hatred increased even more: "His brothers were jealous of him" (v. 11). Three times the narrator has mentioned the brothers' increasing hatred (vv. 4, 5, 8). Now he says they are "jealous of him" — the kind of jealousy that leads to severe punishment (cf. Exod. 20:5; Num. 25:11). The stage is set for a major confrontation.

The narrative conflict is generated when Jacob sends Joseph away from the safety of his father's house to check on the welfare of his brothers. They are pasturing "their father's flock near Shechem" (v. 12), some fifty miles north. Jacob has reason to be concerned about them, for at Shechem two of the brothers had avenged the rape of their sister Dinah by killing "all the males" (34:25). Shechem is a dangerous area for them. So Jacob sends his beloved Joseph. "Go now, see if it is well with your brothers and with the flock; and bring word back to me" (v. 14). We wonder, what will happen to Joseph meeting his hostile brothers so far from home?

Joseph undertakes the long journey from the valley of Hebron to Shechem, but he cannot find his brothers. A stranger finds him "wandering in the fields" like a lost sheep (v. 15). Joseph is completely helpless. How can he possibly stand up against his stronger, older brothers? But at least the stranger knows where the brothers may be found. He had heard them say, "Let us go to Dothan." Dothan is another fourteen miles north. But Joseph doggedly follows the trail to Dothan, still farther from home.

With verse 18 the perspective changes from Joseph to the brothers. This new scene places us in the brothers' camp and allows us to overhear their conversations. His brothers see him "from a distance." How do they know from a distance that it is Joseph? The long robe, of course, with the long sleeves. Seeing that hated robe is enough to make their blood boil. "Here comes this dreamer," they say. "Come now, let us kill him . . . and we shall see what will become of his dreams" (vv. 19-20). The dreams of Joseph still stick in their craw. By killing Joseph they think they can kill his dreams. By repeatedly mentioning the dreams, the narrator provides the clue to understanding the point of this narrative.

The narrative turns the corner to resolution with Reuben's advice not to shed Joseph's blood. As the oldest brother, he will be held primarily responsible for what happens to Joseph. Shed blood cries out to God from the ground (4:10). God will "require a reckoning" for shed blood (9:5-6). Reuben urges, "Shed no blood; throw him into this pit here in the wilderness, but lay no hand on him." Reuben wishes to rescue Joseph later and "restore him to his father" (v. 22). The brothers follow his advice, but first they strip Joseph of his robe — "the long robe with sleeves that he wore" (v. 23, note how the narrator slows the pace to highlight the robe). Then they throw Joseph into an empty cistern (vv. 23-24). Since a cistern is shaped like a bottle with a narrow neck, there is no way for Joseph to escape without help. And not a word in this narrative about Joseph pleading with his brothers (compare his pleading mentioned in 42:21). Joseph is completely helpless! And the brothers sit down to eat as if nothing had happened.

As they are eating, they spot in the distance a caravan of Ishmaelites. This provides brother Judah a way out of the predicament: "What profit is it if we kill our brother and conceal his blood? Come, let us sell him to the Ishmaelites, and not lay our hands on him, for he is our brother, our own flesh" (vv. 26-27). And so Joseph is sold to the Ishmaelites, also called Midianites ("Alternative designations of the same group of traders," according to Wenham's Genesis commentary; cf. Judg. 8:22, 24). Joseph is sold for twenty pieces of silver; "this was the average price for a male slave in Old Babylonian times (early 2nd millennium B.C.)," writes Victor P. Hamilton in his NICOT commentary. These Ishmaelites, significantly, take "Joseph to Egypt" (v. 28).

Reuben, apparently, is elsewhere when Joseph is sold and carried off. When Reuben checks the cistern and finds Joseph gone, he is distraught and does not know where to turn. What will he say to his father?

The brothers go back to plan A, that "a wild animal has devoured him" (v. 20). They slaughter a goat, dip Joseph's robe in the blood, and send it to their father with the message, "This we have found; see now whether it is your son's robe or not" (vv. 31-32).

Jacob recognizes the robe and falls for the ruse. "It is my son's robe! A wild animal has devoured him; Joseph is without doubt torn to pieces" (v. 33). Jacob, "the deceiver," who had deceived his blind father Isaac with his brother Esau's garments and goat's skin on his hands and neck (27:15-16, 23-27), now is deceived by his sons with their brother's garment and goat's blood. Jacob mourns for his beloved son and refuses to be comforted. He says, "I shall go down to Sheol [the abode for the dead] to my son, mourning" (v. 35). Father Jacob is heartbroken. He has given up all hope.

We wonder: Where is God in this story? God is not mentioned even once. But the Israelites who later read this story would have known immediately where God was. God does not have to be mentioned explicitly. Who else but God gives dreams that foretell the future? Think of the dreams of the chief cupbearer and the chief baker; think of the two dreams of Pharaoh (40:1–41:36). "Throughout the ancient world, and Genesis is no exception, dreams were viewed as revelatory, as messages from God," Wenham writes. "Certainly the narrator saw these two dreams as prophetic; the sending of two dreams guarantees their fulfillment (41:32)." Joseph's dreams of his brothers bowing down to him foretell God's plans for his life, as the brothers well understood. Their "Come now, let us kill him [the dreamer] . . . and we shall see what will become of his dreams" (vv. 19-20) is, at bottom, an attempt to kill God's plans. But Joseph's brothers are not successful.

The narrative continues: "Meanwhile the Midianites had sold him [Joseph] in Egypt to Potiphar, one of Pharaoh's officials, the captain of the guard" (v. 36). Joseph is taken to Egypt and is sold as a slave to Potiphar, who has close connections to Pharaoh. Even though Joseph will sink still deeper in Egypt by being falsely accused and imprisoned, eventually he will rise to the highest position in Pharaoh's palace and his brothers will come and bow down to him (42:6; 50:18). Joseph's dreams come true; God's plans are fulfilled. In fact, God's plans entailed much more than the brothers bowing to Joseph. As ruler of Egypt, Joseph will be instrumental in saving his father Jacob and his extended family from death by famine. As Joseph later says to his brothers: "God sent me before you to preserve for you a remnant on earth, and to keep alive for you many survivors. So it was not you who sent me here, but God; he has made me a father to Pharaoh, and lord of all his house and ruler over the land of Egypt" (45:7-8). Still later, Joseph reiterates to his brothers, "Even though you intended to do harm to me, God intended it for good, in order to preserve a numerous people, as he is doing today" (50:20).

The central message of this narrative, therefore, is that the sovereign God can use even the evil deeds of Joseph's brothers to accomplish his plan of salvation. The sovereign God overrules the evil intentions of people to accomplish his goal. In this case God used the evil deeds of Joseph's brothers to keep alive his people Israel — the people out of whom the Messiah would be born. Later Israel celebrated this episode of her history in Psalm 105:16-22. It spoke to them of God's sovereign guidance of his people and of his covenant faithfulness.

O give thanks to the LORD, call on his name,
>   make known his deeds among the peoples.   (Ps. 105:1)

In its history, Israel was frequently perplexed by the evil that befell them. Where is God? This story about Joseph gave them comfort: no matter how dark the circumstances, God is in control! He can overrule the evil deeds of people and accomplish his plan of salvation.

The New Testament story of Jesus has many parallels to the Joseph story, the main one being that Jesus' kin also plotted to kill him. But whereas Joseph remained alive, Jesus died. Was this the end of God's plan of salvation? By no means. Just as God used the evil deeds of Joseph's brothers to save his people, so God used the evil deeds of Jesus' kin to save his people from their sins. Jesus' death accomplished our atonement (Rom. 5:10). The sovereign God overrules the evil intentions of people to accomplish his plan of salvation. In fact, Paul says that "*God* put forward [Christ Jesus] as a sacrifice of atonement by his blood . . ." (Rom. 3:25).

God's people today are often perplexed by the evil that surrounds them and affects them: terrible hatred, persecution, injustice. More Christian martyrs have fallen in the twentieth century than in the preceding nineteen centuries combined. Christians frequently ask: Where is God? How can he allow this evil to affect our lives? The story of Joseph offers them comfort: God is in control; even when evil seems to rule the day, God is in control and can use even evil deeds to accomplish his plan. As Paul writes, "I consider that the sufferings of this present time are not worth comparing with the glory about to be revealed to us. . . . We know that all things work together for good for those who love God . . ." (Rom. 8:18, 28).

Sidney Greidanus

Thirteenth Sunday after Pentecost, Year A

First Lesson: Genesis 45:1-15
(Psalm 133)
Second Lesson: Romans 11:1-2a, 29-32
Gospel Lesson: Matthew 15:(10-20), 21-28

The long narrative or novella about Joseph in Genesis 37–50 has often been used in the church as a moral story, furnishing us with examples of conduct. As Joseph learned humility, goes the saying, so should we. As Joseph forgave his brothers, so should we. As Joseph attributed his successes to God, so should we. Indeed, a few scholars have maintained that the story was originally used in such a fashion to instruct young princes in how to conduct themselves in the court of a king. By such usage, the material is often divorced from the realm of history and made equivalent to any other tale, such as an Aesop fable, whose point is to convey a moral lesson.

We are, however, dealing with history when we talk about Joseph. There is ample evidence of Israelite presence in Egypt at a very early date — even the name Moses is an Egyptian name. And many scholars have located the tale of Joseph in the period when the Hyksos, an Asiatic people of northwest Semitic stock, controlled Egypt, in the seventeenth and sixteenth centuries B.C. The patriarchs, Abraham, Isaac, and Jacob, during those centuries, were seminomadic clan leaders who lived with their people in tents and moved up and down the central hill region and southward into the Negeb of Palestine in search of seasonal pasture for their flocks. Occasionally, some of them made longer journeys into Upper Egypt or Mesopotamia. Camels were unknown at the time, and the forebears of Israel were, like Jacob in our Joseph story, ass nomads, migrating from place. It was a relatively peaceful time, presenting few difficulties to such wandering herdspeople.

On the Sunday that immediately precedes our text in Year A of the lectionary, the story of Joseph has been introduced, using Genesis 37. That reading has concluded with the jealous brothers' sale of Joseph to passing Midianite or Ishmaelite traders (37:28). But the congregation is unaware of Joseph's fortunes after that. In order for the congregation to understand our present lesson, therefore, the preacher will have to review briefly what happens to Joseph in Egypt. He is sold as a slave to Potiphar, the captain of the pharaoh's guard. When he righteously fends off the advances of Potiphar's wife, he is falsely accused of trying to seduce her and is thrown into prison. There his God-given ability to interpret dreams brings him before the pharaoh, who has dreamed of seven gaunt cows eating up seven fat cows. Joseph correctly interprets the dream as a forewarning of seven coming years of plenty followed by seven years of severe famine. He is therefore made the vizier of the pharaoh and given charge over all of the land of Egypt (41:41).

Canaan, too, however, is suffering under the effects of the famine, and Jacob sends ten of his sons down to Egypt to buy grain. When they appear before Joseph, they do not recognize him, but he of course knows who they are. Joseph sells them grain, but he also arranges an elaborate test to see if they have changed in character. He imprisons Simeon as a hostage and insists that when the brothers return, they bring with them Jacob's youngest son, Benjamin.

The story is a superb piece of writing, full of suspense and emotion. It describes Jacob's fatherly anguish; the brothers' long-hidden feelings of guilt over their lies to their father and their hatred of Joseph; the brothers' empathy for their suffering father, who fears he will lose two sons if Benjamin goes to Egypt; and the tearful attempts of Joseph to hide his emotions from his unknowing brothers.

As the final test of the brothers' character, Joseph hides his silver cup (a diviner's device) in the sack of Benjamin, and then accuses the brothers of stealing it, vowing to slay any brother in whose sack the cup is found. When the cup is found in Benjamin's possession, Judah offers to give his life in Benjamin's stead. Seeing this display of readiness for self-sacrifice, Joseph can control himself no longer, and at this point our text for the morning begins.

In tears, Joseph reveals his identity to his brothers. They are struck dumb with amazement and perhaps overwhelming guilt, but the unselfish Joseph hastens to reassure them. First he wants to know if his father Jacob is still alive, so that he may relieve Jacob's anguish also. But then he continues in an extended speech to his brothers. They are not to blame themselves for their deed of selling Joseph into slavery. It was not the brothers' hate that led to their deadly action. Rather, they were acting according to the hidden plan of God. "God sent me before you to preserve life." "God sent me before you to preserve for you a remnant on earth, and to keep alive for you many survivors. So it was not you who sent me here, but God; and he has made me a father to Pharaoh, and lord of all his house and ruler over all the land of Egypt" (vv. 5, 7-8).

Those statements form the central motif of the Joseph stories and are the reason for the inclusion of the Joseph material in our canon. They therefore should be the principal thrust of any preaching from this material. Everything that has happened to Joseph, according to his long and involved story, has not been the result of human initiative alone. Rather, the events have all been moved forward in the plan of God, who has been working silently behind the scene to preserve alive the forebears of his people Israel.

The question is *why*. The Joseph stories, like the rest of Genesis, are finally to be understood in the context of the promise God made to Abraham (12:3), and which was then renewed for Isaac (26:3-4) and Jacob (28:13-14). Part of that promise was God's guarantee that he would make of Abraham and his descendants a great nation. In the time of Joseph, however, Abraham's descendants are threatened with death during the seven years of famine. If the Hebrews die, God cannot keep his promise. He therefore works through the events in Joseph's life to preserve his Hebrew people alive.

The Lord's concern is not simply for the lives of the Hebrew people, however. God also promised the patriarchs that through their descendants he would bring his blessing on all the families of the earth. The Lord's concern in preserving these ancient Hebrews alive, therefore, is for all people. The Lord sets his love on the Hebrews because he loves all folk. And the Lord keeps the Hebrews alive in order finally to bring life and good to all.

It is the manner of the Lord's working in these Joseph stories which perhaps should capture our most careful interest. It is repeatedly said throughout the history of Joseph that the Lord is with him (39:2, 21; cf. 41:16, 38; etc.), giving him the success he enjoys in Egypt. Yet the primary arena of God's working is not in miraculous deeds or cultic manifestations but in his influence over the human heart. God uses the minds and emotions of the various characters to further his purpose — the bragging of the adolescent Joseph, the hatred of the brothers, the perfidy of Potiphar's wife, the forgetfulness of the chief butler, the insight of the pharaoh, the anguish of Jacob, and the guilt of the brothers. Through all of the very human turns of the story, God works his hidden will. It is not that God causes the evil happenings that take place; rather, he uses them to accomplish his own ends.

That may be very much like God's working in our time and place. Not many events that we call miracles take place. Rarely are there new and startling revelations given through worship. But nevertheless, the story of Joseph tells us that God is present and at work, using the seemingly secular events in our lives to move history toward the final goal of his kingdom come on earth.

Certainly that was also like God's working on that spring morning when our Lord was crucified on Golgotha. Seemingly it was a cruel and totally secular execution, wrought by the Roman government at the instiga-

71

tion of a maddened mob. But as Isaiah proclaims, "It was the will of the LORD to bruise him; [God] has put him to grief" (Isa. 53:10). God willed the crucifixion of his Son for the salvation of the world. He therefore worked through the hatreds, the evil, the sin of human beings and used them to accomplish his loving purpose. In our limited understanding, God was totally absent, and Jesus shared even that darkness with us when he cried out, "My God, my God, why hast thou forsaken me?" But God was there, and sin was overcome, and the resurrection was prepared.

Elizabeth Achtemeier

Seventh Sunday after the Epiphany, Year C

First Lesson: Genesis 45:3-11, 15
(Psalm 37:1-11, 39-40)
Second Lesson: 1 Corinthians 15:35-38, 42-50
Gospel Lesson: Luke 6:27-38

It seems clear that the reason we are asked to read Genesis 45 on this day is to illustrate for the Gospel lesson from Luke. "Love your enemies," intones Luke, and in Joseph we are to see a model of one who has done just that. As Joseph reveals himself to his astonished brothers in Egypt as their brother whom they thought long dead, and bids them not be "angry with themselves" for selling him into slavery, so are we to forgive those who have wronged us: "Do to others as you would have them do to you" (Luke 6:31).

But a preacher should resist such an easy connection between texts. Is the Joseph story merely a model for Jesus' famous command to forgive? It is seldom the case in the Hebrew Bible that the narrators of the great stories have simple models for our behavior in mind. How rarely they say, "Be like Moses" or "Act like David." In truth, the stories much more often say "You *are* like Moses" in your impatience, your anger, your unwillingness to follow the call of God, or "You *are* like David" in your self-love, your uncontrolled passions, your heedless lust for power. We are not to strive to be like the heroes and the heroines of the Bible; we are to strive to understand how we

72

too often are like them and attempt to understand how we can avoid or change our similarities to them.

The long story of Joseph is no exception to this general claim, however often he is made out to be a paragon of moral virtue. But if we are to preach from Genesis 45, we must know how we got to this place. Reading Genesis 45 apart from the whole story is like reading one middle chapter of a long novel or only a part of a whole poem. Just what did happen to get us to this point?

Joseph was the much-loved son of the patriarch Jacob. He and his eleven brothers joined their father in the land of Canaan, living the pastoral life of shepherds. Jacob, the favored son of his mother, Rebekah, soon played the same role with Joseph, the child of Jacob's beloved Rachel. To demonstrate his favoritism, he wove for him a marvelous long robe with sleeves, using a large amount of precious cloth to do so. Joseph wore his coat proudly day after day in the presence of his brothers, who soon took a deepening dislike of their young brother.

And if the coat were not bad enough, Joseph is too quick to tell his brothers the details of two dreams that he has. He has already proven himself to be Daddy's favorite by spying on his brothers on the old man's behalf (37:2), but the content of these dreams is too much. Both dreams purport to reveal that Joseph will be a great man in the world, before whom his brothers will one day bow. The second of them places Joseph a little less than God, as the sun, moon, and stars bow down to him, too! Even Jacob, smitten with too much love for the boy, is annoyed at the temerity of this latter dream (37:10).

Soon the other brothers have had their fill of the little twit. They met him far away from the protection of the doting Jacob and plotted his murder. But instead of killing him, Judah urges them to sell him instead into slavery. What profit will they get by killing him? At least his sale can generate a little cash for their pains. But before they are able to offer him to someone, some traders pass by. The brothers pull Joseph out of the dry pit into which they had thrown him, and sell him to the traders bound for Egypt.

In an attempt to cover up, the brothers take that contemptible robe, tear it into tatters, dip it into animal blood, and show it to their distraught father. Jacob concludes that his son has been mauled by wild beasts, precisely as the brothers hoped he would, and wails that he will never find comfort again. Meanwhile, Joseph has been sold into the service of the powerful Potiphar, one of Pharaoh's palace guards.

Joseph soon is put in charge of all of Potiphar's business; the Egyptian has only to worry about his own diet. Unfortunately, Potiphar's wife has a roving eye, and she falls quickly in lust with Joseph. He will have none of her, haughtily rejecting her advances. It is this scene that is often used to portray Joseph as an extraordinarily moral man. However, a careful reading of the text (39:8-9) suggests that his rejection of Mrs. Potiphar is more complex. He begins his speech to her by claiming his extraordinary power in the household, going so far as to say that even Potiphar himself "is not greater in this house than I am." Only after assuring the woman that he could do anything he likes, such power is his, does he say, "How could I do this great evil and sin before God?" It is the speech of a man who knows he has all the power in the situation; it is the speech of a man who is convinced of his greatness, a man of destiny. There is virtue here as well, but virtue is not all that motivates this man.

After Joseph rejects her and runs away naked from her, Potiphar's wife accuses him of raping her, and Joseph finds himself in yet another prison. Just as in Potiphar's house, he soon is running everything in the prison, and because of his wonderful way with dreams he eventually finds himself interpreting the dreams of Pharaoh himself. After his success, he is made second in command of the entire country. The slave Joseph has risen to an exalted height; the power he always dreamed of has come to him.

A famine grips the entire area, and Joseph's brothers are soon forced to travel to Egypt in order to buy grain, usually abundant in the land of the Nile. The brothers are led to negotiate for grain with a mighty Egyptian magistrate who is, we know, Joseph; the brothers, of course, do not know. The scene is important. "When Joseph saw his brothers, he recognized them, but acted like a stranger to them, and spoke to them harshly" (this last word is made from the word for "arrow" — 42:7). He brusquely demands to know where they are from and then accuses them of being spies, coming to search out the land's weak points in order to make possible an attack on the land.

This scene begins an incredible three-chapter assault on the hapless brothers. He first throws them all into prison, then forces them to choose one who will remain behind until they return with their new younger brother, Benjamin. That time their money is surreptitiously placed back in their sacks as they head back to Israel with their grain. Later, after that purchase of grain is exhausted, they must go back to face the mad Egyptian, and over the protests of a grieving Jacob, they take Benjamin with them. But the game of cat and mouse is far from over. After their second purchase of grain, Joseph tells his servant to place his favorite silver cup in the sack of Benjamin, and to run after the departing brothers to accuse them of theft.

Finally, after a heartfelt speech of Judah (44:18-34), we arrive at our passage. But now we may hear Joseph's cries with different ears. "And Joseph said to his brothers, 'I am Joseph! Is my father still alive?' But his brothers were not able to answer him; they were absolutely terrified at his presence" (45:3). We can well imagine the terror of the brothers; the very last human being on the earth that they expected to see was their long-forgotten brother Joseph. But why is Joseph's first question one about the health of his father? Could it be that Joseph knows that the cat-and-mouse game with his brothers would have a terrible effect on the aged patriarch, especially the part where Joseph demands to see Benjamin, Jacob's new favorite. Who better than Joseph knows the pain to be suffered by Jacob at the loss of a favorite?

Joseph's line at verse 5 is the most famous in the entire tale, beloved of preachers for generations. "Now, do not be upset or mad at yourselves that you sold me here; for the preservation of life God sent me before you." Is it enough to solve all of the complex plotting and games that have preceded these words to announce that God had a larger purpose? Do you imagine that the brothers are really only angry at themselves at this moment? Would not that anger and terror be directed at Joseph, the master puppeteer, who has led them on a merry chase for these many months, knowing full well who they were from the very beginning of their entry into Egypt?

Joseph has gotten a sweet revenge in this story. And it is not finally enough to say that God's will has been done. It is Joseph who has piped the tune, and his brothers have been forced to dance. No, the story of Joseph is not merely an illustration of how we are to forgive our enemies, as the lectionary might lead us to think. Joseph is a complex human being, like Abraham and Jacob before him, like Moses and David after him. Our human actions are never simple but are fraught with complex emotions and needs. The Bible's writers knew that fact better than any other peoples in the ancient world, and we do well to remember it as we evaluate our own actions in our own world. How are we like this man Joseph, bent on revenge, filled with our own power, yet convinced that we are called to act on behalf of God? That is the dilemma of the story of Joseph, and it is the dilemma of anyone who would be honest with self and God.

John C. Holbert

Fourteenth Sunday after Pentecost, Year A

First Lesson: Exodus 1:8–2:10
(Psalm 124)
Second Lesson: Romans 12:1-8
Gospel Lesson: Matthew 16:13-20

Exodus is undoubtedly the central narrative of the Jewish faith. Yet it begins, seemingly, without God. Picking up where the book of Genesis left off, Exodus begins with a brief family tree of Jacob's descendants, who are now living in Egypt. Of course, just that fact creates tension: God's people are now *out* of the land promised to Abraham. At least one part of God's covenant is now at best inactive (and at worst imperiled). Yet another threat appears on the scene in the person of a pharaoh who decides the Hebrew folks are a threat. So first he enslaves them, and then he begins a campaign of murder and terror by ordering the Hebrew midwives to do away with all male infants.

But where is God? Except for a brief reference to God in verses 20-21 (where God is said to give Shiphrah and Puah families of their own), God is scarcely mentioned in this lection and appears to be doing nothing. So where is God? What has become of the covenant? The answer to such questions is the key to understanding not just Exodus 1–2 but perhaps a great deal of life before God.

Because the discerning biblical reader is able to locate God in this text. Where is God? He is in verse 9. Pharaoh sizes up the situation of the Egyptians vis-à-vis the Israelites and declares (literally translated), "Look! The nation of the sons of Israel has grown much too big among us." *The nation.* Exodus 1:9 is the first time in all Scripture where the Hebrew word *'am,* or "nation," has been used in connection with the descendants of Abraham, Isaac, and Jacob! The people who could trace their origin back to the childless senior citizens named Abram and Sarai, the ragtag little cluster of people who came to Egypt many years earlier in order to benefit from Joseph's position in the government, have now grown so much that they constitute a nation.

Where is God in Exodus 1? He is to be found in the ordinary coupling of Hebrew men and women and the children those unions produced. Where is God? He's sitting on a birthing stool, the divine hands working in and through and under the blood-slicked hands of Shiphrah and Puah as they grasp the shoulders of newborn Israelite babies and bring yet another life into God's covenant people. God can also be spied in the brave resolve of those two midwives, who refused to carry out Pharaoh's "final solution."

It is striking that the names of these women have been preserved for us in Scripture. In the broad sweep of the Old Testament, it is mostly only the names of the very famous that are recorded (and almost all of even those names are of men, not women). Yet the author of Exodus was savvy in realizing that Shiphrah and Puah deserved a named recognition in the course of salvation history because it was indeed no one less than God himself who was fulfilling his covenant with Abraham through them.

But God's hidden presence in the text extends into Exodus 2. For there we read of the origins of the man who would go on to become the greatest leader Israel would ever have, and yet the story is strangely straightforward and simple. There is no miraculous conception by a woman who had previously struggled to get pregnant. No angels visit to predict great things for this child, and no divinely directed dream in the night gave Moses' mother or father instructions for how to keep the kid alive at a time when many of Moses' would-be nursery mates were floating dead in the waters of the Nile.

Instead we are simply informed that a certain woman got pregnant and, not surprisingly, did her best to keep her son alive. Oddly (though the oddness of this action is perhaps lost on many readers due to overfamiliarity with this story) the mother seemingly puts her child in harm's way by floating him in the same river that is proving to be a source of death for so many other children. Had the average Egyptian seen this baby floating there, he or she would have quickly concluded (as also Pharaoh's daughter will do in v. 6) that it was a Hebrew baby. If so, it would then be a pretty easy task to do in this child by tipping over this little watery basinet and drowning also this one.

Of course, it does not happen that way, and believers have long inferred the providence of God in preventing the death of baby Moses. But such a conclusion is indeed an inference, as the text makes no direct reference to God. So Moses is rescued from the waters of death, which to him become the waters of life, thus setting up what will become (in Exodus as well as throughout the rest of Scripture) the baptismal movement of salvation emerging from the chaotic waters of death.

Throughout Exodus 1 and 2 Pharaoh looms large while God seems in the background (at best). Pharaoh summons leaders, issues decrees, and gets results, while God appears to be doing no more than making sure Shiphrah and Puah get families of their own (a nice gesture, but hardly what the rest of the Israelites needed). Pharaoh creates terror while God seems to provide no comfort to help the people in the midst of this mini-holocaust.

Yet, in the mystery and riddle of faith, God is there after all. He's in a quiet mode, content to work behind the scenes through ordinary means of reproduction and birth, but he's there. (We could also note the irony that Pharaoh ordered the deaths of male children but let the girls live, apparently seeing no threat in daughters. Yet in Exodus 1–2 the *women* are the ones who set into motion what will prove to be the undoing of Pharaoh!)

Soon the power and presence of the one who would reveal himself as Yahweh to Moses at the burning bush would be brilliantly on display, but for the time being (and it was a very *long* period of many decades melting into several centuries) the fulfillment of the covenant marches forward in a most sublimely subtle way. It is not the first time God has taken this kind of tack — after all, the entire covenant got rolling with just that old couple living out in the middle of nowhere with neither children nor realistic prospects for progeny. Eventually the great-great-great- . . . grandchild of Abraham who will be hailed as the Savior of the cosmos will likewise not exactly take the world by storm — instead he will start in a manger and end on a cross. So, in a sense, Exodus 1–2 is a bit *more* typical of God than the miracles and plagues that will come later in this same book.

If we can strip away the layers of waxy buildup which our familiarity with these stories produces, we will likely recognize these narratives as desperately ancient — like some piece of parchment unearthed in an archaeological dig, so these stories threaten to crumble in our hands when we pick them up. (It is curious that when watching some cable TV special about the ancient pharaohs, we are struck by how very long ago and far away and just downright alien the 3,000-4,000-year-old Egyptian culture is. Yet when peering into Exodus, most Christians fail to have a similar sense of sheer antiquity.) But old as this tale is, it points to things which remain the same in all ages.

Like the Israelites languishing under Pharaoh's yoke, so also we may often find ourselves wondering where God is and why he doesn't do something more visible to wow the world with his grandeur. We, too, may wonder why the church looks so weak and ineffective compared to the power structures of the world. It requires faith, of course, to see God at all. But even *with* faith, seeing God's activity and the forward march of his purpose in this world takes practice, and maybe even some imagination.

Barbara Brown Taylor once wrote that as a child she loved those picture books which asked children to "Find the animals hidden in this picture." So she would stare at what looked like a drawing of an ordinary meadow, only to discover the outline of a zebra tucked into the leaves of an oak tree or to discern that the pile of boulders in the distance was really in the shape of an elephant. Children, with the eyes of their imaginations wide open, believe there can always be more to see than meets the eye. Christians believe the same. So faith seeks out the hidden pictures of God in our world, believing that God not only can be active in the most ordinary of circumstances but that he almost always is. Such marvelously disguised yet decisive divine work is the only reason we know about Shiphrah and Puah, Miriam and Pharaoh's daughter. The good news of God's providence is that precisely such folks are all around us today yet, too.

Scott Hoezee

Fifteenth Sunday after Pentecost, Year A

First Lesson: Exodus 3:1-15
(Psalm 105:1-6, 23-26, 45c)
Second Lesson: Romans 12:9-21
Gospel Lesson: Matthew 16:21-28

This text belongs to the broader class of prophetic call narratives (see Judg. 6:11b-17; Jer. 1:4-10; Isa. 6:1-13; 40:1-11; Ezek. 1:1–3:11; cf. also the Gospel lesson [Luke 1:26-38] for the Fourth Sunday of Advent, Year B). These accounts typically contain the six elements outlined below (taken from N. Habel, "The Form and Significance of the Call Narratives," *Zeitschrift für die alttestamentliche Wissenschaft* 77 [1965]: 297-323; see also Walther Zimmerli, "The Form Criticism and Tradition-History of the Prophetic Call Narratives," in Zimmerli, *Ezekiel 1: A Commentary on the Book of the Prophet Ezekiel, Chapters 1–24,* trans. Ronald E. Clements, ed. Frank Moore Cross and Klaus Baltzer with the assistance of Leonard Jay Greenspoon, Hermeneia [Philadelphia: Fortress, 1979], pp. 97-100). Moses is the first of the many figures who receive such calls; his call thus establishes the pattern for the rest. Here too, then, as elsewhere in the Old Testament, Moses' importance and paradigmatic stature are underscored. It should be noted that all of the call elements are complete by 3:12. The account in Exodus continues through 4:17, however, expanding the call with additional objections from Moses and responses from God. The lection itself ends at 3:15, right in the middle of the second of these objection-responses (which ends in 3:22). The homilist may need to reconsider, therefore, the precise delimitation of the unit used for reading and preaching.

1. *The divine confrontation (3:1-4a).* The opening chapters of Exodus (these should be reread) form the poignant backdrop for Exodus 3, which finds Moses in Midian where, exiled from Egypt, he now shepherds his father-in-law's sheep. One day he leads the flock far away — beyond the wilderness — and comes to Horeb, *God's* mountain. Things aren't always what they seem on this mountain! Here Moses meets the divine. The sight of a bush that burns without being consumed is certainly impressive (perhaps foreshadowing the fireworks to follow on this same site) (William H. C. Propp, *Exodus 1–18: A New Translation with Introduction and Commentary,* Anchor Bible 2 [New York: Doubleday, 1999], p. 222) and sparks Moses' curiosity and amazement. Yet it should not be missed that this encounter takes place *in the course of Moses' daily activities.* He is a shepherd, though of someone else's flocks; so, shortly, he will be called to become another (type of) shepherd, this time also of Someone Else's flock. This divine encounter also comes with no time to spare. God's people are in trouble (see 1:9-22); God has seen this and knows it (2:23-25). God must act, and God does so by showing up in a bush on a mountain on the back side of the wilderness. And to a man wanted for homicide, no less! The implications for vocation in this brief narrative, therefore, are obvious, numerous, and compelling.

The wilderness location of the theophany may also have ramifications. Might it be an implicit judgment of Egypt, critiqued as unworthy of such a theophany (see Martin Noth, *Exodus: A Commentary,* Old Testament Library [Philadelphia: Westminster, 1962], p. 32)? If so, this would be further evidence that Yahweh has no part in the oppressive policies of Egypt. He is outside of those practices and, quite literally, dead set against them. More explicitly, however, this encounter is part of the venerable tradition, found throughout Scripture, of the wilderness as a place of trial and test, but also one where God is made manifest to the faithful (see, e.g., Gen. 16:6-14; 21:8-21; Exod. 19; 1 Kings 19:1-18; Mark 1:12-13; cf. Gal. 1:17). God evidently likes to show up in the wilderness, right where we least expect it, but right where (and when) we need it most. Such is the case for Moses, the wanted man, and for Israel, the oppressed people, in Exodus 3.

2. *The introductory word (3:4b-9).* God calls to Moses from the bush. Moses responds with the customary and attentive "Here I am" (see Gen. 22:1; 31:11; 37:13; 1 Sam. 3:4, 6, 8). God instructs Moses to remove his sandals due to the holy nature of the site (cf. Josh. 5:15). This detail is strange: it might be related to the old religious practice of baring oneself or parts of

one's body in the presence of the divine. Alternatively, it might be related to Near Eastern hospitality, which invited guests to remove their sandals before entering the tent (J. Gerald Janzen, *Exodus,* Westminster Bible Companion [Louisville: Westminster John Knox, 1997], pp. 28-29). If this latter option is correct, this God who cannot be approached too closely nevertheless bids Moses welcome and attempts to put him at ease — as much as that is possible in light of the awesome revelation that immediately follows!

Moses is informed that this God is none other than "the God of your father, the God of Abraham, the God of Isaac, and the God of Jacob" (3:6). This is the same God of those saints, the same God who made promises to them, who covenanted with them, who has remembered that covenant (2:24), and who — now — has come down to do something about it. No wonder Moses hides his face!

Yahweh's subsequent speech repeats many of the verbs found in 2:23-25: "observed" (NRSV; the Hebrew is emphatic: "indeed seen"), "heard," "know." The objects of these verbs are equally weighty, however. God sees the Israelites' *misery,* hears their *cry on account of their slave masters,* knows their *sufferings.* The verbs and objects combine to witness to a God of sorrows, deeply acquainted with grief (cf. Isa. 53:3).

And this God wants to do something about suffering. Yahweh intends to deliver Israel from Egypt, to bring them to a good and spacious land where there is freedom and plenty (3:8). This is all well and good, but *how?*

3. *The commission (3:10).* The answer is found in 3:10, though the parallel structure with 3:9 (not apparent in NRSV) should not be missed: "*Now, therefore,* Israel's cry has reached me. . . . *Now, therefore,* come Moses, I will send you to Pharaoh. Deliver my people!" What a non sequitur! The text has emphasized *God's* activity (seeing, hearing, knowing, coming down); why now the onus on *Moses?* Apparently we face here the mystery of God's calling (cf. Walter Brueggemann, "The Book of Exodus: Introduction, Commentary, and Reflections," in *The New Interpreter's Bible,* vol. 1, ed. Leander Keck et al. [Nashville: Abingdon, 1994], p. 713: "In one brief utterance ['Come'], the grand intention of God has become a specific human responsibility, human obligation, and human vocation"). The text does not answer *why;* it is not really interested in that theoretical question. The text is very interested, however, in the *what* of calling. The substance of Moses' calling is to stand before an angry and rebellious Pharaoh (and an angry and rebellious Israel!) and deliver "my people," the Israelites, from slavery (cf. Brueggemann, p. 719: "In our time, the notion of call has often been trivialized, institutionalized, and rendered innocuous as bland calls to 'obedience' and to 'ministry.' Moses, however, knows better than this. A right

sense of call (and its danger) derives from a right sense of Yahweh's intention"). Perhaps more deliverances would happen if the called were more concerned with the *what* of, not to mention *the fact of*, their calling instead of debating the *why*.

4. *The objection (3:11).* Be that as it may, the non sequitur is not lost on Moses. He objects; he is not up to this task. It is too big for the likes of him. Moses' "I" seems puny compared to the huge entities he mentions: Pharaoh, the children of Israel, Egypt. God will respond momentarily, but a critical insight should not be overlooked: the objection is a regular element of the call narratives. When people (especially prophets) are called in the Old Testament, they typically object. Objection is therefore an expected, perhaps even a *required,* element in any true call. These individuals struggled with their calls, disliked them, sought to get out of them. The same is true, no doubt, today. But if we emulate in complaint, we would also do well to direct our objections where they did: to the God who has called. This God is big enough to hear these objections. Of course, if that is true, then this God is probably big enough to respond to them. God's call is not one-sided, therefore, but quite dialogical. But once engaged in the dialogue, the called should be prepared to be convinced! (Note how Jonah, when called, doesn't open his mouth but just flees [Jon. 1:1-3]! He too, however, ends up in Nineveh, though the end of the book would indicate that he remains — to a certain degree at least — unconvinced.)

In the broader unit, this objection constitutes the first of several Moses makes (3:11, 13; 4:1, 10, 13). They tend to degenerate in validity, but each nevertheless serves to highlight or clarify a number of issues crucial for the rest of the story, including: the identity of the God Moses will represent (3:14-15), a strategy for the deliverance (3:16-22) and tools useful for that task (4:2-9), as well as promises of divine and human assistance (4:11-12, 14-17). Here too, then, just as in the Psalms, addressing complaint, struggle, and pain directly to God may actually help engender faithfulness in the long run.

5. *The reassurance (3:12a).* But Moses does have a point: he is a wanted man in Egypt after an ill-fated earlier attempt at deliverance (see 2:11-14). And yet the commission is in line with who he is: that episode in Egypt and the one later at the well in Midian (2:15-17) show he has deliverer in his blood. He is also apparently adept at shepherding someone else's flock (3:1). But God doesn't reassure Moses in these terms. Nor does God indicate that Moses is actually bigger than he thinks vis-à-vis Pharaoh. Instead, God promises simply to be with Moses. So, ultimately, this call really isn't about who *Moses* is. It is about *Who is with* Moses. This Exodus story is about a God

named "Jealous" (34:14) who will stop at nothing to redeem his firstborn child from a wicked pharaoh. Moses certainly plays a key part in this drama, but his isn't the only role, nor is it the most important one. Who exactly Moses is or may be is secondary. But God will be with him and will see to this task. That is enough.

6. *The sign (3:12b)*. Of course, it isn't enough, not for Moses at least, as his continued objections insist. But God also offers a sign to Moses: corporate worship on the mountain once Israel has come out of Egypt. This sign isn't expected: it comes not before but *after* his obedience (but contrast the signs in 4:1-9)! It is, however, a public sign that will authenticate Moses in the eyes of the people and convince them (and himself!) that indeed it is God who has called and delivered. The only adequate response will be worship.

But even after the reassurance and sign, Moses still hesitates. God's response ("I am with you") leads to another question: "Who exactly are you?" Moses couches this as a question he anticipates from the Israelites. That question may highlight Israel's *suspicion* ("And you met this God *where?*"). Even more likely, the question may highlight Israel's *despair*. After all, they had been in Egypt for a long, long time. Their God had not yet delivered them. Maybe their God couldn't. But the question may very well also be Moses' own (cf. 33:18).

Whatever the case, the importance of names in antiquity is crucial for understanding. Knowing and giving names often implied dominance (cf. Gen. 2:19-20; 17:5, 15). Knowing the name of a god or goddess allowed access to that deity, who could then be invoked, summoned, even controlled to some extent. Whether Moses was seeking *mastery* over God is debatable, but the question nevertheless seems to seek *certainty*. Whatever the case, both are rejected in the enigmatic name that God gives: "I AM WHO I AM" (*'ehyeh 'asher 'ehyeh*).

Much ink has been spilled over the exact meaning and significance of this name, repeated in shortened form in 3:14, not to mention the name "Yahweh" (English versions: "the LORD") later in 3:15. Philological analyses of the latter have been inconclusive and are deeply divided. There is no consensus on its meaning, though the two most prominent options are: "he who is" or "he who causes to be" (i.e., creates). Contextually, the narrative seems to connect the name "Yahweh" to the verb "to be" *(hyh)*, with God saying "I am" (*'ehyeh;* first person) but other speakers using the third-person form, "he is" (perhaps originally *yahweh?*). It is difficult to say more, as this is the only text that comments on the name in such a fashion and, with the possible exception of Hosea 1:9, the formula "I AM" is not used elsewhere in the same way.

83

It may be easier, then, to say what the name *does not* mean. Abstract, the-oretical statements of God's existence are not what Moses and the Israelites need to hear at the moment. Ancient peoples believed that lots of gods existed. Egypt had hundreds. And since the Hebrews served the Egyptians as slaves, they might have every reason to wonder if their God — whatever the niceties of his existence — was simply too weak or disinterested to help them. It is doubtful, then, that the name is intended to affirm God's abstract ontological existence. What, then?

Several clues present themselves. First, the name is replete with first-person verbal forms. God remains the Subject of this call. If Moses is seeking certainty or a name by which this Deity can be manipulated, then that is denied (cf. Gen. 32:23-33; Judg. 13). "Who am I? None of your business, Moses." But this cannot be the whole story, given the widespread use of the divine name "Yahweh." A second clue is found in the tense (imperfect) of the verbs used. This tense can be translated as present or future, but is typically used for incomplete actions. "I AM WHO I AM" (or: "I WILL BE WHO I WILL BE") includes, therefore, an openness — especially to the future. All that this God is will only become clear later, as the story — particularly the exodus story — unfolds. "Who am I? Wait and see, Moses. Wait and see."

So, in a very real sense Yahweh has both revealed something critical to Israel (the divine name) and, at the same time, retained his freedom and sovereignty, reserving the right to do more, say more, reveal more in the future. Israel and Moses will learn much, much more of this God as they see the Nile turn red, the sea pile up like walls, the top of Sinai aflame. This burning bush is just the beginning of what "I AM" will be up to. And yet this enigmatic name should also be connected to God's earlier promise of presence, as it is the same verb in the same form *('ehyeh 'immak)*. All that this God will be is not yet clear — has not yet been revealed — but Moses will never have to deliver alone again. He will now shepherd God's flock and will find himself accompanied and supported by the presence of this God who reveals and yet conceals, who is present and yet reserves the right to teach us and show us even more than we already know. A major component of that "will be," then, is that God *will be with* Moses. And if God is with him, then who could possibly be against him (cf. Rom. 8:31)?

Brent A. Strawn

Sixteenth Sunday after Pentecost, Year A

First Lesson: Exodus 12:1-14
(Psalm 149)
Second Lesson: Romans 13:8-14
Gospel Lesson: Matthew 18:15-20

T he reader of the story of Exodus is perhaps surprised when stumbling across this chapter. With its detailed instructions about the Passover sacrifice, it looks more like a section from Leviticus than Exodus. And this surprise is justified. From Genesis 1:1 to Exodus 11, there has been precious little legal revelation, this in spite of the importance of law for Israelite religion. By and large the reader has been treated to narrative upon narrative, many of them gripping in their plot and characterizations. Here, however, the restless advance of chronological time — as evidenced by the advance of the plotline of the stories about the patriarchs — comes to a momentary close, and we are plunged headfirst into the details of ritual enactment. Perhaps this should have been expected in light of the fact that we are now poised at the threshold of those events that will forever define the nation Israel: the deliverance at the Sea of Reeds, the revelation of the law at Sinai, and her formal adoption as God's very own special and holy people. Moses was commanded some time earlier to tell Pharaoh that YHWH had declared that Israel is "my firstborn son" (= my most treasured possession) (Exod. 4:22). Now that office of election is about to be formalized.

Law and narrative. In Judaism, religious devotion is demonstrated by the observance of God's commandments. Not by accident do we designate religious Jews as "practicing Jews" as opposed to the preferred term among Protestants: "believing Christians" (though by adding Catholics into the picture the matter becomes more complicated!). Though sometimes evaluated negatively by Christians, faithful maintenance of the law is not a means of *securing* deliverance ("works righteousness"), but rather a grateful *response* to God's saving (or, perhaps better, "electing") activity. This is entirely in evidence in the present literary context, where the observance of the Passover festival is an act meant to honor the gracious hand of an all-merciful God.

Israel's release from Egypt is not purely an act of "liberation," but liberation toward a specific end. Israel has left the tyranny of Pharaoh's rule, only to enter under the (gentler) yoke of a new king. The harsh and painful legislation of the one is exchanged for the life-giving mandates of the other. By fixing these mandates right in the middle of the story, the author taught the intimate connection between this past historical event and its ever present, contemporary reflex. The effect is not unlike that of putting the words of the institution of the Eucharist in the mouth of Jesus at the Last Supper. The Christian who subsequently hears that story can only separate the historical event from its ritual afterlife with the greatest of efforts.

There is another striking feature of the placement of the ritual. One might have expected that the laws for its observance would more naturally have come at the end of the tale. This would have allowed for a smoother reading of the exodus event. It also would have prevented the confusion as to what actually constitutes the difference between the circumstances of the first celebration and its future reenactment. Our biblical writer eschewed this option. Instead, the story of the exodus was severed in the middle, and anachronistic details like the Feast of the Unleavened Bread were set therein.

Yet this unartful "splicing" of the text has important theological consequences. As Brevard Childs has noted in his *Book of Exodus,* it sets up a profound dialectic between redemption as hope and redemption as memory: "The interplay in vv. 1-20 and 21-28 between the now and the then, between what is to come and what has already happened, is not dissolved after the event, but once again picked up and maintained in a new dialectic between the past and the future. Israel remains a people who has been redeemed, but who still awaits its redemption." This brilliant move, effected by the canonical editors, meant that biblical Israel and, subsequently, the Jewish people themselves (after A.D. 70) never had the option of viewing the exodus as a completely finished event. By placing the memorial for its observance just prior to the deliverance at the sea, those who continue to celebrate the rite in generations to come match themselves up with an Israel still awaiting redemption. And so our story's awkward narrative placement serves well to render the exodus event as both a past event and a present hope. No wonder this text becomes such a rich locus for eschatological expectations in Second Temple Jewish writings and in the nascent church.

The Passover. Behind the entire story of the exodus is a darker undercurrent of two worlds at war with one another: the world of power and nationalistic pretension as represented by Pharaoh, and the more mysterious but ever-sure guiding hand of Israel's God. Although Israel's God is ruler over all creation, the exercise of his power on earth has its limits. It is crucial to realize this to enter fully into the drama of the story. God does not simply transport Israel out of Egypt by divine fiat once he hears of their distress; he demonstrates to Israel and the world the nature of his lordship by a full-scale engagement with the powers that be. As Moshe Greenberg saw well, this whole sequence of plagues leading up to the event of "passover" was designed for a single end: the revelation of God's nature to Pharaoh, the Egyptians, and ultimately to all men and women.

At the beginning of the story of the plagues, we learn of God's overall designs: "I shall harden the heart of Pharaoh and multiply my signs and wonders in the land of Egypt. Pharaoh shall not obey you, so I will set my hand against Egypt and bring my host, the people of Israel, up out of Egypt with *great judgments*" (Exod. 7:3-4). What were those great judgments? Not the first nine plagues, but the tenth: "I will cross over the land of Egypt on this night and slay all the firstborn of Egypt . . . and against all the gods of Egypt I will execute these *great judgments*" (12:12).

The highly anthropomorphic quality of God as he appears in this tale lends tremendous power to the drama. How will he save the people he so treasures from such terrible circumstances? God's power to judge, once it is released, is imagined by our biblical writer to be ferocious in scope and not capable of making fine distinctions (no notion of a "surgical strike" here!). Once he sends for "the destroyer" (cf. 12:23), *all* who stand in his path, both Israelite and Egyptian alike, stand in danger. (This aspect of the divine personality is often neglected by modern persons; as a corrective, see the writings of Luther or Calvin on the topics of "the wrath of God" or "the unrevealed God").

God, in order to protect himself from himself, informs Moses as to how Israel can be saved from the coming cataclysm. "The blood [of the paschal lamb] shall be a sign for you upon your houses, and I will see the blood and *pass-over* [Heb. *pesaḥ*, Aram. *pisḥa'*; so our 'paschal'] you. No plague will destroy you when I smite the land of Egypt." As in many of the Psalms, when a supplicant implores God by fasting or other means to take note of his distress as though he were incapable prior to that moment, so here the blood of the Passover lamb is a ritual protection put in place to remind God of his promise to attend to Israel and not visit her with his punishing hand. In both the Psalms and in the story of exodus, the stress on these "limits" to God's being serves to underscore the *coparticipation* of human beings through prayer and sacrifice in the saving activity of God.

Firstborn. Finally we should attend to the theme of the firstborn. Egypt, because of her contempt for Israel and her God, is put to a severe punishment. She loses all her firstborn, both man and beast. Israel, it would seem, comes through unscathed. But lurking behind this tale is the ancient cultic notion that all the firstborn belong to God, and at any point he can, should he wish, call home his chips (on this see Gen. 22 and the recent work of J. Levenson, *Death and Resurrection of the Beloved Son*). Israel had earlier been designated as God's own firstborn (Exod. 4:22), and here at the Passover she formally assumes that position. Yet Israel's vocation as firstborn is not without its own cost. The firstborn of Egypt are "taken" off to a gruesome death. But Israel, as God's firstborn, is "taken" as well. She too is now the personal property of her God. And along with the privileges come the duties. To fulfill her vocation she must make the will of God primary over her own.

In the New Testament, Jesus Christ assumes the title of "Firstborn." In fulfillment of that office he offers his entire life in obedience to the will of his Father. But as with most of the honorifics that accrue to the Son, they are meant to be passed along to those who bear his image within the church. Several patristic writers were happy to identify the moment of baptism as the time when individual Christians were adopted into the divine family as firstborn sons or daughters. As such, this interpretation closed a circle that began in the Old Testament. If sonship for Israel was initiated by passage through the saving waters of the Sea of Reeds, then sonship for the Christian was to be achieved through immersion in the font of baptism.

Gary A. Anderson

Seventeenth Sunday after Pentecost, Year A

First Lesson: Exodus 14:19-31
(Psalm 114)
Second Lesson: Romans 14:1-12
Gospel Lesson: Matthew 18:21-35

It is good to begin with the placement of this famous episode in the overall story of Israel's formation. In Genesis 11, with the building of the tower of Babel, God gave up, at least momentarily, on the nations of the world. The hubris in building a "city with its tower" led to the dispersal of humankind across the face of the earth and the multiplication of human languages so as to prevent their reaggregation. Enter Genesis 12, and the undoing of this process begins with the election of a single individual, Abraham, who will be the progenitor of a single nation. Through this one people, all the nations of the world will come into divine blessing (Gen. 12:3). Such is the promise God lays down. The election of Abraham looks toward Mount Sinai as it natural fulfillment, for it is there that Israel the nation is formally covenanted to her Lord and the promise made to the individual, Abraham, is given a corporate character. In between these two moments we have the plot of our story: the *descent* of Abraham's progeny into Egypt, their enslavement under the tyranny of Pharaoh (who, unlike almost all other foreign kings in the Bible, however evil they may be, is not graced with a name; an important feature to bear in mind, as Pharaoh is as much a cipher for evil as a flesh-and-blood human being), and their *ascent* from Egypt after a miraculous moment of divine deliverance that takes place against all odds. The language of descending and ascending is significant because its more natural home is in the Psalter, which speaks of descending to the nether-world and being drawn back up (e.g., Ps. 30:1, 9; 1 Sam. 2:6; cf. the Magnificat). The exodus is literally a matter of life and death.

Put this way, I think the purpose of the exodus becomes clear. It is not a legally binding moment like that of the promise to the patriarchs (on its legal force, see Exod. 32:11-14, where only the terms of this "contract" stay God's hand when he intends to slay Israel; Moses uses the promise to hold God accountable to himself), nor is it quite the formal attribution of identity to the people of Israel as God's very own. Although one must concede with respect to the latter, it comes very close to being such. Rather, what the exodus is, is the public demonstration to Israel and the world of just who this God, the Lord (YHWH in Hebrew), is. In this episode we not only see his mighty presence on full display, but by these very actions we see to what great extremes this God will go to realize the promises he had laid down in Genesis.

As we enter the story, both Israel and Egypt are unclear as to just what this God is all about. As Israel races out of Egypt after the slaughter of the firstborn, the Egyptians say: "*What is this we have done* sending Israel out of servitude to us?" (14:5). Israel, seeing Egypt in hot pursuit, nearly mimics these very words, though in a more acerbic fashion: "Is it because there weren't enough graves in Egypt that you brought us out to die in the wilderness. *What is this you have done to us* bringing us out of Egypt?" As the world accounts for things, the events seem stretched beyond capacity. Why should a great nation, a superpower in the truest sense of the word, be afraid of this mixed rabble of indentured laborers? Moses urges Israel not to fear but "to stand still and take in [lit. 'see'] the deliverance of the Lord" (14:13). And this is just what Israel does as the chapter draws to its close: "The Lord delivered Israel on that day from the hand of the Egyptians. Israel saw the

Egyptians dead upon the bank of the water. And when Israel saw the great deed which the LORD had done against Egypt, the people were in awe of their LORD and believed in their LORD and in Moses his servant" (14:30-31).

And their perception was not without effect. It issued forth in one of the most famous hymns of praise in the Bible (Exod. 15). Where there once had been doubt, now there was faith and praise: "Who is like you among the gods, O LORD!"

To appreciate the role of this public demonstration of God's capacity and will to deliver his people, let me quote a famous midrash about the same. It nicely positions this in relation to the next dramatic move in our plot.

> I am the LORD, your God [Exod. 20:2]. [If] the Ten Commandments [were so important] why were they not said at the beginning of the Torah? About this the Rabbis told a parable. To what may this circumstance be compared? To a king who entered a new territory and said to its citizens: "May I be your king?" the people replied: "What have you done for us that we should grant you the right to rule over us?" What did the king do? He built a wall around the city for them, he brought the water supply within the city and fought their battles. Then when he came before them again, [and] said, "May I be your king?" they responded, "Yes, Yes." And so God did for Israel.

The knowledge of the Lord is not limited to Israel alone. It is very much a part of the prophetic hope that the nations will come to know Israel's God, mend their ways, and find their way to Jerusalem in pilgrimage (Isa. 2:1-4; Zech. 14). This theme of "knowledge" frames the story of the exodus, though to a more tragic end. Consider these framing texts:

> Afterward Moses and Aaron went to Pharaoh and said, "Thus says the LORD, the God of Israel, 'Let my people go, so that they may celebrate a festival to me in the wilderness.' But Pharaoh said, "Who is the LORD, that I should heed him and let Israel go? I do not know the LORD, and I will not let Israel go." (5:1-2)

> Then I will harden the hearts of the Egyptians so that they will go in after them; and so I will gain glory for myself over Pharaoh and all his army, his chariots, and his chariot drivers. And the Egyptians shall know that I am the LORD, when I have gained glory for myself over Pharaoh, his chariots, and his chariot drivers. (14:17-18)

[The LORD] clogged their chariot wheels so that they turned with difficulty. The Egyptians said, "Let us flee from the Israelites, for the LORD is fighting for them against Egypt." (14:25)

Pharaoh and his host do come to know the Lord, but only at the midnight hour, in the middle of the riverbed, once matters are beyond repair.

Israel comes to know her God in this stupendous fashion so that she can witness through her praise to his beneficent nature (so Exod. 15), but also so that she can be moved to prayers of petition that God would repair matters when things began to break down. Israel has not simply been liberated from Egypt, she has become her divine Lord's personal and treasured possession. As a treasured child, she can have the temerity to remind God, in moments of crisis and lamentation, of his prior acts of fealty. In these cases the moment of the exodus looms large (see Ps. 77). Moreover, the exodus assumes a large role in framing Israel's hope for restoration after the exile. Second Isaiah in particular sounds this theme most consistently and intensely (51:9-11). In these eschatological texts, the mythic themes of God's contest with darkness and evil come to the fore. The unnamed tyrant "Pharaoh" (for the emotive effect of the lack of a personal name, think of the title "Der Führer" in our own day) is done one better; God's new opponent is the chaos dragon. In patristic writings and in the liturgy of the early church, this dimension of the tale gets fullest play as Pharaoh becomes a cipher for the devil himself, his hold over all humanity, and his hatred of God's beloved Son, the Christ.

Gary A. Anderson

Eighteenth Sunday after Pentecost, Year A

First Lesson: Exodus 16:2-15
(Psalm 105:1-6, 37-45)
Second Lesson: Philippians 1:21-30
Gospel Lesson: Matthew 20:1-16

The party was over. After ten stunning plagues in Egypt, after the wonder at the Red Sea, and after the people's final liberation from the Egyptians, suddenly reality began to set in. The horse and rider had been thrown into the sea, but now what? Miriam's glorious song and dance had been fun, but the echo of her tambourine had now died off, ricocheting off the distant mountains of the desert and disappearing into the wavy haze of wilderness heat.

This was not what they had expected. The travel brochures had said nothing about spending time in a desert with no food or water. And at least some of the people began to feel like victims of one of those real estate frauds which promised beachfront property but delivered a vacant lot in the middle of nowhere. In the throes of disappointment (not to mention the swooning force of the sun beating down on one's head), mind and memory can play tricks on a person. In the case of Exodus 16, Egypt strangely transmogrifies from the "house of bondage and the land of death" into some kind of Club Med.

Egypt became a sparkling land of crystal waters in the river Nile (never mind that their babies had floated dead in that same river once upon a time) and also a place of never-ending buffets of meat and vegetables (never mind that most evenings the people were too tired to bring their hands to their mouths following exhausting days of whip-driven brickmaking). It may all have been a lie, but for the time being the people believed that Egypt had been better than this rotten, arid desert to which Moses had led them. They felt like they had come to a swift dead end. Behind them was the Red Sea and Egypt, in front of them was, not the Promised Land, but a long stretch of wasteland.

Exodus 16 is about one of faith's unhappier surprises; namely, getting saved does not necessarily mean that all difficulty evaporates. The path to the Promised Land leads through the desert. But biblically the wilderness is precisely the opposite of what anyone wants — it is even the theological opposite of cosmos. Genesis 1:1 begins in the primordial chaos of *tohu wabohu*. In the balance of the Hebrew Scripture, *tohu wabohu* becomes a shorthand way to refer to the desert — such wilderness stretches are where the fallenness of this creation is on raw display. As Terence Fretheim notes, in Exodus 16 the people began to think that the whole of salvation was no more than a desert mirage. Their faith and confidence in Moses (and hence in Yahweh) was shifting and eroding like the sand on the dunes all around them.

Why would God redeem his people, only to take them first to so dreadful a place? Small wonder the people grumbled. But in this case (unlike some later instances of similar communal grousing) God appears to understand. His words to Moses are not harsh, nor is there a hint of judgment in this chapter. Instead God swiftly and lovingly responds to the people's legitimate need for food and so richly provides them with quail and manna.

But not before we read one of the most stunning and theologically loaded verses in the Bible: Exodus 16:10. The people are scared and hungry. They see now that the way forward leads through a place of grave danger. Hence they request a reverse course — they suggest rewinding the videotape of salvation history thus far by returning "home" to Egypt. But instead God comes to the people, claps his hands on their collective shoulders, and turns them around. He faces the people eastward, not westward back toward Egypt. He turns their faces east toward the wilderness, and it is *there* that they see the glory of Yahweh! They looked ahead into the hard times, and that is where they found God. They were not in the Promised Land or even within sight of it. Life after salvation was still going to have its share of hardships and heartaches. But the difference that salvation would make was the fact that within those hard times they would never be alone. The glory of God was out there, and in that the people were to find profound hope — not a simple hope that it was smooth sailing from here on out; not a pie-in-the-sky optimism that it was going to get swiftly better; not a health-and-wealth scheme wherein faith equates with successful living. Instead the hope proffered by Exodus 16:10 was at once realistic and deep: God would be with them in the places of danger and death.

An immediate indication of this came in the form of the manna. "What is it?" the people said even as they crinkled up their noses at this strange stuff that had appeared from out of nowhere. "It is the bread Yahweh is giving you to eat," was Moses' simple reply. Later the people would realize that the bread was itself the glory of God's presence and word which alone can sustain the life of faith (see Deut. 8 and its explanation of manna, which will later become Jesus' reply to Satan in Matt. 4). But for now it was an early token of that unique glory of Yahweh which was just waiting for them in the wilderness (of all places!).

Deep down, perhaps most people wish the kingdom of God were, already in this life, like some kind of Disney-ized Magic Kingdom. We wish the kingdom were a place where the streets were always clean, where trash was always swept out of sight, and where nightfall would mean only that the whole place would light up with twinkling lights. But it's not that way. Even for those who know and accept the good news of the gospel, there can still be the wasteland of depression and the scorching sand of cancer. Like the people who passed safely through the waters of the Red Sea, so also we plunge into the death of Jesus through the waters of our baptisms, but even still we find various desertlike experiences on the other side. That is the bad news of a reality-inclusive faith.

The good news is that the presence of such wilderness times does not nullify the presence of God. As in Exodus 16:10, it is possible to peer into the wilderness and see the glory of the Lord. This does not mean that the *suffering itself* is of God (or the same thing as God's presence in a person's life). Nor does it indicate that God glories in our hurts (and that therefore we should revel in them, too). Perhaps it means only that if we look closely enough, we may still find evidences of God's care in the midst of it all. The manna was one such evidence for the Israelites. It was not milk and honey by a long shot, but for the time being it was enough — enough to assure the people that they were not alone, that the covenant was still on track, that a better day really would come (and that when it did, it would be solely and sheerly a gift of grace).

Someone once noted that suffering is so universal that no religion can ignore it. Suffering must be accounted for. Some faiths deny suffering, reducing it to a bad state of mind, even as others try to blame its presence on the poor faith of the sufferer ("If only your faith were stronger, this would not have happened to you!"). Some make God the author of suffering ("Through this God plans to make you stronger"), even as others make God a helpless kind of cosufferer. What no faith can realistically do, however, is simply not deal with this subject at all.

The Christian faith charts a middle way between those who evacuate God from the midst of suffering and those who involve God altogether too much in it all. It is a way that leads through the cross. The cross is that quirky ray of glory that shines in the middle of this world's multiple wildernesses of hurt and sin and suffering. The cross is simultaneously the worst thing that ever happened and yet also a focal point for hope. The cross is that glory in the wilderness which properly prevents believers from responding to suffering by flippantly saying, "Oh well, it really doesn't matter," even as it also prevents us from dumping faith because of suffering by saying,

"To hell with this Christian stuff — if God were real, none of this unhappiness would happen."

The wilderness is not a pleasant place. We would all just as soon detour around it. For now, however, that's not possible. The challenge of faith is to resist the temptation to turn back to the house of bondage and death and to proceed forward, looking for God's glory and, just maybe by grace alone, also finding that glory in the wilderness.

Scott Hoezee

Third Sunday in Lent, Year A

First Lesson: Exodus 17:1-7
(Psalm 95)
Second Lesson: Romans 5:1-11
Gospel Lesson: John 4:5-42

Nineteenth Sunday after Pentecost, Year A

First Lesson: Exodus 17:1-7
(Psalm 78:1-4, 12-16)
Second Lesson: Philippians 2:1-13
Gospel Lesson: Matthew 21:23-32

This Sunday's text is part of a genre of Pentateuchal materials known as "the wilderness traditions." These materials have proved difficult to interpret for several reasons. One is that the stories are sometimes "told twice" (i.e., they are doublets). For our story, see its repetition in Numbers 20:1-13. Another problem is their differing evaluations of the cause and result of Israel's murmuring. In all these stories Israel complains about a particular circumstance she faces. In some cases her complaint is treated like an intercessory prayer; Moses comes forward and is granted a resolution. In other cases the complaint is understood to be a form of wanton rebellion and Israel is quickly punished. Why this variation? Also problematic are the variant characterizations of this period as a whole elsewhere in the Bible. Some texts see the wilderness era as a harbinger of all of Israel's subsequent woes; others see this moment as the time of her true virginal innocence.

Let us begin with the latter problem, the variant characterizations. No doubt this ambiguity is due to the problem of the wilderness itself as a symbolic category. On the one hand, the wilderness can be a spot of uncompromising purity. Unsullied by the vagaries of human culture, pilgrims headed to deserts as spots of repentance and renewal. The most extreme form of this is evident in the early Christian monastic communities that took root in Syria and Egypt. Though postbiblical in origin, those individuals and their biographers appealed (not without warrant!) to figures like John the Baptist and Elijah as biblical models. Perhaps most important for our purposes is Jeremiah's recollection of the wilderness period as one of Israel's chaste espousal of marriage to her divine suitor.

> I remember the devotion of your youth,
>   your love as a bride,
> how you followed me in the wilderness,
>   in a land not sown.
> Israel was holy to the LORD,
>   the first fruits of his harvest.
> All who ate of it were held guilty;
>   disaster came upon them,
>   says the LORD.   (Jer. 2:2-3; cf. Hos. 2:14)

The other way to construe the wilderness is as a spot of uncleanness and death. It is hardly an accident that on Yom Kippur (the Day of Atonement, see Lev. 16) the scapegoat which bore Israel's sins was driven off to the arid desert of Judea. There, far away from the habitation of God and man, it would meet its death. Considered this way, the wilderness was a natural location for Israel to rise up in rebellion against her Creator. And so a very influential stream of the biblical tradition remembers the wilderness period as one of unending rebellion. Indeed, Israel's sorry state is grounded right from the start in an obstreperous rebellion that knew no bounds. Consider the usage of Psalm 95 in Hebrews 4:1-3: "Therefore, while the promise of entering his rest [a metaphor for entering the Promised Land/kingdom of God] is still open [i.e., to 'us,' the newly baptized], let us take care that none of you should seem to have failed to reach it. For indeed the good news came to us just as to them; but the message they heard did not benefit them, because they were not united by faith with those who listened. For we who have believed enter that rest, just as God has said, 'As in my anger I swore, / "They shall not enter my rest"' [= Ps. 95:11]." For further ruminations on the horror of the wilderness period, consider Deuteronomy 9:22ff. and Psalm 78.

To sort through the wilderness texts, then, is not an easy task, but being aware of their literary functions is helpful. The first point to note is that the stories of Israel's murmuring in the desert can take two different literary forms (so Paul Hanson, as expanded by Brevard Childs in his *Exodus*). In pattern I there is recognition of a legitimate need (in Exod. 17, that of water, hardly an extravagance), a complaint by the people, an intervention by Moses, a miraculous intervention by God. In our text the pattern is clear: the people demand water (vv. 1-2), an appeal is made to Moses (vv. 2-3), Moses appeals to God (v. 4), and God brings forth water from a rock (vv. 5-7).

What is the theological significance of this pattern? None other than the *testing* of Israel. God will provide food, drink, and guidance in the wilderness. Israel, for her part, must learn to trust. For good reason numerous early Christian writers understood the appeal for "our daily bread" in the Lord's Prayer as an allusion to the wilderness. The force was this: one prayed only for bread sufficient to a day's work. In this way one would learn to trust in the Lord for each day's provisions (see especially Exod. 16, and note vv. 19-21). And so for our text the demand for water was understandable, but Israel is being tutored in the desert to let go of worries about her own person and to trust the beneficent hand of her God. A tall order to be sure, and so we must repeat this request every day with the hope that we might attain such faith.

The second pattern is more ominous. In this literary variation (see Num. 11:1-3; 17:6-13; 21:4-10) there is a complaint, God's angry reaction and punishment, and finally an act of intercession by Moses and then some sort of reprieve. Most of these texts occur after the giving of the law (Exod. 20–Num. 10). This is significant, for God is naturally more willing to be lenient toward Israel prior to her moral education in the ways of the Lord. It is as though Israel reaches the age of majority when she comes to Sinai. (Consider the significance of the rite of Bar Mitzvah in rabbinic Judaism: at puberty the young male becomes a "son of the commandment," namely, responsible to keep the law.) Before Sinai, she doesn't know any better; after Sinai, she should have learned her lesson.

This typology helps explain the very odd second story about finding water in the wilderness (Num. 20:1-13). Its overall literary shape conforms, by and large, to that of pattern I. But unlike most of the pattern I stories, the murmuring in Numbers 20 takes place *after* Sinai. Because of this particular placement, its ending appears more like pattern II. In addition to the act of gracious intervention (water is provided), it speaks of a horrible punishment: "But the LORD said to Moses and Aaron, 'Because you did not trust in me, to show my holiness before the eyes of the Israelites, therefore you shall not bring this assembly into the land that I have given them'" (Num. 20:12). In brief, this story is a mixed type. Because the story in Numbers takes place at Meribah just like the tale in Exodus 17:1-7, the two traditions are often blended together elsewhere in the Bible (see Ps. 95).

With this in mind we are now in a position to understand the usage of these materials by Paul in 1 Corinthians 10:1-5: "I do not want you to be unaware, brothers and sisters, that our ancestors were all under the cloud, and all passed through the sea, and all were baptized into Moses in the cloud and in the sea, and all ate the same spiritual food, and all drank the same spiritual drink. For they drank from the spiritual rock [Exod. 17:1-7 and Num. 20:1-13] that followed them, and the rock was Christ. Nevertheless, God was not pleased with most of them, and they were struck down in the wilderness." The desert is portrayed as a spot where God's gracious guiding hand led Israel from death to life. They passed through the tumultuous sea into the arid desert. There they were safely sustained by a rock that traversed the wilderness from the edge of Egypt (Exod. 17) to the border of the Promised Land (Num. 20), a miraculous rock that Paul identifies as a type of Christ. However, Israel rose up in rebellion against her God, most poignantly after the giving of the law, and so they were struck down in the wilderness.

Paul's own concluding guidelines are worthy of consideration in pondering the lessons of the wilderness period (1 Cor. 10:11-13): "These things happened to them to serve as an example, and they were written down to instruct us, on whom the ends of the ages have come [i.e., an entering into the 'rest' spoken of in Hebrews]. So if you think you are standing, watch out that you do not fall. No testing has overtaken you that is not common to everyone. God is faithful, and he will not let you be tested beyond your strength, but with the testing he will also provide the way out so that you may be able to endure it."

Gary A. Anderson

Twentieth Sunday after Pentecost, Year A

First Lesson: Exodus 20:1-4, 7-9, 12-20
(Psalm 19)
Second Lesson: Philippians 3:4b-14
Gospel Lesson: Matthew 21:33-46

Third Sunday in Lent, Year B

First Lesson: Exodus 20:1-17
(Psalm 19)
Second Lesson: 1 Corinthians 1:18-25
Gospel Lesson: John 2:13-22

One of the biggest problems for understanding the Ten Commandments is their familiarity. Printed and reprinted hundreds upon thousands of times, these commands always have the danger of becoming tired
old saws.

Yet the Ten Commandments themselves must be understood — if they
are to be understood properly — as a form of revelation. Though they have
some overlap with what moral philosophers call natural law, we must be
wary of understanding them as solely that, that is, a set of moral conventions that the Bible shares with men and women everywhere. God must approach Israel (and, by extension, *us!*) *directly* in order to reveal them. And
such approaches are always fraught with danger.

Who can behold the face of the living God and live? This is a scriptural
maxim we could do well to recover, given the propensity of the present age
to make God an overly "cuddly" creature. When Manoah and his wife — the
parents of Samson — are blessed with the appearance of an angel, they fall
on their faces in fear (Judg. 13). "We shall surely die," Manoah cries, "for we
have seen God." His wife, not doubting the principle, reassures her fearful
husband by reminding him that if this appearance were intended to punish,
certainly it would not have been marked by the annunciation of a miraculous conception.

When Moses sees the bush burning before him, he turns to investigate.
God calls to him, and Moses answers: "Here I am." Then God asks him to remove his shoes, for the ground he is standing upon is holy. Should he stand
there improperly appareled, the presence of the living God may work woe

instead of weal. And lest one think this solely a problem of the Old Testament, consider the response of Peter to Jesus' miracle while they were fishing: "Go away from me, Lord, for I am a sinful man!" (Luke 5:8).

By making the Ten Commandments into a cultural icon, we run the danger of shearing these commandments of their revelatory context and losing the sense of religious awe that attended their first hearing — and our hearing. These are not ten good maxims for living the good life; these are the living words of God himself, which are "sharper than any two-edged sword, piercing until it divides soul from spirit, joints from marrow; it is able to judge the thoughts and intentions of the heart. And before him no creature is hidden, but all are naked and laid bare to the eyes of the one to whom we must render an account" (Heb. 4:12-13).

Those who brought Exodus 19–20 into its final canonical form seemed quite aware of the danger these *general* maxims might fall prey to. And to avoid any such error they have shored up this moral revelation with cultic norms. As Moses made careful preparation for his encounter at the burning bush in the wilderness of Sinai some sixteen chapters earlier, so Israel must prepare herself for the arrival of the deity at this mountain amid the storm and the fire (Exod. 19:10-15). The men and women must abstain from sexual relations for three days, put on clean clothes, and observe carefully the boundaries of the mountain. One should not hear these commandments in a casual fashion.

Now one might imagine that these cultic prescriptions, once followed in all their detail (Exod. 19:10-25), would lead to an appearance of God, as if by formula. "We have prepared ourselves, O God," we may wish to say, "now make your person manifest before us." But the text surprises. And it does so at two levels. The last line of chapter 19 describes Moses descending the mountain to warn Israel one final time. We would expect to read his last instructions beginning in 20:1, but we are surprised. God pulls back his curtain and addresses Israel directly. The close of this story is also unusual. We might expect that the people, in honor of this direct speech, would address themselves somehow to its content. But nothing of the sort happens. The people respond as though they heard nothing. The text says they heard the sounds and saw the lightning and moved to a distance (20:18). The reader is hard-pressed to know whether this response is to the commandments themselves (20:1-17) or to the theophany described earlier (19:16). In any event, their desire at this point is clear: they want Moses to go forward to hear (the rest of) what God will say!

How are we to understand this? One meaning that is clearly conveyed is that the revelation of God cannot be contained by human ritual or convention. In spite of the elaborate preparations of Exodus 19, Moses, Aaron, and the rest of Israel are completely taken by surprise. But there is another possible meaning. The revelation of the Ten Commandments is shortly to be replaced by a far longer set of laws known as the Covenant Code (Exod. 20:22–23:33). And though the reader of the Covenant Code may think he has finally reached the end of the revelation, this code simply broadens itself even further and gives way to the legislation of the Priestly Code (Exod. 25 through the end of Num. 10, and then sporadically until the end of Numbers). And then there is also the recapitulation of the entire revelation in the book of Deuteronomy. Some seventeen verses turn into several chapters which then become dozens of chapters. It is striking how each legal revelation, which looks like a world unto itself, simply cracks open and serves as the introduction for a whole new set of laws. The revelation of the Torah is not a onetime moment, but an ever expanding guide for making one's life holy.

There is not sufficient space to follow the implications of this canonical shaping with respect to every commandment. Let me illustrate by way of one.

The seventh commandment is framed very succinctly: "Thou shalt not commit adultery." And its message would also seem brief: the marital bond is to be hallowed as an inviolable one. But before we conclude too hastily, we should take care not to isolate this command from what follows. For, like Israel, we might wish to ask ourselves whether we really heard this command in its fullness or have been merely thunderstruck by its very brevity.

The very shape of the Sinaitic revelation ought to inform us that it is not that easy. The seventh command is picked up and deepened by what follows. According to Priestly law in Leviticus 18, the failure to hallow the marital bond led to the loss of the land on the part of the Canaanites. And God threatens the same should the Israelites not heed carefully what is revealed.

Why such a concern for the marriage bond? Because marriage was the institution that most closely replicated the bond between Israel and her God. The undying erotic affection of God to become one with his people was to be mirrored in the marital bed. It was an affection that was to have no competitor and be without end. And like the marital bond, the affection of God toward Israel was not closed in within itself but constantly opening to the world around it in the form of progeny. Some Christians are wont to place a cross above their marital bed, not as a sign of prudery, but as a token of their commitment to love each other unto death. To paraphrase Paul: husbands are to love their wives as they do their own bodies, as are wives to love their husbands.

Of course, the marriage bond does not close with the Torah. It opens up into far broader vistas in the writings of the prophets and the Song of

Songs, and returns as a key theme in the New Testament and patristic Christianity.

In sum, what we see in the Ten Commandments are two things. First is the holiness of the legislation. Law does not stand outside God's person. To hear law properly is like meeting God face-to-face. It is a striking thing that the telltale sign of a vigorous monastic movement (and so the font of later mysticism) is the publication of a set of rules. Consider the foundation text of Western mysticism, the rule of Saint Benedict. For moderns the orchestration of amorous feelings through the fulfillment of prescriptions will sound odd. But we best not ignore the testimony of the saints who have gone before us. Love is work. Love, for those who know it well, can be like a precious and fragile seedling. Only with constant care and attention to its details will it grow to a mature and healthy tree.

The second matter to keep in mind is that the Ten Commandments are not a complete summary. If anything, they are a stenographer's shorthand. They need interpretation; they point beyond themselves to an ever expanding revelation. To understand any one commandment properly, one must set the Ten Commandments in the developing trajectory of biblical thought.

Gary A. Anderson

Last Sunday after the Epiphany (Transfiguration), Year A

First Lesson: Exodus 24:12-18
(Psalm 2)
Second Lesson: 2 Peter 1:16-21
Gospel Lesson: Matthew 17:1-9

The Jewish Bible has at its heart the revelation of the Torah, or "law" as it is sometimes rendered in English. And at the very center of this central moment is the descent of God's presence into the tabernacle at the close of Leviticus 9 and the beginning of 10. Indeed, it's not just a thematic climax but a structural one too. Medieval Jewish scholars noted and recorded in the margins of their Bibles that the number of words and verses is divided in half precisely at this point in the story. It is the fulcrum around which the first five books of the Bible turn. And this is not simply a Jewish point; it is also deeply incarnational (on this see the fine essay of Michael Wyschogrod, "Incarnation," in *Pro Ecclesia*). It is here that God's presence descends to dwell among carnal or "fleshly" Israel. Most of Exodus 25ff. and Leviticus can be read as an "owner's manual" of what to do and how to act when in close vicinity to God's "real presence."

I mention this because this act of divine condescension is adumbrated here in Exodus 24, one of the most beloved of chapters of the Bible for the Christian ascetic and mystical tradition. Gregory of Nyssa (Cappadocia, fourth century), in his *Life of Moses,* took a great interest in the story of Moses' ascent to the peak of Mount Sinai and thought of it as a paradigm for the call of every person to approach the divine throne and become like God (the notion of "deification" so crucial to the theology of the Eastern churches). Moses had prepared himself for this moment by a life of moral and physical purity. One can see this through the many warnings he gave the people Israel (Exod. 19:10ff. and 24:2) about being pure in order to witness an epiphany of God. In the middle of Exodus 24 Moses "sees God" with the seventy elders of Israel (vv. 9-11), but then he is called once more (vv. 15-18) to ascend even higher to enter the cloud of darkness (cf. the famous medieval tract, *The Cloud of Unknowing*). Here, in the closest proximity to the divine Presence, Moses must put aside all he had ever thought about God in order to be tutored anew. Abraham Malherbe makes the following point in his *Gregory of Nyssa, "The Life of Moses"*:

> What does it mean that Moses entered the darkness (24:18) and then saw God in it? What is now recounted seems somehow to be contradictory to the first theophany (24:9-11), for then the Divine was beheld in light but now he is seen in darkness. Let us not think that this is at variance with the sequence of things we have contemplated spiritually. Scripture teaches by this that religious knowledge comes at first to those who receive it as light. Therefore what is perceived to be contrary to religion is darkness, and the escape from darkness comes about when one participates in light. But as the mind progresses and, through an ever greater and more perfect diligence, comes to apprehend reality, as it approaches more nearly to contemplation, it sees more clearly what of the divine nature is uncontemplated.

Exodus 24 sits as a midway point between the arrival at Sinai (19:1) and the complete condescension of God to dwell with his people (Exod. 40/Lev.

9). It marks the move from the miraculous and onetime gift of a particular form of divine epiphany (the storm and thunder that precede the giving of the Ten Commandments) to the regular opportunity to meet the living God at the liturgy of the tabernacle (appropriately called "the Tent of *Meeting*"). This link can be established by reading Exodus 24:15–25:1 in parallel with Exodus 40:34–Leviticus 1:1 (also compare Lev. 9:22-24). As Moses enters the cloud in 24:18 to meet God, so the people will meet God through the cloud when the tabernacle is built. As Moses ascends the mountain and enters the cloud in order to hear the word of God, so the tabernacle upon completion will be surrounded by a cloud from which God will begin to reveal his Torah (Lev. 1:1ff.) to all Israel.

And, as if to put an exclamation point on all of this, our writer notes the linkages of this material with the creation imagery of Genesis 1. Moses must wait six days before entering the cloud on the seventh. This is a clear allusion to the Sabbath of Genesis 1. Seven times in Exodus 24 we find the Hebrew word for "to ascend." The tabernacle is completed through seven stages (Exod. 40:16-33) and is finished on New Year's Day (40:2) — the day that marks the creation of the world — and shortly thereafter (eight days) God's presence is revealed to the entire nation (Lev. 9:24).

This moment represents the culmination of creation as the Jewish Bible understands it. Indeed, not a few Jewish sources speak of the creation of the world remaining in an inchoate state until Israel's arrival at Sinai! On this view, one is hardly surprised that John, in his Gospel, characterized the incarnation as the moment when Christ "tabernacled *(eskēnōsen)* among us" (John 1:14). This act of tabernacling, for John, had also been foreshadowed at creation ("in the beginning *was the word* . . ."). All these themes — appearance of the glory, divine condescension, building of a tabernacle — return in the tale of the transfiguration, a set of parallels not lost on the fathers of the church. Indeed, the Greek Fathers were fond of drawing parallels between this epiphany of the incarnate Son and its important forerunner in the Old Testament. What Brevard Childs, in his *Exodus,* wrote in summary of chapter 24 could just as easily be transferred to the moment of the transfiguration: "But in light of God's complete otherness [which occasioned all the concern for purity of body and character — GAA], the all-encompassing focus of the chapter falls on God's mercy and gracious condescension. It is this theme which lies at the heart of the witness of the Sinai Covenant."

Gary A. Anderson

Twenty-first Sunday after Pentecost, Year A

First Lesson: Exodus 32:1-14
(Psalm 106:1-6, 19-23)
Second Lesson: Philippians 4:1-9
Gospel Lesson: Matthew 22:1-14

The larger context for this lection is Exodus 32–34, a narrative complex dealing with the breaching and restoring of Israel's covenant relationship with God. In this first section (32:1-14), the emphasis falls on Israel's failure, the Lord's initial reaction, and Moses' attempt to dissuade God from inflicting ultimate punishment.

Moses had been on the mountain with God for some time (24:12), a delay which made Israel restive (32:1). All of Israel's actions are described collectively. They are a *people* who *congregated themselves* (*wayyiqqahel;* in its nominal form *qahal* is the OT equivalent of "church") in Aaron's presence (Aaron was Moses' brother). As one, they order Aaron to "rise, make us *a* god/gods." They justify this request, which is a direct violation of 20:4, by citing Moses' prolonged absence. But this is clearly disingenuous. Israel's elders had been told explicitly to wait till Moses returned; in fact, Aaron and Hur had been put in temporary charge (24:14). Also underscoring Israel's incipient disobedience is their description of Moses as "the man who brought us up from the land of Egypt." Had Israel forgotten already that Moses was merely the *servant* of the Lord, who was the One who actually had rescued them?

It is unclear whether Israel wanted Aaron to make them *a* god (JPS) or *gods* (RSV). Grammatically, either is possible, since in the Old Testament *'elohim* refers both to one god and multiple gods, depending on context. The issue may be resolved later in the episode.

No less incredible than Israel's demand is Aaron's compliance. Without a single word of protest, he requested that the golden earrings of wives, sons, and daughters be brought to him (v. 2). This command the people obey without hesitation (v. 3)! Once Aaron had fashioned a molten calf, Israel proclaimed: "This is your God / these are your gods, O Israel, who brought you up from the land of Egypt" (v. 4). In this instance the god or gods that Israel requested were apparently not conceived of as foreign deities. Rather, it appears Israel was attempting to construct a concrete (golden!) image of its own God. The problem was the difficulty they were having with Moses' absence, which for them was the equivalent of God's absence. The calf, being identified with the deity who brought them up from

105

Egypt, was the means by which they could "get a handle" on God. If that is so, then the translation "god" rather than "gods" is more probable. Aaron's subsequent actions tend to support this reading. After he built an altar before the calf, he announced: "Tomorrow is a feast to the LORD" (v. 5). By identifying the calf with YHWH, the distinctive personal name of the Israelite God, Aaron shows that Israel is not actually turning its allegiance to another god. Rather, it wants a form of the deity that is simultaneously visible and portable. No golden calf can disappear or show up desultorily!

During the feast on the day following Aaron's declaration, Israel engaged in normal religious activities, only this time with the calf as the focus. Virtually everything they did involved appropriate rites and rituals. In fact, in Exodus 20 Israel had been explicitly commanded to offer burnt offerings and peace offerings (v. 24). But in the same context, the people were warned not to make such offerings to gods of silver or gold. Further, an altar of earth or stone was the place on which these offerings were to be made; indeed, if a stone altar was used, then hewn stones were forbidden since any tool would profane the religious object (v. 25). Thus the one variable to Israel's carrying out God's command was the calf Aaron had constructed. That one act rendered all the other potentially holy acts egregiously profane! Even the eating and drinking described in this story was, under the right circumstances, perfectly appropriate religious behavior (see Exod. 24:9-11).

The one exception to all this potentially appropriate behavior in an unquestionably inappropriate context is the fact that Israel "rose up to play." The reference may be to something as innocuous as "dancing" (so JPS) or as reprehensible as orgiastic rituals. The verb is *leṣaḥeq*, which usually has to do with laughing. In this context, it is probably safe to say that some activity indicative of gross profanation of proper worship is meant. While a sexual connotation is certainly possible, there is insufficient context to be certain about such a meaning in this situation (for a sexual nuance, see Gen. 26:8).

While this bogus feast is going on, the scene shifts to God and Moses on the mountain (v. 7). The Lord's reaction to Israel's behavior was swift, predictable, and sobering. In effect, God's first reaction was to disown Israel! This is indicated by the use of pronouns. The Lord tells Moses to "go down" (i.e., to the scene where the events are unfolding) because *your* people, whom *you* brought up out of the land of Egypt, have sinned so very badly (vv. 7-8). In a sense, of course, Israel was Moses' people, and he had led them out of Egypt. But it cannot be lost on the reader that ultimately Israel belonged to the Lord, who was truly the One who had led them from Egypt. At this point, it is as though God wants nothing to do with the very people he had brought into being!

The remainder of God's description of what the people had done is straightforward, simply confirming what the narrative already indicated (v. 8). But God's judgment for the offense is another matter — it is most severe. Referring to Israel as "stiff-necked," the Lord has every intention of consuming them. This awful consumption is to be complete, for the Lord plans on beginning all over again with Moses: "But of you I will make a great nation" (v. 10). There are few judgment scenes in the Bible more chilling than this one.

Moses' response to the divine outburst is as surprising as the severity of the punishment. He will have none of it! He counters the Lord's demand to stand aside while the divine anger smolders (v. 10). Instead, Moses calls the extent of the anger into question. Then Moses reverses the pronouns, strenuously objecting to the Lord's attempt to disown Israel: "Why does *your* wrath burn hot against *your* people, whom *you* brought forth out of the land of Egypt . . . ?" (v. 11). According to Moses, this people belongs exclusively to the Lord, notwithstanding the strategic role God asked him to play. Moses builds on this argument by pointing out Egypt's likely reaction to God's wiping out Israel in the wilderness, namely, that God was setting them up all along for evil purposes (v. 12)!

Moses' extraordinary argument, which was perhaps as foolhardy as it was courageous, comes to a head when he demands that God put aside the divine wrath and "repent" (!) of the evil (i.e., judgment) that was intended against Israel. Though the word "repent" *(wehinnahem)* in this context does not connote changing one's immoral behavior, it is nonetheless radical. Moses is doing nothing less than urging God in no uncertain terms to change the course of action that had already been determined.

Moses' trump card is the very covenant that YHWH had made with Israel. That's why he calls on God to "remember" Abraham, Isaac, and Israel, the very servants to whom God had once sworn unconditionally to provide progeny and land (v. 13; see Gen. 12:7; 13:14-17; 15:5, 18-19; 17:4-6, 19; etc.). From Moses' perspective, this promise God made to Israel's ancestors was, in effect, unconditional. That is, while Israel might collectively undergo punishment — even severe punishment from time to time — nothing could finally abrogate God's promises to the ancestors. Apparently the deity agreed, for God seemed to accept the logic of Moses' argument and relent from the punishment that only a short time before had been announced.

This startling behavior on God's part was not a function of divine weakness, but of divine grace. In short, in this first segment of these three strategic chapters, God's grace got the best of God's justifiable anger. This is part of a biblical pattern: judgment is never God's final word. Indeed, God's love

107

and gracious attitude toward Israel were such that Moses had the temerity to importune the deity until there was a change of divine behavior. Ironically, later we discover that Moses, who implored God on Israel's behalf, was prevented from entering the land of promise while Israel, whose punishment seemed so deserved, entered it as a function of God's grace.

Frank Anthony Spina

Twenty-second Sunday after Pentecost, Year A

First Lesson: Exodus 33:12-23
(Psalm 99)
Second Lesson: 1 Thessalonians 1:1-10
Gospel Lesson: Matthew 22:15-22

Traditionally, theology works by thinking issues through discursively and analytically, and this takes up one way the Bible does theology. But the Bible often does theology by telling a story, and that is happening in Exodus 32–34. The present passage in particular offers a narrative discussion of the question, What do we mean by saying that God is *with* us? How can *God* be *with* us? How much of God is with us? In what way is God with us? How do we experience God being with us? What difference does it make? Telling a story means that different ways of handling the question can be explored without the author having to decide that one of the approaches is *the* right one. The various angles in the story can contribute to the way its hearers think through the issue and live with it. For, like most of life's important questions, this one does not exactly have *an* answer. We do not so much answer such questions as walk around them and live with them. So the sermon might seek to help the congregation to think about the various meanings we attach to the idea of God being with us, and to test and expand these by Scripture.

When Christians think about how God can be *with* us, we often see the problem as lying in God's *moral* holiness and our sinfulness. Exodus knows that we are sinful, but it also knows that God is inherently gracious and merciful (v. 19) and does not have a problem forgiving people. Exodus is more preoccupied with another angle on the question, which does not concern Christians so much, and may therefore be the angle we need to learn from. It is that God is *metaphysically* holy, whereas we are earthly. In the Old Testament, "God is holy" means God is other than us, transcendent, belonging to the realm of heaven, uncreated, awesomely powerful and majestic. God's presence is like a monarch's presence. It reduces you to silence. You are a being of a quite different status and significance. "Our God," like the God of Sinai, "is a consuming fire" (Heb. 12) — not only in relation to sin but just in being awesomely transcendent. We and God are such different beings that we can hardly imagine being in the same room with God, or on the same mountain (Exod. 19).

So, when asked who will accompany Moses in leading the people, Yahweh answers, "My *presence* will go with you, and I will give you rest." The word for "presence," *panim,* literally means "face." A person's face tells us that the person is with us. It shines out with the person's love and concern. We know the person is "with" us from his or her face. We know the person cares from the face. When someone *looks* with favor, and that person's face thus shines on us, that naturally issues in generous acts toward us (cf. the priestly blessing in Num. 6:22-27). So having Yahweh's face with the people will guarantee that they experience God's blessing and provision and reach their destination (v. 14). At the same time, speaking of Yahweh's "face" being with them avoids implying that the whole of Yahweh is with them. Speaking of the presence of God's face is like speaking of the presence of God's hand or arm or breath or name. It implies a real presence of God, but not a presence of the whole of God that we would be unable to cope with.

When Moses then asks to be allowed to see God's *glory,* the story is taking another run at the question of how we can understand God's presence. A person's glory or splendor is the outward manifestation of the person's intrinsic importance. When sitting at home watching television, a monarch is still sovereign of the realm, but he or she looks less impressive than when robed in regalia and sitting in the state carriage, processing before the people. God's glory is the outward manifestation of God's intrinsic holiness, the holiness that distinguishes God from human beings. So Moses says, "I want to see you as you really are, in all your splendor." It would be a silly request (but perhaps we are not to treat this piece of narrative theology as part of some actual conversation that an actual Moses once initiated). Moses would fry. God therefore offers some alternatives.

First, "I will make all my *goodness* pass before you." "Goodness" sounds more abstract than the Hebrew word *ṭob.* "All my good" would be as fair a translation, which fits with the fact that here we are being given another run at the issue that arose in verses 12-17. The "good" Yahweh intends to give the Israelites is the fulfillment of the purposes that have been announced to them. They will be taken to their Promised Land. That promise's fulfillment is an aspect of Yahweh's splendor that Moses will be able to cope with. The people will know God is with them because they will experience God giving them good things.

Second, Yahweh undertakes to proclaim before Moses that *name* Yahweh. In traditional societies, names often express something about a person's character or destiny, or the vision or hopes the person's parents hold for him or her. The name Yahweh itself spoke of God's character, of who God would be for Israel. It was not just a label, but a revelation.

Old Testament names can be a puzzle — they may not intrinsically have the meaning the Old Testament associates with them. Instead, it is the shape of the name that suggests something. Moses' name does not refer to being drawn out of water, but it looks a bit like a verb meaning that, so it can be given a link with that (Exod. 2:10). Similarly, Yahweh's name is reminiscent of the verb *hayah*, "to be" or "to happen." The short version of the name is Yah (cf. "hallelu-yah"). Perhaps Yahweh is a lengthened form of some such shorter name, as happened when "Abram" became "Abraham." Thus the name Yahweh does not exactly mean "the one who is/will be there," "the one who is/will be with you," but it looks rather like a form of the verb that would mean that. That is therefore the message or the promise that God invites Israel to receive from this name (see Exod. 3). The name means that God will be with you, or (to put it another way) that you will experience God as one who is always insisting on being gracious and merciful (v. 19).

It is in this sense that the name reveals the person and that having the name means you have the person. We might compare the preciousness of the name Jesus. It is therefore entirely appropriate that this narrative discussion of what God's presence means should include a reminder of the name Yahweh. The name mediated the presence of the person, because through saying the name people were saying who the person was. Further, in this particular case the actual name spoke of presence. It is therefore sad that translations deprive us of the name that God graciously revealed and replace it by the patriarchal expression "the LORD."

So in response to the request about seeing God's splendor, God first promises that Israel will see God's goodness and then that they will know God's name. Then we are amazed to hear God adding, "But you cannot see my *face*" (v. 20). Translations obscure the contrast with verse 15 because there they rendered the same word "presence." And in a sense that is right, because evidently the word has some different sense here. Or perhaps the implication of the double usage is that you can *know* God's face is with you but not *see* God's face. We might recall Jesus' exhortation to Mary not to hold onto him, and recall the way in which he disappears as soon as he is recognized (Luke 24:31; John 20:17). And we might recall the frequency with which hymns and songs ask to "see" God, but mean this metaphorically. Israel's leaders did see God (Exod. 24:9-11). Here, seeing God would kill you. Both declarations make important statements about the reality and the limitation of the sense in which we know God's presence.

The story has one other run at the question, one that has often amused people. We cannot see God's face, because it will shine out with that splendor that Moses has asked to see. But we can see God's *back* (vv. 21-23). We cannot see God coming, but we can see God going. Again we are reminded of resurrection stories. Jesus leaves the tomb while the disciples are not looking, and goes off ahead of them to Galilee (Mark 16:7). They had better run if they want to catch him up. We do not see God, but sometimes we see God's back disappearing around the corner and realize that God has just acted.

John Goldingay

Last Sunday after the Epiphany (Transfiguration), Year C

First Lesson: Exodus 34:29-35
(Psalm 99)
Second Lesson: 2 Corinthians 3:12–4:2
Gospel Lesson: Luke 9:28-36, (37-43)

We are at the close of a tumultuous stage in the story of Israel's time at Sinai — indeed, of its relationship with Yahweh. It is a pregnant moment when Moses comes down the mountain with his two stones. They are the "covenant stones" or "testimony stones." They give testimony to the basis on which the covenant relationship between Israel and Yahweh will work in the future. That basis is the Ten Words from chapter 20. These detail for Israel the basic requirements and promises built into that relationship.

Coming down with these stones might itself be enough to make someone's face shine with enthusiasm and joy. Another natural cause of that shining would be the simple fact of having been with God for six weeks. To be in the presence of someone who loves us puts a shine on our faces. Being welcomed into the presence of someone very important can have a similar effect. Both have been true of Moses.

But there is something else going on. "Shine" (qaran) is an unusual word. It is a "denominative" verb, a verb formed from a noun — the opposite to the usual rule in Hebrew, where nouns are formed from verbs. In a case such as this, we work out the meaning of the verb from the noun rather than vice versa.

This noun (qeren) is a much more common word meaning "horn." It refers to

- the literal horn growing on an animal
- such a horn used as a flask or a musical instrument
- something that a horn symbolizes, such as strength and impressiveness
- something horn-shaped (given a little imagination!) such as a tusk, or a hill, or the projections at the corner of an altar, or the rays of the sun

In the only other occurrence of the verb, in Psalm 69:31, it means "to display horns," and in connection with Exodus 34 medieval artists and sculptors portrayed Moses as having literal hornlike projections in his forehead. But the Greek translation of Exodus assumed that here it meant "to shine," and this seems more likely. This involves inferring that the verb took its meaning from the last of the noun's metaphorical usages. The same inference underlies 2 Corinthians 3.

The other passage where "horns" refers to the rays of the sun is the vision in Habakkuk 3. That vision pictures Yahweh coming to act decisively in world history to rescue Israel and its king and to defeat its oppressors. Near the beginning of the picture (Hab. 3:4) is a description of Yahweh:

> The brightness was like the sun;
> rays came forth from his hand,
> where his power lay hidden.

Now it is quite common to describe God as shining like the sun, and it seems that this distinctive statement in Exodus 34 links with that. The implication is that as Yahweh shines like the sun, Moses has "caught" some of that brightness. Rays shine forth from his face that reflect Yahweh's glory.

Naturally enough, Moses is unaware of this, and naturally enough, it has a startling effect on the people. The passage turns out to continue the narrative discussion of what it means to be in the presence of God, which was a dominant theme in passages such as Exodus 33:12-23 (see the comment). There Moses was told he could not see God's glory because that would mean death, yet we had already read about Moses and other people seeing God's face and surviving. These are not so much contradictions as testimonies to the ambiguous nature of the presence of God. Here it is implied that Moses has indeed seen God's glory, and has come home reflecting it. That makes him in turn a danger to the people, who have already expressed the desire that he should go into that dangerous presence on their behalf and then speak on God's behalf to them, rather than that God should speak directly to them (cf. 20:18-21).

It is thus tempting for the people of God not to want to get too near to God. When God acts, it is a scary matter. We long to have an experience of God's awesome presence, but we are also fearful of it. One of the gospel aspects of this story is that God deals graciously with such mixed feelings on our part. God does not cooperate with our desire that we should not have to come too near to God's glory. But God makes allowances for us in the way that glory appears. As 2 Corinthians 4 goes on to note after this passage has been taken up in 2 Corinthians 3, we see the glory of God in the face of Jesus Christ, where it is easier to handle (cf. also John 1:14).

It might also be tempting for leaders to collude with that reluctance to get too near to God and to enjoy the prestige of being the person who embodies the scary presence of God. Moses' response is rather the one that Paul and Barnabas will one day make when they have an analogous experience (Acts 14:8-18). His response is to call the people close, because it is important that they hear what has transpired in his meetings with Yahweh. This is so precisely because those meetings took place for their sake and not just for his. In due course, indeed, God's glory will come to dwell in the shrine that the Israelites will shortly make (Exod. 40:29-35). God's glory will dwell in their very midst and will signify when they are to be on the move and when they are to settle down. They will be guaranteed God's presence, but they will also be protected from it, because it is located in this shrine, and none of them will actually enter it — not even Moses himself.

So Moses shares God's word with them. As usual, one underlying assumption of the story is that discovering God's expectations of them is a privilege and a joy. To know God's commands is no more a burden than when we discover the desires of someone we love or admire or respect. It will be a joy to us to seek to fulfill those desires (perhaps!). Christians often think of the Jewish people as burdened by the commands God has given them, but that is not the impression the Old Testament gives. Nor is it the feeling that Jewish people themselves usually have — any more than Christians feel it a burden that Jesus gave us the Sermon on the Mount.

The rays that emanated from Moses' face were a sign that he had been in God's presence and had received those commands from God. Moses thus spoke with the people with his face unveiled, so that they could see the sign. After he had finished telling them God's words, he put a veil on his face, apparently so that they were not put off from relating to him in everyday life. The next time he went to talk with God, he uncovered his face again, because he did not need to have it covered before God, and once more he would stay unveiled while passing on God's words to the people. That routine obtained as long as the people were at Sinai. We assume that it is a "veil" that he put over his face, though the Hebrew word (masweh) is another unusual one: it appears only here in the Old Testament.

Exodus gives no hint of the idea that Moses wore the veil so that people would not see the glory of his face fading (2 Cor. 3). Paul is perhaps taking up the way the story was interpreted in New Testament times, and simply working with that interpretation. In Exodus itself the point of the story is to convey something of the wonder of the fact that God has given Israel a supernatural revelation. It means it is possible for people to know clearly what God expects of them, and to do it.

Paul draws our attention to the fact that seeing the glory of God in the face of Jesus Christ makes us all bearers of the glory. We are all people who continually shine out with God in the church and in the world, as Moses did. Exodus itself points to a converse fact, that from time to time individuals are the bearers of God's glory to a special degree. They shine out in remarkable ways. A congregation may have someone like that within it. We do well to pay attention to people who seem to have climbed the mountain and come down redolent of God, and even to be open to the possibility of people finding that in us. We might need especially to pay attention to such people when we have previously dismissed them (see 32:1, the first verse of the complex of chapters that 34:29-35 closes off).

John Goldingay

Seventh Sunday after the Epiphany, Year A

First Lesson: Leviticus 19:1-2, 9-18
(Psalm 119:33-40)
Second Lesson: 1 Corinthians 3:10-11, 16-23
Gospel Lesson: Matthew 5:38-48

Leviticus is not the favorite biblical book of most Christians. Neverthe-less, in all of Leviticus, this lection is likely to be well known because two verses from it are quoted in the New Testament:

- 19:2 is cited in 1 Peter 1:16 (and alluded to in Matt. 5:48);
- 19:18 is cited in Matthew 5:43; 19:19; 22:39; Mark 12:31, 33; Luke 10:27; Romans 12:19; 13:9; Galatians 5:14; and James 2:8.

This listing, obviously, does not include the additional echoes of 19:15-17 that are found elsewhere in the New Testament. Leviticus 19 is more impor-tant, then, than it might at first appear. Still, while some of this material might be familiar — even important — its meaning is probably neither for most churchgoers. The preacher who takes up this material must first make it understandable, therefore, before its importance can be grasped. Perhaps nowhere is this task more critical than in the conception of God's *holiness*.

Leviticus 19:2b, "*Holy* you shall be, for *holy* am I, Yahweh your God" (the adjective is in emphatic, first position), could serve as the theme of the chapter, or even of the book — especially as this sentiment is repeated a number of times (see 11:44-45; 20:7, 26). Indeed, Leviticus 17–26 is often called the "Holiness Code," deriving its name from texts like 19:2, not to mention the concern with holiness running throughout these chapters.

In chapter 19 that concern takes its origin in the holiness of the divine nature itself. But what does it mean that God is *holy*? Elsewhere, Leviticus stresses that God's *name* is holy (20:3; 22:2, 32) and that God is the one who *sanctifies Israel* — that is, who makes Israel holy (20:8; 21:8, 15, 23; 22:9, 16, 32). But apart from 10:3, which seems to indicate that God's holiness is manifested in the *judgment of sin*, there is no explicit definition of what God's holiness is in and of itself. Instead, holiness seems to be "intrinsic to God's character" (Gordon J. Wenham, *The Book of Leviticus*, New International Commentary on the Old Testament [Grand Rapids: Eerdmans, 1979], p. 22). God's intrinsic holiness may be underscored by the fact that in 19:2 God's holiness is expressed in a nominal sentence whereas Israel's holiness

115

must be expressed by a verbal sentence. It is something Israel *must* or *will be* but that God *is* (see John E. Hartley, *Leviticus,* WBC 4 [Dallas: Word Books, 1992], p. 312).

Holiness has typically been thought to involve *separation:* the Holy is Wholly Other (the classic study is Rudolf Otto, *The Idea of the Holy: An Inquiry into the Non-Rational Factor in the Idea of the Divine and Its Relation to the Rational,* trans. John W. Harvey [London: Oxford University Press, 1958]).

Anthropological studies have stressed that holiness also involves wholeness (wholi-ness!) and completeness (see, e.g., Mary Douglas, *Purity and Danger: An Analysis of the Concepts of Pollution and Taboo* [London: Ark Paperbacks, 1989], esp. chap. 3: "The Abominations of Leviticus," pp. 41-57). Yet such phenomenological insights must be correlated with and tempered by two critical *textual* insights.

The first of these is to be found in the refrain "I am the LORD," found throughout Leviticus 19 and indeed the whole Holiness Code (see 18:5, 6, 21; 20:7; 21:12; 22:2, 3, 8, 9, 30, 31, 33; 23:22; 24:22; 25:17; 26:2, 45). The phrase occurs some fifteen times in chapter 19 alone (19:3, 4, 10, 12, 14, 16, 18, 25, 28, 30, 31, 32, 34, 36, 37)! This formula is also used frequently in Ezekiel, where it always precedes God's activity and where Yahweh is always the subject. The action that accompanies the phrase "I am Yahweh" there functions to reveal God's person and nature to those who witness that action. These persons, in turn, are to recognize that it is God who has done this thing (see, e.g., Ezek. 24:15-27). Apparently, the same issue is at work in the Holiness Code and its use of this formula. Somehow, in this strange hodgepodge of laws, God's nature and holiness are being revealed. Walther Zimmerli writes: "A comparison of the Holiness Code with Ezekiel 20:7 makes it clear that this indefatigable repetition of *'ny yhwh* ['I am Yahweh'] at the end of individual statements or smaller groups of statements in the legal offerings is not to be understood as thoughtlessly strewn decoration; rather, *this repetition pushes these legal statements into the most central position from which the Old Testament can make any statement.* Each of these small groups of legal maxims thereby becomes a legal communication *out of the heart of the Old Testament revelation of Yahweh.* Each one of these small units offers in its own way a bit of explication of the central self-introduction of Yahweh, the God who summons his people — or better, recalling Leviticus 18ff. (and Ezek. 20), the God who sanctifies his people" (*I Am Yahweh* [Atlanta: John Knox, 1982], p. 12, emphasis mine; cf. Hartley, p. 293: "The role of this formula in Lev 18–26 then is to teach that Israel's distinctive existence as a people rests on Yahweh's self-revelation of his holy character").

The second insight is closely related to the first and, indeed, derives from it. Given the strange collection of laws in Leviticus 19, one might easily wonder whether the God — and that God's holiness — revealed in such is equally strange. What kind of odd God is this? An answer is gained by looking closely at the contents of this chapter. What seems at first to be a formless collection can be organized roughly around three topics: 19:3-8 have to do with regulations concerning God; 19:9-18 have to do with regulations concerning one's neighbor; and 19:19-36 are something of a miscellany of regulations, at least some of which have to do with Canaanite practices that the Israelites are not to emulate.

It would seem, therefore, that these laws — which at first seem so odd and inapplicable — are actually designed to do a number of things that are quite applicable to the contemporary context. Perhaps preeminent among these is that these laws serve to *separate Israel off* and *mark Israel as different* from the outside world. But this separate*ness* is not separat*ism*. These laws are motivated by "I am Yahweh," and that means that God wishes to know and be known by humans via these actions — via *Israel*. The passage is therefore concerned with an ethic that functions both to proclaim something about this holy God and also to communicate that holiness to others who might be watching. "Why don't you gash yourself for the dead?" (19:28). "Why don't you consult mediums and wizards?" (19:31). "Why don't you gather the fallen grapes in your vineyard — why do you leave them for the poor?" (19:9-10). The answer to these questions is because "he is Yahweh" — that is, because Yahweh is our God! (I have developed these ideas further elsewhere. See Brent A. Strawn, "The X-Factor: Revisioning Biblical Holiness," *Asbury Theological Journal* 54, no. 2 [1999]: 73-92.)

Yet, while the *dynamic* at work in Leviticus 19 is one that is quite important for and applicable to contemporary Christian communities, the *specifics* may be less so. Still, the lection's focus on 19:15-18 is reflective of a perspective that this subunit is relevant even in its specifics. The dynamic outlined above, however, should not be forgotten. That is, it may very well be that it is in our treatment of our neighbors that God's holiness is made manifest and proclaimed to the world through us.

19:18b is obviously the most familiar of the laws in this smaller unit and functions as its climax. Here too, however, the context must be kept in mind. "Love" was never an abstract concept in ancient Israel; it was marked by concrete actions. One loved God — as Deuteronomy delights in pointing out — by keeping God's commandments. In context, then, the love of neighbor that is enjoined in 19:18b must be connected with reverence for parents (19:3); compassion for the poor (19:9-10); injunctions against stealing, deceitful dealing, lying, false testimony, fraud, improper payment of wages

(19:11-13; see also 19:35); and proper respect for the physically handicapped (19:14), the aged (19:32), and one's own children — especially daughters (19:29). One loves one's neighbors, that is, by not cheating them in business, by treating them with the proper respect due them, and so forth. (Some have taken Sirach 28:1-7 to be a commentary of sorts on Leviticus 19:18. If so, it contains similar concrete examples of what this "love" entails.)

19:15 focuses particularly on equity in legal matters. The plight of the poor is often highlighted in the Old Testament, which dictates that they be treated with special care (see, e.g., Exod. 22:21-27; 23:6; Lev. 19:9-10; Deut. 24:17-18; 27:19). But not so in matters of justice! Judgments must be made righteously *(beṣedeq)*. Favoritism cannot be shown — not even to the poor. The same holds true for the "great" (cf. James 2:1-9). While God's holy compassion may have a preferential option built into it, God's holy justice apparently does not.

19:16 continues the legal theme of 19:15. "Slandering" (19:16a; also in Jer. 6:28; 9:4; Ezek. 22:9; Prov. 11:13; 20:19) may have to do with speaking falsely in court and would thus connect, not only with 19:15, but also with 19:12. The meaning of 19:16b, "you shall not stand over [or: against] the blood of your neighbor," is uncertain. It may mean to conspire against someone or to neglect that person at an important moment (e.g., in court), or even to profit by his or her blood (so NRSV). The point, regardless, seems to be that one shouldn't put another's life at risk (Hartley, p. 316).

19:17 begins by forbidding hatred for one's kin (cf. Matt. 5:43-47). It then stridently commands (the Hebrew construction is emphatic) that companions must be reproved. Although the terms utilized are different ("kin" vs. "companion"), the thoughts may be related. If one doesn't "reprove" someone for what the person has done, one may end up hating him or her for it. "Reprove" is a term with legal connotations — it means to establish what is right (see Amos 5:10; Isa. 29:21). Hence, "reprove" here may involve taking someone to court. Conversely, reproof may be a necessary step prior to litigation (cf. Matt. 18:15-17). Which option is correct is unclear, as is the exact meaning of the end of the verse: "you shall not bear sin for [or: on account of] him." Perhaps by formally complaining — whether in court or not — one is prevented from taking "justice" into (and the subsequent sin onto) one's own hands. Or it may be that a person is not to remain silent and therefore become an accomplice in another's sin. Sin demands reproof! And if reproof is neglected, the guilt of sin lies as heavy on the one who averted his or her eyes as on the sinner (cf. Ezek. 33:1-9).

19:18a forbids seeking vengeance from and keeping a grudge against "your people." The enemy is often one of our own people. The enemy is often within! As such, and because they too belong to the covenant community, vengeance and grudges are not permissible options. Throughout the Bible, God promises to see to vengeance (Deut. 32:35; Ps. 94:1; Rom. 12:19; Heb. 10:30; Rev. 6:9-11). This should free us up from having to seek it ourselves.

19:18b is the passage most familiar to us. It — like several other injunctions in the chapter — is formulated positively. God's law is not only about restrictions, it also contains proactive commands, like "Love!" This particular verbal construction ("you shall love . . .") is constructed slightly differently in Hebrew than it is elsewhere. Some scholars have correspondingly argued that the love in 19:18b is different, having to do with helping, assisting, or being beneficial to the neighbor. (See, e.g., Hartley, p. 318, who argues that the construction involves one "centering on helpful action that is motivated by concern for another.") It is just as likely, however, that the different construction is purely stylistic or dialectical, and thus carries no significant interpretive weight. Whatever the case, "neighbor" is a broad term that includes both close friends and mere acquaintances. In light of the mention of the "alien" or "sojourner" elsewhere in this passage (19:10, 34), "neighbor" is probably restricted to other Israelites.

The exact significance of "as yourself" is elusive. Some have thought it involves *self-esteem:* one must first love oneself before one is able to love others. However, it is unlikely that ancient Israel had yet developed this sort of psychological insight. It may be that the phrase means that the neighbor is *the same as* the Israelite — he or she is also an Israelite or, at the very least, also human — and therefore deserves love. 19:33-34 would seem to support this latter interpretation. Whatever the case, the contextual insights into what this "love" entails should not be forgotten (see above).

19:18b is, of course, quoted by Jesus as one of the two great commandments. In Luke, Jesus uses the parable of the Good Samaritan (Luke 10:25-37) to redefine and significantly broaden the category of "neighbor." Yet Leviticus 19 already knows this lesson. In 19:34 it enjoins the love of the alien (see also Deut. 10:19) in *the exact same terms* as it enjoined the love of neighbor in 19:18b.

In sum, this very real, very concrete love of one's neighbor *as well as* the foreigner is part and parcel of Israel's responsibility to be holy as its God is holy. Yet one final thing about this holiness — God's and Israel's — must be noted. It is *all-encompassing.* In 19:15-18, several different terms are used ("poor," "great," "associate," "your people," "neighbor," "kin," "children of your people"), underscoring that God's holy nature requires a holiness in Israel that is reflected *in all of its relationships.* But the chapter is about much more than just human relationships, as important as these may be and are.

119

Instead, the "diversity of material in this chapter reflects the differentiation of life. All aspects of human affairs are subject to God's law" (Wenham, p. 264). Hence, as J. H. Hertz has rightly pointed out, "Holiness is thus not so much an abstract or a mystic idea, as *a regulative principle in the everyday lives* of men and women. . . . Holiness is thus attained not by flight from the world, nor by monk-like renunciation of human relationships of family or station, but by the spirit in which we fulfill *the obligations of life in its simplest and commonest details:* in this way — by doing justly, loving mercy, and walking humbly with our God — is everyday life transfigured" (*Leviticus* [London: Oxford University Press, 1932], pp. 190-91, emphasis mine, cited in Wenham, p. 265).

Brent A. Strawn

Fourth Sunday in Lent, Year B

First Lesson: Numbers 21:4-9
(Psalm 107:1-3, 17-22)
Second Lesson: Ephesians 2:1-10
Gospel Lesson: John 3:14-21

After their escape from bondage in Egypt, the Israelites are making their long trek through the wilderness south of Canaan toward the Promised Land. The location of Mount Hor is uncertain, although it may be near the border of Edom. We do know that the king of Edom has forbidden the travelers to pass through his territory by way of the main road, called the King's Highway (Num. 20:14-18). Israel is therefore forced to skirt the west side of Edom, through some very forbidding territory. The desert is traditionally a place of danger in the Old Testament, inhabited by scorpions and vipers and "flying serpents" (Isa. 30:6), a "land of deserts and pits," of "drought and deep darkness" that "none passes through and where no man dwells" (Jer. 2:6). The Israelites have only the sameness of daily manna to feed upon, and they are frequently bothered with thirst. They therefore turn upon Moses and accuse him of bringing them into the wilderness to die. Ab-

120

sent is any recollection of their gracious deliverance by the hand of God. Gone are all thoughts of the covenant they have entered into with the Lord at Mount Sinai. Forgotten is the divine promise that they are to be God's chosen, holy nation and a kingdom of priests. Their present discomfort and suffering rob them of the memory of God's gracious redemption and faithful day-and-night guidance of them.

Forgetfulness of God always brings its consequences, however, and so the Lord sends fiery serpents among them to bite them, and many of the people die. As a result, the people realize that in speaking against Moses, they have spoken also against the Lord. They ask Moses to intercede for them, begging God to take away the deadly serpents. Moses prays on behalf of the people and is instructed by the Lord to make an image of a fiery serpent and set it on a pole. Whenever the Israelites look at the image, they will not die. Moses therefore makes a bronze serpent — perhaps called "fiery" because of its color — and sets it up on a pole, so that anyone who looks at it will live and not die from the serpents' bites.

Few passages in the Old Testament seem more strange to us than this one. It comes across to us as an account of an ancient superstition that has nothing to do with our faith. Yet it is this story to which Jesus alludes in our Gospel lesson from John 3:14-21. As Moses lifted up the serpent to give life to the Israelites in the wilderness, Jesus teaches, so too must he be lifted up on the cross so that whoever believes in him may have eternal life. In short, our Lord takes this story quite seriously. In addition, this bronze serpent erected by Moses is referred to in 2 Kings 18:4 as having had a place in the temple in Jerusalem, until it is removed by King Hezekiah of Judah in the eighth century B.C. For five centuries, Israel preserved this ancient image! Perhaps we should therefore look at our text more carefully.

Certainly serpents have long been associated by many people with healing. The Greek god of healing, Asclepius, was represented by a serpent, and still today the symbol of the medical profession has a serpent entwined about a pole. But long before the Greeks, the serpent was associated with various gods and goddesses in Egypt and Mesopotamia and was depicted in various statues and paintings. In some passages in the Bible, a serpent bears a positive connotation. For example, in the call of Isaiah, chapter 6, the seraphim who hover above the throne of God have serpentine forms.

On the other hand, there are many negative connotations connected with serpents in the Bible. It is a serpent who tempts Eve in Genesis 3, although he is not to be understood there as a figure of Satan. The great sea serpent, which was borrowed from Mesopotamian language and which is often called Rahab or Leviathan in the Old Testament, is a symbol of darkness, chaos, evil, and death (Isa. 27:1; 51:9; Pss. 74:14; 89:10). In addition, the serpent was associated in Canaanite religion with the pagan god Baal, his consort Astarte being represented by a serpent. In removing the image of the bronze serpent from the temple in the eighth century B.C., King Hezekiah was therefore probably eliminating that form of Baal worship from the sacred site.

Despite all such background information, however, we must note very carefully that the bronze serpent that Moses sets up on a pole is not intended as a representation of God. Israelite religion, from its very beginning, forbade all images and representations of the Lord, and that prohibition forms the second of the Ten Commandments: "You shall not make for yourself any graven image" (Exod. 20:4). There is nothing in heaven or earth, or in the waters under the earth, says that commandment, that can represent the being of God. He is an invisible God, who can be worshiped in no person or thing that he has created. (Note that the Nicene Creed is emphatic in stating that Christ is "begotten, not made.")

Further, any magical interpretation of the story in our text is to be ruled out. There was the belief among some ancient peoples that they could rid themselves of some vermin by making images of them. Thus there is the story that the Philistines were rid of an infestation of mice when they made images of the mice and so drove them out of the country. But our text is not dealing in magic. The Israelites are not healed automatically of the snakebites simply because they look at an image of a bronze snake that Moses has erected on a pole. The image has no automatic power in itself, as it would if it were magical. Rather, it has power to heal because God gives it that power. And the healing is effected only if the Israelites believe that God will heal them when they look at the image. In other words, God has punished, but he has also provided the means of healing. And only insofar as the Israelites trust God's provision and take advantage of it are they granted healing from the desert's deadly snakes.

That is also the point we should notice when Jesus refers to this story from Numbers in the Gospel according to John. Our Lord does not say that when he is lifted up on the cross, all persons everywhere are automatically and magically forgiven their sins and granted eternal life. Rather, Jesus says that "whoever believes" in him and the work God is accomplishing by means of the cross will be given life everlasting (John 3:15). God always provides the means whereby we may be delivered from that death which is the wages of our sin. But we must respond to that merciful and forgiving gift. We must appropriate it by faith, reach out for it, grasp it by trust, and thus participate in its saving power. Like the Israelites entrusting their lives to the work of God through that strange symbol of the bronze serpent, so we are to entrust our eternal life and salvation to the work of God in the cross and resurrection. We cannot save ourselves any more than the Israelites in the desert could save themselves. But God does save, in both Old Testament and New, and we are heirs of that merciful grace.

Taking a further tack, it is always rewarding in using the Old Testament to understand the story of Israel as the story of our lives. Israel, in our text, was on a journey between her redemption out of slavery in Egypt and her entrance into the Promised Land, which is frequently referred to in the Old Testament as Israel's "place of rest." In many respects, you and I are on the same journey, traveling between the time of our redemption by the cross of Christ and the time of our entrance into the kingdom of God, which the Epistle to the Hebrews also calls our "place of rest" (Heb. 4:1-13). And Hebrews warns us not to "harden our hearts" as the Israelites hardened theirs in the wilderness (3:15; 4:7). Rather, we are called to the same trust to which Israel was called — trust that despite all of the dangers of our journey, despite any hardships that may come our way, despite all the forbidding landscape of our lives, there is yet One who ministers to our every need and who can guide us safely, surely to his promised kingdom. The dangers of our present wilderness cannot thwart God's purpose for our lives, any more than that dry and wasted land of the desert could thwart God's plan for Israel. God is in charge, despite all our waste places — in charge over sins and hunger, over thirst and anguish, over doubt and deepest fear. Our task is simply to trust him with our salvation.

Elizabeth Achtemeier

Ninth Sunday after the Epiphany, Year B

First Lesson: Deuteronomy 5:12-15
(Psalm 81:1-10)
Second Lesson: 2 Corinthians 4:5-12
Gospel Lesson: Mark 2:23–3:6

This is the first Deuteronomy passage assigned for comment. It therefore provides occasion to make certain points that apply to all. (On the general character and provenance of Deuteronomy, the classic study is still Gerhard von Rad, *Studies in Deuteronomy*, trans. David Stalker [London: SCM Press, 1953]. Or see any standard introduction to the Old Testament published thereafter.)

The preacher's situation with texts from Deuteronomy is determined by the circumstance that Deuteronomy is itself preaching, indeed doubly so. The book is composed as a sermon by Moses to Israel as she is about to enter the Promised Land, and by general scholarly opinion this composition rests on a tradition of actual revival preaching in late monarchical Israel.

It is often said that the preacher's task is to say what the text said, in a new situation. With many texts this is not very helpful advice, since they are not speeches. But with most texts from Deuteronomy it is to the point: we should indeed ask what the earlier preachers wanted to accomplish with their hearers and set corresponding goals for our own sermon. And there are two decisive characteristics of Deuteronomistic preaching that should guide the correspondence.

First, Deuteronomy's preaching is sacramental. Moses is depicted addressing his hearers at the Jordan as the very congregation that had received the Torah at Sinai (5:3), though according to Deuteronomy's own tradition the Sinai generation never reached the Jordan. Moreover, the hearers of the preaching epitomized in Deuteronomy, and the original readers of the book, are themselves addressed as the nation standing before the Jordan, though they lived hundreds of years later and of course knew that. Both within the scenario of the book and in its own historical situation, the past events — known to be past — that the preacher talks about are enacted upon present hearers, by the act of the preaching.

Christian preaching carries on Deuteronomy's tradition. In general, Christian sermons are not supposed merely to talk *about* saving events; they are to communicate them. They are not merely to be about, for example, Christ's crucifixion; they are to set their hearers before or even on the cross.

Using a slogan of recent ecumenical theology, right preaching "re-presents" its matter, it makes the past — or future — reality it talks about present. Preachers will have reason to relax this rule occasionally, for apologetic or catechetical reasons, but with texts from Deuteronomy it is mandatory.

The events re-presented by Moses' imagined sermon, or by the preaching practice behind it, are the giving of the Torah at Sinai/Horeb, the exodus events surrounding it, and Israel's decision before crossing the Jordan. Here there is a theological decision for the preacher to make: When preaching from Deuteronomy to a Christian congregation, are these the events now to be re-presented? Can a usually mostly Gentile congregation be addressed as an assembly of escapees from Egypt, recipients of Torah at Sinai, and imminent entrants into the Promised Land in other than metaphorical fashion? Preachers will be unable to proceed faithfully with texts from Deuteronomy — or much of the rest of the Old Testament — until they have come to some reasoned view of just how the Christian church is one people with canonical Israel.

Let me suppose my own view of the matter, and say: a Christian congregation is indeed to be addressed as very directly one people with Israel, and so, with respect to texts from Deuteronomy, as Israel in the Sinai and before the Jordan. Of course, Christian preachers cannot re-present Sinai and the situation at the Jordan in quite the same way as the Deuteronomistic preachers themselves did, since Christians look back to canonical Israel across Christ's crucifixion and resurrection. The church reads the two Testaments as one narrative in which earlier events prepare for later events. Thus in the church, exodus and Sinai are to be re-presented *as* these events prophesy Christ and the gospel. Working out how this in each case happens is the chief theological preparation for preaching from Old Testament texts.

Second, Deuteronomistic preaching is exhortation to the elect. Scholarship generally holds that some version of the book of Deuteronomy, and the preaching practice behind it, drove and/or reflected Josiah's religious and political reforms (2 Kings 22-23); no more detailed historical reconstruction has won general acceptance, but for our purposes the generality suffices. Deuteronomy is repentance preaching addressed to an elect people in need of reform, indeed in danger of rejecting their election. In Deuteronomy's view, the people of Israel are God's people by God's choice and acts and not by their own; but just so, they do have their own choices to make and actions to accomplish (e.g., Deut. 7:6-11). The choices and actions which Deuteronomy calls for are those appropriate to God's election; those against which it warns are those which defy God's election.

125

Christian preaching from Deuteronomy should address congregations in the same way: as God's chosen in danger of fighting God's choice. As to where the temptations to apostasy now lie, the required analogies are all too easy to draw. Indeed, at central points monarchical Israel's temptations and those of late modern Western Christian congregations are simply the same. The chief temptations against which Deuteronomy fights are self-righteousness, fatalism before an indifferent universe (the "host of heaven"), and worship of the gods of the world's endemic sexuality religion, the Goddess and the Baals.

So to 5:12-15. The passage comprises one of the Ten Commandments and a Deuteronomistic preacher's comments on it. In Deuteronomy's conception, the Ten Commandments are theologically different from the rest of Torah: whereas the "statutes and ordinances" which occupy most of Moses' sermon were spoken just to Moses and are only at the Jordan passed on to the people, the people themselves heard God speak these ten commands from the mountain (5:4) — these then were not "ordained . . . through an intermediary" (Gal. 3:19), however one then deals with Paul's argument.

The congregation at the Jordan, and so our congregations, can and must say: once we ourselves "heard [God's] voice out of the midst of the fire . . . and still live" (Deut. 5:24). We should ask before we preach on one of the commandments: *How* is this confession true in the mouths of Gentile Christians, who are probably most or all of those who will hear the sermon? And then: Why should it be so surprising still to be alive, having heard the commandments? And if death is the predictable outcome of hearing God, what has preserved us?

The particular commandment before us enjoins abstention from labor on the last day of a seven-day week. The positive correlate of the abstention is that the day be kept "holy," that is, set apart, "to YHWH." What was originally done to sanctify the day, we do not know; in later Judaism there are special prayers and ceremonies. Nor do we know the historical circumstance of the Sabbath's beginnings. The Old Testament tells only how canonical Israel understood the Sabbath as she had inherited it.

Obligation to keep Sabbath was understood as a sign of the covenant (e.g., Exod. 31). In later times it and circumcision became *the* marks of Israel's election; how Sabbath came to have this distinction we again do not now know. Our passage derives the obligation from God's freeing the people from Egypt, but the connection is unexplained.

The deepest interpretation is by the Priestly strand of the Pentateuch. In Genesis 1–2:3 (see Claus Westermann's commentary on Genesis), God's six days' action of creation has a "finish" beyond itself, a seventh day set apart from such action, that God declares "holy." This institution of concluding holiness is presented both as a pattern of divine life and as mandated for human life: all laborious action has its purpose beyond itself. God's set-apartness, his rest, is its own goal, and being set apart thereto is the goal and reward of human action.

Preachers on the Sabbath commandment to mostly or entirely Gentile Christian congregations have a notoriously difficult question to answer for themselves: Just what does this word demand of such a congregation? The mainline of the mostly Gentile church has never kept Sabbath, following Paul, for whom the central marks of the covenant, circumcision, and observance of "days . . . and seasons" (Gal. 4:10) were the very practices not to be imposed on Gentiles grafted into God's people. Yet the Sabbath commandment is not one of the "statutes and ordinances," whose nonapplicability to Gentile believers is relatively easy to understand; it is a word spoken directly by God to his people, in one tight set with the prohibitions of idolatry, murder, etc. Moreover, it is exegetically likely (see Westermann's commentary) that Genesis makes the temporal rhythm of labor and sanctifying abstention from labor constitutive not only for Israel's life in the covenant but for human being as such.

The mainline of the church has tried to rescue the Sabbath commandment by generalizing it: by enjoining rest from labor, though not on the Sabbath, and taking the church's holy day, the first of the week, for the purpose, and by reading from the commandment a mandate to worship God, never mind when. Sunday rest is, of course, a forgotten tradition in the mainline American church. Should it be? And indeed, is this whole way of dealing with the commandment satisfactory?

The gloss on the commandment (5:13b-15), mandating extension of Sabbath rest to slaves and strangers resident in Judea, because Israel learned in Egypt what it is to be enslaved and alien, is easier to handle than the command itself and offers obvious homiletic possibilities. But it poses a temptation: to escape into moralisms.

And now we must pose the final question the preacher must answer before preaching: How do the Sabbath, and the divine speech that enjoined it, lead to Christ? A test of a proposed answer will be that it negotiates the difficulties noted just above.

One path is laid out in the New Testament. Hebrews (3-4) cites the last verses of Psalm 95, which end "I swore in my anger, / that they should not enter my rest." Within the psalm, the "rest" is the Promised Land, prohibited to the Sinai generation. Both the old rabbis and the author of Hebrews

127

interpreted the psalm and its "rest" eschatologically: it is a "Sabbath rest" (Heb. 4:9), which on the pattern of Genesis is the goal of all God's works. "That day is wholly Sabbath, in which there is no eating or drinking, no buying or selling, but the righteous will be enthroned with crowns on their heads and delight in the glory of the *Shekinah*" (*Pirke Abot, Rabbi Nathan,* 1). In Hebrews, this final and universal Sabbath is the goal of the church's journey through this world, and is held open by the ascended Christ. "There remains a Sabbath rest for the people of God" (4:9).

Robert W. Jenson

Ninth Sunday after the Epiphany, Year A

First Lesson: Deuteronomy 11:18-21, 26-28
(Psalm 31:1-5, 19-24)
Second Lesson: Romans 1:16-17; 3:22b-28, (29-31)
Gospel Lesson: Matthew 7:21-29

Readers who have not read the first part of the article on 5:12-15 should do so before proceeding to the following. It offers general comments about preaching from Deuteronomy that apply to all but the last of the lectionary's Deuteronomy pericopes.

About our present passage there is an obvious first question: What are "*these* words" of Moses which Israel is to write on doorposts, make children memorize, etc.? The pronoun's immediate antecedent in Deuteronomy's text is in 11:13, "my commandments which I command you this day, to love the Lord your God and to serve him with all your heart and all your soul." That is, "these words" are the "first great commandment" in which Jesus epitomized the Torah; and indeed, Jesus was citing Deuteronomy.

Moreover, Deuteronomy's special corpus of "statutes and ordinances," the particular laws for Israel's behavior in the land now to be entered (see Gerhard von Rad's *Theologie des alten Testaments*), begins only with chapter 12. In our chapter we are therefore still concerned specifically with the Ten Commandments themselves, enunciated in chapter 5. We should therefore understand "these words" also of the commandment to love the "neighbor as yourself," as Jesus epitomized the "second table" of the commandments.

Israel, according to our text, is to lay up the commands of love to God and neighbor, the two tables of the Ten Commandments, in their hearts and souls. Nor is this to be a merely mental act: Israelites are to keep the commandments physically about them, as observant Jews do to this day. Above all, the commandments are to be taught to the young and meditated on by the mature. The goal of Moses' sermon is the creation of Israelites who find their "delight" in Torah and mull over it "day and night" (Ps. 1:2) — and indeed, sages who lived in this fashion, forerunners of the Pharisees and the rabbis who made the Talmud, were probably models from whom the Deuteronomistic preachers drew their inspiration.

We should not suppose that Christian "freedom from the law" opposes this valuation of the commandments or dispenses with inculcating them in the young and meditating on them in maturity. Jesus did not call the Pharisees hypocrites because they rehearsed and exegeted the commandments, but because they bent them to religious self-interest — which can be avoided only in what Scripture calls "faith." Theological history contains few such enthusiasts of Christian liberty as Martin Luther, who nevertheless taught that the whole purpose of the gospel was to enable "passion [*lust!*] and love for all God's Commandments" (*Large Catechism*, to Article 3). And when someone, or Paul's own reflections, suggested to him that we might actually *not* obey the commandments, he could only react with horrified exclamations (Rom. 6:1-2).

However we are to understand Pauline freedom from "the Law," or the Reformation's "justification by faith, apart from works of the law," one thing is sure: any understanding that sets commandments and faith against each other is wrong. The pervading heresy of the contemporary American church in all denominations is what historians call "antinomianism," the notion that since God is above all merciful, and since we are saved by faith, it does not finally matter whether or not we obey these "restrictive" commandments, indeed that we can each make up our own set of "values" and judge ourselves only by them, that if it is "fulfilling" or "loving" it must be good. Any sermon faithful to the present text will directly combat antinomianism. In the view not just of Deuteronomy but of all of Scripture, we are not our own creatures, but God's, and therefore his commands and not our judgments decide what is our good. (There is a "hegemonic discourse," the discourse of law and gospel, because there is in fact a *hegemon*; to its delights, see the following.)

The chief theological question a preacher must answer before preaching on this text, or others like it, is this: Why are God's commandments *lovable?* How could the psalmist sing, "My *delight* is in the Law of the Lord . . ."? Let me suggest some parts of an answer.

We should first understand that when God tells us "You are to be faithful rather than religiously questing, devoted rather than self-fulfilling, chaste rather than liberated" and so forth through the commandments, this is not the heteronomous imposition of a set of rules. For it is by such moral address that God creates and sustains us in the first place. In Genesis's account of creation, the act of creation is at every step a *command,* "Let there be . . . ," aimed at the "good"; and the very existence of the creature is response to the command. Therefore to hear and ponder God's moral address is to hear again the word that creates me in the first place, is to be refreshed in my very being. Luther, to continue with the most reliable possible enemy of justification by "law," expounds the commandments in his catechisms as blessed revelations of the good life, obvious and delightful to follow. This is a first reason to love them.

Next we should note the predominantly negative formulation of the commandments and their nevertheless positive role in the life of Israel and the church. The commandments were given as a special blessing by a specific God to a specific people; we must attend to their integral preface, identifying both their Giver and those to whom they are given, "I am YHWH, your God, who brought you out of the land of Egypt." Yet in their negative formulation they obviously apply to all nations.

For no community can long endure that flouts its religion, whose sexual and generational structure is not enforced, in which the duty of the citizen to faithful witness is sloughed off, in which life and property are not protected, in which greed is an accepted motive. The crimes and vices that the commandments prohibit are those that will undo any community. Therefore it always belongs to the mission of those to whom the commandments are entrusted to preach them to the state and civil society, that is, to remind the world of its own best interest. In this function the commandments may not inspire warm affection; a wise state and society will nevertheless cherish them.

But while communities *survive* by avoiding crime and vice, no community flourishes or gives meaning to its members' lives merely thereby, but by positive communal practices that define it and by the positive virtues it cultivates. Such things are initiated and sustained in the history that has made the community and by memory of that history, by communal telling of the founding and the ancestors and the destiny promised to them. So in the life of Israel and the church the commandments are more than prohibitions of obvious wrongdoing. They have acquired and continue to acquire associations and interpretations by which they become centers of the community's moral meaning. (To this whole aspect of Christian "ethics," see, above all, any work of Stanley Hauerwas.)

Thus, for example, the command not to couple with another's spouse, as a mere prohibition, leaves open many forms and understandings of spousehood, and demands only that whatever form of marriage a community practices is to be enforced. But in Israel and thereupon in the church, marriage came to be seen as a created image of the Lord's faithfulness to his people. It is, as Paul said, "a great mystery," that is, a window into divine reality, and what is seen is the relation of "Christ and the church" (Eph. 5:32). This imaging then of course worked also the other way around: as there is only one Lord and one people of this Lord, so the monogamous marriage of one woman and one man has come to be the form of marriage among God's people, whatever may be permissible in other communities, and faithfulness, like that of God to his people, is apprehended as the great sexual blessing, as it rarely has been otherwise.

As the life of Israel and the church is eschatological, drawn by a fulfillment beyond the conditions of this age, so in Israel and the church the commandments' deepest import is eschatological. Finally, they are a description of the kingdom of God, whose nearness our Lord came to proclaim (Mark 1:15). We are promised a day when God's will for our good is fulfilled; the last purpose of the commandments is to tell us how things will be then. When we teach them to our children and rehearse them for ourselves, we should say, "God is making a world of love to God and each other. What a fine world that will be. We will be faithful to God. We will be passionate for one another. We will be truthful. We will. . . ." And that is the final reason why we must and can love them. If the promise of the kingdom is true, then the commandments are not at the last rules to be obeyed, but promises of blessing.

Having said all that, there is one more — complicating — thing to be said. Paul does after all say that "the Law" is the very power of sin and death — not a very lovable role — and the Reformation knew of a "Law" that only condemns, to open our hearts to the gospel. The relation between this "Law" and the Torah of which we have been speaking is exegetically and even confessionally disputed, but the two can hardly be simply distinct. In this respect, preachers have studying and thinking to do that cannot be adjudicated here.

Robert W. Jenson

Fourth Sunday after the Epiphany, Year B

First Lesson: Deuteronomy 18:15-20
(Psalm 111)
Second Lesson: 1 Corinthians 8:1-13
Gospel Lesson: Mark 1:21-28

Readers who have not read the first part of the article on 5:12-15 should do so before proceeding to the following. It offers general comments about preaching from Deuteronomy that apply to all but the last of the lectionary's Deuteronomy pericopes.

The long central section of Deuteronomy, to which this pericope belongs, comprises "statutes and ordinances" that are to govern Israel's life when it has crossed into the Promised Land and taken possession of it (Gerhard von Rad, *Theologie des alten Testaments,* 2:219). Among the circumstances of her life there will be the absence of Moses, whom the Lord does not permit to cross the Jordan — itself one of the mysteries of Scripture, to which a later pericope will return us.

In the conception of the Deuteronomists, Moses was the first and paradigm of Israel's prophets, that is, of those among God's people who can speak to them directly for him, whose words simply *are* God's own words, and who just so can also turn and intercede with God for the people. The patriarchs, to be sure, had heard God speak and could pronounce blessings in his name (e.g., Gen. 49:1-27), but they did not speak *for* him. At most we may say that as patriarchal Israel was Israel ahead of time, Israel existing by promise of being a nation in the future, so patriarchal revelations and blessings were foretastes of prophecy. With Moses we have the thing itself, one who can say "Thus says the LORD."

Analogues of prophecy appear, of course, throughout the religious world. If, as all observation confirms, a people coheres and perdures only by its relation to a divine moral reality beyond itself, every people must have some access to that reality. Every people will therefore have some way of seeking what the Chinese called "the mandate of heaven" or it will not survive. And we may think that these analogous practices too are means by which the one true God addresses the peoples and so maintains their life. But then we must quickly pair this judgment with recognition that in actual religious practice God's address is routinely distorted and subverted.

Thus in the passage which immediately precedes our pericope and motivates it, the Canaanite nations' divinatory practices are lumped together with their child sacrifice, necromancy, and black magic as "abominable" religious practices. Moses therefore lays it down, "These nations . . . give heed to soothsayers and to diviners; but as for you, the LORD your God has not allowed you so to do" (18:14). It is somewhat to the side of our immediate argument, but preachers may want to ponder the contrast between this biblical view of religion and the late modern American doctrine that a "spirituality" is always good, never mind which. In the far more realistic view of Scripture, much, perhaps most, religious practice is simply wicked.

Divination is "abominable" for Israel in particular because it is a substitute for prophecy, so that for Israel, turning to astrology or crystal gazing or following a Führer is turning *from* the word of God itself; the Barmen Declaration of the church's independence from Hitler was in the genuine Deuteronomistic spirit. By whatever stratagems God may speak to other nations, he gave Israel the prophet, one who could guide their life by directly saying what God intends, so that for Israel to settle for less was apostasy.

But now, when the people cross the Jordan, their prophet is to stay behind. Lest Israel in Canaan be compelled willy-nilly to adopt Canaanite ways of seeking a divine will, Moses promises that the Lord will replace him, will provide someone else to stand between God and the people, to hear God's word and speak it. And it belongs to the statutes and ordinances of life in Canaan after Moses that the people are to heed Moses' replacement as they heeded him.

Who is this "prophet like me"? On a first reading, it is no one person. On this reading, what Moses promises is that there will always be someone to fill the role, that God's people will never be without a speaker of his word. And this is already a considerable theological provocation, with which a prospective preacher on this text should dwell: it is here promised that there is a people to whom the Word of God will always come.

But then the text asks us to read it a second time. The command that the people must heed the prophets as they had heeded Moses is barbed, because of course Israel in the wilderness had notoriously *not* heeded Moses; and readers are expected to feel the irony. Indeed, a chief reason for the revival preaching behind Deuteronomy and for writing the book itself was Israel's by then centuries-long record of actively persecuting the prophets. The promise that there will always be some prophet was double-edged for the audience of Deuteronomy: it also meant that there would always be someone to persecute.

Moreover, Moses raises the likelihood of *false* prophets, of whose actual appearing Deuteronomy's audience had abundant experience; when prophets contradict each other, as crowds of them had been doing for centuries, some or all must be false. Moses does provide a test for false prophets, but as the test works out it only points out the problem, as again we are surely expected to notice. A true prophet, says Moses, is one whose threats and promises come to pass; a false prophet is one whose threats and promises do not. To be sure — but if that is all that can be said, prophecy can be relied upon only after it is no longer of any use. The same criterion in Jeremiah's more or less contemporary polemic against his colleagues was openly cynical: the best chance to be a true prophet is to prophesy disaster, since that is what mostly happens anyway (Jer. 28:8-9).

Thus in the hints and ironies of our passage, the actual history is evoked: the institution of prophecy was frustrated in Israel. And now we should note that it was frustrated in a way parallel to the frustration of Israel's other great institution, the monarchy. The kings were to shepherd God's people in righteousness, which most of them did not do. Prophets were to speak God's truth to the people and the people's truth to God, which most of them did not do or did not survive doing.

As Israel's hope became explicitly eschatological, integral to such hope was expectation of a king who would at last do what Israelite kings were supposed to do, a final "Messiah." And as it was seen that Israel's eschatological hopes could not be fulfilled under the conditions of this age, that a radical transformation of reality is required, so the coming Messiah came to be seen as a king beyond all possibilities of this world's politics (e.g., Isa. 11:1-9). We may expect a parallel hope for a final prophet, and indeed there is one. The question about our text is: Does it contain that hope?

The Servant Songs of Second Isaiah (Isa. 42:1-4; 49:1-6; 50:4-11a; 52:13–53:12) present the vision of one who will do what prophets are supposed to do, speak God's saving truth and stand between God and the people (to this and much of the following, see von Rad, 2:260-70), enduring the suffering that this location must inflict and that in fact marked the lives of true prophets — here, by the way, is a far more reliable test than the one in our text! However the Servant is or is not to be identified historically, his office, like the office of the Messiah, clearly transcends the possibilities of this world. Finally we should note that in Deuteronomy and the Old Testament literature related to Deuteronomy, roughly contemporaneous with Second Isaiah, Moses is regularly and emphatically called "the Servant of the LORD" (von Rad, 2:269-270). So "Perhaps (Deuteronomy 18:13) does after all contain the promise of a new Moses" (von Rad, 2:270).

Is then Jesus, whose resurrection identifies him as the Messiah-King, also the promised Prophet like Moses? The primal church read the Servant Songs and Moses' promise just so. The church did not merely "apply" Isaiah

53 to her Lord; this Servant Song simply *was* her chief and sufficient doctrine of atonement; see the story of Candace's eunuch, who needed only to have this passage explained to have completed his catechumenate (Acts 8:26-40). The baptism that inaugurated Jesus' ministry was initially narrated as a prophet's call-vision and anointing (Mark 1:10-11); those who observed his mission needed little reflection to classify him as a prophet or would-be prophet (e.g., Luke 7:15-38); and he dies in Jerusalem just because "it cannot be that a prophet should perish away from Jerusalem" (Luke 13:33).

Of course, classical historical-critical exegesis thought it absurd to identify the prophet like Moses with Jesus. But perhaps we may now summon the courage to defy standard criticism's prejudices and frequent theological superficiality. If John's and the church's doctrine is true, that Jesus is himself in person the Word of God, then he must in literal fact be the Word which true prophets heard and spoke, the Word that in singular self-identity "came to" all the prophets. The patristic church could read the Old Testament no other way: every prophetic utterance was identified as an appearance of the Word who is Jesus. Christ is, if we may put it so, the Prophet in every prophet, and so indeed the one who does what prophets do when they are true. In that Jesus is risen, his people can never again lack a prophet.

Robert W. Jenson

First Sunday in Lent, Year C

First Lesson: Deuteronomy 26:1-11
(Psalm 91:1-2, 9-16)
Second Lesson: Romans 10:8b-13
Gospel Lesson: Luke 4:1-13

Readers who have not read the first part of the article on 5:12-15 should do so before proceeding. It offers general comments about preaching from Deuteronomy that apply to all but the last of the lectionary's Deuteronomy pericopes.

Deuteronomy 26:1-11 is the object of one of the most famous hypotheses in modern biblical scholarship, proposed by Gerhard von Rad in his *Theologie des alten Testaments*. We will divide von Rad's analysis into steps, since it has partly held up in subsequent scholarship and partly not.

Von Rad observed, as is indeed obvious once pointed out, that 5b-9 is a confession of faith explicitly appointed for liturgical use (5a), and that it and the second article of a three-article Christian creed are in much the same style. Moreover, he isolated confessional formulas with the same basic elements throughout the Old Testament. Some are more starkly creedal and some are more narratively elaborate, varying in this respect much as did the flexible "rule of faith" in the earliest church — a point which von Rad did not note.

Already this first observation is important for the Christian preacher. Whatever may be true of rabbinic Judaism, some of whose representatives claim that Judaism has Torah but no theology strictly so called, ancient Israel had a creedally formulable faith that confessed bondage in Egypt, deliverance from Egypt, and consequent entry into the Promised Land just as the church confesses Christ's death, resurrection, and ascension-return. For Christian theology this poses the question: How are these two "second articles" to be related? One can hardly preach on the prior one without giving some thought to the question.

And it is a troubling question. For the early Christian rule of faith, and the creeds that have succeeded it, move straight from creation to the birth of Christ (e.g., Tertullian, *De Virginibus Velandis* 1: "The rule of faith is . . . to believe in one God Almighty, Creator of the world, and his Son, Jesus Christ"), skipping over the whole history that Israel confessed as salvific. Gentile Christians are so accustomed to this that they hardly notice it, but if, as the church early decided against Marcion, the God of Israel is identical with the God of the church, the omission is surely deeply problematic. Many contemporary theologians, including the present author, are convinced that the theological tradition's effective removal of the exodus from the saving history we confess is a major error, which it is long past time to correct. Christian faith identifies God as "whoever raised Jesus from the dead," which we should always understand as presupposing and including "having raised Israel from Egypt." To the immediate point of preaching: What does it mean for a sermon on this text, i.e., on Israel's exodus confession, that it is in this fashion continuous with resurrection confession?

A second step of von Rad's proposal is again an observation: the long narrative of the Pentateuch is plotted by the very sequence of events recited in the creedal formulas. Thus there is another parallel, between the Pentateuch and the Gospels, for the Gospels similarly are long versions of a story quickly recited by the second articles of the three-article creeds. If bondage-and-exodus and death-and-resurrection together make one confession, so the Pentateuch and the Gospels make one expansive account of what is confessed; preaching on a Pentateuchal text — as our text itself is — should be approached much as we approach a Gospel text.

Finally, von Rad proposed that the Yahwist and the Elohist, the earliest of the documents posited by classical Pentateuchal source-theory, not only have the plot of the confessional recital but came about historically by its gradual expansion. Since this part of von Rad's interpretation has not been upheld by subsequent scholarship, we need not here concern ourselves with it.

We must next note the actual items of Israel's creed. In our particular formulation, the story does not, as often elsewhere, begin with creation or even with Abraham, but only with Jacob's descent into Egypt. Thus it seems that Israel *could* confess what the Lord had done for her without mentioning anything before the exodus and the captivity that occasioned it. Israel could speak meaningfully of the exodus without mentioning creation, but not, as we see in the plotting of Genesis and Exodus, of creation without connecting it to the exodus; Israel's saving history is not there for the sake of rescuing or maintaining the creation, but rather creation is there to begin saving history. Christian theology, which simply takes over the doctrine of creation from Israel, must observe the same order, as some theologies have done more explicitly than others (most systematically perhaps, that by Karl Barth). We should say with Martin Luther, "God created us precisely in order to redeem us" (*Large Catechism,* to Article 3).

Jacob is identified only as "a wondering Aramaean," a surprisingly laconic — and ethnographically accurate — description. The Aramaeans were an ethnic-linguistic group who, coming from the Arabian–southern Mesopotamian steppes, occupied much of Syria and northern Mesopotamia during the latter part of the second millennium B.C.; some scholars have regarded the empire of David and Solomon as the Aramaeans' (brief) big moment in history. It is also notable that God's promises to the antecedently wandering Aramaeans Abraham and Isaac, so determinative in the Pentateuch's fuller story, are not explicitly adduced; for this creed everything before the exodus is so much prologue that it can be omitted.

The recital of the exodus and the entry into the Promised Land is then as we would expect from the Pentateuch, except for yet another and glaring omission: the giving of Torah at Sinai. This is the more remarkable in that enforcing this Torah is the whole purpose of Deuteronomy.

The omission supports two scholarly contentions. First, that 26:5b-9 is indeed a set creedal text as we have been supposing. Clearly the Deuteronomists did not themselves compose this summary of saving events, since it omits the point they would have most wanted to include; they felt bound by the text they found. Second, that the traditions of exodus and of Sinai were once separate traditions, perhaps of different tribal groups who came together to form Israel. What a preacher makes of the second contention will depend on his or her understanding of canonical authority: Is the pre-canonical state of a tradition significant for preaching on it?

However one answers that last question, the omission of Sinai from this creed has considerable theological significance: it was possible, though perhaps barely so, for canonical Israel to confess her faith without mentioning the Torah — if Paul had noticed this, he would surely have made much of it. Our passage offers some support for the legitimacy of reading the Old Testament as the church does, as primarily narrative of saving events and only so as transmission of saving laws, rather than the other way around, as does rabbinic Judaism.

We must finally consider the liturgy for which this creed is stipulated. This is a harvest festival celebrated by pilgrimage to "the place which the LORD your God will choose, to make his name dwell there," bringing token offerings of the harvest.

The text speaks of one sanctuary to which all Israel comes. It was a large part of Josiah's reform program to establish this centralism, to abolish local country sanctuaries, where worship of YHWH could too easily meld with worship of the fertility gods and goddesses native to the places; particularly local harvest festivals were temptations. It was at the Jerusalem temple that Josiah centralized Israel's cult. Nevertheless, our text does not specify Jerusalem, since before David there was no worship of YHWH there and it belongs to the Deuteronomists' picture of history that there had always been a central sanctuary at some site or other.

It is a chief piece of Deuteronomistic theology that, as there is one only true God, YHWH, and one people of this God, so there can be only one place for sacrifice, the temple at Jerusalem or a predecessor. And that remains determinative for Judaism. Indeed, it remains determinative for Christianity, since the body of Jesus takes the place of the temple, at least for Gentile believers (John 2:21). There can be only one church, self-identical wherever the body is gathered. The church as the body of Christ has no branches or varieties; it is the same unique sanctuary wherever it is.

According to our text, the true sanctuary is established in that God makes his "name dwell" there. This is trinitarian theology. Throughout the Old Testament, the Lord's "name" is both the same as and distinct from the Lord himself, as are the "glory" and "angel" of the Lord. As his name or glory or angel, God is an actor *within* the history of his people, while remaining God *of* that history. The Jerusalem temple is where God both is and is not. The second triune identity both is the same God as the Father and is other than the Father. Where we gather as the body of Christ, we both enjoy God's presence and long for his coming.

Finally, the "earth is the Lord's and the fullness thereof." Israel in the Promised Land cultivates the Lord's land and not her own, and she must, like any set of tenant farmers, bring the owner a — in this case token — share of the harvest. Whatever other nations may intend by harvest festivals — celebration of the dying and rising grain or impregnation of mother earth or just feasting while the feasting is good — Israel's was for rejoicing in what the Lord had let them have.

Robert W. Jenson

Sixth Sunday after the Epiphany, Year A

First Lesson: Deuteronomy 30:15-20
(Psalm 119:1-8)
Second Lesson: 1 Corinthians 3:1-9
Gospel Lesson: Matthew 5:21-37

R eaders who have not read the first part of the article on 5:12-15 should do so before proceeding. It offers general comments about preaching from Deuteronomy that apply to all but the last of the lectionary's Deuteronomy pericopes.

It is in this passage that Moses' sermon reaches its dramatic climax. The whole Torah has been proclaimed, both the founding Decalogue which all Israel heard at the mountain and the statutes and ordinances specific for her imminent new life in Canaan. Moses poses the question decisive for that life: Will you follow this Torah or not?

The pericope is hard for preachers — not to mention commentators — precisely because of its simplicity. There is little to add to the manifest challenge of the text; there are few subtleties to track and no obscurities to alleviate. Moses says what he says, and we — whether "we" are Israel or the church — understand him, though we may wish we did not. The points chiefly to be considered by a prospective preacher present themselves without further ado.

First is the appalling clarity of the demanded decision. The people can obey Torah or not obey it; no mediating possibility is offered. Chiefly and decisively, they can worship the Lord or they can worship something else; what they cannot do is worship the Lord *and* something else, for to worship anything else is merely in itself to "turn away" from the Lord (v. 17).

Israel's whole history between exodus and exile can be construed — and that is in fact how the Deuteronomists construed it — as an extended effort to be more sensible about this matter. The rule of that history could have been formulated: "YHWH, to be sure, is our God, but who is to say there is not something true and valuable also in the gods of our neighbors, in the Baalim and Asherah and the host of heaven? And if there is, surely we should give them their due honor." Surely in religious matters it is wiser to be inclusive than exclusive.

It is a characteristic of Deuteronomy we have noted before: it sometimes speaks so directly to Christian congregations in late modernity that no analogies need be drawn. The implicit rule of Israel's idolaters is the explicit dogma of late modernity, and has gained power also in the church. And it is desperate falsehood. Either God is the only God or there is nothing but the little gods and goddesses. The preacher who is unwilling to be bluntly clear at this point should at least not try to preach on Deuteronomy.

Since the gods and goddesses are not the Creator and do not claim to be, they can afford to be accommodating and allow us to select and combine their names and characters as seems good to us, to mix some Zeus with some Baal or Osiris, or maybe some Invisible Hand with some Sophia. For very little rides on the gods' identities. But for the Creator to allow his identity to be dissipated would be to dissipate the determinate meaning of what he creates, that is, of our lives and the universe we inhabit — and that life and the world are meaningless is what polytheist antiquity indeed finally came to think and what late modernity also supposes. It is therefore a message of *salvation* when God says,

> I am *YHWH*, that is my name;
>> my glory I give to no other. (Isa. 42:8)

The decision Moses demands of Israel is the decision Scripture elsewhere calls faith. Religion can be spread around; faith is "Amen" to the first table of the commandments. This becomes quite inescapable with Jesus the Christ: one cannot temporize with a man on a cross, and either he was raised or he was not. Divinity may have many avatars, but Jesus is either the Father's "*only* Son" or he is no son at all and there is therefore no Father.

Second is the equally appalling absoluteness of the decision's consequences. Obeying or disobeying the Lord's Torah results in polar and unmediated opposites: obeying in life, good, and blessing and not obeying in death, evil, and curse. The one somewhat more scholarly help a commentator can give with this pericope is some elucidation of this language, and we will come to that. But for now a first understanding will suffice.

What is at stake in obedience or disobedience to the Word of God, including whatever of the individual biblical laws the synagogue or a Christian theological tradition may think apply, is much more than is at stake in usual religion. At stake is whether we and our communities and our world are gifts of God to one another or a horror. The world described by the commandments, the world of true worship and loyalty and chastity and truth, of love to God and the neighbor, may be the real world, or of course it may not. On which do we bet our lives?

Thus the decision demanded by Moses' peroration is not a "choice" in our ordinary sense. It is not a choice between alternative means to a good end or for the lesser of evils. Confronted by the word of life, good, and blessing on the one hand and by death, evil, and curse on the other, we have nothing to choose. There is only an obedience which is perfectly obvious in itself, or the mystery of iniquity, of our factual ability deliberately to choose our own destruction. Confronted finally by the yet more stringent word of cross and resurrection, we have nothing to choose. One can only say, "My Lord and my God," or go away sorrowful.

Of course, most late moderns, also or perhaps especially those who hear sermons, have never been presented with any decision this serious, and may indeed suppose that the function of their religion is to shield them from such. A sermon on this text must explicitly aim at rescuing its hearers from this avoidance.

Third, when Josiah heard Deuteronomy read — or an earlier or parallel version — he "rent his clothes" (2 Kings 22:11). It was precisely this sort of passage that undid him. For he understood immediately that by the norm of Deuteronomistic Torah, the nation had already chosen death.

The reforms Josiah thereupon undertook were certainly all to the good. But they did not rescue the nation from the curse it had chosen; it was too late for that. The exile came. Nor indeed was the return from exile a triumphant return to life and blessing, grateful though the people were or should have been for the little that was granted. National independence was not restored; the temple did not regain its splendor until the fascist Herod indulged his building complex; and prophets and Deuteronomistic preachers needed to continue their jeremiads.

Thus in Deuteronomy's actual situation, the decision really posed was not between death or life, for death had already happened. What Deuteronomy posed and poses can only be death or *resurrection*. Here is the point where Deuteronomy, in the whole plot of Israel's story, led and leads definitively beyond itself. Can there be resurrection? *Was* there one?

We can turn now to the promised bit of linguistic help, which will also set up a last and perhaps not so obvious gloss on our text. Of the three polar pairs that describe the consequences of obeying or not obeying, "blessing" and "curse" are controlling and are anyway now most in need of explication.

Berakah, "blessing," is the power of life itself to expand and flourish in all ways (e.g., Gen. 1:20-28); a distinction of material from spiritual blessings is not posited. The one who is blessed is just and worshipful, lives long, is prosperous, has many descendants, etc. (Johannes Pedersen, *Israel: Its Life and Culture,* trans. Aslaug Moeller [London: Geoffrey Cumberlege, 1926], I-II:182-212). The notion itself is found in all cultures, in many of which blessing is a sort of free-floating life force, but in Israel blessing is linked exclusively to the Lord: *he* is the blessed one and gives blessing to others. There is a further association, still reflected in our English usage, that "a blessing" is regularly something spoken: it is above all the *Word* of God that brings blessing. Thus the linkage between obeying Torah and deciding for blessing is almost tautological; to hearken to Torah simply *is* to receive blessing.

"Curse," *qelalah,* is the sheer deprivation of blessing: it is enfeeblement, ignominy. Construing from what seems to be the first meaning of the root, to be cursed is to be "lightweight" in every way — the notion is very close to the philosophical idea of nonbeing. It is again nearly tautological that the one who will not hearken to the Word is emptied.

So a fourth and last point. The decision posed by Moses was that faced by Abraham, who believed the Lord (Gen. 15:6) and became the father of faith. We should now note that what Abraham believed was that he would be blessed and be a blessing, *and* that this blessing was finally to extend to all nations (Gen. 12:2-3). It was central to the message of the great prophets just before and during the exile that the inclusion of all nations in Abraham's blessing finally requires an entire new order of things, a "new heaven and new earth," and that nothing less is promised. Here again is Deuteronomy reaching beyond itself to the Christ.

Robert W. Jenson

Twenty-third Sunday after Pentecost, Year A

First Lesson: Deuteronomy 34:1-12
(Psalm 90:1-6, 13-17)
Second Lesson: 1 Thessalonians 2:1-8
Gospel Lesson: Matthew 22:34-46

Whoever wrote this short chapter, or an original core of it, was a great master. Few lines of the world's literature can match "So Moses, the servant of the Lord, died there in the land of Moab, according to the word of the LORD, and (the LORD) buried him in the valley in the land of Moab opposite Bethpeor" or "And there has not arisen a prophet since in Israel like Moses, whom the LORD knew face to face." Just how preachers will reckon with this rhetorical power of the text will vary, but it must somehow be done. Those who read Hebrew may even wish to chant the lines to themselves, for the sheer sound.

Moses is buried outside the Promised Land, because the Lord had sentenced him (5b) not personally to share in the fulfillment to which his life had been dedicated. Why? Deuteronomy gives two not altogether compatible explanations.

Within Moses' sermon itself the recurrent explanation is, "The LORD was angry with me on your account" (1:37; 3:27; 4:21-22). God holds Moses responsible for the rebellions which marked Israel's life in the wilderness, though Moses was rather their victim than otherwise. Thus Moses' exile is seen as belonging to the suffering which defines a prophet. The prophet speaks for God to the people and for the people to God, and so stands between them; thereby his own life becomes the meeting place of the people's rebellion and God's judgment.

Christians understand Jesus as the final fulfillment of the promise in Deuteronomy 18 of a prophet like Moses. Following this out, we can understand Jesus' suffering as the final degree of the suffering attendant on prophetic mediation. Indeed, here is an entire doctrine of atonement, i.e., an interpretation of the saving power of the crucifixion, to which preachers may wish to lead the sermon: death is what must come to an absolutely faithful prophet, who binds God and the people by persisting between them. And if we follow yet further the way in which Jesus' death fulfills Moses' death, we may even wish to note the emphasis Deuteronomy gives to the hiding of Moses' tomb from grave robbers: of the two graves, one is empty and the other presumptively still occupied.

143

In the narrative framing Moses' sermon, a different explanation is given (32:51), according to which it is Moses' own sin that is punished. In Deuteronomy the sin is referenced only as what happened "at the waters of Meribath-kadesh"; we must turn to Numbers 20:2-13 to discover what that was. The people are without water; they complain to Moses and Aaron; these intercede with the Lord and are told to "take the rod" and command water to flow from a cliff face; Moses does this but not only takes the rod but strikes with it, which he was not told to do; water nevertheless flows. According to both passages, Moses' sin has a double aspect.

On the one side, it is a failure of faith. In Deuteronomy itself the verb translated "broke faith" is one used among other things for marital infidelity; in the closely parallel formulation of Numbers, "you did not believe in me," it is a negative of the verb (*'aman*) usually used for "be faithful" or "be reliable" or "trust in [someone's] reliability," and used centrally in the description of Abraham's response to the promise: "And Abraham *believed* the LORD, and [God] reckoned it to him as righteousness" (Gen. 15:6). Moses' sin, the difference between his behavior and Abraham's, is that he thought something more must be needed than the sheer words of God's promise. On other occasions the Lord had commanded Moses to gesture with his rod to accomplish "signs and wonders," but for Moses, on his own judgment, to add this use to what was commanded was to use the rod not from faith in God but as mere magic.

Just thereby, Moses degraded YHWH in the eyes of the people, he did not make him "holy" (32:51b). In both passages the verb is from the root *qdsh.* A fair equivalent in the language of modern anthropology is the notion of "taboo": to be holy is to be marked off from the things of daily experience, and so to be both attractive and dangerous. YHWH is holy because he is a God who both speaks to his people in love and is not to be trifled with. He dwells protectively among his people in the tabernacle or temple; but just so, unauthorized manipulation of, for example, the "ark," the throne of the Lord's presence in both, is fatal (e.g., 1 Sam. 5).

Those who hear and speak God's word, as Moses did, are to make God holy in the eyes of his people; not to do so is unfaith. A preacher should ponder: What rule should someone planning a sermon draw from that?

Moving now to items of the story, we may note that there is not in fact a height from which all the territories can be seen that the Lord "showed" Moses, and that of course Deuteronomy's original readers would know this; already in setting the scene, the narrative transcends the conditions of this world. Nor does the text intend us to suppose that God buried someone with pick and shovel; it deliberately leaves the act itself in mystery. And in general, the narrative insists on the uniqueness and finality of the event. The narrative is thus at least incipiently eschatological, and preachers should exploit that, perhaps in connection with the parallel between Moses' death and Jesus'.

With verse 9 the narrative returns to the course of history. Joshua takes over the role of prophetic leader. The content of this is described: he "was full of the spirit of wisdom." Three points are to be noted about this proposition.

First, in the Old Testament generally, there are two statements of what makes a prophet. One is that the prophet can speak the word of the Lord because that *Word* himself has "come" to him or her (e.g., Hos. 1:1). The other is that God's *Spirit* animates the prophet, making him or her capable of speaking God's word (e.g., 1 Sam. 19:20; Isa. 61:1).

In quick summary, we may say that as the word "spirit" is used in Scripture, someone's spirit is the person's life itself, insofar as this liveliness goes out to move others. The wordplay between breath and wind, in the usage of either *ruaḥ* or *pneuma,* is essential: my spirit is at once my inner breath of life and the force I may exert to agitate things beyond me. God's Spirit is at once the life that God is in himself and the whirlwind going out from God that agitates all being.

The connection between this conception of divine Spirit and prophecy will not be clear until we remember that it is precisely by speaking that YHWH calls forth creaturely actuality, and that except at the very beginning he does this by his prophets. Prophecy does not merely predict what will happen; if it is true prophecy, the Word that is God's, it summons it to happen (famously, Isa. 55:11). The prophet is an instrument of God to keep history moving; that is, the prophet is an instrument of God's Spirit. At a decisive moment in the history of Christian trinitarianism, Irenaeus of Lyon would say that the Word and the Spirit are God's "two hands."

Second, the act of the Spirit to make a prophet was sometimes an unmediated descent; so, for example, Amos had no connection with established prophecy (Amos 7:14). Joshua, however, becomes a prophet by ritualized succession to Moses (Deut. 32:9), indeed by the act of laying on of hands which was to become central in Jewish and Christian ordination; and the Deuteronomists assume that this is the usual event. Preachers will perhaps vary in their use of this observation, according to their confession's understanding of ordination; but also those with "lower" doctrines of ordination and ministry must reckon with it.

Third, the prophetic Spirit is here called the spirit of "wisdom," a central phenomenon in the Old Testament. For the Deuteronomists there is a close relation between prophecy and wisdom. Yet wisdom was in itself a very different phenomenon from prophecy: wisdom is the result of experience and long reflection, and is the virtue that enables governance, whether of kingdoms, of which Solomon is the great paradigm (1 Kings 3:6-14), or of one's own life (most of Proverbs); whereas prophecy is an unlearned gift. By the time of the Deuteronomists, however, an understanding was emerging in which all divinely granted cognition, whether prophecy or wisdom or Torah exegesis, is taken together (e.g., Neh. 9:20); what is emerging, in fact, is the notion of doctrine.

Finally, the preacher preparing to preach on this text should dwell long with the line specifying Moses' uniqueness: he was the one "whom the LORD knew face to face" (v. 10). This is not creatures' usual situation: although Isaiah saw the Lord only in symbolic apparition, he nevertheless could not stand the vision (Isa. 6:1-5); and it is doctrine for John that "No one has ever seen God" (John 1:18). But what of the creature who is personally identical with that "Son" in whom God sees himself? Not only must he be face-to-face with the Father, but even those who have seen him have "seen the Father" (John 14:9). How, then, the prospective preacher must ask, is this Jesus related to Moses?

Robert W. Jenson

Twenty-fourth Sunday after Pentecost, Year A

First Lesson: Joshua 3:7-17
(Psalm 107:1-7, 33-37)
Second Lesson: 1 Thessalonians 2:9-13
Gospel Lesson: Matthew 23:1-12

The event recorded in this passage was a long, long time in coming. Abraham's descendants finally will cross the Jordan River in order to take the land that God had promised to him centuries before. In Genesis 12:1-3 God had told the patriarch that his descendants would be a great nation and that they would eventually come to possess the land of Canaan.

With this motivation, Abraham departed the culturally sophisticated city of Ur and went to the hinterlands of Canaan.

Many years have passed since the time the patriarchs wandered the land, living in tents. Famine had forced them to go to Egypt. God had prepared the way for them in Egypt by using the sinful acts and motives of Joseph's brothers to force him there, where he rose to a position of great prominence and power. However, after the death of Joseph and the pharaoh he had made rich, the children of Abraham had come to be hated and exploited by the Egyptians. Nonetheless, God remembered his promises and raised up a deliverer who brought them out of their slavery. Of course, this hero is Moses, who not only took them out of the land of bondage but also led them toward the land of promise. This deliverance began with an act of God's great power, the crossing of the Re(e)d Sea. As the Israelites had their backs against an impassable body of water, an angry and embarrassed pharaoh bore down on them with his chariot troops. No possibility of escape was possible! This was true, at least from a human perspective. Moses, though, turned to the Lord and raised high his staff, symbolic of the presence of God, with the result that the sea split and the people of God escaped, while their enemies were destroyed by the waters as they tried to pursue them.

This was a great deliverance indeed, but still the arrival into the Promised Land was a long time in coming. As a matter of fact, it would be a whole other generation than the one that left Egypt that would enter Canaan on the day recorded in Joshua 3. The delay was not because of the length of time it took to go from the border of Egypt to Canaan — the journey was relatively short. Even with the events that took place on Mount Sinai (the receiving of the Law and the building of the tabernacle), the trip could certainly have been made within a year. But it was not a year, but rather forty years before they would come to the Jordan River.

The reason for the delay was the sin of the people, and the pivotal rebellion took place at the occasion of the sending of the spies as recorded in Numbers 13–14. Moses ordered twelve spies, one from each tribe, to go up into Canaan to explore the land. When they returned, they had good news and bad news. The good news was that this land was an excellent place, a land "flowing with milk and honey." The bad news was that the land was inhabited by fearsome people, whose presence caused them to doubt whether they could actually take possession of the land. They imagined a great defeat.

This attitude and interpretation of the situation revealed a fundamental distrust in God, the God who had defeated Pharaoh and his troops at the Re(e)d Sea. As a result, God declared that none of that generation, with the

147

exception of the two spies who delivered a minority report — Caleb and Joshua — would be allowed to enter the land. Though the fickle people then tried to force their way into the land, God stopped them by having the people of the land defeat them as they had feared. Thus, for the next forty years, the people wandered in the wilderness under the leadership of Moses, who himself had offended God in the matter of striking the rock (Num. 20:1-13). The book of Numbers has as its theme the death of the first generation and the rise of the second generation of hope. This purpose is why the two census accounts, probably actually troop registrations, structure the book. Numbers 1 lists the troops of the first generation, and Numbers 26 the second.

It is this second generation, led by Joshua, one of the faithful spies, who stand now at the eastern edge of the Jordan about to enter the land to take possession of it by force. It is a crucial moment in the history of God's work among his people. They were about to encounter a fierce and powerful enemy in the Canaanites, beginning with the city of Jericho. Jericho was the oldest city in the area by far, and its walls were legendary. While archaeologists debate the history of habitation of Jericho, which they identify with Tell es-Sultan, we will not treat this question since we will restrict ourselves to the world of the story. The point is that the generation that stands poised to enter the land will encounter a formidable foe, and surely their confidence was challenged by the enormity of the task before them. For that reason, God orchestrates the events of the crossing in such a way as to inform them that the God who was with Moses at the crossing of the Re(e)d Sea is with them now; the same divine warrior who defeated Pharaoh and his troops will bring his power against the Canaanites, whose sin has now called God's judgment upon them.

God shows that he will be with Joshua as he was with Moses by a kind of recapitulation of the dividing of the sea forty years earlier. At the center of this great act is the ark. The ark is the mobile symbol of God's presence. It was built during the wilderness period and normally housed in the Holy of Holies, the most sacred part of the tabernacle. It was considered variously as either God's throne or his footstool. In any case, when the divine warrior moved with the army, this was represented by the presence of the ark. Thus it is God who leads the way into the land. Once the feet of the priests who carry the ark hit the waters of the Jordan, they will stop so the people can step over into the Promised Land on dry ground. As they do so, they are called to remember the events at the Re(e)d Sea. The God of power is still with them!

Some have attempted a rationalistic explanation of this event. It is true that in the past couple of centuries the movement of the earth has caused land slides that resulted in the stopping of the Jordan River, but such explanations do not mitigate the miraculous nature of the event. Certainly God can use secondary causes, though there is no suggestion of such in the text, but the timing would be supernatural if nothing else.

We might also inquire into the particular form of this event to further understand its significance. In a phrase, what is it about God and water? He splits the sea and he causes the rivers to dry up. We are surely to understand that the Bible here exploits a deep-rooted ancient Near Eastern mythological construct that the God of creation shows his power by fighting against the God of the sea. Indeed, Psalm 114, which recounts both events, personifies the waters and treats the events as a defeat of the Sea and a routing of the River. In the same way that God defeats cosmic disorder represented by the Sea/River, so he will defeat sociological chaos represented by the sinful Canaanites. In the psalms, too, the waters are used to represent psychological chaos. As the psalmists feel the hostile elements of life closing in around them, they describe it as water about to overwhelm them, and they call upon God to save them from drowning (Ps. 69).

With this pervasive Old Testament theme in mind, we cannot help but think of Jesus Christ, who calms the waters so that he and those who have confidence in him can walk on the water. The Gospels, particularly Matthew, show us that Jesus' life is patterned on the exodus, wilderness wandering, conquest pattern. His baptism was equivalent to the Re(e)d Sea crossing (cf. 1 Cor. 10:1-6), which is followed by forty days in the wilderness where he was tested in the same way that Israel was (Matt. 4:1-11). Of course, he was obedient while Israel was disobedient. He died on the cross on the eve of the Passover, that great festival of the exodus, showing that he is our Passover lamb (Luke 22:7-30). As a result, those of us who follow him today are in a period of wilderness wandering (Heb. 3:1–4:13). We look forward to the future, when we will finally cross the Jordan and enter the promised land.

Tremper Longman III

Fourth Sunday in Lent, Year C

First Lesson: Joshua 5:9-12
(Psalm 32)
Second Lesson: 2 Corinthians 5:16-21
Gospel Lesson: Luke 15:1-3, 11b-32

Joshua 5:9-12 marks the critical transition from the wilderness period to the conquest of the Promised Land. In this brief Scripture we learn about Israel's circumcision, its celebration of Passover, and the cessation of the manna. The reading, however, starts in the middle of a paragraph, so it is important to place our passage in the broader context in order to understand the significance of the acts recorded there.

The children of Israel had just crossed the Jordan River to enter the land. God had shown them that he was still with them with power through the act of stopping the flow of the Jordan so they could march into the land on dry ground. Of course, this was reminiscent of the crossing of the Re(e)d Sea and just the encouragement the people needed to begin the dangerous prospect of warfare with the formidable inhabitants of the land. Indeed, according to Joshua 5:1, this mighty divine act sent shivers of fright through the inhabitants, with the result that they shrank back from the Israelites, allowing them to perform the necessary ritual preparations with which our passage is concerned.

As a matter of fact, ritual preparation is the main focus of Joshua 5:9-12. First, the Israelites perform a mass circumcision, then they celebrate Passover. We will take a closer look at these acts in a moment, but first let's explore the reason for their timing. After all, they are now in enemy territory, near the powerful city of Jericho, and circumcision, the cutting off of the male foreskin, is a painful and debilitating procedure, especially on adult males. Genesis 34, the story of Levi and Simeon killing the male population of the city of Shechem after convincing the males to circumcise themselves, reminds us of the risk the Israelites are taking in order to fulfill this ritual obligation. However, the truth of the matter is that it would be much more dangerous for Israel to continue without this ritual than with it. If the males were not circumcised at this moment, they would not face the mere anger of fellow human beings, but rather the anger of God himself. After all, they were about to engage in holy war against the inhabitants of the land. God himself, the divine warrior, would be in their midst represented by the presence of the ark. It was absolutely necessary that the army be cultically ready to be in the presence of God.

So, for that reason, the Israelites are circumcised. The ritual was established in conjunction with the Abrahamic covenant (Gen. 17:9-14). Every male among Abraham's descendants was to be circumcised as a sign that he was in covenant with God. Circumcision involved the physical cutting off of the foreskin of the penis, and the ritual appropriately represented a self-curse. That is, the implicit oath at circumcision is that if the person breaks the covenant, he will be cut off from the community just like the foreskin of the penis. It is clear that circumcision was practiced outside of Israel, but as far as we know, only Israel invested the ritual with this religious meaning.

Thus we can easily see why it was important for the Israelites to take on their bodies the sign of the covenant before entering into holy war. What is not so clear is why the males were not circumcised soon after birth. The text does not give us an explicit reason, so we are left to speculate.

It appears that the generation that had left Egypt had been circumcised, but the generation that was born in the wilderness was not, most likely because of the nature of the wilderness wanderings after the events of Numbers 13–14. In these chapters Moses sent twelve spies, one from each tribe, into the Promised Land from their campgrounds in Kadesh-barnea. Upon their return, they confirmed that this was indeed a wonderful land, a land "flowing with milk and honey." However, on the negative side, they frightened the people with their report of the inhabitants, whom they described as unbeatable. This report led to a crisis of confidence in God, and to God condemning that generation to die in the wilderness. The wilderness then became a place of judgment. The second generation, born in the wilderness, was the generation of hope, to be sure, but as long as they were in the wilderness, even they were not privileged with the sign of the covenant on their body.

But the moment has now come. They are out of the wilderness and about to take possession of the land, and so they are circumcised. The paragraph immediately preceding our text describes the ceremony. They use flint knives, as opposed to iron ones, likely reflecting the antiquity of the ritual. The place where the mass circumcision took place apparently was renamed for the occasion, Gibeah-haaraloth, or "Hill of the Foreskins." The site that will serve as battle headquarters for the conquest also receives its name from the significance of the circumcision. Gilgal, located only a few miles from Jericho, gets its name from a verbal root, *galal*, "to roll away." Just like the incised foreskin is rolled off the penis, so the shame associated with the bondage in Egypt rolled away from Israel.

If circumcision is a sign of initiation into the covenant, so Passover is the sign of continuing in the covenant. It is therefore not surprising that Israel next celebrates Passover. We learn about the establishment of the Passover festival in Exodus 12; it commemorates the fact that during the climactic plague against Egypt the angel of death passed over the houses of Israel as he struck down the firstborn of Egypt. Passover was the festival that reminded the Israelites of God's great deliverance of them from slavery in Egypt. Now they celebrate it in anticipation of the victory God will give them in Canaan.

Baptism and the Lord's Supper are rough analogues to the Old Testament practice of circumcision and Passover. Christians may debate over much that has to do with the form and significance of these sacramental rituals, but they clearly are signs of covenant initiation and maintenance, respectively.

Finally, our passage mentions the cessation of the manna as the Israelites begin to eat the food produced in the land of promise. Perhaps nothing could symbolize the transition from the period of the wilderness to the entry of the land better than this. The manna was the food that God provided for Israel in the wilderness. We learn about it in Exodus 16:13-35, Numbers 11:4-9, and Deuteronomy 8:1-20. The manna came with the morning cover of dew. It was something the likes of which Israel had never seen before, so it was named "manna," which means "What is it?" This, apparently, was the question asked by Israel when they saw it. Indeed, it is a question asked by interpreters even today. Some feel that the intention of the text is to describe a miraculous feeding, while others suggest that God used a natural process, for instance, "the secretion of small aphids that feed on the sap of tamarisk trees. When it hardens and falls to the ground, it can be collected and used for a sweetener" (J. Walton and V. Matthews, *The IVP Bible Background Commentary: Genesis-Deuteronomy* [Downers Grove, Ill.: InterVarsity Press, 1997], pp. 102-3). However, this only happens seasonally, and though other natural processes are also suggested, it is clear, as Walton and Matthews would agree, that even if God used a natural process, it was surely understood to be exploited in a supernaturally providential manner. In any case, the manna now ceased and they would eat regular food. A new era has arrived; God's promises are in the process of fulfillment.

Tremper Longman III

Twenty-fifth Sunday after Pentecost, Year A

First Lesson: Joshua 24:1-3a, 14-25
(Psalm 78:1-7)
Second Lesson: 1 Thessalonians 4:13-18
Gospel Lesson: Matthew 25:1-13

As the book of Joshua closes, so does the era of the conquest under the leadership of Joshua. Joshua has been an effective and faithful successor to Moses. God used him to direct Israel in the taking of the land (Josh. 1–12) and also in the distribution of the land to the tribes (Josh. 13–22). The book ends with an account of Joshua's death and burial (24:28-33), but our present text anticipates and tries to prevent the coming crisis that will result from a possible vacuum of leadership. When Moses was about to die, he led Israel in a covenant-renewal ceremony, represented by the book of Deuteronomy, that reaffirmed the relationship that had been established at Mount Sinai, the so-called Mosaic covenant (Exod. 19–24). In a similar fashion, a generation later, Joshua leads Israel to reaffirm their covenant relationship with God and their commitment to stay faithful.

In other words, Joshua 24 is a narrative describing a covenant-renewal ceremony, and therefore has the elements of a covenant document. Before listing these elements, we begin with a description of the covenant concept in the Old Testament. The English word "covenant" partially captures the idea, since "covenant" is a legal term that describes a relationship. However, recent research has shown that the idea is actually closer to what we would call a treaty, and that some biblical texts, including Joshua 24, contain the elements of an ancient Near Eastern treaty. Indeed, archaeologists have recovered and philologists have translated a number of treaties for the second and the first millennia B.C.E., and divine-human covenant texts like Deuteronomy and Joshua 24 have many of the elements that are found in a subset of these treaties we call vassal treaties. Parity treaties are treaties between near equal powers (say Egypt and Hatti), whereas vassal treaties are between a dominant power and a lesser power, a good example being the treaty between Mursilis of Hatti and Duppi-Teshub of Amurru (found in *Ancient Near Eastern Texts*, pp. 203-5). A vassal treaty is more appropriate to communicate the power relationship between God and his people than a parity treaty.

Vassal treaties have six parts, each of which is reflected in Joshua 24 in some fashion. We will describe the passage and its context as a whole as we survey these six parts, after which the ramifications of this genre identification will be spelled out.

Introduction. A vassal treaty begins with the introduction of the two parties involved. In Joshua 24 we do not have the actual treaty document, but we have an account of the ritual that confirms it. It is quite clear from the first verse who the two parties are. On the one hand are the leaders of Israel who will survive Joshua, the "elders, leaders, judges and officials of Israel," and on the other hand is God. Joshua, the mediator of the covenant, will speak for God in this passage. The significance of the site of Shechem, located in the northern hill country, goes back to the patriarchal period. Abraham built his first altar in Shechem (Gen. 12:6), and Jacob later bought land there for his dwelling (Gen. 33:19). Furthermore, in the earlier covenant renewal at the time of Moses, it was anticipated that the blessings and curses of the covenant (see below) would be read from Mount Gerizim and Mount Ebal in the vicinity of Shechem. In fulfillment of this request of Moses, Joshua had earlier traveled up to Shechem to build an altar to God and read the law of Moses (Josh. 8:30-35). So already by the time of our text, the city and vicinity of Shechem was invested with great significance. It is also of contemporary interest that the archaeologist A. Zertal ("Has Joshua's Altar Been Found on Mount Ebal?" *BAR* 11, no. 1 [1985]: 26-43) has uncovered what he identifies as a cultic site on Mount Ebal, which he associates with the activities of Joshua in chapters 8 and 24, though this has been disputed by others.

Historical review. An ancient treaty would often begin with a review of the history of the relationship between the two parties. In secular treaties the great king would lay it on thick by telling the vassal king how wonderful he had been to the weaker nation and how ungrateful the other king had been to him. In Joshua, of course, the historical remembrance is more than manipulative political ideology. God in truth had been overwhelmingly gracious to Israel. The historical review (vv. 2-13) begins with Abraham in Mesopotamia and narrates to the present time when Israel, through God's good agency, have been given a productive land.

Law giving. After the gracious relationship between God and Israel has been firmly established, God gives them the Law. This, too, follows the pattern of the ancient Near Eastern treaties, in which the present obligations of the law spring from the relationship of the past. The covenant renewal here in Joshua 24 assumes a reaffirmation of the Mosaic covenant, but in particular the emphasis is on what is the fountainhead of that covenant, and that is the exclusive worship of Yahweh alone. The transition from historical review to law is often signaled by the word "now," which brings us from the past to the present. 24:14-15 reads "Now fear the LORD and serve him with all faithfulness. Throw away the gods your forefathers worshiped beyond the River . . . or the gods of the Amorites, in whose land you are living." Joshua then affirms his own intention to be obedient in what may be the most well-known words of this chapter: "As for me and my household, we will serve the LORD."

Rewards and consequences. In the next section, the law stipulates consequences for disobedience. In ancient Near Eastern treaties, the great king would inform the vassal that wonderful rewards would follow obedience to his laws while punishment would surely reach the one who disobeyed. In a similar manner, conditions attach to Israel's response. Joshua emphasizes the curse that will result from disobedience: "You are not able to serve the LORD. He is a holy God; he is a jealous God. He will not forgive your rebellion and your sins. If you forsake the LORD and serve foreign gods, he will turn and bring disaster on you and make an end of you, after he has been good to you" (24:19-20).

Witnesses. A treaty, being at heart a legal document, needs witnesses. In ancient Near Eastern treaties, the gods and goddesses of the respective nations often served in this capacity. This need explains Joshua's language about the people serving as witnesses against themselves (24:22). In verses 26-27 Joshua also raises a large stone under an oak which is near the holy place. This stone also serves as a witness. How can this be? Simply by the fact that everyone will know and remember that the stone was set up on the occasion of this covenant agreement. The tradition will be passed down, so that whenever people see the stone, they will remember this agreement.

Deposit of the treaty document. Narratives that describe covenant ceremonies often will describe what is done with the actual document. This is a legal procedure, and it is put down in writing. The recording of this covenant affirmation is described in 24:25-26.

It is very clear that the form and content of Joshua 24 is a renewal of the covenant made at Sinai on the occasion of the crisis precipitated by the impending death of Joshua. The people reaffirm their commitment. However, in its present canonical context, the people's reaffirmation is essentially a self-condemnation. After all, the next book in the canon is the book of Judges, which describes the downward spiral of the people of God. Without a leader ("In those days Israel had no king; everyone did as he saw fit" [Judg. 21:25]), Israel's spiritual and ethical depravity increased as time went on. Eventually, God would judge Israel by sending them into exile. In other words, the curses of the covenant came into effect.

Nevertheless, we must not lose sight of the fact that the covenant concept is one that develops from the very beginning of the Old Testament and extends into the New Testament. Space will not allow a full exposition here, but those interested might consult O. Palmer Robertson, *The Christ of the Covenants* (Presbyterian and Reformed Publishing, 1981). In brief, however, the Old Testament speaks explicitly of a covenant of Noah (Gen. 9), a covenant with Abraham (Gen. 15; 17; cf. 12:1-3), a covenant with Moses (Exod. 19–24, renewed in Josh. 24), and a covenant with David (2 Sam. 7). Jeremiah 31 anticipates a future new covenant, and Jesus speaks of the new covenant that he establishes by his death and resurrection (Matt. 26:28). The book of Hebrews also speaks in the language of the new covenant in Jesus superseding the old covenant, which refers to the collective covenants found in the Old Testament (Heb. 8). The point is that believers today, like those at the time of Joshua, are in a covenant relationship with God, one that fulfills the covenants of the Old Testament.

Tremper Longman III

Twenty-sixth Sunday after Pentecost, Year A

First Lesson: Judges 4:1-7
(Psalm 123)
Second Lesson: 1 Thessalonians 5:1-11
Gospel Lesson: Matthew 25:14-30

Although the first lesson is part of the lectionary's semicontinuous track through the Old Testament, it has a significant point of contact with the Gospel lesson. Properly understood, the parable of the talents is not primarily about whether and how we use what God has given us, but rather it focuses attention on the character of God. Is God harsh, arbitrary, and to be feared, as the third servant suggests (Matt. 25:24), or is God gracious and compassionate, as indicated by the master's incredible decision to turn his whole fortune over to three slaves? The parable suggests the latter — that is, the incredible graciousness and compassion of God.

The issue of God's character is especially relevant in confronting the only passage from the book of Judges in the Revised Common Lectionary, Judges 4:1-7. Judges has frequently been understood to portray a God who is allegedly vengeful and violent, and who seems arbitrarily to favor Israel over all other peoples. A sermon on the story of Deborah is an opportunity to address these misconceptions. To be sure, the story of Deborah is a violent story; and Judges contains plenty of violence. But this too is an opportunity, because it gives the preacher a chance to remind contemporary persons that our world is every bit as violent, if not more so, than the world of Judges. By confronting the violence in this book and by considering God's role in the story, we are invited to a deeper understanding of God and God's justice, and we are also challenged to consider whether we are, in terms of the conclusion to Deborah's story, God's "enemies" or God's "friends" (Judg. 5:31).

The lesson, of course, only begins to tell Deborah's story. We do meet Barak, her colleague, but 4:1-7 makes no mention of Jael, who also is a major character. Thus it will be necessary for the preacher either to keep reading beyond 4:7 or to tell the whole story to the congregation. What is present in 4:1-7 is the pattern that characterizes the book of Judges. The people do "evil" (v. 1; see 2:11; 3:7, 12; 6:1; 10:6; 13:1); they are "sold" to an enemy (v. 2; see 2:14; 3:8; 10:7); and they cry to God for help (v. 3; see 3:9, 15; 6:6). At this point the pattern is broken. Ordinarily there is the notice that God raises up a deliverer (see 3:9, 15), but this is missing in Deborah's story. This may be because there will actually be three deliverers — Deborah, Barak, and Jael — but the effect too is to emphasize that the real deliverer is God (see 4:23).

Thus the altering of the typical pattern also invites attention to the character of God; and indeed, the pattern itself has theological significance. To be sure, it suggests (as do all the books of the Former and Latter Prophets) that there are destructive consequences for failing to worship and obey God, but it also affirms that God hears and responds to the cries of the oppressed, even when their oppression may have been deserved. In a word, this is grace; and each new deliverance in the book of Judges is, in effect, a new exodus. The pattern in Judges, therefore, portrays not a God who is harsh and vengeful, but rather a God who is gracious and compassionate. While there are inevitably destructive consequences of injustice, God regularly acts by grace to restore conditions which make possible life as God intends it. In short, in Judges, as throughout the Bible, God pursues justice by way of grace.

In this regard, it is crucial to notice the situation of the Israelites in 4:1-7. Sisera "had oppressed the Israelites cruelly twenty years" (4:3). At this point Deborah is introduced. Not only is she the only judge that appears to function in an actual legal capacity (v. 5), but she is also "a prophetess"

(v. 4). Deborah speaks the word of God to Barak (vv. 6-7), and Barak subsequently treats her as nothing short of an embodiment of God's presence. As Israel would later go into battle only accompanied by the ark of the covenant (see 1 Sam. 4), so Barak will only go into battle if accompanied by Deborah (4:8-10). Lest the partnership between Deborah and Barak be seen in gender terms as Deborah's need for a man to do the actual fighting, the real hero of the story turns out to be another woman, Jael. While Jael has often been accused of being treacherous and of breaking the ancient code of hospitality, it is actually Sisera who breaks the hospitality rules at every point — by approaching Jael in the first place rather than her husband, by accepting an offer which was not Jael's to make, and by making requests of his host (see Victor Matthews, "Hospitality and Hostility in Judges 4," *Biblical Theology Bulletin* 21 [spring 1991]: 13-21). All this would have served to put Jael on alert, and her killing of Sisera amounts to self-defense. Furthermore, this killing is immediately followed by the notice that "God subdued King Jabin of Canaan" (4:23); and both Deborah and Jael are described in 5:7, 24 in the most exalted of terms.

The effect, again, is to focus attention on the character of God. How are Jael's violent act and Deborah's military leadership congruent with God's will for justice, righteousness, and peace? To begin to answer this question, it is crucial to note, as suggested above, that Deborah's and Jael's actions address a situation in which violence already existed — the institutionalized violence involved in the cruel oppression of the Israelites (4:3). What the story of Deborah, Barak, and Jael affirms is that God vehemently opposes oppression, and that God impels people to dismantle oppressive systems. Lest God's activity in the book of Judges be dismissed as crass favoritism toward Israel and hatred of the Canaanites (and other peoples), it should be noted that the previous judge, Shamgar (3:31), was probably not even an Israelite; and neither is Jael! Furthermore, in the larger context of the canon, when Israel becomes an oppressor, God opposes Israel as well, resulting in Israel's destruction and the exile. In Judges, therefore, the Canaanites and other peoples are a symbol for the way of injustice that leads to death. If God shows partiality, it is partiality only to justice, righteousness, and peace, which means that in situations of cruel oppression the oppressor must be opposed.

This is a message that pervades the Bible, from Exodus to and through Christ. It is revealing that the exalted titles for Deborah, "a mother in Israel" (5:7), and especially for Jael, "most blessed of women" (5:24), anticipate the New Testament. The only other woman who receives such exaltation is Mary, mother of Jesus, who is addressed as "Blessed . . . among women" (Luke 1:42). Not coincidentally, Mary soon sings a song that, like the song of Deborah and Barak (Judg. 5), praises God for opposing oppressors: God "has scattered the proud in the thoughts of their hearts" and "brought down the powerful from their thrones, / and lifted up the lowly," and "filled the hungry with good things, / and sent the rich away empty" (Luke 1:51-53). This is what God characteristically does; it is a manifestation of "his mercy" (Luke 1:54). Mary's song, of course, anticipates the life and ministry of her son Jesus, who proclaimed and embodied the same message.

To be sure, Jesus rejected violence, and without a doubt God never wills violence. But in situations where violence already exists, what do we say and do? As John Hamlin says of Jael: "If we put ourselves in the place of those who have suffered under tyrants like Hitler, Stalin, Samoza, or Idi Amin, we can understand how Deborah would call the woman who destroyed Sisera 'blessed'" (*Judges: At Risk in the Promised Land* [Grand Rapids: Eerdmans, 1990], p. 87).

In the final analysis, the violence of Deborah's story and the book of Judges is a challenge for contemporary persons to place ourselves in relation to the violence of our world. For us, as for the Israelites in Judges, violence already exists. The twentieth century was the most violent century in human history; as for citizens of the USA, we live in a society where violence is a daily reality on our streets, in our schools, and in our homes. The book of Judges invites us to ask ourselves whether the same greed and self-centeredness that has produced our superaffluence is not also systematically teaching us to be violent. And, as for our incredible affluence, Judges also invites us to place ourselves in relation to the poverty of most of the rest of the world. If, as the story of Deborah and the story of Jesus affirm, it is God's character to bring down the powerful, might we not need to be worried? The book of Judges is, after all, a part of the prophetic canon, which generally functions theologically to call people to repentance. Are we the victims of cruel oppression, or are we the perpetrators of cruel oppression?

The name Deborah means "bee"; and in a real sense, when Deborah's story is heard in the larger context of the prophetic canon, it performs a theological sting operation. Readers of the whole prophetic canon are reminded that when the people of God become oppressors, God opposes them too! Thus the story of Deborah finally invites us to consider whether we are "friends" or "enemies" (see Judg. 5:31) of the God who ultimately claims the whole world and all its people as God's very own. Or, in terms of last week's Old Testament lesson, the story of Deborah invites us again to choose whom we shall serve (see Josh. 24:15) — the gods of progress and affluence or the God who mercifully opposes cruel oppression.

J. Clinton McCann

Twenty-fourth Sunday after Pentecost, Year B

First Lesson: Ruth 1:1-18
(Psalm 146)
Second Lesson: Hebrews 9:11-14
Gospel Lesson: Mark 12:28-34

After the horrific conclusion to the book of Judges, where Israel is seen at its worst, the canon offers a counterpoint, the book of Ruth, where Israel is seen at its best. More than a transition piece from the amphictyonic period to the monarchy (and its penultimate model, David, whose genealogy concludes the book), the short story beautifully combines a woman's profound faithfulness and the subtle working of God within human striving. While most of Ruth (one of only two biblical books named after a woman) is concerned with a family's remarkable restoration, this lection describes the deterioration of that family. Women marginalized by widowhood, the loss of male heirs, and foreign birth will find haven in the *hesed* (Hebrew for loving-kindness or caring responsibility) of God even as they seek to practice it themselves.

Because of famine, Elimelech ("my God is king"), his wife Naomi, and their two sons leave Bethlehem to go dwell in Moab, a land apparently on friendly terms with Israel at that time (compare Josh. 24:9; Judg. 3:12; 2 Sam. 8:2). Like hungry others before them, Abraham (Gen. 12:10) and Jacob (Gen. 42:1), they become strangers in a strange land for a time. But Moab is hard on the men of the family, as one tragedy follows another. Elimelech dies, as later do both his sons, ten years after marrying two Moabite women, Orpah and Ruth. Taking foreign wives seems to have been acceptable then, as the strict enforcement of laws against such would not come until the time of Ezra and Nehemiah. Verse 5 makes clear Naomi's situation. In a culture where women without males are quite vulnerable, she has lost both husband and sons.

The narrator names God's active work in verse 6 (the only other such divine intervention comes at 4:13 when Ruth conceives a child) when the famine in Judah is said to have been lifted by God's grace. News of this change at home leads Naomi to head back to Bethlehem with her daughters-in-law. She reflects as she walks and soon decides (or perhaps "judges") (Edward F. Campbell, Jr., *Ruth: A New Translation with Introduction, Notes, and Commentary*, Anchor Bible 7 [Garden City, N.Y.: Doubleday, 1975], p. 58) that it is ill advised for her daughters-in-law to accompany her. She asks God to have *hesed*

(v. 8) on them, and urges them to stay in Moab to seek husbands there (and to return, oddly, to their "mothers'" houses, perhaps suggesting their fathers are dead as well). Although she does not say so, perhaps she fears how they, as aliens, will be received in Bethlehem. Orpah and Ruth affirm that they wish to go on with Naomi. She insists even more that they stay, citing the impossibility of her bearing more sons who might when grown fulfill the responsibilities of levirate marriage (see Gen. 38; Deut. 25:5ff.). Naomi, whose name may mean "sweetheart" (Geoffrey E. Wood, "Ruth, Lamentations," in *The Jerome Biblical Commentary* [Englewood Cliffs, N.J.: Prentice-Hall, 1968], p. 605), declares in Job-like anguish that her life has become utterly "bitter" by the hand of God while there may still be hope for the younger women. Orpah is at last persuaded by this logic and turns back toward Moab.

Seeing Orpah go, Naomi asks Ruth a third time to do likewise (on this threefold repetition, compare Abraham's negotiations with God in Gen. 18:22ff. as well as the story of the call of Samuel in 1 Sam. 3:1ff.). Ruth again refuses her, this time with her well-known and beautifully poetic words of faithful devotion (vv. 16-17). Although saddened, Orpah models prudence and common sense and leaves with Naomi's blessing. But Ruth "ventures beyond human horizons, a human estimation of what is correct or safe. She manifests the spirit of Abraham" (Wood, p. 606). She confesses Yahweh to be her God, and commits herself to live in the spirit of Yahweh's *hesed* toward Naomi. In a world where men rule and women depend on them to survive, widowed and childless Ruth casts her lot in solidarity with an older, widowed woman without surviving male offspring. That is no small act of faith.

The motivation behind Ruth's profession of faith and devotion to Naomi is not clearly specified. While she could make Orpah's choice, she does not do so. Rather, Ruth chooses to be in relationship with Naomi and her God, at once being loyal and becoming more vulnerable than she would be in her native land. She answers a question similar to that which the disciples put to Jesus, "Lord, to whom shall we go?" (John 6:68), by choosing Naomi and Naomi's God as those with whom she will be in relationship. Neither she nor Naomi knows what lies ahead for them, but they will encounter it with one another and their God. The God who ends famines may provide life in new ways for these two women as well.

Ruth clings (v. 14) to her mother-in-law the way Israel, at its best, clings to God in covenant relationship. There is no turning aside for another, even for good and practical reasons. It is not too much to say then that Ruth enters into covenantal relationship with Naomi and her God, as the language of verses 16 and 17 indicates (Campbell, p. 31). It is this embodying of covenantal life which in part elicits faithful, covenantal responses from the community of Bethlehem when the two women return. They will have to be clever, not unlike the Hebrew midwives and other conspiratorial women who delivered Moses in Exodus 2, but they act out of devotion to the calling of God. The marginalized often have to play by a set of rules not always in accord with by-the-book morality, becoming even somewhat manipulative, in order to survive (compare the Canaanite woman's repartee with Jesus in Matt. 15:21ff.).

Although not spoken to directly by God, as was Abraham, Ruth exhibits the same willingness to become a sojourner in a foreign land. She literally "steps out in faith" and becomes the unlikely alien sojourner through whom God acts. And where Abraham became the father of a nation, Ruth will be the mother of its line of kings (Wood, p. 607). For its part, the community of Bethlehem will come to treat Ruth in accordance with Israel's best traditions of compassion toward strangers and widows (see Exod. 22:21ff. and many other similar texts), even a Moabite whose membership in the assembly was forbidden for ten generations (see Deut. 23:3). Rather wonderfully, a rabbinic comment says that Ruth could be welcomed because she was a Moabitess, not a Moabite. Being a woman worked to her advantage in that case.

Ruth's story begins in this lection with her willingness to become vulnerable to a future that she does not have much power to control. Her trust is born in part from what she has seen in Naomi. When events over which she had no control befell her, first a famine and then the death of all the males in her family, Naomi chose a course of action that in both cases involved relocation. She lamented her condition before God, to be sure. But she also chose how she would respond. Naomi's feelings are understandably those of bitterness, but she is able to act, to choose, to exercise what measure of freedom she has. She does not fall prey to immobilizing victimization. Although she is pragmatic in her advice to her daughters-in-law, she also is aware that God may yet act favorably toward her in the future. Though in desperate circumstances herself, she nevertheless asks that God's *ḥesed* be upon Orpah and Ruth. Naomi is a woman who knows herself to be in relationship with God, and she is therefore feisty and open to the future. Hers is the faith that Ruth seems to catch, and finally comes to bet her life on. If "faith is the assurance of things hoped for, the conviction of things not seen" (Heb. 11:1), then this is the faith Naomi and Ruth share in covenant commitment to God and with one another.

Lawrence W. Farris

Twenty-fifth Sunday after Pentecost, Year B

First Lesson: Ruth 3:1-5; 4:13-17
(Psalm 127)
Second Lesson: Hebrews 9:24-28
Gospel Lesson: Mark 12:38-44

In its hurry to establish Ruth as the progenitor of Israel's great king David, the lectionary passes over much of the richness of one of the Bible's most beautiful stories. The preacher may wish to expand the first part of this lection to include verses 6 through 13 of the third chapter or begin the second part at verse 7 of chapter 4. These comments will address the lessons so expanded. It will be helpful to have read the preceding entry on Ruth 1:1-18.

Acting in accordance with the laws concerning gleaning (Lev. 19:9; Deut. 24:19ff.), Boaz, a relative of Ruth's deceased father-in-law Elimelech, has allowed Ruth to glean in his barley fields and thereby shown himself to be a just man. Boaz has gone beyond the law's requirements to provide adequate grain for Ruth and Naomi (2:14ff.). He has taken Ruth "under his wing," and yet sees his action as part of the work of God, "under whose wings you have come for refuge" (2:12).

The lection opens with Naomi addressing Ruth as "my daughter" and seeking to find more lasting security for her (and no doubt for herself as well). She advises Ruth to clean and adorn herself in preparation for seeking out Boaz, which she is to do when he has retired for the night at the threshing floor after a surfeit of food and drink. Ruth is to do what Boaz tells her to do.

In the middle of the night, Boaz awakens to find Ruth at his side. But Ruth, taking the kind of initiative she has seen her mother-in-law take, doesn't wait for his instruction but rather asks him to share his cloak with her as a kinsman should do. She calls upon the righteous Israelite to behave righteously. Boaz, like Naomi, calls Ruth "my daughter" twice, acknowledging her right to make a claim, and expresses his pleasure at her seeking him out. Although another unnamed man has the right of first refusal on Elimelech's property (which includes Ruth), Boaz promises to do all he can legally do to protect Ruth as next of kin.

The first thing the next morning, Boaz gathers elders of Bethlehem to witness the sorting out of legal matters and eventually, by the grace and hand of God, as the narrator wants us to know, secures the right to take

163

Ruth as his wife. This arrangement not only pleases Boaz, who has been drawn to Ruth, but also serves to maintain Elimelech's name and of course provides the security sought by Naomi and Ruth. Such a remarkably satisfying conclusion could only be wrought by God in concert with people like Boaz acting justly and with *ḥesed* (Hebrew for loving-kindness or caring responsibility), and women like Ruth and Naomi acting with *chutzpah.* As would be expected in a small town like Bethlehem, there are many witnesses to this joyous moment. Ruth is compared to Rachel and Leah, the matriarchs of Israel (perhaps because of the tradition in Gen. 35:19 that Bethlehem is the burial site of Rachel). The Moabite outsider has found full acceptance in the house of Israel. God is asked to bless the couple with children, like Judah and Tamar, in acknowledgment of how the intention of levirate marriage (see Deut. 25:5ff.) has been fulfilled in an unexpected and grace-filled way, in part because of the faith and wits of women.

For only the second time in the entire narrative, God makes a direct appearance in making Ruth conceive (4:13, the other being God's relief of the famine noted in 1:6). Boaz and Ruth become parents to Obed, who, remarkably, is named by the women of the community rather than by his father. The women praise God and celebrate with Naomi for at last having kin and the continuance of her family insured against tremendous odds. And Ruth is cherished, remarkably, as "your daughter-in-law who loves you, who is more to you than seven sons." *Inclusio* piles upon *inclusio* as the tragedies that opened the tale are overcome. And yes, through this family shall come the great king David, who was not a purebred Israelite but had a Moabite great-grandmother of astonishing faith and love.

Ruth is a paragon of love and loyalty without question. But these qualities do not in and of themselves insure happy endings to life's tragic circumstances, as the story's hearers surely know. In this story, such admirable qualities "become the vehicle by which Yahweh is enabled to do dramatic and wonderful things, not just for the women of Elimelech's family, but for all Israel — indeed, for all humankind" (Walter Brueggemann, Charles B. Cousar, Beverly R. Gaventa, and James D. Newsome, *Texts for Preaching: A Lectionary Commentary Based on the NRSV — Year B* [Louisville: Westminster/John Knox, 1993], p. 579). There is a partnering in this wondrous tale between God and God's people that parallels the partnering of Ruth and Naomi. In both instances the relationship is built on *ḥesed,* on faithful, loving, caring, responsible living in and under covenant. Life is not always, or even often, this way. More often than not, human sinfulness temporarily thwarts the redemptive intentions of God. And sometimes God is about purposes much larger than securing "happily ever after" endings for our lives. But the book of Ruth is a blessed and shining example of what life in God's inbreaking kingdom looks like. It is a story populated with people taking risks out of faith in God's future action, people seeking to live righteously in community according to time-tested traditions and at the same time being open to surprising new ways of God that break down boundaries between insiders and outsiders. Perhaps the story's most remarkable aspect is what is never said. No one ever suggests that God could not work through a single, widowed, childless foreigner. Those who know Scripture will see that God has worked again and again through outsiders, strangers, and the marginalized in order that we will not mistake life's wondrous moments as being solely of our own creating. Not only was Jesus born of a woman like unto Ruth, he cited and told stories of such people again and again (e.g., see his use of Naaman in Luke 4:27ff. and the parable of the Good Samaritan in Luke 10:29ff.).

Ruth's faith is not a matter of submission to a set of doctrinal propositions. It is born of joining herself to Naomi, to Naomi's God, and to Naomi's community for better or worse. What Ruth knows of the God of Israel has been incarnated in the people of that God whom she knows — the dramatic, wily, steadfast, don't-quit-on-God-even-as-you-lament Naomi; the righteous, beyond-the-letter-to-the-spirit-of-the-law Boaz; and the people who weep, rejoice, and make space for Ruth in their shared life. As is often said, the lifestyle of the faith community communicates. In proclaiming the story of Ruth in a culture obsessed with individualism, it will be important to focus not only on her but also on the community that welcomes, accepts, witnesses, celebrates, and praises. Bethlehem is the town where newness is born — in David, whose origins this story wants to name, and in Jesus, who opens new possibilities where none seems to exist. Ruth is a woman of gift and insight, but it is in the context of a faith community that those gifts unfold to the glory of God. Indeed, "God's activity [here] is very much that of the one in the shadows, the one whose manifestation is not by intervention but by a lightly exercised providential control" (Edward F. Campbell, Jr., *Ruth: A New Translation with Introduction, Notes, and Commentary,* Anchor Bible 7 [Garden City, N.Y.: Doubleday, 1975], pp. 28-29). So it is in our own world for those who have eyes to see, faith to live by, the courage of hope, and life in *ḥesed* community.

Lawrence W. Farris

Twenty-sixth Sunday after Pentecost, Year B

First Lesson: 1 Samuel 1:4-20
(1 Samuel 2:1-10)
Second Lesson: Hebrews 10:11-14, (15-18), 19-25
Gospel Lesson: Mark 13:1-8

As always, the Bible begins one of its greatest sagas with a small, domestic scene. We are about to hear of the rise of kingship in the newly forming community. If this were a Hollywood script, we might expect blares of trumpets, marching soldiers, the clash of arms. Not at all! We hear of a "certain man" named Elkanah (Hebrew for "God creates"). This Elkanah was so nondescript a man that his great-grandfather's name was Tohu (Hebrew for "waste"!). But from such an unpromising father will come one of Israel's greatest figures, the prophet Samuel. So it often is in the surprising world of God in the Bible.

Elkanah had two wives, as was common in this long-ago time. His first wife was Peninnah, a name whose meaning is not clear. His second wife was Hannah, a name built from the Hebrew word for "grace." The text is very clear about the stark differences between the two women: Peninnah was fruitful and presented her husband with children year after year; in contrast, Hannah was barren.

It was a terrible fate to be barren in a patriarchal world. It was bad enough if one were the only wife; lack of children, after all, could be the fault of the husband. But for Hannah the taunts and false pity would have been unbearable. In a world controlled by men, a woman's unique ability was childbearing; if she could not do that, of what use was she? In verses 1-3 the stage is set for a delightful and mysterious drama of God and Hannah, the woman of grace.

Every year Elkanah would leave his village in the hill country of Ephraim and journey to Shiloh (a trip of some ten miles) in order to perform appropriate sacrifice and worship of Yahweh. Whenever Elkanah brought sacrifice to Shiloh, he would give portions of that meat sacrifice to his wife Peninnah and to all her sons and daughters (v. 4). "But to Hannah he also gave one portion only, because he loved her, even though Yahweh had closed her womb." The NRSV translation speaks of a "double portion," implying that Elkanah attempted to make up for Hannah's barrenness by giving her more than Peninnah and her children. The Hebrew text says pointedly "one portion," suggesting that Hannah received no more than the youngest child of Peninnah did. That single portion could only have added to the despair of the childless woman, as her cowife's growing brood each delightedly ate their equal slice of meat.

Not only that! Peninnah never missed the opportunity to lord it over Hannah, pouring abuse on her, irritating her, because of her barrenness (v. 6). Every year it was the same: the same measly piece of meat, the same haughty scorn (v. 7). No wonder Hannah was reduced to tears and refused to eat that wretched meat! Elkanah's attempts to comfort Hannah (v. 8) could be heard in two ways: either he is genuinely solicitous of her tragic plight, offering her his own person and his own support as a substitute for her lack of sons, or he is the very king of male chauvinist pigs, saying with feckless foolishness, "Am I not better for you than ten sons?" Each reader must determine how this sentence may be heard.

Hannah says nothing in response to Elkanah's words, but her actions suggest that she was not going to be satisfied with anything he might say. After the family meal she headed right to the temple. Though we are told that Eli, high priest at Shiloh, was sitting on a seat near the temple door (v. 9), Hannah walked right by him, anxious to speak directly to Yahweh. "Her life was bitter, so she prayed to Yahweh with deep sobs" (v. 10). Her prayer was a vow, a sacred oath. "O Yahweh of hosts, if you will look clearly at the misery of your servant, and remember me, and not forget your servant, but will give to your servant a male child, I will present him to Yahweh a consecrated one all the days of his life; no razor will ever touch his head" (v. 11).

Hannah refers in her oath to the Nazirite vow detailed in Numbers 6:1-20. She promises that the child Yahweh will give her will be a special servant of Yahweh his whole life, eating or drinking no product of the grape, never approaching a corpse, never getting a haircut. This is a radical vow. Numbers 6 describes in detail the rituals involved when a Nazirite has finished his limited time of service; Hannah vows that her son shall never finish his time.

While Hannah prayed in the temple before Yahweh, old Eli enters the building and watches her. Observing her distress, he quickly concludes that she has had too much to drink and accuses her of being a public drunk, demanding that she "reject her wine"! Hannah corrects the holy man. "No, my lord. I am a woman of pierced [she uses the word for 'bow'] spirit; I have drunk no wine. I have been pouring out my life before Yahweh. Do not think that your servant is a bad woman; I have been speaking out of great distress and misery all this time!"

Eli's response to her, after Hannah has told him the truth, is curt. "Go in peace, and may the God of Israel grant the request you have asked" (v. 17). Why doesn't Eli ask what her request was? Why doesn't he offer some pastoral care to a woman much aggrieved? Why doesn't he ask for her forgiveness for thinking she was an evil woman? Hannah shows magnanimity in the face of the priest's reply and, punning on her own name, asks that "she find favor ['grace'] in his eyes." Eli has seen "grace" right before his eyes, but he has not really seen it or she who bears it.

Though the rest of verse 18 is difficult to translate, we can say that Hannah left the presence of Eli and once again ate food. After rising early in the morning, the family worshiped again and returned to Ramah. Hannah and Elkanah made love, and Yahweh remembered her. She conceived and bore a son. She named that son Samuel because, she said, "I have asked him of Yahweh" (v. 20). This is a most peculiar sentence, because the name Samuel clearly is built on the Hebrew verb "hear," not on the verb "ask." We would expect her to say "because Yahweh has heard me." In fact, the verb "ask" lies at the base of the name Saul, perhaps a foreshadowing of the difficult relationship between Saul and Samuel that the ensuing story will tell.

The end of chapter 1 is important for the meaning of the story. After Hannah gives birth to Samuel, she no longer attends the yearly sacrifice at Shiloh with the rest of the family, staying at Ramah to nurse her son, saying she will attend the sacrifice only when he is weaned. After the weaning, she goes alone to Shiloh with Samuel, bringing appropriate sacrificial offerings to the temple. Presenting the boy to old Eli, she proudly proclaims, "For this child I prayed; Yahweh has granted me the request I made. As a result, I offer [based on the verb above translated 'ask'] him to Yahweh; all the days he has he is offered to Yahweh" (vv. 27-28).

From the unlikely wife comes the great Samuel. Of Peninnah's special children we know nothing, not even their names. Husband Elkanah has faded in our memories and is little known in the Bible. Old Eli is destined to be remembered as a failed father (1 Sam. 2:22-25 and 3:13), a poor priest (2:29-36), dying in grief and agony, blind and fat (4:12-18).

Just as the Bible's human story begins with a man and a woman in a garden; just as the choice of a nation begins with a beautiful wife and her weak husband; just as the saving of that nation from slavery begins with a reluctant murderer at a bush; just as the entry into the land of promise begins with two spies and a prostitute; just as the Christian story begins with a humiliated man and his much-too-young pregnant girlfriend, so this story of kingship begins with an insensitive husband, a foolish priest, an arrogant cowife, and a barren woman who dared to demand from God that which would give her dignity and respect. Such domestic tales which lead to such grand actions! Our God indeed moves in mysterious ways God's wonders to perform!

John C. Holbert

First Sunday after Christmas, Year C

First Lesson: 1 Samuel 2:18-20, 26
(Psalm 148)
Second Lesson: Colossians 3:12-17
Gospel Lesson: Luke 2:41-52

I t is very easy to come to this day in the church year and this text feeling a little weary and let down. And who could blame you? After all, how are you going to match the excitement of Christmas and the celebration of our Savior's birth? The trumpets are still ringing in your ears. The choral anthems and the children's voices singing your favorite hymns still stir your heart. The crowds, the anticipation, the preparation, the joy, the decorations — it is all so magnificent and uplifting. Ah, but that was "yesterday." Today, things begin to return to normal. Almost overnight, the tree has started looking a little dry and must soon come down. People may even be a little tired of seeing it. The choirs have all decided to take a break to recover from their busy week. And the crowds? Well, the crowds have scattered to wherever crowds go when they think the party is over, and that in itself may be disheartening.

The readings selected for this Sunday, at first glance, may seem to signal something of a letdown as well. The Gospel lesson, Luke 2:41-52, certainly doesn't have the emotional appeal or the drama of the Christmas Gospel, Luke 2:1-14. Already, in fact, the narrative has moved us twelve years forward from the day of Jesus' birth, and that jump in worship themes might leave us a little disoriented. Nevertheless, here we find Jesus in the temple, much to the chagrin of his worried parents, discussing the Scriptures with the leaders and amazing everyone with his understanding. (It would be very easy at this point, in fact, to preach a sermon about children obeying their parents — in itself quite a "downer" after the lofty themes of Christmas.) At any rate, we get a glimpse of the promise of Jesus, so prevalent at the story of his birth, now coming into fulfillment. "Didn't you know I had to be in my Father's house?" he asks suggestively. And the text hints at even greater things when it concludes: "And Jesus grew in wisdom and stature, and in favor with God and men." Otherwise, it is a rather "quiet" text.

However, read in connection with the Old Testament lesson, something surprising jumps out. This has happened before! When we jump back to 1 Samuel, a pattern to all this can be discerned! First, the circumstances surrounding the *birth* of Samuel are narrated in great detail. In 1 Samuel 1 we are introduced to Hannah, whose womb Yahweh had closed (v. 5) and who is in great distress because of it. Before even telling us, the narrative suggests to us that Yahweh is going to give a child to this woman. It will be a miracle birth, so to speak — one directed by Yahweh. And the reader can already surmise that the child will play a special role in Yahweh's plan. (In fact, the reader is well acquainted with such "miracle births." See Gen. 21; 30:22; Judg. 13.) And, upon the blessing of Eli, Hannah does conceive and bear a son.

Hannah rejoices over Samuel in song (1 Sam. 2) and delivers the child to Eli at the tabernacle as she had promised. Miracle birth — song of praise — child in tabernacle. That is very much the way Luke records the events of Jesus' early life. His was a *miracle birth* (born of a virgin!) — angels sang songs of praise — Jesus was presented at the temple for circumcision, and then — at age twelve — he was in the temple, his Father's house. Our text concludes with these words: "And the boy Samuel continued to grow in stature and in favor with the LORD and with men." Luke makes a point of saying the same thing about Jesus: "And Jesus grew in wisdom and stature, and in favor with God and men."

The Old Testament text should be read in connection with the surrounding context because Samuel doesn't simply end up in the tabernacle for no reason. The narrator is quick to contrast Samuel with Eli's sons who were serving as priests. The author of Samuel takes pains to describe the wickedness of Hophni and Phinehas. These two men "had no regard for Yahweh," and they showed their unbelief in the way they handled the sacrifices of the people. In 2:12 the author labels them "wicked men" (literally *sons of Belial*), and in 2:17, following a description of the way they desecrated the "holy sacrifices" in Yahweh's house, he reiterates: "This sin of the young men was very great in the LORD's sight, for they were treating the LORD's offering with contempt." Eli's sons were putting the very faith of the entire people at risk with their practices. If it is true that *lex orandi lex credendi* (i.e., the way we worship is the way we believe), then the faith of the entire nation was in great danger because of these two men.

But Yahweh would not let their sin go unpunished. In contrast to Eli's sons, our text describes Samuel in positive terms. He "was ministering before the LORD — a boy wearing a linen ephod." In contrast to Hophni and Phinehas, who slept with "women who served at the entrance to the Tent of Meeting," Samuel "continued to grow in stature and in favor with the LORD and with men." The tabernacle, you see, is the focus of Yahweh's concern, and it is in connection with the tabernacle that Samuel will carry out his mission. In essence, by placing Samuel and Eli's sons in juxtaposition, the author implies that Samuel's job will be "to cleanse the tabernacle."

And so, the text serves as something of a prelude to what will happen next. Yahweh has a plan for Samuel and his people, Israel. And in the first part of the book, up to chapter 8, we see that Samuel plays the most prominent role as Israel's leader. In 3:20 the author says all Israel recognized that Samuel was the Lord's prophet. The Lord was with him, and none of his words proved unreliable or false. In chapter 7 Samuel interceded for the people and delivered them from the Philistines. Samuel proved to be a faithful leader, and Yahweh was with him in all that he did. The early promise of Samuel in our text proves to be true.

However, beginning in chapter 8, Samuel begins to fade from the scene. As Samuel grows older, the people want a king, and Yahweh obliges by giving them Saul. Saul and then David become the focus of the rest of the book. Samuel, it becomes clear, was not Yahweh's final word to Israel. The text is a prelude to the rest of Samuel's life, but Samuel himself was only a prelude to someone greater, someone already foreshadowed in the kings who rose after him, especially David and his descendants.

And so the question before us today, as we consider the connection between Samuel and Jesus, is this: Do Jesus and his work "fade away" in the face of someone greater as Samuel did? Is Jesus only another "Samuel" who was great, but not the greatest? Indeed, on this Sunday after Christmas, it is tempting, as said above, to allow the glory of Jesus and his birth to fade away as we turn to other — greater — concerns. In other words, the temptation is to read the text as a "postlude" — the end of a great story.

However, that is not the point of the readings! Of course Samuel and Jesus are "connected." Luke is suggesting that Jesus' advent is not an entirely different thing. Yahweh has not suddenly changed the way he works or reinvented the wheel. The Old Testament has manifested the pattern for the way Yahweh deals with his people. Purely out of grace, he sends "saviors" (cf. the book of Judges) to rescue and redeem his people.

But Jesus is not simply "prelude" to something greater, and Luke and the other Gospels make that abundantly clear. That's why Jesus doesn't "give way" to another king in the Gospel narratives. In fact, just the opposite happens. The focus remains on him and his ministry up until his death and then his resurrection, something that doesn't happen to Samuel. He dies, but he has not yet risen. The Gospels make it clear that Jesus is the King of kings. Ironically, the placard on his cross read, "This is the king of the Jews." And so he is. He is the one who saves. And his death and resurrection are the means by which his kingdom is established and salvation comes to all men. As David Holwerda has suggested, Jesus' ministry around the temple suggests that even the temple was fading in significance before the Lord who "tented"

171

among us (John 1:14), who is the perfect High Priest (Heb. 7) and the once-and-for-all sacrifice (Heb. 10). (For more detail see David Holwerda, *Jesus and Israel: One Covenant or Two?* [Grand Rapids: Eerdmans, 1995], pp. 59-82.)

The Old Testament reading for today, therefore, is indeed exciting. It is not "postlude," but "prelude" to an even greater salvation. Yahweh saves his people. Jesus is one even greater than Samuel. Not only did he minister in the temple, he has made it insignificant. In him we, the nations of the world, have an everlasting hope.

Timothy E. Saleska

Second Sunday after the Epiphany, Year B

First Lesson: 1 Samuel 3:1-10, (11-20)
(Psalm 139:1-6, 13-18)
Second Lesson: 1 Corinthians 6:12-20
Gospel Lesson: John 1:43-51

Second Sunday after Pentecost, Year B

First Lesson: 1 Samuel 3:1-10, (11-20)
(Psalm 139:1-6, 13-18)
Second Lesson: 2 Corinthians 4:5-12
Gospel Lesson: Mark 2:23–3:6

Eli seems to have been a decent enough man, but, not to put too fine a point on it, he also bore a striking resemblance to Milquetoast. When Hannah properly used God's temple as a place to pour out her heart in prayer, Eli accosted her as a drunk. "God's house is not a detox center, lady!" But when Eli's sons improperly turn God's house into a brothel (actually having sex with women in the doorway to the Tent of Meeting), all Eli could manage to do was limply scold them in ways Hophni and Phinehas found easy to ignore. Most famous of all, perhaps, was the night Yahweh called out to Samuel three times before groggy Eli realized that just maybe this was the Lord God himself calling to the boy (they were in God's temple, after all!).

As Walter Brueggemann has noted, the story in 1 Samuel 3 is fodder for a typical Sunday school story of childlike faith. Any number of children's sermons can spin (and have spun) out of this story, often arriving at a bottom line of application which tells the boys and girls something like, "You see, God loves children, too," or "You see, maybe God is calling to you right now, too. Will *you* listen the way Samuel did?"

In truth, however, this is no children's story. The immediate context is filled with tawdry degradation in the antics of Hophni and Phinehas as well as pathetic ineptitude in the person of Eli. The larger setting is equally grim, as we are still in the period of the judges, replete with the evil and sordidness with which the book of Judges ended (that time during which "everyone did what was right in their own eyes"). Not surprisingly, therefore, when young Samuel does finally ask God to speak, what Samuel hears is a dreadful oracle against the house of Eli. Samuel represents the hope of a new beginning, but a terrible ending must come first. The word of God to Samuel is a disruptive, devastating word which would have dreadful consequences.

The lectionary has assigned this reading for two Sundays, both of which come at a time of potential anticlimax. 1 Samuel 3 is what we turn to *after* the high points of Christmas and Epiphany have come and gone. This is the lection we read *after* Pentecost's celebration of God's Spirit is over and done with for another year. As such, perhaps this is a text which can remind us that even (or perhaps especially) during ordinary, in-between times the Word of God continues to call, to speak, to reveal, and sometimes also to disrupt. The high points of the church year are not the only times God has something to say. (Indeed, we legitimately arrive at the high points *only* when we travel regularly with God's Word.)

There can be little doubting that the concept of God's Word is the central theme in this chapter. Verse 1 swiftly sets the stage by stating baldly that "the word of the LORD was rare; there were not many visions." In short, Israel, like old Eli, had grown deaf and blind. They did not hear from God. They saw no visible evidences of God. Long gone were the days of manna on the ground and cloudy pillars going up ahead of the people. Leaders of great stature like Moses and Joshua were also just a memory. It was a dark time.

But things are about to turn around. Before they do, however, verse 3 throws in an intriguing detail: "The lamp of God had not yet gone out." *Not yet.* The lamp in question was the golden menorah which God long ago had instructed Moses to craft. God's instructions stated that this lamp was to be

173

fueled by oil which the people were to bring to the temple even as the priests were charged with tending the lamp. It is not clear from the biblical texts whether the lamp was to burn twenty-four hours a day or only during the dusk-to-dawn overnight period (texts for both possibilities can be found here and there in the Old Testament). In any event, the lamp was clearly a sign of God's abiding presence in the temple (and so with God's people) such that this lamp was never merely to flicker out.

Yet in 1 Samuel 3:3 it appears the lamp is flickering. Of course, it is possible, as some commentators point out, that this reference is only a temporal marker for the story. Telling readers that the lamp had not yet gone out may simply be a way to indicate that God's call to Samuel came shortly before dawn. In that case, telling us that the lamp had "not yet gone out" may be the equivalent of saying "The alarm clock had not yet gone off." But in the wider context of 1 Samuel 3 and its focus on the scarcity of God's word in Israel, perhaps one can read both distress and hope in those two little words "not yet."

God's word was rare. Visions had become uncommon. Even Eli was so unaccustomed to hearing from Yahweh (despite living within a stone's throw of the ark of the covenant!) that it was only after the third call of Yahweh to young Samuel that Eli tumbled to the notion of a revelation from God. The presence of God had grown tenuous, the divine light a bare flicker. It was a dangerous time, but not without some measure of hope as well. After all, the lamp of God had *not yet* gone out. Indeed, it was soon to flame back with a renewed brightness.

God calls to Samuel, and although the message God delivers is an R-rated word of disruption (and not the G-rated homily of the flannel-graph versions of this tale), nevertheless the word of God is returning in ways that give hope. By the end of 1 Samuel 3 we have moved from God's word being rare to God's word coming fast and furious. The concluding verses of this chapter (which range just beyond the verses included in the lectionary) assure us that because Yahweh is with Samuel, God "let none of [Samuel's] words fall to the ground" (v. 19). Samuel is then attested throughout Israel as a prophet (v. 20), in that God continued to reveal to Samuel his word (v. 21), and so Samuel's word comes to all Israel (4:1). Three times in as many verses the reality of God's word is mentioned. The lamp of truth is burning brightly once more.

Preaching on this text gives pastors an opportunity to foster hope. Dark though the times were in the days of Samuel, and flickering though the presence of God among his people had become, the fact is that the lamp of God had *not yet* gone out. The promise of Epiphany's light and Pentecost's

Holy Spirit is that this lamp will *never* go out. The light of the world that shines at Epiphany still shines after Epiphany. Those tongues of flame that danced on Pentecost still flare forth with God's truth a couple Sundays later.

Here is a reassuring word from the Lord which people need to hear, particularly during the kinds of topsy-turvy changes which have become the norm of the postmodern world. Change is constant now. Yesterday's technological wonder is tomorrow's junk. Politics keep changing globally, resulting in maps and globes which, though accurate ten years ago, are now outdated. Everything seems up for grabs.

Heady and exciting as such times can be, they also produce fear. Such anxiety has also been evident in Christian communities in recent years. Suspicion has led to ecclesiastical splits. Some North American ideological disagreements have been characterized as a kind of "culture war," with "winner" and "loser" rhetoric attendant to that metaphor (and thus raising the specter that if the war goes badly, God's Word could lose). Gender-inclusive versions of the Bible have been branded "stealth Bibles," borrowing the language of espionage to give voice to the fear of vast conspiracies.

In such a time people need to be reminded that as in Samuel's day, so all throughout God's history with his people: the lamp of God's Word has *not yet* gone out. It cannot! The Bible, God's written Word to his people, concludes with a lone apostle, exiled on an island, living through what could be accurately labeled a very dark time indeed (then again, has the church ever endured singularly bright times?). Yet while on that island, the Spirit of Pentecost lifted up John's chin and pointed him to a vision of Jesus, the Lamb of God, ruling the cosmos in glory, the lamp of truth blazing brightly in his hand. It has not yet gone out. And it never will.

Scott Hoezee

Third Sunday after Pentecost, Year B

First Lesson: 1 Samuel 8:4-11, (12-15), 16-20; (11:14-15)
(Psalm 138)
Second Lesson: 2 Corinthians 4:13–5:1
Gospel Lesson: Mark 3:20-35

N ow begins the great experiment of early Israel: the beginning of kingship. As always, the Bible is not content with a simple story of success or failure. It knows, as no other ancient, and few modern, documents know, that significant cultural change is fraught with ambiguity and complexity. And these facts have both a social and a human face.

The period of the judges lasted some two hundred years. The book that bears that name indicates something of the period. It was a time of great confusion and discord, marked by much violence during periods of anarchy. Leadership came from the unexpected anointing of the divine spirit, a spirit that fell on the great (Deborah) and the less than great (Samson). Each judge (or "warrior leader") had a time of success, followed by a time of failure and disaster which then awaited the appearance of another divinely appointed ruler. It was an uncertain way to govern an emerging nation. This lack of stable leadership was bound to create dissension.

The last judge of Israel was Samuel. It could rightly be said that he was more than a judge. At the height of his power Samuel controlled every aspect of the culture: economic, political, religious. As we begin chapter 8, the superjudge has grown old, so "he gave his sons to Israel as judges." The aging prophet/priest/ruler clearly has in mind a dynasty with his sons as his rightful heirs. Surely no one would deny the mighty Samuel the right to determine his successors. After all, he has led Israel well. Who better than the great man's sons to follow his sterling example?

The name of his eldest son is Joel, meaning "Yahweh is God"; his second son is Abijah, "Yahweh is my father." Splendid names for budding leaders of Israel! While Samuel was still able, he had wisely established his boys as judges in Beersheba, the far southern deserts of the land, the better to give them experience for the greater task of ruling the whole land after Samuel's death. All seemed set to create the Samuel dynasty, a sort of permanent judgeship with son following son as long as Israel lasted.

But there is a huge problem. "His sons did not walk in his ways. They sought plunder, taking bribes, twisting justice" (v. 3). Samuel had given his life for the stability of Israel, apparently reaping few rewards for himself.

176

But now his appointed sons and heirs are infamous for violence and evil. Surely these louts must not be allowed to rule! Surely the wise Samuel will see that something different must be done!

The leaders of Israel can wait no longer, for the old Samuel may die at any time, leaving these monstrous boys in command. In great alarm they approach Samuel at his home in Ramah and say, "You are very old, and your sons do not walk in your ways! Appoint for us a king now to govern us like all the other nations!" (v. 5). This is a very reasonable request. Samuel himself has already begun a process to circumvent the two-hundred-year-old way of establishing the leaders of Israel by attempting to start a dynasty of his family. Why not go all the way and establish a kingship, like all the other nations, so that stability of authority may be fixed and Samuel's disgusting sons will never get their grubby hands on power? The people's demands are not obviously a rejection of any religious sort; they merely want stability and a way to stop Joel and Abijah.

"The thing was evil in Samuel's eyes when they said, 'Give us a king to govern us'" (v. 6). Samuel's anger at the people's demands is complex. First, their demand for a king must have rankled the old prophet who had spent his life in service for them, never asking to be king. Second, their desire to be "like the other nations" must have infuriated the one who saw Israel as the special people of Yahweh. And third, Samuel must have been enraged that these ungrateful wretches had rejected him and his sons, calling him old and his sons trash. In boiling anger, Samuel prayed to Yahweh. However, Yahweh's answer was not quite what Samuel had hoped.

"Listen to the voice of the people, to everything that they say to you. Surely, they have not rejected you. Rather, they have rejected me from ruling over them. Just as they have done from the time I brought them out of Egypt until this very day, forsaking me and serving other gods, so they are acting with you. I repeat, listen to their voice. Only, be certain to warn them; tell them of the king's ways who will rule over them" (vv. 7-9).

Yahweh twice tells Samuel to listen to the people and to do exactly what they have asked. In short, Samuel must make them a king! Only the most reluctant of divine servants could have missed the command of Yahweh. Unfortunately, this servant hears only the final words of the command. Samuel is all too ready to warn the people about the coming king. Verses 10-18 describe a monarch out of control, a petty tyrant ready to despoil the people in any way he can imagine. Samuel concludes this catalogue of royal evil with a closing blast: "You will cry out on that day in the presence of the king whom you have chosen for yourself, but Yahweh will not answer you on that day!" (v. 18).

The furious Samuel heard Yahweh tell him to warn the people about their proposed king, and no one could deny that they have been warned! But concerning Yahweh's twice-uttered command to make them a king, Samuel says and does nothing. It seems more than obvious that Samuel's personal feelings of rejection, of him, of his sons, of his dynasty, have so clouded his judgment that only venom against a king can stream from his mouth.

The people are not convinced; they did not listen to Samuel. "They said, 'No! We will have a king over us, so we will be like the other nations, that our king may govern us, and go out before us and fight our battles'" (vv. 19-20). Again they are looking for stability, and they are rejecting the specter of Samuel's chosen heirs. And again the enraged prophet, perhaps further angered by the failure of his salty attack against kings to change their minds, resorts to prayer to Yahweh. Surely Yahweh will see how mad this kingly experiment is; surely Yahweh will affirm the dynasty of Yahweh's favorite, Samuel. But Samuel is again disappointed. "Listen to their voice. Set a king over them" (v. 22). For the third time Yahweh commands the prophet to make Israel a king. And again, astonishingly, the prophet refuses. He turns to the people and says, "Everyone go home" (v. 22).

The storyteller's brilliance and insight shine brightly here. In the story Yahweh sees the need for a king, however dangerous such a move may prove to be. And of course, Yahweh and Samuel are proven right to be leery. Saul is a terrible failure as king. David, however overtly and publicly successful his kingship may be, is a personal disaster as father and husband. And Solomon fulfills nearly to the letter all the warnings that a furious Samuel voiced before the first king was crowned. The people's felt needs are matched by Yahweh's responses and warnings. Samuel, caught in the middle, tries to survive, and perhaps save face, by doing nothing at all. But in chapter 9 Yahweh will finally force Samuel to make a king by bringing the man right to the prophet's door; Samuel will finally not be able to wriggle off Yahweh's hook.

This story is about the complexities and ambiguities of power and the felt realities of a needy culture. A terrified people are there, a reluctant prophet is there, and God, as always, is there. How these three interact at the crucial moments of decision is the stuff of the story. How the three interact at the crucial moments of our decisions is the stuff of our stories. No decisions may be made purely, certain of the approbation of God, certain of the applause of the people. This three-thousand-year-old tale reminds us again that decision making is never easy, that hard choices are always there, and that the will of God in all of that is never simple to discern.

John C. Holbert

Fourth Sunday after Pentecost, Year B

First Lesson: 1 Samuel 15:34–16:13
(Psalm 20)
Second Lesson: 2 Corinthians 5:6-10, (11-13), 14-17
Gospel Lesson: Mark 4:26-34

This passage ends one of the most difficult periods in the early history of Israel. Saul, the first king, a handsome and towering man, a deeply religious man, a man of genuine courage, has been publicly humiliated and dethroned by the prophet Samuel. The prophet claims that Saul has failed to follow the express command of Yahweh by refusing to annihilate (*herem* in Hebrew) the forces of Amalek (1 Sam. 15:1-33). Though Saul twice (vv. 15 and 20) claimed that he had saved the very best of the victor's spoils, along with the great prize of King Agag of Amalek, in order to sacrifice them at the shrine of Gilgal, thus completing Yahweh's command with a spectacular, religious ritual, Samuel rejects Saul's argument and drives the king mad (vv. 24ff.). A now pathetic Saul begs the prophet's forgiveness, grabbing for the furious old man as he leaves Saul sprawled on the ground of Israel's victory. Saul tears the prophetic robe, and Samuel, never one to miss a preaching opportunity, thunders that "Yahweh has torn the kingdom of Israel from you this very day, and has given it to your friend who is better than you" (v. 28). Exactly who this "friend" (or "neighbor") is we are not told, just as we are not told precisely when Yahweh made such a choice.

The better to seal Saul's public fate, Samuel calls for Agag to be brought before him. The captured king comes "in a lordly way" (one possible reading), saying to himself, "Surely the bitterness of death is past" (v. 32). He apparently imagines that he is about to be set free, but Samuel has something else in mind. After a poem of fury, announcing the judgment against him, Samuel hacks Agag to death at the holy shrine of Gilgal, completing the work that Samuel believed Saul should already have done.

With that bloody deed finished, Samuel heads home to Ramah as Saul returns to his home in Gibeah. The shocking events at Gilgal leave Israel in an ambiguous position. Saul is still king in name by virtue of his earlier coronation by Samuel (1 Sam. 11). Yet, that same Samuel has proclaimed Yahweh's rejection of Saul, saying that one of Saul's "friends" has been chosen king. Well, just who is this friend? Where is he? If Saul is not king, then who is? Verse 35 claims that "Samuel did not see Saul again until the day of his death." This is not strictly true, if 19:19-24 be read as a confrontation between Samuel and Saul. More importantly, there is irony in the line. The most famous future meeting between Samuel and Saul will be after *Samuel's* death when, at the cave of the woman of Endor, Saul hears again the announcement of doom, this time by the ghost of Samuel (1 Sam. 28). Thus the final "his" in verse 35 may refer to Samuel rather than the more obvious referent, Saul.

The middle of verse 35 is often translated "but Samuel grieved over Saul." This reading suggests a picture of the crusty prophet in mourning over the fallen king, a highly unlikely occurrence given the amazing scene we have just witnessed at Gilgal. The verb surely means "to mourn," but the preposition is rather unusual. I would suggest its meaning here (and in 16:1) is "because of." Samuel does not mourn *for* Saul; he mourns because of Saul's actions, his refusal, according to Samuel, to follow the commands of Samuel and Yahweh. Samuel mourns in the same way that the gates of Jerusalem mourn because of the injustice of the city (Isa. 3:26). There is as much anger in this mourning as sorrow.

"And Yahweh was sorry to have made Saul king over Israel" (v. 35). Yahweh has changed Yahweh's mind, something that happens in other places in the Hebrew Bible (see Exod. 32:14 and Jon. 3:10). The Hebrews believed in a God who could change, either in response to the cries of the people (so the Exodus and Jonah passages) or because of human action (so this passage). The God of Israel is no static, unchanging deity.

Yahweh determines that the unfounded cries of Samuel about a "friend" of Saul should be made real. So Yahweh demands that Samuel cease his grieving about Saul, about the mess that the nation is in, and get about the business of finding a replacement. This is not the first time Yahweh has had to help Samuel find a king. In 1 Samuel 8:22 Yahweh expressly demands that Samuel "set a king over" Israel. At first the prophet flatly refuses, sending all the people home. Yahweh finally has to lead the candidate Saul to Samuel in chapter 9 before the coronation occurs. Once again, Yahweh must coerce Samuel to choose a king.

This time he is to head for the tiny village of Bethlehem to the home of an unknown man named Jesse, one of whose sons Yahweh has chosen. At first, Samuel refuses, whining that he is afraid that Saul will kill him if he hears about Samuel's plans. Is this the Samuel who just confronted the mighty Saul at Gilgal, shouting in his face that he was no longer king, furiously dispatching Agag in a theater of gore? Samuel is again very reluctant to crown a king, but Yahweh will have none of his excuses. The prophet is to use the cover story that he has come to make sacrifice at Bethlehem and that he is to invite Jesse and his sons to join him. "I will show you what you shall do; you shall anoint for me the one whom I name for you" (16:3). The reader receives the strong opinion that Yahweh needs to be especially direct with this Samuel, who seems none too eager to follow the divine command.

As Samuel approaches Bethlehem, sacred heifer for sacrifice in tow, the elders of the city approach him in terror. They know what he has done and said at Gilgal, and they fervently wish he would take his grisly show to some other place. Has he come in shalom, they ask? He has, he says, and asks all of them, especially Jesse and his sons, to "sanctify themselves" for the sacrifice (vv. 4-5).

As Jesse's firstborn, Eliab, approaches the sacrificial table, Samuel thinks to himself, "This surely must be Yahweh's messiah" ("anointed," v. 6). There follows one of the Bible's most famous lines. "Yahweh said to Samuel, 'Do not look at his appearance, especially his height; I have rejected one like that. Yahweh certainly does not see as humans see; they see with their eyes, but Yahweh looks at the heart'" (v. 7). Yahweh apparently can see things about us that we cannot see, because we have only our eyes with which to see one another and are able to make judgments only on that seeing. There is enormous and often sad truth in that sentence. We humans do indeed too often make judgments only on what we see; racism in our world is only the worst of the results of that limited sight.

Samuel now watches as all seven of the sons of Jesse who were present at the sacrifice pass before his eyes, eyes now warned that Yahweh sees somehow differently. Samuel rejects all seven. In surprise, he asks Jesse if all his sons are present (v. 11). The father responds, "Well, there is still the youngest, but he is tending the flock." The implication of Jesse's answer is that the prophet can surely not imagine that his shepherd boy, the eighth son, could possibly be of interest to the mighty Samuel. But he is wrong. "Send for him! Bring him here! We will not sit until he comes!" So he is sent for and brought in, and the storyteller works some sly magic at his entrance.

"He was ruddy [i.e., 'red complected'], with beautiful eyes, and handsome ['good for seeing']." Immediately, the thing we and Samuel were warned against, namely, looking only with our eyes, the storyteller forces us to do! We are enchanted with the magnificent David before he says or does a thing! Are we not concerned with his heart? Do we not want to know more of him than his beauty? This great beauty will cause the adult David no end of trouble, both with his women and with his own sons. The storyteller warns us when first we catch sight of this remarkable man. Though he is Yahweh's chosen (Samuel anoints him in the presence of his brothers), and though Yahweh's spirit is mightily with him "from that day forward" (v. 13), this man will be no simple man, no easily understood man. To be sure, he will shatter half of the Ten Commandments in one incredible story later in his life (2 Sam. 11)! This David will be unforgettable, both famous and infamous, both deeply devoted to Yahweh and more often deeply devoted to his own desires.

Two crucial ideas arise from this seemingly simple story. Once again, our God has chosen the unlikely one to be the chosen one. And second, we are warned that our seeing is not Yahweh's seeing, our choices are not God's choices. Just who is God choosing now? Two answers can be given with certainty: it is an unlikely choice, and it is almost certainly not one we would make!

John C. Holbert

Fourth Sunday in Lent, Year A

First Lesson: 1 Samuel 16:1-13
(Psalm 23)
Second Lesson: Ephesians 5:8-14
Gospel Lesson: John 9:1-41

This story features the prophet Samuel anointing David as Israel's king in the wake of the failed kingship of Saul. Prior to this episode, there have been only a couple of veiled allusions to David, never by name. The first occurred when the Lord told Samuel that Saul had been rejected and that the Lord had sought out a successor who was a "man after his heart" (13:14). The second took place when Samuel informed Saul that God had not only torn the kingdom from him, but had also given that kingdom to a "neighbor of yours, who is better than you" (15:28). At this point in the story, one is inclined to think that Samuel knows whom God has in mind. After all, the Lord had informed Samuel beforehand that Saul had been divinely chosen (9:16-17). But we will soon discover that this time around even the great prophet Samuel was in the dark about the next king's identity.

The Lord did tell Samuel that Saul's successor would be one of the sons of Jesse — but which one was not specified (16:1). Samuel was afraid of the task that God had given him, thinking that Saul — who was still exercising rule even though he had been formally denounced and in effect deposed — would surely kill him when he learned that the prophet was about to anoint a rival (v. 2). As a counter, the Lord encouraged Samuel to hide the true intentions of his mission behind the facade of a sacrificial ceremony. By using this pretext, Samuel would be safe while the Lord would still be able to point out which of Jesse's sons was to be anointed. Samuel complied with these directives (v. 3). In addition to Jesse and his sons, he invited the elders to the feast, who were themselves fearful, presumably because they were worried about being caught in the middle of a power play between Samuel and Saul (v. 4). In any case, during the whole episode Saul does not appear. The "pious ruse" worked.

Samuel's ignorance about which of Jesse's sons he should anoint becomes immediately obvious. As soon as the prophet saw Jesse's son Eliab, he figured he was by all means the Lord's anointed (i.e., messiah; v. 6). But the Lord's instant rebuke dispels that notion. The Lord goes on to lecture Samuel on what the criteria of selection should be. Appearance and height are not important, according to the Lord, for these are "outward" signs that may be impressive from a human point of view but do not reveal the "inward" signs more important to God (v. 7; cf. 13:14). Should we see in this statement an allusion to Saul's own appearance and stature (9:2; 10:23), which indeed were impressive but hardly indicative of the qualities required for being Israel's king? Perhaps, but one cannot go too far in this direction since Saul had been chosen exclusively by the Lord — the people were only informed of God's decision (10:17-24). Given his experience with Eliab, Samuel quickly rejects the next of Jesse's sons who appeared before him, though the basis for his reluctance this time around is not mentioned (v. 8). Jesse parades his third son — Shammah — by Samuel, but he does not "make the cut" either; Samuel simply "knows" that the Lord has not chosen this son (v. 9).

Eventually, Jesse has seven of his sons pass before Samuel, none of whom is selected (v. 10). At this juncture Jesse's behavior is curious. Does he have only seven sons? Surely there is another, since the Lord had said one of Jesse's sons would be anointed, but none has so far been found acceptable. Further, why would Jesse not have been anxious to make sure that all his sons were considered by Samuel? Our only clue to the answer to these questions emerges when Samuel asks Jesse, "Are all your sons here?" (v. 11). To this query Jesse says he does, in fact, have one more son, the youngest, but he happens to be shepherding sheep. This is a strange posture on Jesse's part. Was taking care of the sheep so crucial in his eyes that he would not ask this son to take a little time off so that Samuel could evaluate him? Or was it the case that in Jesse's perspective, being a shepherd was somehow not an appropriate occupation for a potential king of Israel? However we answer these questions, Jesse's behavior regarding his youngest son remains anomalous. But Samuel is undeterred. He insists on waiting until David is brought forward. Regardless of whether David is seen as an unconventional option from Jesse's vantage point, Samuel demands that the candidate appear.

For all that the Lord had said about the irrelevance of the anointed one's appearance, the narrator unabashedly describes David's winsome features. He was ruddy, with attractive eyes, and handsome (v. 12). Besides his being with the sheep — and the two allusions already mentioned above — we have been told nothing else about David. To some degree his introduction in this account is mysterious and enigmatic. Nevertheless, at his appearance the Lord immediately says, presumably to Samuel, "Arise, anoint him, for this is he" (v. 12). There can be no doubt about the validity of the choice of David in this instance. The Lord, and only the Lord, had chosen David. Not even Samuel, the prophet through whom the Lord has been consistently speaking, had a hand in the selection of David. In this instance Samuel was little more than a functionary doing the Lord's bidding.

According to the text, when Samuel anointed David, he did so "in the midst of his brothers" (*beqereb 'eḥaw*; v. 13). At first glance, this appears to be an innocuous and perhaps redundant statement; one supposes that his brothers who had not been selected were standing around watching the proceedings. But it is likely that this phrase is pregnant with meaning, since it calls to mind a similar phrase occurring in the famous "law of the king" found in Deuteronomy 17:14-20. In that passage Moses outlines to Israel the sort of king that will be appropriate to them when they arrive in the land of promise. Naturally, Israel's king will be someone "the LORD your God will choose" (v. 15). Equally, the king is to be "one from among your brothers" (*miqqereb 'aheka*; v. 15). The only difference in the two phrases is in the pronouns. Moses uses "your" as he addresses all Israel; the narrator of 1 Samuel uses "his" as he narrates in the third person. But one cannot mistake that in terms of intrabiblical exegesis, David is to be seen as the "ideal" king who fulfills the standards Moses sets forth in this strategic passage in Deuteronomy.

Indeed, this may to a degree explain Jesse's hesitation, for David turns out to be an unconventional choice. Moses' stated ideals also underscore the unconventional. Moses asserted that the Israelite king chosen by the Lord must not (1) multiply horses for himself, or cause the people to return to Egypt to multiply horses; (2) multiply wives for himself; or (3) multiply for himself silver and gold (Deut. 17:16-17). Surely horses is a cipher for military power, wives are indicative of international relationships (kings marry the daughters of other kings to cement their dealings with other countries), and silver and gold are signals of the wealth needed for a king to support a lavish court and run a powerful nation. These are all the conventional ingredients of kingship. But Israel's king was to be utterly unconventional. He was to sit on the throne, write a copy of "this law" (i.e., Torah), from which he would regularly read and learn to obey God, and thereby learn how to be a king with a very different set of standards (vv. 18-20). It does not take much imagination to see in the negatives outlined by Moses in the "law of the king" the figure of Solomon, who did multiply horses (even from Egypt!), wives, and money. This is why Solomon could never be the model of Israel's messianic king, as was David.

Once the anointing was completed, God's Spirit "came mightily" on David from that time forward (1 Sam. 16:13). The Spirit of God had come on Saul also (11:6), but due to a series of mishaps Saul no longer could be led by that Spirit (see 16:14). Things had changed. God had made this time an unconventional choice for king: one who was before anything else a shepherd. This "unconventional David" was the model of Israel's messiah. Initially, not even Samuel, the great prophet, had been able to see that. But God did.

Frank Anthony Spina

Fifth Sunday after Pentecost, Year B

First Lesson: 1 Samuel 17:(1a, 4-11, 19-23), 32-49
(Psalm 9:9-20)
Second Lesson: 2 Corinthians 6:1-13
Gospel Lesson: Mark 4:35-41

Few biblical stories are better known than "David and Goliath." In fact, this account has arguably become a literary classic, even in secular circles. David in this story is the patron saint of underdogs! Of course, from a strictly biblical point of view, overcoming seemingly insurmountable obstacles is possible only with God's help, not merely superhuman effort and resolve.

Regardless of the role this episode has assumed in the lore of Western culture, we need to ask whether the "underdog" take on the story is warranted. Granted, many places in the Bible teach that with divine aid one may tackle any difficulty, no matter how formidable it appears. But is this account one of those? If not, then 1 Samuel 17 prompts the following question: Is the "David and Goliath Story" a "David and Goliath Story"? That is, does the narrative purport to teach us to rely on God when challenges seem beyond our natural capabilities?

With many familiar stories, sometimes the "lore" about them deviates from the actual nuances of the text. That appears to be the case in this instance. For one thing, Goliath is never referred to as a "giant." Twice the text refers to him as "the man of the betweens" (vv. 4, 23). This is the only place in the Bible where this curious phrase occurs. It is usually rendered "champion" (so RSV). If the phrase is to be understood literally, perhaps it suggests a person willing to stand alone between two armies. To the extent that "champion" connotes an able and tested warrior who knows no peers, it is perhaps acceptable.

At the same time, a "champion," regardless of prowess, is not the same as a "giant," especially when the latter is seen in virtually cartoonish terms. To be sure, Goliath's height is given as "six cubits and a span" (17:4), but that is the only reference to his size in the whole account. Instead, it is not Goliath's size but his impressive armament that the text emphasizes. In contrast to the singular reference to his height, the text spends fully three verses on the warrior's armor. He wore a bronze helmet and was outfitted with a coat of mail weighing five thousand shekels of bronze. In addition, he had bronze greaves on his legs. For firepower, he sported a bronze javelin and a spear. The shaft of the latter was as thick as a weaver's beam; its head weighed six hundred shekels of iron. To top this off, the man was preceded in battle by a shield bearer (17:5-7). In short, the Philistine "champion" (if that is the word we should use) is presented as one whose conventional power and weaponry are incomparable.

This stress on Goliath's superior conventional strength is put into bold relief when one compares him to King Saul, who is surely to be seen as this man's Israelite counterpart. When Saul was first presented to Israel (10:20ff.), he was described as "taller than any of the people from his shoulders upward" (10:23). When he appeared, the prophet Samuel said, "Do you see him whom the LORD has chosen? There is none like him among all the people" (v. 24). This does not necessarily mean that Saul was Goliath's physical match. But it does mean that we are wrong to see Saul as a "mere mortal" while viewing Goliath as a legendary giant of titanic proportions. Still, the fact remains that in terms of conventional power Saul and the Israelite army were seriously "outgunned."

To see this in context, we must remember that Saul was divinely selected as king when Israel had demanded a king "like all the nations" (8:5). Among other things, that meant that Israel wanted a king who could fight their battles for them (8:20). This is precisely what Saul is attempting to do in the Goliath episode. But Israel was not supposed to have a king like all the other nations. That is, Israel's king was to have more than conventional power at his disposal. Conventional power works only so long as it exceeds rival conventional power. Moses had made very clear in Deuteronomy 17:14-20 what the requirements for an Israelite king were. And these requirements had nothing to do with *conventional* power and everything to do with *unconventional* power, the power that was a function of Torah and grounded in God's will for Israel. The people had seriously miscalculated when they thought that a king like those of all the other nations would supply them with sufficient conventional power to solve their problems. The David and Goliath story illustrates that Israel's conventional power was useless in the face of Philistia's far greater conventional power.

Goliath's role as the quintessence of conventional power is underscored by numerous references to "the Philistine." In fact, the warrior is only called "Goliath" twice (1 Sam. 17:4, 23). Otherwise, he is "Goliath the Philistine" (21:19; 22:10) or just "the Philistine" (vv. 8, 10, 11, 16, 23, 26, 32, 33, 36, 37, 40, 41, 42, 43, 44, 45, 48, 49, 50, 51, 54, 55, 57; see also 1 Sam. 18:6; 19:5; compare 2 Sam. 21:17). This phrase occurs so often that it should be viewed as a virtual technical term. Sometimes translations obscure the force of the phrase; for example, the RSV has Goliath say, "Am I not *a* Philistine?" (v. 8), when the Hebrew text has "*the* Philistine." This phrase underlines Goliath's role as the representative of Philistia. It also stresses that what he represents is not simply a people, but conventional political power. In other words, this story has the effect of demonstrating that Israel's role in the world had nothing to do with conventional power.

Two other features in the story confirm this interpretation. One is the utter inability of either King Saul or any single Israelite warrior to meet *the Philistine's* challenge. Note how angry Eliab, David's oldest brother, was that David was on hand to witness Israel's humiliating nonresponse to *the Philistine* (v. 28). Also, it is a great irony that when David volunteered to take on the challenge, Saul insisted that David wear the king's armor (vv. 38-39).

Clearly, the armor was useless to Saul! Neither the Israelite army nor Saul had the conventional ability to counter Goliath's dare.

A second feature of the story illustrative of this theme is the manner in which David's own unconventionality is constantly stressed. Just previous to this incident, David's father Jesse had to be prodded by Samuel the prophet to present the youth as a candidate for king. Jesse had withheld David because he was "with the sheep" and apparently not suited for the crown (16:11). From a conventional perspective, Jesse had a point. David's connection to sheep also plays a role in this episode. Jesse had ordered David to take provisions to his three brothers who were serving in Saul's army. By contrast, David "went back and forth from Saul to feed his father's sheep" (vv. 13-15, 17-18). His brothers were conventional soldiers; David still dealt with sheep. The narrator even goes out of the way to mention that David left his sheep with a keeper before heading for the front lines where his brothers were (v. 20). Equally, Eliab disdains his brother's occupation when he arrives where the army is encamped: "And with whom have you left those few sheep in the wilderness?" (v. 28). Further, David presented himself to Saul as capable of taking on Goliath by appealing to his prowess, not as a warrior, but as a shepherd (vv. 34-37)! Explicitly rejecting conventional arms (vv. 38-39), David met *the Philistine* armed with a shepherd's implements: sling and stones (v. 40). After David felled Goliath, we are reminded that David was not conventionally armed: "There was no sword in the hand of David" (v. 50). A shepherd accomplished what no conventionally armed Israelite could accomplish.

David expresses the conventional-unconventional motif in theological terms. At first Goliath had been utterly dismissive of David. From the perspective of conventional power, a person like David was hardly to be taken seriously. More than that, Goliath actually equated conventional power with divine power, which is why he cursed David "by his gods" (v. 43). But David boasted of divine power also, except that this power was not expressed in conventional terms. It did not have to do with sword and javelin, but with the name of Israel's God. David put the contrast as sharply as possible. He wanted "this assembly" to know that "the LORD saves not with sword and spear; for the battle is the LORD's" (v. 47).

This story is not about an underdog's victory. It is about contrasting forms of power, one conventional, the other unconventional. From a conventional point of view, sufficient conventional power provides security. Shepherds are no match for soldiers. But from a "biblical" point of view, what the world sees as abject weakness may be in the final analysis utter strength. In God's kingdom, the *weak* are strong while the *strong* are weak.

Frank Anthony Spina

Sixth Sunday after Pentecost, Year B

First Lesson: 2 Samuel 1:1, 17-27
(Psalm 130)
Second Lesson: 2 Corinthians 8:7-15
Gospel Lesson: Mark 5:21-43

David's lament over Saul and Jonathan is both a turning point in the ongoing story of David and a haunting elegy for the fallen king and prince of Israel. Both the context and the beauty of the poem are worth attention.

Within the story of David, and for those preaching the Year B cycle which follows the highlights of this story, the context of the lament is crucial. Saul's and Jonathan's deaths represent the moment when a long-simmering tension is resolved. Since the time the prophet Samuel announced the Lord's rejection of Saul's kingship (1 Sam. 15:26) and anointed David as the newly chosen king (16:13), there have been two kings in Israel. Saul, the transgressing and rejected king, has seen his kingdom, his family, and his sanity fall apart. In David's career as outlaw and military vagabond, he has gained strength, followers, and a power base even while running from Saul's murderous wrath (1 Sam. 17–30). In the event which prompts the lament, Saul and three of his sons, including his heir Jonathan, fall in battle against the Philistines while the Israelite army is routed (1 Sam. 31). Now only David remains as the yet-to-be crowned king.

2 Samuel opens with David far from the scene of the disastrous defeat of Israel's army. He is in his power base in southern Judah where Ziklag is located (v. 1). There he hears the report of Saul's death from an Amalekite messenger who tells David that he himself was the one who finished off the dying Saul (1:2-16). Perhaps expecting a reward from a relieved David for delivering Saul's royal paraphernalia, the Amalekite instead receives a death sentence for killing King Saul. David reiterates a point that he has made in the past — the Lord's anointed commands respect and loyalty, not treachery (1 Sam. 24:6; 26:9). No matter that David knew he was to be king instead of Saul, he cannot publicly condone the killing of the Lord's anointed king.

The portrait of David mourning for the deceased king and prince of Israel reveals several thematic highlights within the ongoing story. As just noted, respect for God's will necessitates respect for God's anointed from David's point of view. This makes a point about David's righteousness even as his own political wisdom and events propel him in creating an alternative to Saul's leadership. It is also a sound political judgment, since *he* is now the Lord's anointed king!

This scene also displays a theme which has been developed throughout the portrayal of Saul's downfall and David's rise. The ancient writers took care to avoid any suspicion that David undermined Saul or was guilty of any wrongdoing in regard to succeeding him as king. Since 1 Samuel 15–16, the writers have made clear that Saul's rejection is based on his own actions and that David, while chosen, has not been responsible for any of the troubles which plague Saul. While political misgivings and historical judgments might suspect otherwise, the story has made clear that David was in no way party to the battle or the death scene. David is shown as loyal to the king, blameless even when events fall to his benefit.

The narratives about David also address the issue of the interactions between the will of God and human decisions. The story of David as a whole contains the ancient community's memory of and reflection on the ways in which human choices and historical events interweave with God's purposes. The story is framed within the Lord's will for Israel's kingship, and the writers emphasize that the Lord has been the initiator of the whole chain of events. Yet, most of the narrative attends to the actions and decisions of human agents. With only the knowledge that God has chosen him, David must face threats from Saul, prepare for his own ascension as king, and remain blameless against Saul all at the same time. The moment of Saul's and Jonathan's death captures these conflicting agendas with no direct indication from God as to how David should react. David here and throughout displays a blend of political astuteness and faithful loyalty to God while demonstrating patience in the face of the sometimes inscrutable enactment of God's will. As modern readers, we might note David's ability to see and trust a larger providence despite the current and clouded swirl of circumstance.

This passage catches David just at the critical and poignant moment of the king's death. Before he continues his own path to kingship, he leads the mourning for Saul and Jonathan. The poem of lamentation is a moving elegy; it marks their death in words that must be said for the community to express its grief publicly and for David to express his grief personally. A combination of words, images, and repetition conveys the complex reality of death, especially a king's death, which changes both the world and individual lives.

David takes on himself the role of chief mourner as he laments a lament; this repetition in verse 17 is deliberate in Hebrew to emphasize the mourning and the mourner. The lament is first of all a recognition of those who died, of who Saul and Jonathan were in life. The focus remains on them, and their names are repeated throughout the passage (vv. 17, 21, 22, 23, 24, 25, and 26). They were mighty (19, 21, 25, 27), courageous in battle (22), beloved and lovely (23, 26), stronger and swifter than the most majestic of animals (23), victorious and beneficent (24). In a verse which overlooks the tensions between Saul and Jonathan over David, they are remembered as united in life and now in death (23). These words and images recall the best of those memorialized by the poem.

The lament likewise is a recognition of the dead in their roles for, and relationships with, others. Both Saul and Jonathan individually are remembered. Saul's public role as king is remembered in his provision of riches for his people (24). For Jonathan the memory is more personal, as David mourns the loss of deep friendship and loyalty, which are the primary overtones of the "love" between them. The primary role of both men, king and prince, as Israel's defenders in the desperate fight against the Philistines and other aggressors is conveyed in the powerful imagery of the weapons of war — the shield (21), bow and sword (22), and all the weapons of battle (27). In an ancient context, the role of warrior was glorified and honored because war was a constant and cruelly necessary part of life. The more universal element that David celebrates is Saul's and Jonathan's dedication to their calling, their ability and willingness to respond to what their times demanded.

Besides preserving the memory of those who died, the poem is a recognition of the brutality and finality of death. The ugly details of violent death are faced honestly in the imagery of battle, blood, and defilement. The haunting and magnificent repetition, "How the mighty have fallen!" (19, 25, 27), both honors the slain and makes real their death. In David's words, the community cannot and must not escape its grief-filled reality for the sake of its ability to move on after the mourning is over.

The lament accomplishes one more task, that of recognizing the impact of death on those that survive. The gloating of the victors is proscribed (20), even though it was inevitable in a battle setting. But the people of Israel and Judah are called to recognize their role in remembering and grieving for their dead. Set against the rejoicing of the Philistines' daughters, the daughters of Israel are called to weep in their role as mourners for their community's loss (24). The introduction to the poem (18) instructs that it be taught to the people of Judah; it was preserved by its inclusion in the Book of Jashar (an unknown book of poetry mentioned in Josh. 10:12-13 and the Septuagint version of 1 Kings 8:12-13). David as the one lamenting reveals his personal grief both in his words about Jonathan (25-26) and in his framing of the whole poem. Even the environment is called to play a role. The mountains of Gilboa are enjoined to mirror the community's grief in the cessation of life-giving waters and fruitful fields (21).

This story of David's reaction to Saul's and Jonathan's deaths achieves a number of goals with economy and elegance. It resolves the narrative tension of having two kings of Israel. David honors the Lord's anointed while he distances himself from any blame or hint of gain in their death. The narrative also portrays the writers' reflections on David's trust and God's providence. David's poem itself focuses on the reality of death, in recognizing the best of the ones who have died and in celebrating their life and their dedication to their community and their calling. The lament acknowledges death, and thus paves the way for true grief and recovery beyond grief. And it recognizes the impact of that death on those that survive. The lament thus does beautifully what a public elegy in all ages must do for the community that mourns.

Patricia Dutcher-Walls

Seventh Sunday after Pentecost, Year B

First Lesson: 2 Samuel 5:1-5, 9-10
(Psalm 48)
Second Lesson: 2 Corinthians 12:2-10
Gospel Lesson: Mark 6:1-13

The ongoing David story reaches a climax in chapter 5 of 2 Samuel. Along with the next two closely related passages in the lectionary cycle in 2 Samuel 6 and 7, significant events are related in the story of David's rise and reign. These three lessons together contain a cluster of concepts important theologically within David's story and within the larger biblical narrative.

The anointing of David as king over Israel in chapter 5 continues and climaxes the story of David's rise from the unknown shepherd boy of 1 Samuel 16 to the first king of a united Judah and Israel. The first part of that story was resolved in 1 Samuel 31 when the *other* anointed king of Is-

rael, Saul, who had been rejected by God for disobedience, was killed in bat-
~~tle along with his heir, Jonathan. Since that time, several key events have~~
happened that have allowed David to come to the point of becoming Israel's
king.

First, and significant in its own right, David was anointed king by the
people of Judah (2 Sam. 2:1-4a). Visible here is the underlying division of the
tribes into a southern component (Judah) and a northern group (the other
tribes called, collectively, Israel). David was from Judah and had retreated
into its southern wilderness and established a home and power base there
when Saul sought to kill him. His status changed from warrior outlaw after
Saul's death when he was anointed king by the people of Judah in Hebron, a
major southern city.

Intervening events, narrated in 2 Samuel 2-4, then clear the way for David to become king of the northern tribes as well. The issue and outcome are
clear in 2 Samuel 3:1: "There was a long war between the house of Saul and
the house of David; David grew stronger and stronger, while the house of
Saul became weaker and weaker." Both the heir to Saul's throne, Ishbaal,
and Saul's powerful commander, Abner, are murdered, leaving Israel with
only one clear choice for leadership — David.

The northern tribes now come to petition David to become their king.
"All the tribes of Israel," a phrase connoting northern unity, make three arguments (5:1-2). First, they present themselves as David's "bone and flesh,"
which is not a biological connection but a phrase highlighting covenantal
loyalty. They recall that, even when Saul was king, it was indeed David (the
Hebrew text uses an emphatic form) who was their military leader, the one
who was "leading out and bringing in Israel." Finally, they quote to David a
word from the Lord that he would one day "shepherd" God's people and be
their "leader" or "ruler." The translation of this last term is uncertain; it is
distinguished from the term for "king" but means something like "king-
designate" or "prince."

The elders of the tribes, that is, the heads of the most powerful households and clans, then actualize the petition to David by entering into a covenant (v. 3). This "covenant" was probably an agreed contractual arrangement, like a pact between a lord and vassals, in which various responsibilities
and allegiances are stipulated. Parallels to this type of agreement are found
in cultures throughout the ancient Near East. In an indication that David is
the more powerful member of the covenantal agreement, he makes a covenant with the elders. That this agreement is understood as religiously based
is signaled by its being made "before the LORD." The elders, now the initia-
tors of their part of the bargain, anoint David "as king over Israel."

An interruption in the narrative flow in verses 4-5 provides the official formula for a king's reign in biblical history writing. Similar to the usual "regnal formula" found in the book of Kings, it is placed in the narrative immediately after the king assumes the throne. In this context in the David story, it makes the point that David has indeed become king "over all Israel and Judah."

It is true that this narrative bit seems too brief to be the capstone of the story of David's rise. Yet it carries that weight because the account is shaped to highlight key political and theological concepts which are built into the overall story. The story has shown David to be a mighty warrior, the one who can truly lead the troops in battle, repeating three times the victory chant, "Saul has killed his thousands, / and David his ten thousands" (1 Sam. 18:7; 21:11; 29:5). Within the story, key figures have confirmed that David will be "prince" and "king" — Samuel both in person at the initial anointing and in ghostly form (1 Sam. 28:17), Abigail (1 Sam. 25:30), and even Saul himself (1 Sam. 24:20). The Lord through Samuel anointed David to be king (1 Sam. 16); now that choice has become a political reality when Judah and Israel anoint him as Saul's legitimate successor. The youthful shepherd of his father's flocks has, in the Lord's word reported by the tribes, become the "shepherd" of God's people, symbolizing the leadership and care he must carry out for Israel and Judah.

However, the attributes of David and the kingship he has received and shaped raise even larger issues within the biblical narrative. In a larger framework that stretches back to 1 Samuel 8–12, real questions about kingship as an ambiguous institution, and theological concerns that a human king might replace God's kingship, have been raised. Despite these concerns, David's story shows that a human king has been found who is God's choice and has fulfilled the promising future seen for him as leader, king, and shepherd. David's story and the biblical story will go on to reconsider and reevaluate aspects of these concerns and concepts in narratives and poetry about kings and kingship, prophets and prophecy. Based in the David story and climaxing here, these political and theological concepts have potential for thoughtful reflection on how God's will is carried out in human affairs and by human leaders.

The lectionary reading goes on to pick up two verses about the conquest of Jerusalem as David's capital. The reading omits several verses on the actual capture of the Jebusite city which are difficult to interpret. But the point that David took the stronghold and renamed it as his own city is clear (v. 9). In terms of ancient Near Eastern cultures, establishing a capital is a natural and expected act for a new king. David's political brilliance is shown in the choice of city for his capital. Jerusalem is between the two "halves" of his kingdom, yet belongs to neither and so can be claimed for the king's name and allegiance alone. David immediately begins to build up the city to be a worthy capital. It will become so in time and, in the next lectionary passages, will also become a holy city.

The final verse of the reading acts as a summary of the passage and the story to this point. As with numerous concepts that can be traced throughout the David story, both the idea of David's greatness or success and the fact that God was with him confirm notices found in earlier narratives. The reader has been told about David's success in an early phase of his relationship with Saul, when he was leading Saul's army (1 Sam. 18:14-15, 30). God's presence with him has been confirmed at his initial anointing (1 Sam. 16:13, 18) and three times during the time of his successful military actions under Saul (1 Sam. 17:37; 18:14, 28). The summary statement placed here by the writers thus rings true as a culmination of a brilliant career that was initiated and accompanied always by God.

This passage clearly summarizes the David story to this point and reiterates important theological aspects from the story. But this little reading also looks forward to much more extensive themes within the overall biblical narrative. Theological realities within the David story initiate and anchor some of the most significant themes in wider Old Testament, and later New Testament, theology. The first of these broad themes centers on "king" and "kingship." Rooted in early Israel's understandings of themselves as God's people and as an emerging state, this theme will evolve to include reflections on the utility and futility of human kingship and the possibilities for a king who truly fulfills God's will. In a related way, the idea of "the anointed one" (Heb. *mashiah,* "messiah") begins here to be associated with a king of David's line and will in later times develop into a figure with the stature and function of the one who brings God's deliverance to God's people. In the most incipient way as well, Jerusalem emerges here for the first time as a chosen city and will evolve into a symbolic complex of great power in certain strands of later Old Testament and New Testament theology. These ideas and several more related overarching themes emerge in the next two lectionary passages as well.

Patricia Dutcher-Walls

Eighth Sunday after Pentecost, Year B

First Lesson: 2 Samuel 6:1-5, 12b-19
(Psalm 24)
Second Lesson: Ephesians 1:3-14
Gospel Lesson: Mark 6:14-29

In the ongoing David story that the lectionary traces, the next move in David's consolidation of his kingdom occurs in this reading. David brings the ark of God up to his new capital city, Jerusalem, in a procession filled with political and religious significance. The occasion is an opportunity for great rejoicing and one that builds toward David's and Israel's future.

The reading follows closely on the previous one in chapter 5, yet several significant events have occurred in the meantime (5:11-25). David has used imported cedar wood to build himself an appropriately magnificent royal palace. He has enlarged his group of wives and concubines and had more sons and daughters (see also 3:2-5). And he has decisively defeated the Philistines in two battles. While these events may not be related here in strict historical order, the narrative makes the theological point that David is fulfilling his role as the Lord's chosen king. Indeed, it was Abner, King Saul's commander, who had made one particular promise known: "The LORD has promised David: Through my servant David I will save my people Israel from the hand of the Philistines" (3:18). So David has made a start on consolidating his royal privileges and status, including a harem, dynasty, palace, and military success. But for all his success, David must not, and does not, forget God. When David brings the ark to Jerusalem, he literally brings God into the center of his kingship.

The ark of God was the most powerful symbol of the Lord's presence with Israel at that time. The container for the tablets of the commandments had accompanied the people for years on their journey toward the Promised Land and during their time of settlement on the land. The ark was more than a box; it was a visible symbol of God's awesome presence for and with the people. The ark was flanked with cherubim, mythical beasts that held God's invisible throne (6:2). The tabernacle tent which contained the ark had been shrouded in cloud and fire while it guided the people during their wanderings in the wilderness (Num. 9-10). The ark had been brought across the Jordan into the land with great ceremony by Joshua and lodged at Shiloh, a hill country sanctuary (Josh. 3-4). As a visible reminder of the

Lord's might, it had led the people into battle during their struggles to occupy the land. It had been lost to the Philistines during battle, but they desperately returned it to Israel when its power had created a plague among them (1 Sam. 4–6). It had stayed in Kiriath-jearim, an alternate name for Baalah of Judah, all during the time of Saul's kingship (1 Sam. 7:1-2). Now David brings this potent symbol of God's power and might up to Jerusalem.

Note that the narrative helps the reader understand the import of what David does. Using the technique of repetition to emphasize points, the story here is shaped to convey several aspects of the event. The phrase the "ark of God" or just "ark" occurs nine times in the reading, constantly reminding the reader that this is the center of attention. And "David" himself, by name or pronoun, occurs eighteen times in the passage! The narrative thus claims for David the initiative and righteousness of being the one who fulfilled the key role of bringing the ark to the city of David. The inclusion several times of the phrases "all the people" and "all Israel" in the description of the event makes clear that David has done this not just for himself nor by himself. Also, in describing the event, liturgical and religious language abounds. There are all the accoutrements of a religious celebration — a new cart, attendants, music, instruments, rejoicing, offerings and sacrifices, and a feast. David wears the "linen ephod," a garment worn by the priests when officiating. A ceremonial shofar, or trumpet, is blown and the ark is installed in a tent prepared by David. Even the grammar enhances the picture. In the verses describing the procession (vv. 3-5, 13-16), participles abound ("driving," "dancing," "singing," "bringing," "leaping"), giving a sense of a rolling party of joy surrounding the slowly moving ark.

The selection of verses in the lectionary reading leaves out two peripheral story lines. As the ark is first on its way from Abinadab's house (vv. 6-12a), Uzzah, one of its attendants, reaches out to steady the ark when the oxen jar it. The "anger of the LORD" is aroused, and Uzzah is killed on the spot for daring to touch the ark. This scene reflects the ancient understanding of the absolute, untouchable, and dangerous holiness of God and everything associated with God. David in turn is angry and afraid and abandons his project for three months, leaving the ark at a nearby house until he learns that the house has indeed been blessed. Then he returns to his original plan to retrieve the ark. The scene where Michal, daughter of the late king Saul, sees and scorns David's unseemly dancing (v. 16) is the only negative note to the whole joyous day, but her perspective incidentally confirms the enthusiasm of David's actions. Michal's reaction and her subsequent conversation with David (vv. 20-23) are best understood within the larger narrative's story line about the ambiguous relationships between David and Saul's family.

David's actions within the story are shaped to accomplish a number of important objectives, both political and religious, although these categories overlap quite a bit in an ancient context. On the more political side, as a new king, David must demonstrate his allegiance to God and to the traditional religious symbols and institutions he has inherited. By adopting and moving the primary visible representation of the tribes of Israel during their wanderings and early years in the land, David has shown he will keep faith with tradition. At the same time, he has added the stability and orthodoxy the ark represents to his reign and his new capital city. It is likewise important for a new king to demonstrate God's favor and approval for the initiation of his reign. Successfully installing the ark of God helps to make this point. Finally, David must do all this in the most public and celebratory way. The constant presence and participation of the people of Israel, the long and joyous procession, and the feast that includes everyone remind the people that David is king *for them*.

The more religious motivations underlying the bringing of the ark are also important for the new king who was the primary intermediary between the earthly and divine realms in the ancient world. David has dramatically established that the Lord is in the midst of the people by bringing the ark to Jerusalem. His actions have proved as well that he is leading the Lord's people faithfully. This new institution of kingship, and he himself as king, will serve God, not just the exigencies of politics. The depth and completeness of the liturgical celebration have demonstrated that this king knows the appropriate religious actions for a ceremony such as this, and that he and the people honor God in celebrating with singing, dancing, offerings, and feasting. Finally, his enthusiasm, while daunting to the representative of Saul's house, Michal, has shown how thoroughly and faithfully David will commit himself, even relinquishing his respectability, in the service of God. He is truly the Lord's servant.

However discerning David may have been about the political and religious outcomes of moving the ark to Jerusalem, the writers who preserved and handed down the story are no less so. For both ancient and modern readers, the shaping of the story reminds us of significant statements and values. David's story shows that political and religious realities overlap in complex ways; humility and wisdom are required to understand and carry out one's allegiances and commitments to both. The story makes clear that placing God in the center orients the rest of a people's life and institutions in faithful ways. The portrait of David as an astute yet faithful king lends weight to the narrative's insistence on qualities of leadership that truly serve God.

As with the lectionary passages before and after this one, larger themes in the overall biblical narrative are anchored here. The developing theme of kingship in service to God has received a concrete example in David's actions. That value will be a constant criterion for kingship, both human and messianic, in wider biblical theology. Jerusalem, which had previously been only David's political capital, has been confirmed as a religious center for the first time. This city is now God's chosen place, not just David's chosen place. Soon it will also be much further on its way toward being a long trajectory of significance and symbolism as the city of God.

Patricia Dutcher-Walls

Fourth Sunday of Advent, Year B

First Lesson: 2 Samuel 7:1-11, 16
(Luke 1:47-55)
Second Lesson: Romans 16:25-27
Gospel Lesson: Luke 1:26-38

The seventh chapter of 2 Samuel contains the fullest narrative account of God's covenant with King David and the Davidic line of kings in the Old Testament. The Old Testament lectionary text comprises only a portion of the chapter, namely, the part that focuses specifically on the promises of God to David. In the narrative of 2 Samuel, David has finally acquired "rest from all his enemies around him" (7:1) and decides that it is time to build a house (a temple) for the Lord. The Lord's ark, the symbol of the divine presence, was residing in a tent in Jerusalem (6:17). With the help of the Phoenician king, Hiram of Tyre, David constructed a great palace of cedar in the capital city (5:11; 7:1). King David felt that such difference in lifestyle — he in a cedar palace and the ark in a tent — was hardly commensurate with the way affairs should be.

David proposed building God a "house," and this theme forms the backdrop for the subsequent promises of God to the king. The narrator plays on the double meaning of house, signifying both temple, in the case of

God, and dynasty, in the case of David. The king's plan was submitted to the prophet Nathan, who first approved the temple construction but then withdrew approval after a nighttime consultation with God (7:2-7). With God's disapproval of the construction of a temple, the focus shifts from God's house to David's house and from David's desires to the divine promises. Several features are noteworthy in God's promises to David.

1. David is reminded of his humble origins as a shepherd from which he was elevated to become prince over Israel (v. 8). Here one finds a common motif of the Bible: God's special concern for the lowly and compassion for the humble. Over and over again this theme reappears in Scripture. One can recall the aged Abraham and Sarah without a child; Moses as a baby floating on the Nile River; oppressed slaves laboring in Egypt; and, as Advent approaches, a Babe in a manger. In all of these, the meek and powerless for whom God has special concern find their ultimate status a reversal of their original state.

2. David is reminded of his conquest over his enemies (see 2 Sam. 8). He is also reminded that his reputation will be like that of the great ones of the earth and that his name will be remembered forever (v. 9). This is, of course, a theme that reappears in the emphasis on Jesus' name in the New Testament. For example, the Christ hymn in Philippians 2 describes Jesus as one who

> emptied himself, taking the form of a slave,
> being born in human likeness.
> . . . obedient to the point of death — even death on a cross.
> Therefore God also highly exalted him
> and gave him the name that is above every name,
> so that at the name of Jesus every knee should bend,
> in heaven and on earth and under the earth.

3. David's success and greatness would be shared by his people Israel, who would live in tranquility in their own place (vv. 10-11a). The God who is described as constantly wandering (v. 6) promises the people a place where they will be planted, and the humble David, who is elevated, has a people with whom to share the glory of the newly acquired state.

4. Above all, God promises David that his family will be established forever. There is no house for God, who dwells in the temporary mobile home of a tent. But for David there is an eternal house! The continuity of David's family and the eternity of its rule are promised in general terms in verse 16, which highlights and summarizes the central promise to David — a dynasty,

a kingdom, and a throne, forever. All subsequent Jewish and Christian expectations of the coming Messiah were fed in one way or another by this text.

5. Verse 12 focuses on the immediacy of the promise. One of David's immediate offspring will succeed him; his dynasty will not be replaced like that of Saul (v. 15). Here, of course, the narrator and reader anticipate David's son Solomon, who would come after David and build God a house (v. 13).

6. Finally, David's son will also be God's son. "I will be his father, and he shall be my son" (v. 14). The ancient Israelites did not think of this parent-child relationship in terms of physical or biological descendance but in terms of an adoptive relationship. David's son and God would be like Father and son, parent and child. Sonship in this text, however, involves not so much special privilege as the promise of special responsibility and of God's punishment of the son for disobedience. Here the narrator anticipates the eventual lack of complete obedience on Solomon's part and the subsequent disruption of the kingdom at his death (see 1 Kings 11).

2 Samuel 7 has a central programmatic function within the larger corpus of the so-called Deuteronomistic History, which runs from the book of Deuteronomy through Joshua, Judges, 1-2 Samuel, and 1-2 Kings. This large corpus seems to have been shaped by similar vocabulary, themes, and editorial techniques (e.g., insertion of key speeches by leaders), so that it appears to have been carried and shaped within one tradition within ancient Israel, the so-called Deuteronomistic tradition. The structure of the Deuteronomistic History is marked by certain key turning points. In Deuteronomy 31 Moses commands the conquest of Canaan and the distribution of its land to the Israelites. The book of Joshua recounts the obedience of the people and their victorious conquest. However, Judges 2:1–3:6 indicates that ultimately the Israelites break the covenant with God and God resolves to allow the Canaanites to remain in the land as a constant test of Israel's faithfulness to God. The second major turning point in the Deuteronomistic History is Nathan's promise to David of an eternal dynasty in 2 Samuel 7. The promise is fulfilled in Solomon (1 Kings 8). However, ultimately the united kingdom falls apart and both the kings of northern Israel and the kings of southern Judah disobey God and cause Israel to sin and lose their land in forced exile by a foreign empire (2 Kings 17).

But it is important to note that the Israelite kingship does not end in "final failure" at the end of 2 Kings. The notion of a human king in Israel is not extinguished. At the very end of the Deuteronomistic History in 2 Kings 25:27-30, the narrative offers some small glimmer of hope of the possibility of the ongoing life of the Israelite kingship. The empire of Babylon has destroyed Jerusalem, exiled the people of Judah, and arrested the Israelite king of Judah named Jehoiachin. However, the Babylonians release King Jehoiachin from prison, speak kindly to him, and allow him to eat with the Babylonian king. Although the political institution of kingship ended for Judah with the death of Jehoiachin, this ending to the Deuteronomistic History, combined with the promise of 2 Samuel 7, opens up the future to an expectation of the possible reemergence of a king in Israel, a Messiah, an "Anointed One" who would rescue God's people from their oppressors. This hope for the Messiah grew increasingly eschatological as the expectation was forced to a distant time of fulfillment in an increasingly apocalyptic mode for some traditions within Judaism. There were some Jewish groups in the time of Jesus who looked for a more immediate and political/military Messiah who would overthrow Roman rule. Other Jewish groups at the time of Jesus expected a Messiah of a more dramatic and apocalyptic nature who would signal the transformation of the world.

In any case, it is the promise of 2 Samuel 7 that has been the primary fuel for this flame of messianic hope throughout the centuries within both Jewish and Christian traditions. Its expectation of the eternal rulership of the house of David is the fountainhead for all messianic hopes about the revival of David's rule after the fall of Jerusalem in 587 B.C.E. As part of the readings for the Advent season, it looks forward to him who is the David to come. In the Gospel reading for this Fourth Sunday of Advent in Luke 1, the angel announces to Mary, "Do not be afraid, Mary, for you have found favor with God. And now, you will conceive in your womb and bear a son, and you will name him Jesus. He will be great, and will be called the Son of the Most High, and the Lord God will give to him the throne of his ancestor David. He will reign over the house of Jacob forever, and of his kingdom there will be no end." 2 Samuel 7 is the seedbed for the angel's promises to Mary.

Dennis T. Olson

Ninth Sunday after Pentecost, Year B

First Lesson: 2 Samuel 7:1-14a
(Psalm 89:20-37)
Second Lesson: Ephesians 2:11-22
Gospel Lesson: Mark 6:30-34, 53-56

In many ways this passage is a key point in the David story and in Old Testament theology. The narrative of Nathan's oracle to David develops important theological, thematic, and political ideas all while presenting God as a punster! Indeed, the passage is built around an extended pun on the word "house" which is integral to the passage's meaning and significance.

In the ongoing story, David has reached a crucial moment. He has been anointed as king over Judah and Israel (2 Sam. 2:4 and 5:3); he has captured and reinforced Jerusalem as his capital city (5:9-10); he has the marks of royalty in a harem, descendants, and a palace (5:11-25); and he has established the symbol of Yahweh's presence, the ark, in Jerusalem (6:1-19). As with other ancient kings, his next most important task was to build a temple for the God who had established his throne. Generally, temples were built to serve and worship the high god of any nation and in turn functioned to legitimate the king who built them. Ancient Israel shared this cultural background, and yet invested its king and temple with its own significant theological meanings.

So David resolves to do something about the fact that the ark of God is still dwelling in a tent (7:2). As he was already settled in his own "house," that is, a palace, he will build a "house" for God to dwell in, that is, a temple. Thus, the immediate issue at the core of the narrative is, Will David build a house for the Lord? At first, Nathan the prophet gives the culturally expected answer, of course "do all you have in mind, for the Lord is with you" (v. 3). But then a surprising answer comes in a word of God to Nathan that night — in fact, David will *not* build a house for God. Rather, the LORD will make a "house" for David, that is, a dynasty (vv. 11b-12). And it is the offspring of David's house who will be the one to build a house for the Lord. Here the extended pun reaches three layers: "house" is used as house of the king (palace), house of the Lord (temple), and house of the royal line (dynasty). A number of English translations bury the pun under secondary words ("palace," "temple," "dynasty"). It would be good to respect the Hebrew narrative's depiction of God's ability to make a pun.

But the passage does more than resolve the issue of who will build a house for the Lord. Built into the narrative are wider perspectives that set the immediate issue into the scope of past and future relationships between God and God's people. First, the oracle remembers the past, when God was moving about in a tent with the people on their journey (vv. 6-7). Following that, the past personal history of David with God is remembered (vv. 8-9a). Then the oracle turns to address what God is about to do for David (v. 9b) and what God will do in the future for the people (vv. 10-11a). Finally, the oracle comes back to what God will do for David (v. 11b) and for David's offspring in the future (vv. 12-14a).

The most significant themes of the passage are woven into this survey of past and future, all of which are embodied in this moment of revelation to David and actualized in David's reign and its future. For example, God's gracious provision of peace and rest for the people can be traced back to words of Moses in Deuteronomy where God promises such rest in the land (Deut. 12:9-10; see also Josh. 21:44). Verse 1 of our passage notes that the Lord had given David rest, and Nathan's word from God promises future peace for the people and David (vv. 10-11). God's protection and care in providing rest for God's people is a word of comfort to all who hear in any age.

More significantly, the provision of a house for God also has roots in the past and is brought to fruition in Nathan's oracle. The building of a house for the Lord, a place for God's name to dwell, as Deuteronomy phrases it, had been first mentioned in Moses' commands to the people as they were about to enter the Promised Land. When the people came into the land, they were to "seek the place that the LORD will choose as his habitation" and bring their offerings to the place which God has chosen as a dwelling for his name (Deut. 12:5, 11). Yet the Lord remembers in his words through Nathan the long years when a tent and tabernacle were the movable place and sign of God's presence with a wandering people.

While questioning David's presumption that God needs a "house," the oracle nonetheless assures him that his own offspring will indeed build the place where God's name will dwell. In this way the narrative directly anticipates the story of Solomon building the temple in 1 Kings 5–8, which is the central event of his reign. However, Nathan's oracle raises theological issues which we do well to consider. The contrast between a tent, a movable place of presence, and a temple, a permanent one, resonates with questions about where and when God is present with the people and the extent to which God's presence can be assured and established in any one place. The Old Testament explores through its narratives the common but dangerous assumption that God's presence is automatically assured to any particular place. Jeremiah's "temple sermon" is a case in point (Jer. 7:1-15).

Human kingship in the context of God's sovereignty is the final major theme that resonates within the passage and beyond. David becoming king of Judah and Israel has been traced in the story for many chapters, since his anointing in 1 Samuel 16. And the ambiguities about kingship as the leadership pattern for Israel have been raised since the people first came to Samuel the prophet demanding a "king like other nations" (1 Sam. 8). Even back in Deuteronomy, the laws included limitations on kings (Deut. 17:14-20). But the initiation of a dynasty raises further questions. Like the judges and prophets, a king can be chosen and designated by *charismatic validation,* by the spirit of the Lord being with him. Indeed, this had been the theological assumption about legitimate leadership under Yahweh for generations, from Joshua (Josh. 1:5, 9) and the judges (Judg. 2:18) through to Samuel (1 Sam. 3:19) and David himself (1 Sam. 16:13). But a dynasty means that the next king is chosen and designated not by God but by *human agency,* by the will and political power of the previous king and his advisers to choose a successor among his sons.

This passage in 2 Samuel 7 plays an important role in showing that indeed God was the initiator and validation for the Davidic dynasty. While individual kings would no longer be charismatically chosen, the line of David had been chosen by the Lord to be rulers of God's people. This significant alteration in the theology of kingship could not be accomplished on human terms, but only by God declaring that the throne and kingdom of David's offspring will be firmly established. That David's offspring will become God's own is signaled by the adoption language in verse 14. That the promise is irrevocable is signaled by the term "forever" and the language (in v. 15) of God's faithful, covenantal love never being taken from David's heir.

In an overall survey of biblical theology, this unconditional covenant with one dynastic line is in some ways at odds with other Old Testament understandings of God's choices and grace. In a number of places, warnings are given to God's people and their leaders that only by living out the intentions and purposes of God, only by keeping the commandments, can one live a blessed life as God indeed intends for humanity (1 Sam. 12:13-15). The tensions between these two senses of God's covenantal faithfulness, the unconditional and the conditional, are played out in the stories of the Old Testament, especially where kings act on the common but dangerous assumption that God's presence can be automatically assured to any particular person, regardless of that person's actions.

The most significant themes which are rooted in the David story and will span the larger biblical narrative are now in place. God's people have seen their leadership roles develop from charismatic judges and warriors to an anointed king to an established throne, kingship, and dynasty. A particular king and a particular dynasty have been anointed as the bearers of the Lord's faithfulness forever. Through the twists of history the idea of the Lord's anointed, the Messiah, a king of David's royal line, will endure as hope for the people, coming to fulfillment for Christians in Jesus of Nazareth. David's city has become more than a political capital. Now it has become the place where God chooses to dwell, where the temple will be built, the city of God in the midst of the people. In Old Testament theology, Jerusalem will in time become the source and symbol of God's presence and consolation for both God's people and the nations. For Christians, the symbolism of Jerusalem will in time transcend the limits of history and space to become the new Jerusalem of God's final reign.

Patricia Dutcher-Walls

Tenth Sunday after Pentecost, Year B

First Lesson: 2 Samuel 11:1-15
(Psalm 14)
Second Lesson: Ephesians 3:14-21
Gospel Lesson: John 6:1-21

The lectionary includes only the first fifteen verses of the whole story, but no preacher can avoid the entire chapter as the appropriate material from which to preach. Here we find David, remembered as the greatest king in the history of Israel, acting little better than a mafioso don! This David, chosen one of Yahweh, conqueror of Goliath, charismatic leader of a united Israel, descends here to the level of a thug, a lying, murdering, repulsive monster.

The one who would preach from this story must begin by asking the question: Why is this story told at all? Would it not have been far more politic, far less embarrassing, to have consigned this tale to the lost pages of a great life? The Bible itself provides a clear example of at least one writer who tried that very tactic. The author of the books of Chronicles retells the story of the early monarchy and, when the life of David is recounted, makes no mention whatever of today's account. If one were to read only Chronicles about David, one would conclude that he spent his days writing psalms, worshiping God, and directing choirs! However, the Bible's compilers decided that the unforgettable and terrible story of 2 Samuel 11 could not be excluded.

The story begins with a martial flourish. "It happened at the turning of the year [i.e., spring], the time when kings march forth, that David sent Joab out, along with his officers, the whole army of Israel. They destroyed the Ammonites and besieged Rabbah. But David remained in Jerusalem" (v. 1). It is immediately striking that after we are told that "kings go forth," it is said quite pointedly that David did not. Why? No explanation is forthcoming, but we know as the story begins that all is not as it should be.

"It happened [because David has remained home] one early evening that David arose from his bed and strolled on the roof of the palace" (v. 2). There is chance here. David is on the roof of his house, perhaps in the attempt to catch the afternoon breeze. He has napped and arisen at his leisure, a most unkingly thing to do at the very time his armies are fighting the king's enemies in the field. So the king arose from his afternoon snooze and with sleep-swollen eyes gazes down on his city, the city of David, the capital of his expanding empire.

"He saw from the roof a woman bathing, and the woman was very beautiful" (v. 2). A naked woman catches the indolent king's eye; a quick question to a servant establishes that the woman is Bathsheba, daughter of Eliam, the wife of Uriah the Hittite. Eliam is one of "the Thirty," the private force David has to protect his person (see 2 Sam. 23:34), and Uriah is one of David's foreign generals. Both father and husband are significant members of David's most senior inner circle. With no comment to this information, David sends for the woman and sleeps with her. Whether it was a onetime fling or a rather longer affair, the result is Bathsheba's pregnancy.

The reader might pause at this point and wonder what David might now do. Earlier stories of the wily David (see the two stories of 1 Sam. 21, for example) suggest that he has a plan to solve this little problem. Verse 7 reports a chatty conversation between a good soldier, following the commands of his superiors, and the commander in chief. David politely asks Uriah about Joab and the warriors and the progress of the battle. He then says, "Go down to your house and bathe [the same word that got David in trouble in the first place] your feet" (v. 8). Because "feet" in the Hebrew Bible is often a euphemism for genitals (see Isa. 6 and Ruth 3, for example), this is a bit of "foxhole" talk between two old fighting men. David digs a friendly elbow into Uriah's ribs and rather unsubtly commands him to go home to his comely wife and sleep with her.

And with that the plan becomes clear. Once Uriah is seen entering his home, and once the door is closed, the child will be Uriah's and no one will be the wiser. Uriah leaves the throne room, and David sends after him a nice kingly present to ease his way to his house. But something quite unexpected occurs; Uriah sleeps in the streets with David's servants and does not even come close to his house. When the surprised and certainly very disappointed king is told, he asks the general incredulously, "Haven't you just come from a trip? Why didn't you go home?" (v. 10). General Uriah provides a clear explanation. "The ark along with Israel and Judah are living in temporary shelters; my lord Joab and the servants of my lord are camping in the open field. Should I go home, eating and drinking and sleeping with my wife? On your life, on your very life, I will not do such a thing" (v. 11)!

One can only imagine the look on David's face as he hears Uriah's grand speech. And one can only imagine how many plans flew through his mind. He simply had to get Uriah into his house with Bathsheba! He commands that Uriah stay in Jerusalem one more day, and the next day David invites him to a drinking session in order to make the general drunk. But even in a drunken stupor, Uriah does not head home but sleeps once again in the street.

So now David, great king of Israel, becomes a murderer. He writes to his faithful Joab the following command: "Put Uriah at the place of the most dangerous fighting, and have everyone draw back from him in order that he might be struck down and die" (v. 15). Because he can trust the faithful Uriah, David hands the letter to him to take back to Joab. He is carrying his own death warrant.

Of course, the plan that David has devised is ludicrous. The wily David's cleverness has deserted him, perhaps because of his desperation to rid himself of the more virtuous Uriah. If Joab is to follow the king's command, he will place a force of his soldiers, including Uriah, at a dangerous spot and will arrange a signal to fall back, a signal not told to Uriah. What will the retreating men think when their general stands alone to be slaughtered by the enemy?

Joab has a wiser plan. He assigns Uriah to an especially dangerous place, but he also makes certain that Uriah's death is not the only one to occur; Joab sacrifices a number of David's warriors, the better to cover over the death of Uriah (v. 17). Joab's better plan works; Uriah is killed and no warrior can guess that it was the will of the king.

But now the king must be told of Uriah's demise. No one, aware of David's past relationships to messengers bringing bad news, would leap at the chance to inform the king (see 2 Sam. 1). Nevertheless, the king must be told, and Joab has a carefully designed plan to do so. He meticulously instructs the messenger, "When you finish telling the king about the fighting, it could happen that the king's anger may rise." If it does, "just say, 'Oh. Your servant Uriah the Hittite is dead, too'" (vv. 19-21).

It is obvious that Joab knows David well. He knows that David will have to put up a good front upon hearing of the death of Uriah, and he expects him to do so. But he must warn the messenger about the king's great passion so that the man will not be terrified in the king's presence. When the messenger comes to David, he is not quite able to follow Joab's instructions. He speaks of the battle, and the nearness to the wall, and the death of some of the king's warriors. But he does not wait for the anger of the king; he blurts out a direct quote from Joab: "Oh. Your servant Uriah the Hittite is dead, too" (v. 24).

But there is no passion from the king, no history lesson from the annals of warfare about the dangers of getting too near to walls in battle, no emotion about the dead warriors. The king is completely calm. His words in the face of the news are among the most chilling in all of literature. "Say this to Joab, 'Do not let this thing be evil in your eyes [the literal Hebrew]; the sword devours now this one, now that one. Press your attack against the city and overthrow it.'" And then to the messenger David adds, "Encourage him" (v. 25)!

Note very carefully what the king has said in this terrible speech. The euphemistic translation of the NRSV, "Do not let this matter trouble you," is correct, but it does not catch well the grim double edge of the Hebrew. The thing done is clearly "evil" in everyone's eyes, and no command or comment from the king can make it otherwise. "War is hell," says David, killing now one and now another. The statement is true, but not here. This was plainly murder. David's final words to the messenger to encourage Joab say, in effect, "Nice going, my clever general. I can always count on you!"

The story ends quickly. When Bathsheba hears of the death of her husband, she mourns for him, but when the proper mourning time is over, she moves in with the king, marries him, and gives birth to the child conceived sometime before the marriage. If any tongues were wagging in Jerusalem, we are not told!

By one count, David breaks the last five of the Ten Commandments: he murders Uriah just as surely as if he had done it himself; he commits adultery with Uriah's wife; he steals her from Uriah; he lies about it several times;

he covets her enough to act upon his desire. With this remarkable story about the mighty and memorable David, the text wants to remind us of two things: David is a human being, all too human. Do not expect him to act like a god, because he is not one. There is only one God in the universe, and David is not that God. Secondly, David can be our model, but that does not mean that we ought to strive to be like him. It rather means that we *are* all too often just like him. Like David, we love our God; it is just that too often we love ourselves more.

John C. Holbert

Eleventh Sunday after Pentecost, Year B

First Lesson: 2 Samuel 11:26–12:13a
(Psalm 51:1 12)
Second Lesson: Ephesians 4:1-16
Gospel Lesson: John 6:24-35

So now there comes a reckoning for the enormous evils of King David in his affair with Bathsheba and the murder of her husband. After Bathsheba made an appropriate period of lamentation for the dead Uriah, "David sent and added her to his household; she became a wife for him." In 1 Samuel 11:4 we read that "David sent messengers, and she was taken and came to him." But after the murder, David sent and "added" her to the household. The verb used implies that Bathsheba has become a member of the royal harem, certainly not David's only wife. He adds the pregnant Bathsheba to his already long list of royal women (Michal, daughter of Saul, Abigail, former wife of Nabal, and Maacah, among others). By so doing, he legitimizes Bathsheba as a royal spouse, the affair between the two is covered over, and life in Jerusalem appears to return to normal.

But a potent and quite unusual sentence concludes chapter 11. "But the thing that David had done was evil in the eyes of Yahweh." Very rarely in the long stories of Samuel, Saul, and David does the storyteller break into the tale to pronounce such a direct judgment on the activities narrated. All the more reason to take with great seriousness this powerful indictment from God. The reader can only agree at this point in the story that the actions of the king have been monumentally heinous; Yahweh, who was generally silent after the death of Samuel and Saul, has apparently had a divine fill of the odious behavior of the most recent choice for king of Israel.

But the way Yahweh chooses to confront the foul monarch is noteworthy. Nathan is sent to David to deliver Yahweh's displeasure. Just who is this Nathan? What role does he play in the royal court? How was he chosen for this task? We have met Nathan earlier in the story. In 2 Samuel 7, after David completes his royal palace, he determines to build a great temple for Yahweh. He announces his intentions to the prophet Nathan, who quickly accedes to the king's desires, saying, "All that you have in mind, do, because Yahweh is with you" (7:3). But that very night the prophet is warned by Yahweh that David is not to build a temple. Rather, Yahweh will build David's house, and one of his sons will build the temple. Thus, already we see that Nathan is called to contradict the desires of the king.

And at the end of the long story of David, as he lies on his deathbed (1 Kings 1–2), Nathan, in consort with Bathsheba, again goes against what David has apparently planned. His son Adonijah has declared himself king, and Bathsheba's son, Solomon, will be at best banished and at worst killed when his brother ascends the throne. So she "reminds" the aged David that he had promised to make Solomon king, though there is no mention of this supposed fact anywhere in the tale. After Bathsheba makes her plea to David, Nathan sweeps into the bedchamber and adds the divine seal of approval for a Solomonic rule.

So, now here. Each time Nathan meets David, he demands that the king do something different than he proposed to do. This fact leads to two important conclusions concerning Nathan's relationship to David and the court. First, Nathan is independent of royal authority. He has every right, and the apparent duty, to countermand the desire of the king when he is commanded by Yahweh to do so, something he does on three separate occasions. Second, he has ready access to the king, who listens carefully to the prophet and never contradicts the prophetic word.

This remarkable relationship leads to a very significant and far-reaching conclusion for contemporary religious life and for preaching: when Nathan strides into David's throne room to deliver the divine word, we witness the origins of the crucial idea of the separation of church and state. The independent prophet, heeded by the sovereign temporal authority, sets the pattern for that delicate balance between earthly and heavenly powers that has bedeviled nations for all of the three thousand years since the writing of this scene. The fact that the prophet *is* fully independent announces to all who name the Bible as some sort of supreme authority in the arrangements of human affairs that Yahweh's will is supreme in life, and that no earthly ruler, however magnificent, however powerful, can possess final authority to decide her/his own actions apart from that authority. As Nathan speaks, and as David listens, human government is put on notice that its power is forever limited by a power that is forever greater than its own.

The form of Nathan's sermon to David is also significant. We preachers would say it is a narrative sermon with a decidedly direct didactic conclusion. The prophet wins his way into the ears of the king by means of a story. As do we all, David loves stories, and gives Nathan his rapt attention. The prophet tells of two men who lived in a city, the one rich and the other poor. The rich man had countless flocks and herds, while the poor man had only one ewe lamb which he had scraped the money together to buy. He brought the little creature up himself. He helped it to grow as he helped his own children. When they ate, the lamb got her share. She slept close to him on the cold nights; she was nothing less than a daughter to the poor man.

A visitor came to the rich man's house, and of course a proper meal was needed. The rich man did not desire to take one of his own sheep to serve his visitor, so he grabbed the poor man's little lamb and served her to his guest. Thus ends the sermon of Nathan.

He has no time to "drive home the point," to "make the meaning plain." David does it for him. "David was furious with that man and said to Nathan, 'As Yahweh lives, the man who has done this is a child of death. [David means that the rich man has effectively killed himself by acting in such a disgusting manner.] That lamb he shall restore four times over, because he did this thing and because he was without pity.'" Nathan's response to David's outburst has echoed down the ages: "You are that man!" You have acted without pity. You have stolen what was not your own. You have murdered Uriah, and though you did not push in the blade yourself, the sword of the Ammonites performed the evil deed at your express command. You have then taken Uriah's wife to be your wife. And all this, says Nathan, was done in spite of the incredible gifts that Yahweh has given you: salvation from the fury of Saul, the kingdom of Israel to govern, Saul's own daughter as wife.

"And I would have added as much more," wails the prophet on behalf of Yahweh. But David's evil will first result in the death of the child of adultery, then the public humiliation of his wives. These two events happen in due time, but even more is in store for the king. David will be thrown out of his own city by his own son, Absalom, and his final days will be marked by a lack of heat, a lack of real authority, and an ignominious death as he spouts a demand for revenge on an old and feeble enemy. The affair with Bathsheba and the subsequent evil that ensues are the watershed events in the life of David, after which his existence spirals down to a series of tragedies for his own children and family.

To be sure, David announces in the face of Nathan's onslaught, "I have sinned in the presence of Yahweh" (12:13), and Nathan says Yahweh has pushed that sin aside in such a way that David's life is spared. But as the reader can see, from this point on that life is a grim one, punctuated by sorrow and capped by a pathetic death.

This tale wishes to remind us that there is in fact an accounting for evil, and that God does not take kindly to a wanton abuse of power, whether done by king or commoner. And confessions of sin, however heartfelt, do not automatically make things right once again. Cruel deeds, such as King David performed, are hardly snuffed out with a few choice religious words. Our deeds certainly do follow after us — a stone dropped into the pond creates an ever widening series of circles whose end no one can actually see.

Some preachers of this text will need to take great care so as not to turn its power into a simple "God always pays us for our sins" message. It is all too true that sin does create great rifts in the fabric of God's universe, yawning tears that are difficult to mend. David's life and death are proof enough of that fact. But we all know that sometimes it is more than difficult to see just exactly how evildoers are in fact given their comeuppance. Remember the terrifying words of old Job: "Why do the wicked live on, / reach old age, and grow mighty in power?" (Job 21:7). Why indeed? We must not reduce David's story to a simple one of reasonable retribution for evil.

Also, other preachers will want to offer reflection on the issue of church-state relationships, especially in our time when the divide between church and state seems all too often ready to be breached: by flag-bearing patriots or by those who would pray only certain prayers in schools filled with students with other prayers, or no prayers, in their hearts; or by sincere religious people who would stamp their deeply held convictions on all the people; or by politicians who would baptize their own policies in the font of religious certainty. To be sure, the David story and its cast of characters contain ideas and insight for far more than a short season of sermons!

John C. Holbert

Twelfth Sunday after Pentecost, Year B

First Lesson: 2 Samuel 18:5-9, 15, 31-33
(Psalm 130)
Second Lesson: Ephesians 4:25–5:2
Gospel Lesson: John 6:35, 41-51

A moment of intense grief, filled with the possibilities and failures of a lifetime — this is what this lectionary passage offers. David has been on the throne of Judah and Israel for many years, a canny and determined ruler. But here he is reduced to a sobbing, almost inarticulate cry, "O my son Absalom, my son, my son Absalom!" In this moment, the text prompts reflections about the story of David, this moment of grief, and the working out of the Lord's purposes in human events.

For those preaching this passage, the context in the ongoing story of David is important. Much time has passed narratively since the David and Bathsheba story (2 Sam. 11–12), the starting point of this section of the story and the source of the previous two lectionary readings. In the six chapters since then, covering more than eleven years, the narrative has been working out the consequences and implications of Nathan's prophecy which was God's response to David's sins of adultery and murder. Besides the immediate consequence of the death of the child conceived by David and Bathsheba, longer-term realities were announced. David was told that the sword would never depart from his house, and that God would raise up trouble against him within his own house (12:10-11).

The story then traces the sad and sordid history of David's adult children playing out their ambitious and violent struggles against each other and against David. The heir to David's throne, Amnon, callously raped his beautiful half sister Tamar (13:1-19). Absalom, Amnon's half brother and full brother to Tamar, bided his time before setting up the murder of Amnon in revenge for the rape (13:20-39). Absalom fled and stayed in southern Judah for three years. Only the crafty intervention of Joab, David's army commander, using a wise woman to present his case, could convince David to bring back Absalom, who was now heir to the throne (2 Sam. 14).

Absalom's return became dangerous, however, because he turned to preparing to seize the throne from his reigning father and in time revolted outright against David (15:1-12). David the king was forced to flee from Jerusalem. Even as he and those still loyal to him mourned the disastrous events, David placed supporters back in Jerusalem to try to bring down Ab-

214

salom (15:13-37). Both Absalom and David prepared for war, positioning their forces, gathering supporters, and planning for a battle that could only have a bitter outcome (2 Sam. 16–17). Nathan's prophecy has come full circle: there could be no greater trouble from within David's own house than for him to be forced to fight Absalom. Tragically, the story of David has shown the once brilliant and beloved king brought to the event where he must use his power and brilliance against his own son.

Chapter 18 narrates the final confrontation between king and heir. The story's perspective is from within David's camp in a nearby city. We see him sending out his battle-seasoned troops in three sections to surround and confound his son's forces. Emphasis is given to David's final instructions to all his army, that they should "treat with gentleness the young man Absalom" (v. 5). After giving all the detail of preparations, the text treats the battle itself with economy, with two verses that describe a slaughter of Absalom's "men of Israel" by the king's troops, "the servants of David," in the forested wilderness (vv. 7-8). It seems that even the natural order itself participates in events, for the forest "devours" more victims than the sword, and a single tree plays a role in Absalom's death.

More narrative attention is given to the death of Absalom, who unexpectedly is caught, first by his head in a tree and then by Joab and his men. The almost bizarre image of a warrior trapped in the snare of tree branches is a detail set in relief to the background of general slaughter. But it is the detail that the whole narrative has been working toward since Absalom first rebelled. Caught between being heir to the throne and the power on the throne, caught between two opposing armies, caught by a tree and left suspended between "heaven and earth," he is caught between life and death (v. 9). Joab, David's general who has never flinched from murder for the king's sake (Abner, 3:27; Uriah, 11:16-17), strikes Absalom and then his men finish him off (v. 15). In doing this, Joab has disdainfully dismissed David's concern that his son be treated gently, which the story has taken pains to show that he had heard (vv. 5, 11-14). The death of the rebellious son finally ends the battle, and he is ignominiously buried (v. 17).

Even greater narrative attention is paid to delivering the news of Absalom's death to the king. With fine detail we are told that two messengers are dispatched and come running to the city where David waits in the gate. We watch with David as he sees the messengers approaching, already knowing as readers the message he awaits. Both messengers carry the good news that the rebellion is over and the battle won. But David has ears only for one concern: "Is it well with the young man Absalom?" (vv. 29, 32). When the first messenger, the son of one of David's priests, cannot bring himself to reveal the awesome and terrible news, the second messenger, who is a foreign mercenary, does so (vv. 31-32). David, the successful commander, retreats in grief to mourn with a heartrending cry, "O my son Absalom, my son, my son Absalom! If only I had died instead of you — O Absalom, my son, my son!"

In this narrative and especially in this moment of grief, all attention is focused on David and Absalom. In chapter 18 the words "David" or "the king" are used thirty-four times; Absalom is mentioned twenty-six times. All the other characters and events circle around these two, for it is only their relationship that drives the poignancy of the story. Finally, the story centers on David mourning the immense and complicated loss of his son and heir. It seems that David's relationship with Absalom has always been profoundly ambiguous, including a range of emotions from yearning love (13:39), to silent judgment and apparent reconciliation (14:24, 33), to intense fear and bitter grief (15:14, 30). At the news of Absalom's death, the king who could have celebrated a rebel's downfall mourns the loss of a son. The father who might have simply mourned the loss of a son grieves over his own culpability in precipitating the tragedies that arose within his own house. David's grief is real, yet it bears all the conflicts and questions of David's lifetime. The text here suggests reflections on the ambiguities and complicated relationships which mark human life and so often create complex layers of emotions in moments of grief.

All the while David and Absalom and the other characters pursue their own strategies and purposes, the purposes of God are seemingly silent in the telling of the story. It appears that human agents largely act on their own and that this sad history is merely the working out of its own consequences. Yet the text makes a powerful if subtle statement about the Lord's presence in human affairs. The whole story of trouble within David's house had been set in motion by Nathan's prophecy of the Lord's word against David. Once that is powerfully stated, God is referred to only a few key times in the story. As David flees from Jerusalem, he prays that the counsel of Absalom's esteemed adviser, Ahithophel, be turned "to foolishness" (15:31). And indeed, this prayer is answered. In the briefest of notes, the intentions of God in the whole complicated affair are revealed: "For the LORD had ordained to defeat the good counsel of Ahithophel, so that the LORD might bring ruin on Absalom" (17:14). The Cushite messenger who brings to David the news of the battle and Absalom's death has it right: "The LORD has vindicated you this day" (18:31). Yet the story makes clear that David can only count the cost of such vindication: "O my son Absalom, my son, my son."

While the human characters in the David story do indeed make their own choices and initiate actions and reactions that make sense within their own perspectives, throughout all that occurs the intentions of God are inexorably working themselves out. The story seems to be making the theological point that God is not heavy-handed in intervening in human affairs, yet is still sovereign over human life. Human choices and God's will are intertwined in enigmatic ways, yet, if David's story reflects truth, then God's providence is the context of our lives.

Patricia Dutcher-Walls

Christ the King, Year B

First Lesson: 2 Samuel 23:1-7
(Psalm 132:1-12, [13-18])
Second Lesson: Revelation 1:4b-8
Gospel Lesson: John 18:33-37

The first thing one notices about this text is that it is out of place. It is identified as "the last words of David," but David doesn't die after saying it. In fact, much of David's story remains to be told, and it is not until 1 Kings 2:10 that he actually dies, after giving final instructions to Solomon, the new king.

Obviously, the author of the book of Samuel was not interested in a chronological ordering alone. He put the last words of David here for different reasons. This text follows the "Song of David" (2 Sam. 22), much like the "Blessing of Moses" follows the "Song of Moses" in Deuteronomy 32–33. Thus poetic material is sandwiched in between the narrative. On each side, the author narrates the story of David. That story is a "rags to riches" story. It is a story of victory and defeat, triumph and tragedy, rebellion, salvation, love and lust, sin and grace. Sometimes it is unbelievably bloody and cruel. Sometimes it is tender and touching. In the middle of it all is David, and with David — through it all — stands Yahweh.

This poetic material in what is called the appendix to the book of Samuel (chaps. 21–24) emphasizes that at the heart of it all, David was a man of unshakable faith in Yahweh, the God who had so graciously saved him. In

2 Samuel 22, David praises Yahweh for the deliverance he had given him from all his enemies. Yahweh, David's rock, his fortress, his salvation, had saved him from every enemy, even when death herself threatened him (22:1-7). Throughout the psalm, David acknowledges that Yahweh is the one who had given him the strength to overcome. Yahweh ensures that David's foot will not slip (22:37). Yahweh ensures that every enemy is subdued under David. Yahweh had avenged him from all his foes (22:48). In the last verse of the psalm, David remembers the covenant that God had made with him (2 Sam. 7). It is for the sake of the covenant that Yahweh had given David so much success in the past. But the covenant also directs David's thoughts forward to Yahweh's care in the *future* for David's descendants as well. Thus he says:

> He is the tower of salvation to his king,
>> and shows mercy to his anointed,
>>> to David and *his seed* forevermore. (22:51)

This turn to the future and to thought of the covenant connects with the words of the text where David also calls himself the anointed one (v. 1) and recalls the covenant God had made with him (v. 5). As the song in chapter 22 praises Yahweh for his salvation in the past and for the covenant he had made, so these last words of David look to the future and to the salvation that would come, also on the basis of the covenant with David. And so the author places both discourses together in order to emphasize Yahweh's grace in David's life and the hope that it gives to his people.

The idea that 2 Samuel 23:1-7 is future oriented is based on a reading of a text that holds many difficulties for the interpreter, and that accounts for the variety in the translation and commentary of this passage. Nevertheless, certain points can be made which will be useful for one preaching this text. First, the expression in verse 1 translated by the NIV as "the oracle (of David)" *(Ne'um Dauid)* is an expression that occurs by and large in prophetic contexts. The phrase in which it occurs here is similar to that used by Balaam in Numbers 24:3, 15 before his prophecy concerning Israel, which was also given when the Spirit of God came upon him (Num. 24:2). David may have had that incident in mind here. At any rate, the phrase implies that David is not about to speak his own words, but as a prophet, the words of Yahweh. Indeed, verses 2-3 reinforce that conviction. In the four cola, David reinforces the idea that he was not speaking his own words: "The Spirit of Yahweh spoke with me, and his word is on my tongue, the God of Israel spoke, to me the Rock of Israel said. . . ."

The following statements (vv. 3b-4) are the words that Yahweh speaks through David the prophet. The NIV is typical of how most translators understand the somewhat obscure wording of the text. They connect the two verses together as follows:

> When one rules over men in righteousness,
>   when he rules in the fear of God,
> he is like the light of morning at sunrise
>   on a cloudless morning,
>   like the brightness after rain
>   that brings the grass from the earth.

In other words, here Yahweh describes the "ideal ruler" and "godly leaders," as one commentator says.

However, a number of points can be made against this interpretation. First, it can be observed that such an understanding seems anticlimactic after the buildup of the previous verse that Yahweh himself was speaking through David. It weakens the force of the word introduced as "the word of God." Read in this way, Yahweh doesn't say anything that isn't rather obvious already. Second, this understanding of 3b-4 removes the connection between the covenant Yahweh made to David in 2 Samuel 7 and these words of Yahweh to David. Since the covenant Yahweh made with David is such a "fundamental reality" in David's life and theology (cf. the comments above), it would be strange for David to speak of something else in this passage introduced as "David's last words." Third, this interpretation leads one to understand verse 5 as introducing a new thought. After Yahweh's message, David turns to the covenant. But if this is the case, the connection between the two verses isn't entirely clear.

However, the Hebrew of verse 5 begins with a *ki*, which more naturally should be understood as referring to the preceding expression and giving David's reason or explanation for what Yahweh has just said. Verse 5 is the commentary that reflects back on verses 3b-4. As David explains in verse 5, Yahweh's words refer to the covenant that Yahweh made with David's house in 2 Samuel 7. Read in this way, verse 5 can be understood as follows: "For is not my house *thus* [referring to Yahweh's words] with God? For he has given to me an *eternal covenant,* arranged in detail and guarded [guaranteed]. For in regard to all my salvation and all my [or perhaps 'his'] delight, will he not surely make it sprout?" (On the image pictured in the last expression, see especially Isa. 11:1-5; Jer. 23:5-6; 33:15-16.) In connection with this translation, note specifically Yahweh's words to David when he gave David the covenant in 2 Samuel 7:11-12: ". . . and Yahweh will tell you that a *house* Yahweh will make for *you*. When your days are filled, and you lie with your fathers, I will raise your seed after you who will come out from your loins, and I will establish *his kingdom. He* will build a house for my name, and I will establish the throne of his kingdom forever." David also reflects on this promise in his prayer following Nathan's words to him (7:18ff.).

Yahweh's words in 3b-4 are of much greater moment when they are seen to refer to this "seed of David" whose kingdom will never end. In verse 5, therefore, David reflects upon the significance of Yahweh's (obscure) words in verse 4 by referring them to the covenant Yahweh had made with him. (*Nota bene:* It does seem that throughout the OT, those passages traditionally regarded as messianic always seem to contain some obscurities about them which makes their interpretation "ambiguous." It is as if one either sees the messianic reference or one does not.) At any rate, based on the above remarks, 3b-4 can reasonably be translated as follows: "[There will be/come] a righteous ruler over mankind, one who rules in the fear of God. And he will be [or 'it will be,' i.e., his reign will be] like the light of the morning when the sun shines — a cloudless morning. From [his] brightness and [his] rain grass [will spring] from the earth." (For an explanation of this translation and other details of the text, see H. N. Richardson, "The Last Words of David: Some Notes on II Samuel 23:1-7," *Journal of Biblical Literature* 40 [1971]: 257-66.) This last phrase appears to express in figurative language the blessings that this righteous ruler and his kingdom will bring to the earth. The language parallels that of Psalm 72:6-7, which is also understood as a messianic psalm:

> He shall come down like rain upon the mown grass,
>   like showers that water the earth.
> In his days the righteous shall flourish,
>   and abundance of peace.

It is worth noting that the Targum on the Former Prophets also interprets this passage messianically. Seen in this light, David's "last words" function not only to comfort him but also to comfort us. What do people think about when they are about to die? All of us are going to have "last words." What will we say? Where will we look? Some people cannot take their eyes off the world — even as they are about to be torn from it and torn in half, that is, soul from body. It is said that P. T. Barnum was interested in money until he drew his last breath. His last words: "How were the receipts today at Madison Square Garden?" Many people have nothing to say. After all the "words" of their life, death finally leaves them silent — without excuse — without argument. After all, you can't argue with death.

And that is why, from our perspective, David's "last words" are so highly ironic. Here was a man who had lived life to the fullest. There was almost no experience or emotion that David had not had. His life had been wonderfully blessed. And yet he does not linger over it. At death — at life's end — David does not have to look back. He does not have only the past to cling to, like so many of us. Yahweh had promised him a future and his people a future, and it is that promise that is on David's mind and lips as he breathes his last.

From David's house, Yahweh promised a righteous ruler. A ruler who would bring light to this dark world like the sun on a cloudless day. A ruler who would change everything, as the sun and rain change the landscape and cause the earth to bear its fruit. David clung to that promise and found hope. But it is really a promise that is just as much for us. It is a promise that Yahweh of course fulfilled in Christ.

Christ is the righteous one (as Isaiah says, "the righteous sufferer") who rules over our greatest enemies, up to and including death. He is the "light of the world" who offers hope even as the last moments of our life fade away. His blessings, like light on a cloudless morning, like brightness after the rain that brings grass on the earth, are spiritual — forgiveness, life, peace, hope — and eternal. His kingdom will never end, and by God's grace we are part of that kingdom. We are redeemed from the curse of the Law (death) and promised us his salvation.

That means that when it is time for our "last words," we don't have to cling to the past. Like David, we are promised a future in the Son of David which will never end. As David is dying, his words comfort us, for they speak of a Savior. In them, even in life's darkest moments, we find comfort too.

Timothy E. Saleska

Thirteenth Sunday after Pentecost, Year B

First Lesson: 1 Kings 2:10-12; 3:3-14
(Psalm 111)
Second Lesson: Ephesians 5:15-20
Gospel Lesson: John 6:51-58

David, while far from perfect, was a king who loved God, and God used him to accomplish many important tasks in the building of his kingdom. For instance, he completed the conquest by defeating the Philistines, and he established Jerusalem as his capital, preparing it to be the place where the temple would be built. God, in turn, blessed David by promising him a dynasty of kings. This promise is expressed in the form of a covenant and is found in 2 Samuel 7.

Now David is dead, but in answer to the promise, his son Solomon takes the throne. Solomon's very name is a tribute to David's kingdom work. The name relates to the common Hebrew word *shalom*, which means peace, and indeed the beginning of his reign is characterized by peace. Our passage introduces us to Solomon as he ascends the throne, and we find that he is a very perceptive and spiritually sensitive ruler.

Solomon's love for the Lord took him to Gibeon. We need to remember that the temple had not yet been built and Gibeon, about seven miles north of Jerusalem, had an important shrine dedicated to God. Solomon went there to worship God, and the text tells us that he offered numerous sacrifices at this time. In response, God appeared to Solomon in a dream with an incredible proposal: "Ask what I should give you" (3:5). Imagine the possibilities! Carte blanche from God himself. Reflect on what you might request if you got the opportunity. Solomon could have asked for staggering riches or unlimited power. But he doesn't. Instead he asks God for wisdom. He apparently recognized the tremendous responsibility involved in ruling God's people, and he was aware of his own inadequacy. Accordingly, he turned to God and asked for practical knowledge and insight to rule.

God was pleased with Solomon's answer, for the king had asked for something that would help him carry out his God-given task, the kingship, and not for something that would promote his own glory.

The Lord was so pleased, in fact, that he also promised to grant wealth and honor to his servant Solomon. As we read on in the books of Kings and Chronicles, we see that it was precisely through Solomon's divinely given wisdom that he received riches and glory.

222

Before proceeding, however, let's inquire a little further into what the Old Testament means by wisdom. We in the modern West, influenced by classical thought, prize intelligence, an amassing of facts. Intelligence is measured by IQ and has nothing to do with ethics or even competence. The Old Testament conception of wisdom, however, is much more practical and is closer to skill than to intelligence. However, even the concept of skill does not quite handle it, especially when describing the kind of wisdom that God gave Solomon.

Wisdom begins with relationship, and in our text Solomon clearly enjoys an intimate relationship with God. In the Old Testament, the book of Proverbs is the most distinctive example of the literary genre of wisdom we have. In the light of the historical traditions we are studying, it may be no surprise that the book is explicitly associated with Solomon (Prov. 1:1). In that book, which more than any other helps us understand Old Testament wisdom, we find this motto repeated (with variations) throughout: "The fear of the LORD is the beginning of knowledge" (1:7). This again emphasizes the relational aspect of wisdom.

Furthermore, wisdom has an ethical component, at least in how it is used in the Solomon text we are studying and in the book of Proverbs. Lady Wisdom, the personification of Yahweh's wisdom in Proverbs 8, hates "pride and arrogance and the way of evil and perverted speech" (8:13). Embracing wisdom leads to life. Lady Folly, on the other hand, butchers her disciples (9:13-18).

Wisdom thus involves far more than intellect. It is a relational, ethical, and also emotional category. As many proverbs indicate, those who are wise know how to express their emotions in a reasonable fashion, appropriate for the context. In sum, biblical wisdom is much more like what today goes by the name of emotional intelligence than IQ.

We can see the practical effect of Solomon's divinely given wisdom by a look at 1 Kings 3, the narrative that immediately follows God's giving wisdom to Solomon. Here we have a court case involving two women. Solomon wisely solved a dispute over a child, a case made difficult because no witnesses were present to speak on behalf of either woman. With understanding for motherhood, Solomon ordered the child cut in two so that each woman could have half. Solomon knew that the true mother would rather give up the child than see him die. As a result of this ruling, Israel marveled "because they perceived that the wisdom of God was in him, to execute justice" (3:28).

Solomon's wisdom, however, extended far beyond the borders of Israel. His widespread fame is evidenced in the story of the queen of Sheba (10:1-

223

13). Sheba was a wealthy country because of its trade in spices and precious metals. While its exact location is disputed, the best guess places it at approximately the same area as modern Yemen. This identification means that the queen traveled about fourteen hundred miles to meet Solomon in Jerusalem.

We don't learn the content of the discussion between the queen and Solomon, but we know that the queen was amazed by Solomon's wisdom and his wealth. Solomon's wisdom caused this Gentile queen to praise God: "Blessed be the LORD your God, who has delighted in you and set you on the throne of Israel! Because the LORD loved Israel forever, he has made you king to execute justice and righteousness" (10:9). She also increased Solomon's wealth by giving him an abundance of gold and spices.

One of the mysteries of the Bible is that someone as wise as Solomon foolishly turned his back on God. In spite of his wisdom, Solomon was not perfect; he loved foreign women more than he loved the Lord, and he worshiped their idols. Indeed, it is interesting that 1 Kings 3 drops hints about the later problem even as it is talking about the early Solomon seeking wisdom. The chapter is introduced with a note about the marriage to Pharaoh's daughter and the fact that Solomon sought God at a "high place," both anathema to the narrator of Kings. In any case, because of his foreign love and resultant foreign worship, God became angry with Solomon, and because of Solomon's sin, God caused the Israelite empire to crumble.

Solomon's failure reminds us that a human being is neither the origin nor the prime example of wisdom. When we think of wisdom and wish to seek it, we should not look to the man Solomon, but rather to the one he anticipates, Jesus Christ.

In Matthew 12:38-45 we read that religious leaders pressed Jesus for a miracle. They wanted Jesus to prove himself by doing something extraordinary. Jesus responded by pointing out their blindness. They should recognize who he is. "The queen of the South will rise up at the judgment with this generation and condemn it, because she came from the ends of the earth to listen to the wisdom of Solomon, and see, something greater than Solomon is here!" (12:42). A Gentile queen (the reference is to the queen of Sheba) recognized Solomon's divinely given wisdom, but the religious leaders could not recognize one greater than that king.

As Christians we know that Jesus Christ, unlike Solomon, is consistently wise. When we need wisdom, when we need guidance in how to live our lives, we seek Jesus Christ, "in whom are hidden all the treasures of wisdom and knowledge" (Col. 2:3).

Tremper Longman III

Fourteenth Sunday after Pentecost, Year B

First Lesson: 1 Kings 8:(1, 6, 10-11), 22-30, 41-43
(Psalm 84)
Second Lesson: Ephesians 6:10-20
Gospel Lesson: John 6:56-69

Ninth Sunday after the Epiphany, Year C

First Lesson: 1 Kings 8:22-23, 41-43
(Psalm 96:1-9)
Second Lesson: Galatians 1:1-2
Gospel Lesson: Luke 7:1-10

The setting of these two readings is the dedication of the temple that Solomon built for the Lord. To correctly interpret our passage, we must first of all understand the function of the temple in the Old Testament. In a word, the temple was a space rendered sacred by the presence of God. One Hebrew phrase used for the temple in the Old Testament was "house of God"; the structure, in other words, was the place where God was thought to reside on earth. As such, it was surrounded by all kinds of taboos and restrictions of who could go where within the temple area.

This thought seems strange to us who know the pervasive biblical teaching that God was everywhere (Ps. 139; Jonah). How could he live in a particular location; how could he have a house? Solomon will address this theological problem in the context of his dedicatory prayer.

But first, let's realize that the temple was a long time coming. Construction on it began in the fourth year of Solomon (1 Kings 6:1, ca. 966 B.C.E.) and was completed seven years later (6:37). David had wanted to build the temple, but was blocked from doing so by Nathan the prophet, who was speaking on behalf of the Lord (1 Sam. 7). Among the reasons given was that he was a "man of blood" (1 Chron. 22:8; 28:3). We misunderstand this phrase if we take it in an ethical sense, because in large measure God ordered the holy war that resulted in David's military activities. On the contrary, there is a redemptive-historical motivation behind this statement. The temple, as opposed to the tabernacle, was a permanent architectural structure. It symbolized the fact that Israel had rest from its enemies and was firmly established in the land. In other words, while David was the conquest completer, Solomon, whose very name means peace, was the one commissioned to build the structure that represented a new era of God's people. Thus the dedication of the temple represents a climactic moment in the history of God's people, and the dedicatory speech, given by Solomon, expresses the theology that stands behind the temple building.

At the focal point of the temple was the ark of the covenant that had been in the Holy of Holies in the tabernacle. The ark was a simple box 33/4 feet long, 21/4 feet wide, and 21/4 feet high (see the description in Exod. 25:10-22). It was a small but incredibly potent symbol of the presence of God. It also had rings attached to the sides through which were slid poles that were used to carry the ark. While the construction design was simple, its composition was not. The poles and the box were made of precious acacia wood, and both were covered with gold. Indeed, the box was covered with gold both inside and outside. Furthermore, the cover to the ark is given a separate special description and said to be made of pure gold. It is also said to be the place where atonement takes place. At each side of the ark were to be placed gold statues of cherubim. The cherubim are especially powerful spiritual beings who served the role of protectors of God's holiness. They are at the sides of the ark with their wings outstretched and touching each other, while their heads are bowed (1 Kings 8:6-7). The reason for their posture is that the ark is a potent symbol of God's presence in the tabernacle. Indeed, it is seen as the footstool of his throne (1 Chron. 28:2), perhaps even occasionally as the throne itself (Jer. 3:16-17). God the king sits in his earthly house on his throne, and the cherubim, whose wings support him, look to the ground to shield their gaze from the radiance of his glory. The ark was also a container. In 1 Kings 8:9 we are reminded (see Exod. 25) that it is the place where the stone tablets of the covenant were held. Indeed, the presence of these tablets is surely the reason one of the most common names of the ark is the "ark of the covenant." Recent research has shown that the conceptual world behind the Old Testament concept of covenant is a treaty between two nations, represented by their kings. In a typical treaty, two copies were made and deposited in the one sanctuary. In the case of the covenant between God and his people Israel, there is, of course, only one God, and both copies were deposited in the one sanctuary, as happens here with the ark. At the heart of the covenant idea is the fact that God promises to be with his people. Thus the ark is connected to the covenant as a concrete token of the divine presence.

The ark was placed in the most holy place of the temple, as it had been in the tabernacle beforehand (1 Kings 8:6). While the temple was a magnificent, ornate, luxurious building, befitting its role as the house of God, by modern standards its dimensions were not overwhelming. According to its description in 1 Kings 6, it was a building ninety feet long and thirty feet wide, thus its total interior was 2,700 square feet, again not a gigantic building. Its height too was not excessive, being forty-five feet. While not large, however, the quality of the workmanship was unsurpassed in ancient Israel. It was made of the finest woods and metals; as contrasted with the tabernacle, no cloth materials are mentioned in its construction. The building was divided into two parts by a partition that separated the back area, constituting a third of the total area, from the rest of the interior. The back was where the ark of the covenant was kept, and its dimensions are given in 1 Kings 6:20 as thirty feet long, thirty feet wide, and thirty feet high — a cube, in other words. This room was the most magnificent part of the temple compound, as we would expect since it housed the ark. Its ceiling and its walls, as well as its floors, were made of precious cedar wood, which was covered with pure gold.

As mentioned, the temple, like the tabernacle, symbolized God's presence with his people. Accordingly, we find heavenly imagery, like the cherubim, in the Holy of Holies, and garden imagery, connoting Eden where God walked with the first human couple, throughout the inside and the outside. We can also observe an intensification of precious materials, like pure gold, as we move toward the specific place where God was thought to have his throne.

In addition, however, we find innovations as we compare the temple and the tabernacle. Interestingly, they all point in the same direction, to the transition to a new era in the relationship between God and his people, that is, their establishment in the land. In this way they support what we have already seen in terms of the timing of the building of the temple.

In the first place the temple, quite simply, is a permanent house, whereas the tabernacle was a portable tent. This important yet simple architectural feature indicates the transition from a wandering people to an established kingdom. The pillars enhance this understanding of the symbolism of the temple. Pillars not only make a structure more grand; they impart the impression of permanence. The names Jachin and Boaz ("He has established" and "By his strength") encourage this understanding.

Finally, the name of the basin of water, the sea, has obvious significance. Throughout the Bible the personified Sea is often seen as God's rival, representing the anticreation forces of chaos. God fights the Sea and controls its dangerous power. This image goes deep in the psyche of the ancient Near East and is found in Canaanite as well as Mesopotamian creation texts. Here, the temple is bounded, controlled right outside the temple, which represents

God's throne. This seems to represent the fact that God has defeated the former inhabitants of the land and has firmly established his people there.

1 Kings 8:10-11 describes the scene after the ark had been placed in the temple, when the priests filed out. At this moment God filled the temple with a cloud which prevented the priests, we presume only temporarily, from performing their duties at the temple. The cloud is a well-known symbol of God's presence as well and an appropriate symbol for an invisible, mysterious deity because, while it is tangible, it also obscures sight. The cloud both reveals and conceals, since one sees it but cannot penetrate it to know what lies inside or behind it. The cloud also filled the tabernacle in the wilderness (Exod. 40:34-38), where it also guided the Israelites during the day. Later writings refer to this cloud as the Shekinah and closely associate it, as does the Bible, with God's glory.

Now that we understand the significance of the temple and its central symbol, the ark, we understand the gravity of the occasion of its dedication. The temple was God's house on earth, replete with images of heaven and Eden. Solomon understands that the building of the temple represents the fulfillment of divine promises made years before to David, and implicitly before him to Abraham as well (1 Kings 8:22-24). God promised by means of a covenant relationship that he would give Abraham many descendants as well as a land. Further, Abraham would be blessed and be a blessing to many (Gen. 12:1-3). While the possession of the Promised Land began with the conquest under Joshua, it was not completed, as we mentioned above, until the time of David. Solomon's reign is the first that begins with rest from all the internal enemies, and the temple symbolizes establishment in the land. God had further promised David, Solomon's father, that his heir would build the temple (2 Sam. 7:12-13). It is within the context of this Davidic covenant that he also promised that king that one of his descendants would perpetually sit on the throne in Jerusalem (2 Sam. 7:14-17), and Solomon continues his dedicatory speech by reminding God of this promise (1 Kings 8:25-26).

At this point in his speech, Solomon acknowledges that the temple, the house of God, is a symbol of God's presence and not his literal residence. God does not live in the temple as human beings live in their homes. "But will God indeed dwell on earth? Even heaven and the highest heaven cannot contain you, much less this house that I have built!" (1 Kings 8:27). In modern theological language, God is transcendent as well as immanent. However, later Israel will make the mistake of believing that God had to be perpetually on their side, never allowing their military defeat, because he lived in Jerusalem. In his famous temple sermon, Jeremiah (Jer. 7) charged the people with presuming on the presence of the temple as they shrugged off his calls to repentance on threat of exile. Indeed, Ezekiel 9–11 envisaged the glory of God leaving his throne in the Holy of Holies, mounting a cherubim-driven chariot, and abandoning the temple on the eve of its destruction.

Solomon then implores God to listen to the prayers that would be directed toward the temple. The text specified by the reading focuses on the prayer of the foreigner. This reminds us that even in the Old Testament the non-Israelite was a hoped-for participant in the divine promises. After all, the Abrahamic covenant alluded to above declared that all nations would be blessed through the promises directed to the patriarch's heirs. And we learn of God's good dealings with certain Gentiles, and these are probably the tip of the iceberg: the mixed multitude coming up from Egypt, Rahab, and Naaman. Solomon thus rightly calls on God to hear not just the prayers of beleaguered Israel, but also of the foreigner in their midst.

Finally, as we contemplate this passage, we need to look beyond it and ask how it fits into the broader canonical story. The temple was a symbol of God's presence with his people, as was the tabernacle before it, and individual altars before the tabernacle. They all hark back to a time when no special place was needed to meet with God, the Garden of Eden, which was truly heaven on earth. The Solomonic temple lasted several hundred years until the armies of the Babylonian Nebuchadnezzar destroyed it in 586 B.C.E. The temple was rebuilt in the Persian period, being finished in 515. This temple lasted over half a millennium and existed, aggrandized by the building efforts of Herod the Great, during the time of Jesus. Jesus treated the temple with the respect it deserved, most famously cleansing it of mercenary money changers (John 2:12-17). However, it was also of this temple that Jesus proclaimed, "Not one stone will be left here upon another; all will be thrown down" (Mark 13:2). The destruction of the Second Temple took place in 70 C.E. as the Roman general Titus put down a Jewish revolt. It was said of Jesus that he claimed that the temple would be rebuilt in three days (Mark 14:58). Though this testimony is garbled, there is no question but that the writers of the New Testament understood that the presence of Jesus rendered the temple superfluous. After all, when Jesus was present, God was present (John 1:14).

But even this is not the end of the story. For that we have to turn to the last two chapters of the book of Revelation where we get a highly symbolic picture of the time of the end. In the new Jerusalem, it is specifically mentioned that there will be no temple. Why? "Its temple is the Lord God the Almighty and the Lamb" (Rev. 21:22). We are back to Eden, even heaven itself.

Tremper Longman III

Third Sunday after Pentecost, Year C

First Lesson: 1 Kings 17:8-16, (17-24)
(Psalm 146)
Second Lesson: Galatians 1:11-24
Gospel Lesson: Luke 7:11-17

E lijah has just been introduced in the previous passage (17:1-7). He springs on the scene with the minimum of an introduction. God simply announces to him that he was instituting a drought in Israel. This drought served an important theological purpose. Ahab, the king of Israel, had married Jezebel, the daughter of King Ethbaal of the Sidonians, and she had lured Ahab's heart toward the worship of the god Baal. This led him to construct worship sites for Baal in the heart of his empire. He likely did not abandon the worship of Yahweh altogether; he simply combined it with the worship of Baal. What could be wrong with a little tolerance in one's religion, after all?

God, though, is a jealous God (Exod. 20:4-6), and he countered this move toward his rival Baal with a drought. A drought attacked Baal worship at its center. After all, Baal was a fertility god. He was thought to be the personal force behind the rains, the dew, thunder, and lightning. In effect, Yahweh is challenging Baal to come through for his worshipers. He refuses to provide the rain because the people will attribute its produce to Baal.

Our passage is set in the midst of the resultant famine. If there is no rain, then there is no food. Elijah himself survived well beside the Kerith Brook for a while. Ravens brought him food and the brook provided him water. But after a while the brook dried up, necessitating a move.

Elijah must have wondered what God was up to when he was left without water, and must have been doubly surprised when he heard God's marching orders: "Go now to Zarephath, which belongs to Sidon, and live there" (17:8). This city was on the coast of the Mediterranean between the great Phoenician cities of Tyre and Sidon. Indeed, as we mentioned above, the wicked Jezebel came from this general region. While a Sidonian goes to Israel and works much mischief there, we now see God sending a faithful Israelite prophet to Sidon, and much good will result.

If we go back to the Abrahamic promise in Genesis 12:1-3, we will observe something that Israel constantly forgot. In its selfish appropriation of the promises, Israel often forgot the outward face of these promises. Not only would the direct descendants of Abraham be blessed, but "all peoples on earth will be blessed through you" (Gen. 12:3b). God would use Israel to bring many people to himself. During the period of the Hebrew Bible, we get occasional glimpses of this. Some of the more obvious include Rahab the Canaanite (Josh. 2) and Naaman the Syrian general (2 Kings 5). Here Elijah is sent not to an Israelite widow, of whom there would have been many suffering the same fate during the drought, but to a foreign widow.

And we should also pause to consider the fact that Elijah is sent not just to any woman, but to a widow. This is in keeping with a basic concern throughout the Hebrew Bible for those who are powerless. Widows and orphans had no natural human resources to turn to when they were in trouble, so God took special care of them and protected them by his law (e.g., Exod. 22:22). Here God will protect this widow and her son by a wonderful miracle that provides them with sustenance in the midst of famine.

When Elijah first met the widow, he must have seemed anything but a glimmer of hope in a difficult world to her. Not only did he not immediately help her, but he put an additional burden on her life. She was out gathering sticks for a fire on which to cook the last meal for herself and her son. She only had a little left, and they were going to eat it and then wait for death to come. Elijah saw her and immediately asked her for water, and then, as if that were not enough, he added, "Bring me a morsel of bread in your hand" (17:11). At this she demurs, protesting that she had little to bring. How could she bear it?

However, Elijah then reveals his purpose to her. If she makes him a cake, then never fear, there will be food enough not only for the day but for the duration of the famine! God would miraculously provide sustenance for her and her son.

The demand that the prophet be fed first allows the widow to demonstrate faith in God. If she is willing to give up what little she has, then she can expect much from God. This, of course, is contrary to all appearances, and that is why it is an act of faith.

The narrative records her obedience and its result in a simple, straightforward manner: "She went and did as Elijah said, so that she as well as he and her household ate for many days. The jar of meal was not emptied, neither did the jug of oil fail, according to the word of the LORD that he spoke by Elijah" (17:15-16).

By so doing, God demonstrated that it is he and not Baal who provides life. Fertility and food are the gift of his hand. God here does it miraculously in a way that authenticates the divine word. And this is an important point. God doesn't perform miracles to be sensational, but to confirm a prophetic word (Heb. 1:1; 2:4). Furthermore, miracles have a redemptive purpose.

They restore what sin has torn apart. The famine was a result of the sin of idolatry. The miracle overcomes the ravages of famine in the life of the widow and her son.

We will see many parallels between Elijah and Elisha and the life and ministry of Jesus. Jesus' message too went beyond the confines of Israel to reach the Gentiles. Indeed, when he ran into resistance in his hometown of Nazareth, he anticipated the reception he would get from the Gentiles by reminding the people that Elijah went to a widow in Zarephath, though there were many hungry widows in Israel (Luke 4:24-27). Jesus also showed that he had divine power by feeding the hungry miraculously (Mark 6:30-44; 8:1-10). Jesus is even greater than Elijah, since he is life itself.

Like the widow, we may be asked to give up what little we have in service to God. We may be suffering as she was, but still be ready to give as well as to receive. We must be careful not to fall into the temptation of seeking the apparent power of our idols, whether money, power, pleasure, but rather to seek the source of real power, God himself. He is the source of life and is sovereign over death.

The next account continues with this general theme, yet with a new twist. It is one thing to be brought back from the brink of starvation, and another to be brought back from death itself. The unnamed son of the widow got ill and died. Imagine the effect on the widow. God had saved her son from the famine only to allow him to die of some illness. It is not hard to see why she blamed Elijah and by implication God himself for this tragedy.

Baal didn't even claim to be able to raise the dead. In the Aqhat epic, the goddess Anat tempts Aqhat to turn over his composite bow to her by offering him eternal life. He scoffs at her offer: "Don't lie to me, girl, your lies are despicable to a real man. What afterlife can one obtain? What can a man obtain hereafter?" (translation from W. W. Hallo, ed., *The Context of Scripture*, vol. 1 [Leiden: Brill, 1997], p. 347). Neither Anat nor Baal could overcome death for Aqhat. As a matter of fact, Baal could not even overcome death (Mot) himself. In the Baal epic, the god Death (Mot) swallows him up. It is true that the text implies that Baal is later raised, but nonetheless for a season death had its way with Baal himself. Not so Yahweh. Indeed, he swallows death (Isa. 25:8). Elijah lies on the widow's son, and God restores life to him. Again, God is the victor over death.

The parallels with Jesus are, of course, striking. Jesus raised the dead. We think of Lazarus three days in the tomb but springing to life again at the word of Jesus (John 11:38-44). But even more remarkable is his own resurrection from the dead. Indeed, that resurrection is the firstfruits of the general resurrection described in 1 Corinthians 15, which culminates with a quotation from Isaiah 25:8 combined with Hosea 13:14: "'Death has been swallowed up in victory. / Where, O death, is your victory? / Where, O death, is your sting?' The sting of death is sin, and the power of sin is the law. But thanks be to God, who gives us the victory through our Lord Jesus Christ" (1 Cor. 15:54b-57).

Tremper Longman III

Second Sunday after Pentecost, Year C

First Lesson: 1 Kings 18:20-21, (22-29), 30-39
(Psalm 96)
Second Lesson: Galatians 1:1-12
Gospel Lesson: Luke 7:1-10

Our text occurs at the climax of one of the most dramatic passages in Kings, if not the whole Bible. In order to understand the meaning and impact of the specified verses, we must understand the passage in its context. The broader context is the reign of Ahab, the king who married Jezebel, the daughter of the king of the Sidonians. She was a worshiper of Baal and had convinced Ahab to worship Baal in addition to Yahweh. Baal was the head of the Canaanite pantheon and was a specialist in fertility, which included being the god of rain, dew, thunder, and lightning. Yahweh, Israel's true God, responded by closing up the skies so there would be no rain and, of course, no fertility in the land (1 Kings 17:1).

1 Kings 18 takes place sometime after the beginning of the drought, and therefore the "famine was severe in Samaria" (v. 2). People were hungry, and Ahab commanded Obadiah, one of his palace officials, to help him search the land for grass as food for the animals. Obadiah is identified as someone who risked his life to save some of the prophets of the Lord from Jezebel, the queen who was intent on promoting Baal worship at the expense of Yahweh worship.

It was during his investigation of the land that he encountered the prophet Elijah, who insisted that he tell Ahab that he wanted to meet him.

233

Apparently, Ahab had wanted to find Elijah for some time, but every time he is about to catch up with him Elijah disappears, frustrating the king, who wants to harm him. Obadiah worries that Elijah will disappear before the king comes, and if that happens it is Obadiah who will feel the anger of the king. However, after assurances from Elijah, Obadiah fetches Ahab, who greets the prophet with the ominous "Is it you, troubler of Israel?" Elijah had not troubled Israel, however, but rather Ahab and his policy that promoted foreign religion in the country. Elijah had not come to debate but to demonstrate the power of Yahweh over that of Baal, so he told the king to gather together the prophets of Baal and Asherah to Mount Carmel for a contest of power.

Once the prophets of Baal and Asherah were gathered, Elijah spoke the challenge that constitutes the first part of our passage. He accuses the people of "limping with two different opinions" (v. 21). From the context, it is clear what he means. These people were not worshiping Yahweh as he desired. They combined the worship of the true God with the worship of Baal, a false god. The people of Israel were thus falling into the practice of the people of the broader Near East. They were polytheists, after all. They did not have to reject Yahweh in order to accept Baal. They simply grafted the worship of Baal onto the worship of Yahweh. However, Yahweh is a "jealous God" (Exod. 20:5); he does not want to be one among many; he wanted to be the one and only ultimate concern of their lives.

We often forget or even repress the biblical teaching of God's jealousy in the Bible. We rightly strive to be tolerant of people whose beliefs are different from our own, but that does not mean we participate in that belief. We don't serve the cause of the true God by incorporating elements of the worship of other gods into our lives. The Bible, Old and New Testaments both, is clear in its insistence on the worship of the true God alone.

In any case, God's jealousy is an energy that propels him to fight for his people. Behind Elijah's challenge of the prophets of Baal and Asherah is God's challenge of Baal himself. What is most remarkable about this challenge is that it takes a form that pinpoints Baal's divine specialty. The object of the challenge is to light the altar fire. Both parties will prepare an altar fire, but they won't light it. Instead, they will call on their god to light the fire from heaven. Remember — Baal is a rain god. He is a specialist at throwing fire (lightning) from heaven. Indeed, in one well-known ancient artistic representation of Baal, he stands upright throwing an object that is best interpreted as lightning. If Baal can do anything at all, he can light this altar fire.

Furthermore, we should note how the deck is stacked against Elijah from the start. In the first place, the numerical advantage goes to the forces of Baal. There are 450 prophets of Baal and 400 prophets of Asherah (18:19). In addition, the king is against him and the people are "limping with two different opinions." Though Obadiah may be privately rooting for him and the Lord, Elijah basically stands alone. Second, they go first. If the altar fire is lit, then the contest is over. Yahweh will not even get a chance to bat.

In spite of all this, however, nothing comes of the fervent appeals of the prophets to their god. They ask, but they get no answer; the altar fire stays unlit. Elijah simply makes fun of them. From a human point of view, the forces of Baal seem overwhelming, but their impotence wins only laughter (cf. Ps. 2). From a biblical point of view, Baal worship was exploitative and abusive. Jezebel had systematically persecuted those who followed God. In this light, celebration of their failure makes perfect sense, even the type of ridicule that Elijah levels at them.

We only truly understand the significance of the self-mutilation of the prophets of Baal and Asherah if we know something about their mythology. In the Baal myth, recovered from the ruins of ancient Ugarit, there comes a point where Baal is overcome by Mot, the god of death. Baal is swallowed by Mot and fertility comes to an end. At this point the god El, mourning Baal's death, cuts himself in a way very similar to that of the prophets here. They are not throwing in the towel as such, but rather acknowledging that Baal is dead. The myth, though broken, implies that Baal is later revivified, thus reflecting the seasonal cycle. But in any case, for the purposes of this text, it is clear that Baal is impotent.

It is now God's turn. As if circumstances were not already set against Elijah and his God, the prophet now ups the ante by having the altar virtually flooded with water. Nonetheless, in response to Elijah's prayer asking God to demonstrate his power to the people, God sends fire from heaven that leaves no doubt as to his existence. The people climactically respond: "The LORD indeed is God; the LORD indeed is God."

God's mighty acts in history are not done to appeal to human sensationalism, but rather to attest to his great redemptive acts. From our present vantage points, we look back in history to the greatest attestation of God's power in the cross and resurrection. As we read and believe the Gospel accounts of the work of Christ, we too are led to exclaim: "The LORD indeed is God; the LORD indeed is God."

One last observation is well worth mentioning. Notice how God communicated his presence and his power in the language of the culture, even a culture that was inimical to him. Today, some Christians withdraw from culture and create a virtual subculture. Thus, when they speak to the culture, they look like fish out of water. However, it is God's desire that, though we are not "of the world," we be "in the world." Acts 17 is a New Testament analogy to 1 Kings 18 as to how God's people should speak with the craftiness of a serpent in a hostile culture.

Tremper Longman III

Fifth Sunday after Pentecost, Year C

First Lesson: 1 Kings 19:1-4, (5-7), 8-15a
(Psalms 42 and 43)
Second Lesson: Galatians 3:23-29
Gospel Lesson: Luke 8:26-39

T he narrative of Elijah's flight from Ahab and Jezebel unfolds in three scenes: Jezebel's threat and Elijah's journey to Beersheba (vv. 1-3), his time in the wilderness (vv. 4-8), and his encounter with God at Mount Horeb (vv. 9-18). Omitting verses 5-7 and ending the story prematurely at verse 15 interrupts the movement of the story, and the preacher may well want to embrace the whole narrative (through v. 18) in order to deal with its richness.

Having just triumphed in his contest with hundreds of the prophets of Baal and Asherah at Mount Carmel, Elijah draws the wrath of Jezebel and finds himself the subject of a death warrant to be executed immediately. In short order he goes from the mountaintop to the wilderness, heading to Beersheba, at the edge of the more deserted wastes, where he may find refuge from royal power (Walter Brueggemann, *1 Kings,* Knox Preaching Guides [Atlanta: John Knox, 1982], p. 87).

He journeys but a day before collapsing beneath a broom tree, the high exaltation of his recent victory swept away by his fear of Jezebel. Having not improved on his ancestors' faithfulness (probably Moses, Joshua, and Samuel), Elijah experiences himself as a failure. Curiously, in his despair he asks God to do unto him what Jezebel seeks to do — to end his life. By not dignifying this request with a verbal response, God affirms that seeking death is not the answer to Elijah's despondency. In the midst of deep sleep that night, he is awakened by the touch of an angel, who does as ravens did earlier (compare 17:1-7) in providing nourishment, here cake and water. Given the string of miracles Elijah has recently experienced, his unremarked acceptance of an angelic visitation is perhaps not surprising. Elijah sleeps again, and is awakened a second time; this time he learns that the provided nourishment is for a journey. Indeed, it will be sufficient for a journey of forty days and nights to Mount Horeb, "the mount of God," the sacred place where Elijah's standing in the Mosaic covenant will be renewed.

Finding Elijah in a cave at the holy mountain, God inquires of the prophet, "What are you doing here?" Elijah responds with a declaration of his faithfulness, of Israel's lack of response, and of his utter isolation in his task. God commands Elijah to stand on Horeb to witness God's presence (compare Moses' similar experience in Exod. 33:12ff.). A great storm, an earthquake, and a fire mark God's passing by as elsewhere in the Old Testament (compare Pss. 18:12-14; 68:8; Isa. 30:27), but God is not identified with these dramatic events. Surprisingly, it seems the prophet has disobeyed and has not come out of his cave as instructed, for it is only the "sound of sheer silence" that claims his attention and draws him to the mouth of the cave. Perhaps he has had enough drama from God of late and is so utterly numbed by his despair that only the quiet can pique his interest.

God poses the same question again, asking for an explanation of Elijah's presence, and receives, remarkably, the exact same lament as earlier. Has the prophet not been affected at all by the divine pyrotechnics? God makes no more powerful gestures, but instead gives new instructions to the prophet concerning his role as kingmaker. As a final reminder, offered as counterpoint to the prophet's insistence on his unique and lonely faithfulness, God notes that there are seven thousand in Israel who have not gone after other gods (v. 18).

Nothing unimportant happens on mountains in Scripture (e.g., Ararat, Moriah, Sinai, Carmel, Sermon on the Mount, Mount of Transfiguration), and the significant number forty (e.g., the flood, years in the wilderness, Jesus' temptation) also calls attention to the story's significance. What begins as flight from a tyrant soon becomes a journey to God led by God. God's persistent calling to renew Elijah's identity and vocation is present in the midst of flight, fear, sleep, wilderness, a long journey, and finally in both word and silence. Like the man healed by Jesus at the pool of Bethsaida (John 5:2-9), Elijah does not readily embrace the offer of new life extended by God. He has been sorely cast down by the death-dealing Jezebel, so much so that the life-giving presence of God is almost missed. The prophet is fleeing not only the queen but also his vocation that has brought him into conflict with her power. The tension in the narrative is between whether Elijah will be defined by his fear of Jezebel or by his faithfulness to God. God's twice-repeated question is, in essence, "How can you fulfill my purposes if you are not where I need you to be?"

Elijah's repeated, self-righteous lament marks the depth of his despair. He seems almost past caring. Even the haunting silence does not change his defensive words. He has not moved at all in his understanding of himself in relationship to God. If the action on Mount Carmel will not persuade Israel nor intimidate Jezebel and Ahab, what will (compare Luke 16:31, where Jesus says if his hearers will not believe Moses and the prophets, they will not believe by virtue of the resurrection)? Fear has frozen his mind and heart profoundly. Elijah has come to the place, to the sacred place, where it is not dramatic demonstrations of God's power that are needed (compare Mark 15:32, where Jesus is taunted to come down from the cross), but God's presence and guidance. God does not speak through the storm, earthquake, fire, or silence, but rather directly, perhaps a bit impatiently, to the exhausted and despairing prophet. Elijah is converted back to his prophetic vocation by having his fear-driven flight given new direction, not unlike the disciples' experiences in meeting the resurrected Christ (John 20 and 21). Because of God's refusal to give up on him, Elijah is called back to his role in God's work to subvert the destructive and oppressive regime of Ahab and Jezebel.

This compelling story speaks to many crucial aspects of the Christian experience. It is an exploration of God's work in the midst of human fear, despair, isolation, sense of failure, and loss of identity (Richard D. Nelson, *First and Second Kings* [Louisville: John Knox, 1987], p. 129). Remarkably, it is neither the experience of God's dramatic nor quiet presence, for which many so long in the midst of such feelings, but in attending to the work at hand and needing to be done through which life is renewed. A successful therapist once admitted, almost sheepishly, that what she mostly did with clients was to listen, and then ask, "And what are you going to do?" Action, rather than feeling, is the arena in which humans have freedom to choose. Elijah is called back to action, to the fight into which God has enlisted him, not because he feels like it but because it's what needs doing that he can do. Where else is he going to go? Elijah has lost his vocational identity, as so many do in the midst of life's vagaries (and perhaps people are most vulnerable to such loss after a "mountaintop" moment such as Elijah had on Mount Carmel). Recovering a vocation may well come from being reminded of God's action in the past (as Elijah is given an experience previously known only to Moses) and by being given specific actions or next steps to take.

Furthermore, Elijah's lament is heard. But part of the price of being heard by God is that he is somewhat humbled, not so much by the majesty of

God, although that is certainly evident, but rather by having to acknowledge he is not alone. There are others he has not recognized but with whom he can be in community. Immediately following this narrative, God will graciously give him Elisha as companion and heir. No longer is Elijah to be the heroic figure acting alone. And so, he must also surrender the egotism associated with that role in order to be in deeper communion with God, who is the principal actor. Faithfulness can lead to loneliness at times, but one's sense of loneliness cannot be allowed to become a perverse source of ego gratification ("no one understands me"). Ultimately, that is the path to deathly despair.

One of the essential marks of Jesus is his clarity about his identity. Although labeled in many ways — as glutton, drunkard, Sabbath breaker, blasphemer — he remained clear about and faithful to his vocation through his relationship with God and his community of disciples. He did not try to go it alone, and in fact formed a community as his first act of ministry. In this narrative Elijah has lost his vocational identity by his acceptance of Jezebel's label "enemy of the state" and his own label of "failed to outdo my ancestors." All believers will be challenged from time to time about who they are and what they are to do, and will have to resist false voices, even their own, as did Elijah, in pursuit of faithfulness in order to hear finally the voice of God. Waiting upon, rather than fleeing from, the Lord will open the path to be walked.

Lawrence W. Farris

Fourth Sunday after Pentecost, Year C

First Lesson: 1 Kings 21:1-10, (11-14), 15-21a
(Psalm 5:1-8)
Second Lesson: Galatians 2:15-21
Gospel Lesson: Luke 7:36–8:3

In this passage, Ahab is king of Israel. As king, he should be a paragon of faith and virtue. According to Deuteronomy 17:14-20, Israel's kings should not be like the kings of the surrounding nations who seek their own wealth and glory. Rather, they should be ruled by God's law, because, after all, they are a reflection of the true King who lives in heaven. Furthermore, though they have important responsibilities, they should not put themselves above "other members of the community" (17:20). By the time we come to 1 Kings 21, however, we already know Ahab as a king who does not desire the best for his God or for his people. We also know his wife Jezebel, the daughter of the royal house of Sidon (1 Kings 16:31), a woman who is an outspoken advocate for her god, Baal. Already we have seen this pair in action in the contest on Mount Carmel with the prophet Elijah (1 Kings 18).

The chapter opens by introducing Naboth, who lives in the city of Jezreel, and continues by informing us about his vineyard in that city. While Samaria was the main capital of the northern kingdom at this time, Jezreel was the location of a new winter palace, and according to the text, Naboth's vineyard backed up to the king's house. Ahab wanted to expand his grounds and develop a vegetable garden on the site of Naboth's vineyard. We must first acknowledge that Ahab's initial approach to Naboth seems quite reasonable. He proposes a transaction, not theft or blackmail. He will give Naboth a better plot of land or even money for the vineyard. Naboth's response, though, is unhesitating: "The LORD forbid that I should give you my ancestral inheritance" (21:4). Ahab then returned home, which probably means Samaria, where he was so depressed that he just got into bed and neither talked nor ate.

Questions arise in this initial scene of our story. In the first place, why was Naboth so adamant? He seems almost unreasonable. It's not a matter of survival; he could even get ahead of the game from a financial perspective. But there is something much more fundamental at stake, and we are alerted to this by his referring to the land as his "ancestral inheritance," signifying that this was the land that his ancestors received at the time of the entry into the land. Leviticus 25:23 succinctly states the underlying theology of Naboth's assertion: "The land shall not be sold in perpetuity, for the land is mine; with me you are but aliens and tenants." In essence, God owns the land. He brought Israel into the land by defeating the Canaanites. They would not have the land if it were not for his power. He gave the land to the people, and they were always to have the land in their possession. They could rent out the land or sell it temporarily, but not permanently. Naboth understood Ahab to be asking for a permanent sale, and Naboth rightly refused. Indeed, the religious nature of Naboth's refusal is earmarked by the beginning of the sentence "God forbid. . . ." If he had sold it, it would be an offense against God himself. Indeed, as Provan (*1 and 2 Kings,* New International Bible Commentary [Peabody, Mass.: Hendrikson, 1995]) tells us, there may be a sinister symbolic meaning to Ahab's desire to change Naboth's vineyard into a vegetable garden. Deuteronomy 11:10 tells us that Egypt was like a vegetable garden, whereas Israel frequently is likened to a vine (Isa. 3:13-15; 5:1-6). Ahab is a king that wants to transform God's land into a land of bondage.

Secondly, Ahab's reaction to Naboth's rejection appears odd, out of all bounds with the occasion. Indeed, it seems quite a trivial matter in which the king is involved, and then, when rejected, he goes home and pouts like a disappointed baby. It is precisely, however, because the matter is so trivial that Ahab is so distressed. After all, he is king, and he cannot even persuade a local landowner to give him a vineyard that he wants. Ahab is fully aware of the power of neighboring kings; indeed, in the next scene Jezebel will give him a primer on royal power. Kings do not ask; they take! Ahab's power is limited in Israel. Certainly that is the way God wanted it. The king was to be a mere human reflection of the divine King. However, even at the institution of kingship, when Samuel anointed Saul, that prophet anticipated the exploitation that human kings would foist on God's people (1 Sam. 8:11-18). God may have wanted his kings to serve in the interests of his people, but Ahab was only interested in his needs.

Nonetheless, apparently Ahab felt powerless to do anything about his disappointment except to mope. His Sidonian wife, Jezebel, will now take charge. She will give him a lesson in kingship, in good ancient Near Eastern style! She first of all inquires into his depression. She must have been mystified why her husband the king felt so powerless; her father wouldn't have had the same problem. That seems to be the effect of her rhetorical question to him, "Do you now govern Israel?" (21:7). As a matter of fact, subtle hints indicate that Ahab may have been more than a little nervous around his strong-willed wife. Notice that as he tells her about the offer he made to Naboth, he subtly leaves out the fact that it was a *better* vineyard that he offered for his vineyard. Such condescension might have put Jezebel over the edge.

She acts in Ahab's name as she arranges a conspiracy that will result in the death of Naboth. In the first place, she demands that local officials proclaim a fast. Now in the Old Testament a fast was called at times of distress, the threat of war, a drought, or the like. The text may assume some kind of manufactured crisis where there is then a meeting at which Naboth plays a prime role. The fact that he is seated in a prime location may be because he is under suspicion already. Two "scoundrels" (lit. "good-for-nothings") are in place to bring the accusation: "Naboth cursed God and the king" (21:13). There are two scoundrels because witnesses had to come in pairs in order to be credible according to Deuteronomy 19:15-21. Such a crime deserved death (Lev. 24:10-23; Exod. 22:28), and Naboth is taken outside the city and stoned. The report of the deed was then relayed to Jezebel.

Jezebel then informed Ahab that Naboth was out of the way, and Ahab seized the vineyard and presumably turned it into a vegetable garden. To be honest, scholars are not quite sure why Ahab was now allowed to take the vineyard. After all, if there were other relatives, it would have become their ancestral inheritance. But perhaps there weren't other relatives; we just don't know. In any case, Ahab and Jezebel seem to have gotten away with an incredible injustice against a fellow human being and, as the story will emphasize in its conclusion, an even more important offense against God.

God dispatches Elijah to confront Ahab. One very important role of the prophet in the Old Testament is to be the conscience of the king. We can see this in the relationship between Samuel and Saul as well as Nathan and David. When they go astray, kings are confronted by prophets. In this case, though, the relationship between Elijah and Ahab is more like guerrilla warfare. The former confronts the latter abruptly and then leaves. Elijah publicly rebukes Ahab for his injustice against Naboth and declares that the penalty for the sin will be severe. Both Ahab and Jezebel will meet violent deaths, and their bodies will be abused. Furthermore, Elijah declares that God will end Ahab's dynasty.

But an amazing thing happens. In this case, Ahab repents! If we understand 1 Kings 22 to be sequential with the present story, it is a temporary repentance, but nonetheless it causes God, who will reverse or delay a judgment because of his overwhelming grace, to delay the denouement of the Omride dynasty of which Ahab is a part. Nonetheless, in keeping with his word, both Ahab (1 Kings 22:29-40) and Jezebel (2 Kings 9:30-37) die horrible deaths. Indeed, the final chapter of the story takes place when Jehu rebels against Ahab's descendant Jehoram, also known as Joram. Jehu not only has him killed, thus bringing the Omride dynasty to a close, but has his body thrown on the land where Naboth's vineyard stood (2 Kings 9:25-26).

The story of Naboth and Ahab fits into the broader story of Israel as presented in Samuel and Kings. This history has a debated compositional history, but most scholars are convinced that it was given its last major redaction during the exilic period. It presents the story of Israel with the intention of answering the question: "Why are we in exile?" This story of royal betrayal is just one of a number of events that illustrates the deep sin of Israel that led to the punishment of exile. In particular, Samuel and Kings narrate how Israel and its kings betrayed the laws of Deuteronomy with the result that the curses of Deuteronomy came into affect.

Ahab was yet another king that let the people down by not pointing them to God. Even the best kings of Judah and Israel — David, Solomon, Jehoshaphat, Josiah, to name a few — had their deep flaws. They were flawed reflections of God's rule and anticipations of that future perfect Davidic descendant, King Jesus.

Tremper Longman III

Last Sunday after the Epiphany (Transfiguration), Year B

First Lesson: 2 Kings 2:1-12
(Psalm 50:1-6)
Second Lesson: 2 Corinthians 4:3-6
Gospel Lesson: Mark 9:2-9

There are very few persons in any congregation who understand this Old Testament text when it is read as one of the stated lessons for Transfiguration Sunday. The passage comes across as opaque and mysterious, and perhaps that is a fitting reaction to it, for it is indeed full of mystery.

Let us first establish some of the facts about the passage. Its setting is the ninth century B.C., between the reigns of the northern kings of Israel, Ahaziah (850-849 B.C.) and Jehoram (849-842 B.C.), during the time of the early, nonwriting prophets. Its central focus concerns the inheritance of the prophetic office of Elijah by Elisha (v. 15), and therefore the reading of the passage should probably proceed to that point, if not to the end of the chapter. We know already from 1 Kings 19 that the prophet Elisha is to be the successor of Elijah (19:16) and that the ultimate mission on which Elijah is sent by God is to topple the great Omri dynasty in Israel by fomenting a prophetic revolution that will place Jehu on the throne.

The repeated phrase "the sons of the prophets" (vv. 3, 5, 7, 15) refers to those bands of early, nonwriting prophets in Israel who carried on the initial fight of the Yahwistic faith against the absolute claims of the monarchy and against the incursions of fertility Baal religion into Israelite society. Such prophetic bands lived together in closed colonies near the various shrines about the countryside. Some of these prophets were married, some had their own houses. Frequently they traveled about on errands, answering the questions of the people when persons "inquired of the LORD" and delivering oracles from God. In contrast to the later inspiration of the writing prophets by the Word of God, the source of inspiration for these early prophetic bands was the Spirit of God, and often they were drawn into ecstatic states by that Spirit (cf. 1 Sam. 10:10-11). There is no certain evidence, however, that Elijah was a member of such bands, though he had frequent contact with them.

The journey on which Elijah leads Elisha in our story is rather pointless. Gilgal is very near the Jordan, which is Elijah's final destination. Jericho is a few miles from Gilgal, but the trip there is interrupted by a detour to Bethel. The route seems to have no purpose other than to illustrate Elisha's determination to remain with Elijah and to show that Elisha hears the same words from the sons of the prophets at each of the shrines. Nevertheless, the journey does serve to build suspense in the story.

The mantle of Elijah, which is a long, loose cloak, recalls his mantle in 1 Kings 19:19, and the crossing of the Jordan on dry land reminds of Joshua's parting of the Jordan's waters as well as the crossing of the Reed Sea in Exodus.

When Elijah asks his disciple what he can do for him before he dies, Elisha replies that he wishes to inherit a double share of Elijah's spirit of prophecy (v. 9). Elisha is not asking to be greater than his master. Rather, Elijah is Elisha's "father," a term of greatest respect, and according to the law of Deuteronomy 21:17, Elisha is simply asking for the inheritance which was granted the firstborn son. In order for Elisha to inherit Elijah's spirit and thus to be his successor, he must first pass a test, however. Elisha must see Elijah as he is being "taken up" (v. 1) or "taken from" (v. 10) him.

Those terms are never explained, and contrary to an early reading in Sirach 48:9 and to popular tales and artistic depictions of this event which has traditionally been called "the translation of Elijah," that prophet is not conveyed to heaven in the chariot of fire (v. 11). Rather, he is taken up in a whirlwind, which is elsewhere associated with the revelation or action of God (Job 38:1; 40:6; Isa. 29:6; Nah. 1:3; Zech. 7:14). Verse 12 makes it clear that Elisha sees Elijah as he disappears and so passes the test given to him.

The strange exclamation in verse 12, "My father, my father! The chariots of Israel and its horsemen!" is found again only in connection with Elisha's death (13:14). And, of course, the question is, What does that signify? Certainly horsemen and chariots were symbols of the power of a king (Gen. 41:43; 2 Sam. 15:1; 1 Kings 1:5). Chariots were usually manned by three "horsemen," one the driver, the second the weapon bearer, and the third the shield bearer. But the horsemen and chariots in our passage are not ordinary. They are chariots and horsemen of "fire," which is so frequently associated with the divine in the Old Testament (1:10-14; Deut. 33:2; 1 Kings 18:24, 38; Isa. 30:27; etc.). We find these fiery agents again in 2 Kings 6:17 and 7:6-7, where they are revealed to make up part of God's unseen army against his and Israel's enemies. Significantly, in 6:17 they are revealed only to the eyes of faith. We might say, therefore, that these horsemen and chariots of fire are God's secret weapon. We might even equate them with some of God's hosts of heaven, with which he does battle against his foes.

There is a prominent so-called "holy war" tradition in the Old Testament that the Lord fights for his people (Deut. 20:1). Thus at the time of the exodus, and throughout the period of the judges and Joshua, very often Israel's battles are in actuality God's battles, in which he fights with supernatural weapons, confusing the enemy, turning their swords against one another, throwing down stones from heaven, and employing cosmic forces to gain victory.

But why, then, are God's weapons of the fiery chariots and horsemen associated with his prophets Elijah and Elisha? Probably because the prophetic word from God is also the Lord's weapon. God uses his word, given to Elijah and Elisha, to challenge monarchs, to defeat the Syrians, and even to topple a royal dynasty. The word of God does not just convey information; it is a mighty force that effects that of which it speaks. In the words of Jeremiah, it is a "fire" burning in his bones (Jer. 20:9), a hammer that breaks rocks in pieces (Jer. 23:29). And the fact that Elisha is allowed to see the forces, the hidden army, the horsemen and chariots of the word, means that his prophetic word, too, will be a weapon in God's warfare against his foes. Indeed, it is finally Elisha who completes the revolutionary mission given to Elijah, to put Jehu on the throne of Israel (2 Kings 9–10).

Such are apparently the facts connected with this difficult text. But we are still left with the sense of mystery that surrounds the whole, and everything in the passage contributes to that sense. There is Elijah's seemingly pointless journey in which he appears driven by some inner compulsion, and at every point along the way he apparently wants to separate himself from the ordinary world. He tries to get rid of Elisha, but that disciple clings fast to his master. The sons of the prophets know, apparently from the Spirit, that Elijah is going to be taken away, but they are forbidden to speak of the fact. And when the place on the eastern side of the Jordan is finally reached, Elijah and Elisha are separated from each other by those fiery manifestations of God's power.

More than that, the story is deliberately set in timelessness, much like the story of the transfiguration, *between* the reigns of kings Ahaziah and Jehoram, although in earthly human history there was no "between." And the place on the far side of the Jordan is a private place where no human eye except Elisha's can watch. Following the story, the sons of the prophets have no idea what has happened to Elijah; they have not seen his translation, and they go in search of him.

In short, we deal in this story, as we do also in the story of the transfiguration, with another realm where there is no time or place. We deal with the realm of eternity, the realm of God, the unseen world behind and above ours, where there is great power and death is no more, and from which the Father sends his Son and his Spirit to work miracles upon the earth. We hear of that realm in other stories about the prophets — in 1 Kings 22:19-23 and Isaiah 6, in Jeremiah 23:18 and Isaiah 40:1-8. All speak of a transcendent reality that is hidden from ordinary eyes but is glimpsed, if still imperfectly, by the eyes of faith. And we learn from the Scriptures that the final destiny of this ordinary, workaday world of ours will be shaped by the God who inhabits that timeless reality, who defeats all his foes, and who wills nothing other for us but life and good everlasting.

Elizabeth Achtemeier

Sixth Sunday after Pentecost, Year C

First Lesson: 2 Kings 2:1-14
(Psalm 77:1-2, 11-20)
Second Lesson: Galatians 5:1, 13-25
Gospel Lesson: Luke 9:51-62

Second Kings 2 marks the transition from Elijah to Elisha. Indeed, it is the only place where we see one prophet replacing another upon the latter's death. Prophecy, unlike kingship or priesthood, is not a matter of biological descent, but rather a matter of God's choosing and anointing with the Spirit. As a matter of fact, God had already alerted Elijah that Elisha would succeed him as prophet in the next generation, as is recorded in 1 Kings 19:15-18. Since Elisha's succession was announced in advance like this, we wonder why Elijah seems to cast doubt on the process. In 2 Kings 2:10, in response to Elisha's request that he receive a double portion of Elijah's spirit, Elijah tells him that he has asked a "hard thing," the granting of which is conditional on whether or not Elisha sees Elijah's end. Furthermore, Elijah does his best to lose Elisha as he moves from Gilgal to Bethel to Jericho. What is going on here?

The text does not tell us explicitly, and there is more than one possible motivation for Elijah's actions here. Perhaps he knows that Elisha will succeed him and to succeed him he must be with him, but Elijah is trying to avoid his fate by not being in the same place at the same time with his successor. Whatever the reason, however, we certainly learn from this that Elisha is determined to be Elijah's successor as he goes everywhere that Elijah goes. He desires the calling to be Elijah's successor and so is determined not to let the older prophet out of his sight. And certainly Elijah cannot escape the divine appointment of his end, about which everyone in his circle, including the broader group of disciples, knows will take place that very day (2:3).

Why do we learn so much about Elijah and Elisha in the book of Kings? In fact, we learn more about them than any other nonwriting prophet. The answer to this question also helps us see the importance that a strong person like Elisha succeed Elijah. God raised them up during a perilous moment in Israelite history. While many of the kings of Israel as well as Judah strayed from the Lord, few were as determined and systematic about it as Ahab. Ahab had married Jezebel, a daughter of the Baal-worshiping Sidonian king. She was an aggressive evangelist for her religion, and many, many people were turning away from the Lord and toward Baal at this time. God was using Elijah, and now will use Elisha, to turn the tide of apostasy.

As a matter of fact, many of the miracles that surround the ministry of Elijah and Elisha were shaped as polemics showing the powerlessness of Baal worship, and the form of Elijah's transition to heaven is no exception. The expectation and the fulfillment was that Elijah would be caught up into heaven by a whirlwind. When this great event actually took place, Elisha cried out, "Father, father! The chariots of Israel and its horsemen!" (2:12). To modern readers this expression seems odd, even out of place. However, we must remember that Baal was thought to be the cloud-riding deity. The cloud was his chariot in which he went into battle as a warrior. But here God is teaching Israel that it is God who is the power in the storm and the rider of the chariot.

As mentioned, Elisha requested of Elijah a double portion of his spirit.

This does not mean twice as much. The reference is to the inheritance of the firstborn. The firstborn heir would receive twice as much as any other heir (Deut. 21:15-17), and that is Elisha's request. Unlike many prophets, most notably Moses and Jeremiah, Elisha desired to be used of God in his prophetic work.

The prophet's clothing plays a very important role in this story. The focus is on a word which is variously translated cloak, robe, or mantle. It is an outer garment, and the Hebrew word suggests that it is a quite magnificent item of clothing. In any case, it is a symbol of the prophet's charisma. It is not magical, but rather symbolic. Already in 1 Kings 19:19, at Elijah's first meeting with Elisha, the former had put his garment over Elisha, foreshadowing the succession. In the present story the garment makes its appearance as Elijah rolls it up and strikes the waters of the Jordan. This episode is highly reminiscent of Moses leading the people across the R(e)ed Sea and, to a lesser extent, Joshua leading the people across the Jordan. Indeed, it may be a way of signaling to the reader that both these men are in succession from Moses, the paradigmatic prophet, the one from whom all other prophets derive (Deut. 18). The robe functions here like Moses' staff, again not magically but as a symbol of divinely given prophetic power.

In any case, when Elijah is taken up into heaven, his garment is left behind and taken by Elisha. The continuity of divine power is indicated by the fact that Elisha now takes it and strikes the Jordan's water and passes back into the Promised Land on dry ground. Elisha is now ready to be used of God as he battles the forces of evil resident in the worshipers of the false god Baal. The miracles of Elisha that are reported in the following passages authenticate Elisha as a worthy successor to Elijah.

The manner of Elijah's end and the language that describes it leave us in some ambiguity over what is intended by the biblical author. Nowhere does the text say that Elijah died, but rather that he was taken up into heaven (2:3, 5, 9, 10). This terminology is reminiscent of Enoch, about whom it is said, "Enoch walked with God; then he was no more, because God took him" (Gen. 5:24). For this reason, some have suggested that Enoch and Elijah were taken up into heaven alive. This is probably what led to the expectation that Elijah would one day return as a herald of the messianic age. According to Malachi 4:5-6, God announces: "I will send you the prophet Elijah before the great and terrible day of the LORD comes. He will turn the hearts of parents to their children and the hearts of children to their parents, so that I will not come and strike the land with a curse."

With this passage in mind, it is interesting to note the similarities between Elijah and John the Baptist. As the Malachi passage suggests, Elijah and John the Baptist both serve the role of forerunner to the final day of judgment. They even dress alike (2 Kings 1:8 compared to Matt. 3:4). They both preach about the coming kingdom of God to their respective generations. Indeed, John the Baptist is identified as Elijah by an angel (Luke 1:11-17) and by Jesus himself (Matt. 11:1-19; 17:11-13). This does not mean that John is Elijah; rather, it is a figurative connection. So too the book of Revelation sees Elijah as one who will appear before the final judgment at the second coming (Rev. 11:1-12).

Tremper Longman III

Sixth Sunday after the Epiphany, Year B

First Lesson: 2 Kings 5:1-14
(Psalm 30)
Second Lesson: 1 Corinthians 9:24-27
Gospel Lesson: Mark 1:40-45

Seventh Sunday after Pentecost, Year C

First Lesson: 2 Kings 5:1-14
(Psalm 30)
Second Lesson: Galatians 6:(1-6), 7-16
Gospel Lesson: Luke 10:1-11, 16-20

The story of the Aramaean (Syrian) military officer Naaman is about conversion. Naaman is introduced as a commander of the king's army, a "great man" before his lord (i.e., the king) and highly decorated (2 Kings 5:1). But that is not all. Through him none other than the Lord (YHWH) — Israel's very own God! — has made Aram victorious. Apparently, this officer is so special that Israel's personal deity has helped him, not to mention Aram. There is only one downside to Naaman's life. In spite of his being a mighty man of valor, he had a grievous skin disease (v. 1).

249

Conventionally, this disease *(meṣoraʿ)* has been translated "leprosy." Perhaps that is correct, but more important than the medical character of the disease is what it represents in religious terms. Two full chapters are devoted to this disease in Leviticus (chaps. 13-14), a book that emphasizes holiness. According to Leviticus, if this disease is not properly treated medically and ritually, then the afflicted person is to be quarantined for seven days. Obviously, a person so confined would not be able to worship in public. Thus this disease has the potential of blocking access to God in a congregational setting.

Given this introduction, Naaman has been presented as a man at the furthest possible remove from Israel. He is an Aramaean, a foreigner; he is highly positioned in an army which was constantly in conflict with Israel (e.g., 1 Kings 15:16-20; 20:1-34; 22:1-36). Moreover, he had a skin condition which would have prevented his access to Israel's God even if he had been an Israelite! Even more galling from an Israelite perspective, this man who was so distant from Israelite values and concerns had actually been aided by Israel's God. Nevertheless, circumstances would pave the way for this Aramaean military man who was also ritually unclean to convert to Israel's God. In fact, there may already be an adumbration of the conversion in the double entendre of the word "victory" in verse 1 *(teshuʿah)*, for this is also the most common word for "salvation." The strange line intimates at the outset that Aram and Aramaeans are eligible for "victory/salvation" as proffered by Israel's God.

As the episode unfolds, there is a decided emphasis on the contrast between conventional and unconventional power. An unnamed Israelite girl *(naʿarah qetannah)* who had been captured during an Aramaean raid and placed in the employ of Naaman's wife (v. 2) informed the woman about "the prophet who is in Samaria" who could surely heal this skin condition (v. 3). When Naaman relays this to the king, he responds in completely conventional terms. Urging his officer to go to Israel, the monarch sends a letter to his royal counterpart — the prophet in Samaria is completely ignored! Further, when Naaman travels to Israel, he takes with him the sorts of gifts common in diplomatic exchanges: silver, gold, and garments (v. 5). True to form, Naaman goes straight to the Israelite king and presents the letter, which demands that the king — not the prophet! — heal Naaman (v. 6). Clearly, the letter reveals that the Aramaean king saw all effective power as residing in the royal office; at no point did Naaman object to this viewpoint.

Equally, the Israelite king was as clueless as the two Aramaeans. He recognized that he was powerless in this situation. Indeed, he figured that such an absurd demand was designed to provoke a military encounter. Being the weaker in this confrontation, he did the only thing he knew to do: rip off his clothes as a gesture of lament, anger, and frustration (v. 7). Ironically, it turns out that at least one of the festal garments that Naaman had brought along could be put to immediate use! In sync with the Aramaeans, the Israelite king never once thought of "the prophet who was in Samaria."

But Elisha, who *was* the prophet in Samaria, heard about the incident. Subsequently, he puts a simple question to the hapless king: "Why have you torn your clothes?" Then he summons Naaman, though not by name: "Let him come now to me, that he might know that there is a prophet in Israel" (v. 8). The Aramaeans were well aware that there was a *king* in Israel. But that was beside the point, for the king had no effective power for Naaman's condition. Power of another sort was required.

Naaman went to the prophet, but still in conventional mode: on his horse and with his chariot (v. 9). In stark contrast, Elisha paid no attention whatsoever to this pomp. He did not so much as invite Naaman in; rather, he sent a messenger with the instruction that Naaman was to wash seven times in the Jordan, after which his flesh would be restored and he would be ritually clean (v. 10). Naaman's response to this affront was completely predictable from the point of view of established power. He got mad! The reasons for his anger are most revealing: "I thought he would by all means come out to me, stand, invoke the name of YHWH his God, wave his hand over the place, and heal me of the disease" (v. 11). The Aramaean was anxious for flamboyance and spectacle. While he was no longer in the setting of either a royal court or the military, he wanted comparable ceremony. Underscoring his complete failure to realize he was dealing with an alternate source of power, he complained that Aram's rivers were superior to Israel's, as though the quality of the water were at issue. He then walked off in a huff (v. 12). Elisha remained silent (v. 8).

At this point the narrative makes a stunning reversal. Naaman's aides — who are themselves Aramaeans, of course — attempt to reason with him. They are shown to have considerable insight into his makeup. Though appropriately deferential — they address him curiously as "my father" — they remind Naaman that he would have willingly done some "great thing" had the prophet asked that of him. Why, then, not do this implied "little thing" of washing and becoming clean (v. 13)? Amazingly, with no explanation for Naaman's change of mood, he takes his servants' advice: "So he went down and dipped. . . ." Following the prophet's instructions to the tee — "he dipped seven times as the man of God had said" — his flesh was restored to that of a little boy and he was rendered (ritually) clean (v. 14). When we are told that his flesh was restored to that of a "little boy" *(na'ar qaṭon),* we cannot help but recall the "little girl" (*na'arah qetannah* [v. 2]) whose matter-of-fact mention of the prophet in Samaria set this whole episode in motion. That "little girl" understood unconventional power in a way that two kings and a highly decorated military officer did not. Even Naaman's aides seem to have had a better grasp of this alternate source of power.

Afterward, Naaman returned to Elisha and made a confession of faith. He now knew that there was no God in all the earth except for Israel's God (v. 15). It is not clear whether Naaman's desire to give a present at this juncture was a slight reversion to conventional thinking or an act of simple gratitude. In any case, Elisha would have none of it, even when Naaman insisted (v. 16). This was an act of grace, not a service provided for a fee. However, if Elisha would not accept a present, perhaps he would give one. Naaman wanted to take home with him two donkeyloads of soil. This strange request had to do with the Aramaean's resolve to offer sacrifices from now on only to Israel's God (v. 17). Apparently he wanted to worship on good Israelite turf! This is an instructive detail. Had Naaman been superstitious about what had happened to him, he might have requested "holy water" from the Jordan. But he was interested in worship. He would remain an Aramaean citizen and an Aramaean military man, but in terms of faith he would be an Israelite.

But Naaman requested more than dirt. He also asked for advance forgiveness. Since he was obligated to assist his king when the monarch worshiped in the house of Rimmon, Aram's deity, Naaman wanted the Lord to forgive him when he bowed low — he made clear that he would be bowing only to support his king, not as an act of obeisance (v. 18). As we saw, when Naaman truly worshiped, it would be on Israelite soil (v. 17). Elisha granted the request with the words "Go in peace" (v. 19).

Though this lection ends with verse 14, the story proper continues through verse 27. In that segment Elisha's aide Gehazi's greed gets the best of him as he persuades Naaman to leave some of the gift that the prophet had initially refused (vv. 15-16, 20-24). Naturally, Naaman was happy to oblige. Eventually, Elisha confronts Gehazi, who compounds his sin with deception (vv. 25-26). In the end, Gehazi contracts the disease that Naaman had had (v. 27). Thus the conversion story is concluded with an "excommunication" story. The "outsider" Naaman became an Israelite "insider," religiously speaking, while the "insider" Gehazi became an Israelite outsider. This same motif is present in Jesus' appeal to this story in Luke 4:27-30.

Frank Anthony Spina

Third Sunday after the Epiphany, Year C

First Lesson: Nehemiah 8:1-10
(Psalm 19)
Second Lesson: 1 Corinthians 12:12-31a
Gospel Lesson: Luke 4:14-21

A ccording to the traditional date of Ezra's mission, the events of the text happen around the middle of the fifth century B.C. Israel is still alive and kicking, but just barely. A little over a hundred years have passed since the first volunteers, under the leadership of Sheshbazzar and then Zerubbabel, returned to their decimated homeland from Babylonian exile. Those hundred years have been marked by hardship, poverty, and discouragement. At times the morale of the community has sunk to depressingly low levels. As long as seventy-five years after the first return, Jerusalem itself had remained largely unpopulated and in ruins (Neh. 7:4).

According to the prophet Haggai, in the early years of the resettlement the crops suffered from blight, mildew, and hail. Many people had inadequate food and clothing. Their neighbors in Samaria were openly hostile. In such conditions, even getting the temple rebuilt was a work of major proportions. After a number of delays, that task was finally completed some twenty-two years after the first return from Babylon. But even that accomplishment was mixed with bitter disappointment because the new temple suffered badly in comparison with the former temple.

Difficult years followed the completion of the temple. However, groups continue to return to the homeland. Scholars estimate that by the mid–fifth century the population of Judah may have been around fifty thousand. Towns around Judah are becoming populated once again. Yet, as John Bright describes it, the spiritual situation of the community is precarious: "Disappointment had led to disillusionment and this, in turn, to religious and moral laxity. . . . The danger, in short, was real that if the community could not pull itself together, regain its morale, and find direction, it would sooner or later lose its distinctive character, if not disintegrate altogether" (*A History of Israel* [Westminster, 1981], p. 378).

Into this environment come Nehemiah and Ezra. Nehemiah is an officer in the court of Artaxerxes I (465-424 B.C.) who, after hearing of the terrible conditions in Jerusalem, receives permission to come and help in the restoration. Appointed governor of the province, he sets himself the task of rebuilding the walls of Jerusalem (cf. especially Neh. 2:11-18). His work has

253

proceeded rapidly, and in fact he finished the work in fifty-two days, on the twenty-fifth day of the sixth month (Neh. 6:15). This event forms the immediate context to our text from Nehemiah 8, because it is only a few days later (on the first day of the seventh month) that Ezra reads the Torah to the assembly.

It has long been recognized that Nehemiah's great contribution was to the physical safety of the postexilic community. He brought organization, political status, and security to the people. However, the spiritual reform, the spiritual revival, was left to the scribe Ezra. Ezra's mission is stated in Ezra 7:12-26, but scholars note that it is far from clear what the parameters of his authority were and to what degree he was successful. Most agree that he completed his work within a year. Perhaps the most important insight into Ezra and our text is seen in the words of Ezra 7:10: "For Ezra had prepared his heart to seek the Torah of the LORD, and to do it, and to teach statutes and ordinances in Israel."

This is what Ezra does on this day. Upon the completion of the city walls, during the celebration of the Feast of Trumpets (Lev. 23:23-24), to "restoration people" who needed (spiritual) restoration, Ezra brings the word — the Torah — of Yahweh.

Behind the people (in the distant past) is the great saving event of the exodus/conquest. Then God had delivered his people with great "signs and wonders" never before seen. With a mighty hand he had redeemed them from slavery and brought them safely into the Promised Land where he had defeated their enemies. God's presence, his power and glory were seen by all. In the more recent past, God had again acted in a marvelous way in a "second exodus" — the return from Babylonian exile. Once again the people could see God's power working in their lives.

And yet they knew that Yahweh wasn't finished with them. As the above background sketch well illustrates, the return from exile had not fulfilled the glorious promises foreseen by Isaiah (40–66) and other prophets. The people still looked forward to the time when Yahweh, through the Davidic King, would bring his glorious kingdom and reign to them.

The point of all this is that now the people were living "between the times." On the one hand, they look back to the exodus for assurance that Yahweh has indeed elected them (cf. Deut. 7). On the other hand, they look forward to Yahweh's return when he would bring his kingdom of peace and righteousness to all nations (cf. Isa. 11; 42). In between these two glorious comings, we find Israel on this day, without "glory," without much prosperity. Their lives are ordinary, mundane, even routine. There is no pillar of fire. No manna from heaven. No Sinai with the thundering voice of God. There is no divine Warrior scattering the enemies in miraculous ways. These are average people struggling to stay alive in a hostile environment. They certainly could have used the visible presence of God now — signs like those he performed in Egypt.

But instead, what they get is the scribe Ezra reading the Torah of Yahweh. What a contrast! From God speaking on Sinai and from his presence in the tabernacle, to Ezra in a wooden pulpit reading the Scriptures. What a letdown! Surely God has abandoned his people. These people who are gathered around a book are surely deluding themselves.

And yet, that is not how the text describes things. God has not abandoned them. Rather, we see that God's word is sustaining them. In this text we see not so much what the word of God is, but rather what it *does*. First of all, the word of God attracts the people. The text says the people gather "as one person" and ask Ezra to read the word to them (v. 1). The written and read word is not a disappointment at all. The people long to hear it. That's a powerful word.

Second, the text says that when they hear the word and when the Levites and Ezra's assistants explain the reading to them, the people start to weep. God's word can make grown men cry. The story of the life and death of Israel is not just a history lesson to these people. It is their story — their life and their death. The story of God's infinite love and their own pitiful rebellion brings them to their knees. That's a powerful word.

Third, there is the visible "word of the day" urged upon the people by Nehemiah and the other leaders. He reminds them that the day on which they are gathered (the Feast of Trumpets) is a holy day to the Lord. As Moses describes it in Leviticus 23:24-25, it is a "Sabbath rest" and a memorial with trumpets and convocation, and the people are to do no work. The people rest — that's a good word indeed. The day is a visible reminder of God's grace in their lives. He brings rest. He brings all good things. And so Nehemiah invites the people to feast on rich food and drink. It is not a day of fasting, but a day of feasting and celebration. He says, "Do not grieve because the joy of Yahweh is your strength." Though the phrase is often taken as an objective genitive, it could also be understood to mean that Yahweh is the one who works joy in the people, that is, "the joy that the Lord gives is your strength." In other words, the point that Nehemiah is trying to make is that through this holy day Yahweh gives his people joy, and that joy strengthens people. That's what the day is for — not tears but laughter. And as this section concludes, we note that the people's weeping is turned to joy: "And so all the people went to eat and to drink and to send portions and to make great joy because they understood the words which they made known to them" (v. 12). That's a powerful word. Through the word of the day, tears are turned into great joy. The word, so to speak, both cuts the people and then heals them.

From this perspective, the text certainly speaks to us today. We too live "between the times." That is, we too look back to our own exodus in the redemption Christ accomplished at the cross (Luke 9:31). There in the second person of the Trinity, God was present in all his power and glory (John 1). There he rescued us from slavery to death and Satan and brought us into glorious freedom (Rom. 8). Now we are his chosen people, his special treasure (1 Pet. 2:9). We look back to Christ's redemption for our assurance of God's grace and mercy much as Israel looked back on the exodus.

That message, again like that to Israel, gives us hope for the future. God's promise fulfilled in Christ assures us that he will come again and manifest his kingdom for all to see. It is a kingdom in which we are the heirs along with Christ (Rom. 8:17). We long for that day.

But now, we live "between the times." There is no pillar of fire. No Moses. No resurrections. Miracles few and far between. We are ordinary people struggling to live in a hostile culture. Has God abandoned us? Not at all. We too have God's word to sustain us. That word is not just a history lesson to us, nor is it a dry list of rules we have to follow. It is our story. It is the story of our life and death and resurrection in Christ. It is a story with the power to make us weep and fill us with joy. In other words, the word does for us what it did for ancient Israel. It gives life. And, like the postexilic community, we gather around the word on our "day of Sabbath rest," our Sunday. It is a day of feasting on the Lord's Supper and celebration of the resurrection and our resurrection hope. It is a day of joy when we are reminded of the Lord's grace in our lives and in which we receive strength to live "between the times."

Through the word, then, God does a great work in us. Note the power of the word in the following: OT: Isaiah 55:10-11; Jeremiah 5:14; 23:29; Ezekiel 37:7; NT: Luke 4:32; John 6:63; Romans 1:16; Ephesians 6:17; Hebrews 4:12. Until Christ comes again, he has left us with his word. And so we, God's people in the "time in between," attend to it. We preach it. We proclaim it. We meditate on it. We share it. We do all this because God has put his almighty power in it. In its proclamation souls are saved, hopes are revived, sagging spirits are strengthened.

Though the text seems to be so far removed from us, we see that it really is not. Ezra the scribe read and preached the word, and the people came to life. We would do well to do the same "until the day dawns and the morning star rises in our hearts" (2 Pet. 1:19).

Timothy E. Saleska

Nineteenth Sunday after Pentecost, Year B

First Lesson: Esther 7:1-6, 9-10; 9:20-22
(Psalm 124)
Second Lesson: James 5:13-20
Gospel Lesson: Mark 9:38-50

The story of Queen Esther and the Jewish people of the Persian Empire is a story of deliverance from death. In this event from Israel's history, God fulfills a promise made to his people centuries before, not through miraculous intervention but through the ordinary actions and morally ambiguous motives of human beings. In a biblical book totally lacking any direct mention of God, he nevertheless shows himself to be a greater king than all the powers that be in one of the world's mightiest empires.

This highly charged scene is about who gets life and who does not. It begins innocuously enough with: "So the king and Haman went to dine with Queen Esther." Little did either of them know what awaited them there! The king repeats a question he had previously asked Esther, "What is your petition? . . . What is your request?" (5:3). Her reply is structured exactly as his question: "Grant me my life — this is my petition. And spare my people — this is my request." By framing her response using the king's rhetoric, Esther is identifying her life and the life of her people as one and the same. Her destiny is one with her people.

When Esther reveals Haman as her mortal enemy, she at the same time reveals herself to be Jewish. In so doing, she not only indicts herself for living as a pagan in the harem of the king (2:10), she also brings herself under the irrevocable decree of death that Haman had instigated against the Jews with the king's approval (3:8, 9). Driven by uncontrollable pride and arrogance, Haman had plotted to slaughter the entire race of Jewish people because his lust for power over others could not be satisfied as long as Mordecai the Jew refused to bow to him (3:5).

Haman does not appear to be anti-Semitic in the modern sense of the word, for he would probably have been willing to commit genocide against any population if it satisfied his megalomaniac pursuit of honor and power. His plan to take revenge on one man by annihilating his entire race was an evil of demonic proportions, regardless of who those people were. The enormous stature of Haman's evil is pictured in the seventy-five-foot height of the gallows he unknowingly constructed for himself.

But the story holds particular theological significance because the people Haman targeted happened to be the people the Lord God had chosen as his own centuries before. When Haman is first introduced in the story, he is identified as an Agagite (3:1), implying that the enmity between the Jews and the Agagites is mirrored in the personal enmity between Mordecai and Haman. Agag was the king of the Amalekites at the time Saul was the first king of Israel (1 Sam. 15). The Amalekites had the dubious distinction of being the first people of the world to attack and try to destroy God's newly formed covenant nation at the time of the exodus many centuries before. Because of this, God promised Moses that he would completely erase the memory of the Amalekites from under heaven and would be at war with them from generation to generation (Exod. 17:8-16). When Saul became Israel's first king, God instructed him to wage holy war on the Amalekites, to "attack the Amalekites and totally destroy everything that belongs to them," and "to put to death men and women, children and infants, cattle and sheep, camels and donkeys" (1 Sam. 15:1-3). Saul did attack, but he took Agag their king alive and spared his life. This act of disobedience disqualified Saul from being Israel's king. Over the following centuries, other perennial enemies of Israel were called Agagites even if they had no ethnic relationship to the Amalekites. In the Persian period, Haman the Agagite wore the signet ring of the Persian king, endowing him with the king's authority. He effectively acted as the king of the enemies of God's people.

In the Diaspora setting, God no longer fought holy war through Israel's king and army, for Israel no longer had either a king or an army. Would God's people still be protected by his covenant promises, or would they themselves receive the same fate promised to God's enemies? By designing the death of Haman, the "king" of God's enemies, Queen Esther has succeeded where her ancestor King Saul failed. Esther wore the crown of the queen of Persia, making her the ruling monarch of the Jews of that time. Queen Esther killed Haman with her cunning as surely as King Saul could have, and should have, killed Agag with the sword. In her action God was fulfilling his promise of destruction against those who oppose his redemptive work.

It is fitting that Mordecai should write down the events that fulfilled God's covenant promise of protection to the Jews in Persia. In response to God's great deliverance of his people from Haman's edict of death, the Jews of Persia agreed to continue the celebration of that event with annual days of feasting and joy called the Feast of Purim. Purim is still celebrated today to commemorate the inviolability of the Jewish race by those who live only a generation or two after a modern expression of Haman's evil, the Holocaust. Throughout history the book of Esther has been read not as an isolated episode in Jewish history, but as symbolizing the final salvation of God's people at the end of time. Esther reveals that life and death are determined by identification with a people. Therefore the book of Esther forms a link between the covenant God made with his nation at Sinai and the eschatological destiny of God's people in the kingdom of God.

The book of Esther is part of the spiritual heritage of Christians bequeathed to us by Jesus Christ. The first occurrence of Purim was a spontaneous celebration of the joy of finding oneself still alive on the day after an irrevocable death decree was executed. Instead of sorrow there was joy, and instead of mourning there was celebration among God's people. The eschatological reality foreshadowed by Purim was realized in the resurrection of Jesus Christ, who announced, "Because I live, you also will live" (John 14:19). In New Testament theology, life and death are also shown to be by identification with a people who are joined to the resurrected Christ. As the apostle Paul writes, "As in Adam all die, so in Christ all will be made alive" (1 Cor. 15:22). The work of Jesus Christ is the consummation of God's redemptive work begun in the covenant promises to ancient Israel. Thus the ultimate fulfillment of God's promise to his people for protection from death is found in Christ. Those identified with Christ constitute a people who will be delivered from death and live forever, just as Jesus was.

When the church gathers for worship each Sunday, it has every reason to celebrate the resurrection of Jesus Christ with joy and feasting, with expressions of goodwill and affection for one another, and with gifts to the poor. Our sorrow has been turned to joy, and our mourning to celebration. Just as the Jews of Persia were delivered against all odds from the destiny of death to the destiny of life, we too, who should expect nothing but death, have seen the ultimate reversal of human destiny. Because of the death and resurrection of Jesus Christ, our destiny has been reversed from death to life against all expectation. This is the heart of our Sunday celebration.

Even in our darkest hours, when joy is far from our hearts, we can be assured of our final destiny of life with Christ. Christians can face even the most threatening circumstances with hope because we share in the resurrection of Jesus Christ. It is that destiny we celebrate in worship even on those Sundays when sorrow and mourning seem all too present. Despite our circumstances, where Christ's people gather for worship, the feast of Holy Communion commemorates our deliverance from death. Where the gospel is preached, the decree of everlasting life is proclaimed. We come together in Christian worship to identify ourselves as the people of God in Christ who were dead but who are alive forevermore. Rejoice!

Karen Jobes

Twentieth Sunday after Pentecost, Year B

First Lesson: Job 1:1; 2:1-10
(Psalm 26)
Second Lesson: Hebrews 1:1-4; 2:5-12
Gospel Lesson: Mark 10:2-16

Preaching effectively on the four selections from the book of Job calls for an understanding of the entire book (forty-two chapters!) from which they have been drawn. Preachers may recall from seminary lectures that many theories have been proposed concerning the genesis of the book — for example, that the author used a story about a holy Job (chaps. 1-2; 42:7-17) into which he inserted a lively dialogue between Job and three friends before having the Lord deliver the speeches of chapters 38-41. It is perhaps possible that chapter 28, on wisdom, and the reaction of Elihu (chaps. 32-37) have been inserted. But the best preparation for preaching is to try to understand the book as a whole, in its present form. What does it say to us? Its point is not the proverbial "patience" of Job (correctly rendered in the NRSV for James 5:11 as "the endurance of Job"), nor is the book a treatise on theodicy. It probes the mystery of suffering, which is not solved but is accepted by Job as the result of his final encounter with the Lord (42:5). The work is a cleverly wrought literary composition, not the script of a live debate between Job and the three friends. Such magnificent poetry is not tossed off casually while dying, as Job seems to be, sitting "among the ashes" (2:8). The following observations concerning the whole book should be noted; they describe a context that will enable both preacher and audience to better understand it. For a summary I recommend Roland E. Murphy, *The Book of Job — A Short Reading* (New York: Paulist, 1999).

1. Nowhere else in the Bible is such a fundamental question about human existence brought up as in 1:9, "Does Job fear God for nothing?" The Lord accepts the challenge concerning Job's loyalty and the first test is inflicted, to be followed in chapter 2 by a second test. How does the preacher understand the horrendous decisions of the Lord?

2. What is to be made of the reactions of Job in chapters 1-2? Is this image of Job merely part of the traditional story of a "holy" Job (cf. Ezek. 14:14)? How does it function in the book? It is essential to the development in the book that Job remains blameless.

3. The dialogue between Job and the three friends is precipitated by Job's outburst of *why* in chapter 3. Neither they nor Job knows what has

transpired in chapters 1-2. The friends present orthodox views on retribution, emphasizing the connection of suffering with (Job's) putative sinfulness. If Job would only repent and appeal to God, he would be restored. But Job is blameless (as the Lord has stated in chaps. 1-2), and his very integrity demands that he reject such theology. The terrible treatment he has received leads him to question his relationship to God. Why is God treating him this way? He is moved to attack God with wild words (part of the verisimilitude the author is bent on achieving). Thus he runs the gamut between faith and despair. He cannot understand this God he always knew, with whom he was in a gracious relationship (cf. chap. 23). He *never* asks to get back what he lost. What is God doing to him?

4. How does the poem in chapter 28 on the "place" of wisdom (only with God!) fit into the whole?

5. Beyond detailing the "medicinal" character of suffering (33:15-30; cf. 5:17-18), Elihu adds little to the views of the friends, although his words about creation (36:24-37:24) seem to anticipate the Lord's speeches.

6. The speeches of YHWH from the whirlwind (chaps. 38-41) are relatively mild, considering the wild rage in Job's previous statements. The Lord does not "answer" Job, but draws him into the greater mystery of dealing with all creation.

7. Regarding Job's surrender (42:1-6) to God: (1) He admits that he dealt with things "too wonderful" for him to know. (2) He finds some kind of relief in *seeing* God, as opposed to mere knowing (42:5). (3) The translation of 42:6 is difficult. Job does not "repent in dust and ashes" — the sense is that he is comforted, being but dust and ashes (i.e., human). It is clear from the Lord's verdict in 42:7 that only Job spoke "what is right" (and has, therefore, nothing to repent of), and hence the friends are to offer a sacrifice to the Lord, with Job's intercession.

8. Job's restoration (42:7-17) is *not* the point of the book. God can do what God pleases, and can rehabilitate Job. The double compensation may be associated with the double restitution for thievery specified in Exodus 22:4.

*   *   *

The preacher must note the essential description of Job in 1:1, the judgment of the narrator which is repeated by the Lord in 1:8 and 2:3: blameless and upright, fearing God (the meaning of "fear of God/Lord" in the Old Testament = devout, awesome reverence and obedience), and avoiding evil. This characterization fits the mention of Job in Ezekiel 14:14, 20, where he is paired with the righteous Noah and Daniel. These were outstanding heroes of holiness in the ancient world. In Ezekiel the Lord announces that not even their holiness would be enough for the land of Israel to be spared the punishment the Lord intended to inflict on the people. Their righteousness would save only themselves; it could not have the vicarious effect of sparing the people (see the deliberations of Abraham and the Lord in Gen. 18:22-33). Noteworthy also is the fact that Job (as well as the three friends) is not an Israelite; he was from the desert area, either northeast or south of Palestine. Chapters 1–2 are quite dense and far from naive. They set the scene for the dialogue by letting the reader in on events that Job and the friends know nothing about. There is a literary balance: 1:1-5, Job's service on earth; 1:6-12, a view of what is going on in the heavenly court; 1:13-21, Job's losses and his virtuous reaction; 2:1-6, a second encounter of the satan with YHWH in the heavenly court; 2:7-13, back on earth, Job's suffering and reaction to his wife's words; the reaction of the three friends who come to comfort him. This information provides needed background for the preacher, to be used as needed in developing the sermon.

For some unknown reason the lectionary skips immediately to 2:1-10, which describes the second test of Job, his *personal* suffering. At first this looks like a repetition of chapter 1, but it is not; it is an intensification of those events. The reader is once more swept into a scene in the heavenly court in which the Lord musters his "family," the "sons of God." In the biblical view, these members of the heavenly court serve as the divine entourage, worshipers who praise him (Ps. 29) and messengers ("angels") who serve him. The question-and-answer style between YHWH and one of these, called the satan, or adversary, reveals his function. His purpose is to roam the earth, presumably in the interests of the Lord, observing human beings. In response to the Lord's question about Job's integrity, he had expressed severe doubt, "Is it for nothing that Job fears God?" (1:9). The implication was that Job's piety was self-centered. Should he lose his possessions, he would surely curse God. The Lord accepted this challenge, and not only Job's possessions, but his children, were destroyed. Job's reaction is framed in those memorable words: "The LORD gave, and the LORD has taken away; blessed be the name of the LORD" (1:21). Now in chapter 2, the Lord takes the initiative with the satan (as he also did in 1:8; does the author describe the Lord as boasting about Job?) and points to Job's fidelity, even though the destruction of everything was "without reason" (2:3). That phrase plays an important role in the narrative. It is on the lips of the satan in 1:9 where it is translated "for nothing" (NRSV). Now in 2:3 the Lord admits that the satan has incited him to destroy Job "for nothing." But the satan will not give up. Humans will do anything to save their skin; Job's person is unscathed. If his "bone and flesh" are struck, he will surely curse God to his face. And so it happens; Job is afflicted with a disease we cannot identify exactly, but he sits among the ashes scraping himself with potsherds. (The reaction of Job's wife may be either sarcastic, repeating the words of God in 2:3, or practical in that cursing God would ensure Job's death and release from suffering.) Job does not swerve — he acknowledges that both good and bad come from the *hand* of God (v. 10; in v. 5 the satan had asked the Lord to "stretch out your *hand* now and touch his bone and his flesh"). The author notes explicitly that Job did not sin (v. 10). The reading ends here, but attention may be given to the three friends, also non-Israelites, who have an important role in the book. Their genuine grief at Job's suffering is given striking expression in their seven days of silence. They will speak only after Job's outburst in chapter 3, but none of the lectionary readings mentions them!

The above paragraph lays out a fuller understanding of the drama that underlies the lectionary reading. But it is the preacher who must decide in what direction to go.

Little is to be gotten by developing the figure of the satan; that should be saved for a lecture; it is true that there is a development through the Old Testament (cf. 1 Chron. 21:1; Zech. 3:1-2) until the real devil (Satan) emerges in New Testament times. Many people incorrectly assume that the satan in Job is to be identified with the devil of the New Testament. Not so; it is clear from the conversation between the Lord and the satan that he merely does the Lord's bidding.

What about the figure of YHWH? This is a truly difficult problem. On the one hand, the Lord comes off looking like a pitiless tyrant authorizing the destruction of Job's family and possessions and afflicting him a second time with physical suffering. Surely the Lord of heaven and earth knew that Job was a loyal servant, and even his reply to the satan admits that this first test was "without reason" (2:3; cf. 1:9). Yet YHWH goes on to deliver Job to the satan's "power" (hand). A second test?! Why did not the Lord accept the first trial as adequate proof, especially when he seems to boast in 2:3 that Job remained steadfast. On the other hand, one can examine the scene in another way: Suppose God had said no to the satan's question in 1:9, or to the second challenge in 2:4-5 (the author is clearly ratcheting up the predicament). Then there would have been no book of Job. Then also it could appear that the Lord had doubts about his servant Job: Was he "God-fearing" only because of what he got out of it, as the satan claimed? So there is a divine dilemma, and the question of the satan in 1:9 turns out to be central. Is God afraid to trust creatures to serve and love him without profit? God is, as it were, damned if he does and damned if she doesn't. The author/editor of the book clearly felt no need to invoke divine omniscience as a solution to the situation. Nor did he operate with the notion that God "allows." It will be recalled that all that happens is under the "hand" of God. This is really the hand of the satan, as the Lord tells him to stretch out his hand against Job (1:12); the satan asks God to stretch out God's hand in 2:5, and God decides that Job is in the satan's "hand" (or "power"; NRSV, 2:6). In 2:10 Job clearly says that all comes from the hand of God. The Lord's prerogative and responsibility are not lessened by handing off to the satan the power to afflict Job.

Even if it is on the lips of the satan, the question in 1:9 is perhaps the most important question in the Old Testament, and certainly it is central to Christian life. Why does one serve/love/adore/worship God? How much self-interest is involved? Is it because God is "good" to such a person? Or does the biblical phrase "fear of God" mean that one acts only out of fear and not out of love? Such questions as these are prompted by the conversation between the satan and YHWH, and they are central to the Christian concept of the love of God. Why do you love God? In his famous work on the love of God, Saint Bernard of Clairvaux described degrees of love, and we can easily recognize such degrees of love in our own life experience: the demanding and self-centered love of children for parents; the considerate and outgoing love as children mature; the sacrificial love of which adults are capable; etc. The question of the satan provokes a salutary examination of conscience. Ultimately, is genuine love, even between humans, possible without sacrifice? How does one tell?

The above exposition of the text has gone beyond the intention of the liturgical shaping of the reading. The selection (Job 1:1; 2:1-10) highlights only the virtue and fidelity of Job despite his suffering. This is clear from the description in 1:1 and in the tone of Job's resignation in 2:10, the first and last verses of the reading. However, to preach only about the "holy Job" of the prologue is to be unfaithful to the spirit of the entire book. The reply of Job in 2:10 (and in 1:21) would appear unrealistic to a modern person. These opening chapters are not intended to be a sop to the sufferer. They are an introduction to one of the Bible's most profound wrestlings with the problem of suffering, and the congregation is not to be shielded from a serious consideration of this matter.

The preacher should not shirk the responsibility of going beyond the limits of the liturgical when this is necessary for the understanding of a pericope.

Roland E. Murphy

Twenty-first Sunday after Pentecost, Year B

First Lesson: Job 23:1-9, 16-17
(Psalm 22:1-15)
Second Lesson: Hebrews 4:12-16
Gospel Lesson: Mark 10:17-31

C hapter 23 is the only selection made by the liturgy from the dialogue be-tween Job and the three friends (chaps. 3–31). It does not convey the flavor of the repartee to be found in their exchange. This chapter is more of a monologue or soliloquy on Job's part. Again, the choice of verses deliberately shapes the message: in verses 1-9 Job gives voice to confidence that the Lord would hear and acquit Job could he only come before him and plead his case. But alas, Job cannot find him at any point of the compass. The intervening verses, 10-15, in which he complains of God's arbitrary reaction ("whatever he wills, he does," v. 13) and indifference to his fidelity, are omitted. The last two verses are an expression of quiet despair that, in context, is the result of the failure to find God. Indeed, the terror at God's presence that Job fears in 23:15-16 might seem to cancel out his initial desire to find God and confront him; but Job has expressed such fears before. The most poignant lines are in 13:20-22:

> Only grant two things to me,
> > then I will not hide myself from your face:
> withdraw your hand far from me,
> > and do not let dread of you terrify me.
> Then call, and I will answer;
> > or let me speak, and you reply to me.

The author's description of Job's situation is twofold. On the one hand, Job has every reason to dread any confrontation with God. Up to his present moment he has been visited with one disaster after another. He wants to escape from God's gaze:

> Will you not look away from me for a while,
> > let me alone until I swallow my spittle? . . .
> > Why have you made me your target?   (7:19-20)

On the other hand, he summons enough courage to challenge God. Job *wants* a confrontation; he will risk a lawsuit against God, and he even has moments of certainty of victory:

> I will defend my ways to his face.
> This will be my salvation,
>> that the godless shall not come before him.　　　　(13:15b-16)

How ironic this bravado is! In a deeper sense it is not mere bravado. It is the truth, because the Lord has acknowledged in chapters 1–2 that Job is innocent and blameless, but of course Job does not know that.

The choice that confronts the preacher is the wisdom of following the intention of the liturgical shape of the reading or the entire chapter in the context of the book. If the first option is followed, one can develop a portrait of fidelity through the agony of suffering and of divine distance, a kind of "dark night of the soul." The last two verses are a mild comment on this pitiful situation. Will Job eventually find or be found by YHWH? Will errant human beings find or be found by God? These questions might be further developed by referring to the eventual appearance of YHWH in the narrative, when he speaks to Job out of the whirlwind in 38:1. (For comment on chapter 38, see the Twenty-second Sunday after Pentecost, Year B.) I find this a doubtful way to proceed; there is the danger of delivering a phony message. In fact, one is hardly being faithful to Job 23 in using it as background for such a sermon. Perhaps, although one is departing from the point of Job, one could simply take up the search for God as the general topic of the sermon, without arriving at any contrived "happy ending." It is possible to develop the idea that God is present when he is also absent. The elusive divine presence can be illustrated by events at critical junctures of life. In the case of Jesus Christ, the cry of Psalm 21, "My God, my God, why have you forsaken me?" (Mark 15:34; Ps. 22), is testimony to the "hidden God" theme *(Deus absconditus)* that was a favorite of Martin Luther.

There are two reasons for going in another direction. First, the omission of verses 10-15 is fatal. Job is searching for a confrontation with God in order to prove his innocence. For him it is not a question of seeking some divine consolation; it is a matter of justice, and Job would "come out like gold" because he has "not departed from the commandment of his lips" (vv. 10-12). Second, Job recognizes this as a vain hope. God does as God pleases, and this inspires terror in Job's heart.

If the first option is chosen, the preacher can probe the manner in which Christians determine the presence or absence of God in the lives of ordinary churchgoers. Both aspects should be developed. How is God present to us? What reasons can we give to believe that? Moreover, what do we mean when we complain of God's absence? Is God absent, or is it we who are absent to God? Job felt confident, as 23:6-7, 10-11 indicate; on what might we be able to base a similar confidence?

If the second option is chosen, the sermon is being more faithful to the intent of the text. The text is not a comfortable one. It reflects the many doubts that Job has had about God (vv. 13-17), despite Job's affirmation of his own integrity. Ultimately the spirit of this chapter is one of Job's frequent waverings between hope and despair. He registers a belief that God will recognize his loyalty (vv. 7, 10-12), if only he could confront God. But he also ends up on a despairing note; in fact, he is terrified at his presence (v. 15; lit. "before his face") and is filled with dread (the NRSV footnote to v. 17 indicates there is no certain translation of that verse). At this point the preacher might throw up his/her hands. No one wants to preach despair. But despair in the context of the book of Job is a salutary despair. Job does not remain there; he moves. His "despair" is balanced by many contrary assertions of faith (e.g., 13:15, construed as an affirmation of hope; 19:25; 27:2-6). Such a mixture reflects human reality: the continuous movement between hope and despair at various moments of life. Herein lies fruitful material for a sermon: the fluctuation between faith and despair, between fidelity and revolt, between fervor and lukewarmness, etc., that characterizes human lives.

Roland E. Murphy

Twenty-second Sunday after Pentecost, Year B

First Lesson: Job 38:1-7, (34-41)
(Psalm 104:1-9, 24, 35c)
Second Lesson: Hebrews 5:1-10
Gospel Lesson: Mark 10:35-45

The reply of YHWH from a whirlwind has an attractive ironic touch. In 9:14-20 Job complained how unfair any contention with God would be, for he would crush him with a "whirlwind" (translated as "tempest" in 9:17) and multiply his wounds "without cause" (the very phrase the Lord used against the satan in 2:3, "for no reason"). Now the meeting that was so often contemplated (13:18-24; 19:25-27; 31:35-37) takes place. But it is surprisingly mild and calm. The opening lines find a partial echo when the Lord gets his second wind at 40:7 (cf. 38:3):

> Gird up your loins like a man;
>   I will question you, and you declare to me.

He does accuse Job of darkening "counsel" and "words without knowledge," but the Lord's questions are in fact easy for Job to answer. Of course Job was not present at creation, nor does he have any power over the created things. Indeed, Job never claimed to have such knowledge. Mainly, he wanted to know *why*.

From one point of view the questions of the Lord seem hugely irrelevant. The narrator is not interested in going back to the events of the prologue that inaugurated the action. Instead he borrows ideas that were current in Israel's view of creation and lays them out before Job. The preacher can see this by comparing chapter 38 with Psalms 104 and 107. In both psalms human beings are part of the picture, although not a major concern as in Genesis 1–2. The striking thing about Job 38 is the total absence of reference to the creation of human beings; it is almost as if they were not a concern of the Lord, who describes in great detail the complexities of his creative and sustaining activity in favor of animate and inanimate things. There is even a certain quaintness about the Lord's work. He has made room for the stupidity of the ostrich (39:13-18), yet that bird is gifted with speed and "laughs at the horse and its rider." Part of that universe, too, are the birds of prey, like the hawk and eagle, whose young suck up the blood of the slain (39:26-30). This "carnival of the animals" comes to a climax with the creation and taming of the redoubtable Behemoth and Leviathan, symbolic powers of chaos.

Is this a reply to the provoking cries of the steadfast Job? Obviously, it is not a satisfactory "answer" for the modern reader. Paradoxically, it represents an experience of Job that is sufficient to change him, as his reaction demonstrates (40:3-5, taken up in the reading for the Twenty-third Sunday after Pentecost, Year B, 42:16). Yet it has left many a reader nonplussed. Why? Because they were expecting something else, even demanding something like a clean answer to the problem of suffering. Would it have been simpler if the narrator simply had the Lord describe to Job the events of chapters 1–2? We have seen in our analysis above of these chapters that the position of the Lord in the whole affair is rather a shaky one, and no satisfactory "answer" can be derived from the wager between the Lord and the satan (who has disappeared from the scene, it should be noted, having fulfilled his role).

In his poem about Job, "The Masque of Reason," Robert Frost skirts this nonsolution by a humorous reference to God's showing off to the devil. But Frost recognizes that the point of Job lies elsewhere when he has the Lord acknowledge to Job that Job set him free to be God. Before that, he had to reward good and punish evil, but Job changed all that and set God free to reign. Job's sufferings? It was essential that they be without meaning in order to have meaning, that Job could not be able to understand them. Frost's rather free interpretation of the book has a lot to recommend it, and in particular it suits the mood of chapter 38.

Were preachers to restrict themselves merely to the verses indicated for this Twenty-second Sunday after Pentecost, there might be a tendency to give a sermon on the marvels of creation. But even the questions of 38:2-3 should be an indication that more is at stake than a creation poem. Such a distant view of creation is hardly fitting in the mouth of the Lord at this point. Is God praising and boasting about his own creation? Far from it. The questions in verses 4ff. about earth, sea, abyss, darkness, light, rain, etc., are by design a reply to Job, and the preacher should be faithful to that. If one is going to preach on the marvels of creation, choose one of the psalms that have been mentioned.

It is important to capture the proper tone of this chapter. It has been likened to the Lord saying to Job: "You know that I know you know these things. . . ." Outside of the gruff beginning, the only frankly sarcastic remark is 38:21:

> Surely you know, for you were born then,
>   and the number of your days is great!

Of course, Job was not born then. Interestingly, the only one born then was Lady Wisdom, whose birth and presence at creation are celebrated in the liturgy for the First Sunday after Pentecost (Trinity Sunday), Year C. Overall, chapter 38 is an astonishingly mild response to Job. Indeed, one might ask if Job "learned" anything new from it. Probably he could have pondered the mysteries of creation if he were not sitting on the ash heap. From the earlier Job speeches it is clear that Job was no mean theologian. And in 12:7-8 he challenged the three friends to look at creation for instruction:

> Ask the animals, and they will teach you;
>   the birds of the air, and they will tell you;

ask the plants of the earth, and they will teach you;
and the fish of the sea will declare to you. . . .

It is fair for preacher and reader to insist on asking what this chapter, despite its loose association with the context, is really saying.

The answer to that, unless I am being as mysterious as the author, is that the design of the YHWH speeches is to lead Job out of his own horrendous predicament into a greater mystery — the difficulties the Lord has in his many concerns for *nonhuman* creatures. It is almost as if the Lord were enlisting Job's sympathy, if not understanding. This is not an "answer" (as we conceive answer) to Job. However, it is consonant with 40:8-14, which is the only passage in the divine speeches where the issue of the book is joined. It is an interesting altercation. The Lord now accuses Job in 40:8 of denying the divine right — the very charge Job had made against God in 27:2, 5. The shoe is on the other foot. With all of Job's declaiming, can he deal with the proud and the wicked? Only if he can pull that off will the Lord acknowledge him, quoting from Psalm 98:1, that his right hand has won him victory. This seems to be a sarcastic gibe at Job, reminding him that the issue is not power. Clearly the Lord is all-powerful, as the YHWH speeches imply. But God has his own way of running things, his own freedom to act as he pleases. No human being such as Job has any right to judge him and run his universe. We are confronted with an old wisdom commonplace that was already expressed in Job 28:12, 20, that only God knows the place of wisdom, and by Qoheleth in Ecclesiastes 3:11; 7:1; 8:17, that no human being can understand what God is doing. But perhaps the best answer to the question is Job's reaction to the speeches of the Lord (see the Twenty-third Sunday after Pentecost, Year B).

Roland E. Murphy

Twenty-third Sunday after Pentecost, Year B

First Lesson: Job 42:1-6, 10-17
(Psalm 34:1-8, [19-22])
Second Lesson: Hebrews 7:23-28
Gospel Lesson: Mark 10:46-52

One wonders why verses 7-9 were eliminated from the reading, since verse 7 is a pivotal verse in the chapter and in the book itself. Instead, we are given in verses 10-17 a long description of Job's restoration, replete with the proper names of Job's daughters in verse 14, in case anyone was awaiting this revelation with breathless interest. Again, a certain type of sermon, or perhaps two sermons, is shaped by the selection. First, one can recognize Job's surrender, a surrender begotten by a vision of God (v. 5), and an "appropriate" restoration of the poor man. Thus a "happy ending" is provided for this intensely dramatic and violent book. Second, two sermons can possibly be made out of the selection: (1) Job's surrender is a matter of repentance (hence a lesson for sinners who are as rebellious as Job); (2) the repentant Job is rewarded with double what he lost and everyone remained happy forever after. Obviously I agree with none of the above, and I urge the preacher to be faithful to the book and include verses 7-9, even at the expense of losing the details of Job's later life!

Let us begin at the beginning. Verses 2-6 contain Job's answer to the Lord's speeches. It is not the first reply he has given; that can be found in 40:2-5. But there is an overlap. 42:3a quotes the beginning of the YHWH speeches, the Lord's question asking who it is that "speaks without knowledge." Verse 4b quotes 38:3b (cf. 40:7b) about question and answer. These opening lines present a restrained, humble Job who accepts the mild divine reproof. He admits in verse 3,

> I have uttered what I did not understand,
> > things too wonderful for me, which I did not know.

That admission seems to have been brought about by the lengthy speeches he has just heard in chapters 38–42. What is interesting is the spirit in which he now receives them — the spirit of Psalm 131:1, "I do not occupy myself with things / too great and too marvelous for me." Job does not vouchsafe any particulars that he has learned, but his capitulation is clear. And when one looks back at the tough language and challenges that Job put to God, one realizes that his surrender is not frivolous. The encounter with the Lord enabled him to acquiesce, when all the orthodox arguments of the three friends failed to move him — indeed, only pushed him into his violent and passionate language. It should be emphasized that Job expresses no sorrow. He recognizes that he has gotten in over his head. Even his opening line (42:2) contains nothing new, but simply reflects on the omnipotent will of the Lord.

However, verse 5 is stunning. It is an explanation of the effect that the encounter of the Lord has had upon him:

> I had heard of you by the hearing of the ear,
>   but now my eye sees you.

There is a contrast between hearing and seeing, and naturally the emphasis is on sight. Job knew of the Lord, by hearsay as it were, but now the vision has occurred and he is transferred to another level of existence. It is true that the encounter involved words in chapters 38–41, but words were the only tool for the author to convey the impact of a meeting with God; those speeches are a literary presentation of a unique spiritual experience. There is little difference if one does not insist on a contrast. The parallelism in the verse guides us to recognize the seeing in verse 5b as an intensification of 5a; words yielded to vision. There is no greater avenue for approaching the Lord than sight. Yet, to see God was to die, as the Lord advised Moses: "You cannot see my face; for no one shall see me and live." But the Lord makes this concession to his favorite: "See, there is a place by me where you shall stand on the rock; and while my glory passes by I will put you in a cleft of the rock, and I will cover you with my hand until I have passed by; then I will take away my hand, and you shall see my back; but my face shall not be seen" (Exod. 33:20-23). The frequently repeated sight of God's face in the Psalms is to be understood as contemplating God's "face" or presence in the temple (e.g., Ps. 42:2).

Verse 6 is the problem. There is no certain translation of this verse, and the preacher can verify that by examining various versions. However, one thing is certain. Job does not repent of any wrongdoing. Yet this is the sense conveyed by so many translations (e.g., NRSV, "repent in dust and ashes"). Why can one be so apodictic in rejecting such a meaning? (1) Job has been pronounced blameless by the Lord in chapters 1–2, and it is inherently necessary for the consistency of the following chapters that he remains so. It is not a reply to this to claim that Job repented of his extreme language. There is no sign of that. The "dust and ashes" are not an automatic signal of a penitential rite. Here they are a symbol of the human condition, as in Job 30:19 and Genesis 18:27. Such a claim is invented to defend a view that has become somewhat traditional, a kind of pardon for Job's rage. (2) The verdict of the Lord in verse 7 (eliminated along with verses 8-9 in the liturgical reading!) settles the problem. The Lord says to Eliphaz: "My wrath is kindled against you and against your two friends; for you have not spoken of me what is right, as my servant Job has." So Job, not the three, was in the right, and he spoke rightly about the Lord. Those who cannot or refuse to recognize the validity of human complaining against God have much to learn from verse 7. There is also the delicious irony that those who lectured Job in a somewhat sanctimonious style must offer a sacrifice for themselves and request Job's prayers, which the Lord will hear. The final irony of the book is that the author has used a traditional story about a holy man, a non-Israelite named Job, to explore the mystery of suffering in a very untraditional manner. The preacher would do well to read the various translations explained by Carol Newsom in her commentary in the *New Interpreter's Bible* (Nashville: Abingdon, 1996), 4:629. The Hebrew text is admittedly ambiguous, and the following can be suggested: "Therefore I retract and change my mind, being but dust and ashes" (repent means "change of mind," as in Gen. 6:6; Jon. 3:9-10). Another possibility: "I yield, and am comforted, being but dust and ashes." In any case, there is no "repentance" for wrongdoing.

The restoration of Job (vv. 11-17) follows upon a significant observation in verse 10: "The LORD gave Job twice as much as he had before." Such a statement seems to give comfort to those who deride the Job story as simplistic. But how is the restoration to be evaluated? First of all, the doubling. There seems to be here a subtle reference to the legislation in Exodus 22:4, according to which a thief had to provide double restitution for what was stolen. Was the author bold enough to hold the Lord to this law in Exodus? Second, it provides closure; the trial is over and a traditional expression of Job's relationship to God can be expressed. Job did not cease to cling to God. It would make little sense for the Lord to simply walk away after the verdict in verse 7; some sign of divine blessing, originally granted to the human race in Genesis 1:28, is in order.

There is nothing in the restoration that calls for particular comment, except the notion itself. Some would interpret this as the point of the book. In the end, a holy person will be rewarded, despite suffering in life. It is difficult to see how one can arrive at such a simplistic conclusion after the agony of chapters 3-31.

*　　　*　　　*

At the conclusion of the cycle of Job readings in the lectionary, it is profitable for a preacher to contemplate the presuppositions contained within the book and also within oneself.

1. The Bible generally sees a connection between sin and suffering. This is most obvious in the laments of the Psalter, where the pray-er asks for relief from some distress that he understands to be due to sinfulness.

2. However, the above observation is not to be absolutized. There are too many exceptions to it. Even among the psalms, there are stout claims to personal justice and cries to God to honor that justice (e.g., 26). Moreover, the universal recognition of the existence of the poor and oppressed, whose condition could not be simply due to sinfulness but clearly to the sins and oppression of others (condemnations of oppressors especially in the Prophets), also points to the mystery of suffering.

3. It follows that the so-called deed/consequence mentality (a good deed produces a good result; a bad deed produces a bad result) is an inadequate and misleading summation of biblical thought. The Israelites applied human standards of justice to the Lord. They could do no other. But they were also painfully aware that the mysterious YHWH was not to be so easily programmed. In the case of Job, the author has pilloried the idea that one can infer wrongdoing from misfortune.

Roland E. Murphy

Seventeenth Sunday after Pentecost, Year B

First Lesson: Proverbs 1:20-33
(Psalm 19)
Second Lesson: James 3:1-12
Gospel Lesson: Mark 8:27-38

Where shall wisdom be found? Where do we find that practical ability to make our way wisely through the world? We live in an age where many stumble, lose their way, trip up and fall down. How is it possible to negotiate the uncertainties of life in a manner that is prudent and discerning without being merely cautious and calculating? Wherein is wisdom?

A man I know did a study of mission statements from American colleges in the late twentieth century. He noted that most of these colleges began by promising students that, if they studied at this college, they would eventually acquire "wisdom." By midcentury colleges had become more modest in their claims, saying they were places that dispensed "knowledge." By the end of the century, colleges had scaled down their sights even more, now promising to give aspiring students "information." In a few years colleges may be little more than places that contain and disseminate "data."

Our text arises from a different age, an age where there were still teachers of wisdom, those who loved the young into adulthood by sharing with them that practical, prudent, discerning virtue they called "wisdom."

Proverbs 1–9 consists of long addresses — I count twelve in all — concerning the worth of wisdom, or speeches that are made to Dame Wisdom herself. This is a quite different mode of literature than what we encounter later in Proverbs 10–30, that compendium of pithy folk wisdom that we know as proverbial. There we find strings of proverbs, most of them disconnected from one another. The text, Proverbs 1:20-33, is of a quite different mode of wisdom literature.

Our text is a clearly crafted, unified composition. Perhaps it was used by some ancient sage, during Israel's wisdom literature renaissance, to instruct students in the characteristics of wisdom. The text falls into two parts. The introduction (vv. 20-21) personifies Wisdom as a woman who "cries out in the street" (1:20). Wisdom is a woman who is selling her wares. "How long, O simple ones, will you love being simple?" (1:22). Here is Wisdom, not as a set of passive principles to be taken or left at the student's discretion. Here is Wisdom as that teacher who actively, passionately, resourcefully seeks out students, attempting to entice them into the sphere of her instruction. In the hands of Wisdom, all education is public education, that pedagogy that dares to intrude into the realm of politics, business, and commerce like the marketplace and the city square. We find a similar personification of Wisdom speaking and seeking in Proverbs 8–9.

Wisdom cares enough about these scoffing fools who hate knowledge (1:22) to go out looking for them in the nooks and crannies of the city, to get in their face, to demand a hearing.

> I will pour out my thoughts to you;
> I will make my words known to you. (1:23)

Most really good teachers are good at intruding upon their students' lives. The wise teacher loves the material enough, and loves the student enough, to use every means possible to win a hearing from the student. The poor teacher sits back, assuming that teaching is a matter of sticking to the facts, letting the students take or leave those facts.

When Wisdom speaks, she speaks first in the second person (vv. 22-27), then shifts (in vv. 28-33) to the third person. Wisdom thus moves from direct address (in the manner of a teacher addressing a group of students) to sweeping exhortation as "you" moves to the more impersonal "they." Perhaps the shift denotes a change of tone in Wisdom's speech in which Wisdom becomes gradually more incensed at the stupid behavior of her students.

As Wisdom continues to speak, she does seem to become more angry, more wrathful and judgmental. Earlier (1:26) she had warned that she would "laugh at your calamity" and "mock when panic strikes you," the calamity and the panic brought on by foolishness and lack of wisdom. By the time we get to the concluding verses of our text, Wisdom sounds like Jeremiah the prophet in his most condemnatory mood. When disaster strikes, as it always does to those fools who stumble along in their foolishness, in that day they shall cry out to Wisdom, "but I will not answer" (1:28). Then it shall be too late for lessons, too late for careful discernment, too late.

Foolishness and disaster do not always walk hand in hand in life; sometimes good things do happen to foolish people, and sometimes wise folk perish. Yet not in this text. Wisdom, using every means at her disposal to get her students' attention, is not above using the motive of fear. Her goal appears to be to change hearts, minds, and souls. Real change often requires forceful rhetoric, and that is what we have here. Wisdom's threats and warnings are in service of a message to those who are "simple," so her admonitions are direct, straightforward, and unequivocal.

It is my impression that contemporary Christian communicators are a bit squeamish about a one-to-one correlation between wisdom and a good life, or between foolishness and failure. We tend to be more interested in why bad things sometimes happen so unjustly to such good people like us, than we are in the somber fruit of foolishness.

Perhaps therefore we ought to admit that Lady Wisdom has a point in her tirade against the simple and the foolish. Sometimes, not always, but sometimes stupid, foolish lives do result in (in her words) "calamity," "distress," and "anguish" (1:27). Not all of the bad things that happen to people in life are the fault of their own foolishness, but many are.

Somewhat exasperatingly, Wisdom tells us almost nothing about the content of this wisdom she so highly praises. What does wisdom actually look like? How might we know it if we saw it?

This failure to be specific about wisdom is quite typical of the sages. Perhaps these first chapters of Proverbs are meant only to motivate us in our search for wisdom while the later chapters give the content of that wisdom, those strings of proverbs that allegedly tell us what to do on most every occasion in life.

We are told that fools tend not to "choose the fear of the LORD" (1:29), but even then we do not know exactly what that means, at least not in this passage.

Perhaps the greatest challenge for our understanding and interpretation of this passage is that few of us contemporary folk really believe there is a direct correlation between our actions and our consequences. Verses 29-33 are therefore a great challenge for us. Most of us are more comfortable with the questions and challenges posed by Job than with this thinking of direct moral calculus where stupid behavior always leads to painful results. Nowhere does our text claim that God will wrathfully bring malefactors to grief. God doesn't need to. Their own misdeeds bear with them their own bitter consequences. There are, in the old words of Scripture, certain "wages" of sin. Our foolishness will be paid, sometimes in the awful consequences of our sad and confused lives.

Wisdom loves to speak in "either-or" terms. Before we forsake Wisdom's straightforward instruction to the simple as being, in its stark polarities, too simple for the contemporary church, let us at least admit to the possibility that her praise of the way of wisdom is a challenge to our moral and intellectual slovenliness. We all know folk whose sad lives validate Wisdom's claim that "waywardness kills the simple, / and the complacency of fools destroys them" (1:32). We also know those souls who, late in life, are able to look back on their lives with gratitude that they played by the rules, lived by what was right, and tried to walk wisely.

Ethicist Stanley Hauerwas, speaking to a group of pastors who were debating the morality of abortion, said, "There is a prior question, even to asking, Is abortion right or is it wrong? That question is, what sort of person would you like to be when you are sixty-five? That is the question that frames all of our questions about right and wrong. Who would I like to look like when I grow up?"

It was the sort of statement of which Wisdom might approve. Our actions, our decisions, our deeds do have consequences. As we are acting, deciding, and doing, we are being formed into certain sorts of persons who live in the world in a certain way. Will we live as fools, or as those who are se-

277

cure and living at ease, safe in the knowledge that we are pursuing the way that ends in a life well lived?

William H. Willimon

First Sunday after Pentecost (Trinity Sunday), Year C

First Lesson: Proverbs 8:1-4, 22-31
(Psalm 8)
Second Lesson: Romans 1:1-5
Gospel Lesson: John 16:12-15

It is quite obvious that the feast of Trinity Sunday has dictated the choice from Proverbs 8 as the first reading. It is not so obvious that a Christian preacher would want to dig back into the Hebrew Scriptures for material for such a distinctively Christian feast. The mystery of the Trinity itself, from a New Testament and Christian point of view, would seem to be more than enough to handle in one sermon. Yet the Old Testament reading is important, not only in itself, but because of the role it played in the development of the doctrine of the Trinity. In the early centuries the Arians fastened on the phrase "the LORD created me" (Prov. 8:22) to establish their understanding of Jesus Christ as subordinate to the Father. There is a long journey from the personification of Woman Wisdom in the Hebrew text of Proverbs 8 to the Word of John 1:1-14, to the second person of the Trinity and the council of Nicaea in A.D. 325. The feast provides an opportunity for preachers to revisit their understanding of Christian doctrine, and also to ask why the lectionary chose this Old Testament reading. It is the purpose of this entry to examine *why,* and thus to provide a biblical-theological basis for the doctrine.

The book of Proverbs is generally divided into two parts, chapters 1–9 and 10–31. The first part is characterized by relatively long wisdom poems that form a kind of narrative containing lessons that the wisdom teacher wanted to communicate (the address from father to son is frequent). The second part consists of individual sayings or aphorisms; these are also wisdom teachings, phrased in neat, pungent proverbs of two parallel lines that were also part of the traditional teaching (e.g., 10:1, "A wise child makes a glad father, / but a foolish child is a mother's grief"). For our purposes, chapters 1–9 are important.

These chapters are regarded as an introduction to the disparate proverbs that follow. Usually a father is depicted as giving advice to "my son" regarding "fear of the Lord," i.e., the avoidance of evil and the doing of good. That is the way to cope with life. There is a ready equivalence between wisdom and virtue, folly and evildoing. In three instances Wisdom is introduced as speaking directly: 1:20-33; 8:4-36; and 9:4-6 [11]. Thus, Wisdom is personified, i.e., portrayed as a being who requests human beings to follow her and so acquire all blessings. The personification is most sharp in chapter 9, where Wisdom is opposed to Dame Folly, another personification, who invites youths to her deceitful banquet ("Stolen water is sweet, / and bread eaten in secret is pleasant," 9:17). Indeed, it can be said that the personification of Wisdom is the most striking and extensive personification in the entire Bible. Significantly, too, she is portrayed as a woman. This is not simply due to the fact that the Hebrew term for wisdom, *ḥokmah*, is feminine, or that the wisdom teachings seem so male oriented. The teachings are destined and applicable for all, male and female. We really have no answer as to why wisdom is personified as a woman, although some have claimed that a goddess lurks behind this figure.

In 1:20-33 Wisdom speaks in a prophetic mode, castigating those who are unfaithful to her teachings. In 9:2-6 she appears as a host inviting all the "simple" or immature to her meal of bread and wine. In 8:4-36 she gives her longest speech. She addresses everyone, encouraging them and launching into a description of her gifts. Her teaching is more precious than gold or silver because it is true, and righteous, leading to prosperity. The lectionary reading begins at 8:22 where Wisdom describes her origins from the Lord: created, begotten, brought forth. She is a firstborn, aware of the divine activity in creation. Indeed, she was beside the Lord "like a master worker"; the NRSV footnote provides another possible meaning, "little child." One can conclude either that she assisted in the divine work or was a child who gave pleasure to God. The preacher would do well to emphasize two factors: Wisdom's preexistence to creation and her delight "in the human race" (v. 31). These two items also emerge in later wisdom literature, as in Sirach 24:3 ("I came forth from the mouth of the Most High") and 24:8, where she receives a command from the Lord to dwell among creatures; in Jacob/Israel she is to "pitch her tent." Although Jewish tradition did not accept Sirach within the canon (as Roman Catholics and Orthodox do), it followed Ben Sira's identification of wisdom with Torah or law (Sir. 24:23).

But this urge to identify wisdom or *sophia* continues into Christian tradition. Paul describes Jesus as one "who became for us wisdom from God" (1 Cor. 1:30); he is "the power of God and the wisdom of God" (1:24). The most vivid presentation is given in the opening lines of the Gospel of John. Here the term *logos* (Word) replaces *sophia*, but the inspiration of John 1:1-14 comes from the background of the personification of Wisdom. The Word was in the beginning with God, and was God. He "pitched his tent" (John 1:14; NRSV, "became flesh") and dwelt among us, just as wisdom dwelt in Israel and ministered to God in Zion (Sir. 24:10).

What does the above description do for the Christian? It describes some major steps in God's revelation of self to humanity. The mysterious figure of Woman Wisdom, begotten of God, and indeed speaking in divine tones (Prov. 8:35, "whoever finds me finds life"), provided a biblical basis for the early Christians to grasp the identity of Christ. As Christian theology developed, he was understood to be, in trinitarian terminology, the second Person, the Logos or Word, who existed with God from all eternity. He is not identical to Woman Wisdom, but the figure of Woman Wisdom provided an opportunity to enter into the mystery of God who was also present in the man Jesus Christ. Thus far, the reading bears on the mystery of the Trinity. But if Christ is the "wisdom of God," as Paul writes, there is another dimension: to see Christ as a wisdom teacher (his sayings and parables); but that is a sermon for another day.

This reading also suggests a lesson in hermeneutics or interpretation. That is to say, by what right can one move from the Old Testament to the New and beyond? There are presuppositions here that a Christian should make explicit. Thus there is the assumption that God's revelation to Israel is not a static thing. It grew throughout the years of Israel, and the Old Testament was the Bible that nourished the first Christians. They adopted and adapted the biblical text to their own reality; they "actualized" the word of God, applying it to their own day and to their leader, Christ. Today's Christian is also challenged by the Scriptures, both Old and New. In a special way, the Christian needs to become aware of his or her roots in the Old Testament and experience the biblical heritage. The Revised Common Lectionary does mount such a challenge, since no Sunday escapes without an Old Testament reading. What are your roots in the Bible?

Roland E. Murphy

Sixteenth Sunday after Pentecost, Year B

First Lesson: Proverbs 22:1-2, 8-9, 22-23
(Psalm 125)
Second Lesson: James 2:1-10, (11-13), 14-17
Gospel Lesson: Mark 7:24-37

Proverbs: short, pithy, everyday wisdom condensed into a series of memorable one-liners as lessons in daily living, steps along the way to the good life. In seminary we were taught never to preach from just one verse of the Bible, to consider the text as a whole. But Proverbs is a large collection of small sayings, stand-alone truths that stick in the mind and need not be argued, only asserted. "A penny saved is a penny earned." "Early to bed, early to rise, makes one healthy, wealthy, and wise." Ben Franklin charmed a young America with such proverbial wisdom.

Proverbs 10–31 is a conglomeration of these pithy folk sayings. While one searches in vain for some organizing principle for these proverbs, the lectionary's selection of 22:1-2, 8-9, 22-23 is a systematic grouping of proverbs that have to do with the perils of riches, the pitfalls of wealth, and sympathy for the poor. Tradition attributes this sort of wisdom to Solomon, the wisest of all the wise. Contemporary scholars note that Proverbs tends to lump together very ancient wisdom, sayings that were known throughout the Near East, with wisdom teachings that were devised during the later period when wisdom was in fashion in Israel.

Read by the church in early September, as the Revised Common Lectionary places Proverbs 22:1-2, 8-9, 22-23, most congregations will think of school. In September children return to school after the summer holiday. Few biblical texts are as pointedly scholastic as this one. When Proverbs 22 is read in the congregation, church becomes a school, a school where the old tell what they know to the young who do not yet know. Israel loved its young enough to show them the way, to provide them with memorable little guides for better living, proverbs to point the way. Here is literature that arose in a culture where those who were older, experienced adults felt a responsibility to share what they knew with the young, where the young were not forced to reinvent the wheel, ethically speaking. By comparison, our own culture seems remiss in the area of careful inculcation of the young. Too often, what we call "education" is a matter of the young being forced to discover for themselves truths that ought to be lovingly told to them. They are urged to dig down deep in themselves for the way to live rather than being shown that way by adults who care that the young not stumble.

Lately among us there has been an upsurge of proverbial wisdom. Bill Bennett's *Book of Virtues,* as well as collections of proverbs and folk wisdom like the popular Chicken Soup series of books, speak to people's need, in an often confusing and pathless age, for someone to show the way. We long for wisdom that is sharp and memorable enough to fit on a poster in the office or to be engraved on a bracelet. Proverbs specializes in that sort of philosophy.

Some of the proverbs contained in this collection of 22:1-2, 8-9, 22-23 appear to be gleaned from everyday experience and restated as general truth. Here is the proverbial way to make sense out of the world in which we must live. This is how we ought to relate to one another within human society. The truths here sound like general exhortations. They do not seem to be limited to the faith community, nor do they appear to arise out of the particular faith of Israel and the church. While it might not be possible to put the Ten Commandments on the wall of a classroom in a public school, due to the particular context out of which the commandments arise, one could tack up almost any of these proverbs in a public place and get away with it in a pluralist society. Most proverbs could begin with "Everybody agrees that. . . ."

It takes someone like us, living in a permissive, at times seemingly valueless society like ours, to note that most proverbs do not shrink from making judgments about value.

A good name is to be chosen rather than great riches,
    and favor is better than silver or gold. (22:1)

Proverbs delights in these "better than" comparisons. In the world, there tend to be two ways: the way of foolishness and folly, the way of wisdom and life. Proverbs dares to assert that one way is "better than" another. Here is teaching that takes a stand, that dares to assert that all ways in life are not of equal value. Proverbs tends to render life as a series of choices along the way, daring to choose this way rather than that one.

To stand up in the average North American congregation — people swimming in a sea of affluence, folk working themselves to death in order to accumulate more and more — and assert that something, anything, is "better than silver or gold" will take some theological fortitude. While most of us have some qualms about giving our lives for the state, or risking death in behalf of Jesus, scores of us seem to have no reservations whatsoever in laying down our lives for cars, vacation homes, and assorted accumulations.

"A good name . . . is better than silver or gold." In our context, where there appears to be little that is better than silver and gold, the particular proverbial wisdom dons combat fatigues, seems combative, revolutionary. Biblical texts ought to be read in context. Context helps to determine the reading of a text. When our context is a thriving capitalist economy, this proverb sounds abrasive. "Better than"? How curious that proverbial wisdom — a product of Israel's time of national contentment, the establishment, conventional knowledge of the old told to the young — presents such a challenge, a critique to our settled arrangements with wealth. The rich and the poor are not as divided as they sometimes think, says Proverbs. "The LORD is the maker of them all" (22:2). Both the rich and the poor stand before the judgments of God, a God who, as maker of all, has the right to assert that one way of life is distinctly "better than" another.

"Those who are generous are blessed, / for they share their bread with the poor" (22:9). This is more than a lead-in to the annual church fall stewardship campaign, this is a countercultural assertion that generosity toward the poor is a source of blessedness. In a society in which all that I have is called "mine," openhanded generosity becomes a way of resisting the powers that be. Most of Poor Richard's proverbs, devised by Ben Franklin, stress prudent management of wealth, cautious care of riches, the way of economic progress. These biblical proverbs assert another way of life where riches tend to be perilous and the Lord takes sides with the poor, despoiling the lives of those uncaring, ungenerous rich "who despoil them" (22:23).

This particular collection of proverbs ends with judgment. Having been told that one way is "better than" another, there is judgment for those who foolishly follow the other way. Our proverbs move from "better than" to the directly imperative "Do not . . ." (22:22). We are not to rob the poor, to crush the afflicted. If we do, God promises to rob and afflict us, or at least to "despoil" those who dare to despoil those whom a holy God has created and dearly loves.

It is a rather rare event for the lectionary to dare to admit to the righteous judgment of God, as it does in including Proverbs 22:23. The lectionary often sanitizes or excludes passages that speak of divine wrath and judgment. In saying that one way of life is "better than" another, Proverbs also dares to speak of what happens to those who foolishly follow the way that is wrong. It is the nature of this God to punish those who despoil the poor. One might have expected God to punish those who abuse Scripture, or who believe false doctrine, or who fail to follow correct liturgical procedure. No, this God is very particular about the poor. Being the God who is the "maker of them all" (22:2), this God has a claim on the poor. They are

283

none other than God's cherished creation. Therefore God is not nice to those who rob, crush, and despoil the life of those who have so little. The poor have it hard in life, not necessarily because God meant it that way, for God means for those who have to be generous toward those who do not have (22:9). It is the will of God that all have bread; therefore, it is God's will that those who have bread share with those who do not (22:9). Because God cannot be good without being righteous, without hating injustice, those who sow "injustice will reap calamity" (22:8). Faithful reading of the text requires the contemporary interpreter to be honest and up front about the impending judgments of God upon the uncaring, ungenerous rich who despoil the poor.

Our venture into Proverbs, which began with claims that Proverbs is conventional, pithy, everyday wisdom, helpful hints for the good life, has ended with hard talk about judgment, wrath, and the severe punishments of a righteous God. Tough talk from a book of the Bible that is usually known for its rather modest claims.

Whether this proverbial talk of judgment is good news or bad depends on which path one is following. If one is on the path toward silver and gold, miserly self-aggrandizement and insensitivity toward the poor, then what we have here is bad news indeed. On the other hand, if one is poor, oppressed, hungry — good news, God is on your side and God is not pleased by present arrangements. A lawyer none other than the Lord himself pleads your cause (22:23), a judge none other than Yahweh promises one day to get those who have so cruelly gotten you.

Good news or bad? It all depends on where you happen to be standing when you hear the proverb.

William H. Willimon

Eighteenth Sunday after Pentecost, Year B

First Lesson: Proverbs 31:10-31
(Psalm 1)
Second Lesson: James 3:13–4:3, 7-8a
Gospel Lesson: Mark 9:30-37

What we have here is the only possible text for the church on Mother's Day. Until the Revised Common Lectionary, it had never appeared in the lectionaries of the church. A good woman is hard to find — Proverbs 31:10-31.

What we may have here is one of the most problematic texts in the Old Testament. We do well not to assume that we know what is going on here until we give it a careful, contextual reading.

First, we ought to note that this is the text that concludes the long book of Proverbs. In a book of the Bible just filled with hymns to Wisdom, as well as long, sometimes tedious maxims for daily living, this is the grand finale, this hymn to the "capable wife" who is "far more precious than jewels" (31:10). Wisdom has been, in Proverbs, repeatedly personified as a woman. One might think that, for the final hymn of praise, Wisdom would be the woman being lauded. No, the woman praised here is a wife. The bridge that brings us here is Proverbs 31:1-9, which the careful interpreter would do well to read, the so-called oracle of King Lemuel's mother where vulnerable men are warned against the evil of giving one's "strength to women" (31:3).

In the Hebrew, each line of this song to the good wife begins with a successive letter of the Hebrew alphabet. As poetry, it isn't much, for in its present form it reads like a shopping list of desirable traits in the allegedly "capable wife."

The poem begins with a rhetorical question, "Where can one find a capable wife?" If you find such a woman, she is more valuable even than rare jewels (31:10). She is amazingly productive; therefore, "her husband trusts in her." Because of this, she does "not harm" for as long as they live. Then begins an almost laughable list of all the tasks at which this productive woman excels: she works in both wool and flax, brings in food from "far away." Rising when it is still dark, she gets to work. She is an expert in real estate, grape cultivation. She has strong arms and her lamp never lacks oil. Spinning, giving generously to the poor, clothing members of her own household in crimson — she does all that. For herself, she prefers "fine linen and purple," which she sometimes sells at a profit. We thus see what a woeful understatement the ancient sage made when he (surely he was a he) declared, "A capable wife . . . she is far more precious than jewels" (31:10).

This domestic dynamo still has time, amid all her household tasks and mercantile activity, to be a wise teacher (31:26). It is interesting that this mention of wisdom, such a prominent commodity in the book of Proverbs, must wait until all these other domestic tasks have been praised before it appears.

Need we note that we are reading the paean of a decidedly patriarchal society? This is the woman who is every man's dream, every man who believes that the chief virtue of a woman is in service of a man. What shall we do with such a text? Does its patriarchal quality render it useless to the contemporary church?

It is always a dangerous thing to place ourselves in a superior position to biblical texts. As Christians, we are to be subservient to these texts, to obey them rather than make excuses for them or dismiss them. Yet interpretive work is called for with a text like this one for a number of reasons.

We ought to be bothered not only because this praise of a woman is measured almost exclusively in terms of her value for others, particularly men, but also because the standards of measurement are ridiculously high. The husband of such a wife may have "no lack of gain" (31:11), for she has great monetary value for him in her prudent management of the household. But surely we ought to wince at this characterization of a good wife as being a valuable commodity for her husband.

One sometimes hears this text read at the funeral of a woman. In such a context it always seems to me odd. After all, no matter how industrious and productive the deceased woman may have been, there is no way she could have measured up to this superwoman who excels at so wide a range of endeavor. Furthermore, most of her great virtues are domestic in nature, the skills of housewives who rule the private space of the home so that their husbands may engage in more important public work like "taking [their] seat among the elders of the land" (31:23). She stays home, from morning to night, working like a slave, so that the husband may take pride in his valuable wife and so that he may be about more important work near the "city gates."

Perhaps we ought to admit that all of us, both men and women, at one time or another have this desire to be served rather than to serve. As Christians, Christ calls us to serve others, but not to mere servility. One wonders where this woman's children are when she is rising before dawn to work for her family. Where is her husband? Has he any responsibilities for marriage and the family other than periodic praise of his relentlessly hardworking wife (31:28)? Is this woman doing her family a favor by bearing all of their burdens, working from before dawn to well past dusk, while they merely praise her for being such a good woman? Ought we to join our voices in praising her? Or ought we to question how her self-sacrificial life may be warping the lives of her children and her husband, relieving them of their God-given responsibility to serve and to create?

In most congregations there are always some people, and often they seem to be women, who shoulder far too much responsibility. We praise them for their hard work, their dedication to their families and to the church. We find that we call on them repeatedly whenever there is tough work to be done. But ought we to do so? When does our praise of them for their hard work become a subtle form of abuse?

Or perhaps we are meant to marvel that in a Near Eastern, patriarchal society, we have this example of such extravagant praise for a woman? Proverbs has personified wisdom, which it says is the highest human achievement, in feminine form. Proverbs ends with this praise of a woman who does all things and does them well. She manages well in the domestic sphere, but she also holds her own in the tug and pull of economic life, astutely wheeling and dealing, assuring economic security for her family. About the only thing her husband contributes is sitting with the elders and heaping occasional praise upon his capable wife. How this woman, in the days before electric dishwashers and trash compactors, still manages to be a real estate tycoon (31:16) is a wonder.

While her gifts are remarkable, I am still hesitant to join this tough woman's children and husband who rise up to call her happy and blessed. I have known too many people, both women and men, who know no limits on their activity, who take upon their backs too much responsibility for making their families work, who say yes to every request for help, and who eventually pay dearly for what the rest of us hail as remarkable capability.

There is no mention of this woman keeping Sabbath in her weekly round of activity. If there were, then we might be able to join in the chorus of praise, led by her grateful children and husband, and call her truly blessed. Until she learns to "fear the Lord" by keeping Sabbath, we ought to praise her, but with some serious reservations.

William H. Willimon

Fifteenth Sunday after Pentecost, Year B

First Lesson: Song of Solomon 2:8-13
(Psalm 45:1-2, 6-9)
Second Lesson: James 1:17-27
Gospel Lesson: Mark 7:1-8, 14-15, 21-23

Although it is late summer when Song of Solomon 2:8-13 occurs in the Revised Common Lectionary, our text from the Song of Solomon is all spring, and newness, and love.

In exegeting this text, we ought first to remind ourselves that we are reading poetry. In our investigation of this text, we will take care not to kill it by dissection. Poetry is better experienced than explained. Poetry has an immediate impact. Poetic metaphors tend to wilt when they are pushed too far or analyzed too exactingly. The history of interpretation of the Song of Solomon demonstrates a tendency not to analyze this book of the Bible but to allegorize it, sailing quickly past its amorous content and allegorizing its images in service to the church. Dear Chrysostom was the master at making the Song of Solomon serve Christ and the church, no matter what its originating purpose might be.

The Song of Solomon is a collection of at least two dozen poems or parts of poems. Thus the designation of this book as Song of Songs or Canticles makes sense. Throughout, a man and a woman take turns praising the physical characteristics of one another, and in the greatest and most excruciating detail. Metaphor is pushed to the limit in this book, sometimes to almost laughable limits. Body parts are described with reference to palm trees and various sorts of animals. I picture the lovers as young and infatuated, perhaps enjoying first love, certainly young love, delighting in the sheer wonder of one another's body and personality, but mostly body.

What all this body-talk has to do with Christians and the church has long been a matter of consternation for Christian communicators. Most of them seem to have been embarrassed by the literal language of physical love and therefore sought to stretch the language to apply to Christ and his church. This move, to allegorize the Song of Songs, began in Judaism. Hosea had previously compared God's love of Israel to that of a man and a woman (Hos. 2:16-19). Later the man and woman were Christ and his church, a treatment that finds echoes in places like Revelation 21:2-9.

Most of us experience this rather odd book of the Bible at weddings, if at all. That makes sense, since some contemporary commentators believe the book to be a collection of Hebrew wedding songs. Some have heard, in the sensuous cadences of this book, hints of the pagan fertility religions that were practiced by Israel's neighbors. Some feminist commentators see the woman who appears throughout these poems as a personification of Sophia, goddess of wisdom, or some early pagan goddess of love.

It is in keeping with most contemporary interpretation to focus upon the plain, more literal meaning of the text. Here we have an unabashed, exuberant Hebrew poem of love. Let us enjoy it in that sense, marveling that the Bible is big enough to include such mundane, utterly human (and usually utterly delightful) concerns within the confines of its canon. With all the other serious — sometimes so deadly serious — concerns of Scripture, is it not a delight to encounter a book of the Bible that takes time to marvel at the wonder of the human body and the joy of human love?

As you know, God is not mentioned in the Song of Solomon. The book thus offers Christian interpreters, and their congregations, a sort of vacation from our usual Sunday concerns. How fortuitous that the lectionary offers us this text in the doldrums of late summer!

So much of contemporary piety is moralistic, a matter of doing this or that to promote human betterment, or to bring us closer to God. Preachers who enjoy the use of imperatives, filling the air with "should," "ought," and "must," will find this text to be a theological stretch, but one that they do well to attempt. Some Scripture does have definite ethical intention, the urging of this or that behavior. Other texts try better to inform us of the ways of God.

The Song of Solomon has, it seems to this interpreter, more doxological intent. I find no greater purpose in these poetic lines than the joyful praise of human love, the wonder of relations between men and women, romance, sex, beauty, and other pointless joys of the life God has given to us on this earth. I personally know preachers who would not dare to preach from this text. All I can say is that their congregations are the poorer for it.

In our text, first the woman speaks. She praises the glory of her beloved (2:8-10). This she follows with remembrance of his words to her (2:10b-13). In other words, the woman takes the lead and all that we know of the man comes to us, at this point, through the words of the woman. It is a joy, in Scripture or in our society, to hear a woman given the first word, to hear a woman assign significance to the man. She lies in her room and, upon hearing the voice of her beloved, imagines his approach, seeming to her as that of a gazelle or a young stag who bounds toward her. Vitality and virility are evoked by such images.

The beloved takes his place outside her window. The moonlight balcony meetings of Romeo and Juliet are brought to mind at this point. He speaks, he calls to her to arise, to come away with him. It is spring, not only in the world, but in their hearts. If there are places in the Song of Solomon that seem to be concerned with marriage, this is not one of them. This is all romance, infatuation, courtship, and love. When two people are in such love, it really is as if the whole world has changed, has risen up to meet them in their love. Thus he sings that "the winter is past, / the rain is over and gone" (2:11). Whereas she has spent most of her lines describing him, he expends most of his words on the way the world now looks, now that love has come. There are flowers, singing, the song of the turtledove, lush fig trees, and the sweet smell of spring blossoms.

The sensuousness, the luxuriant and lush fertility of it all, is what impresses. For those in love, for those who have found someone to love, and to return their love, it often is as if a desert has burst into blossom. In love, the boundary between the self and the world is bridged. Those in love simply cannot believe that the whole universe does not rejoice in their love. It all seems so perfect, so right. The flowers that bloom have burst into bloom, just for them. The birds that sing, sing only for their delight. It is spring all over.

Thank God, Israel and later the church, in their collective wisdom, retained this unusual but beautiful book in the Bible. This world, our bodies, the blossoms and the breasts, the gazelles and the leaping stags — they are all spectacular creations of an abundantly creative Creator. The greatest sin would be, not to celebrate their beauty too much, but not to notice. As these two ancient lovers lovingly recount every detail of the arms, legs, lips, and voice of their beloved, they thereby bid us to notice ourselves and others and the world. When someone is in love with someone else, the lover tends to love every inch of the beloved, tends to marvel at the way sunlight falls upon the hair or the funny little way a lip upturns. To love is to notice God in the details, to notice is to love. The lovers of the Song of Solomon help us, particularly us older types in the summer or fall of our lives, to remember, to notice, to rejoice.

What are we to do with this ancient love poetry, this Hebrew celebration of romance? In one sense, nothing. That is, we are to drop our prosaic, dull utilitarian disposition that makes us want to turn everything into a means of self-enhancement and simply relax, rejoice, revel in the glory of young love and its extravagance. This is a text to be done as doxology, as praise to God from whom all blessings flow, particularly the blessing of romantic love. The Song of Solomon does not mention God, does not need to, for how could there be such young love, and such beauty, and such a world, unless it were divine?

In another sense, we are to be reminded that we, and this world, are

God's loving, lovable creations. Just as there is room in the canon for such a sensuous book of useless poetry, so there must be room in Christian theology and the life of the church for all the blessings of God, including the physical, romantic love of a woman and a man. The feelings with which we are sometimes blessed, in the spring of the year, in the spring of life, are not to be despised. There is certainly enough confusion abroad concerning the gift of romantic love for there to be at least one occasion when the church considers this subject from a godly perspective. Why should Hollywood always have the first and last say on love?

On other Sundays, there will be an opportunity to speak of the dangers of being overly exuberant about these matters. There will be the occasion for reminding young people of their responsibilities for their feelings and their bodies. Then we can speak of the ethical implications of our Christian view of love, and how important it is to be careful, prudent, and responsible in our use of God's gifts, including the gift of sexuality.

But this Sunday, if you accept the invitation of these two young lovers, relax, revel, lighten up, and praise God for blossoms, and leaping stags, and silly young fools, and all the rest. How much the poorer we would have been without this frivolous book of the Bible, how much the poorer our lives would be without these gifts of God.

William H. Willimon

Twelfth Sunday after Pentecost, Year C

First Lesson: Isaiah 1:1, 10-20
(Psalm 50:1-8, 22-23)
Second Lesson: Hebrews 11:1-3, 8-16
Gospel Lesson: Luke 12:32-40

The book of Isaiah stands at the beginning of the Bible's collection of prophetic writings. The biblical editors of these books had a reason for placing Isaiah at the beginning. Anyone wishing to read the prophets, this arrangement says, ought to start by reading Isaiah.

The lectionary testifies to the importance of the Isaiah book in the history of preaching and teaching in the Christian church. According to the Revised Common Lectionary, there are some sixty-nine texts assigned to various Sundays and holidays in the church year from Isaiah. This is in comparison to twenty-seven from Jeremiah, twelve from Ezekiel, and thirty-three from all twelve of the "minor prophets" (Hosea through Malachi). In fact, in the entire Bible, Isaiah is second only to the book of Luke, which provides seventy-three texts for lectionary selections.

Welcome to the Prophets! The first sentence in the book introduces the prophet and all the prophetic writings. It reads: "The vision of Isaiah son of Amoz, which he saw concerning Judah and Jerusalem in the days of Uzziah, Jotham, Ahaz, and Hezekiah, kings of Judah" (1:1). This sentence links the material that follows with a particular person (Isaiah), a particular place (Jerusalem), and a specific time, during the administrations of four kings of Judah: Uzziah (also called Azariah; see 2 Kings 15:1-7; 2 Chron. 26) reigned from 783 to 742 B.C.E. He was succeeded by his son Jotham (742-735; 2 Kings 15:7, 32-38; 2 Chron. 27), who was in turn succeeded by his son Ahaz (735-715; 2 Kings 16; 2 Chron. 28). Ahaz was followed by his son Hezekiah, who gets the most coverage in the biblical historical books and who had many interactions with Isaiah (715-687; 2 Kings 18–20 and 2 Chron. 29–32). Since Isaiah began his work in the year that King Uzziah died (Isa. 6) and continued it into the time of Hezekiah (Isa. 39:1-8), it would seem that this initial sentence is directing us to consider the historical situation in the years of these kings, in other words, in the second half of the eighth century B.C.E. (about 750-700). In his introductory remarks to reading Isaiah, published in his Bible translation, Luther wrote: "[I]f one would understand the prophecies, it is necessary that one know how things were in the land, how matters lay, what was in the mind of the people — what plans they had with respect to their neighbors, friends and enemies — and especially what attitude they took in their country toward God and toward the prophet, whether they held to his word and worship or to idolatry" (*Luther's Works,* vol. 35 [Philadelphia: Muhlenberg, 1960], pp. 273-74).

The way it was in Isaiah's day. How were "things in the land" at the time Isaiah carried out his work?

On the international scene, thoughtful observers were worried about Assyria, a new power arising in the east, in the land of the Tigris and Euphrates Rivers. Under Emperor Tiglath-pileser III (745-727), Assyria would soon conquer all the smaller nations in the area and in fact push all the way into Egypt. Israel would be crushed and fall to the Assyrian armies in 722, and Judah would be nearly wiped out in 701. But the time of the Assyrian

Empire was also the time of Isaiah. Just a few years after Tiglath-pileser took charge, a prophet was called to begin his work, in Jerusalem (Isa. 6).

Internally the nation of Judah continued to enjoy the prosperity brought about by Uzziah (note, e.g., 2 Chron. 26!). Some of Isaiah's sayings reflect the spirit of the time. The wealthy were buying up small farms and consolidating them into big ones (Isa. 5:8). We hear of those in Isaiah's day who revel in luxury, with live music and wine accompanying their all-night parties (5:11-12). We even catch a glimpse of the women of Jerusalem, wealthy and exceedingly well clothed (3:16-23). And religion? The places of worship were busy, with people bustling about with sacrifices, bringing offerings, burning incense, and offering prayers (1:10-15).

Jerusalem just past mid-eighth century B.C.E. was a place where the economy was booming, the elite were basking in the prosperity of the Uzziah years, and ecclesiastical institutions were buzzing with sacrifices and songs. But beneath it all, something was wrong. A terrible sickness was eating away at the heart of the nation. Isaiah had seen it, and tried to warn his people about it before it was too late!

Religion and life. This opening chapter of the book of Isaiah collects prophetic sayings from various occasions. After the title in verse 1; an opening lament about rebelling children, that is, the people of Judah and Jerusalem (vv. 2-3); and a description of the suffering of these children (vv. 4-9), verses 10-17 offer a critique of what is going on at the temple and some instruction about getting life back in order. Verses 18-20 are an invitation to debate with the Lord, and verses 21-31 offer a lament for the city (vv. 21-26) followed by some short sayings (vv. 27-31).

The setting for this prophetic sermon is the Jerusalem temple, where people have gathered to offer sacrifices, burn incense to the Lord, and pray (vv. 11-15). The prophet identifies his words as "teaching," indicating that the purpose of this sermon is going to be to instruct. The sermon begins with words that would have been shocking: his hearers are addressed as people of Sodom and Gomorrah, the notorious sin cities of that time (see also Gen. 19:1-29; Deut. 29:23; Isa. 13:19; Jer. 23:14; and others). Hardly a sermon introduction designed to win the favor of the audience!

Verses 11-15 continue with the prophet's words that nothing of what is going on in the busy temple is acceptable to the Lord! The offering of sacrifices was a way of paying for sins that had been committed. Offerings and incense were also a part of the routine of religion in the temple. Festivals were held at the time of the "new moon," when the moon was not visible and people were unusually anxious. But all of this has become an abomination (v. 13) and a burden to the Lord (v. 14). Then, in a statement that surely was shocking to these people gathered to worship the Lord in the temple, the prophet, speaking in the Lord's name, says, "When you pray, I will not listen!" A reason is given for this refusal: the hands that are stretched out for prayer are covered with the blood of the innocent (v. 15).

This short sermon ends with a series of imperative verbs, commands, telling the people what they ought to do. This includes cleansing themselves from evil, learning to do good, and seeking justice. This last imperative is spelled out: to "do good" and "seek justice" means to rescue those who are being oppressed, and to care especially for the orphan and the widow.

To summarize: the prophet says these people had arranged their lives in two compartments. One was marked "religion" and involved participation in the ceremonies and rituals of the temple. It appears that the services there were well attended! The other compartment was marked "life." In their day-by-day lives, these people were neglecting the orphan and the poor. In other words, they were *not* doing justice and defending orphans and widows, as the prophet called them to do.

Monday morning in the implement shop. I recall as a boy going pheasant hunting with my father and some of his friends. It was a crisp fall afternoon. The hunting for the day was finished. We sat eating lunch, and the men told stories. I remember that someone asked a question: "I need a new combine. Where is the best place to buy it?" "Buy it from X," someone said. "He is a member of our church." Then a crusty old farmer took a cigarette out of his mouth and commented, "Don't buy from him. Yes, he goes to church every Sunday, he even goes twice! But don't go to his implement shop on Monday morning! He'll take you for all you've got!"

This recollection from decades ago makes the point that the prophet was making in this sermon. Religion can't be separate from everyday life. It's not "religion and life" but "religion in life," which includes honesty in buying and selling. Why did the Lord not delight in the worship, the hymns, the songs of the people? Not because the choir was out of tune or the liturgy was not performed correctly; not because of what happened in the temple on the day of worship. But because of what was happening every other day of the week, in the shops, on the streets, and in the homes of a people who had forgotten that religion has to do with the ordinary things of everyday life.

James Limburg

First Sunday of Advent, Year A

First Lesson: Isaiah 2:1-5
(Psalm 122)
Second Lesson: Romans 13:11-14
Gospel Lesson: Matthew 24:36-44

F ew biblical texts have enjoyed the popularity and public exposure of the "swords to plowshares" sayings in Isaiah 2 and Micah 4. The words of Isaiah 2:4 are engraved in large letters on the wall opposite the United Nations headquarters in New York City:

> THEY SHALL BEAT THEIR SWORDS INTO PLOWSHARES AND THEIR SPEARS INTO PRUNING HOOKS: NATION SHALL NOT LIFT UP SWORD AGAINST NATION. NEITHER SHALL THEY LEARN WAR ANY MORE. ISAIAH 2.4

In the north garden area of the United Nations grounds stands a nine-foot sculpture of a muscular blacksmith beating a sword into a plowshare. On the base appear the words WE SHALL BEAT OUR SWORDS INTO PLOW-SHARES, with a reference to Micah 4. In Washington, D.C., at Indiana Avenue and Fourth Street, NW, stands a remarkable sculpture. Welded to a sixteen-by-nineteen-foot steel plowshare are thousands of disabled handguns confiscated by the Washington Police Department. The label for the sculpture reads, "Guns into Plowshares." Finally, the words of verse 4 in Hebrew are sung as a song of peace throughout the world: *Lo yisa goi 'el goi hereve, v'lo yilm'du 'od milhama* [nation shall not lift up sword against nation, neither shall they learn war any more].

A portrait of peacemaking. The location of this saying in Isaiah signals its importance. The first chapter introduces the entire book. After this, 2:1 introduces the collection of sayings "concerning Judah and Jerusalem" in chapters 2–12. This leadoff piece in the collection is oriented toward the future, speaking of Jerusalem "In days to come. . . ."

2:1-5 may be divided into a core saying (vv. 2-4, paralleled closely in Mic. 4:1-4) and a frame (vv. 1 and 5). 2:1 is obviously the work of the editor, signaling the start of the 2:1-12 collection. 2:5 is also the work of an editor, addressing and applying the core saying to the listening congregation, the "house of Jacob." The editor of Micah, as we shall see, adapted the core saying to a new context by means of a concluding frame (Mic. 4:5). The core saying in verses 2-4 is a *vision* and, as such, is more a portrait than a photograph, transcending reality with vivid imagery.

Walking the walk. There are three main themes in the core saying. First of all, there is an *all nations* or ecumenical dimension to this text. This is a vision of a future time ("in days to come") when "all nations" and "many peoples" will stream to the house of the God of Jacob (vv. 2, 4). With this "all nations" concern, it is quite appropriate that the texts in both Isaiah and Micah find themselves on display at the United Nations headquarters. Isaiah 12, which closes the 2–12 unit, also has an eye on the nations of the earth in the future (12:4, 5).

Second, there is an *instructional* theme in verses 2-4. Verse 3 tells why the nations are coming to Jerusalem. They are not making a pilgrimage to bring gifts (as in Isa. 60 and Hag. 2:7-9), nor are they coming to take part in a festival in Jerusalem (Isa. 56:6-8; Zech. 14:16). These people are coming to receive instruction (the Hebrew word is *torah*, v. 3), specifically theological instruction ("that he may teach us"). Since "he" is the Lord, this is a description of a future theological conference. This anticipated instruction is not just head knowledge. Those enrolled in this schooling expect to be taught the "ways" of the Lord, and then expect to "walk" in those ways. Here is no split between theology and everyday life. This instruction provides both programs to study and paths in which to walk. Theoretical knowledge and practical action are of one piece.

Isaiah 2:3 indicates the place where the instruction originates. Centuries ago, instruction went out from Mount Sinai (Exod. 20). In the future, instruction will go out from Mount Zion. At Sinai it was the Lord who spoke; from Zion, that which is spoken will again be "the word of the LORD" (v. 3). This will not be the last time instruction in the ways of peace is given in a mountain setting (see Matt. 5:9 and the discussion below).

The climax of this prophetic portrait of the future comes in verse 4 with a description of *peacemaking*. The *all* nations theme recurs, with the mention of the Lord working among "the nations." Once again, word and act will be combined when the representatives of the nations return to their home countries to put into practice the results of these diplomatic discussions. That practice will result in massive programs of disarmament, transforming weapons of war into implements of peace. Even the war colleges and other places devoted to instruction in methods and tactics of warfare will be shut down: "neither shall they learn war any more."

What of the frame in verse 5? Upon hearing the description of this portrait read in a worship setting, a person in Jerusalem might think, "A marvelous vision, vividly portrayed, using relevant and concrete imagery!" One could imagine the gathered people complimenting the prophet for the creative and challenging sermon! But the prophetic word has not yet come to a conclusion. Now, for the first time, the hearers, the "house of Jacob," are addressed directly. These words are not for those nations that will one day in the future stream to Jerusalem. They are aimed at the community living in the hard realities of the present. The appeal is doubled, using the same verb twice, for emphasis: "O house of Jacob, / *walk* (Heb. *halak*), let us walk / *(halak)* in the light of the LORD!"

With verse 5 the beautiful vision of verses 2-4 is brought down to earth. The hearers are invited to get this marvelous picture of peacemaking out of the realm of the imagination and into the realities of everyday life. The prophet paints a picture of peacemaking but also exhorts the people to get busy at that activity. These people ought not only think the thoughts or talk the talk about peacemaking, but they are challenged to walk the walk as well.

Micah's version. The core saying about peacemaking finds another context in the book of the prophet Micah. Once again the core saying (vv. 1-3) has been provided with editorial comments. The *all nations* dimension is intensified with the addition of the words "many . . . strong . . . far away" (v. 3). The editor's conclusion in verses 4-5 provides clues for interpretation and application. The message about peace is individualized in verse 4, and the saying is theologically certified with the formula "for the mouth of the LORD of hosts has spoken." Instead of the brief exhortation of Isaiah 2:5, Micah's version acknowledges the religious pluralism of the day, "for all the peoples walk, / each in the name of its god" (5a), and then invites all hearers to join in making a resolution, "but we will walk in the name of the LORD our God / forever and ever" (5b).

In Micah's version of this saying, the core saying has received additions and has also been expanded to enable the entire saying to be used as something of a liturgy with congregational response.

Blessed are the peacemakers. The "swords to plowshares" saying is not quoted directly in the New Testament. There are, however, words about peacemaking. Our core text envisioned instruction going out from Mount Zion on some future day to nations gathered there. The author of Matthew portrays another mount (Matt. 5:1) where instruction is once again being given, and that Gospel concludes with an account of Jesus' final instruction to his disciples, instruction once again delivered on a mountain (28:16-20).

We have noted the themes of the Isaiah text: (1) *all nations* will come to Jerusalem to hear (2) *instruction* that leads to action. (3) That action has to do with *peacemaking,* which involves a program of disarmament. As we look at the scene in Matthew 5–7, we observe:

1. The purpose of the gathering on the mountain is *instruction:* "Then he began to speak, and taught them, saying: . . ." (5:1). As in Isaiah, this is the kind of instruction that leads to action. Jesus' "sermon on the mount" ends with a story encouraging the audience to be not only hearers, but to act on these words (7:24-27).
2. Jesus pronounces a blessing on *peacemakers* (5:9) and gives an example of individual peacemaking (5:38-42). Could he have pronounced those blessed who beat their swords into plowshares?
3. The audience Jesus addresses does not consist of "all nations" as envisioned in Isaiah 2, but rather of the disciples and others listening in. But this instruction is not for "insiders" only. The disciples are to be the salt of the *earth,* the light of the *world* (5:13-16). And at the conclusion of the book, they are charged to "Go therefore and make disciples of *all nations . . .*" (28:16-20).

James Limburg

Thirteenth Sunday after Pentecost, Year C

First Lesson: Isaiah 5:1-7
(Psalm 80:1-2, 8-19)
Second Lesson: Hebrews 11:29–12:2
Gospel Lesson: Luke 12:49-56

The Old Testament text for this Sunday offers an excellent opportunity to preach about social justice. The prophetic message is in the form of a song that packs a powerful punch about "doing justice," that is, about caring for the widow, the orphan, and the poor.

A song about a friend and a vineyard. We could imagine a festival celebrating the harvesting of the vineyards during a time when there was still peace and prosperity in Judah, before the times of warfare beginning with Ahaz in 735 B.C.E. The festival takes place somewhere in the neighborhood of Jerusalem. Vineyards were a central part of the agricultural life of Israel and Judah. Teachers referred to vineyards in illustrations (Prov. 24:30-34; Matt. 21:33-

43). Isaiah used the image both in sayings (1:8; 3:14) and in song (27:2-5 and here).

Harvest time in Judah, like times of harvest the world over, was a time of celebration. There would be singing, dancing, and wine for all. The fall festival of *sukkot,* or booths, was a weeklong celebration of the grape harvest (Deut. 16:13-15; see also Neh. 8:14-18) and is still a major Jewish festival. Judges 9:27 describes a harvest festival: "They went out into the field and gathered the grapes from their vineyards, trod them, and celebrated." See also Nehemiah 8:14-18.

Great expectations (5:1-2). In the midst of such festivities, the young man Isaiah steps forward, perhaps with the eighth-century-B.C.E. equivalent of a guitar in his hand. "Let me sing a song," he announces, "a song about my friend and his vineyard." The crowd is attentive. The song begins: "Listen while I sing you this song, a song of my friend and his vineyard: My friend had a vineyard on a very fertile hill. . . ." (Note: The *Good News Bible (Today's English Version)* is preferred, because the translation "friend" is better than "lover," as in the NRSV.)

The emphasis in the first two verses is on all the work the "friend" had expended on the vineyard. The verbs pile up: he dug, cleared, planted, built, hewed out. Finally, this vineyard farmer expected some good grapes as the result of his labors! But, surprisingly, the grapes were worthless (lit. "stinking"; the same word is translated "stench" in Amos 4:10; Isa. 34:3; Joel 2:20)! The friend's great expectations were disappointed. And here the song ends.

The song is about you (5:3-7)! Verses 3-4. The song is ended. Now the prophet turns to his hearers and engages in a bit of role play. Instead of speaking about the "friend," he takes the role of the friend. He addresses the audience directly, as if they were a jury. "And now, inhabitants of Jerusalem and people of Judah, judge between me and my vineyard," he says. He invites the participation of the audience. He asks a pair of questions that demand a response: Could I have done anything more for this vineyard of mine? The implied answer: "Of course not! After all, you cleared all those stones, dug up the ground, planted those vines, built that watchtower!" Why did the vineyard produce such a worthless crop? Clearly, the fault did not lie with "the friend"!

Verses 5-6. The prophet continues speaking in the role of the "friend." He imagines the audience as a jury. Now he will announce the sentence. The vineyard is still "my vineyard" (v. 5). But what can this farmer do? He announces that he will take away the vineyard's special protection. He is going to stop pruning and hoeing and let it go to waste and to weeds (see Prov. 24:30-34). And then comes a final, ominous note. This "friend" says he will command the clouds so that they do not rain on the vineyard! But who is this "friend" whose role the prophet is taking? Who could this be that can command the clouds?

Finally, in verse 7, comes the punch line, the application. It is delayed until the last possible moment. The prophet drops the mask and reveals the identity of this "friend." No longer does he speak in the form of a parable, but in plain, ordinary language:

> For the vineyard of the LORD of hosts
>   is the house of Israel,
> and the people of Judah.

He concludes with a pair of puns in Hebrew, which make his message unforgettable: The Lord expected justice (Heb. *mishpaṭ*), but the Lord found bloodshed *(mispaḥ)*. The Lord expected righteousness *(ṣedaqah)* but instead heard only a cry *(ṣeʿaqah)*, like that of an abused widow or child crying to the Lord because there is no one else to help (Exod. 22:23-24; Job 34:28).

Doing justice, prophetic style. This text provides the opportunity to sketch the shape of the prophetic notion of doing justice.

First, justice is the expected *response* of God's people to what God has done for them. The pattern of the song is a reminder of what God has done (vv. 1-2) and then a judgment on the people for failing to respond as they ought to (vv. 3-7). This is also the pattern of the Ten Commandments, which begin with a reminder of what the Lord had done in the event of the exodus (Exod. 20:2) and continue by spelling out the expected response of the people (Exod. 20:4-11).

Secondly, as we look at the word "justice" or the verb "do justice" in other passages of Isaiah and Isaiah's contemporaries, we see that justice is properly something that a person does. The biblical way of speaking is to "do justice." There is, in other words, a *dynamic* dimension to this notion. Amos once called for the people to "let justice roll down like waters, / and righteousness like an ever-flowing stream" (Amos 5:24). The image of justice is not a scale held by a blindfolded woman so that everything is quiet, stable, and in balance. The prophetic image is rather a mighty stream, rolling and roaring through the land, cleansing and cleaning up everything in its path. Isaiah's contemporary Micah spoke of justice, once again in dynamic terms. He said,

> What does the LORD require of you
> but to do justice, and to love kindness,
>   and to walk humbly with your God?   (Mic. 6:8)

Finally, as we listen to Isaiah's preaching, we discover that doing justice means taking up the role of *advocate for the powerless*. In Isaiah's preaching about justice, one keeps running into people in need, specifically the widow and orphan (Isa. 1:17, 23; 10:2) and the poor (3:14-15; 10:2). These are the powerless, who have no clout in society. The widow has no husband, the orphan has no parent, and the poor have no money. To "do justice" according to the prophets is to take up the cause of these persons and act as their advocate. People and political leaders alike are exhorted to do so (1:17). The failure of leadership to act as advocates for the powerless caused once-faithful Jerusalem to become a faithless whore of a city (1:21-23). The politicians have enacted legislation that discriminates against the powerless, and those unfair laws will be the end of these legislators (10:1-4).

Taking up the advocate role. These prophetic texts that speak of doing justice can provide guidelines as we seek to work for justice in our own time. We recall the shape of "doing justice" that we have noted:

Doing justice means the people of God's *response* to what God has done for them. The prophets recalled God's mighty acts such as the exodus; as Christians, we need only recall what God has done for us in Jesus Christ, through his death and resurrection. "We love because he first loved us," said the writer of 1 John (4:19; see also 4:7-12). Note how Paul's letters begin with a reminder of what God has done (Rom. 1–11; Eph. 1–3) and then continue by giving directives for the expected response (Rom. 12–15; Eph. 4–6). Luther put it this way: "It is true that we are justified by faith alone without works, but I speak of the true faith which after it justifies does not snore lazily, but is active in love" (see George Forell, *Faith Active in Love* [Minneapolis: Augsburg, 1954], p. 89).

What form should this response take? The Bible gives no specific answer on how to vote on abortion, housing, busing, or tax reform. Nor are there any programs or blueprints for social welfare. But one thing is clear. If we as a people of God are interested in doing justice in the prophetic style, we are asked to act as *advocates for the powerless*, lobbyists for those who have no clout in the public arena. Just as Jesus went through his ministry as both Messiah and Man for Others, so we who call ourselves Messiah's people (that is what "Christians" really means) are called to be a people for others. Our calling is to respond to the good news by acting as advocates for the powerless.

James Limburg

First Sunday after Pentecost (Trinity Sunday), Year B

First Lesson: Isaiah 6:1-8
(Psalm 29)
Second Lesson: Romans 8:12-17
Gospel Lesson: John 3:1-17

"The president is dead! John F. Kennedy has been assassinated!"
Many of us remember very well hearing those words from a newscaster in Texas, as whatever television program we were watching was interrupted for a special news bulletin. It was a crisp fall day in November. The date is permanently etched in our memories: November 22, 1963. The country's mood quickly became one of confusion, perplexity, uncertainty about the future: Was this part of a communist plot? Or did the assassin work independently? What sort of world will our children grow up in?

The sixth chapter of Isaiah also remembers the death of a powerful leader. It begins with the words "In the year that King Uzziah died. . . ." The Bible indicates that if we are going to understand the words of this chapter, we have to begin by learning something about the historical setting. What was the situation in Isaiah's Judah at the time of the death of King Uzziah, about 742 B.C.E.?

"Hear ye! King Uzziah is dead." The Uzziah years, beginning about 783 B.C.E., had been good years for Judah, marked by peace and prosperity. For a summary of the accomplishments of Uzziah, read through 2 Chronicles 26! Uzziah's long and prosperous rule was balanced by that of Jeroboam II in Israel to the north, who led that country from 786 to 746.

But then with the death of Jeroboam II, things began to unravel for Israel. There was a disastrous period of intrigues, assassinations, and finally the fall of Samaria, the capital city, to the Assyrians in 722. Judah enjoyed something of a calm before the storm under King Jotham, who succeeded Uzziah (742-735), but then experienced warfare and invasions under both Ahaz and Hezekiah (735-715, 715-687).

Behind these events was a new Assyrian empire, under the leadership of the vigorous emperor Tiglath-pileser III (745-727). He drove a powerful war machine which pushed into the west, conquering one city or country after another, until the empire stretched from Mesopotamia all the way into Egypt.

A king dies (Uzziah) and a new empire comes to life (Assyria). Up to this time, the histories of Israel and Judah had been spun out in a great power

302

vacuum, with little interference from Egypt or the powers of Mesopotamia. But now, just when Isaiah began his work, things were different. The parade of foreign rules over Jerusalem and Judah was beginning: Assyria, then Babylon, Persia, Greece, and Rome.

When they heard the crier announce "King Uzziah is dead . . . ," parents in Jerusalem must have wondered: "What kind of future will my children have?"

The call of a prophet. Chapter 6 may be divided as follows:

6:1-4   Isaiah see the Lord as the Holy One
6:5-7   Isaiah sees himself as sinful (v. 5) and then forgiven (vv. 6-7)
6:8-12   Isaiah hears a call and volunteers for a mission

6:1-4. The Song of the Seraphs. Isaiah's ordinary routine apparently included attending worship services at the temple. As he was worshiping, in the prophet's mind the smoke of the sacrifices being offered became the Lord's robe. "Seraphs" were huge winged creatures, carved on the sides of the throne in the temple. In the prophet's imagination, these creatures came to life and began praising the holiness of the Lord. "Feet" as used here is a euphemism for genitals, as in Isaiah 7:20 and Exodus 4:25.

Of central importance is the triple "holy, holy, holy." The fundamental idea of the Hebrew word translated "holy" *(qadosh)* is "separate" or "removed." The word may refer to God (Ps. 99:9) or to God's name (Pss. 99:3; 111:9) or to the place where God resides (Exod. 15:13) in heaven (Deut. 26:15). On earth, "holy" may designate a place where God has appeared (Exod. 3:5). Vessels used in worship (1 Kings 8:4) as well as the Sabbath day (Exod. 20:11) can be designated as "holy" or "separate," related to God in a special way. In modern Israel, a location with special historical religious significance is marked with a sign that says *maqom qadosh,* or "holy place."

This song contains another very important word: "glory," in Hebrew, *kabod.* The basic meaning of this word is something that is heavy or weighty, such as Moses' hands when he had to hold them up continuously (Exod. 17:12) or Absalom's hair at the time of his annual haircut ("it was *heavy* on him," 2 Sam. 14:26) or a cloud that is *thick* with rain (Exod. 19:16). The word can also have the sense of splendor or pomp (Esther 1:4; the splendor is illustrated in v. 6). The sense in this Isaiah text is that the Lord's glory is like a mighty cloud, heavy with rain, covering the earth, magnificent in its splendor.

6:5-7. Isaiah sees himself as sinful and then forgiven. "My eyes have seen the *King,*" said Isaiah. This King imagery was a typical way of speaking about

God in temple services. Psalms used in the temple speak this way: "For the LORD is a great God, / and a great *King above all gods*" (Ps. 95:3; see also 91:1; 93:1; 96:10; 97:1; 47:2, 6-8). In this visionary experience, the prophet first understands himself to be guilty, then as forgiven. But the encounter with the heavenly King does not end here. This is not some sort of religious "high" to which the prophet has attained. The religious experience is not an end in itself. There is work to be done, and the prophet is asked to be a part of that work.

6:8-13. Mission impossible? While the lectionary cuts off the text with verse 8, the remainder of the chapter must be considered to put the first eight verses in context. Isaiah is described as having a visionary and auditory experience of the Lord's "divine council," that is, a gathering of those beings surrounding the Lord in heaven and waiting to carry out the Lord's commands (see also Gen. 1:26; 1 Kings 22; Job 1:6-12; Jer. 23:18, 22).

On this occasion of his initial call to prophetic ministry, Isaiah is told in advance that he will experience failure! He will preach, but the people will not listen! There will be a 90 percent destruction in the land! But there is *some* good news. The destruction will not be total. There will be a remnant that remains.

Why did Isaiah preserve a record of his call to be a prophet? The first-person style indicates that the piece must have come from the prophet himself. This was his certificate of prophetic calling, his credentials as a prophet. He was told from the beginning that his work would not all be smooth sailing. He knew that although he might have succeeded at another vocation, he had to be a prophet. He knew that he had been called and sent, as God's messenger.

A word for our time. Here are suggested a few directions for application of the text to our own time:

1. Claus Westermann has suggested that this chapter reflects the basic pattern for Christian worship. First is the encounter with God, then the conviction of sin and the experience of forgiveness. But the worship experience is not an end in itself, as in some sort of mysticism. The text concludes with the Lord asking for a volunteer for a mission, and the prophet offers to take up that challenge (*A Thousand Years and a Day* [Philadelphia: Fortress, 1962], pp. 212-25).

2. In a sermon addressed to theological students, Paul Tillich once said: "There are many amongst us who believe within themselves that they can never become good theologians, that they could do better in almost any other realm. Yet they cannot imagine that their existence could be anything other than theological existence. Even if they had to give up theology as

their vocational work, they would never cease to ask the theological question. It would pursue them into every realm. They would be bound to it actually, if not vocationally. They could not be sure that they could fulfill its demands, but they would be sure that they were in its bondage. They who believe these things in their hearts belong to the assembly of God. They are grasped by the Divine Spirit. They have received the gift of knowledge. They are theologians" (*The Shaking of the Foundations* [New York: Scribner, 1948], p. 121).

3. In the Bible, a visionary experience is never an end in itself, but rather leads to mission. See Acts 9:3 and 9:15; 22:6-21, and note verses 10, 15, 21; Acts 26, noting the Lord's words in verses 16-18; and Paul's quotation of this passage in Acts 28:25-28.

4. Here the Lord is portrayed as holy, as "wholly other," as "high and lofty." Isaiah 55:6-9 illuminates Isaiah 6. The Lord is holy, but the Lord is also the One who stoops down to rescue a hurting people (Ps. 113), and finally to send a Savior (John 3:16; Phil. 2; the New Testament message).

James Limburg

Fifth Sunday after the Epiphany, Year C

First Lesson: Isaiah 6:1-8, (9-13)
(Psalm 138)
Second Lesson: 1 Corinthians 15:1-11
Gospel Lesson: Luke 5:1-11

This famous text follows the pattern of prophetic call narratives that is first established in the Old Testament in the calling of Moses (Exod. 3:1-12; see the first lesson [Exod. 3:1-15] for the Fifteenth Sunday after Pentecost, Year A, for further details). This pattern, outlined below, would indicate that the optional verses, 9-13, ought to be included in the lection (contrast the first lesson [Isa. 6:1-8] for the First Sunday after Pentecost [Trinity Sunday], Year B). This is further warranted by even a bipartite division of the unit into *commission* (6:1-8) and *message* (6:9-13). Messengers are, after all, commissioned with a message. However, given the precise nature of this message (see below), it is not surprising that the church has often left 6:9-13 aside!

1. *The divine confrontation (6:1-2)*. The power of Isaiah's vision, which may have taken place in the temple itself during worship (note the terms and symbolism in 6:1-4, 6) — the chapter has often been seen as an outline of true worship — should not overshadow the historical notation that at first seems out of place in this supernatural setting. Isaiah had this vision "in the year that King Uzziah died" (6:1a). The exact year is unimportant, but the event is significant nevertheless. According to Chronicles, Uzziah (called Azariah in Kings) was a good and righteous king who ruled over Judah during a very long and prosperous period (2 Chron. 26:1-15; cf. 2 Kings 14:21-22; 15:1-7). His death would invariably raise questions: What direction would the nation take? Would Uzziah's successor, his son Jotham, continue his good legacy — both religiously and politically? What if he did not? With the fate of the *kingship* in question, Isaiah has a vision of *the King*, the Lord of hosts (6:5).

And what a vision it was! Isaiah, like Micaiah ben Imlah before him (1 Kings 22:19-23) and Ezekiel (Ezek. 1:4–2:1) after him, has a vision of God in the heavenly throne room. God sits in state, on a high and lofty throne. The throne is not the only large thing: the royal robes are so massive that the bottom hem was enough to fill the temple (6:1). This gigantic God is served by fantastic creatures: the seraphim (NRSV: "seraphs") are fiery, winged creatures who were probably pictured like the winged serpents familiar in Egyptian and Syro-Palestinian art (cf. also 14:29; 30:6). (Artistic representations of such winged serpents also sometimes depict them with legs. It is thus not entirely certain that "feet" in 6:2 [covered by a pair of the seraphim's wings] should be taken as a euphemism for the pudenda.) Such creatures were typically protective, their wings outstretched to protect the deities they served. But in Isaiah's vision the seraphim must hide their own faces lest they see Yahweh (6:2)! God's power and might, therefore, are underscored throughout these opening verses.

2. *The introductory word (6:3-7)*. But this power and might is further defined in 6:3 where the seraphim sing God's praise. The Lord of hosts is holy — thrice holy (cf. Rev. 4:8) — and glorious: the whole earth can barely contain his glory. Everywhere you turn, there it is! The temple shakes with the reverberations of these praises (6:4). The whole scene is too much for Isaiah. He is immediately grasped with his own inadequacy vis-à-vis this holy God (this vision may be the origin of the epithet of God used frequently in Isaiah: "the Holy One of Israel" [see 1:4; 5:19, 24; 10:20; 12:6; 17:7; 29:19, 23;

30:11, 12, 15; 31:1; 37:23; 40:25; 41:14, 16, 20; 43:3, 14, 15; 45:11; 47:4; 48:17; 49:7 [twice]; 54:5; 55:5; 60:9, 14). Visions of pure holiness have a tendency to do that: they have a nasty habit of highlighting our own unholy sin.

Isaiah realizes this, and his "woe" indicates that his life is in danger (6:5). "I am lost" continues this theme, though the verb could be taken from a different root and translated "I am silenced." This latter option could be connected to the fact that Isaiah confesses unclean lips, the seraph cleanses his lips (6:7), and this subsequently permits him to say the message God gives him (6:9). Deciding between the two options may be unnecessary; perhaps both were intended.

Isaiah confesses his own *individual* sin ("I am a man of unclean lips"), but is equally aware of the sins of his community and his participation in that ("I live among a people of unclean lips"). Today we would call this *corporate* sin. Here is additional evidence that the prophet is not above the prophetic "law" — that is, the message that the prophet proclaims. Judgment falls on the community of God, and the prophet is the bearer of that news. As such, the prophet is also the first to feel it.

It is interesting that because of what Isaiah's *eyes* have seen, he confesses the sins of his *lips*. Momentarily his *mouth* will be cleansed and he will be able to *hear* God, who will call him to a mission involving the *hearing, sight, heart, ears,* and *eyes* of the people. Visions and missions of the Holy God involve the total person — no part is left untouched.

Isaiah may be "undone" (KJV), but God has the means to undo Isaiah's undoing. One of the seraphim — the fantastic creatures who inspired awe and fear earlier — now serves Isaiah. The seraph takes a burning coal from the altar and approaches Isaiah (6:6). It is hot enough that even a fiery seraph must use tongs to take it from the altar, but Isaiah feels its burn directly on his mouth and lips (6:7). No one said forgiveness was painless. But, while it may have been extremely painful, it was also entirely efficacious: Isaiah's iniquity is turned aside, his sin covered. He is now prepared to hear what comes next.

3. *The commission (6:8-10).* For the first time God speaks, or perhaps only now Isaiah is able to hear God, as he almost seems to come in on God in midsentence. Evidently, this august assembly has met for a reason. God seems to have a task and apparently needs some assistance with it. God seeks a messenger to commission ("Whom shall I send?"); at the same time, this individual will be a volunteer representing Yahweh and his entourage ("Who will go for us?"). Without even knowing what this mission entails, perhaps still flushed with his newfound purity and forgiveness, Isaiah inter-

rupts the Lord. He steps forward ("Here am I") and, as if this interruption wasn't enough, dares to command God ("Send me!")!

Such a response is unparalleled in the other prophetic call narratives and has won Isaiah an eternal place in homilies throughout the ages. What courage! What obedience! What sensitivity and willingness to serve! But such praise — while certainly not undeserved — should not go unqualified. One might surmise that Isaiah was given this vision for the express purpose of his commissioning. This sort of thing, after all, doesn't happen every day! If so, his volunteerism, while admirable, would not be integral, as God typically talks prophets into these tasks, no matter how they feel about it. More to the point, however, is that Isaiah doesn't yet know what he is in for. His commissioning isn't done yet. He has volunteered, and that is well and good. But the task is set forth in 6:9-10, and when Isaiah hears it, he objects like all the other prophets — attempting to get out of this task.

In one very real sense, then, 6:8 is *not* the ideal response to a calling — coming, as it does, *before* Isaiah even knows what the calling entails! (A more ideal response is found in Luke 1:26-38 where, *after* Mary learns of the things to befall her [her *mission,* as it were], she *nevertheless* responds, "Here am I, the servant of the Lord; let it be with me according to your word" [1:38]. See further the Gospel lesson [Luke 1:26-38] for the Fourth Sunday of Advent, Year B.) Still, Isaiah's eagerness — while naive — nevertheless continues to fascinate. The newly forgiven are often eager — perhaps to a fault! The trick is to teach them what must be done — including its gravity — without quenching their fire.

In this text, what must be done is more than enough to take the wind out of Isaiah's sail. The impressiveness of the vision of God is matched by the despair of the mission of God. And what a mission it was! God commands Isaiah to go with a message of futility for the people. No matter how long they listen they will not understand; no matter how long they look they simply won't get it. This is bad enough, but God is not done. The imperatives that Isaiah is to address to the people are matched and made much worse by the imperatives directed to Isaiah himself. He is to make the heart of this people fat (i.e., dull), their ears heavy, and their eyes sealed over (i.e., unable to hear or see) *with the express purpose* that they *will not* be able to see with those sealed-up eyes, hear with those heavy ears, or understand with those insensitive hearts. Still worse is the fact that this blindness, deafness, and ignorance is *divinely willed* so as to *prevent* the people from turning and being healed! God doesn't want these people turning back, doesn't want their healing. Indeed, God wills their unhealing (Walter Brueggemann, *Isaiah Volume 1:1–39,* Westminster Bible Companion [Louisville:

Westminster John Knox, 1998], p. 61: "God wills an unhealed people! This is not what we might expect, but of course prophetic assertion is most often not what is expected. This is indeed a countermessage, countering official religious assumption that God always wills good").

Surely this is one of the many "hard sayings" in Scripture. Its difficulty did not stop the early church from drawing on it numerous times in the New Testament (Matt. 13:10-17; Mark 4:10-12; Luke 8:9-10; John 12:37-43; Acts 28:17-28). Each of these passages deserves attention; they should not be simplistically lumped together or categorically explained. Still, perhaps Brueggemann is on the right track when he writes that in such sayings it is clear "that the purposes of God are at work in the midst of severe human obduracy" (Brueggemann, p. 63). More will be said on the Isaianic passage below.

4. *The objection (6:11a).* Isaiah, having realized what he has gotten himself into, now interjects again: "How long, O Lord?" Thus, like the other prophets before him and after him who are called in this fashion, Isaiah objects to this call. The expression "how long?" is often indignant in tone (see Exod. 10:3, 7; Num. 14:27; 1 Sam. 16:1; 2 Sam. 2:26). It is, moreover, similar to lament phraseology (cf. Ps. 13). "How long," therefore, carries with it connotations of torment and impatience. These speakers are not politely inquiring about the duration of the task. Rather, they want release from their situation. Isaiah's earlier rush to be a part of God's plan was — quite literally — a rush to judgment: God's judgment. He now realizes that he was rash. Now that he knows the details of that plan, he wants no part of it.

5. *The reassurance (6:11b-13).* Though the element that follows the objection in the call narrative form has been termed "the reassurance," one might well wonder if it is misnamed in the case of Isaiah 6! God responds to Isaiah's "How long" (Heb. *'ad matah*) with an "until" (Heb. *'ad 'asher*) that governs the rest of verse 11 and verse 12. That "until" is bleak: *until* cities lie waste without inhabitants, *until* houses are similarly abandoned, *until* the land is utterly desolate, *until* Yahweh sends everyone far away, *until* the emptiness is vast in the midst of the land. *Until,* that is, the end. There is not much reassurance here! If Isaiah hoped for a respite from his task, he will get none. Or, to be more exact, he will get one but it will be a grim one: it will come when the end has come, when everyone and everything — city, house, person — has a respite, when all of this rests . . . in peace!

Even so, there *is* a limit on this judgment. Isaiah won't have to preach doom forever. There will be an end to this end. While hardly "good news," this is at least an indication that this somber and serious task to which Isaiah is called is divinely delimited. It should also be noted that while the

309

commission in 6:9-10 was full of imperatives to Isaiah, delineating what he was to do and say, Yahweh now takes responsibility in 6:11-13, particularly in the explicit mention of Yahweh's activity in 6:12. This dark task which lies heavily on Isaiah's shoulders will not be shouldered only by him. To be sure, this is a bitter "reassurance," but it may nevertheless confirm and affirm the prophet in some significant ways.

A final glimmer of relief and hope might also be seen in 6:13b, though the whole verse is quite difficult and uncertain in the Hebrew (see the textual note to NRSV). The sense of the verse seems clear, though, even if the details are not. This hope, too, is muted and is a costly one. It comes only after 6:13a, which promises that even if there is a remnant — a tenth left over — it will again be burned. All that will be left of the magnificent oak will be the eyesore of a stump. But even stumps can sprout shoots! And this new growth is "the holy seed" — the hope of a purified remnant (note the glimpses of hope in 2:1-4; 4:2-6; 7:3 [Shear-Jashub means "a remnant shall return"], 10-25), cleansed of its sins (cf. 1:2-20) — like Isaiah himself! — and ready, like him, to carry out a mission: to be God's people and a light to the nations (see 5:1-7; 42:6; 49:6). Perhaps that is the reason for felling this tree in the first place, and for the calling of this prophet . . . to obtain the seed.

Brent A. Strawn

Fourth Sunday of Advent, Year A

First Lesson: Isaiah 7:10-16
(Psalm 80:1-7, 17-19)
Second Lesson: Romans 1:1-7
Gospel Lesson: Matthew 1:18-25

If a preacher uses this text simply as a prophecy of the virgin birth of Jesus Christ and jumps immediately from Isaiah to Matthew, the preacher will have missed the vast sweep and import of the text. This is a text that has to do with international relations, with kings jockeying for power and armies clashing and the lordship of God over all nations. It is but one section of the prophecies collected together in Isaiah 7:1 through 8:22, and the term "Immanuel" occurs again in 8:8, 10. What is going on here?

We have to start with 7:1-9, which immediately precedes our passage. When Tiglath-pileser III rose to power over the empire of Assyria in 745 B.C., he began systematically swallowing up the small states west of the Euphrates in order to gain access to Egypt, to southwestern Asia Minor, and to Mediterranean commerce. Syria and the northern kingdom of Israel stood in his path. Their kings, Rezin of Damascus and Pekah ben Remaliah (737-732), formed a military coalition in order to turn back the Assyrian tide and wanted Judah to join them, but Ahaz of Judah (735-715), who had only recently ascended to Judah's throne, refused. Rezin and Pekah therefore gathered their armies and marched on Judah, intending to put a puppet named Tabeel on Judah's throne. They closed in on Jerusalem from the north (2 Kings 16:5). At the same time, Edom to the south regained its freedom from Judah, and the Philistines mounted attacks from Judah's west, conquering towns in the lowlands and the desert. Judah was thus attacked from three sides.

It is at this point that Isaiah 7 begins. King Ahaz is outside the walls of Jerusalem, inspecting access to the city's water supply, because Jerusalem had no natural spring inside its walls and water was carried by aqueduct from the spring of Gihon. In the remarkable verse 3, the Lord gives the prophet Isaiah highway directions in order to find Ahaz — how specific is the Lord! And the word of the Lord that Isaiah carries is that Ahaz should not fear or let his heart faint before the onslaught of Rezin and Pekah. After all, they are just men, "smoldering stumps of firebrands" (v. 4), who will soon be extinguished, whereas the Lord God is the defender of Jerusalem, and he has given his promise that the Davidic throne, of which Ahaz is heir, will be established forever (cf. 2 Sam. 7:13; 23:5). If Ahaz will trust that promise and rely on the Lord's protection — if he will believe — he will be established. Such is Isaiah's foreign policy. But if Ahaz will not believe, his kingdom will fall to Assyria.

The prophet Isaiah, we must understand, knows that the course of nations is finally determined by God. Assyria, Isaiah 10:5 tells us, is the "rod" of the Lord's anger and the "staff" of his fury, and the Lord is using that great empire to carry out his divine will. Therefore, Ahaz should trust the Lord, who holds the fate of nations in his hands.

Now our text for the morning begins. In order to guarantee the truth of the word that he has delivered from the Lord, Isaiah even promises to give Ahaz a visible sign. Ahaz can ask for anything possible or impossible. But Ahaz demurs. He has already summoned Assyria to come to his aid, and so he piously replies, in accordance with the law of Deuteronomy 6:16, that he will not put the Lord to the test. Nevertheless, the Lord will give Ahaz a sign. A young woman will bear a son and call his name Immanuel, which means "God with us" (v. 14), and before the child is old enough to eat solid food, Syria and Israel will be destroyed by Assyria (vv. 15-16).

Jewish interpretations of verse 14 read it in the present tense: "A young woman has conceived." But all scholars, except for the most conservative, agree that the Hebrew word for "young woman" is not the term for a "virgin." That reading of the verse comes only from the Greek version (the Septuagint) of the Old Testament, although that is the reading that Matthew 1:23 adopts in order to view the birth of Christ as the fulfillment of the Isaiah prophecy. That is not really an invalid use of the Isaiah text, because "God with us" is used in a messianic sense in Isaiah 8:10, leading up to the messianic prophecy in 9:1-7.

In the original Hebrew, however, it is clear that only a young woman of marriageable age is intended. It is also most likely that the young woman is known to both Ahaz and Isaiah. She may be the wife of Ahaz, or of the prophet himself (cf. 8:3). As in 8:3, Isaiah gives to his children names full of meaning (cf. Hosea's names for his children, Hos. 1:4, 6, 8, a prophetic practice). But it is the designation of the child as "Immanuel" that is to serve as a sign for Ahaz.

In the passages that follow our text, the name Immanuel is shown not necessarily to be comforting. In 8:8 Judah, the land of Immanuel, will be flooded by the waters of Assyria, in the judgment of the Lord upon it for its injustices (cf. 10:1-2). In 8:9-10, however, the defeat of Assyria is promised because God is with Judah. Immanuel, the sign of God with us, can signal either judgment or salvation.

That is true also for us, is it not? We always interpret "God with us" as a comforting word, assuring us of the love, the forgiveness, the mercy of the child born at Bethlehem. That is the predominant note of our Christmas celebrations. Indeed, sometimes we very glibly and pridefully believe that God is with us, on our side, always ready to bale us out of any difficulty in which we find ourselves. But have we really stopped to consider what it means that God is with us in Jesus Christ? Can your life stand up to the scrutiny of the Lord? Can mine? Is our society as full of injustice and faithlessness as was Judah's? And do we expect that God-with-us overlooks all of that? In the Gospel according to Luke, Simeon, inspired by the Holy Spirit, prophesies that the child Jesus is "set for the fall and rising of many" (Luke 2:34). And so, does God-with-us come to us as our promise of rising? Or of falling? Certainly Judah, in the time of Isaiah, was set for fall.

312

In this season of Advent, perhaps if we ponder all of that, we shall be better prepared to approach the manger at Bethlehem, for we can truly receive the birth of Immanuel, not in glib assurance of our own righteousness and faithfulness, but only in the humility of those who know that they have no plea before a God who is pure righteousness and who does not countenance the persistence of sin among his people. We can truly receive the birth of Immanuel only with the prayer of "Lord, be merciful to me a sinner," undeserving of any grace of forgiveness and yet offered it in full measure by a God of love.

But that takes faith, does it not, the same faith to which Isaiah called King Ahaz in the eighth century B.C.? Later, in 30:15, our prophet tells another king, "In returning and rest you shall be saved; in quietness and in trust shall be your strength." That is the heart of Isaiah's message to his people, and that is also the principal word of God that comes to us from our text for the morning. Trust. Trust in the promise and lordship of God. If we will believe, we shall be established.

That trust is to embody reliance on our Lord not only in our own individual situations, however. When Isaiah calls for trust from Ahaz, he is dealing with empires and international relations and military conquests. He is calling for trust in a world where armies are clashing and national fortunes are at stake, and we know all about such a world, don't we? We too live in a time of international tensions and disputes, and so often we think that only the politicians and multinational corporations and military are in charge. But the God of the prophets is bigger than that, and the God of Israel, who is also the Father of our Lord Jesus Christ, is the Lord over all empires and peoples. That revelation is one of the principal gifts that the prophetic preaching brings to us. God is in charge of all history and all nature. And so despite the turbulence of our times, or of any time, the people of faith know that earth's petty powers will never have the last word. After all, Jesus Christ was born when Caesar Augustus ruled, and Caesar is now dead, but Jesus Christ lives. We celebrate at this Christmastime the birth of the King of kings and Lord of lords. And we are called to trust him.

Elizabeth Achtemeier

Third Sunday after the Epiphany, Year A

First Lesson: Isaiah 9:1-4
(Psalm 27:1, 4-9)
Second Lesson: 1 Corinthians 1:10-18
Gospel Lesson: Matthew 4:12-23

*H*istorical and literary background. The chapter division is notoriously difficult here; Isaiah 9:1 in the English Bible is 8:23 in the Hebrew text. In some ways the English division is helpful, as the shift from gloom to glory seems to form the major turning point at the end of chapter 8. The preceding section includes the so-called Book of Immanuel (chaps. 7–8), where the sign of the Immanuel child was largely a word of judgment against the lack of faith on the part of King Ahaz (7:9, 17-25; 8:5-8).

Yet there is a positive word as well. The series of texts that directly speak to the meaning of "God with us" close with a final assertion that man may propose but that God will dispose (8:9-10). Thereafter, however, the rest of chapter 8 takes a turn for the worse. Isaiah seems to go away in a bit of a God-directed huff to wait on the Lord and to leave the people to their own impending doom. Words of doom and gloom are piled upon one another in 8:22.

Against that backdrop, the expectation that darkness will turn to light is striking. Further, assuming some connection between the Immanuel child and the announcement of a scion to the Davidic throne (9:7), the text that now follows in chapter 9 moves the message of the royal child forward from judgment to promise and hope. In Isaiah's own day, confidence in the Davidic king was certainly called into question by the faithlessness of King Ahaz in the face of the Syro-Ephraimite threat, which in turn was a response to the rising power of the neo-Assyrian empire in the second half of the eighth century. There was no doubt much uncertainty as to whether the house and lineage of David would stand or fall, and the central message of the text in 9:1-4 (concluding in v. 7) is clearly an affirmation of God's commitment to the Davidic line.

Textual notes. The lectionary has limited this text only to the initial verses, stopping short of the clear references to the throne of David. What is intriguing in the text is that these initial verses focus not on the Davidic throne in Judah but on the northern territories of Galilee. In fact, the region highlighted is not simply the northern kingdom but the northern fringes of the northern kingdom Israel, which would be the first to experience the onslaught of foreign invasion (especially the inevitable "foe from the north," as Jeremiah would put it). It may well be that the threefold citation of geographical regions at the end of the verse is a reference to the territories already lost to Assyria at the time of the Syro-Ephraimite war. The point made is not simply that light would follow darkness but especially that the light would come first to those who know the deepest darkness, and that the first to fall in gloom will be the first to rise in glory. This observation is certainly not lost to the Gospel of Matthew in noting the significance that Jesus began his ministry in these very Galilean regions.

A further theme may actually be a subtle corrective against the Davidic monarchy at least of Isaiah's day. As this text describes the joy and victory of the premonarchic period, both by its citation of the old tribal territories and by referencing the day of Midian (Judg. 8), it alludes to a time when Israel was more directly under Yahweh's leadership. At the time of the rise of the monarchy, the dangers of kingship were well noted, with the greatest concern "that they have rejected *me* as their king" (1 Sam. 8:7). So it would be with a kingship "like the nations," which would inevitably not be the kingdom of God. That any glorious future in Isaiah's day might lie with a recapitulation of the days *before* the rise of the monarchy may well have served as a reminder that the house of David was subject to Yahweh's judgment like any other king "like the nations."

At the same time, the confirmation of God's faithfulness to the throne of David at the end of this pericope would suggest that the reference to the northern territories is an assurance that the promise to David is a promise once again to all Israel, as before the kingdom was divided. This is consistent with prophetic words of restitution that envision the future as a time when Israel and Judah would be reunited as one common people under Yahweh.

Textually, there are several translational problems. Two broken construct chains, both interrupted by the preposition "in," are striking and odd ("dwellers of *in* a land of darkness" in 9:2b, Hebrew 9:1b, and the phrase "like the joy of *in* the harvest" in 9:3b, Hebrew 9:2b). The noun *ṣalmawet* in 9:2b (Hebrew 9:1b) is really not the compound noun "shadow of death" as previously thought (cf. also Ps. 23:4), but a form of the noun "shadow" with an intensifying suffix, "deepest darkest shadow." Finally, the opening line of 9:3 (Hebrew 9:2) is a text-critical crux. The negative *(lō')* is amended to the prepositional phrase "to him" *(lô)* by the Masoretes, although it is quite probable that the form is simply a textual corruption for the noun *haggilah*, which would form excellent parallelism with the entire rest of the verse: "you have multiplied the joy, you have magnified the gladness."

If verse 9 is a recollection of the victory of Gideon over Midian, then the second half of the verse may well include an allusion to the deliverance from Egyptian bondage, since the word "oppressor" *(nogesh)* is the same participle used somewhat distinctively for the Egyptian taskmasters. The point, however, is that the strife is over, the battle won, even though the image is one of a bloody battlefield left for the burning of loot and garments.

Homiletical application. The text essentially makes two assertions: darkness will be turned to light, and this divine enlightenment will begin in the most unlikely place: Galilee of the Gentiles. That the Gospel of Matthew recognizes these words as fulfilled in the early ministry of Jesus of Nazareth is precisely the point of this Epiphany proclamation. God's light has come into the world, but in a most unlikely place and fashion.

Nevertheless, even as the text seems to move from Galilee to Jerusalem, so the very life and ministry of Jesus moves from his early ministry in Galilee to when he sets his face for Jerusalem. There it is his mission to fulfill the ultimate destiny of the house of David as a king who came, not like the nations, and not as one to be served, but as one who would serve and even give his life as a ransom. Darkness leads to light, but first the Epiphany light must lead to the darkness of the Lenten journey to the cross. But that, too, is not the end of the story. In the latter time (the "end of the story"), those living in darkness will have seen a great light!

Andrew H. Bartelt

Nativity of the Lord (Christmas Day), Years A, B, C

First Lesson: Isaiah 9:2-7
(Psalm 96)
Second Lesson: Titus 2:11-14
Gospel Lesson: Luke 2:1-14, (15-20)

The chief exegetical problem in dealing with this text from Isaiah 9, one could observe, is the violins. That is to say, who can read through verse 6 without hearing the violins in Handel's *Messiah* striking up the introduction to "For unto us a child is born . . ."? That oratorio has been a good part of the reason why these words from the ninth chapter of Isaiah are among the most well known in the entire Bible.

The lectionary marks off the reading as 9:2-7, but in order to understand this text one ought also consider 8:21–9:1 as part of the unit. The piece then divides as follows:

8:21-22 Distress and darkness
9:1-7   Salvation and light
    9:1-3   Past sorrow and future joy
    9:4-7   Reasons for that future joy

Gloom and anguish, distress and darkness (8:21-22). A grasp of the historical **A** situation lying behind this prophetic saying as described in Isaiah 7 provides the clue for understanding it. Isaiah 7 tells the story of Syria and Israel attacking Judah in 735 B.C.E. King Rezin of Aram (Syria) and King Pekah of Israel were trying to force King Ahaz of Judah to join in an anti-Assyrian coalition. When Ahaz refused, Rezin and Pekah came down with their armies from the north, seeking to force Judah to join in. When Ahaz heard of this coming invasion, he was scared to death (7:2).

At this time the prophet Isaiah, taking his son along, went to meet Ahaz. He told him to trust in the Lord, who would not allow Jerusalem to be taken (vv. 4-9).

But Ahaz did not trust in the Lord. He preferred, rather, to trust in Assyrian artillery, and asked the Assyrians for help against Syria and Israel (2 Kings 16:5-9). In response, the Assyrians marched westward and soon captured Damascus, the capital of Syria (in 732), and continued southward into Israel, finally capturing Samaria in 722 (2 Kings 17).

The words in Isaiah 8:21-22 describe the situation of those people in the northern kingdom, Israel, who had experienced the ravages of the Assyrian war machine as it moved through their territory toward Samaria and eventually Jerusalem. These citizens of Israel are described as distressed, hungry, enraged, and cursing both "their king and their God" (RSV). They look about them and see only gloom, distress, anguish, and thick darkness. The prophet's words which follow in chapter 9 now address these discouraged, broken people.

Joy and celebration, peace and justice (9:1-7).

9:1-3. The words here are concerned with the territories of Zebulun and **B¹** Naphtali, territories to the north and west of the Sea of Galilee. These territories were precisely in the path the Assyrian armies had taken as they marched from Damascus toward Samaria and Jerusalem. These were the people who had taken the brunt of the Assyrian invasion.

In verse 1 the prophet sets up a series of contrasts, the "former time" referring to the prophet's present, and the "latter time" referring to the future. One could sketch a chart with two columns labeled *Present* ("former time") and *Future* ("latter time"). In the present time, says the prophet, the territories in the north, the ancient tribal holdings of Zebulun and Naphtali, have been humbled (NIV) by the invading armies. In the future they will be made "glorious" (NRSV) and experience "honor" (NIV).

The contrasts continue. The prophet uses a device in Hebrew called the "prophetic perfect," which refers to the future and can better be translated as "The people who walked in darkness will see a great light. . . ." More contrasts follow, with the present "deep darkness" contrasted with the future "light has shined" (v. 2).

Verse 3 is all about future joy, now set in contrast to the gloom, anguish, and deep darkness of the present time. The prophet uses pictures to illustrate the sort of joy that can be expected. Those who have experienced life on a farm or in an agricultural setting will understand the reference to the kind of joy that one experiences at harvest time (see also Pss. 4:7; 65:13; 126:6). Any persons who remember the celebrations by the Allies after the end of World War II, or who have seen films of such celebrations, will understand the prophet's second illustration. This refers to the joy that accompanies a victory, when the things captured from the enemy are divided up (see also Ps. 119:162; Prov. 16:19).

9:5-7. The prophet expresses reasons for this future joy in three statements, each beginning with "for." First, the oppression of the cruel Assyrians will be broken. That oppressive power of these cruel conquerors is pictured as a yoke on the necks of the people, like the sort of yoke one puts on oxen. Or that oppression is described as a rod, of the type that a slave owner would use to beat a slave. The prophet assumes that his hearers are familiar with the great stories of God's works of deliverance in the past. Here he refers to the Lord's deliverance from the oppression of the Midianites; under the leadership of Gideon, the Israelites used a select army and devices of psychological warfare (torches, trumpets) to defeat them (Judg. 7:15-25).

A second reason for joy is the fact that the war will be over. The battlefields will be cleaned up and all the military equipment burned (v. 5).

The final reason for joy is again introduced by "for" (v. 6) and continues through verse 7. Its position as third in the series, and its length, clearly indicate that here is the climax, the major reason for this promised future joy.

It all has to due with the birth of a son. While some have understood this as referring to a king taking a throne as God's son (see Ps. 2:7), it seems that here the reference is to the birth of an actual child. This promise then links up with the promised birth in Isaiah 7:10-17 (see especially 7:14). The child will grow up to be a great king, whose rule is described in verses 6b-7. This is a king from the line of David (v. 7) who will be especially concerned for the establishment of justice and righteousness, qualities the prophet saw as woefully lacking in his own day (Isa. 1:16-17, 21-26; 5:1-7; 10:1-4, for example). This king will be a "Prince of Peace" (v. 6) who will bring about peace among his people (see also Ps. 72:3, 7). This peace will in fact be endless (v. 7). The "expectation of peace" theme is further expanded in Isaiah 2:1-5 and 11:1-9. This will be a superking, whose authority and kingdom will continually expand and who will in fact rule forever (v. 7)!

Hope for a Messiah. In expressing these extravagant promises regarding the coming Davidic ruler, the prophet is saying nothing new. He is taking up the themes expressed in the Royal Psalms from the days of King David. These were psalms designed to play a role in the life of the king, such as a king's wedding (Ps. 45), or a coronation (2; 72; 101), or a time before battle (20). After the monarchy, when there were no more kings, they projected into the future a portrait of an ideal king to come.

Isaiah attended worship services in the Jerusalem temple (Isa. 6!) and knew these psalms well. They became a seedbed for messianic hope. The picture that these psalms painted of a coming ruler became a portrait of a future "anointed one" or, in Hebrew, Messiah. Gerhard von Rad wrote in his *Old Testament Theology:* "It was therefore a magnificent purple robe which the royal psalms laid on the shoulders of the young successors of David at their accession."

But king after king proved a disappointment, unworthy of that magnificent garment. Thus that robe awaited another, of whom it would be said, in the language of these psalms, "You are the Messiah, the Son of the living God" (Matt. 16:16).

The Messiah has come. Perhaps the best commentary on Isaiah 9 is to be found in the oratorio *Messiah* by George Frideric Handel. He captured the drama of the text with the shift from the dark, minor mode of 9:2 ("The people that walked in darkness," Air for Bass, #11) to the major key of 9:6 ("For unto us a child is born," Chorus, #12).

It is the conviction of the New Testament that these ancient promises about a coming Messiah find their fulfillment in the person of Jesus of Nazareth. Matthew sees the work of Jesus which began in the territory of Zebulon and Naphtali as the fulfillment of the promise in Isaiah 9 (Matt.

319

4:12-17). Luke records the promise of a child made to Mary, a promise using the language of Isaiah 9 (Luke 1:26-35; 2:11). Matthew, Mark, and Luke all report the incident at Caesarea Philippi, where Peter confessed Jesus of Nazareth to be the Messiah (Matt. 16:13-20; Mark 8:27-30; Luke 9:18-20).

James Limburg

Second Sunday of Advent, Year A

First Lesson: Isaiah 11:1-10
(Psalm 72:1-7, 18-19)
Second Lesson: Romans 15:4-13
Gospel Lesson: Matthew 3:1-12

Historical and literary background. The winds of change and uncertainty blew across the Middle East in the second half of the eighth century like a hot, desert wind. After a half-century of peace and prosperity, the rise of Assyria under Tiglath-pileser III had destabilized the entire region and brought all nations under the threat of Assyrian dominance. Unlike their predecessors, Assyria no longer built empires simply by international extortion. Their mode of conquest sought to destroy the very infrastructure of society and culture, which is what happened to the northern kingdom Israel in 722.

The situation in Judah proved no less perilous, and the future of the Davidic dynasty seemed much more precarious. Isaiah's prophetic ministry seems to have begun in "the year in which King Uzziah died" (6:1), after a long and prosperous reign. The economic boom in the middle of this eighth century is reflected in the earlier chapters of this first major section of the book of Isaiah (1:11; 2:7; 3:18; 5:8-23). However, even with Uzziah's son Jotham already in place as co-regent, the "house and lineage of David" would face at least two generations of decline and uncertainty. Threatened by a coalition of Israel and Syria to join their defensive alliance against the rising power of Assyria, Ahaz actually became a vassal of the dreaded and pagan enemy Assyria (2 Kings 16:7; Isa. 7–8).

This insecurity which now characterized the throne of David, threatened both from without and from within, stands as a powerful backdrop to Isaiah's words in chapter 11. Against both the threat of foreign nations and the timidity of the Davidic king, Isaiah has already offered words of divine comfort, assurance, and promise. Concerning the nations, Isaiah has asserted that they stand under the ultimate power and control of Yahweh, the God (and true King) of Jerusalem. In the "latter days" (i.e., the eschatological future), the nations will even flow (uphill!) to Zion, there to be instructed in Torah and the word of Yahweh (2:2-4). Even mighty Assyria lies under the control of Yahweh, first as a rod of angry discipline against God's own people Judah (10:5) and then under God's direct wrath and judgment for Assyria's arrogance and asserted independence (10:12-15).

Concerning the future of the Davidic dynasty, Isaiah has already been reminded that the kingdom of David is really the kingdom of God, and that the true king is alive and well, seated on the heavenly throne even as he touches his earthly kingdom in the temple throne room (6:1). The earthly Davidic king rules only at the good pleasure of this heavenly king, yet Yahweh's promise of 2 Samuel 7 (vv. 12-16) remains in force. In spite of words of judgment and punishment even against the house of David (Isa. 7:18-25; 8:6-8), the literary unit of Isaiah 2–12 concludes with words of promise and security, of a future and a hope. Assuming that the Immanuel child is, in fact, a Davidic scion (although the identity of the child is much debated in the commentaries), the birth (or coronation) of the royal child in 9:1-6 and now the powerful words of hope in chapter 11 all indicate Yahweh's faithfulness to the Davidic kingdom over which he himself remains as king.

Textual notes. Even if cut down, the family tree of the house of David will retain life in its roots, sending out a shoot from the "stump" of Jesse (cf. 6:13). It may be that the reference to Jesse is simply an allusion to the family tree, but it may also suggest that the hope of the Davidic line does not lie simply in another son of David but in a "radical" return to the very roots of the family, to a new and second David. The central theme of this entire text speaks not just of a restoration of a righteous and faithful David in contrast to the faithless Ahaz (7:9b), but rather of a much more glorious day and a kingdom described in terms of perfect righteousness, justice, faithfulness, and peace. In terms of biblical theology, this is the eschatological new age, announced both by John the Baptist and then by Jesus himself in their inaugural proclamation that "the kingdom of God is at hand."

At the time of Isaiah, these words stood in sharp contrast to the realities of the kingdom as they knew it. Hopes for a utopian kingdom may well have accompanied every royal birth and coronation, but they were probably dashed rather quickly (perhaps within the "first hundred days" of his tenure!) by the realities of yet another self-serving human king. Even the Davidic kings were all too often much more "like the nations" than an under shepherd/king to the great and good shepherd/king who was Yahweh himself (Ps. 23:1).

Verse 2 speaks of the "resting" (Hebrew verb *nuaḥ*) of the spirit of Yahweh *(ruaḥ yhwh),* who brings three pairs of "spiritual gifts" (like the three pairs of wings on each seraph in chap. 6). The first pair deals with discernment for good governance (wisdom and understanding), the second pair with the authority to rule (counsel and might). The third pair is grammatically different, two nouns in the construct state, both bound to the divine name Yahweh, who likely extends grammatically to be understood as the source of all the gifts.

Verse 3a is a crux of translation. In form the verb is a hiphil infinitive construct of the verbal root *riaḥ.* The verb means "to smell," usually used in the sense of God's smelling the "sweet savor" of a proper sacrifice. Derivatively, this could lead to the traditional translation that "he will delight in the fear of Yahweh." On the other hand, it may be that Isaiah has actually generated a hiphil verb form of the noun *ruaḥ* (which would then make seven uses of this vocable within the chapter), here as the "seventh gift" of the spirit. If the suffix is subjective, one could translate, "he will 'in-spirit' [him] in the fear of Yahweh." In any case, the series concludes with the focus on a proper "fear" of Yahweh, which is biblical idiom for a true understanding of Yahwistic faith.

Verses 4-5 speak to the full and proper completion of the royal job description, to do "justice and righteousness" *(mishpaṭ* and *ṣedaqah).* This entailed a concern for the needy, poor, and other disenfranchised and vulnerable persons within the people of God at the same time that the king was to execute justice against the wicked. The theme is the same as that with which this larger section began in 2:2-4, where Yahweh himself would serve as judge between the nations.

Verses 6-8 describe the eschatological reign of peace, what could rightly be called "Paradise Restored," consummated in the new heavens and a new earth (Isa. 65:17ff.; Rev. 21) but inaugurated with the messianic age and the proclamation that "the kingdom of God has come." (The notation in Mark 1:12 that Jesus was with the wild animals under the power of the Spirit at the time of his temptation may well be an allusion to this text.)

Verse 9 locates this earthly restoration of paradise on the holy mountain of God, which is the royal city and temple not so much of the Davidic king as of Yahweh himself. Yet while located in the temple, this sacred and special place of peace is intended to be for all nations, including even the dreaded Assyrians. On "that (eschatological) day," this root of Jesse will stand as an "ensign" *(nes)* for the peoples; the nations will see the banner and rally to Zion (cf. 2:3). The promise of a new and ultimate David will result in a resting place that is not just "glorious" but a place of God's glory itself (the Hebrew word *kabod* is the noun, not the adjective). Yahweh's "holiness" and his "glory," located in the earthly temple (6:3), now stand as a rallying point for all the nations, even as God's glory moves out to fill all the earth so that it will be proclaimed among the nations (66:19-21).

The same theme continues through the rest of chapter 11 as Adonai reclaims the remnant and restores them to Zion by means of his holy highway back from Assyria, as from Egypt, and from wherever the Diaspora may be found.

Homiletical application. The text clearly speaks words of hope and promise to the people of God at a time when they were threatened by hostile forces from without and by fear and faithlessness from within. Such characteristics are hardly unique to the people of God in the latter half of the eighth century B.C. As an Advent text, the lectionary makes the christological connection to the person and work of Jesus the Christ, the greater and final David who came both as David's son and David's lord. With his advent the kingdom of God has indeed come, even as it continues to come whenever the Word of Yahweh goes forth among the nations. In Christ, the righteous rule and reign of God has come to earth in a kingdom yet "not of this world" and certainly not "like the nations." A restoration of God's perfect peace and the privilege of unclean sinners standing on God's holy mountain come only through atonement and forgiveness of sins (cf. Isa. 6:5-7), accomplished once for all by God's new David, a king who came not to be served but to serve and to give his life as a ransom.

Andrew H. Bartelt

Third Sunday of Advent, Year A

First Lesson: Isaiah 35:1-10
(Psalm 146:5-10)
Second Lesson: James 5:7-10
Gospel Lesson: Matthew 11:2-11

*H*istorical and literary background. Isaiah 34 and 35 form parallel (though antithetical) pieces: judgment, curse, and bane against the nations and specifically Edom in chapter 34; blessing, promise, and restoration for the redeemed and ransomed of Yahweh in chapter 35. The position and role of these chapters within the final form of the book of Isaiah are debated in the commentaries. It was long assumed that they formed an eschatological conclusion to so-called First Isaiah, but more recent scholarship has suggested that the book divides after chapter 33, with chapters 34 and 35 forming the introduction (or at least transition) to chapters 40ff. Clearly the connection of the holy highway in chapter 35 (for the people of Yahweh) is related to the royal highway (for Yahweh himself) in chapter 40 (cf. 62:10-12, where both Yahweh and his people come home on the highway).

What is clear is that Isaiah 34–35, somewhat like Isaiah 11 (last Sunday's lesson), continue the focus on the final and eschatological day of both judgment and salvation. In 34:8 the day of the Lord is proclaimed as a time of retribution for Zion and for judgment and destruction against Edom as an archetype of all those opposed to the kingdom of God and his righteous rule on earth. Chapter 35 does not speak specifically of the new creation, but it is clear that the imagery suggests a transformation of nature from its time of groaning (cf. Rom. 8:20-22) into a time of rejoicing.

God's Old Testament people, whether in the eighth century or the sixth, before, during, or after the Babylonian exile, certainly lived between the polarities of hope and despair. With every new king, Davidic hopes were likely raised anew. With the end of the Davidic kingship and the exile to Babylon, such hopes seemed dashed once and for all. The return from Babylon, to which both chapters 35 and 40ff. speak powerfully, no doubt raised hopes and joyful anticipation anew, but they were lowered again and again by unfulfilled expectations and unrealized eschatology. This sense of waiting, whether before, during, or after the proclamation that "your God will come," is a major theme of the Advent season. Heightened expectation that God will come is as much a part of New Testament proclamation as it was of Old.

Textual notes. Verses 1-2: It is one thing for hopeless people to rejoice; it

324

is remarkable indeed for nature to be transformed from desert into marsh-lands, from desolation into rejoicing. The God who was coming, however, is the creator God who "has measured the waters in the hollow of his hand" (40:12) and to whom his creation responds. The poetic lines are well crafted here, although there is no compelling reason to move the final word of verse 1 ("like the crocus") into the second line simply for metrical uniformity. Words for joy and gladness are multiplied, and the "glory" *(kabod)* of Leba-non, which stands as a symbol of the greatest expression of natural beauty, is surpassed by the "glory" of Yahweh, even as the "splendor of Carmel" is surpassed by the "splendor of our God." In chapter 40 "all flesh" will see the glory of Yahweh; here in chapter 35 it is the creation, not just the creatures.

Verses 3-4: Yet the restoration goes beyond nature to its effects on God's special creatures whose hands are feeble and knees unsteady, and whose hearts are "hurried" (a more literal rendering of the Hebrew). The impera-tives are plural, presumably addressed to the same people as 40:1, who are told to "comfort my people." Ironically, the imperatives may well be directed to the same nations who are addressed in 34:1, in which case the nations who were to bring judgment and destruction (cf. Assyria and Babylon) would now be God's agents to bring restoration and renewal. More tradi-tionally, it is assumed that these commands are addressed either to the di-vine council and heavenly messengers or to the prophets themselves.

In any case, the reason to exhort God's people "to be strong and do not fear" is that "your God will come." "Vengeance" and "recompense" are not the most felicitous translations, as both Hebrew words, *naqam* and *gemul*, in-dicate justice and the proper work of God to do (and accomplish) what is good and right, including vindication for his people.

Again, the poetic lines are well crafted. Verses 4b and c are exactly paral-lel with a weaving together of linear and chiastic parallelism (*hinneh//hu'*, chiastic; *'elohekem//'elohim*, linear; *naqam//gemul*, chiastic; *yabo'//yabo'*, lin-ear). What is noteworthy is that the final word (*weyosha'akem*) is left hang-ing at the end of verse 4c, almost as a final statement in and of itself. The nonconsecutive use of *waw* may indicate either a strong indicative state-ment or possibly a purpose clause; "he will come, and he will save you" or "he will come so that he may save you."

Verses 5-7: the use of "then" (*'az*) seems emphatic (and repeated at the beginning of v. 6). This restoration of full health and wholeness (cf. the bib-lical concept of shalom as peace and wholeness) will happen *then*. The trans-formation and restoration of human health shifts back to the restoration of nature itself, as deserts turn into marshlands and hot burning sand be-comes a pool and bubbling springs.

Verses 8-10: Finally, the text turns to the holy highway now no longer defiled by anyone unclean or endangered by wild beasts. In the context of the Old Testament history, this is the highway back from exile, the second exodus through the wilderness, which, as also in 40:3-5, will be much more a superhighway than a circuitous way of wandering as was the first exodus. Presumably there will be no unclean or fools upon this road because all of the people of God will have been cleansed and sanctified by Yahweh's redemptive presence (v. 4).

This holy processional returns to Zion with singing and with joy. The vocabulary forms an *inclusio* with verse 1, with the addition of the wonderful phrase *śimḥat ʿolam ʿal ro'sham*, "everlasting joy upon their head." The people of Yahweh now echo the expression of joy that was introduced by a renewed creation itself.

Homiletical application. The Third Sunday of Advent traditionally emphasizes the theme of joy (including the pink Advent candle if such a wreath is used). The joy of this text is overwhelming, starting with the restoration and renewal of creation and continuing to the ransom and redemption of the people of God. The reason for such joy is clear: "your God will come." No matter how dark the hopelessness or dry and dusty the feeling of despair, there is confidence and joy in knowing that God will not leave his people abandoned. He will come to rescue and redeem them.

Further, the renewal of creation extends also to human health and wholeness. These are signs of the presence of God and the inauguration of the messianic age. Jesus himself appealed to this text in response to the question from John the Baptist as to whether Jesus were truly the Messiah or not. The healing miracles of Jesus are seen as signs that Isaiah 35 was being fulfilled in the person and work of Jesus of Nazareth. Modern proclaimers of this text are able to strengthen feeble hands and steady weak knees with the proclamation that in Christ, "your God has come!" To be sure, his righteous reign may lie hidden behind realities that are still of the old order, but signs of peace and joy within the people of God are manifestations that God has indeed "ransomed captive Israel."

God's people march in holy procession along the holy highway, safe in the presence of God even amidst the fears and dangers of this world. Liturgically, the holy highway of God is made real every Sunday. Led by the processional cross, the people of God are bold to come into God's holy presence, to approach him with an offertory procession and in prayer, and even to come near in sacramental participation, all as they enter Zion with singing. And then they are bold to extend that highway out from Zion as the ransomed and redeemed of Yahweh walk the road of life in full confidence that everlasting joy will crown their heads and that sorrow and sighing will indeed flee away, when *our* God and Savior will come again.

Andrew H. Bartelt

Second Sunday of Advent, Year B

First Lesson: Isaiah 40:1-11
(Psalm 85:1-2, 8-13)
Second Lesson: 2 Peter 3:8-15a
Gospel Lesson: Mark 1:1-8

This passage is actually made up of two proclamations, the first in verses 1-8, the second in 9-11. The whole forms the beginning of the book of Second Isaiah (chaps. 40–55), who delivered his message among the Babylonian exiles of Judah sometime between 550 and 538 B.C. While the passage does not have the form of a prophetic call narrative, nevertheless it tells of Second Isaiah's summons to his prophetic ministry.

The setting in the passage is the heavenly court of the Lord, where God is enthroned as king and where all of God's heavenly servants and messengers are gathered together to await his directions for their missions on earth. For a portrayal of the heavenly court, see 1 Kings 22:19-22 and Job 1:6-12. That court also is the setting for Isaiah 6 and for the visions in the first six chapters of Zechariah. Jeremiah tells us in 23:18 that true prophets are those who are allowed to stand in the heavenly court and to hear its deliberations.

The ones addressed by God's opening words in verses 1-2, therefore, are his heavenly messengers. The verbs are all plural imperatives, as in the KJV (comfort *ye*), and the heavenly hosts are commanded, literally, to "speak tenderly to the heart of Jerusalem," who personifies the whole of Israel. They are to announce three glad messages. The first word in each of the announcements is the Hebrew *ki,* which has the meaning of "for," or "because," and which gives the reason for the preceding statement. Thus the heavenly beings can comfort Jerusalem "because," first, its warfare or time of punishment for sins is ended. The Israelites were sent into Babylonian exile because of their faithlessness to their covenant with God, and that punishment is elsewhere understood by the prophets as the time of the Lord's "warfare" against his people (cf. Ezek. 13:5). But now, secondly, the Lord has forgiven his people and put aside his weapons of war. Indeed, third, Israel has received double punishment for its sins, a fact that will be illumined in Isaiah 52:13–53:12.

The forgiveness of Israel means that God will return to be with his people, because it is sin that separates us from God. Therefore, in verse 3 another heavenly being cries out to the heavenly hosts to prepare a king's highway for God, reaching from Babylonia to Jerusalem. The heavenly beings are to make a straight road and to fill in every valley and level every mountain, in order that God's way may be swift and unimpeded. And when God does return, all nations, "all flesh," will see his effulgent, glorious presence returning to his people in a universal revelation. Moreover, his return is absolutely certain because *(ki)* the Lord has promised it.

A different heavenly being then turns attention to the prophet and commands him to "Cry," that is, to preach (v. 6). But Second Isaiah replies, "What shall I preach?" The following verses, 6c-8, detail the message that the prophet is to proclaim. In a series of stunning repetitions, the waywardness and inconstancy of human devotion are set forth. The Hebrew word for "beauty" in verse 6 is *ḥesed,* which has the connotation of "covenant faithfulness and love." And we do have our moments of dedication, don't we, when we feel ourselves fully committed to the Lord. But our faithfulness is like the flower of the field, beautiful at the moment but rapidly failing when trouble and distraction come upon us. Yet, "but," nevertheless (that last pregnant word in v. 8), in contrast to our inconstancy, God's faithfulness is not inconstant. His word stands forever. He never takes it back. God keeps his promises.

That assurance that the Word of God stands forever is the same message with which Second Isaiah ends in 55:10-11, and it forms the overarching theme of this prophetic book. God never lets his word return to him empty. He always fulfills it. That is the most comforting message of all for the Israelites. It means that the promises given in the preceding verses will come to pass. God will indeed forgive his people and return to be with them. He will in fact reveal his glory among all nations. But there is much more than that in the way of comfort here. The fact that God's word does not return to him void means that all of God's promises to Israel in the past will also be fulfilled. To be sure, God is doing a "new thing" in the life of the exiles (43:19), but that new thing will also gather up all of God's promises of the past and bring them to fulfillment. So, in Second Isaiah, there will be a new multiplication of the population, a new exodus, a new wilderness wandering, a new gift of the Promised Land, a new covenant of David, a new revelation to the world, a new universal people, bringing all of Israel's past history to its final realization.

Having been given that sure word of promise, Second Isaiah therefore takes up his preaching in verses 9-11. Jerusalem has heard the comforting words that the heavenly beings have announced to her. Second Isaiah therefore calls upon her in his preaching to become the herald of the good tidings that have been told to her. Here we have the first mention of an evangelist in the Bible, that is, one who is a herald of good tidings (cf. 52:7). An evangelist brings good news, and it is very good news indeed that Jerusalem will once again know the presence of her God with her. Apart from God's presence there is no good or life or future. Jerusalem has lain in ruins since her destruction by the Babylonian armies in 587 B.C., populated only by a meager citizenry of peasants, leaderless and as good as dead (cf. Ezek. 37:1-14). Now God's return will mean possibility and life.

The evangelist Jerusalem or Zion is not to keep the good news to herself, however. She is to tell it to all the cities of Judah (v. 9). She is to summon them to look up and to see. Behold! Look! There comes your God! Do you not see him, there on the King's highway? Here he comes!

And what a God he is! He is mighty. His mighty arm is going to defeat the Babylonians by means of Cyrus of Persia (cf. Isa. 44:28; 45:1-3, 13) and restore Jerusalem and the cities of Judah. "They shall be built, / and I will raise up their ruins" (44:26), says the mighty God. Cyrus shall perform the counsel that you have heard from the heavenly host and fulfill all my purpose (44:26, 28). Jerusalem "shall be built," and the foundation of your temple "shall be laid" (44:28). God's arm will rule, and no other.

But the mighty God is not coming alone. Behold! Look! He is accompanied by a "reward," a "recompense" — the exiles from Babylonia. He is leading them back to their own country. And when they have arrived in Judah, God will be a shepherd over them. His mighty arm that is raised in victory will also be lowered in tenderness, so that he will gather the lambs in his arms and carry them in his bosom, and gently lead the mothers with their children.

We must not sentimentalize that picture of God the shepherd, however, no matter how tender it is. In the Bible, the shepherd of a people is their king, and God the shepherd is a royal figure. But it is a familiar figure in the Bible, and one that is promised in an abundance of Old Testament texts (cf. Ezek. 34:11-31; 37:24-28; Pss. 23; 78:52; 80:1; Jer. 31:10), as well as in the New (John 10:11; 1 Pet. 2:25).

When dealing with the Old Testament, we must always ask, What became of its ancient promises? Did God keep his word, proclaimed through his prophet Second Isaiah? Certainly Israel's liberation from bondage in exile in Babylonia came to pass, as God worked his redeeming will through Cyrus of Persia. By a 538 B.C. edict, Cyrus allowed whoever wanted to, among the exiles, to return to Palestine and rebuild their ruined Jerusalem and its temple. But what of that "new thing" that God was going to do, when he would return to his people and at the same time gather up all his past promises to Israel and bring them to completion?

Surely the Lord does work in surprising ways to fulfill his word. We now anticipate once more on this Second Sunday of Advent the birth of God-with-us in Jesus Christ. And he comes to us as the Davidic king, redeeming us as he redeemed Israel, multiplying us into a universal people called the Christian church, leading us in freedom out of our bondage to sin and death, renewing his covenant with us through his cross, and giving us a future full of goodness and hope. In truth, the Word of God does stand forever. And that is very good news. That is our gospel.

Elizabeth Achtemeier

Fifth Sunday after the Epiphany, Year B

First Lesson: Isaiah 40:21-31
(Psalm 147:1-11, 20c)
Second Lesson: 1 Corinthians 9:16-23
Gospel Lesson: Mark 1:29-39

The precise limits of the text are somewhat unclear. There is widespread agreement that chapters 40–66 come from a period much later than 1–39 and hence from a different prophet than Isaiah, the son of Amoz, of Jerusalem (1:1; 2:1). Chapters 40–55, specifically, are generally termed Second (or Deutero-) Isaiah and are thought to date to the period of the Babylonian exile, perhaps shortly before the capture of Babylon by Cyrus (539), who is referred to by name in 44:28; 45:1, 13.

The opening verses of chapter 40 announce Second Isaiah's theme: comfort to the people, tender speech to Jerusalem (40:1-2). What hopeful words to a people suffering the effects of God's judgment in exile far away from God's land! 40:1-11 is something of an introduction, then, to Second Isaiah as a whole, and may in fact contain the call narrative of this anonymous prophet. If so, 40:12-31 is the first speech of this newly commissioned prophet. It belongs to the prophetic speech form of *disputation*, where a prophet quotes opponents and then offers a reply which shifts from accusation to direct reproach (see, e.g., Mic. 2:6-11). But 40:12-31 is a different type of disputation. Indeed, only 40:27-31 is a true disputation; the preceding units are preparatory for these final, climactic verses. (Hence, to begin with 40:21 is against the flow of the text, despite the fact that verse 21a is echoed in 28a.) But even the disputation of 40:27-31 is unique insofar as it *does not condemn* the people but is designed to *give them hope*. This, in short, is a disputation *of grace*.

The three units (40:12-17, 19-24, 25-26) preceding the climactic finale deserve some attention. In 40:12-17 the prophet introduces a series of rhetorical questions that serve to highlight the incomparable nature of God. God is the Creator — no one can claim to do the things God has done (40:12), nor can anyone claim to have taught God, as if God should need a tutor (40:13-14; 1 Cor. 2:16)! When compared to the Creator, even the greatest things imaginable — be they waters, the heavens, the earth, the mountains, the hills — are minuscule. If this is true of the natural world, it is no less true for the political one. The nations are like a drop from a bucket, barely affecting God's cosmically precise scale (40:15). Indeed, the nations are as "nothing" *('ayin),* as "less than nothing," and as "emptiness" *(tohu)* (40:17). The last term is the same used to describe the earth at the time of creation (Gen. 1:2): *tohu wabohu* (NRSV: "a formless void"). To the One who made everything from nothing, everything still bears a strong resemblance to the nothing from which it came!

The prophet further underscores God's incomparability in 40:18-24. "To whom then will you liken God?" The answer should be obvious in light of the preceding, but the prophet entertains a rhetorical possibility: Perhaps an idol? Be serious! Idols are nothing at all (cf. 1 Cor. 8:4) — they cannot save, and those who believe in them will be put to shame (42:17; 45:16, 20). Indeed, such persons *deserve* that shame because they should know better: idols are created things but not God-created (as creation); they are even less — *human*-created. 40:19-20 is a warm-up for the intense anti-idol polemic that will follow in subsequent chapters (44:9-20; 46:1-7).

In place of idols, the prophet praises the God who "sits above the circle of the earth" (40:22). The earth's inhabitants are like insects from such a perspective, and, if the nations were infinitesimally small and as nothing before God (40:15, 17), so now the princes and rulers suffer the same fate — this time at God's own hand! They are *brought* to "naught" *('ayin)* and *made* as "nothing" *(tohu)* (40:23). God has only to blow on them, and these seemingly strong and deeply rooted individuals (along with their institutions?) are blown away in what seems — to them, at least — nothing less than a tempest (40:24).

In 40:21 Second Isaiah shifts from rhetorical to nonrhetorical questions (also in 40:28). These three questions chide the exiles: Didn't they know all of these wonderful things about God? Hadn't they heard about this God "from the beginning"? Didn't they understand these truths "from the foundations of the earth" about the God who laid those selfsame foundations? The prophet apparently assumes that Israel *did* know, *had* been told, and *had* understood — or at least *should have.* Presumably, at least some of that knowledge, information, and comprehension was available to the exiles in their worship — specifically the hymns of praise that celebrated God in terms very similar to those Second Isaiah has been using (see, e.g., Pss. 33; 90). Hence, the prophet is attempting to revive the exiles' "forgotten praise" (Claus Westermann, *Isaiah 40–66: A Commentary,* OTL [Philadelphia: Westminster, 1969], p. 49; see also pp. 50, 56). As Westermann states: "All that is to follow [in Second Isaiah] depends upon God's becoming once more great in his chosen people's eyes" (Westermann, p. 49). This praise serves to do just that.

But the prophet realized that the exile raised some very real questions that must be answered. The political realities — nations, princes, rulers — should not be underestimated: Israel suffers in exile at their hand. But in the ancient world politics and religion were inseparable. The Babylonians' destruction of Judah and Jerusalem in 597 and 586 could only mean one thing: their gods were stronger than Yahweh. And their gods were, among other things, astral deities — Marduk, for instance, the Babylonian creator god, associated with, among other things, the sun. So the prophet returns to rhetorical questions and the issue of comparison in 40:25-26. But this time the Holy One asks the questions directly! And it is as if God can read the exilic mind. These astral entities (the heavenly "host" included the sun, moon, stars, etc.) — that were so often deified in the ancient world — are *created things. God* created them! They are no deities, rivaling Israel's God in power and deserving Israel's worship. Instead, as created things they are no more worthy of reverence or fear than the idols mentioned earlier. Only the Creator is worthy of praise — this Creator who not only made these phenomena but who also named them. (Genesis 1 also describes the creation of these astral bodies, and there the sun and moon are not even named, further polemic against their divine status throughout the ancient Near East.) The reason they exist and continue to do so is only because of God's great strength and mighty power (40:26). (Westermann writes: "Spoken in a region where the Babylonian astral cult held sovereign sway, the boldness of the oracle is quite amazing" [p. 58].)

Now comes the coup de grace. The prophet draws the various questions and issues that have been addressed throughout the passage and faces them directly. Or, perhaps better, he forces Israel to face them directly. For the first time the exiles are engaged by name: "Jacob, Israel" (40:27a). The terms are somewhat unexpected since it is the people of Judah who are in exile in Babylon. Perhaps the names are reflective of the prophet's vision of a completely restored Israel or a completely dedicated people of God. Whatever the case, they are frequently used in Second Isaiah (e.g., 41:8, 14; 44:1).

The exiles are not only directly *addressed,* they are also directly *quoted.* The prophet inquires as to why they say "my way is hidden from the LORD" and "my right is disregarded by my God" (40:27b). These statements are clearly related to the laments found elsewhere in the Bible, especially in the Psalms (e.g., Pss. 13; 22; 44). As such, these sentiments capture the pathos that was felt by the exiles. That pathos is filled out by attention to the *content* of this particular lament.

The two statements constituting the lament are two parts of one poetic line, but the thoughts expressed in each are not identical. This may be underscored by the fact that the Hebrew is chiastically arranged (not evident in NRSV): "*hidden* (is)-**my way**-*from Yahweh//and my God*-**my justice**-*passes over.*" The first part asks after Yahweh's *ability* to help the exiles. "Can God even see our way?" The second part asks after God's *willingness* to help the exiles. "Has God purposefully passed over our need for justice?" In light of the preceding praise, it should be obvious that Yahweh is powerful enough to do whatever he wants. But does Yahweh want to help the exiles? The response is clear: Yahweh is both willing and able (see Ralph W. Klein, *Israel in Exile: A Theological Interpretation,* Overtures to Biblical Theology [Philadelphia: Fortress, 1979], esp. chap. 5: "Yahweh Willing and Able: Second Isaiah's Response to the Exile," pp. 97-124)!

In a standard disputation, it is after the prophet cites his or her opponents that she or he proceeds to judgment *(mishpaṭ).* But if Israel wondered if God had "passed over" (NRSV: "disregarded") their "justice" *(mishpaṭ),* Second Isaiah "passes over" the opportunity to condemn them and instead engages them yet again by asking another pair of direct, nonrhetorical questions: Had they not known? Had they not heard (40:28a; cf. 40:21a)? Again, it would seem that they did know and had heard, but in the face of their dire situation could benefit from hearing it again! So the prophet repeats it again, again praising God in a way that confirms the previous units and coheres with their theological claims. Yahweh is not limited — not by temporal or spatial categories, nor in physical or cognitive capacities (40:28b).

- *Temporally unlimited:* Yahweh is the everlasting God — a sharp contrast with the temporal nature of the nations, princes, and rulers of the earth (40:15, 24).
- *Spatially unlimited:* God is the creator of the "ends of the earth." There is no place that God can't see or get to — including the ghettos of Babylon where bands of displaced, oppressed exiles huddle together trying to remember (but forgetting!) their heritage, their tradition, their God.
- *Physically unlimited:* This has been obvious throughout the passage from God's creation power, but is here phrased negatively: God does not tire or grow weary. The Lord is thus the perfect person for the faint and exhausted, which is an apt description of human beings — even at their prime (40:30).
- *Cognitively unlimited:* God's understanding is unfathomable, unsearchable. No one teaches or tutors God (cf. 40:13, 14). The corollary is equally apposite, however: God may be up to some things that Israel just won't be able to understand. Perhaps the exile is one of those things.

In this light, 40:28 answers the first of the exiles' questions definitively. *Could* God help them? Definitely. There can be no doubt that God has the power to help the exiles.

In 40:29 the prophet turns to the second question: *Would* God help them? Absolutely, for this God apparently delights in giving power to those who lack it and strength to those without any. It should be noted that this language, too, is descriptive praise (see Westermann, pp. 49, 59, 62, for further information). The prophet doesn't promise that such things *will be* true about God. They *simply are* true. As surely as God is *creator* of the ends of the earth (40:28), God is *giver* of power to the faint. (The forms for both terms are the same [Qal active participles]. One might also note that the same form *and* the same verb [*natan*, "to give"] are found in 40:23, though the form in 40:23 has the article *hannoten* — lit. "the one who gives [i.e., sets, makes]" the rulers to nothing. Cf. 40:27: "Giver [*noten*]" of power to the faint.)

334

Surely "faint" and "powerless" are apt descriptions of the exilic community! Hence, God is not only *able* to help them but is also *especially concerned* to help people just like them. Indeed, even at their prime (40:30: "youths, young"), humans are marked by fatigue and inability. One wonders if this sudden turn to the young is for more than rhetorical effect — might it be a comment directed sideways to the second generation? No one is without need of God's help. Whatever the case, there is a way to counteract the inevitable failure of human strength. It is by *waiting on* (or *for*) the Lord. The waiting implied here is a state of being. Waiting is, therefore, a *lifestyle* or *disposition* — *the* ethic for the exilic community (see also 49:23). They do not know the specific nature of Yahweh's plans — his understanding is, after all, unsearchable — but they are called to put themselves and their futures at his disposal.

This is certainly no quick fix. Much is uncertain about this future that they await. But there are also some things that are certain: those who wait for God renew their strength (the same term translated "power" by NRSV in 40:29). They will mount up with wings like eagles (see also Ps. 103:5) — perhaps an allusion to Exodus 19:4, where God brought the covenant community on eagles' wings out of Egypt. The allusion — if present — ties in with other passages from Second Isaiah that describe the return from exile as a second, new-and-improved exodus (see, e.g., 43:14-21; 51:9-11). Finally, those who wait for God will run and not be weary, walk without growing faint — a marked contrast to 40:30! Those who wait, therefore, begin to take on some of God's own characteristics (see 40:28). Even more importantly, those who wait are given the strength and abilities necessary to get them back home. Someday their waiting will pay off. And it did!

Brent A. Strawn

First Sunday after the Epiphany (Baptism of the Lord), Year A

First Lesson: Isaiah 42:1-9
(Psalm 29)
Second Lesson: Acts 10:34-43
Gospel Lesson: Matthew 3:13-17

Historical and literary background. This Sunday and the next present the first two of the four so-called "servant songs" found in Isaiah 40–55, and they could be paired with each other as well as with the Gospel lessons provided by the lectionary for these first two Sundays after the Epiphany. Although the servant theme is not unique to these texts (and commentators are less certain today of their demarcation and segregation from the larger literary context), and although the servant is mentioned already in 41:8, there is in 42:1-9 a distinct focus on the person and work of this "servant of Yahweh."

Within the literary and historical context of the book of Isaiah, the identity of the servant is elusive. Interpretations tend to focus on the prophetic persona and his apparently vain and futile mission to a people who seem to have not ears to hear or eyes to see, or on the identity of Israel herself, who is otherwise blind and deaf (42:19) yet enlightened to be a light to the nations (60:1-3), a very dominant Epiphany theme. That both the prophetic role and the historical identity and mission of God's people Israel come together in the messianic expectation and fulfillment is precisely the point of the citation of this text at the baptism of the Lord. By describing a prophetic mission to Israel at the same time that these servant texts speak directly to Israel as a corporate people, this text also speaks about the identity of Christ as one commissioned *to* Israel at the same time that he embodies the corporate identity *of* Israel. And all those who are brought together "in Christ" become, both individually and corporately, the very body of Christ. Christian identity, itself grounded in baptism, finds its common source in the one who came from Galilee to the Jordan to be baptized by John.

Speaking to a time when the people of God were in exile, questioning the very justice of a God who would have allowed his people to suffer so, words about justice (v. 4) and freedom (v. 7) would certainly serve to "comfort my people" (40:1).

Textual notes. The person of the servant is clearly chosen and designated by God himself. This is not just anyone or everyone, but a certain one, who

336

is identified and empowered by the very spirit of God (cf. also the Davidic child of Isa. 11:1 and its application as the reading for the Second Sunday of Advent, a fortuitous liturgical *inclusio* around both Christmas and Epiphany).

The end of verse 1 introduces the theme of justice *(mishpat),* which forms a major theme reinforced by the poetic structure of these lines. Within the three pairs of bicola that make up verses 1-4, the clause "he will bring forth justice" occurs in the fourth colon of the first pair and the first colon of the last pair, with the order of object and verb reversed. The final bicolon begins with a third assertion that "he will not grow weak / until he has established *justice* in the earth."

The concept of *mishpat* refers to a positive sense of God's "law and order": a peaceful and whole life in relationship with God, with others, and with all creation. God's justice itself is a two-edged sword, and *mišpāt* could just as easily be translated "judgment" as "justice." Most people tend to long for justice, unless they are in fact guilty.

God's justice involves both condemnation and vindication, as even Israel and Judah had learned through the crucible of the exile. As with the prophet Isaiah himself (6:5-7), the presence of God brings judgment on sin. Yet repentance and confession bring God's touch of forgiveness. And so also corporate Israel has been comforted in the proclamation that

> her iniquities are declared forgiven
> and that she has received from the hand of Yahweh
>   a double portion for all her sins.   (40:2)

Unlike most human attempts at justice, however, the servant's work will not be simply through political or military forces, nor does he come with pompous fanfare and a media entourage. He goes about his business quietly, gently, with care and concern for those who are bruised and weak (v. 3). Yet he accomplishes his mission with faithfulness. Perhaps because his mission is so distinctive and even unique, even the distant islands (representative not just of the nations but of the distant nations to the ends of the earth) wait with anticipation for his Torah teaching (v. 4c, a theme introduced already in 2:2-4 as a sign of the eschatological "last days," when the nations seek out God's people in Zion for God's Torah truth).

That God can do what he has promised is anchored in the theology of creation (v. 5). Against all pagan ideologies and creation myths, to which Israel would easily fall prey both in Canaan and in Babylon, the prophet asserts the sovereignty and supremacy of "the God *(ha'el)* Yahweh" as the creator of heavens and earth as well as the giver of breath (*neshamah;* cf. Gen. 2:7) and spirit *(ruaḥ)*. The God of creation is also the God of re-creation and restoration for a people captive in prison and sitting in darkness (v. 7). God's creation and election, applied personally to the servant (v. 6), are also a word of hope corporately to captive Israel. Those who had not eyes to see (6:9-10) have now come to understand what blindness and darkness really are. To those who are thus humbled in helplessness comes a message of light and liberty.

What is remarkable is that the mission of the servant is to bring justice not only to Israel but also to the nations, presumably to replace the apparent injustice done to God's people Israel but apparently also for the sake of the nations themselves. More than simply to ransom captive Israel, the mission of the servant extends the covenant theology between God and Israel also to the nations (see also next week's lesson, where this Epiphany theme is expanded). The God who created the earth and all that is in it is, by implication, the God of all the nations.

Finally, the pericope closes with an additional assertion of absolute monotheism: there is no other God, no other name, no one to whom God will give his "glory" *(kabod)*. (Note the contrast between the glory of Yahweh and the glory of human beings in 40:5-6, as well as the glory of God that fills all the earth in 6:3.)

This same creator God now promises to replace the "former things" with "new things" that have yet to come (cf. 43:18-19). The former things are usually understood to mean the message of judgment and destruction which was fulfilled in the Babylonian captivity, now to be replaced by the new exodus and restoration. It is likely that the words speak beyond the return of Babylon, however, and anticipate even greater things yet to come, ultimately the new heavens and the new earth of Isaiah 65:17. Thus the text pulls the reader ever forward toward a yet more glorious day.

Homiletical application. So where is the sovereign Lord in the midst of human suffering, especially within the turmoil and tyranny imposed on God's very own people? The historical context of the book of Isaiah spans the darkness from Assyria to Babylon, yet God's people at the time of the baptism of Jesus were still a "people walking in darkness" (see Matt. 3:16). God's people throughout time are often distanced from the power brokers and all who would establish a kingdom like the nations. Of course, darkness and blindness extend beyond social and political forces; they are a sign and symbol of sinfulness, whether recognized as such or not. One message of the book of Isaiah is the need for even God's people to recognize their blindness as sinful arrogance against their God. Yet it is precisely to those who acknowledge such blindness that the prophetic message of justice, peace, light, and freedom is proclaimed.

But God's way of justice is unique. The servant is distinctly chosen by Yahweh and endowed with the Spirit. He brings forth justice calmly, quietly, gently, yet faithfully and without falter or fall — ways completely unlike those of the world.

So who is this servant who both fulfills the prophetic proclamation and embodies the very identity and mission of Israel? The link to today's Gospel asserts that in the baptism of Jesus, he was announced to be the one in whom God delights and through whom all righteousness will be fulfilled. Here God is doing a new thing greater than all former things and still in anticipation of something yet to come. That this servant would establish justice by bearing God's judgment upon himself is truly distinctive, unique, and the glorious work of no other God. That we might claim a role as humble messengers of this justice and as heirs to the very identity of God's people Israel is our liberating and enlightening "new thing," accomplished through our baptism into the life, death, and resurrection of this same Jesus.

Andrew H. Bartelt

First Sunday after the Epiphany (Baptism of the Lord), Year C

First Lesson: Isaiah 43:1-7
(Psalm 29)
Second Lesson: Acts 8:14-17
Gospel Lesson: Luke 3:15-17, 21-22

It is the near universal conviction among scholars that the unnamed prophet we call Second Isaiah delivered and wrote his words toward the end of the period of the Babylonian exile of Israel, a period that covers some sixty years, from the first deportation in 597 B.C.E. to the return to Jerusalem in 539. Because the prophet knows the name of Cyrus, king of Persia (44:28), and knows that Cyrus has decreed that the Israelites living in Babylon are free to return to their homeland, his work must have occurred in that last year of exile or soon after. In order properly to understand and to

339

appreciate the force of Isaiah's words, we must be aware of the social setting in which they were given.

When the armies of Babylon finally destroyed Jerusalem in 587, the last king, Zedekiah, a direct descendant of the great David, was blinded right after witnessing the murder of his sons. With his exile the Davidic line disappeared after some 400 years. Along with that end came the destruction of the temple of Solomon, which for over 350 years had served as the center of the religious and cultural life first of a united Israel and, after the kingdom's division, of Judah. With the temple's end came the end of the priesthood which had served the temple and all those who sought its ministrations. And, perhaps worst of all, the very land of Israel, promised by God to the ancient worthy Abraham to be a chosen land for a chosen people for all time, was now under the complete control of a distant enemy, first Babylon and then Persia. These fatal blows to the long-held social and religious convictions of a people were bound to raise painful questions about God's purposes for the world and for this special people.

As the leaders of Judah trudged off into exile, leaving thousands of Judean peasants behind to survive as best they could, questions arose in their troubled minds. Why has this happened to us? What is our future now? Where is Yahweh in all of this? Perhaps Marduk, city god of Babylon, is in fact the real god of all the world? The prophet Jeremiah, who witnessed the end of Judah and had warned of that end, wrote a letter to the exiles urging them to settle down in Babylon and to pray for the city's safety. It was Yahweh's will, he said, that Judah go to exile and remain there for a long time. In Babylon's shalom is your shalom, he said, and Yahweh still had a future in mind for the chosen people (Jer. 29). Well, maybe, the exiles thought, but how long? What about now? And just exactly what sort of future did Yahweh have in mind?

The exiles lived in Babylon for about fifty years, and some even a bit longer. When Cyrus, after his defeat of the Babylonian Empire, announced that all Babylonian captives could return to their homes, how many of the Judeans who left Jerusalem would still be alive? Surely not many. The great majority of Judeans would have been born in the city, and many of those would have become acclimated to the place, would have taken on the look of Babylonians, would have spoken the local language; the memory of Jerusalem and all that it had meant would have faded. Why should we go back to a place few of us have ever seen? Besides, the last view of the city, for the few old ones who remember, was a place in ruins. Would it now be rebuilt? The historical fact is that when Judah was given its freedom from Babylon by Cyrus, many Jews stayed in Babylon, forming the Babylonian Jewish community, one of the most important communities of the far-flung faith for the next thousand years.

Into this complex setting Second Isaiah spoke his words. To a Judean community long familiar with Babylonian life and culture, this prophet announced that Yahweh still had big plans for them, plans that outstripped their wildest imaginings. The very first words of his book say that Yahweh's anger, real as it has been, has now passed.

> "Comfort, comfort, my people,"
>   says your God.
> "Speak to the heart of Jerusalem
>   and tell it
> that its time of service has ended."   (40:1-2)

Judah has been punished, the prophet says, for the evils it was warned against by all the earlier prophets. But now Yahweh has another word to say to the chosen people. Yes, they still are God's chosen ones, and Yahweh still has a mission for them, however small they see themselves, however uncertain they may be about their future. Though the exiles have little hope of recapturing the great promises of land, temple, king, and priest, Isaiah attempts to kindle the fire of the future in them once again.

His poetry is among the loftiest in the Bible, his vision among the most grand. He literally sees cosmically, demanding that the exiles raise their sights beyond survival, beyond a continued life in a foreign place, beyond a trivial sense of their place in the world of Yahweh. In the famous 49:6, he exhorts the exiles to recognize that even some of their desires to go back to Jerusalem to begin the old institutions once again are not visionary enough for their God. No! Yahweh wishes to send them as "a light to the nations / in order that Yahweh's salvation may reach the ends of the earth." Heady stuff indeed! How in the world could a tiny pack of Judeo-Babylonian exiles possibly do such a thing as that, to impact the whole world for Yahweh, to bring the shalom of God to everyone?

43:1-7 offers Isaiah's answers to those questions.

> (1) But now, thus says Yahweh,
>   the one who created you, Jacob,
>   the one who formed you, Israel:
>   Do not be afraid, for I have rescued you;
>   I have called you by your name.
>   You are mine!

This passage says several important things. Yahweh is creator and shaper of Israel. The word translated "formed" is the same word found in Genesis 2 as Yahweh molds the human being to live and work in God's garden; as Yahweh formed Adam, Yahweh formed Israel. Do not be afraid, is Yahweh's persistent assurance to those Yahweh calls to service. Fear is driven out because Yahweh is redeemer, rescuer, savior of the people. And Yahweh knows them by name. Just as Adam named the animals in the garden and thereby established a kind of power over them, so Yahweh's naming of Israel announces Yahweh's ownership of them.

What does this rescue mean?

> (2) When you pass through the waters, I am with you;
> through the rivers, they do not drown you;
> when you walk through fire, you are not burnt;
> the flame does not devour you.
> (3) Surely, I am Yahweh, your God,
> the Holy One of Israel, your Savior!

I translate the verbs as present tense (present and future are identical grammatically in Hebrew) because Isaiah wishes to say to the exiles that whatever water and fire there have been and will be, Yahweh will be with them to save. The obvious references to water are the Egyptian miracle at the Sea of Reeds (Exod. 14) and the crossing of the Jordan River into the land of promise (Josh. 3). But whatever dangerous waters there may be, past, present, or future, Israel need not be afraid. So, too, with fire. Whether it be the fires that consumed Jerusalem or some imagined fires of the future, Israel need not fear. Any fears are swallowed in the conviction that Yahweh is the Holy One of Israel and their savior.

The first part of verse 4 may be the most important claim Isaiah has to make.

> (4) Because you are of great worth in my eyes,
> honored, and I love you,
> I give a people in exchange for you,
> nations in exchange for your life.

All of Yahweh's continued care for the exiles is based in the simple fact that Yahweh is deeply in love with the precious Israel. As Deuteronomy 7:8 makes plain, Yahweh rescued Israel from Egyptian bondage because Yahweh loved them. In like manner Yahweh will rescue Judah from Babylon precisely because they are loved, not because of anything they have done.

Yahweh will bring the far-flung exiles back to the Holy Land, from north and south, both sons and daughters, because Yahweh loves them and because Yahweh created them "for my glory" (v. 7). The role of Israel has always been, from the time they first saw light as people of Yahweh, to show forth Yahweh's glory, to proclaim in word and action that Yahweh was their God and no other. Now, says Isaiah, Judah is being called again to show forth Yahweh's glory by returning to Israel and serving as Yahweh's light to all the nations, for many still do not know of the saving power and the continuous call for justice and righteousness of this God.

It is hardly an accident that this text appears on the day when the church celebrates the baptism of the Lord. This Lord, the Son of the Yahweh described in Isaiah 43, announces in his ministry the saving power and demand for justice and righteousness made plain to the exiles of six centuries before. And so it is with all those who would follow this one. We, too, are called to be beacon lights to the world, announcing the glory of God in the gift of the Christ.

John C. Holbert

Fifth Sunday in Lent, Year C

First Lesson: Isaiah 43:16-21
(Psalm 126)
Second Lesson: Philippians 3:4b-14
Gospel Lesson: John 12:1-8

This passage forms the first strophe (stanza) of the long, three-strophe salvation oracle contained in Isaiah 43:14–44:6. Because there is a prophetic formula ("thus says the LORD") in both 43:14 and 16, some scholars have maintained that verses 14-15 belong to the beginning of some other poem that has been misplaced. In addition, the Hebrew of verse 14 is indecipherable, although the RSV reading is probably as good an emendation as is possible. However that all may be, we will deal with the passage as it stands.

This announcement of salvation forms part of the proclamation delivered by Second Isaiah (chaps. 40–55) to the Judean exiles in Babylonia, sometime between 550 and 538 B.C. God used the armies of the Babylonian emperor, Nebuchadnezzar, to send the Judean remnant of Israel into exile in 587 and 582. But now the Lord has raised up Cyrus of Persia as his instrument to defeat Babylonia and to release the captive Israelites to return to Palestine (cf. 44:28; 45:1-3, 13). Liberation is on the horizon. Such is the background of our text.

We need first to examine the names by which the Lord is called at the beginning of our text. In both verses 14 and 15, the name of God is "the Holy One" or "the Holy One of Israel." That is a frequent divine name in the Isaiah books, as well as in Jeremiah, Ezekiel, Hosea, and Habakkuk. In prophetic usage it is another way of saying "God," because God's holiness is his qualitative difference from all other persons, gods, and things. Especially in Second Isaiah, God's holiness is his absolute incomparability. "To whom then will you liken God, / or what likeness compare with him?" asks our prophet (40:18). The nations are as nothing before him (40:17); all nature is under his control (40:12, 22). He reigns as absolute Creator and Lord over history and the natural world.

God is therefore Israel's king. Long before the time of the monarchy, God ruled Israel's life (cf. Exod. 15:18), delivering his people from bondage to the Egyptian pharaoh and entering into a royal covenant with them (Exod. 24). As king, God established the Davidic throne (2 Sam. 7), though the Davidic heir languishes in the Babylonian court (2 Kings 25:27-30). But God is still king over his people and all people.

The Lord not only rules Israel's life, however; he also began Israel's life. He is their creator. There was no people of Israel when they were slaves in Egypt. They were simply a ragtag bunch of seminomadic Semites, a "mixed multitude" (Exod. 12:38), some of them heirs of Jacob, some of them not, toiling in the mud pits of Rameses II and looking for help from any quarter. But the Lord saw their affliction and heard their cries (Exod. 3:7) and set his love upon them, adopting them as his son (Hos. 11:1), as his family member, and delivering them out of slavery. With that act by God, Israel was formed as a people who had all been redeemed together. That became their founding story and the basis on which they then pledged their loyalty as one people to one Lord in the Sinai covenant.

So God was also Israel's redeemer, which means that he was the relative who bought back his family member, Israel, out of slavery. Such was the law of redemption (Lev. 25:4-50). The fact that the Lord was Israel's redeemer is found in nine other passages besides this one in Second Isaiah, and is most often joined with the title of God as the Holy One of Israel. Thus the memory of the exodus is foremost in this prophetic book. God in his incomparable power and rule over nature and history delivered Israel from the house of bondage. That act was foundational for Israel's life — the deed of love and mercy apart from which Israel would have had no existence. Indeed, throughout the Old Testament the exodus deliverance from Egypt is considered the principal redemptive act of God, paralleling the importance of the cross in the New Testament.

Given those considerations, the words that follow in our text are astounding. First, in verses 16 and 17 the exodus event is recalled. The Lord made a way through the sea, that is, the Reed Sea, for Israel to cross on dry land to freedom. The pursuing Egyptian chariots and horsemen were drowned in the returning waters of the sea, quenched by the almighty Lord as easily as one snuffs out a burning wick (Exod. 14:21-30). The repetitions in verse 17 emphasize the absolute nature of the victory.

But then Second Isaiah, speaking God's words, tells the Israelites,

> Remember not the former things,
> nor consider the things of old. (v. 18)!

Throughout his preaching, Second Isaiah recalls the exodus and names God "Redeemer" on the basis of it, viewing it as the Lord's primary redemptive act. But now, here in our text, the Lord says "don't remember it"! That seems totally puzzling, and comparable to having someone tell us to forget our redemption out of slavery to sin and death by the cross of Christ. Should we ever forget that redemption? Surely we would be "no people" then, just as Israel was "no people" if she ever forgot the exodus redemption (cf. Hos. 1:9). Our common deliverance from slavery is what makes us a people, the community of the Christian church. That's what binds us together. Should we then forget our founding story?

To answer the questions, perhaps we need to consider Israel's situation in exile. Yes, Israel remembers God's deliverance of her in the past. Yes, she knows that was a mighty act of mercy that made her a people. Yes, those were memorable events when God came to Israel's aid out of love for her and redeemed her out of bondage. But that was all in the past, wasn't it? Now, as she languishes in exile, Israel believes God has forgotten her. "My way is hid from the Lord," she mourns, "and my right is disregarded by my God" (Isa. 40:27). God is through acting on her behalf, is Israel's thought. He has forgotten his people, and Israel is as good as dead.

But now the glad announcement follows.

345

> Behold, I am doing a new thing;
> now it springs forth, do you not perceive it? (v. 19)

God is not through acting. He has yet a new act of deliverance in store for his people. As in Israel's first deliverance and journey in freedom through the wilderness, so now, once again God will make a way in the desert for his people, giving them water as he gave them before, sustaining them on their way. God formed Israel as the people who would praise him for his mighty acts of love. Now once again, in a merciful recapitulation of sacred history, Israel will be able to praise and honor her Lord for his salvation. Indeed, not only the people of Israel, but even the wild beasts, will be led to honor God for this new act of mercy.

It is that new act that Second Isaiah elsewhere tells Israel to expect and to await (40:27-31). Your way is not hid from the Lord, the prophet announces. God is an everlasting Lord who does not grow weary of his work. He will redeem you from bondage once again. Therefore wait for him, because if you do, your strength will be renewed and you will mount up with wings like eagles. You shall run and not be weary. You shall walk in new-found freedom and not faint.

Certainly, in our piety we are very much like the exiles in Babylonia. We know God redeemed us from sin and death by the cross and resurrection of Jesus Christ, and we cling to that knowledge of God's past saving acts. We argue over them. We defend them. We teach and proclaim them to all who will listen. But do we expect God to do anything else? Do we believe that the God who acted in Jesus Christ is the same Creator, King, and Holy One who is continuing to act in our lives here and now? Or have we become purely secular people, like the rest of our society, who say, "Sure, I believe in God, but I don't think he does anything" (cf. Zeph. 1:12)? Is God doing anything in your life now? Do you know him now? Do you trust him to act now? And do you wait in expectancy and faith for that action? Or have you set out on your own to make the best of your situation by your own powers and plans? We are never to forget God's redemption of us by the cross and resurrection, any more than Israel was ever to forget her redemption in the exodus. But like Israel, we also know that God presses on in his purpose, and that there are yet new acts that will come forth from the love and might revealed to us in Jesus Christ. God is not done with our lives until his kingdom comes. Therefore, wait for him and upon him — in prayer, in Bible study, in worship, in obedience. Then we can soar, and run, and walk, good Christians, and never fall or faint.

Elizabeth Achtemeier

Seventh Sunday after the Epiphany, Year B

First Lesson: Isaiah 43:18-25
(Psalm 41)
Second Lesson: 2 Corinthians 1:18-22
Gospel Lesson: Mark 2:1-12

The future for Judah-in-exile will be a glorious gift from God. It will begin a most miraculous way — so miraculous that it will lead the people to forget the stories told about God's deliverance of their ancestors. The prophet affirms that God is about to do something that will completely reverse the fortunes of the Jewish exiles. This reversal will be as miraculous as transforming the desert into a place of waters abundant enough to slake the thirst of every creature (vv. 19-20).

The prophet uses such inflated rhetoric to encourage the Jews who have been in exile for more than fifty years. While many were clearly disheartened by the loss of their native land (see Ps. 137), their situation in Babylon was tolerable. They were not held as chattel but had some freedom, though they were settled in marginally fertile areas, which they were to farm. A few of them even held positions in Babylon's bureaucracy. The prospect of returning to Judah and Jerusalem, which many had never seen, was not enticing to many of the exiles. After all, they were living at the center of a great world empire. Judah was an out-of-the-way province whose political and economic prospects did not appear to be very bright. The prophet's goal was to change his people's attitude about the restoration, which he believed to be imminent.

Separating Babylon from Judah was an impassable desert whose utter aridity made it a barrier that was impossible to cross. The prophet assured his people that their restoration to the land promised to their ancestors would be no problem for God. After all, he asserted, God's power can transform the desert into a well-watered refuge where both animals and people will find refreshment. God will transform Judah's prospects. This miracle will be akin to turning the desert into a well-watered garden.

Though the prospect of an imminent restoration ought to have led the Jews to confess the mighty power of God, they failed to do so. The prophet criticized their failure to see God's purpose in the events that would soon end Babylon's power. Many of the exiles regarded their ancestral religious traditions as relics of the past that had little relevance to their present. Though God did not require the sacrificial worship that was impossible given the destruction of the temple (vv. 23-24), God did expect the exiles to still "call upon" their God through prayer (v. 22a). Instead of praising God, the people burdened God with their sins (v. 24a).

Verse 25 begins God's response to the people's indifference. Yahweh announced that the people's new failure will not frustrate God's new creative action. God's transformation of the exiles' world will go on despite their complete lack of enthusiasm. For the exiles, their religious traditions were about the past — about mighty acts of God done in the past. Their present circumstances make the remembrance of those acts painful and pointless. The prophet's words, however, affirm that the exiles ought not look to the past but to the future: God is about to do something quite new (vv. 18-19). God's saving acts have not come to an end.

This lesson serves to illuminate Jesus' new moral imperatives given in the Sermon on the Mount. Jesus teaches a moral code based not on obligations and minimalism. He calls on his contemporaries to move beyond the commandments to a new level of generosity. God's new movement in the life of the exiles calls them to a new enthusiasm for the praise of God. God's new movement in people's lives through Jesus calls for a new moral response, one not limited by the old obligations of the Law, but whose only limitations are people's generosity and commitment.

Both the prophet and Jesus spoke to people who belonged to traditional societies. In such societies change does take place, but gradually, over a long time. Innovation is regarded with great skepticism. Continuity with the past is a very important value. The prophet's problem was that the exile undercut the basis of Judah's religious beliefs. What he had to do was show the continuity of God's action in the world. What he affirms is that Yahweh always was and always will be Israel's redeemer. While Israel's religious traditions and worship focused the people's attention on God's act of redemption in the exodus, new circumstances required a new act of redemption as miraculous as the splitting of the Red Sea and the guidance through the wilderness of Sinai. In 43:16-17 the prophet makes an obvious reference to God's victory at the Red Sea, and the first part of today's pericope (vv. 18-21) alludes to the wilderness tradition. The prophet wants to energize the exiles to renewed faith in Israel's redeemer.

Jesus faced an even greater challenge as he called people to go beyond the obligations of the Torah in shaping their response to God's movement in their lives. The Torah was the embodiment of traditional Israelite morality. The Jews believed that living according to Torah brought God's blessing while ignoring Torah brought a curse. The quality of one's obedience to Torah then determined the future. Jesus did not reject this belief. He did, however, call people to move beyond the obligations of Torah as they shape their response to God's saving action on their behalf. Focusing on minimal obligations can lead to trivializing the Torah through casuistry. Jesus' call to go beyond the minimal commandments of the Law prevents this. The only limitation on the disciples' response is the level of their commitment to the ideals preached by Jesus.

The prophet did manage to lead the exiles to believe in the future that God was creating for them. They survived the loss of their state, dynasty, temple, and land with their faith in God intact because of this prophet's ministry. He was able to persuade his fellow exiles that they had reason to hope. The foundation of this hope was in their God — their Creator and Redeemer. One stimulus for the prophet's optimism about the future was the new international climate occasioned by the rise of the Persian Empire and Cyrus, its vigorous leader. The prophet was certain that Yahweh was controlling the events that would eventually lead to Judah's restoration. But more than this, he was able to lead his fellow exiles to that same certainty. The person who proclaimed these words to the exiles was responsible for the very survival of the Jewish people as a believing community.

Preachers have a task similar to the one so ably accomplished by the prophet. They are to help their congregations experience continuing relevance of an ancient faith. They are to show how the biblical tradition can shed light on the issues that believers face today. Like the prophet, preachers have to persuade people to see that the faith directs their attention to the future rather than the past. It is Christianity's vision of the future that ought to give shape to believers' life in the present. That future is determined not by human sinfulness but by the saving power of the God who does not remember our sins (see v. 25).

In the eyes of many of the prophet's fellow exiles, the destruction of the temple, the end of the Judahite national state and dynasty, and the loss of the land promised to Israel's ancestors proved that their religious traditions were about a past that was no longer pertinent to their actual life situation. The days of the Israelite national states living under the patronage of Yahweh were gone and likely never to return. Babylon and its patron deity, Marduk, achieved dominance over the nations of the world. Still, the prophet was convinced that the fall of Jerusalem and the exile of its people could not be God's final word to the descendants of those whom God freed at the Red Sea. The rise of Persia, a new world power, convinced the prophet to announce that God had new plans for the Judahites in exile. There would be a miraculous restoration by the One who has always proven to be Israel's redeemer. Not even the people's sins will frustrate God's plans. When Jesus

349

teaches about the proper response to God's saving action in people's lives, he challenges people to go beyond the minimal obligations that the Law specifies. Following the lead provided by the prophet and by Jesus, the preacher today will acclaim a God who leads believers to a glorious future. The believers' response to that proclamation cannot be limited by minimal obligations. That is why Jesus calls his followers to a generous response that goes beyond the Law.

Leslie J. Hoppe

Second Sunday after the Epiphany, Year A

First Lesson: Isaiah 49:1-7
(Psalm 40:1-11)
Second Lesson: 1 Corinthians 1:1-9
Gospel Lesson: John 1:29-42

Historical and literary background. Following upon the first so-called servant song which was last Sunday's lesson, this second Sunday after the Epiphany focuses on the second such poem. Since the servant theme is not limited to the "songs," it may be worth noting that in the poetry between 42:1-9 and this pericope, the servant of Yahweh has been decried as deaf and blind (42:18), identified as Jacob and Israel, described as formed by Yahweh in the womb (44:1-2), chastised for sin and faithlessness (43:22-24; 48:1-11), and assured of God's faithful love and forgiveness (43:25ff.; 45:22-25). In 49:1-7 the servant is most clearly and already identified as Israel (v. 3), but then is immediately described as a third party who has a mission to Israel (v. 5).

As elsewhere in Isaiah, the relationship of Yahweh to Israel is placed into the larger perspective of the relationship of both Yahweh and Israel over against the nations. This text is, in fact, addressed to the far-off nations, the coastlands and the peoples who otherwise should have little interest in either Israel or her prophets. Yet the message of this text is one for all to hear, whether born of the house of Israel or the object of Israel's great commission to make disciples of all nations.

To Israel in exile this must have seemed outrageous, even ludicrous, as it no doubt did also to the less-than-full complement of Jewish disciples on a mountain in Galilee (Matt. 28:16). *Cui bono* might well have been the question of the exile as well as of Isaiah himself and his successors, who only saw their prophetic warnings unheeded and God's people fall deeper into the abyss of their sin and God's judgment. And if a message of judgment would go unheeded, then certainly words of joy and restoration would fall on deaf ears (49:4).

Yet God's plan looks beyond what is seen and behind what may seem all too futile to that which is unseen and unexpected. There is something even greater yet to come.

Textual notes. What you don't see is what you get! Even before birth, God had given identity, purpose, and plan to the otherwise yet-to-be identified servant (v. 1). Like the sanctified mouth of a prophet, the servant's mouth was sharpened as a sword into an effective and efficacious tool. But with a description similar to the quiet work of the servant in 42:2-4, this effective weapon was hidden, its power restrained, its potentiality unseen (v. 2).

Nevertheless, in spite of having lost its sense of identity and purpose in the Babylonian exile, Israel would show forth the very splendor of God. The hithpael verb (*'etpa'ar*, "I will show forth my glory") at the end of verse 3 is significant: it is God who will display/declare his own glory and splendor in and through Israel.

The reaction in verse 4 is both dispirited and yet strangely confident. To be sure, there seems to be no good purpose in what has happened to Israel or to her prophets. Yet as with the very people of God, and with preachers of God's word, there is little more to do when one has spent and been spent than to leave both mission and ministry in the hand of God for his purpose and vindication. Interestingly, the Hebrew word for the justice *(mishpaṭ)* that the servant would bring forth to the nations in 42:1-4 is that which now rests as vindication in a very personal way with "Yahweh my God."

Verse 5 recapitulates the argumentation up to this point in the text even as it introduces something new and greater with the introductory "and now." This same Yahweh who was active even in the womb and who had commissioned the servant to restore and gather Israel — a mission in which the servant would "be glorified (niphal of the root *k-b-d*) in the eyes of Yahweh" — now is given something even greater to do.

That Israel, who had been used and abused by the nations and now completely destroyed and enslaved into captivity, would become a light for the very nations that had subjected her to darkness is a most remarkable reversal of circumstance. Yet the message is clear and consistent: Yahweh's salvation rests with Israel alone. Like the sharpened arrow, God's purpose lay hidden even behind the destruction and exile that was Israel's punishment. Yet through such judgment God would bring salvation not only to Israel but through Israel also to the very ends of the earth!

The "Holy One of Israel" (v. 7) is one of the major motifs and names for Yahweh throughout the book of Isaiah. Holiness is a two-edged sword, bringing both judgment and sanctification (cf. chap. 6). Here the "Holy One" is identified also as "Israel's redeemer," who would reverse the fortune and the future of those who had become servants of rulers. Now kings would see and arise, only to bow down in worship, not because of Israel but because of Yahweh's own faithfulness. As 42:5 linked *creation* to God's claim on all the nations, here it is the *redeemer* God who restores Israel and makes her a light to the nations. It is almost as though the first assignment is too easy, or at least not nearly enough. Israel's salvation is a wonderful event in and of itself, but the greater mission is "to be my salvation to the end of the earth."

Homiletical application. The hiddenness of God's plan and purpose stands in stark contrast to the Epiphany themes of light and mission. The mission of Israel simply to be the people of God empowered by the past act and by the future promise of redemption was no doubt lost in the futility and darkness during the exile. Into that despair the prophet brings a message not only of restoration but also of proclamation to become a light to enlighten the Gentiles. The first must have seemed impossible; the second preposterous.

Yet God declares that it is too easy a thing "just" to restore the tribes of Jacob. If that is a good and gracious work of God, then "you ain't seen nothing yet!" In spite of the work of the nations to bring Israel to her personal and collective knees, God now declares that Israel would be God's means to bring salvation to the ends of the earth.

Some would think it hard enough just to restore God's promises to Israel. Salvation itself is not only difficult, it is impossible except for the God of redemption. Once accomplished, it is too easy: the humility of faith stands opposed to human pride and desire to take some credit for ourselves. So God's servant comes to be baptized by John and then to invite John's disciples to "come and see" (John 1:39). In this rabbi from Galilee, Israel is identified anew both individually and corporately. But God's purposes are not completed if salvation comes only to the lost sheep of the house of Israel. That was the "easy" part! There is more to be done. God's salvation extends to the end of the earth.

Andrew H. Bartelt

Eighth Sunday after the Epiphany, Year A

First Lesson: Isaiah 49:8-16a
(Psalm 131)
Second Lesson: 1 Corinthians 4:1-5
Gospel Lesson: Matthew 6:24-34

The people of Judah find it impossible to believe the prophet's assurance that the days of their exile will soon come to an end. They respond to the prophet's description of their imminent restoration as a miraculous manifestation of God with a lament. Clearly, they find the prophet's words beyond belief.

The prophet characterizes the days during which he spoke in the name of God as "a time of favor" (v. 8). He was certain that Babylon was going to fall to Cyrus, who was threatening it. Nabonidus, the last Babylonian emperor, flitted away all popular support because of his religious and personal idiosyncrasies. He promoted the worship of the moon god Sin in place of Marduk, the patron deity of Babylon, thus alienating the priests responsible for the national cult. Even more unpopular was Nabonidus's edict that the statues of gods worshiped in all Babylonian cities be taken from their shrines and sent to the capital. He believed this would rally the people to the defense of that city. Actually, it had the opposite result. In the end, the city of Babylon opened its gates to Cyrus because its people tired of the incompetents that ruled them. The Babylonians regarded Cyrus not as a conqueror but as a liberator.

The prophet saw all this coming and recognized in these developments the very hand of God (44:28; 45:1). Their ultimate purpose was to make the restoration possible. This was the time that the people of Judah were praying for. God was answering their prayers and would soon restore them to Zion. The word that God has for the Jews exiled in Babylon is "Come out!" (v. 9). The return to Jerusalem will be less a wearisome trek and more a procession led by God, who will guide the people as a shepherd, an image found also in Exodus 15:13-17; Psalm 78:52-55; and Isaiah 40:10-11. Jewish exiles from all over the world — not just Babylon — will stream toward their ancient homeland (49:12; Syene is modern Aswan in Upper Egypt).

Inanimate nature recognizes Judah's restoration for what it is: a miraculous demonstration of God's power. The response of nature is uninhibited joy (v. 13a). The restoration of the Jews to Zion then would be no mere political event. The cosmos is caught up in this redemptive act of God that re-

353

stores the Jews not merely to their homeland but especially to their unique relationship with God (v. 13b). The people have suffered because of their infidelity, but God's compassion will not allow God's justice to have its full effect on Israel. Judgment was not God's last word to Israel. The prophet sees the people's redemption on the horizon. Nature too sees this and rejoices in a restoration whose effects are not limited to a small group of exiles but encompass the cosmos.

How do the exiles react to the momentous events in which they are caught up? How do they respond to the prophet's words of hope? Unlike the heavens and the earth, which recognize the significance of God's action, the people of Judah utter words of disbelief (v. 14). The exiles consider the prophet's words too good to be true. Perhaps they considered them the product of an overwrought religious personality.

To counter the exiles' disbelief, the prophet uses a very poignant metaphor. He asserts that God's love for the people of Judah exceeds that of a nursing mother for her child. While some biblical metaphors can be obtuse, the image in verse 15 is impossible to misinterpret. It is difficult to find a more touching image of God's love anywhere else in the Bible. It underscores the unbreakable bond between God and Israel. While this bond did not exempt Israel from experiencing divine judgment for its infidelity, God's commitment to Israel remains secure. The phrase in the first part of verse 16 ("See, I have inscribed you on the palms of my hands . . .") may refer to tattooing, another image of the permanency of God's commitment to Israel.

The affirmation of God's commitment to Israel is not an example of "cheap grace." Before the exile, the prophets railed against those who blithely touted the tradition of God's election of Israel as excluding the possibility that Jerusalem would fall. God chose Israel, David, and Jerusalem. It was a matter of divine honor for God to maintain the Judahite national state and dynasty. Such a belief, though it had the veneer of faith, prevented the people from seeing their actual state before God. The unjust social system created in Judah and maintained by the people of means was under divine judgment. It had to be dismantled, and Babylon was God's instrument of judgment. Once Jerusalem fell, once the Davidic dynasty came to an end, once the temple was destroyed and its priesthood scattered, once the Judahite national state ceased to exist, once its people were in exile, it became impossible to ignore Judah's infidelity. The judgment was so severe that those who survived the fall of the Judahite state believed that God had utterly forsaken them. Their response to the prophet's message of restoration is a lament (v. 14). They are utterly incapable of any other response.

Paul cited Isaiah 49:8 to urge the people of Corinth to respond to God's grace at work in them (see 2 Cor. 6:2). Like the apostle and the prophet, the preacher is to persuade the people of God's gracious activity in their lives. Discouragement can immobilize believers as it did the exiles in Babylon. The prophet whose words are preserved in Isaiah 40–55 is regarded among ancient Israel's greatest prophets precisely because he was able to move the exiles beyond their discouragement and despair. Without his efforts, the people could have lost not only faith in their ancestral religious traditions but also faith in their very future as a people. A most important duty of a pastoral minister is to stand with people in times of crisis so that they can remain convinced of God's continuing love for them.

Another important feature of this passage is the prophet's use of the maternal metaphor in verse 15. While masculine images for God are far more frequent in both Testaments, the prophet's bold comparison of God to a mother is most appropriate as he was trying to encourage his people to believe that God's love for them had not come to an end. Indeed, it could not possibly come to an end. Sooner would a nursing mother forget the cries of her baby than could God ignore the laments of God's people in exile. This usage is a reminder to pastoral ministers to move beyond the exclusive use of masculine images when speaking about God. This passage shows how powerful a feminine metaphor can be.

Also significant for our culture in which religion has become something personal and private is the response of inanimate creation (v. 13a) to the prophet's affirmation of an imminent restoration for Judah. Redemption involves all creation. Just as sin has warped God's creation, so Christ's redemption will restore it. Redemption, then, has cosmic significance. The result of the preaching of the gospel is not simply the conversion of individuals but the transformation of the cosmos. Because of Christ, the universe will become what God had always designed it to be. It is no wonder that the prophet depicts the heavens and earth exulting and the mountains singing at the approaching liberation of God's people and their restoration to Judah and Jerusalem. This text gives the preacher the opportunity to push people to see the cosmic dimensions of Christ's saving work. These cosmic dimensions call believers to become engaged in the liberation of all creation from the effects of human sin. This text provides an opportunity to speak about environmental issues as calling forth a response from those who have experienced God's salvation so that *all* creatures may join in the praise of their Creator and Redeemer.

The prophet wants to convince his people that the approaching political and military triumph of Cyrus over Babylon is much more than it appears to be. It is nothing less than God's liberation of the Jewish exiles. Their return to Zion will be so miraculous as to lead inanimate creation to join in the praise of God. Judah's discouragement ought to melt before the warmth of God's maternal love — a love that can never fail.

Leslie J. Hoppe

Palm/Passion Sunday, Years A, B, C

First Lesson: Isaiah 50:4-9a
(Psalm 31:9-16)
Second Lesson: Philippians 2:5-11
Gospel Lesson (Year A): Matthew 26:14–27:66
Gospel Lesson (Year B): Mark 14:1–15:47
Gospel Lesson (Year C): Luke 22:14–23:56

The Old Testament text for the sixth Sunday in Lent is the third of four so-called "suffering servant" passages in Isaiah 40–55. Those four passages include 42:1-4, 49:1-6, 50:4-9, and 52:13–53:12. Second Isaiah is a series of rhetorically artful and persuasive poems and oracles which seek to persuade a downtrodden community of Jewish exiles in Babylon to have hope in God's promise that they will return home to Jerusalem. It was a tough sell. The attitudes and resistance of Second Isaiah's audience to such a message are revealed in the exiles' words:

> My situation is hid from the LORD,
>   my case escapes the notice of my God. (40:27)

But Zion [inhabitants of Jerusalem now in exile] said, "The LORD has abandoned me, my Lord has forgotten me." (49:14)

The servant poem in 50:4-9a should be seen as part of an extended speech aimed at a dispirited exilic audience. The larger speech begins with 50:1 and ends at 51:8.

The text: Isaiah 50:4-9a. This section of the prophet's speech has affinities with a genre or form called the psalm of thanksgiving in the book of Psalms. Psalm 34 is an example. The psalmist describes a time of distress but then reports God's rescue from the suffering or enemies. The report typically includes an exhortation to the listeners to join the psalmist in trusting God, to listen to his teaching, and to obey God's righteous commands. As we shall see, earlier sections of the so-called First Isaiah (chaps. 8 and 30) also provide traditions from which this text in Isaiah 50 seems to draw.

Verse 4. Here the prophet or servant recognizes that his mission is given to him by God. The mission involves the tongue, speaking words, teaching "the weary with a word." Each day ("morning by morning") God wakens the servant's ears to listen to the divine teacher like a student, a disciple. And now the servant in turn will teach members of the community who will hear his word from the Lord. The image of the teacher/disciple reaches back to First Isaiah, especially 8:16-18 and 30:8-14. These texts come from an earlier time, in the eighth century B.C.E. in Judah, before the exile to Babylon. First Isaiah had become so frustrated by the people of Judah and their refusal to listen to his warnings and oracles of impending judgment that he had his oracles written down on a scroll, sealed up, and kept with his disciples. Then when the judgment (i.e., exile) would come, First Isaiah's disciples would open the scroll and know the truth of the judgments promised in his oracles (chaps. 1-39). Isaiah 8 predicts that the judgment will be deep darkness and distress (8:22). But the darkness will be followed by a time of great light (9:1-2). Second Isaiah, in 50:4, sees himself as one of these disciples/teachers. For him, now is the appropriate time to open the scroll and preach and teach about the movement from darkness to light. The judgment has already come and the promised deliverance is soon to follow, although its signs may not be apparent. 30:8-14 suggests that in First Isaiah's time, the people of Israel were not yet ready to hear or understand. But Isaiah's words were inscribed in a book "so that it may be for the time to come / as a witness forever" (30:8). For Second Isaiah in 50:4, "the time" is now when the teaching of the book and its words must begin.

Verse 5. Throughout this section, the prophet or servant functions as a pioneer, a precursor who goes ahead of the community and shows the way for them. Here the teacher/disciple (he is a disciple of God, a teacher to the community) provides a model of faithful learning: God opens his ear, and he does not rebel or turn away from the words but accepts them as true and faithful.

Verse 6. The disciple/teacher/servant/prophet is persecuted because of his teaching. But the servant does not run away or hide his face. Rather, he

357

"gives" his back to his tormentors. He willingly submits himself to their humiliations without protest.

Verses 7-9. The servant/prophet is able to stand confident and strong ("set my face like flint") because he knows "the Lord GOD helps me" (v. 7). The one who vindicates (declares him righteous) "is near" (v. 8). The servant/prophet boldly invites anyone who wishes to stand up against him to do so. One might imagine a raucous scene in the area near the city gates where court cases were typically tried in the ancient world. A jeering audience surrounds the prophet. The prophet invites anyone who wants to plead a case against him to come forward and start arguing the case. The prophet/servant knows it is God who stands with him both as defense attorney and as the one and final judge in any such dispute.

> It is the Lord GOD who helps me;
> who will declare me guilty?   (v. 9)

In light of the larger speech of 50:1–51:8, the bold confidence and trust in God exhibited by the prophet/servant in the face of persecution, rejection, and torment becomes a sign of the way the exiled community of Israel will move forward in hope. In spite of its weakness and suffering and lack of visible signs of hope, the exiled community can stand boldly without shame and disgrace as they trust God to deliver God's people in the future, just as God delivered Israel in the past.

The following are theological themes that may be considered in reflecting on this text:

1. Second Isaiah is a strong witness to the power of God's word as it is proclaimed and taught with artful poetry, daring images, powerful persuasion, and rhetorical deftness. The human tongue is God's instrument of salvation in the world. One of its central purposes in times of exile and despair is "to sustain the weary with a word" (50:4).

2. The humiliation and persecution of the individual servant/prophet who yet trusts in God for ultimate vindication becomes the model for the whole community. Often our natural inclination when we are hurt by others through words and actions is to strike back. We may feel shame or disgrace. A psychologist who studies shame and our reactions to it suggests there are four compass points in how we deal with unresolved and severe shame. At the north end of the compass, we strike out at others in hateful and hurtful revenge. At the south end we may do the opposite and strike out at ourselves in self-destructive behavior. At the west end we may throw ourselves into the community and inflate our ego and sense of self, deluding

ourselves and denying that we feel any shame. And at the east end we may do the opposite and withdraw entirely from the community, consumed by our shame with no sense of self or worth. Interestingly in our text, the servant/prophet has been helped by God to avoid all these destructive tendencies in the face of persecution and resistance. He does not strike back in revenge at others, nor does he hurt himself. He does not run away but stays within the community. He asserts his innocence and worth as a disciple of God and stands confident and assured that God will declare him to be righteous, innocent, and vindicated. The servant's confidence does not come from his own abilities or resources, but he relies on "help" from the Lord and depends on God alone for vindication. All other resources, both for and opposed to the servant, "will wear out like a garment; / the moth will eat them up" (50:9; see 51:6, 8).

3. 50:10 describes the servant/prophet in our text as one

who walks in darkness
    and has no light,
yet trusts in the name of the LORD
    and relies upon his God.

In what times and contexts have we or our communities had to walk in darkness where there was no light? For many, such times bring only despair, hopelessness, the kind of sentiments expressed by many in Second Isaiah's audience that we noted above. But sometimes God sends into our paths those individuals who must walk through the valley of the shadow of deep darkness (Ps. 23), and yet they maintain their trust and rely on God and God's promises.

Dennis T. Olson

359

Nativity of the Lord (Christmas Day), Years A, B, C

First Lesson: Isaiah 52:7-10
(Psalm 98)
Second Lesson: Hebrews 1:1-4, (5-12)
Gospel Lesson: John 1:1-14

Jerusalem has been waiting for the day of its liberation and restoration. Those who guard the city's shattered buildings and nearly empty streets are scanning the horizon. They have to be especially wary since the Babylonians undermined the city's walls, leaving Jerusalem defenseless against those that would plunder it. Suddenly, off to the east, they spot someone at the crest of the Mount of Olives. They can barely make out the person's faint cries. As he makes his way down the Mount of Olives, his words become clearer: "Your God is king!" (v. 7). It is a messenger from Babylon. He has made the five-hundred-mile trip across the desert to bring wonderful news to Zion. As soon as the city's guards are able to decipher the messenger's cries, they join him in cries of exultation, for the Lord is returning to Jerusalem, making the city holy by the divine presence. When the messenger arrives in the city, he summons the very ruins of the city to join him in praising God: "Break out in song" (v. 9).

The victories of Cyrus the Persian led to this wondrous scene. His conquest of the Babylonian Empire was complete with the capture of its capital city. Jerusalem's conqueror has itself been conquered. In consolidating his victories, Cyrus departed from earlier practice. The Babylonians pacified their domains by shifting populations from one part of their empire to another. They exiled all those who could have threatened their rule. Cyrus, however, allowed exiles to return to their native lands. The new ruler demonstrated his authority by becoming the patron of the local cults in his empire. He ordered that the Jews return to Jerusalem, rebuild the temple, and resume the worship of Yahweh according to their ancestral traditions (2 Chron. 36:22-23). Cyrus's religious policy was based on his belief that the gods of the nations were local manifestations of the god he worshiped: Ahura Mazda. Whatever Cyrus's intention might have been, the prophet saw Cyrus as God's "messiah" (see Isa. 45:1), chosen to begin the restoration of Zion. The miracle is now taking place on the very streets of Jerusalem.

Isaiah 52 is one of those biblical texts that have helped so many people articulate their experience of God's presence and action in their lives. The early church saw its own proclamation of Jesus Christ as the bearing of "good news" to the waiting world. The Hebrew word *mebaśśer,* "good news" (v. 7), was the inspiration for the use of the Greek word *euangelion,* or "gospel," by the first Christians. Paul cited this text in Romans 10:15 in describing his ministry. Clearly he saw himself as the messenger sent by God not only to Zion but especially to the nations. Jesus too likely understood his own mission in terms inspired by Isaiah 52. That is probably one reason for his journey to Jerusalem. He wanted to announce to the people of the Holy City the fulfillment of the prophet's vision, since Jerusalem was still awaiting God's final and decisive act of restoration and liberation.

The inspiration of the liturgy's use of this passage is the angels' proclamation to the shepherds at the birth of Christ (Luke 2:8-14). The Evangelist depicts the shepherds as guarding their sheep in the hills near Bethlehem. As they gaze toward the hills, they too see a messenger (= angel) from God who brings them "good news" of great joy. The angel announces the final fulfillment of the prophet's vision. Zion's restoration will now be complete. While the temple had been rebuilt, the Davidic dynasty was not returned to Jerusalem's throne. This was something that the Persians could not allow despite their generosity toward the Jewish exiles. The angel proclaims the dawn of God's reign with the birth of the Messiah. Christians, then, believe that in Jesus God has returned to Zion (v. 8) to comfort Israel (v. 9) and complete its restoration as the people of God. The nations have witnessed what God has done for Israel and join in the praise of the Lord who brings salvation to the ends of the earth (v. 10).

This lesson affords the preacher an opportunity to explore the relationship between the two Testaments and the significance of that relationship for Christians. First, it is clear that the Evangelists all expressed their experience of Jesus in terms of Jewish religious tradition as expressed in the religious texts of that tradition — both those that have been accepted as authoritative by later Jewish and Christian believers and those that did not achieve that status (e.g., Jude 14-15). Sometimes the writers of the New Testament expressly cite these texts to assert their belief in Jesus. For example, Matthew uses a formula ("All this took place to fulfill what had been spoken by the Lord through the prophet . . ." [e.g., Matt. 1:22]) to make explicit the continuity that he believed existed between the hopes of ancient Israel and their fulfillment through the life and ministry of Jesus.

Luke's story of the angel's annunciation of Jesus' birth to the shepherds (2:8-14) does not expressly cite a text from the Old Testament, but it is clear that the story itself is shaped, in part, by Isaiah 52. In the prophetic text "the good news" comes to those who are guarding the ruins of Jerusalem, while in Luke "the good news" comes to shepherds guarding sheep in the hills surrounding Bethlehem. The message in Isaiah is "Your God is king!" The angelic messenger in Luke identifies the newborn child as "the Messiah," a royal title. The child will be the ideal king who will sit upon the throne of David in Jerusalem (see Luke 1:32-33) and complete the city's restoration. In Isaiah the guardians of the city shout for joy because they see the fulfillment of God's promises to Zion before their very eyes (v. 8). In Luke the angel characterizes his message as "good news of *great joy*" (Luke 2:10). In the prophetic text the messenger commands the very ruins of Jerusalem to break into song (v. 9), and in Luke "a multitude of the heavenly host" praise God for the salvation that is coming to Zion and to the world through Jesus (Luke 2:13-14). Luke's creative use of Isaiah 52:7-10 shows that he saw Jesus as both the heir and reinterpreter of ancient Israel's religious traditions. The writer of the Third Gospel, then, did not see Jesus as simply fulfilling the prophetic word but fulfilling it beyond the wildest dreams of the ancient visionaries of God's people.

The challenge for the preacher is to present the incarnation as fundamentally continuous with the revelation found in the religious traditions of ancient Israel and, at the same time, transcending those traditions. The incarnation offers believers a paradigm of divine activity in the world: God surprises people. The incarnation shows that God's saving action is unpredictable — in the most positive sense of that term. From the vantage point of Christian faith, the author of Hebrews concludes that the religious traditions of his ancestors embodied a "fragmentary" revelation from God that is completed through the coming of the Son, "the exact representation" of the divine in the world (Heb. 1:1, 3). This should give believers pause as they try to comprehend the divine in their own experience. Believers today should be ready for surprises.

Despite the New Testament's assertion that the coming of Jesus was the fulfillment of ancient Israel's religious hopes for the future, religious Jews find the Christian celebration of Christmas based on a belief that stands in direct opposition to the most fundamental of Jewish tenets: the oneness of God (see Deut. 6:4). Still, the church continues to find in the Old Testament words of spirit and life. Today's lesson from Isaiah reaffirms the church's belief that judgment is not God's final word. The good news is that God's movement into our lives is to accomplish salvation (v. 7). The experience of ancient Israel exemplifies that "good news." The judgment that Israel experienced as a consequence of its infidelity was not God's final word, for God comes to comfort Judah and redeem Jerusalem (v. 9). The coming of Jesus, then, needs to be understood against the backdrop of ancient Israel's religious experience. It is the decisive movement of God in the world, insuring that the world will become what God always intended it to be. God will not allow our selfishness and sin to frustrate the divine will for creation. In Jesus, God has become part of creation to transform it from within. God's self-communication, begun in creation and continued through the experience of ancient Israel, comes to perfection in the incarnation. In Jesus, God has become a human being. That is the "good news" that the church proclaims today.

Leslie J. Hoppe

Third Sunday in Lent, Year C

First Lesson: Isaiah 55:1-9
(Psalm 63:1-8)
Second Lesson: 1 Corinthians 10:1-13
Gospel Lesson: Luke 13:1-9

"Come and get it!" When I was a child, this was an imperative that my mother only had to say once. As soon as we heard the words, my brothers and I would quit our basketball or baseball games in midplay in order to crowd around the dinner table for the meal that my mom had prepared. We didn't respond so quickly because the imperative was a threat, nor did we think of it as a demand being made of us. (My mom could certainly do that too!) Rather, the words were music to our ears! They were good news. They were an invitation to come and fill our hungry stomachs — an announcement that there was good food available *for us.*

That's how Yahweh speaks to his people in the text. The passage before us is thick with imperatives: "Come to the water!" "Come! Buy and eat!" "Come, buy without money and without means of exchange, wine and milk!" "Listen carefully!" "And eat well!" "Delight yourself in the fat!" "Stretch out your ear and come to me!" "Listen and your soul will live!" "Seek the LORD while he allows himself to be found!" "Call on him while he is near!" But the imperatives are not a series of dreary demands. Yahweh is not speaking to his people as a master speaks to his slaves. These imperatives are invitations to a feast! Yahweh speaks as a man might speak to his friend. He is inviting his people to a banquet as his honored guests.

Yahweh issues the invitation here because in the previous chapters he has been preparing the meal for his starving people. They are people exhausted by enemy and exile (40:2; 42:21-25), desolation and death (40:7; 54:6ff.). As Isaiah describes it, they have received from the Lord's hand "double" for all their sins (40:2). Yahweh previously gave his people up to robbers and spoilers because they sinned against him (42:24). In his overflowing wrath, Yahweh hid his face from them (54:8). They are called "afflicted," "storm-tossed," "not comforted" (54:11).

Yet, Yahweh does not abandon his people, and he does not break his promises. The text reminds us of the covenant that Yahweh made with David. Isaiah calls it "an eternal covenant" *(berit 'olam),* and he describes it further as the "sure" or "certain" "mercies" given to David (v. 3). The key words here are "eternal" and "certain." For in them is the promise that even though the people might abandon Yahweh, Yahweh will not abandon them because he will not break the promise he made to David.

Psalm 89 is one psalm which elaborates on that promise. For the psalmist, the covenant Yahweh made with David is a promise in which he and the people also participate. The promise to David blesses everyone. And that's why he will sing of Yahweh's "mercies" (the same word as in Isa. 55:3) in relation to the covenant. And when he describes Yahweh's apparent abandonment of David, he laments (Ps. 89:38-48). According to the psalmist, Yahweh promised that he would establish David's "seed" forever and his throne for all generations (89:5, 35-37). In other words, his kingdom would be an eternal one — a kingdom founded on righteousness and justice (89:14), a kingdom whose joyful people walk in the light of Yahweh's face (89:15), a throne which is as certain as the sun and the moon (89:37-38).

This kingdom is one that will be established by the work of the servant described in the chapters leading up to our text in Isaiah 55. He is the one through whom Yahweh keeps the covenant he made with David. In his work, the mercies promised to David are brought to fulfillment. And so, in imagery similar to that found in Psalm 89, he is described by Isaiah as the one who brings justice to the nations (42:1, 4), who opens blind eyes and frees prisoners (42:6-7), who is a light to the nations and who brings salvation to the ends of the earth (49:6). The servant accomplishes all of this work — he brings his kingdom of righteousness and salvation to all people — through his own suffering and death. As Isaiah says:

He was wounded for our transgressions,
    crushed for our iniquities;
upon him was the punishment that made us whole,
    and by his bruises we are healed. (53:5)

The righteous one, my servant, will justify many [i.e., this is how he
brings the promised righteousness],
and he will bear their iniquities. (53:11)

Now, in the text we hear the great news that this meal is for us! This
banquet of salvation, this feast of victory, is not exclusive but inclusive! For
all of us who are burdened by life's failed expectations, by our own inadequacies, and by our sin, God says, "Come and eat!" For us who are afraid of
death and who often feel as if we are slaves to circumstances beyond our
control, God says, "Come and eat!" For everyone who is thirsty, here is water. To all of us who have no money — nothing to give — Yahweh still says,
"Come and eat!"

This is indeed precious food. Not only do verses 1 and 2 invite all those
who have nothing and have no means of their own, but in effect it says:
"Your money is no good here anyway." "Come, buy wine and milk without
money and without means of exchange." That doesn't only say, "those who
have nothing can still eat," but also that the meal is *not available* for money
anyway. No one can offer anything to get it because it is *priceless* — it has no
price and is beyond price! That is, this meal of priceless value cannot be purchased by us, but as we see in the work of the servant, it was purchased at
great cost to someone else. This is all meant to be almost unbelievably good
news. Only Yahweh would do such a loving thing for such sinful people.
The text says as much: "My thoughts are not your thoughts, and my ways
are not your ways."

The imagery of the text, the wording inviting us to "eat and drink"
Yahweh and his salvation are brush strokes in the picture that all God's
prophets are painting. The picture is of manna raining down from heaven
for people to eat — the bread of angels, the psalmist calls it (Ps. 78:25). It is
the riven rock gushing water in the desert. And the words of Moses: "Man
does not live on bread alone but on every word that comes from the mouth
of the LORD" (Deut. 8:3). And the psalmist:

How sweet are your words to my taste,
    sweeter than honey to my mouth! (Ps. 119:103)

And David:

> You prepare a table before me
> > in the presence of my enemies.
> You anoint my head with oil,
> > my cup runneth over. (Ps. 23:5)

And Wisdom herself:

> Let all who are simple come in here. . . .
> Come, eat my food
> > and drink the wine I have mixed. (Prov. 9:1-6)

And Isaiah again: "'The LORD, the LORD is my strength and my song; / he has become my salvation.' With joy you will draw water from the wells of salvation" (Isa. 12:2-3).

> For waters shall burst forth in the wilderness,
> > and streams in the desert.
> The parched ground shall become a pool,
> > and the thirsty land springs of water. (Isa. 35:6-7)

> On this mountain the LORD Almighty will prepare a feast
> > of rich food for all peoples,
> > a banquet of aged wine —
> > the best of meats and the finest of wines. (Isa. 25:6)

And when the picture is finished, it is, of course, a picture of Christ: "If anyone is thirsty, let him come to me and drink" (John 7:37). "I am the living bread that came down from heaven. If anyone eats of this bread, he will live forever" (John 6:51). "Like newborn babes, crave pure spiritual milk, so that by it you may grow up in your salvation, now that you have tasted that the Lord is good" (1 Pet. 2:2). In the end, Yahweh serves up Christ for us. In him we find compassion and pardon and eternal life. In him God keeps the covenant he made with David, and we receive the mercies of his eternal kingdom. He feeds our hungry souls and fills us with good things, all at no cost to us (remember, the feast is priceless) but of course at great cost to him.

And so, in Christ the meal is ready. He brings us the precious gifts of forgiveness and eternal life. And he wants us to come. As the text says, "Seek him while he allows himself to be found [tolerative niphal]! Call him while

366

he is near!" The meal is ready now. Now is the time of salvation. In his word and the proclamation of it and in his supper in which he offers his very body and blood, the God of pardon and peace and eternal life is to be found. In Christ, the work of the servant is freely offered. Come and eat!

Timothy E. Saleska

Eighth Sunday after the Epiphany, Year C

First Lesson: Isaiah 55:10-13
(Psalm 92:1-4, 12-15)
Second Lesson: 1 Corinthians 15:51-58
Gospel Lesson: Luke 6:39-49

T his passage is an appropriate ending to a collection of prophetic speeches that promised the Jewish exiles a miraculous restoration and a glorious future (Isa. 40–55). Today's text begins by assuring the exiles that they can have confidence in the promises made to them by the prophet because they are the very word of God (vv. 10-11). It may appear as if the fortunes of the exiles are changing because of the rise of Persia, the new imperial power that displaced Babylon. But the prophet has made it clear that the God of Israel chose Cyrus, the Persian king, to be the instrument of Judah's liberation and Jerusalem's restoration (45:1-7). The changes that are occurring in the political sphere are the result of God's decision to bring an end to the people's exile.

To underscore the divine purpose in Cyrus's victory over Babylon, the prophet uses an analogy from the natural order. The fertility of the land was absolutely dependent on water. In Mesopotamia where the Jewish exiles were farming, there was a system of canals that channeled water from the Tigris and Euphrates Rivers into the valley between these two rivers. Still, everyone recognized that the water that flowed in these rivers came from the snow and rain that fell in the mountains far to the north. Farmers in Judah were more conscious of their need for water from the heavens since Palestine has no river system comparable to that of Mesopotamia. The location

367

of the Jordan River and the Sea of Galilee in the Rift Valley made large-scale irrigation virtually impossible. The water needed to make the land fruitful had to come directly from the heavens. In years when the rainfall was inadequate, famine was a genuine possibility. But when the rains did come, the land's fertility guaranteed a bountiful harvest. Enough grain was produced to feed the people and provide seed for the next year's planting (see v. 10b). God, who gave the rain, was responsible for the land's bounty. For the prophet, God's promise of a restored Judah was not simply a profound hope but a veritable certainty. What God wills God accomplishes. Judah can depend on that.

The prophet who spoke these words did not believe that he was merely conveying information to the exiles about their future, though he was clearly doing that. What makes the prophetic word unique is that the word of God is the very instrument through which its fulfillment will take place. In that sense it is like the rainwater that comes from the heavens. It is the water that makes the earth fruitful, and it is the prophetic word announcing Judah's restoration that brings that restoration about. When God speaks, things happen. The prophetic word is itself the guarantee of its fulfillment. At the same time, people have it within their power to accept the prophetic word or reject it. God's word does not work like magic, just as the rain does not. For the rain to work its miracle, the ground must be prepared and the seed sown. For the prophet's message to do what God designed it to do requires that people accept the word of salvation. The prophet's powers of persuasion are critically important. He must keep the Jewish exiles from doubting or disdaining God's word, thus rendering it ineffective. For the prophet is able to lead people from doubt to faith and from despair to hope that God's word will accomplish its purpose.

Despite the prophet's assurances about the fulfillment of God's promises, the return of the Jewish exiles to Jerusalem was not a triumphal procession through a desert that had been transformed into a garden (see 40:3-5). Still, the divine word was fulfilled, though Judah's restoration did not proceed as the prophet led the exiles to expect. The oracles found in Isaiah 56–66 are, in part, a response to the disparity between the prophetic vision of Judah's restoration and the historical shape of that restoration. In spite of this disparity, the magnificent poems of Isaiah 40–55 were treasured by believers because they came to recognize that God always fulfills God's promises, but in ways that transcend human expectations.

The prophet's visions end with an appeal to the exiles to leave Babylon with joy (v. 12). As he did earlier, the prophet again engages in a flight of rhetorical fancy as he describes the return to Jerusalem. It will be a miraculously guided procession through a desert that God will transform into a garden full of evergreens (vv. 12b-13a; see 40:3-4; 42:14-16; 43:19-21). The desert that had become a garden will remain as a "memorial" to the triumph of Israel's God (v. 13b). The book of Joshua tells the story of a similar "memorial." After the Israelites crossed the Jordan under Joshua's leadership, God ordered the people to set up twelve stones to commemorate their miraculous crossing of the river. Questions raised by later generations about the meaning of the twelve stones would provide an opportunity to recount the marvelous acts of God on behalf of Israel as it was poised to enter Canaan (Josh. 4:6-7). Israel must never forget what God has done to defeat the forces that were opposed to its coming into the land and to its return to that land.

Hope for the people's return to their land and faith in God's power to effect this restoration were the engines that drove the prophet's ministry. He is now directing his fellow exiles to leave Babylon with the joy of one who is returning home after a very long time away. The restoration may appear to be a consequence of Cyrus's victory over Babylon, but it is really the sovereign act of the Creator, as is evident in the transformation of the desert. The whole of creation shares in the joy of those set free:

> The mountains and the hills . . .
>> shall burst into song,
>> and all the trees of the field shall clap their hands.　　(v. 12)

Nature then is to share the joy of the redeemed.

The striking imagery of this prophetic text offers the preacher an opportunity to reflect on the transformation of creation that flows from the redemption of God's people. The biblical paradigm that has shaped the attitude of the Christian West toward creation derives from Genesis 1, in which God gives "dominion" of all creatures to humankind (Gen. 1:26). In actual practice, this dominion has often degenerated into exploitation, robbing creation of its participation in redemption (see Rom. 8:19-23). The prophet's words remind readers today that all creation is to be a participant in the transformation that will ultimately lead to a "new heaven and a new earth."

In the Gospel lesson for today (Luke 6:39-49), Jesus approaches the created world from a perspective different from that of the prophet. Jesus uses analogies taken from people's experience of the natural order to undergird his moral teaching. The images of the good and bad trees, the figs and thorns, and the rushing floodwaters were familiar enough to Jesus' audience to help them appreciate Jesus' teaching. For the prophet, the transformed desert, its springs and rivers, its trees, and the mountains and hills that surround it are not blind and mute witnesses to the wondrous restoration of Israel to its land. On the contrary, they not only join in celebrating the restoration, they also stimulate the people to appreciate what God is doing in their lives. The prophet, then, anticipates the belief in a sacramental understanding of creation whereby God's creation reflects God's own glory. The prophet understands creation as reflecting God's redemptive movement in the exiles' life. Creation witnesses this and cannot but sing and clap for joy, stimulating the people of Judah to join in the praise of God. Will the exiles begin the procession back to Jerusalem and join creation in the praise of God for this glorious restoration?

The prophet ends his message to his fellow exiles in Babylon that God has uttered the word of liberation and restoration. This word cannot help but accomplish Judah's restoration since God's word never returns without accomplishing the task God set for it. The prophet sees his own ministry of proclaiming that word as the first step in the fulfillment of God's decision to end Judah's exile in Babylon. To this end God raises up a political and military leader to accomplish this goal. Cyrus, that chosen leader, has already begun to act. The fulfillment of God's promises is just a matter of time. Judah's redeemer is also the world's creator, so creation also has its role to play in the fulfillment of the divine word. Taking full poetic license in proclaiming the divine word to Judah, the prophet assures the people that creation itself will be transformed as God's word finds its fulfillment. What the prophet is hoping for is faith in that word on the part of his fellow exiles. Can they believe in a God who is sovereign over creation and history — a God who wants to comfort them and lead them home?

Leslie J. Hoppe

Fifth Sunday after the Epiphany, Year A

First Lesson: Isaiah 58:1-9a, (9b-12)
(Psalm 112:1-9, [10])
Second Lesson: 1 Corinthians 2:1-12, (13-16)
Gospel Lesson: Matthew 5:13-20

Newer approaches to the book of Isaiah call for a different way of understanding 58:1-12. According to the traditional consensus, it is a part of Third Isaiah (chaps. 56–66), which is supposedly a block of material written by the followers of Second Isaiah (chaps. 40–55) to articulate the disappointing situation after the return from exile when the glorious vision of Second Isaiah had failed to materialize. These followers had apparently been excluded from participation in community life by a priestly establishment, and 56–66 supposedly expresses the pain of this prophetic group.

While this consensus is credible, it fails to discern the unity of the book of Isaiah. Edgar Conrad, for instance, argues that the book as a whole is addressed to "survivors" (see 1:9; 66:19, although the Hebrew words differ) who, having experienced defeat by Babylon, are waiting for a new act of divine deliverance. These survivors can wait confidently because they know of God's earlier defeat of the Assyrian oppressor, narrated in Isaiah 36–39. As Conrad points out, while chapters 40–66 anticipate deliverance from the Babylonian captivity, this deliverance is *not* narrated in the book of Isaiah. The effect is to leave readers of the book in waiting, while grounding their hope in the conviction of God's universal sovereignty and God's ultimate establishment of peace among all nations (see 2:1-14; 52:7-10). The effect of Conrad's discernment of the unity of Isaiah is to invite and facilitate appropriation of the book by each new generation of God's people (*Reading Isaiah* [Philadelphia: Fortress, 1991]).

In this regard, Conrad maintains that the Babylonian captivity may be heard metaphorically as well as historically. In either case, the Babylonian captivity meant the end of the monarchy, so the book of Isaiah invites the whole people of God in every generation to participate in the role formerly entrusted to the kings — namely, the establishment of justice and righteousness toward the goal of international peace (see Ps. 72:1-4, 12-14; cf. Isa. 42:1-9; 49:1-7; 55:3-5). Participation in the establishment of justice and righteousness lies at the heart of the message of 58:1-12. In short, Conrad's approach encourages us to hear Isaiah 58 not only as an artifact of an ancient dispute between priests and prophets, but also as an invitation to entrust ourselves and our futures to God. When we do, then our liturgy and our lifestyle will embody the justice and righteousness which God wills for all people, and which forms the foundation of enduring peace among individuals and nations.

Given that the conviction of God's universal sovereignty is programmatic for the book of Isaiah (see 2:1-4; 52:7-10), it is noteworthy that the announcement of God's reign elsewhere is accompanied by the sound of "a trumpet" (v. 1; see Pss. 47:5; 98:6). The proclamation of God's reign regularly includes also the announcement of God's will for justice and righteousness (see Ps. 98:9, where "judge the earth" would better be translated "establish justice on earth"). In Isaiah 58:2 "righteousness" and "justice" (NRSV's "ordinance" in v. 2 is the Hebrew word normally translated "justice") are clearly in view; the problem is that the people are *not* practicing them. Instead, they are going through the liturgical motions with no practical effect. Liturgy and lifestyle do not cohere. Quite appropriately, therefore, the opening "shout out" has the character of a prophetic commissioning, even though the addressee is unclear. In short, somebody needs to tell the people of their "rebellion" and "sins." A similar message about the emptiness of worship in the presence of injustice occurs in Isaiah 1:10-17 (see also Hos. 6:6; Amos 5:21-24; Mic. 6:6-8). The people have the audacity to expect God to care for them when they fail to care for one another (see Isa. 1:15).

The first part of the divine response to the people's misguided questions in verse 3ab comes in 3c-5. The Hebrew word translated "own interest" (NRSV) in 3c is the same one earlier translated "delight" (twice in v. 2), and this repetition highlights the problem. What the people think is legitimate worship is really nothing but selfishness. As always, selfishness has adverse effects on others, as the divine response points out — oppression and hostilities that result from the people's inflated opinions of themselves (vv. 3d-5). Worship that glorifies ourselves instead of God eventually results in injustice that breeds violence rather than in the justice and righteousness that foster peace.

As the divine response continues, verses 6-7 articulate what God wills, and indeed, what God is described elsewhere as doing (see, e.g., Exod. 21:12; Pss. 107:9, 14; 113:9; 116:16; 146:7; Jer. 34:14). Proper worship will not be self-centered but God-centered; and the outgrowth of proper worship will be opposition to injustice, liberation from oppressive systems, the sharing of resources, and the growth of community. Or, in short, loving God will also mean loving one's neighbors (see Matt. 22:37-40).

The final portion of the divine response (vv. 8-9a) depicts the new situation which will prevail when God's will is enacted. The appearance of "Then" at the beginning of verses 8 and 9, as well as the subsequent "If . . . then" series in 9b-14, seems to suggest a sort of mechanistic, works-righteousness scheme. But the literary context of Isaiah 58 indicates otherwise. God's availability — God's presence or "glory" (v. 8; see 40:5; 60:1-2; 66:18-19) — is a gracious gift to the people. Proper worship, accompanied by the embodiment of justice and righteousness, will not earn God's favor. Rather, it will put the people in touch with God's abiding presence with them. In other words, the people's own self-centeredness and injustice meant that they were cutting themselves off from God. In the act of denying themselves and thus embracing the other in God's name, the people will hear what God was and is always saying: "Here I am" (v. 9a; see 52:6; 65:1). Life with God promises a brighter future, both for Israel (v. 8; see v. 10; 42:16; 60:1-3, 19) and, by way of Israel's servant ministry, for the whole world as well (42:6-9; 49:6; 51:4; see also Matt. 5:14-16, part of the Gospel lesson for today).

To hear Isaiah 58 in the context of the whole book of Isaiah motivates us contemporary readers to ask ourselves how we, as individuals and congregations, may be opposing the will of God, even as we profess to worship God. As much in our day as in ancient Israel and Judah, worship can be fundamentally self-serving and can function primarily to provide an aura of divine sanction for an unjust and oppressive status quo. When this is the case, worship does not put us in touch with God's presence nor glorify or please God. What worship properly involves is the profession that God rules the world, that God claims our individual and corporate lives. Because the fundamental attributes of God and God's reign are justice and righteousness, those who acknowledge God's claim will be just and righteous — that is, they will be like God. Psalm 112, the psalm for the day, makes this truth remarkably clear, especially when it is heard with its intended companion, Psalm 111. While Psalm 111 focuses on God's righteousness, which involves grace and mercy (v. 4) and "endures forever" (v. 3), Psalm 112 asserts that those who acknowledge God's claim upon them — that is, those "who fear the LORD" (v. 1) — will also be gracious and merciful (v. 4) and *their righteousness* endures forever" (v. 3). In short, when God's people acknowledge that God rules the world, they will be like God! As suggested above, Isaiah 58:6-7 points to the same conclusion.

Being like God is, in essence, what Jesus means by the "righteousness [which] exceeds that of the scribes and Pharisees" (Matt. 5:20, part of the Gospel lesson for the day). It derives from acknowledging God's rule, or in Jesus' words, repenting and entering the reign of God (see Matt. 4:17). Not surprisingly, like Isaiah 58, Jesus was concerned with ritual activity, including fasting, that appeared to be proper but was really a manifestation of selfishness (see Matt. 6:16-18, as well as 6:1-15). Not surprisingly either, Jesus' teaching clearly echoes the message of Isaiah 58:6-9a. In particular, Matthew 25:31-46 suggests that God's presence is experienced precisely in feeding the hungry, welcoming the stranger, giving clothes to the naked, and generally being available for the least of our sisters and brothers. The primary actor in this passage is identified as "the king," and the actions "the king" commends are precisely those which Isaiah 58 identifies as righteousness and justice, the essence of worship that glorifies God instead of exalting the self.

In conclusion, let us return to the two approaches mentioned above to the book of Isaiah. They have a primary feature in common: both present a community in conflict. For the traditional approach, it's the priestly party versus a prophetic group. Conrad refuses to label the groups, but he asserts that the "survivors" had opponents within the community itself. In either case, what is suggested is that God's will for justice and righteousness is opposed in every age by elements of God's own people. In an era when the North American church is beset by conflict, it is perhaps somewhat encouraging to realize that God's people have always been conflicted; however, more to the point, Isaiah 58 prompts us to ask whether a major dimension of our problems is that our worship expresses and reinforces our "own interest" (v. 3) rather than glorifying God and inviting submission to God's will. If our worship, mirroring our narcissistic culture, is simply an expression of our "own interest," then it is no wonder that congregational board meetings often end up as shouting matches and that denominational assemblies frequently amount to little more than political maneuvering among factions that are each attempting to impose their will upon the whole church. In the final analysis, Isaiah 58 is a call to repentance — an invitation to set aside our "own interest" and to offer ourselves for the sake of the world as God offers God's own self for the sake of the world.

J. Clinton McCann

Note: Portions of the above appeared originally in substantially the same form in *No Other Foundation* 16, no. 1 (summer 1995).

Epiphany of the Lord, Years A, B, C

First Lesson: Isaiah 60:1-6
(Psalm 72:1-7, 10-14)
Second Lesson: Ephesians 3:1-12
Gospel Lesson: Matthew 2:1-12

*C*hurch time and collateral texts. This is the season of Christmastide. The Gospel reading, the story of the Magi (Matt. 2:1-12), drives the celebration of the Word on this special day. The date of Epiphany is derived from this reading of the church's tradition. Speculation about Jesus' date of birth places the date of the Magi's visit on January 6. For some churches Epiphany, not Advent, is the beginning of the church year. Historians of Christian liturgy remind us that Epiphany has even earlier attestations than does Christmas. It augments what has started on Christmas, namely, the anniversary of the incarnation, with the anniversary of the first recognition by certain Gentiles that Jesus is Christ and Lord.

Ephesians 3:1-12 is a prayer for wisdom, which connects well with the themes of the other readings. The Magi are traditionally connected to metaphors for wisdom, typically Gentile wisdom, which fit the day.

Introduction. Isaiah 40–55 is a collection of songs of renewal; Isaiah 56–66 is a collection of songs concerning the implementation of the renewal. We will examine the first section (60:1-9). However, this also introduces the description of the rebuilding of the city of Jerusalem (vv. 10-14), which leads into the recounting of the changes to Zion (vv. 15-18) and the alterations to the cosmos (vv. 19-22).

First part. The irony of the Epiphany is that it is at core about a learning experience that is external: epiphany is a learned relationship. The first imperatives are in verse 1: "Arise and shine." This is the Christmas season, but it anticipates the season of Epiphany, that is, the coming of the three kings. But we saw the theme of the epiphany of God already in Judges 5:4-5 and Psalm 18:7-17 (Eng. 8-16). This is not strictly an announcement but rather a summons. The emphasis is on movement. The call "arise" is set off by the imperative form of the verb "be light." The translation "Arise and shine" reminds many of the old church camp song "Father Abraham," whose chorus rings in our ears: "Rise and shine and give God the glory, glory."

The imperative has a context set off by the conjunction "for": the audacious act of rising and shining needs a cause, a context. This time the context is the coming of light, a light that is related to the hearing community.

Hence the writer uses the second-person singular to mark the close tie. The glory of God is what is to come. The Hebrew word *kabod* means "heavy" or "weighty." One might think of this as an approaching air mass in which the barometric pressure changes. It is as if the air has become weightier. This weightiness comes upon the community that is being addressed. And the weightiness rises. Thus the writer begins and ends the verse with the "rising": first the rising of the listeners, which is prompted by the rising glory of God.

The mood changes with the next verse, and at first the reader is struck by a change in tone. But this misses the double-edged quality of the presence of God. On the one hand, it is a blessing; on the other, it is a danger. The reference to the darkness sends the reader back to the creation story in Genesis (1:4, 18). The quality of the darkness is set in opposition to the light. In this regard, the Genesis material becomes an interesting parallel to our passage in Isaiah 60, which begins with "light" language in verse 1 and then moves to "darkness" language in verse 2. However, as in the Genesis passages, God is the author of both the light and the dark. Verse 2 uses synonymous parallelism: we get "the primordial darkness" (Gen 1:4, 18) parallel in this line with the image of a dark cloud (see also Job 22:13). In similar fashion, the verb "covers" matches the repetition of the verb "rise."

The rising of God happens to the believing community. The "shining" of verse 1 is now displaced by the "seeing" at the end of verse 2. Verse 3 brings us back to the Gentile issue: in this section we find a new entity, namely, the peoples, and now we are moving beyond the believing community. The "coming" in verse 1 is the coming of God; in verse 3 it is the coming of the nations. The attraction for the nations is the light, and we can see why this text captured the imagination of the lectionary editors who were seeking an Old Testament passage. The light to which the nations come can now be understood as the star. Over the course of years of Christian interpretation, this has become part of the prophecy-fulfillment style of reading the Old Testament.

Before we move on, we should note the common English phrase "coming to the light" as a metaphor for understanding or epiphany. The use of parallels in verse 1 and verse 3 brings this stanza to an end. We should pause and note that just as there is the contrast between light and darkness, so also there is a contrast in Matthew 2 between the Gentiles who get it, namely, the Magi, and the Gentile Herod who does not see the light. The Isaiah 60 passage describes only the former, those Gentiles who see the light.

Second part. We find imperatives that set the tone in verse 4. The catchword of "seeing" connects the first and second stanzas. This passage echoes an earlier passage in Isaiah (49:18), a poem concerning the restoration of Jerusalem. Isaiah 60 wishes to describe the restoration of Jerusalem, but always in the context of the change in human history. What is true of the nations is true of their kings as well. This time the complementary verbs are "seeing" and "coming." The text connects the seeing of the believing community and the coming, which is an acquiescence of the Gentile community to the vision of the believing community. The text uses the catchword strategy again; this time the catchword is "coming." And this time the Gentile community is replaced with the children of the believing community. The sons come from a distance, and the daughters are carried in the arms. The text uses the two extremes to set forth the holistic redemption of the children. We must keep in mind that children and Gentiles were marginal in the postexilic Jewish community. Now they are brought into the circle of faith and knowledge.

"Then you will see." This time the imperative is replaced by a simple indicative. The epiphany of the Gentiles now becomes the catalyst for the epiphany of the people of Jerusalem. Those who were designated as the "other" now become a symbol of the reign of God. In other words, the unbelieving community enables the believing community to faith. The believing community will see anew; for the unbelieving community has come to see and believe.

The language is quite picturesque: "You will see and burn." The NRSV translates the latter verb as "radiate." Both meanings are true: it means to "burn" but also to "shine." The first two verbs, "see" *(ra'ah)* and "burn" *(nahar),* pair off with two other verbs. The pair of "see" and "burn" sets up another pair that affects the heart. Now the heart trembles in awe *(pahad)* and grows *(rahab).*

Verse 6 provides the strongest connector between the Isaiah passage and the Magi tradition. We find in this verse the camels, gold, and frankincense. The items gold and frankincense occur seldom in the Old Testament (Cant. 3:6; Jer. 17:26; 41:5). This epiphany marks an awareness of the broader world. The intersection of the Matthean and Isaianic traditions used this week is the way they make the case for the Gentile "other" as grasping the theological import of an event that many in the so-called believing community have missed.

Third part. Who are these peoples from other nations? The question in verse 8 is a turning point in this passage. What we see in Isaiah 60 is that these outsiders represent the world catching on to what God is doing. If these outsiders can get it, shouldn't we? And if we get it, how can we not arise and shine and give God the glory?

Stephen Breck Reid

Third Sunday of Advent, Year B

First Lesson: Isaiah 61:1-4, 8-11
(Psalm 126)
Second Lesson: 1 Thessalonians 5:16-24
Gospel Lesson: John 1:6-8, 19-28

The Old Testament lesson for the Third Sunday of Advent from Isaiah 61 addresses a time after the return of the Jewish exiles from Babylon back to their homeland, a time of persecution and internal division and severe disappointment for the small community who saw themselves as an extension of the true tradition of the prophet Isaiah. Isaiah 61:1-4 makes a bold interpretive move. It reaches back into its treasured tradition of Second Isaiah from two generations before (chaps. 40–55). It claims that the promise of Isaiah 40 of comfort and justice and of a special servant of the Lord who would bring such justice can now be applied to a new servant of the Lord. The identity of this new servant figure seems to oscillate between the small persecuted community behind Third Isaiah itself and an individual leader of the community. Like the previous servant in Isaiah 42, this new servant would receive the Lord's Spirit (61:1), would proclaim justice and comfort to the oppressed (61:1-3), would not seek the servant's own self-interest but rather would seek "to display [the LORD's] glory" (61:3). The mission of the servant would be specific and concrete, literally bricks and mortar — building up ancient and devastated ruins and repairing destroyed cities and communities (61:4).

Much of the content of the proclamation in verses 1-4 is depicted in political rather than spiritual terms. Part of the original meaning of the liberty of captives and the opening of prisons suggests a political act. The political character of these actions has led some interpreters to suggest that the Persian ruler named Cyrus may have influenced this presentation since he freed many who had been exiled in foreign lands by the Assyrians and Babylonians. He is the ruler responsible for freeing the people of Judah from their Babylonian captivity. Frequently ancient Near Eastern kings proclaimed amnesty to those enslaved and imprisoned when they first rose to the throne. But the liberation of captives is an indigenous value deeply held within the tradition of ancient Israel itself. The "year of the LORD's favor" is best understood as a reference to either the coming of a sabbatical year or the year of Jubilee. The sabbatical (or seventh) year was a time when slaves were freed and debts were canceled (see Exod. 21:1-11; Deut. 15:12-18). The

Jubilee, the fiftieth year in a cycle of seven times seven years (a sabbath of sabbath years), was the time when slaves were freed, debts canceled, and the landholdings redistributed to their original owners (see Lev. 25). The sabbatical and Jubilee years were years of God's favor when human misfortune was reversed and a new beginning was proclaimed and realized. This act of freeing those who are in bondage is rooted in the ancient memory of the exodus out of Egypt: "Remember that you were a slave in the land of Egypt, and the LORD your God redeemed you; for this reason I lay this command upon you today" (Deut. 15:15; see Lev. 25:42).

Isaiah 61:8-11 continues the theme of promise and strengthens it in several ways. The servant of the Lord's commitment to justice stems first from the nature of God: the servant acts for justice since "the LORD love[s] justice." What the Lord loves is what the servant does. Moreover, God makes "an everlasting covenant" with the people of Israel. The promise of an everlasting covenant had been given individually to King David and his dynasty (see 2 Sam. 7 — the OT text for the next Sunday, the Fourth Sunday of Advent). However, Isaiah 55:3 had already "democratized" this everlasting covenant to David and extended its promise to the whole people of Israel. 61:8 continues this trajectory, promising again that "I will make an everlasting covenant with them." God also promises that nations will come to see Israel as divinely blessed (61:9). The text assures us that the future arrival of the promise of God's righteousness and praise is as certain as a garden growing up from seeds or the earth bringing forth its vegetation in springtime (61:11). Although God promises an everlasting covenant with Israel and Israel receives the special blessing of God, the goal is finally that "the Lord GOD will cause righteousness and praise / to spring up before *all the nations*" (v. 11). Just as one of the earliest promises given to Israel through Abraham and Sarah had affirmed that their blessing would be for the sake of "all the families of the earth" (Gen. 12:1-3), so too here Israel's blessing and joy are for the sake of righteousness among human relationships and the praise of God among all the nations.

Themes to be considered through this text might include the following:

1. This text explores what true and deep joy is. In Advent and Christmas we sing "Joy to the World." Yet this time of year often generates the highest frequency of incidents of depression and heartache for many. Joy in this Isaiah text is not about personal pleasure, a surface emotion of happiness, or the possession of a gift already unwrapped. Joy in Isaiah 61 is rooted in a deeply held assurance that the struggles and disappointments of the present will one day be resolved by a fundamental experience of being freed by a God who will not disappoint, no matter what. Such joy knows the reality of

being burdened and oppressed. But the good news is that God will send a servant who will act to bring a freedom and peace that passes all understanding. It is this profound sense of assurance and confident hope which looks forward to the time when "I will greatly rejoice in the LORD, / my whole being shall exult in my God" (61:10). Such joy is in contrast to the frantic pushing and shoving of a department story cash register line or the fatigue and boredom on the faces of those strolling down the shopping mall corridor. The true joy of this text is marked by song and dance, by concrete actions energized to "build up the ancient ruins" and "repair the ruined cities" (v. 4), and by the celebration of a wedding feast with a bride and groom dressed with "garments of salvation" and "robe[s] of righteousness" (v. 10).

2. In the history of biblical interpretation, this text soon became associated with the promise of a Messiah, God's promised deliverer. In the scene of Jesus' first inaugural sermon in Nazareth at the beginning of his career in the fourth chapter of Luke, Jesus stood in the synagogue and read this text from Isaiah 61. And then Jesus proclaimed, "Today this scripture has been fulfilled in your hearing." By that proclamation Jesus was implicitly affirming his mission as God's Messiah or Christ who had come to save and free God's people. And true to that promise, Luke 7 reports the concrete actions of Jesus: "the blind receive their sight, the lame walk, lepers are cleansed, and the deaf hear, the dead are raised up, the poor have good news preached to them" (Luke 7:22). Jesus' ministry of healing and freeing and preaching became the definitive sign of God's coming into the world in a new and definitive way in the form of Jesus, Isaiah's Spirit-filled and anointed servant of the Lord. In Jesus, the messianic age had dawned.

3. The theme of God's overturning of the realities and power arrangements of this age is deeply rooted in the biblical tradition. In Genesis it is the younger who supersedes the older sibling. In Exodus it is the God of the ragtag band of Israelite slaves who defeats the powerful Egyptian empire and the forces of Pharaoh. In Joshua it is this group of Israelite wilderness wanderers who defeat the armies and fortified city-states of the Canaanites. The barren woman is given children. The exiles are returned home. Jesus proclaims that the first shall be last, those who mourn shall be comforted, and those who are hungry shall be filled. Isaiah 61 joins in this theme, promising those who mourn a garland worn at a festive party instead of ashes heaped upon the head at the death of a loved one (v. 3). The oil of gladness is the anointing oil poured upon an honored guest which replaces the mourning of an oppressed slave (v. 3). Ultimately, God will redeem the world through the death and life of an executed criminal, a crucified Messiah. God's ways are not our ways. God's future will be very different from

the present realities suffered by those under various forms of bondage, oppression, and brokenhearted tragedy.

Dennis T. Olson

First Sunday after Christmas, Year B

First Lesson: Isaiah 61:10–62:3
(Psalm 148)
Second Lesson: Galatians 4:4-7
Gospel Lesson: Luke 2:22-40

Isaiah 61:10 to 62:3 can be an overshadowed passage. The discernment of literary units in Isaiah 40–66 has been a matter of consternation to biblical scholars for years. Furthermore, the way this lectionary passage is cut is somewhat troublesome. "The spirit of the Lord GOD is upon me . . ." (61:1, NRSV) dominates the Christian consciousness. Verses 10ff. are the elegant and natural conclusion to the call set forth in the early verses of the chapter. Therefore, the selection of 61:10–62:3 as a unit is not only artificial but leads to overlooking that conclusion. If the preacher consistently uses the Revised Common Lectionary in Year B, the congregation has already heard 61:1-4 and 8-11 during the Third Sunday of Advent, which contributes to the fact that this passage gets lost in the shuffle. (62:6-12 is Propers II on Christmas Day, and 62:1-5 is the reading for the Second Sunday after the Epiphany in Year C.)

It shall never again come to mind. The Gospel reading for this Sunday is the story of Anna and Simeon (Luke 2:22-40), which generally captures the attention of the preacher and once again overlooks Isaiah 61:10–62:3.

One strategy might be to reconstrue the unit and treat it as Isaiah 61, if it has received limited attention during the Third Sunday of Advent. Another strategy might be to examine Isaiah 62 as a unit. A third strategy might be to address what happens as two broken units become a new unit created by the common lectionary. Since the preacher is presumably skilled at the first two strategies, I will examine the third strategy, namely, addressing the artificial unit created by the lectionary. To unpack this, the preacher must determine the structure and genre of Isaiah 61 and 62 and then ask what structural aspects of those literary units are maintained in the new unit.

The structure of Isaiah 61 involves four pieces: the first is the call (vv. 1-4); the second section, which does not appear in the Revised Common Lectionary, recounts the role of the strangers as servants (vv. 5-7); the third section is a series of first-person declarations (vv. 8-10); finally, there is a declaration of the triumph of the called one and the transformation of the earth (v. 11).

Isaiah 62 is a Zion hymn in the tradition of the Psalms. This chapter begins with the first-person declaration for the sake of Zion, which is Jerusalem (v. 1a). The adverb "until" begins an announcement of salvation (vv. 1b-3). The temporal clause "no longer will it be said" introduces the description of the past in contrast to the bright future (vv. 4-5). Verse 6 returns formally and linguistically to the introduction. It marks the return to first-person speech and also the theme of "not being silent" (vv. 6-7). The final section is a divine oath (vv. 8-12).

The lectionary's new unit grafts together a call speech (Isa. 61) and a Zion salvation announcement (Isa. 62). It connects the first-person speech of the one anointed (61:10) with the first-person speech in the Zion salvation oracle. The combination of the two chapters knits together the prosperity of the earth described in 62:11 and the prosperity of Zion/Jerusalem elaborated throughout Isaiah 62.

The language of thanksgiving in 61:10a is interesting. The first exultation, "I greatly rejoice," has no clear parallel in the Hebrew Bible. But the later exultation, "my whole being exults" (JPS), finds an interesting parallel in Psalm 97:1, which is one of the YHWH MLK ("the LORD reigns") psalms, while it is clear that the first-person speech in Isaiah 61:10 is the anointed one. The occasion for the thanksgiving is a coronation: the speaker receives a new suit of clothing. This is typical of transformation stories in the later prophetic books, such as Zechariah (see Zech. 3:1-5). The clothes represent a military as well as a domestic category, and they are described through a genitive relation, namely, "garments of triumph" and "robe of victory."

In addition to the coronation's military aspects, we also discover a multiplicity of domestic imagery here. The language of bride and groom makes clear the marriage background; and if we follow the verbs and objects, we see something more: the verbs that describe the action of the groom and the bride are used for both the marriage festival and the priestly actions. Likewise, the objects of the sentences, "turban" and "jewels," are used in cultic contexts in other parts of the Old Testament (Ezek. 44:18; Exod. 35:22) as well as in the marriage context described here. This lifts up the multiple contexts of hope that this verse gets at, namely, the military connoted by the salvation context, the legal connoted by "righteousness," and the priestly and marital as described above. The careful reader will note that the military language is described explicitly; then the marriage image is connected to it with the use of simile.

References to garments connect this passage to earlier parts of the book of Isaiah, such as 52:1, where Jerusalem is encouraged to put on beautiful garments. This has a more ominous tone in 59:17, where these are garments of vengeance. The use of garments here probably plays on both the idea of garments as vengeance on the one hand (59:17) and those of beauty on the other — in the salvation and restoration of Jerusalem (52:1).

The passage moves us beyond an anthropocentric view of salvation: the text describes human salvation in verse 10 and then turns to the parallel in the natural world in verse 11. This is signaled in the NRSV by the preposition "for," the translation of the Hebrew word *ki*. Here the verbs focus on generativity. The language of "sprouts" in this verse overwhelms us: in the course of this single verse we find three different forms of the word for "sprout," which arises out of the seed. Finally, the text makes the point that the seed itself is righteousness. In this respect, Isaiah 61 replays the hope of Isaiah 45: here, in this passage, God causes righteousness and praise to sprout. This sprouting is seen to be over against the Gentile nations. As a verb, this term means "to be conspicuous"; as an adverb or preposition, it is often rendered "in front of, opposite to" (a more vernacular rendering might be "in the face of"), which points to the vis-à-vis nature of this community of faith in relation to the Gentile nations. As such, it provides a good segue into the psalm of Zion that begins in Isaiah 62.

Isaiah 62 begins with a conjunction of intercession, namely, "for the sake of." The focus of intercession is Zion, which is synonymous with Jerusalem. Isaiah might be called the book of Zion: the term occurs some thirty-six times in the book — twenty-three times in 1–39 and thirteen times in 40–66. Ben Ollenburger has demonstrated that Zion in passages like this provides an idealized place of God's salvation and thus is synonymous with Jerusalem. However, it can also function as the concept that forever critiques Jerusalem for falling short of what it should be as Zion.

More particularly, in 62:3 the term connects the reader to the previous chapter (see 61:3). In Isaiah 62 the mourners in Zion find comfort; we recognize this in the turnabout language indicating that they shall receive beauty for ashes. The synonymous parallelism characterized in the objects finds itself in the verb used in this passage as well: the word for "keep silent" occurs

383

six times in Isaiah, all of them in chapters 40–66. Most often it is God who is the subject of the verb (42:14; 57:11; 64:12; 65:6). Sometimes the silence of God or the salvation of God provokes a human inability to keep silent (62:6).

The Gentile community will observe the light. Once again the reader encounters the language of metaphor and simile, such as "like the brightness." The brightness is modified by the terms "righteousness" and "salvation." Both of these belong to Zion, which in this case is also Jerusalem. "Burning" is the same word used in Exodus 3 for the burning bush. Burning is a typical theophanic element, so the careful reader is not surprised that the next verse begins with the verb "see." The ones having the visions are the Gentile nations; what they are observing is the righteousness and honor.

The fire of salvation opens the conclusion of the passage that returns us to the theme of rejoicing and gladness.

Stephen Breck Reid

Second Sunday after the Epiphany, Year C

First Lesson: Isaiah 62:1-5
(Psalm 36:5-10)
Second Lesson: 1 Corinthians 12:1-11
Gospel Lesson: John 2:1-11

Historical and literary background. This text continues the powerful themes of reversal, renewal, and restoration. Speaking to the exilic community, the text offers a sense that God's ultimate purposes for his people Israel have not yet reached their final goal. If the prophets could look beyond their proclamation of God's judgment as punishment to an even greater action of God in restoration and in salvation and renewal, then certainly the exilic and postexilic communities could be encouraged even when the anticipation of their return from Babylon and the restoration of the glories of Jerusalem were not confirmed by the somewhat disappointing realities of the decades (and even centuries) that followed. So it is in any age.

Confident in the plan and purposes of a God whose vision for the future extends far beyond what human eyes can see, God's people are confident in the hope that the realities and disappointments of life (and its earthly joys, successes, and blessings) are only the *penultimate* realities. Yet even now, as then, or at any time and in any age, in any place and under any circumstance, God's people are bold to give lively and living testimony to the joy of their relationship with the God of both creation and redemption. Through his people on earth, God's light is reflected in a *present* expression of God's righteous rule and reign of peace and glory.

Isaiah 60:1-6 has already set such a tone for the entire Epiphany season. Following the exhortation to repentance (59:12), the prophet has asserted that there was no one but Yahweh himself to work justice and salvation (59:16) and to lead the way (indeed, *make* the way) back to Zion, reestablish his covenant promises, and give a renewal of his spirit (59:20-21).

Then God's glory will rise upon Zion and be reflected for all the nations to see (chaps. 60–61). These chapters include what many consider to be a fifth servant song in 61:1-7, itself an Epiphany text in its application by Jesus of Nazareth to the early manifestation of his own identity and mission (Luke 4:16ff.).

The theme of putting on new clothes (applied to Yahweh's role as Savior already in 59:17) is now extended to God's people (or the person of the servant?) in 61:10-11, which is the appointed reading for Christmas (new clothes for Christmas!). In 62:1ff. the Epiphany themes of glory and splendor point forward, muted only by the implication that their fulfillment still lies in the future, yet powerful in the anticipation that such a future is imminent and that God (or the prophet/servant?) will not be silent or still until all that God has promised will come to be.

Textual notes. It seems most likely that the first-person pronoun belongs to Yahweh, although it is possible that the one who "will not keep silent" is the prophet or even the anointed evangelist of 61:1. In any case, the proclamation cannot be held back, the word of the Lord cannot be restrained.

Yet it is for Zion's and Jerusalem's sake that this good news is proclaimed, not only because it is Zion herself who will be renewed but also because it is Zion who needs to hear that her hope and expectation for God's salvation are not in vain. In spite of her sin and God's righteous judgment, it is her righteousness and her salvation that will shine like the dawn and give light like a blazing torch. It is, of course, *Yahweh's* salvation and righteousness (61:10) given to her, which Zion now wears as her own. She offers humble gratitude to the one who has saved her from the shame of nakedness, abandonment, bereavement, and barrenness. The latter are characteristics of women in that culture who had lost the complement of husbands and children (see vv. 4-5 below).

Yet it is not for the sake of Zion alone that righteousness and salvation are given. The nations, even Assyria and Babylon, who were used by God to punish and destroy, will now be witnesses of Jerusalem's glory and light. Not only will they recognize that the God of Jerusalem has not, in the end, abandoned his people, but those outside Israel would also come to realize that true salvation and righteousness are located in Israel also for them and for all.

For Israel, this message of righteousness and glory comes with a change of character and even identity. No longer perceived as abandoned by God, God's people will now be renewed and renamed. The giving of a name — and the changing of a name — is a sign of a change of identity, and it is from the mouth of Yahweh (v. 2b).

The opulent trappings of monarchy are now bestowed directly upon the corporate people of God as a whole, who are here described more in terms of a queen to King Yahweh than those under the human leadership of a Davidic monarch. All the paraphernalia of a woman's "splendor" (tip'eret), which Adonai had promised to remove from clothes and closet in 3:18-24 (twenty-one items, all defined by the construct noun tip'eret), will be replaced by a diadem of splendor (the Hebrew term has sound play, 'eteret tip'eret) now in Yahweh's hand and not in anyone's personal jewel box. It is probably worth noting that back in chapter 3, the male leadership is also removed and destroyed, so that the bereaved women are left to fend for themselves (4:1). Although a sensitive issue in our contemporary culture, the concept of a barren woman or a widowed wife as a symbol of despair was very real indeed. In this pericope, it serves as a backdrop for the metaphor of Yahweh as bridegroom and husband.

In verse 4 this metaphor is extended to the land, described as a woman whose name is "desolate" or "abandoned." This vocabulary of shemamah and 'azubah recalls the prediction in 6:11. In response to the prophet's question, "How long, O Lord?" (lit. "until when"), God answers, "until . . . the land is a desolation (shemamah) and a great abandonment ('azubah)." In Isaiah 62, the word of God (and/or his prophet) cannot be held silent until . . . the people/land will no longer be a 'azubah or shemamah.

The new names, now to be given by the very mouth of Yahweh, continue to mix the metaphor between woman and land. The wife figure will be called Hephzibah, the actual name of Hezekiah's queen (2 Kings 21:1) and an allusion that may recall the brief and precarious interlude between the Assyrian and Babylonian threats (cf. Isa. 36–39). Literally, the name means "my desire [is] in her," and one is tempted to consider the other references to the "desire" (ḥepeṣ) of Yahweh in the context. In 44:28 it is Cyrus who will carry out God's "purpose," which is to overcome Babylon (48:14), an intent that will come to pass because the God of Jerusalem is the only true God (46:9-10). In 53:10 it is the "desire" of Yahweh to crush the servant yet prolong his days so that the "purpose" of Yahweh will succeed. That God's purpose can extend from darkness to light, and even pass from death to life, brings remarkable comfort that God's Word and promises will, in the end, accomplish that which is his "purpose" (55:11).

In 62:4 the name "my ḥepeṣ is in her" may combine these themes of Yahweh's ultimate purpose for his people with the good pleasure and joy that he receives because his queen/bride is in a wonderful relationship of love and marriage. Like the bride, so the land is also "married" (be'ulah, the passive participle of the verb b-ʿ-l, "to marry, to become husband") and no longer without abandonment or hope.

The metaphor of bride and groom then carries over into the concluding verse 5, which is somewhat the Old Testament's version of Ephesians 5:22ff. In Ephesians the relationship between Christ and his bride the church is the model for marriage; in Isaiah 62 the metaphor of marriage is used to describe the relationship of God to his people. The awkwardness of the expression "your sons will marry you" is most likely simply an extension of the metaphor of marriage to the land and its future. The attempt cited even in some English Bibles to emend the vowels from "your sons" to "your builders" is neither necessary nor improves the sense, although there is interesting wordplay between the vocabulary for "son," "build," and "house." The point seems to be that the generations returning from exile will continue to inhabit the land and maintain the name change from "desolate" to "married" (as in v. 4).

Finally, with all the talk of joy and gladness in so many of these passages, 62:5 adds the wonderful observation that God himself will also rejoice over his people. The joy of God's people on earth is commingled with the joy of God in heaven in a grand and glorious celebration of this life-giving and life-renewing relationship.

Homiletical application. One of the greatest problems within the exilic and even postexilic period, and one that confronts people of faith in any age, is the question whether God has abandoned his people. Optimism can lead to hopes and expectations that may remain unrealized, and even a faith that is securely anchored in the word and promise of God can run up against realities that seem to contradict the way things ought to be. In this text it is clear that God will not sit still until the full glory of his life-giving renewal is revealed. So, too, the "epiphany" of God's glory in Christ. Early indications of his person and message, through proclamation, through acts of healing, and even through a sign such as at the wedding at Cana (see the Gospel reading from John 2:1-11), led to expectations that seemed crushed by the cross. Yet God's ultimate plan — and the full manifestation of his glory — will not be deterred.

Baptized into both the death and resurrection of Christ, God's people receive a new name and with it a new identity. Celebrating a marriage feast even greater than that at Cana, God's people are given to drink a wine far greater than any made with ordinary human hands. And even amidst the disappointments and unrealized eschatology of life in a not-so-good land, we anticipate a yet more glorious day when the new Jerusalem will appear as a bride beautifully dressed for her husband (Rev. 21:2).

Andrew H. Bartelt

Nativity of the Lord (Christmas Day), Years A, B, C

First Lesson: Isaiah 62:6-12
(Psalm 97)
Second Lesson: Titus 3:4-7
Gospel Lesson: Luke 2:(1-7), 8-20

B oth the traditional consensus about the book of Isaiah and newer ap-proaches to it are helpful in understanding Isaiah 62:6-12 (see the exegesis of Isa. 58:1-9a, [9b-12]). The traditional consensus is that Isaiah 56–66, Third Isaiah, was written by the followers of Second Isaiah (chaps. 40–55) to articulate their disappointment after the return from exile when the glorious vision of Second Isaiah failed to materialize. The followers of Second Isaiah had apparently been excluded from participation in community life by a priestly establishment, and 56–66 both expresses the pain of this prophetic group and articulates their alternate vision.

This consensus helps to explain one of the puzzling features of 56–66. Third Isaiah can be magnificently universal in welcoming all peoples and nations, as in 62:10-12 (see also 56:3-8; 60:1-3), but it can also sound extremely narrow and exclusive (see 65:11-16; 66:24). This seeming contradiction is best explained as both an attempt to remain faithful to Second Isaiah's vision of God's universal reign (52:7-10) and an expression of the disappointment the Isaianic followers experienced at being excluded and oppressed by the priestly establishment. In any case, there was a sharp contrast between the glorious promises of Second Isaiah and the realities of life in the restored nation, especially for those who may have been excluded from full participation (see Isa. 58, which mentions hunger, homelessness, and nakedness). Indeed, this contrast enables us to frame what must have been central theological questions for the disciples of Second Isaiah: What happened to the "gospel" proclaimed by our master? Where is our salvation? Does God still reign? Is God still with us?

The existence of such questions means that the community of Third Isaiah would have lived eschatologically — that is, continuing to affirm the sovereignty of God amid circumstances that seemed to deny it. In other words, the community would have lived in hopeful anticipation of God's ongoing activity in their midst. It is at this point that the traditional consensus on the book of Isaiah converges with more recent attempts to discern the unity of the whole book. Edgar Conrad, for instance, points out that, although deliverance from Babylon may be implied (as in 62:6-12), it is *not* explicitly narrated. Thus, he concludes that the book of Isaiah leaves its readers in waiting, living hopefully toward a future entrusted to God and living in pursuit of God's purpose of peace among all nations (see *Reading Isaiah* [Philadelphia: Fortress, 1991]). On Christmas Day we celebrate Christ's birth as a sign of God's sovereignty, and yet we do so in the midst of a troubling and troubled world. As God's people, we are still living eschatologically, not unlike the community portrayed in 62:6-12.

Verses 6-7, along with 61:1-3, seem to offer a glimpse of how the community of Third Isaiah understood its situation and its task. Both 61:1-3 and 62:6-7 recall a key passage in Second Isaiah, 52:7-10. Isaiah 61:1-3 repeats the key word *basar*, "bring good news/good tidings," from 52:7 (see also 40:9; 41:27; by way of its Greek translation, *basar* underlies the English word "gospel/good news"). The concept of "sentinels" from 52:8 is picked up in 62:6-7. There are significant contrasts, however, between the sentinels in 52:8 and those in 62:6 (which may explain why a different Hebrew word is used in each case). In 52:7-10 the sentinels "lift up their voices" (v. 8) and sing joyfully (vv. 8-9). They have good reason to sing, because they have seen "the return of the LORD to Zion" (v. 8). In 62:6-7, on the other hand, the speech of the sentinels is no longer the joyful proclamation of good news, but rather the poignant and persistent intercession for a Jerusalem which is yet to be established (see also 62:1). The sentinels have nothing to see nor proclaim. Their task is continually to "remind the LORD" to act (v. 6).

The implication is that God is not present, even though the return from exile has occurred and Jerusalem has been reoccupied. It remains for the sentinels, the prophetic community of Third Isaiah, to continue to watch and wait and pray. According to 62:6, "they shall never be silent" (see also 62:1). The implication is clear: the prophetic community "shall never be silent" even though they perceive God to be silent. The prophetic community is also enjoined to "take no rest" (v. 6) or "give him [God] no rest until he establishes Jerusalem" (v. 7). Again, the implication is that the prophetic community cannot rest because God is resting. God, it seems, is on leave.

Verses 8-9 highlight the problem. Because the apparent exclusion of "foreigners" (v. 8) seems to contradict the anticipated gathering of the peoples in verses 10-12, verses 8-9 are sometimes viewed as a later addition. But the contradiction is more apparent than real. If the promise in verses 8-9 is understood as the reversal of the covenant curses in Deuteronomy 28:30-33 and Leviticus 26:16, and if the meal described in verse 9 is understood as a covenant meal, then verses 8-9 envision God fully dwelling in Jerusalem with the people again (see Elizabeth Achtemeier, *The Community and Message of Isaiah 56–66* [Minneapolis: Augsburg, 1982], p. 99). This is precisely what the prophetic community was watching, waiting, and praying for.

Verse 10 assumes that Jerusalem has been reoccupied. The command to "go through the gates" encourages returnees to leave Jerusalem in order to work at preparing the way for more of "the people" to enter the city. Are "the people" or "the peoples" Judeans or foreigners? The answer to this question is related to the meaning of "reward" and "recompense" in verse 11, as well as the identity of "they" in verse 12. The end of verse 11 is an exact quote of a portion of 40:10, where it is clear that "reward" and "recompense" designate those returning from Babylon. That could also be the case in 62:11, assuming the return from Babylon spread out for several years following 538 B.C. Achtemeier (pp. 101-2), however, proposes an alternative. In view of the mention of "peoples" (v. 10) and "the end of the earth" (v. 11), she suggests that "reward" and "recompense" refer to foreigners who will come to Jerusalem to worship God. Thus in verse 12 "they," "the Holy People," and "the Redeemed of the LORD" would also refer to this international gathering.

Because all the peoples of the earth will recognize God's reign and will come to Jerusalem to worship, Jerusalem will be "Sought Out" and "A City Not Forsaken" (v. 12; see 62:4). This interpretation has much to commend it. It is in keeping with the universalistic scope with which Third Isaiah begins (chap. 56); it is faithful to Second Isaiah's vision of Israel as "a light to the nations" (42:6; 49:6); and it is congruent with 2:1-4, which Conrad identifies as the programmatic vision for the entire book of Isaiah. It is important to note that Second Isaiah's description of Israel's mission to be "a light to the nations" occurs in two of the servant songs (42:1-9; 49:1-6). In light of 62:10-12, especially when heard in conjunction with 61:1-3 (which is often identified as a fifth servant song; see also 50:4-9; 52:13–53:12), it seems likely that Third Isaiah understood the oppressed prophetic community to be fulfilling the role of the Suffering Servant — being a light to the nations for the salvation of the whole world.

Christians, of course, find the fulfillment of 62:6-12 in Jesus, both the Messiah who proclaimed and embodied God's reign and the Suffering Servant who offered salvation to the world. It is revealing that Luke 4:16-21 records that Jesus began his ministry by reading Isaiah 61:1-3 and saying, "Today this scripture has been fulfilled in your hearing" (Luke 4:21). Here Jesus is cast in the role apparently assumed by the prophetic community of Third Isaiah — Suffering Servant for the salvation of the world (note too how Jesus goes on in Luke 4:22-30 to tell two stories of how the mercy of God is extended to non-Israelites). It is with solid canonical warrant that Isaiah 62:6-12 is the first lesson for Christmas Day.

Affirming that Jesus is the fulfillment of 62:6-12 and the whole Isaianic tradition appears to answer the questions that confronted the disciples of Second Isaiah (see above). We say that Jesus is God's good news to the world (see Mark 1:1; Rom. 1:1). Jesus is our salvation. Jesus is the sign and embodiment of God's reign. Jesus is Immanuel, God with us (Isa. 7:14; Matt. 1:23). These profound and true affirmations, however, should not be taken as facile and simplistic answers. In a real sense, we stand at Christmas, and in all seasons, right where the prophetic community of Third Isaiah stood; and we confront the same hard realities as we proclaim Jesus' birth. For we still live amid the bad news of hunger, homelessness, and the pain of oppression in many forms. We hear more about death and destruction than we do about salvation and life. Terror seems to reign instead of God. We are haunted by the suspicion that we are alone in the universe.

In other words, the church still lives as an eschatological community, affirming the reality of God's reign amid circumstances that seem to deny it. Amid various scenarios for the future (some of them quite catastrophic and even popularly labeled "apocalyptic," such as a nuclear winter or the greenhouse effect), we dare to affirm that the future belongs to God. Affirming that God reigns, we do in the present what the prophetic community of Third Isaiah did and what Jesus did. We watch, we pray, and we assume the role of Suffering Servant for the sake of the life of the whole world and all its peoples. Or, in terms of the second lesson for Christmas Day, we "become heirs in hope of eternal life" (Titus 3:7).

J. Clinton McCann

Note: Portions of the above appeared originally in substantially the same form in *No Other Foundation* 10, no. 1 (summer 1989).

First Sunday after Christmas, Year A

First Lesson: Isaiah 63:7-9
(Psalm 148)
Second Lesson: Hebrews 2:10-18
Gospel Lesson: Matthew 2:13-23

This is an in-between time. Advent and Christmas are over but Epiphany, typically the last Sunday of the year, has not yet started. The preparation for the new year already presses on people in the congregation, who have breathed a sigh of relief but also have experienced a certain letdown after the celebration of the birth of Christ.

If the congregation has been following the Revised Common Lectionary, the first readings have come from Isaiah and the Gospel readings have come from Matthew. The collateral readings for the week are quite interesting. The Psalms passage (Ps. 148) is one of the Hallel psalms (Pss. 145-50): these psalms of praise provide an important crescendo for the praise that is part of the first reading. The connection to the Gospel reading is no less compelling: the beginning of the Isaiah reading that recounts and remembers the redemptive activity of God seems right in line and a helpful liturgical context for God's call to Joseph to take his family to Egypt to escape the murderous Herod (Matt. 2:13-23). The connection to the Epistle reading of the day is more distant: Hebrews 2:10-18 points to the role of Christ as pioneer. One could make connections to the other texts, but it would take remarkable creativity, for the natural valences are tentative.

The first reading is but a snippet; therefore, it becomes all the more important to understand the literary context of the passage. First, one should note that this passage occurs in one of the most often-quoted Old Testament books in early Christianity. Isaiah 63 is usually considered part of either Second Isaiah or Third Isaiah. But the potential problems with this identification are numerous. First, should one speak of the hypothetical Second Isaiah or of Isaiah as a continuous testimony? Second, if one posits a Second Isaiah, what are the limits of that book? That is to say, can one establish that there was in fact a Third Isaiah? Third, if one can establish that there is a Third Isaiah, can it be said to have enough coherence to provide a literary context?

These are not solely academic questions; in fact, they shape our preaching. Despite injunctions not to be double-minded, the preacher will want to make a double affirmation here that might seem contradictory. First, note that the passage is part of the Isaiah school and as such is heir to the promises and the admonitions of earlier Isaiah passages. The preacher will observe that for the community of Qumran there was just one Isaiah. There was not a second Isaiah scroll or a third Isaiah scroll — just the Isaiah scroll. The Isaiah school is like a tradition of jazz: the new composer or arranger builds on the classics inherited. At the same time, the historical and social location of Isaiah 63 stems from the postexilic reconstruction. This social location may resonate with the congregation. Christmas is over; this is the Sunday before the calendar changes the year, and now it is time to think about reconstruction and restoration.

Isaiah 59 is a call to repentance that introduces poems of the glory of Jerusalem (60:1–62:12). The mood changes with chapter 63. First there is a poem of divine vengeance (63:1-6); then the counterpoint to that divine vengeance is the psalm of intercession for the believing community (63:7–64:12). The passage under discussion does not include all of the psalm of intercession.

One of the first things that the careful reader observes when examining 63:7-9 and its immediate literary context is the shift in voices. There is not a change from first-person speech; nonetheless, the first-person speech has moved from divine first person (63:1-6) to human first person (63:7a). This first-person speech is a vow typical in Hebrew poetry. The vow was a staple of the complaint psalm (Pss. 22:25; 56:12; 61:5, 8) but was also sometimes used in the context of celebration (Ps. 108:1-4). The verb used in this passage is not the word for "vow" but the term for "cause to remember," which the NRSV renders "recount" and the NIV "tell." This obscures the Hebrew root for the word "remember" (zakar), which figures prominently in Isaiah: one form or another of this word occurs twenty-nine times in the book.

393

Isaiah 63 blends prophetic and poetic genres. As a key to understanding the structure of the chapter, one should track the term "memory." This points to the fact that the selection of the reading for this Sunday (vv. 7-9) ignores the poetic structure (63:1-19). Structurally the chapter begins with the poem of divine vengeance (vv. 1-6), followed by the intercession (vv. 7-9); then one encounters the transition, which is also an indictment and announcement of judgment (v. 10); and then the term "remember" sets the tone for the rest of the chapter and poem (vv. 11-19).

The call-to-remember vow that begins the prayer of intercession sets in motion the remembrance of verse 11. This passage is a call to remember the salvation of the Lord, but also the disobedience of the people of God (Pss. 78; 106; Neh. 9:16ff.; and Isa. 63:7ff.). The call-to-remember is a vow in form-critical terms, and the vow to remember has parallels with other public confessional behavior: the vow to praise (Pss. 7:17; 9:2; 109:30; 111:1) occurs often; in the penitential prayer we find a vow to teach (Ps. 51:13); the vow in Psalm 51 is part of the penitential element of the psalm. If one notices the function of the remembrance in Psalm 106 and Nehemiah 9:16ff., one can detect the role of public confession. However, we notice that confession has two parts: recital of salvation and recital of disobedience.

Another element of confession is represented in the parallel passage, Psalm 78, where the process of remembering is validation for the rejection of Ephraim. If confession includes the recital of divine grace and human disobedience, it also includes an awareness of the contingency of election. The temptation is to say that God is too good for the contingency to exist, so humans prefer to deny the contingency. A more accurate assessment would be that God's grace is sufficient to come to terms with the reality of the contingency.

The recital of salvation uses a number of rhetorical devices. For example, in the phrase "all which the LORD deals bountifully with us, moreover, much good to the house of Israel," "deal bountifully" and "much good" are in synonymous parallelism. The next passage repeats the phrase "deal bountifully," only this time as a participle. The next phrase repeats the modifier "much." So one sees God's abundant loyalty paralleling God's abundant goodness in the previous line. The third-person description of divine action in verse 7 connects to verse 8, which marks the confession part of the passage. The psalmist quotes a divine speaker as a confession of faith in the salvation history. The actions of verse 7b are based on the divine speech quoted in 8a. Here one might play with the notion of the connection between the speech of God and the action of God, a theme that fits well as we approach the beginning of the year. God's speech announces that this is God's own people. The verse continues as it describes what it means to be the people of God.

> And children do not deal falsely.
> For God has become savior for them.

Morality and community forge a bond in this verse.

The seam of verse 7 and 8 forges the bond of God's action of salvation, divine speech, and human ethics. Verse 9 welds together the salvation acts of God with God's identification with the afflictions of humans. The word often translated "afflictions" includes what might also be called oppression. The metaphor that comes to mind is the "press that makes stress." God takes on every oppression of humans. This reminds us of the teaching of Gregory of Nazianzus (329-89 C.E.), the Cappadocian Father who said that what is not assumed by Christ is not redeemed by Christ. Verse 8 makes the point that God has assumed every oppression of humans, that is, those of the community of faith.

The salvation is mediated through the messenger of God's presence. The salvation language of verse 9 echoes that of verse 8, where the subject is clearly God. The point here is that the messenger is the extension of God. This would be an interesting place to reflect on divine agency and what it means to be an angel or messenger. The parallelism of prepositional phrases is more important than the reader might initially notice. The verse begins with "in all their affliction"; later in the verse comes another prepositional phrase, "in the love and pity of God." This syntactical parallelism makes the point that the suffering of God is an outgrowth of the love of God. In Hebrew grammar and syntax there is a notion of hendiadys, which refers to a single concept that is expressed in two words connected with the word "and." This is the only place where love is so fused with mercy.

The church has associated the messenger with the Messiah, the one who redeems. The redeemer is now described as the one who lifts and carries his people. The redemptive support the community received from God was perceived as long-standing, and this was all the more reassuring to the community in exile. This short passage underscores our vulnerability and God's willingness to take on that vulnerability.

Stephen Breck Reid

First Sunday of Advent, Year B

First Lesson: Isaiah 64:1-9
(Psalm 80:1-7, 17-19)
Second Lesson: 1 Corinthians 1:3-9
Gospel Lesson: Mark 13:24-37

Two background issues should be noted about this text, one historical and one literary. Historically, the passage belongs to a part of the book of Isaiah (chaps. 56–66) which had its origin among the Jewish exiles who had returned from forced exile in Babylon to their homes in Jerusalem and Judah. They sought to restore a holy and pure people back in their homeland. But their efforts were resisted by ruling groups who had taken over the rebuilding of the temple and worship according to their standards, which were not true and faithful to God. This part of Isaiah, Third Isaiah, which encompasses chapters 56–66, has been termed "proto-apocalyptic" material. That is, its themes and motifs and style begin to approach that of apocalyptic literature, known best in the Old Testament in the book of Daniel and in the New Testament in the book of Revelation. This is material focused on the hope of God's radical transformation of the present. It is typically produced by small, persecuted communities who feel powerless against the strength of present oppressors. These small groups survive through their faith in God's future and their diligence in remaining true and pure in their faith. They are self-critical, confessing their own sin but also asking God to overturn their present situation in a dramatic and radical way.

From a literary perspective, Isaiah 64:1-9 functions as part of a larger unit, an extended lament offered by or on behalf of the community (for similar communal laments, see Pss. 44; 74; 79). The larger unit begins in 63:7 and ends in 64:12. A lament is a prayer to God for help in time of need. The petitioner offers reasons why God should intervene and remedy the situation. Lament is disputation, an argument with God. It may be that the lament will change God's mind and reverse God's plans as Moses did on Mount Sinai after the golden calf (see Exod. 32:14; see also Num. 14:10-20). The one making the lament is certainly not guaranteed the desired result. But the faithful petitioner is guaranteed a hearing, a listening. Israel's God is a God who pays special attention to the cry of the oppressed (Exod. 3:7; Deut. 24:15; Judg. 3:9). The extended lament in Isaiah 63:7–64:12 forms the content of the unrelenting cries of the sentinels or guards the prophet has set up on the city walls surrounding Zion in 62:6-7. These sentinels will not give God any rest until God responds to their pleas:

> Upon your walls, O Jerusalem,
> > I have posted sentinels;
> all day and all night
> > they shall never be silent.
> You who remind the LORD,
> > take no rest,
> and give him no rest
> > until he establishes Jerusalem
> > and makes it renowned throughout the earth. (62:6-7)

The substance of what these sentinels are to cry out to God comes in the extended lament of 63:7–64:12, which forms the larger interpretive context for 64:1-9.

The movement of thought in this larger unit of 63:7–64:12 may be outlined as follows as we note the particular role of 64:1-9 (the lectionary text) within the larger community lament:

- A remembrance of God's "gracious deeds" and Israel's innocent youth (63:7-9).
- BUT Israel rebelled and God became their enemy (63:10)!
- Where is the God who acted to deliver God's people so many times in the past (63:11-14)? — an appeal to God's external work in history.
- Where is God's zeal and might, God's heart and compassion, to deliver God's people (63:15)? — an appeal to God's internal character.
- A first affirmation of assurance: "You . . . are our father; / our Redeemer from of old" (63:16).
- Why has God made us to stray and hardened our hearts? Turn back, O God . . . (63:17).
- The first description of the distress: enemies have trampled down the temple (63:18-19).

[The lectionary text begins at this point.]

- O that you, God, would tear open the heavens and come down to make your name known to the nations (64:1-4). God should come not in some quiet or hidden way, but with decisive force as God did before when God caused mountains to quake and fire to blaze forth (see Exod. 19:16-18; Ps. 114:3-6).

397

- A second description of the distress (64:5-7).
- A second affirmation of assurance (64:8) — "YET you are our Father." To address God as divine Parent is a claim to be God's children in spite of all the evidence.
- Do not be exceedingly angry: consider we are your people (64:9).

[This is the end of the lectionary text.]

- A third description of the distress (64:10-11) — Jerusalem is in ruins (64:10-11).
- The climactic plea to God: "After all this, will you restrain yourself, O LORD? / Will you keep silent . . . ?" (64:12).

The important paradoxes and pairings in this extended lament generate a number of theological reflections.

1. There are two great disjunctions in the lament. The first is in 63:7-10 where God deals graciously with an innocent and young Israel, BUT Israel rebels. The second disjunction is in 64:8, in which the one speaking the lament acknowledges Israel's sin and rebellion. "We have been in our sin a long time . . . we are unclean . . . polluted . . . faded, blown away . . . abandoned." And then comes a powerful YET (64:8). That "yet" is the basis of Advent, a *yet* against all the present data, a *yet* based only in the person of God in whom we hope and to whom we belong. YET God is Israel's "Father" and thus should not abandon Israel, even though Israel is rebellious. The prophet lives between these two great disjunctions in the tug between God's righteous judgment on Israel's constant rebellion and God's obligation to save Israel as Israel's divine Parent.

2. Israel's present distress is described in both external and internal terms. On one hand, the cause of Israel's distress is external and visible for all to see. God's temple is trampled, and Jerusalem is ruined (63:18-19; 64:10-11). On the other hand, Israel's distress is described as residing in the inner character of the people, who are sinful and unclean (64:5-7). The outer realities are symptomatic of a deeper and inner distress within the community and within Israel as a whole.

3. Similarly, the lament appeals both to God's external acts of deliverance in past history (63:11-14) and to God's inner character and qualities such as zeal, might, compassion, and heart (63:15) as the reasons why God needs to act now to save God's people.

4. The refrain "You are our Father" is repeated three times in the lament (two times in 63:16 and once in 64:8-9), and thus forms the most important

basis for the prophet's urgent request for God's dramatic intervention to deliver the people from their time of crisis, chaos, and pain. We begin in Advent by knowing whose we are. As we begin to await the coming birth of the Christ child, we are reminded that we are not abandoned orphans. Nor are we self-sufficient adults. We are children of a divine Parent. It may be that some have not sensed the immediate presence of this Parent lately. But in the midst of pain and chaos and confusion, we desperately and passionately cling to the assured future coming of God into our midst.

5. On one hand, the prophet asks God to "look down from heaven and see" (63:15). Here is a more transcendent view of God. Just by looking down from heaven, God may be able to turn this time of crisis around. On the other hand, the prophet, with yet stronger images in 64:1-3, asks that God tear apart the heavens and come down to rescue Israel. The distant God should come near. The agony of the present situation demands a dramatic rupture in the fabric of reality so that the divine enters into the historical realm of human reality, creating a cosmic disturbance of quaking mountains, crackling fires, and boiling waters. It is not enough for God to see from afar. God must enter intimately into the here and now.

6. Advent, like Isaiah 64:1-9, is concerned with human alienation from God and with the drastic consequences of human sinfulness. But like this text, Advent looks beyond these to God's intervention from heaven (64:1) in the incarnation of God-made-flesh in Jesus, who entered into and overcame human sinfulness and sorrow. Mark's Gospel picks up Isaiah's images of ripping open the heavens in the scene of Jesus' baptism (Mark 1:10-11) and the passion story with the tearing open of the temple curtain, the divide between heaven and earth (Mark 15:37-39).

Dennis T. Olson

Twenty-sixth Sunday after Pentecost, Year C

First Lesson: Isaiah 65:17-25
(Isaiah 12)
Second Lesson: 2 Thessalonians 3:6-13
Gospel Lesson: Luke 21:5-19

The Twenty-sixth Sunday after Pentecost marks the approach of the end of the liturgical year. Christ the King Sunday follows the next Sunday. This is the last gasp before the pressures of Thanksgiving and Advent.

The passage begins with a connection to the preceding passage, which closes with "for the former tribulations should be forgotten" (Isa. 65:16b). Isaiah 65:17-25 describes why such a forgetting is possible: the answer is the new creation. The key verb form that sets the pace for this passage occurs only in Second Isaiah, with echoes in Third Isaiah (Isa. 40:28; 42:5; 43:15, 18; 57:19; 65:17, 18). The verb *bara'*, which we encounter for the first time in Genesis 1, is connected to God's unique work of creation. The form here is a participle, whose predominant use is to connote a continuing action. So the JPS translates this, "I am creating." However, the same form can indicate imminent action. Hence the NRSV uses the phrase "I am about to create." The task of the preacher would not necessarily be to decide in favor of one or the other of these two functions, but to play into the question of whether this creation is continuing action or imminent action.

The object of creation once again sends the reader back to Genesis 1, to the new heaven and earth. The language of new heaven and earth has no parallel in the Hebrew Bible; but the New Testament parallel is well known (Rev. 21:1): "Then I saw a new heaven and a new earth; for the first heaven and the first earth had passed away, and the sea was no more."

This text invites us to pay attention to those times when the no can be the most profound yes. The rest of the passage is dominated by no fewer than ten negatives. The first is "do not remember." This not-to-be-remembered language has interesting parallels in Ezekiel (18:24; 33:13, 16), where the forms are the subjects of the verb actions. This indicates that the "former things" refers to, as they say in the legal profession, "previous bad acts."

It shall never again come to mind. The process of remembering is more than an abstract detachment; on the contrary, it is an expression of wholeness. The language of "come to mind" in the NRSV, which could also be translated "come upon [the] heart," reminds the reader of Jeremiah 3:16, which describes the fruit of repentance. The remaining question is how to translate *leb:* some interpreters translate it closer to "mind," while others prefer "heart." In either case, *leb* should indicate the heart as the seat of the will.

The collateral reading for this Sunday (Luke 21:5-19) is an apocalyptic teaching of Jesus that has parallels in other apocalyptic texts. Revelation 21 points to the complete transformation of everything; it is right that we call this process of envisioning a new church "transformation." The passage points not only to the new creation but also to the end of chaos. From Genesis to Revelation, the sea is consistently used as a metaphor for chaos and evil. In an earlier passage, Isaiah 57 suggests that idolatry will be no more; thus the negative is taken away. Here Isaiah 65 invites us to pay attention to those times when the no can be the most profound yes.

The yeses connect God and the people of God. For the people there is delight; for God there is rejoicing in Jerusalem. If these are the yeses of the passage — the yeses of God — then what are the corresponding noes?

Never again shall there be heard weeping and wailing. It would be worthwhile to tarry a moment to allow the congregation to experience what we mean by the term "weeping." Weeping is a full-bodied cry that leaves us exhausted; many humans know this level of grief. It shall be no more.

No longer will it be that people live out less than their full time on earth. "Full days" is more than simply a length of time; it is a quality of life. The theologian Paul Tillich suggested that we rethink our notions of "eternal": we should not think of it only as infinite in length (the person who dies at 100 years of age shall be "reckoned as a youth"), but as infinite in quality. This means meaningful work and restful and stimulating retirement.

The yeses continue the theme of meaningful and productive work: the people get to live in the houses they've built; they plant gardens and eat and enjoy their fruits. Today, as we note the disparity of wealth in North America, it is not unusual for those who keep the lawns to lack the money to buy the houses that rest on those lawns. Those who build and repair homes often cannot afford to buy those homes. This text assures us of a time when there will be a correspondence between work and reward.

The yeses have their corresponding noes. "They shall not build for others to live in, nor will they plant for others to enjoy." They shall not work without purpose. Work does not go away; rather, it is transformed. The generativity of the people, that is to say, their work and their offspring, will come to fruition.

One of the most compelling noes for us is the end of terror: "No longer will they bear children in terror." Fear predominates in North American culture; the statistics on violent crime may go down, but the sense of safety in cities still remains tenuous. Thus purposeful work has a parallel in the definition of the good life: the safety of the children. Across the continent today there are parents who fear for their children. Some parents fear because of random violence against minority groups, others because of the random violence between persons, and others because of domestic violence. This passage echoes Micah 2 (". . . and none shall make them afraid").

The yeses of God continue. The text describes a world of God's attentiveness and of peace among the nations. Prayer will be answered — which refers us to one of the recurring themes in Hebrew laments, the inattentiveness of God. This passage makes the bold claim that God will answer every prayer. Peace will replace the world of predators. The new heaven and earth is a place where the lion and the lamb will lie down together. Truly a new era!

These texts remind us that God is optimistic, and in God we are optimistic about what we can be and what the church can be. But it doesn't just happen by itself. Rather, we are called to start working on this wonderful project of God — building the church and the people of God.

Stephen Breck Reid

Fourth Sunday after the Epiphany, Year C

First Lesson: Jeremiah 1:4-10
(Psalm 71:1-6)
Second Lesson: 1 Corinthians 13:1-13
Gospel Lesson: Luke 4:21-30

Fourteenth Sunday after Pentecost, Year C

First Lesson: Jeremiah 1:4-10
(Psalm 71:1-6)
Second Lesson: Hebrews 12:18-29
Gospel Lesson: Luke 13:10-17

The Creator does not keep his truth to himself, forcing his human creatures to grope in the darkness trying to imagine or construct what their Maker thinks. Nor does he locate his truth in some far-off, inaccessible place. Rather, in an "incarnational way" the Creator reveals himself and brings his truth into space and time, into our world. To do that God uses human language. Only God does not speak directly and immediately — he did that once at Mount Sinai, but the people could not handle it, and thereafter God used Moses as his mouthpiece and mediator (Exod. 20:18-21) — but he speaks through certain individuals called prophets. The Old Testament lesson narrates the call of one such prophet. His name was Jeremiah, and his call came to him in the thirteenth year of King Josiah, 627 B.C.

After the superscription in 1:1-3, the book opens with Jeremiah's autobiographical account of his call to be a prophet to the nations. The narrative has two very specific characters, not some generic deity and an unnamed human being but Yahweh, the God of Israel, and Jeremiah, the son of Hilkiah, of the priests in Anathoth, in the land of Benjamin. The language is that of space-time history and not timeless myth. The account presents itself as a dialogue between Yahweh and Jeremiah in which the focus belongs to the three poetic speeches of Yahweh:

- God calls Jeremiah to be a prophet to the nations.
- God sends Jeremiah to speak without fear.
- God gives Jeremiah God's destroying and upbuilding words.

God called Jeremiah to be a prophet to the nations. The initiative began with God. Jeremiah did not appoint himself; he did not seek the job. In fact, he even objected, "Ah, Lord Yahweh, look, I do not know how to speak, for I am only a boy." The word "boy" means that he was probably about twelve or thirteen years old, just a boy in a culture where adulthood began at twenty (Num. 14:29). Surely God can find others more qualified, others with eloquent speaking ability, since a prophet must speak and orate in public. Jeremiah's objection reminds us of the objections Moses made to his call, one of which was "I am heavy of mouth and heavy of tongue" (Exod. 4:10).

However, God does not typically choose only the best and the brightest. That is not God's usual way of operating. On the contrary, God chooses the lowly to shame the wise and mighty (1 Cor. 1:27-29). One thinks of lowly persons such as Moses; Samuel, who also was only a boy when called; and even Israel itself. One thinks of lowly things such as human words, water, bread and wine. And then there is the lowest of the low, Jesus of Nazareth on a cross.

So God called Jeremiah in spite of Jeremiah's lack of speaking ability and young age. The call from God is based on God's free and gracious choosing rather than on any deserving virtue or quality found in human be-

403

ings. In Jeremiah's case the call happened long before he proved himself worthy in any way. The word of Yahweh came to Jeremiah:

> Before I formed you in the belly I knew you,
> and before you came forth from the womb I consecrated you;
> a prophet to the nations I made you.

God the creator was the one who, like a potter, "formed" Jeremiah in his mother's womb (Ps. 139). Yet before this happened, before there even was a Jeremiah, God "knew" Jeremiah and "consecrated" him and "made [him] a prophet." To "know" here means to "choose" (cf. Amos 3:2), and to "consecrate" means to "set apart unto God for divine service." In 627 B.C. Jeremiah was informed of his call, but the call itself took place long before then. No other prophet had such an advance call. The closest parallel is the apostle Paul (Gal. 1:15).

Jeremiah was to be a prophet "to the nations." The universal scope receives emphasis again later in the pericope: "See, I have appointed you this day over the nations and over the kingdoms. . . ." The God of Israel is not limited to Israel but has authority over all the nations. Yahweh is their Creator, Lord, and Judge, the one to whom they must give an account, the only one they should worship (cf. Jer. 10). Therefore, Yahweh's prophets typically had messages that concerned other nations in addition to Israel. See, for example, Isaiah 13–27, Ezekiel 25–32, Joel 3, Amos 1–2, Obadiah, Jonah, Nahum, and Zephaniah 2. In the book of Jeremiah one may observe this universal horizon in numerous places, such as chapters 12, 18, 25, 27, and 46–51. Today the word of Israel's God continues to claim authority over all people throughout the world, everyone without exception. The scope of the church's mission extends and must always extend to all nations, as she makes disciples by baptizing and teaching.

After Jeremiah raised his objection, Yahweh replied by gently dismissing the objection and continuing his address to Jeremiah:

> Do not say "I am only a boy."
> For on all which I send you you shall go,
> and all which I command you you shall speak.
> Do not be afraid because of them,
> for I am with you to rescue you.

God had called Jeremiah from long ago, even before Jeremiah's existence. Now God sends him to speak without fear. He is to go where God sends him and to proclaim what God commands him. Moreover, God promises to be with him and to rescue him from his enemies. Jeremiah should stop objecting because God is the one who runs the show. God determines who will be a prophet, where the prophet will go, and what the prophet will say. God receives the focus of the prophetic ministry. If the people reject the prophetic word, their real disagreement is with God. The prophet is only God's messenger, God's mouthpiece.

Nevertheless, the assignment of being a prophet to the nations is a bit intimidating, to say the least. So Yahweh adds the promise. There is no need to fear the nations because Yahweh is with Jeremiah to deliver him from his enemies. The promise is repeated in Jeremiah 1:19 and 15:20. It echoes the promises of abiding presence made to others such as Isaac (Gen. 26:3), Jacob (Gen. 28:15), Moses (Exod. 3:12), and Joshua (Josh. 1:5).

The autobiographical account continues by stating that Yahweh extended his hand to touch Jeremiah's mouth. Then Yahweh explained to Jeremiah what just happened: "Look, I have put my words into your mouth." By touching Jeremiah's mouth Yahweh gave him the divine words to speak. Jeremiah is not sent to speak what Jeremiah thinks about things. That is what characterizes false prophets; they speak from their own mind and imagination (Jer. 23:16). Jeremiah is to speak what God commands him and, in fact, the very words God puts into his mouth. Thus Jeremiah will be a prophet like Moses, as promised in Deuteronomy 18:18: "I will raise up a prophet like you for them from among their countrymen, and I will put my words in his mouth, and he shall speak to them all which I command him."

Yahweh then clarified the purpose of Jeremiah's prophetic mission:

> See, I have appointed you this day over the nations and
> over the kingdoms:
> to uproot and to break down
> and to destroy and to overthrow,
> to build up and to plant.

Jeremiah was appointed over nations and kingdoms for a purpose. The purpose of his mission is given with six infinitive verbs; the first four designate the negative purpose and the last two the positive purpose (cf. Jer. 12:14-17; 18:7-9; 24:6; 31:28, 38-40; 42:10; 45:4). But how can Jeremiah do this task of destroying and building up? He does it with Yahweh's powerful words.

Postmodernism contends that human communities construct and create reality by the language they use. Yet, Yahweh is the only one who truly is postmodern, whose words are truly able to construct and create reality. They are the words of the almighty Creator who brings into being what he says, whose words accomplish mighty deeds. They are like fire and like a hammer that shatters a rock (Jer. 23:29). As the two verses that follow our pericope emphasize, Yahweh watches over his word to do it.

The destructive task was necessary because the status quo was so completely unacceptable to God. Sin ruled not only over the other nations but even over God's own covenant people. The preaching of Jeremiah repeatedly tried to convince the people how unacceptable everything was. Because they had forsaken Yahweh and had become hardened in their rebelliousness, they were under divine judgment. Sinners must be put to death; they are unable to reform themselves. So Jeremiah's first task was "to uproot, break down, destroy, and overthrow" with the powerful divine word. And God fulfilled that word with the Babylonian exile. The God of Israel put Israel to death just as Jeremiah had announced. God's word still fulfills this task as it crushes proud, self-righteous, idolatrous hearts.

But that was only a penultimate step, the first stage in a two-stage process. God's ultimate purpose was not destructive but constructive, "to build up and to plant," to bring about a new creation, a new Israel with a new heart and a new covenant. This activity of building up and planting reverses the earlier activity of uprooting and breaking down. Note how the final two verbs occur in reverse order from the first two verbs in an *abba* pattern: "to uproot and to break down//to build up and to plant." God accomplished this great reversal. He brought the exiles back, who then rebuilt the temple and the city walls of Jerusalem. God planted them in their land. But the ultimate fulfillment came in the fullness of time, when God sent his only Son into the world, to the very land of Jeremiah. There Jesus of Nazareth repeated and fulfilled Israel's history. He was uprooted and broken down, destroyed and overthrown, on a cross outside the walls of Jerusalem. On the third day he was built up and planted again. And all for us, so that we might have life with God as God's holy people.

The text highlights the theology of the divine call. The call from God was one of the things that distinguished true prophets from false prophets (Jer. 23:21, 32). What Hebrews 5:4 says about Old Testament priests applied to prophets as well. Individuals could not presumptuously take this office to themselves; they had to be called and appointed by God. Our text still speaks to the church today. Unlike Jeremiah's call, which came to him directly in an unmediated fashion, today the call comes mediated through the church. But it still comes from God. The church's called and ordained ministers bring God's word to people because God has called and sent them (Rom. 10:15). When they feel inadequate or meet resistance, their call from God can reassure them. When the church is tempted to emulate corporate America and to treat her ministers as employees to be hired and fired, the church needs to be reminded of the divine call. The ministry of her shepherds is not based on their own personal charisma or dynamic leadership skills but on being called and sent by the Chief Shepherd (1 Pet. 5:1-4; Acts 20:28).

The text also applies to the whole church in her mission. When the church meets resistance and hears the smear tactics of the world — "Stop proselytizing and imposing your religious opinions on others" — then the church must remember her commission. The crucified and risen Lord, the one sent by the Father into the world, has commissioned and sent us into the world (John 17:18; 20:21). We do not intend to coerce people or impose anything on them, but we are under orders to bring Christ's word and gifts to all people; we have no choice. We are not ashamed of the gospel. Furthermore, just as Yahweh promised to be with Jeremiah, so Jesus Christ has promised to be with us even unto the end of the age (Matt. 28:19-20). His calling, sending, and abiding presence gives us confidence and boldness in the mission as we bring his strong word to the nations.

Paul R. Raabe

Fifteenth Sunday after Pentecost, Year C

First Lesson: Jeremiah 2:4-13
(Psalm 81:1, 10-16)
Second Lesson: Hebrews 13:1-8, 15-16
Gospel Lesson: Luke 14:1, 7-14

Though he was a native of the town of Anathoth in the northern territory of Benjamin, Jeremiah carried out his prophetic ministry between the years 626 and 586 B.C. in the southern kingdom of Judah and principally in Jerusalem. Our passage comes from his earliest preaching between 626 and 621, during the reign of the good King Josiah. As is well known, after a scroll of Deuteronomy was discovered in 621 while the temple was being repaired, Josiah instigated a covenant renewal on the basis of the Deuteronomic law and carried out a massive reform movement in Judah that was

407

designed to eliminate all traces of foreign syncretism and idolatrous Baal religion in his country (2 Kings 22–23). Our text for the morning illumines the apostasy of the Israelites before that reform, in which Jeremiah undoubtedly participated, was undertaken.

The passage is such a model of Hebrew rhetoric that an examination of its structure serves to uncover its principal message. It is made up of four strophes or stanzas, verses 5-6, 7-8, 9-11, and 12-13. The language in verses 9 and 13 reveals that it is a court case of God against the Israelites, with God the plaintiff presenting his case and the heavens acting as the jury. The sentence of the court is contained in verse 13, where God also acts as judge.

The theme of the passage is presented immediately in verse 5, where it is said that the ancestors of the Israelites "went after worthlessness, and became worthless," that is, they went after other gods. At the end of the second strophe, verse 8, the thought is repeated: the prophets prophesied by Baal and "went after things that do not profit," that is, that are worthless. The same words are repeated at the end of the third strophe, verse 11: "my people have changed their glory / for that which does not profit" — once again, what is worthless. Finally, at the end of the last strophe, verse 13, the people have "hewed out cisterns for themselves, / broken cisterns, / that can hold no water," in other words, that are worthless. So the principal thought runs through the whole passage: by committing their loyalty to other gods than the Lord, the Israelites have gone after worthlessness that will profit them nothing. With so prominent a theme sounding from the text, that surely should be the main thrust of the sermon built upon it. It is no coincidence that this Old Testament text is paired in the lectionary with an Epistle and a Gospel lesson that also deal with the outcome of life, with that which profits it and that which does not.

When Jeremiah speaks of Israel's "fathers" or ancestors in our text, he is referring to Israel's actions after she entered into the Promised Land. As the immediately preceding verses, 2:1-3, show, Jeremiah shares Hosea's view that Israel's time in the wilderness was the time of her "honeymoon" with her divine husband, the Lord, when there was no Baal to come between them (cf. Hos. 2:15). But as soon as the Israelites entered into Canaan, they forgot the Lord because they did not remember what he had done on their behalf. They forgot that the Lord delivered them out of bondage in Egypt and led them through the terrors of the wilderness, "a land of deserts and pits," "of drought and deep darkness," where "none passes through" and "no man dwells." Instead, Israel's ancestors turned to the worship of the fertility gods of the Canaanites, because they thought it was the Baals who gave them "the grain, the wine, and the oil" (Hos. 2:8). They thought that the Lord, who had led them in the wilderness, could not furnish them the means of life in a sown land. And so they turned to the gods of agriculture and fertility. What a person worships, however, is what he or she becomes. And so they "went after worthlessness and became worthless" — worthless in the purpose and plan of God.

Yet, the God who led Israel through the dangers of the wilderness also provided for Israel's life in the Promised Land. God brought them to a land "flowing with milk and honey" (Exod. 3:8) — as Deuteronomy puts it, "a good land, a land of brooks of water, of fountains and springs . . . a land of wheat and barley, of vines and fig trees and pomegranates, a land of olive trees and honey, a land in which you will eat bread without scarcity, in which you will lack nothing" (Deut. 8:7-9). As the Lord provided Adam with a garden to enjoy, so he provided Israel with the fruits and good things of Canaan, and he thought that Israel would enjoy such gifts. God owned the land (note "my land" in v. 7), but he lent it to Israel. Instead, the Israelites "defiled" God's land. They polluted it.

We think of pollution of the natural world as having to do with acid rain and unclean water, with smog and the loss of wetlands and oxygen-giving forests to bulldozers and shopping centers. But in the Bible God's land is polluted by sin (Lev. 18:24-30), by murder (Num. 35:33-34), by the breaking of the law and covenant (Isa. 24:5), by adultery (Jer. 3:1), and especially by idolatry (Jer. 3:2, 9; 16:18; Acts 15:20). Indeed, says Leviticus, such sins are such an abomination to the Lord that the land will "vomit" out the persons committing them (Lev. 18:28), as the inhabitants of Judah were in fact to be "vomited" out in 587 B.C.

Jeremiah is very specific about the sins of the Israelites in his time. The priests neither remember the Lord nor teach his law (v. 8). But by "law" Jeremiah means much more than simply statutes and ordinances. Rather, the law or Torah was the sum total of all of Israel's traditions about the works and words of the Lord, and two groups in Israel were responsible for passing those on to the people, namely, the priests and the prophets. Like some clergy in every age, however, the priests know nothing of a living relationship with God, nothing of his character and works and will, and the prophets are preaching not the Word of the Lord, but simply what they hear in the cult of Baal. As for the rulers before Josiah (lit. "shepherds"), they transgressed all the just requirements of the covenant law.

With these indictments against his people, the Lord takes Israel to court (v. 9). And he finds the Israelites' actions, in the light of all that he has done for them, simply astounding. Has anyone ever heard of such a thing before, God asks, that a people would exchange their God who is their glory for "no gods"? Go to other nations and find out, God says. Go out into the Arabian Desert and look in Kedar, or cross the Mediterranean to Cyprus. Have those people exchanged their gods for deities who are worthless? Such actions are nonsensical and incredible.

The Lord therefore turns to the jury, to the heavens, in verse 12, and commands that they should be appalled and shocked at Israel's senseless actions. But then the sentence of God the judge is pronounced. "Be utterly desolate," the Lord commands; that is, be dried up and give no rain or moisture of any kind. In Jeremiah 14:1-10 we therefore find the result of that command: Judah languishes in a severe drought in which there is no water to be had.

Israel has committed two sins against her God, and she suffers the consequences. First, the Lord declares, "they have forsaken me," even though I am "the fountain of living water," the source of life that never fails in good times or bad. Second, in a figure of speech most telling in the arid Near East, God says Israel has dug for herself cisterns that are cracked and can hold no water, no source of life whatsoever. That is, Israel has turned to the worship of the fertility gods of Baal who have no power to provide their worshipers with the necessities of living.

If we set our text in its full context of the canon and turn to the New Testament, it is clear from whom we can find a fountain of "living waters" that sustains our life forever (John 4; 10). In the Fourth Gospel Jesus tells the Samaritan woman, "Whoever drinks of the water that I shall give him will never thirst; the water that I shall give him will become in him a spring of water welling up to eternal life" (John 4:14; cf. 7:37). It also is clear that it is worthless and profits us nothing to forsake our Lord and go after other gods and goddesses of our own desire and choosing. "For what does it profit a man," Jesus asks, "to gain the whole world and forfeit his life?" (Mark 8:36). As he did for Israel, God has delivered us from our slavery, finally to sin and death, and has given us good gifts beyond measure. To abandon such a love, shown forth in Jesus Christ, is worthless, profiting nothing but death. Let us instead choose Christ and life.

Elizabeth Achtemeier

Seventeenth Sunday after Pentecost, Year C

First Lesson: Jeremiah 4:11-12, 22-28
(Psalm 14)
Second Lesson: 1 Timothy 1:12-17
Gospel Lesson: Luke 15:1-10

In the first visions narrated after his call, the prophet Jeremiah receives the message that, contrary to appearances, God is about to act in the history of his people (1:11-12). The second vision, that of a boiling pot tipping its contents "from the north," is elaborated in the remaining verses of the opening chapter of the book. Disaster is coming "on all the inhabitants of the land" (v. 14), at God's instigation (v. 15), because of "all their wickedness in forsaking me" (v. 16). This message of judgment against his people dominates the message of Jeremiah, at least until after the first deportation of the people of Judah to Babylon in 597 B.C. Its essential elements are expressed in a series of textual units in 4:3–6:30. Their atmosphere may well indicate that after 597 and the later siege and destruction of Judah's capital, Jerusalem, in 586, the message was carefully edited in the hope that those now reading it could learn from pondering the prophet's earlier warnings. Not predicting but explaining why and how God works in and through disaster is certainly the main focus of our passage.

In these sayings of Jeremiah, an enemy from the north is described as invading and devastating Judah (e.g., 4:6; 6:1, 22), and the reason given is that it is God's punishment for being faithless, not listening to God's words, and not being remotely interested in truth and justice. Jeremiah probably gave this message many times over the forty or so years of his prophetic ministry. Not for nothing has the term "a Jeremiah" passed into the English language. In the eyes of the self-assured and complacent, anyone giving such a gloomy message is bound to be a pessimist and, moreover, an object of scorn:

> I have become a laughingstock all day long;
>> everyone mocks me.

The picture of someone who cannot seem to cry anything other than "Violence and destruction!" (20:7-8) is, after all, rather comical.

It is a searing expression of this message that appears in 4:11-12. The people will finally believe it when the blistering sirocco wind rips through

411

their land. The prevailing winds in Israel come from the west, across the Mediterranean Sea. To be dreaded, however, is the wind from the east, whose strength and heat are exhausting and paralyzing. Unlike other winds, which are useful for winnowing the harvest (Ps. 1:4) and enriching the land, the sirocco is entirely destructive (Hos. 13:15). The same point is made in the imagery which follows in Jeremiah 4:13. Good and bad alike are ruined by the undiscriminating whirlwind (cf. Jer. 23:19). Evil sets a process in motion and nothing can stop it. As Hosea puts it:

> They sow the wind,
> and they shall reap the whirlwind. (Hos. 8:7)

A recurrent theological difficulty surfaces here in absolute form. Disaster is the punishment inflicted by God for wrongdoing. Yet, in reality, when the destruction comes, be it in wind or nuclear explosion, it brings down everyone and everything in its wake. It leaves only a drab gray world. There is, however, worse to come. Soon there will be no world at all.

This is the upshot of the terrifying picture in 4:23-26. But first comes the explanation again. What we are offered in verse 22 is a basis for understanding the past and laying foundations for the future. This is summed up in the term "knowledge of God." The Hebrew for this carries the sense of both intellectual knowledge as understanding God's requirements and also spiritual commitment as having a practical relationship to God. This is precisely what is missing in the people who are addressed by the prophet (cf. Jer. 8:7; Isa. 28:9; Hos. 4:6). They seem incapable of grasping things. This sort of "foolishness" is often contrasted with wisdom, notably in the book of Proverbs. The only sort of wisdom they possess is the cynical, destructive capacity for "doing evil." Thus, in belief and action they have rejected God at the deepest levels. They have "rebelled" (Jer. 4:17), and the consequences will be truly catastrophic.

"I looked," says Jeremiah, or perhaps better "I saw," as in other prophetic visions, and — nothing. What we have in verses 23-26 is far more cosmic than the sort of national disaster described in verses 11-12. It is the complete dismantling of creation. Step-by-step creation is reversed. Though the pattern and order are different, this passage is surely a deliberate echo of Genesis 1–2:4a, the first account of creation. There are parallels also with the second creation story in Genesis 2:4-24 (the allusion to wilderness, for example), but essentially Jeremiah 4:23-26 is a vision of chaos returned. The "waste and void" (a superbly evocative phrase in the Hebrew) which Jeremiah envisions correspond exactly with the starting point of Genesis 1:2.

The first creative act of God was to create light (Gen. 1:3), but when Jeremiah looks "to the heavens" the light has gone. Sun, moon, and stars, we must conclude, are no more.

Mountains and hills were the most abiding reminders of God's creation of the world (e.g., Pss. 46:2; 65:6), but now even these are reeling (Jer. 4:24). As the climax of creation, God made human beings (Gen. 1:27). Now he has unmade them (Jer. 4:25). There is absolutely no human race, a recurrent prediction of Jeremiah (e.g., 2:14; 4:7, 29). Nor, in contrast to Genesis 1:20 and 22, are any birds to be seen, a sign of destruction if ever there was one (cf. Jer. 12:4). A "fruitful land" is what God's people inherited (Jer. 2:7), but now it is a barren wilderness and its cities are in ruins (Jer. 4:26). The act of creation had concluded with God resting (Gen. 2:2-3), satisfied that everything was good (e.g., Gen. 1:25). Now he is full of "fierce anger," on the rampage until he has undone everything and has achieved total wipeout. It is as if creation had never happened.

In case we have still not got the message, verse 27 announces: "The whole land shall be a desolation." Then suddenly we have a complete contradiction in "yet I will not make a full end." Though various suggestions have been made to render the Hebrew more consistently, such as "I will make a full end in relation to her" or "and none of it [the land] I will remake" or "I have not made an end yet [to the destruction]," the most obvious explanation seems to be that we have here an alteration from an editor who could not accept Jeremiah's complete nullification of life. He has introduced a "mitigating gloss" — "I will not make a full end."

Then, in verse 28, we are straight back into unmitigated disaster. A sort of cosmic funeral is envisaged with the whole earth in mourning and the heavens in black. At the beginning God spoke the irrevocable word of creation. Now he has spoken the irrevocable word of destruction. We should not attempt our own version of a mitigating gloss by balancing out the destructive with the creative word of God, as in Jeremiah 1:10. There is in chapter 4 no building and planting, but only plucking up, pulling down, destroying, and overthrowing. As in verse 12, it is God's purpose which is at stake. In the light of the utter obtuseness of his supposed people (4:22), he cannot revoke the disaster now in train.

We should take the absoluteness of this theology seriously. In the Christian tradition there is "the unforgivable sin," which similarly takes its nature from the attitude of its perpetrators. Jeremiah's contemporaries were quite brazen — arrogant, secure, and scornful in their many manifestations of unfaithfulness to their covenant partner. Jeremiah is surely suggesting that people need to remember God as creator (cf. Eccles. 12:1). If they do not, God judges and will destroy what is malfunctioning. This Old Testament passage, as indeed much of Jeremiah, states an unequivocal link between historical and natural flourishing, between personal and ecological responsibility, between individual and social sin. Not many decades have passed since it was fashionable to mock those who warned of nuclear destruction as the Jeremiahs of our time. Perhaps now the equivalent are those who warn of ecological disaster, be they theist or atheist in their interpretation of life. Let us not assume that the clear-sighted are always religious people, for it is sometimes they who mock the heralds of disaster. Jeremiah clearly encountered many such people. He warned that no place on earth was so sacred that it could not be destroyed if what went on there betrayed God (7:8-15). Says the writer of Lamentations:

> The kings of the earth did not believe,
>   nor did any of the inhabitants of the world,
>   that foe or enemy could enter the gates of Jerusalem.   (Lam. 4:12)

Who are today's equivalents and where are they to be found? The opening chapters of 1 Corinthians show Paul similarly challenging his readers about where true wisdom lies.

It has been said that human history will now be divided between pre-2000 and post-2000, because on June 26, 2000, the human genome was discovered. When asked why American and British scientists had announced the discovery when they predicted at least two years' work before the map of the human gene was final rather than in draft, a spokesman replied that society would need that time for thinking carefully about how to use the information. The accusation against geneticists that they "play God" is surely facile. What does it mean? And what does it mean to be a true partner in God's creation? These are the questions we should be asking. Not everyone, even within one particular religious tradition, is going to agree on what is permissible and impermissible. But everyone with a religious faith must surely seize such critical times as these to determine what it is to know God.

Christine E. Pilkington

Eighteenth Sunday after Pentecost, Year C

First Lesson: Jeremiah 8:18–9:1
(Psalm 79:1-9)
Second Lesson: 1 Timothy 2:1-7
Gospel Lesson: Luke 16:1-13

Jeremiah is in many ways the most remarkable of the prophets of the Hebrew Bible. That is so not only because of what he says; his prophetic targets are similar to those of many of his colleagues: idolatry and injustice head the list. It is, however, the person of Jeremiah that is so striking and unforgettable. He is a man of deep passion, burning anger for the evil evidenced by his people, and deep pain at the destruction they have brought on their heads. Unlike Amos, who manifests no genuine discomfort at the harsh words Yahweh has given him to say, Jeremiah is grieved to his heart because he has been chosen to speak the word of Yahweh's fury at a people bent on evil.

Focusing on the person of Jeremiah, however, should not cause the preacher to psychoanalyze the prophet, making him out to be some sort of manic-depressive, excited about his status as called of Yahweh but at the same time desperate to do anything else but that. To be sure, he is a man possessed by the word of his God and finds himself incapable of doing anything other than speak it, no matter the consequences. And those consequences are dire: prisons, pits, no friends, no family, public rejection and humiliation. Jeremiah is a warning to all who would blithely don the prophetic mantle; being a genuine prophet of God is not likely to win many friends nor influence many people. In fact, after reading Jeremiah, any so-called prophet who lives in luxury and basks in the pleasant glow of the adulation of the multitudes is called into the most serious of questions. Just what sort of "prophet" might this be?

Still, Jeremiah would not wish us to focus merely on his person; he wishes us to hear what he has to say. However, as is the case with most of the prophets of the Hebrew Bible, very few persons are anxious to hear such words! As noted above, Jeremiah spends the first part of his book assaulting his own people of Judah for three basic crimes, all finally crimes against Yahweh. (1) Idolatry. 5:7:

> How can I pardon you?
>> Your children have abandoned me
>> and have sworn by those who are no gods.

The mere fact of worshiping another god is not the real problem. The deeper concern is the resulting behavior of such false worship. (2) Injustice in the community. 6:13:

From the least to the greatest,
   everyone is greedy for unjust gain;
from prophet to priest
   everyone deals falsely.

The cause of the widow, the poor, the orphan, the stranger is forgotten in the headlong drive the community leaders have for power and wealth. (3) Perhaps worst of all, the communities' major religious leaders are themselves no better than those they profess to lead. 5:30:

A repulsive and horrible thing is in the land:
the prophets prophesy falsely
   and the priests function on their own authority.

In other words, no prophet or priest bases her/his work on Yahweh.

Jeremiah's fury is clear enough; he attacks his own people in potent phrase and in sarcastic and often off-color tone. Read his extended metaphor in 2:23-24, where he likens the evil people to camels and donkeys in heat who can always be depended upon, at least monthly, to satisfy their lusts. So, too, are the people of Israel who are ever lusting after gods who are no gods. But the uniqueness of Jeremiah is found in his personal response to these intemperate tirades.

To whom shall I speak, and offer warning
   that they may hear?   (6:10)

I am full of the wrath of Yahweh;
   I am tired of holding it in.   (6:11)

He *must* speak in Yahweh's name (see 20:9 for the most famous expression of this truth), but it causes him the most painful grief to do so.

Today's passage is clear witness to that reality.

I have no joy; grief is upon me;
   my heart is sick.   (8:18)

Jeremiah utters these disconsolate phrases immediately after one of his most strident attacks on the evils of Judah (8:4-17). But his cruel words have brought him at least as much pain as he hoped they would bring to the people. When Jeremiah describes his heart as "sick," he means the very center of his will and intelligence, the Hebrew conception of "heart." The evil of Judah and its inevitable coming destruction have corrupted the life of the very one who announces both; his identity *with* them is complete, hence his pain *for* them is real and agonizing.

That is why he says,

> Just listen! The cry for help from my people (lit. "the daughter
> of my people")
> from far and wide in the land:
> "Is Yahweh not in Zion?
> Is its king not in the city?" (8:19)

Yahweh has absented the center of Judah's life and hope, Jerusalem. In Jeremiah's anguished vision, he hears the dying community cry out for Yahweh, but Yahweh is silent at first. Then Yahweh's angry indictment is heard again:

> Why have they incensed me with their images,
> their foreign nothings?
> Then the people cry out again:
> The harvest has ended; the summer is over,
> but we have not been saved. (8:20)

The time of God's salvation of the people, so evident throughout the history of Israel and Judah, represented here by abundant harvest and the turn of the seasons, is past due. The time is quite literally "out of joint" in Judah, but the plaintive cries of the people are too little, too late.

And Jeremiah is anguished because of it all.

> Because of the shattering of my people, I am shattered!
> I mourn! Horror has seized me. (8:21)

There is no pleasure for Jeremiah in watching the fall of his own people, in witnessing their rejection of Yahweh and Jeremiah's words from Yahweh. He too is deeply moved by their pain, so moved that he cries out, as they have, for a sign of healing. If Yahweh has left Zion, perhaps some healing may be found elsewhere.

417

> Is there no balm in Gilead?
> Is there no doctor there?
> Why has the health of my people
> not been restored? (8:22)

Gilead appears to have been a place known for a healing balm (Gen. 37:25 and Ezek. 27:17), and perhaps was a place one could go for healing. Jeremiah's desperate cry for healing appears to be rhetorical; there are in fact no balms or doctors for Judah in Gilead or anywhere else.

And Jeremiah's desperation deepens in the light of his people's desperation. There is no healing for them, no Yahweh to comfort them. They are doomed, and the prophet is overwhelmed at the prospect.

> If only my head were waters,
> my eyes a fountain of tears,
> that I could weep day and night
> for the fatal wounds of my people! (9:1)

The word I have translated "fatal wounds" often means "profaned/defiled." Perhaps Jeremiah implies both meanings. The people's wounds are fatal because they have polluted and defiled the gifts of Yahweh, the land, the poor, and finally themselves.

Jeremiah does not gloat over the fall of Judah. He does not glory in his role of harbinger of doom. He does not puff himself up with the power that Yahweh has given him to announce divine displeasure. On the contrary! His own pain is very real, his own wound incurable, his own agony uncomforted. In short, Jeremiah so identifies with the people he is called to address that he becomes one with them in their defeat.

And in that reality of the prophet we find a significant reality for us who would play the role of prophet in our own day. No preacher has the right to assault the people she/he has been called to serve, forgetting that he/she is one of them. How easy it is to assume that since one is called to preach, one has the right and duty to speak the "uncompromising word of God" (as it is often called by these preachers), forgetting that the preacher is always included in the audience of every sermon. We preachers need the word of truth as much or even more than our congregations. Jeremiah's very real pain, along with his unwillingness finally to divorce himself from his people, makes him a genuine model for any modern preacher who would speak the harder truths of the gospel.

It also should be said that only the preacher who remembers her/his need of the gospel has the right to speak it to anyone else. Paul's wonderful simile in 2 Corinthians 4:7 is appropriate here: "We have this treasure [the gospel] in clay jars, so that it may be made clear that this extraordinary power belongs to God and does not come from us." I like to translate "clay jars" as "cracked pots," since I have often seen myself, and more than a few of my church friends, as every sort of crackpot! God has chosen us, us pots, to proclaim God's gospel. Jeremiah knew himself to be one of God's special pots, but he knew also that he was no more than that. Thus the passionately pained Jeremiah can become a model for us, we who are passionate and pained in our fallen world.

John C. Holbert

Sixth Sunday after the Epiphany, Year C

First Lesson: Jeremiah 17:5-10
(Psalm 1)
Second Lesson: 1 Corinthians 15:12-20
Gospel Lesson: Luke 6:17-26

The Old Testament lesson consists of two parts, 17:5-8 and 17:9-10. The first part, which corresponds well with the appointed Gospel reading, will be the focus of my comments. It sets forth a contrast between two types of people, those under Yahweh's curse and those under Yahweh's blessing. The second part speaks of the depravity of the human heart, how deceitful it is and how only Yahweh knows the heart and judges accordingly. Both units are connected by the key word "heart," which generally in the Bible designates the seat of thinking and willing rather than the seat of emotions. That same key word connects our pericope with the opening unit in 17:1-4:

The sin of Judah is engraved upon the tablet of their "heart" (v. 1).
The "heart" of the cursed one turns away from Yahweh (v. 5).
The human "heart" is deceitful (v. 9).
Only Yahweh can probe the "heart" (v. 10).

419

The context implies that Judah has become a prime example of one cursed by God. Because Judah has turned away from Yahweh and instead relies on its own political smarts and alliances, Judah will be like a juniper bush in the desert, without fruit and soon to pass away. But there is still hope. If Judah turns to Yahweh in trust, it will flourish like a tree by the water.

The first part of the pericope clearly presents two subunits, a curse (vv. 5-6) and a blessing (vv. 7-8). The two subunits generally mirror each other in an antithetical way, and some of the individual lines closely parallel each other, as a literal translation shows:

"Cursed is the person who trusts in human beings	A
and makes flesh his arm	B
and from Yahweh his heart turns away.	B
He will be like a juniper in the Arabah.	C
It/he will not see when the good comes.	D
It dwells in scorched places in the desert,	
a salt land without inhabitant.	
Blessed is the person who trusts in Yahweh	A
and whose trust is Yahweh.	B
He will be like a tree planted by water,	C
which shoots out its roots by a stream.	C
It/he will not fear when the heat comes.	D
Its leaves will be luxuriant.	
In a year of drought it/he will not worry.	
It/he will not cease from bearing fruit."	

The passage divides all humankind into two categories, an either/or contrast. There is no third category, no half-and-half. The word translated "person" might denote a "strong person" and not simply a common person. In either case, the passage is general enough to apply to everyone, not only the common folk but also the high and mighty, not only ancient Judah but also people today.

A person is declared by God to be either "cursed" or "blessed," that is, either under God's disfavor or under God's favor. The one is like a juniper bush in the Arabah, the desert land south of the Dead Sea. It dwells all alone in places scorched by the sun, a salt land that is uninhabited and uninhabitable. Such a bush in such an area does not flourish. It may temporarily flower and yield berries in good times, but in a parched and salty wasteland it will soon dry up and die. It will not endure long enough to experience the rains if and when they come. The person blessed is like a tree planted by water and with roots extending to a stream (cf. Ps. 1). This tree will remain leafy and green; even in a severe drought it will continue to bear fruit.

A wordplay reinforces the contrast. The one soon perishes and will not "see" (*yir'eh*) or experience the benefits if and when the rains come. The other will not "fear" (*yira'*) when the hot desert winds or times of drought come. It will continue to be healthy and vibrant.

What makes the juniper bush in the desert so fruitless and transient? What makes the tree so fruitful and enduring? It is not that a desert shrub is so bad or that a tree is so great. We need to go to the "roots" of the issue in order to discover the key distinguishing feature. The shrub in the parched wastelands, in the uninhabited salt lands, has no continual source of water to nourish it. Without water even the good times are like a drought. Without water it can only expect to wither up and die. Contrast the tree. The tree does not plant itself; it has been planted or transplanted by Someone Else. Located near a water source and with roots in a stream, the tree flourishes. The water is what nourishes it, gives it life, and makes it fruitful even during a drought.

Jeremiah's simile reveals that there are two and only two types of people. And they are opposites. Some trust in themselves, in "human beings" (*'adam*). They make weak, fragile, and transient "flesh" their arm of strength. They look to themselves instead of Yahweh for their security and hope and righteousness. They are curved in upon themselves. In short, they deify themselves. Others trust in Yahweh; they have the God of Israel as their life, security, hope, strength, and righteousness. They look outside of themselves and away from themselves, and instead they rely on their Maker and Savior. The difference is not that some believe and others do not. Everyone believes. The difference lies in the object of their faith, themselves or Yahweh.

We live in a culture that highly values individual autonomy and self-sufficiency. Our text warns against adopting those values in any ultimate sense. Self-reliance, self-sufficiency, and self-autonomy amount to self-idolatry, and self-idolatry is a recipe for burnout. It has a curse pronounced upon it. You will endure and bear fruit only if you can sustain yourself and nourish yourself. And none of us can do that. Each of us individually and all of us collectively make for a pretty weak god. Those who rely on themselves cannot give themselves life, cannot save themselves or help themselves in any significant way, certainly not when the trials of life come around.

But on those who trust in Yahweh, who have Yahweh as their source of strength and hope, our text pronounces a blessing. When Yahweh is the object of faith, there is a continual source of water to enliven and nourish, come what may. Yahweh is "the fountain of living water" that never dries up (Jer. 17:13), the living and life-giving water.

What kind of God is the God of Israel? He is the God who abounds in steadfast love even for his arrogant and idolatrous creatures. In fact, God so loved his world that in the fullness of time he sent his only Son to live our life and to die our death. Jesus Christ redeemed us from the curse pronounced upon us by becoming a curse for us, as it is written, "Cursed is everyone who hangs on a tree" (Gal. 3:13). On the third day God raised Jesus Christ from the dead to be the living and life-giving Lord. Through the life-giving waters of baptism the Lord has pronounced us "blessed," and he promises to sustain and nourish us through his Word and Supper. With the cross and the open tomb we see what kind of God we have, a much better God than we could ever be. So let us turn away from ourselves and turn to him in faith. Then we will bear much fruit even when the tough times come around. Then we will be like a tree and not a desert shrub.

Paul R. Raabe

Sixteenth Sunday after Pentecost, Year C

First Lesson: Jeremiah 18:1-11
(Psalm 139:1-6, 13-18)
Second Lesson: Philemon 1-21
Gospel Lesson: Luke 14:25-33

Pottery was for the ancient world what steel is for our world. Its importance for the people of antiquity can hardly be overestimated. Among the household objects manufactured in clay were mud bricks, lamps, toys, spindle whorls and loom weights, ovens, roof tiles, figurines, tableware, storage jars, cooking pots, and even jewelry. Large pieces of broken pottery were salvaged for use as writing material (ostraca). Because of the need for earthenware objects, pottery making was one of the earliest, most widespread, and most familiar of all the crafts in ancient Israel. The oldest ceramic forms found in the region date to the seventh millennium B.C. The pottery of Jeremiah's day was of good quality when compared to the coarse and simple forms molded by hand during the Late Stone Age. The pottery of seventh-century-B.C. Jerusalem was mass-produced on pottery wheels in a variety of forms that were both utilitarian and attractive.

Jeremiah exploited the widespread familiarity with pottery making in an allegory that is the heart of this pericope. This allegory exploits the potter's freedom to rework a vessel while it is still on the wheel. In the prophet's day, most potters used the "fast wheel" to shape the objects they were forming. The fast wheel, invented in the latter part of the Middle Bronze Age (1650-1550 B.C.), consisted of two circular stones socketed into each other. The potter shaped the clay on the smaller of the two, which revolved on top of the larger and heavier one. The centrifugal force of the smaller stone allowed the potter to shape the wet clay into the vessel with the hands. After this was completed, the vessel was allowed to dry. The dry clay form would be placed on the wheel a second time for more delicate shaping. Finally the vessels were fired in a kiln (see Sir. 38:29-30). The firing changed the clay's chemical composition and physical characteristics. Clay became synthetic stone suitable for a variety of uses.

The allegory makes the prophet's intention transparent. He teaches that God's freedom to deal with Judah and the nations is like that of potters shaping vessels on the wheel. If they are dissatisfied with the way the vessel is taking shape at their hands, potters will simply start over. The process of manufacturing ceramic forms is irreversible only after the pottery has been fired in a kiln. The point the prophet makes in this, the only specific reference to the potter's wheel in the Bible, is that Judah's fate and that of the nations are not fixed. Just as the potter can rework a vessel while still at the wheel, so can God alter the fate of both Judah and the nations (vv. 1-6). Given Judah's desperate situation, this emphasis on God's sovereignty offers hope. Despite the acute circumstances of Judah's political and military situation, God's power can change these as easily as a potter reshapes wet clay.

Verses 7-10 shift the emphasis off the absolute power of the potter over the clay. Here the focus centers on the clay and the way it determines how the potter will act. It is the quality of the vessel that determines whether the potter continues the process of manufacture. If the molded clay vessel has a pleasing shape, the process will continue. But it is at this point that the allegory breaks down. The prophet encourages the "vessel" to make certain that it is worth keeping — something that is, of course, impossible for a molded piece of clay. Jeremiah calls Judah to please the "potter" who formed it by making the correct choice between obedience and disobedience — a choice whose consequences are life and death.

423

While the first part of the allegory (vv. 1-6) underscores divine sovereignty over Judah and the nations, the second part (vv. 7-10) affirms that the people of Judah control their fate. This is quite an assertion given the political and military realities that indicate the opposite. The key to Judah's future is that the people embrace the traditional Israelite morality — something they have neglected for too long. If they continue to neglect their moral responsibilities, they can be sure that God will effect their destruction. The passage ends with the prophet pleading, in God's name, for Judah to repent. The prophet, however, offers no guarantee that the amendment will be effective. Will the potter start over with the lump of clay that is Judah or simply abandon the project entirely?

While the lectionary does not include verse 12 in the lesson, it is necessary in the book of Jeremiah. Judah fell to the Babylonians in 597 B.C. Ten years later, after an ill-advised uprising against Babylon, Jerusalem was sacked, the temple destroyed and its priesthood scattered, the semblance of Judah's political independence ended, and many Judahites were taken away into exile. Verse 12 has the people rejecting their opportunity to amend their ways. What happened to the city, the temple, and the Davidic dynasty, then, is perfectly understandable. The potter simply abandoned his work.

Prophets like Jeremiah, who preached before the fall of Jerusalem, spoke to people they assumed were in control of their destiny. The prophets were countering a mythological worldview which held that human destiny was determined by events in the world of the gods. In that world, the gods vied for supremacy. The outcomes of these contests were visible in the ascendancy of one nation at the expense of others. If Babylon was the dominant world power, it must mean that Marduk, its patron deity, was dominant in the heavenly sphere. Most Judahites believed that Yahweh controlled their future in accord with the promises made to David. Judah's flourishing temple rituals recalled those promises and assured the people about their future.

Jeremiah wanted to demythologize the way most Judahites thought about the future of their nation. That future — the prophet emphasized — was firmly in their hands. The clay, in fact, controlled the potter. The people of Judah controlled their destiny. The gods did not determine the future — people determined it by the moral choices they made. The prophet had already condemned Judah's moral failures. Still, he assures his listeners that like a potter who scraps an ill-formed clay vessel to reshape it, they can reshape their future — if they amend their ways.

It will take little reinterpretation to have the prophet's words speak to the "not me" generation. People today have become adept at finding some

424

way to evade taking responsibility for the effects their moral choices have had on themselves and others. There is always someone or something else to blame: parents, genes, society, diet, music, peers, international corporations — the list can go on. The task of the preacher is to lead people to accept their moral responsibility for creating the world we live in — just as Jeremiah was trying to lead the Judahites to accept responsibility for their world. The prophet's purpose, however, is not simply to assign blame but to offer hope. He assures the people of Judah that they can have a great future if only they repent — if only they choose obedience. While the prophet begins by affirming divine sovereignty, he ends by underscoring the power of moral choices. If the clay changes, the potter will change.

The lectionary uses this text from Jeremiah to accentuate the choice Jesus calls prospective disciples to make in the Gospel lesson (Luke 14:25-33). Jeremiah calls the people of Judah to act in accord with traditional moral norms. Jesus, however, appears to ask his disciples to go beyond these norms. He asks people to make a choice that appears to make no sense. Disciples are to hate the members of their families and even their lives. They are to give up their possessions. While the prophet was speaking about what the Judahites were to do to maintain their political independence and national identity, Jesus was speaking about something that transcends these concerns, so the response he asks of his disciples transcends what the prophet demands of the Judahites.

Still, both the prophet and Jesus assume that people can make choices. They have effective control of their future. The prophet has to demythologize a worldview that effectively absolved people of responsibility for creating their future. Too many Judahites believed they had no control over their future. All was in the hands of the gods. The people of Jesus' day were not burdened with the mythological views of some of their ancestors. Still, Jesus had to persuade them that living in accord with traditional morality — while commendable — was not enough to respond to God's new movement in their lives. This new situation demanded bold and decisive action. It involved making choices that seemed to make no sense. But from the perspective of God's reign, the renunciation that Jesus demanded of the disciples was true wisdom. Like the prophet, Jesus challenges people to shape their future by the choices they make in the present.

Leslie J. Hoppe

425

Christ the King, Year C

First Lesson: Jeremiah 23:1-6
(Luke 1:68-79)
Second Lesson: Colossians 1:11-20
Gospel Lesson: Luke 23:33-43

A t this point in the book of Jeremiah, one would expect an oracle against King Zedekiah, since the previous chapter comprises Jeremiah's verdict on each of the preceding kings during whose reign he prophesied: Josiah, Jehoahaz, Jehoiachin, and Jehoiakim. Instead we have an overall comment on rulers of the past, followed by a description of what a king should be like.

That those who do not care for God's people (v. 2) are to be identified with the kings of Judah is not made explicit. Some scholars prefer to entertain a wider context, thinking that Jeremiah might be envisaging new forms of leadership, such as Gedaliah, who was appointed governor of what was left of Judah after the Babylonian Nebuchadnezzar had done his worst. Perhaps even unspecified modes of leadership are countenanced, and Jeremiah's point is then that God's people must move with the times and not cling to tradition, however precious. Many factors lead to the more probable conclusion, however, that it is kings who are coming in for the fierce criticism of verses 1-4. These all revolve around the use of the term "shepherd" in the Old Testament.

Jeremiah himself criticizes rebellious "shepherds" along with ignorant priests and unfaithful prophets in 2:8. Here, as elsewhere, his target is the leader of the nation, and in ancient Israel, kings are the most obvious as holders of office in a grouping with priests and prophets. More specifically, Jeremiah threatens "captivity" to "shepherds" in 22:22, following a denunciation of King Jehoiakim.

More generally in the Old Testament, the shepherd is a common image of the king (e.g., 2 Sam. 5:2; Ps. 78:71). A parallel indictment to Jeremiah 23:1-2a is Ezekiel 34 (cf. Zech. 11:4-17). The whole of the Ezekiel passage rests on the metaphor of sheep for the people of Judah, and verse 23 identifies one who will take care of them, that is, be their shepherd as "my servant David," though admittedly the following verse calls this figure "prince" rather than "king." Ezekiel similarly condemns the ruler who looks after himself rather than the weak, the sick, the crippled, the strayed, and the lost (vv. 2-4). Harsh and forceful rule leads to the scattering of the sheep. Shepherds are meant to protect from destructive forces, but when they renege on this duty they inevitably promote destruction.

As a result of the shepherd's neglect, the flock is scattered. This is the consequence also of the stupidity of the shepherds mentioned in Jeremiah 10:21, whose crucial mistake is that they "do not inquire of the LORD." As God's representative, the king needs to be inspired to take careful stock of what God requires (Isa. 11:2-3). God himself is depicted as shepherd in Psalms 23:1; 95:7; 100:3; and Isaiah 40:10-11. So here in Jeremiah 23:3. Yet, according to the next verse, God will raise up human shepherds. The apparent tension here (cf. Ezek. 34:23 and 24) may be resolved in a number of ways. One is to say that Jeremiah at this stage totally despairs of the Davidic dynasty and goes on to envisage something truly different. Certainly the roots of the emergent messianic hope lie in the dawning realization that only God himself can fulfill the ideal of a just rule (v. 6). Another is to say that God always needs human agents to implement his will. Both lines of interpretation are taken up in the New Testament, notably in John 10, where Jesus is variously the gate of the sheepfold and the Good Shepherd himself.

Further tensions, even contradictions, characterize Jeremiah 23:4. While these can be used creatively, some scholars think there is an incoherence about the passage and believe that only verses 1-2a represent Jeremiah's own message. Once the hope kicks in at verse 2b, what we have is an amplification of that message, originating in an author or editor keen to provide an affirmative theological stance. In this view, it is unlikely that any of the three promises in this chapter (vv. 2b-4, 5-6, 7-8) derives from Jeremiah. Significantly, however, the hope that God will "gather" the flock reverses the damage done by the inattentive shepherds who "scatter" it. Unless one denies all hope to Jeremiah — as do some scholars on the ground that his task is essentially one of denunciation, whether or not it is too late for those denounced to make any sort of amends — then it makes a degree of sense to see destruction being followed by restoration. Might it not be the prophet's task to see hope where others see despair? That God can destroy and re-create is the point of the vision Jeremiah has of the potter remolding the clay (18:1-6), and it is certainly a key contention of the Jeremianic tradition if not of Jeremiah himself.

Another link between the "woe" of verses 1-2a and the "weal" of verses 3-4 rests on a play on the Hebrew word *paqad*. This verb is used more in Jeremiah than in any other prophet (e.g., 11:22; 29:32; 46:25, where it is usually translated "punish"). It carries the connotations: attend to, visit, take care of, but the sense of these verbs, even in English, can be positive or negative.

427

Because they have not "attended to" *(paqad)* their flock, God will "attend to" *(paqad)* them. The rendering "visit" is similarly two-edged, since one can visit for good or for ill, though "attend to" is the more appropriate translation with regard to both the shepherd's taking care of his flock's welfare and God's taking care of, that is, punishing, his shepherd's "evil doings" (v. 2).

The second promise sharpens the first in that it asserts with complete certainty ("the days are surely coming") the coming of a king whose just reign will ensure safety for the people. With its more prosaic parallel in 33:14-16, 23:5-6 is the most explicit Davidic promise of the Jeremianic tradition. (See the exegesis of "righteous branch" in First Sunday of Advent, Year C.) It differs from that passage in two particulars. One is the explicit mention of the wisdom of the king (v. 5), and the other is the application of the play on words in "The LORD is our righteousness." In chapter 33 the Hebrew for "LORD" and the Hebrew for "righteousness" are combined to apply to the city of Jerusalem. Here they apply to the king himself. Most scholars see this as the literal reversal of the two elements of the name of the actual king, Zedekiah, which means "the LORD is my righteousness." This was the official name given to Mattaniah (his given name) when he became king. 2 Kings 24:17 relates that this took place when the Babylonian administration deported King Jehoiachin, whose given name was Coniah (see Jer. 22:24-30). 23:6 suggests that Zedekiah would have been better without the name of his office since he did not live up to it. It was the task of the Israelite king to execute justice, especially for the maltreated (e.g., 21:12), but Zedekiah is more concerned to appease his Babylonian overlord. It is his shortsighted foreign policy that leads to the final crisis when Jerusalem is destroyed in 586 B.C. In the play on his name, the Hebrew for "LORD" comes first before *ṣedeq,* "righteousness," in an emphatic declaration that the coming king will do what he is meant to do. He will place all his trust in God.

Continual disappointment with Israelite kings is what led to the development of the messianic hope in terms of a specific figure who would draw all his inspiration from God. Though Jeremiah 23:5-6 has similarities with Isaiah 9:2-7 (e.g., the idea of naming in v. 6), it is in Isaiah 11:1-11 that we see the most illuminating parallels. There will be new growth from the family of David (Isa. 11:1). God's hand will be upon the ruler (v. 2). His rule will be wise and just (vv. 2-5). He will restore his people (v. 11) and ensure their security (vv. 6-9). Specifically, in Jeremiah's judgment, Zedekiah sought some miraculous intervention (Jer. 21:1-10) yet experienced only defeat and death. By contrast, the new king will truly succeed and deliver his people.

That our passage is read on the Sunday of "Christ the King" (as also is its parallel in Ezek. 34) indicates the fulfillment of the promise in the Christian tradition. This develops the Israelite tradition in which every king was "anointed" literally with oil but was seldom seen to match with one who was anointed with God's spirit. That the king's whole purpose is to care for his people is elaborated supremely in John 10, where the Old Testament metaphor of the shepherd who gathers his flock is taken up. One of the most vivid ways in which Jesus declares his central task of seeking the lost is the shepherd who is determined to regather all his sheep (Luke 15; cf. Mark 6:34). Not only are fear and dismay banished, but none will "be missing" (Jer. 23:4).

In Jewish tradition, the importance of "the land" to which the exiles are "ingathered" continues. In Genesis the land is promised. Genesis is further echoed in verse 3 in the words "be fruitful and multiply" (cf. Gen. 1:22, 28; 9:1). In Exodus the land is the goal. In Joshua and Judges the goal is realized. In the Prophets the loss of the land is attributed to disobedience for which God is obliged to punish his people. Some scholars see a conflict in our passage between divine punishment and royal culpability as the explanation for dispersion. Others, however, see a continuity in verse 4, where the verb *paqad* again appears. While its form in that verse is best taken as "be missing" as applied to the sheep, it could also be taken as "attend to," as in its second use in verse 2. Once the kings properly fulfill their role, God will no longer attend to them in the sense of punish. Either way, the tension between human and divine shepherd is artificial, since God can only work through human agents. His rule is most fully seen where his agent reflects God's own right dealings in the way he actively promotes the well-being of every person. The emphasis is on no vague feelings of benevolence but on using position and talents with a constant eye for those who seem to miss out on life. Whether in Jewish or in Christian interpretation, our passage is a useful corrective to the notion that religious hope centers on "pie in the sky when you die." The needs of a flock are very down-to-earth.

Christine E. Pilkington

Twenty-first Sunday after Pentecost, Year C

First Lesson: Jeremiah 29:1, 4-7
(Psalm 66:1-12)
Second Lesson: 2 Timothy 2:8-15
Gospel Lesson: Luke 17:11-19

I f ever a passage needed a historical context for its significance to be appreciated, it is this one. So the opening verse states clearly the situation; namely, that Nebuchadnezzar, king of Babylon, has deported elders (v. 2 adds other important figures) from Jerusalem to Babylon. It is to them that the prophet Jeremiah writes a letter, the chief contents of which are given in verses 4-7. Amplification of the context and a further exchange of correspondence take up the rest of chapter 29.

The first deportation under Nebuchadnezzar occurred in 597 B.C. It was followed by a second, after the destruction of Jerusalem in 586, and a third in 581. As is apparent from chapter 24, which has the same historical backdrop as chapter 29, the obvious conclusion for those seeking any kind of theological explanation for the shock of deportation was that the refugees were the ones who were being punished for their unfaithfulness to God. Conversely, those so far remaining in Judah were being rewarded for their faithfulness. In the vision narrated in chapter 24, this interpretation is turned on its head. It is with those in exile that the future lies. God's punishment always has a purpose, and this purpose lies in his reforming his people so that they will live faithfully (24:5-7). That land was given to their ancestors is indeed significant, but there are still those who have to be exiled from it (24:8-10).

Stressing the history of the time, however, is not meant to preclude an imaginative interpretation of the passage. On the contrary, recognizing both the context and the purpose of the text may help us get inside its still-unfolding meaning. Approaches which go under the heading of "reader response," which seek to engage the reader with all his or her own responses, may well be nearer to what we have in much of the prose material in the book of Jeremiah than a view which gets bogged down in historical detail, as if chapter 29, in this instance, offered a blow-by-blow account of what happened. "Narrative criticism" which stresses story line, plot, and character may also have much to contribute to our understanding of this passage. Certainly, while the structure of the chapter is not altogether clear, the various characters do stride on to the stage quite vividly and utter lines with passionate conviction.

Outside our particular verses, there are the characters of Ahab and Zedekiah, who are busy telling the first deportees that they will soon be back home (v. 21). These men are prophets already in Babylon, and their Judean counterparts are represented in Hananiah, who plays a dramatic role in chapter 28. He too thinks the exile is but a temporary interruption to Judah's successful survival and the power of Babylon will be broken within two years (28:3-4). By contrast, Jeremiah counsels subservience to Babylon on the ground that it is working out God's purpose of punishment and renewal (27:11; 28:14). There is, therefore, one almighty standoff between these two prophets, as they have diametrically opposing views about how God is working in the history of their nation. Jeremiah warns of further deportation of people and treasures from Jerusalem (27:20-21) and says, on God's behalf, that they will stay in Babylon "until the day when I give attention to them." Then and only then will God "bring them up and restore them to this place" (27:22). The issue is essentially one between true and false prophecies, and this is what connects our chapter to chapters 27–28. How is one to distinguish the truth when rival versions of it come from equally plausible claimants?

It is surely not surprising that the exiles of the first deportation wanted to believe the more reassuring prophets. Yet, in 29:9 Jeremiah is adamant that they lack the vital mark of the true prophet, namely, God's commissioning. He does not mince his words in dismissing them as deceivers, dreamers, and liars (vv. 8-9). No wonder the exiles get a letter from Jeremiah. They desperately need an interpretation of their experience, bewildering and disorienting as it must be, which goes beyond a sort of whistling in the dark.

The interpretation Jeremiah offers them is that they must accept their predicament and try to see it in positive terms. The key to this lies in believing that God, in spite of appearances, is still in control. He is still "the God of Israel," who deserves the title "LORD of hosts." This is sometimes taken as referring to "heavenly hosts" in the sense of the moon and the stars — the cosmos — and sometimes to "military hosts" in the sense of great armies. Either derivation gives it the connotation of power. In chapter 27 Jeremiah speaks of Nebuchadnezzar as the servant of this Lord (v. 6), and what lies behind his contention, as he opens his communication to the exiles, is that it is God who has sent them from Jerusalem to Babylon (29:4; cf. 29:7).

If they can make some sort of sense of their new situation, then perhaps they can throw themselves into it rather than counting the days until it is over. "Live in the present" is the crux of his advice. This means living normally, with long-term projects of building houses and planting gardens

431

(v. 5). "To build" and "to plant" represent the creative activity of God himself in the account of Jeremiah's call (1:10). Now the people have to recognize this activity in "a foreign land" (cf. Ps. 137:4) and cooperate with it in their small way. "Lay foundations" in every possible sense is the gist of it. Grow your own food. Marry and have not only children there but also grandchildren (v. 6). In other words, their generation will live out their lives in exile. They should, therefore, do this not reluctantly but enthusiastically, recognizing Babylonian welfare as their own (v. 7). In this final verse of our passage, they are enjoined to pray on Babylon's behalf. In the cold light of biblical exegesis, this might sound a rather obvious thing to do, but against the white heat of bitter disappointment and ethnic animosity which marks any deportation, it is surely remarkable.

Many scholars, even those most skeptical of how far we can posit a real figure of Jeremiah behind the prose and even the poetry of the book, rate the contents of this passage highly. So Robert Carroll, in his commentary, says: "This is civil religion at its very best." He judges it to be a rare combination in the Bible of "domesticity and devotion, hard work and prayer," all contributing to the welfare (*shalom*) of everyone who is bound up together in normal existence. He goes on: "Unique though the prescriptions may be in the Bible, they are a remarkably acute assessment of the situation and a blueprint for millennia to come" (*Jeremiah: A Commentary* [London: SCM Press, 1986], p. 556).

Carroll's words take on a peculiar force as I write in the year of his own sudden and premature death and the turn of a millennium. "Life goes on" is not only a cliché, but also patently untrue. For some, life does not go on, and for many a drastic change — especially when it involves major loss — makes life as it has been known a thing of the past. The loss of their land, their people, and their precious temple which had spelled security, even if of a somewhat misguided sort (cf. Jer. 7:4), must have made the exiles inherently skeptical of, if not downright hostile to, receiving advice about continuity and stability.

The single most astonishing aspect of this advice lies in the command to pray for Babylon. In the book of Jeremiah, not only are there oracles against the nations, but also specific appeals to God to zap one's personal opponents. We see in 17:18 and 18:21, for example, the natural expression of Jeremiah's hostility. Yet in 18:20 he reminds God that he has interceded for his "adversaries." In the perpetual contrast popularly made between Old and New Testaments, Jesus is held up as the first to enjoin prayer for one's enemies (Matt. 5:44) and to pray for his own (Luke 23:34). This is clearly not so. Not only Jeremiah but also the servant of Isaiah 53:12 did so. Jeremiah's outpourings reflect something of the struggle in offering such prayer with any degree of sincerity.

Of all the remarkable words of this letter to the exiles, it is this injunction to pray which is the most instructive. It is central to his notion that religious faith, if it is at all genuine, must be transferable — from land to land, from circumstance to circumstance. Houses would normally be dedicated (Deut. 20:5), as they still are in Judaism. Firstfruits would be offered to God (Deut. 26:2). The clear implication of Jeremiah 29:5 is that such devotion must continue. The prophet Ezekiel, himself deported in 597, gives us the impression that the exiles were left free and unmolested to lead the lives they chose (Ezek. 3:15; 8:1; 14:1; 20:1). Lead them then, says Jeremiah. Ignore the spurious promises of the prophets whose religion is root-bound in Jerusalem and its temple. Fanatics are always in a hurry. Entertain the prospect of a stay of seventy years (29:10) rather than two (28:3). Whether specific or a generally round figure, seventy years means a long haul.

God is to be found in all this upheaval, and he is still the same God seeking all that is best, shalom, for his people, not the superficial shalom of 6:14 and 28:9. For their part, people must live their lives and practice their faith. They must not look back resentfully, asking: "How could we sing the LORD's song / in a foreign land?" and vengefully cursing: "Happy shall they be who pay you back / what you have done to us!" (Ps. 137:4, 8). Rather, they must widen the horizon of their prayers from peace on and in Jerusalem and Israel (cf. Pss. 122:7; 125:5; 128:6) to peace on and in Babylon. They must develop a faith independent of land and temple and ensure that their growing belief and practice are transplanted. They must share Jeremiah's conviction that "I know the plans I have for you, says the LORD, plans for your welfare and not for harm, to give you a future with hope" (Jer. 29:11).

Christine E. Pilkington

Second Sunday after Christmas, Years A, B, C

First Lesson: Jeremiah 31:7-14
(Psalm 147:12-20)
Second Lesson: Ephesians 1:3-14
Gospel Lesson: John 1:(1-9), 10-18

C hapters 30–33 of Jeremiah have become known as "the book of consolation," contrasting the generally hopeful collection of oracles referred
to in 30:2-3 with an earlier collection (36:2-3) in which little hope surfaces.
Our passage contains two poems linked together by their common theme.
This theme is one that sums up the message of Jeremiah at this later stage in
his ministry. Already deported to Babylon in 597 B.C., the Judean exiles need
confidence that they will be rescued. The verbs used express the mixed emotions of people wrestling with the conflicting experience of becoming refugees while believing they are essentially a chosen people. Interspersed with
exuberant celebration is poignant appeal. With the injunctions to "sing
aloud, raise shouts, proclaim, give praise" comes the cry: "Save, O LORD,
your people."

They are to celebrate because God has "ransomed" and "redeemed"
them (v. 11), and yet somehow this saving work has yet to occur. The theological words employed here are so rich in the Christian understanding of
salvation from sin that it is easy to miss the richness they have in the Old
Testament. Strikingly, they carry an intensely practical significance. "Ransom" is characteristically used by the Deuteronomists of the exodus from
Egypt (e.g., Deut. 7:8; 21:8). "Redeem" is used repeatedly in Isaiah 40–55,
usually with reference to the return from exile (e.g., 43:1; 48:20).

The links, both in content and in style, between Isaiah 40–55 and our
passage are so close and so frequent that many scholars think Jeremiah
31:7-14 must be secondary, that is, not from Jeremiah himself. It has either
to be composed late in the exilic period like Isaiah 40–55 or after the exile,
when it could easily have been influenced by these passages. A reasonable
conclusion would be that here is an essentially Jeremianic oracle, but one
which was brought into the final collection by an editor, drawing on the vocabulary and the ethos of Isaiah 40–55.

Whatever their provenance, the words clearly reflect a transformation
and the sort of joy which can be experienced only by those who have known
the intense opposite — whether in the form of physical pain, deprivation,
disorientation, or loss. So all-embracing is the joyful description that it can

434

be taken to refer to a final consummation of God's purposes, the eschato-logical banquet of Isaiah 25:6-9. The big picture is that of restoration: physical, emotional, spiritual, and ritual.

Israel began as "chief of the nations" in the sense that God chose it (Deut. 7:7-8; 32:8-9). Now that it is only a remnant, it needs "saving" (Jer. 31:7). Having been exiled, the people need gathering; having been scattered, they need reuniting so that they can again be "a great company" (v. 8). This reverses the success of the invading army of Jeremiah 6:22, which is "a great company" and came from "the north," the same words being used now in 31:8. "The blind and the lame, those with child and those in labor" are mentioned to emphasize the miracle of restoration (cf. Isa. 35:5-6; 42:16), possibly with the added force that they would normally be totally unfit in military terms. Yet, entirely dependent on God, they will return from a northern land. (Though Babylon is, in fact, east of Jerusalem, the route into Judah would be from the north.) This relationship is described in terms of father-son (as in Hos. 11:1) and then even more tightly in terms of "the firstborn" (Jer. 31:9), suggesting God's particular choice of Ephraim either above his older brother Manasseh (Gen. 48:5, 17-20) or above the other nations (Ps. 89:27). Later in the chapter (Jer. 31:18-20), Ephraim's repentance is indicated. Here the nation will return "with weeping" and "consolations." Verse 9 could similarly be an expression of regret for disobeying God. Then the "straight path" could be understood to mean the "right way." "Consolations" could, of course, refer more to the comfort God gives, and "straight path" could be less figurative than a literal description of an easy route, level (as in Isa. 40:3-4) and with water to hand. Both physical and metaphorical interpretations could well go together, as in the experience represented in Psalm 23:2, 3.

That a second poem begins at 31:10 is indicated by an introductory formula different from the so-called messenger formula of verse 7. The comprehensive depiction of renewal, however, unfolds. The prophet of Isaiah 40–55 and Ezekiel understand that in the eyes of "the nations" Israel's defeat and dispersal indicate not only her shame but also God's weakness. Far from it, says the author of 31:10. God is the faithful shepherd (cf. Isa. 40:11), and this must be announced far and wide.

And now the explanation for it all emerges, introduced by the crucial word "for." Before the future tenses return in verse 12, this verse declares God's deliverance with supreme certainty by using what are known as "prophetic perfects." Uniquely in the entire passage, the past tense is used to describe God's activity. It is as if the redemption has already happened. The word translated "ransom" contains the notion of "price" (e.g., Lev. 19:20),

435

while the word translated "redeemed" has a legal background and expresses the responsibility of the next of kin to "buy back" a person or land, as in Ruth 3-4 and Jeremiah 32:6-15. "Redeem," while common in Isaiah 40–55, does not otherwise occur in the poetic oracles of Jeremiah, yet there is no inherent contradiction between the doom-ridden message of Jeremiah and this hope for the future. That a prose narrative has Jeremiah redeeming his family plot at a time when the Babylonians were overwhelming the whole land of Judah should not be dismissed as romantic insignificance. Even if, as many maintain, an editor has played a part in at least the arrangement of such a narrative, it is hard to see why Jeremiah should have bothered proclaiming anything at this apparently hopeless time unless he genuinely did believe that "houses and fields and vineyards shall again be bought in this land" (32:15).

In consequence of God's activity, all the good things of life will flow. The people of Jeremiah's times, like Hosea's, made the mistake of attributing agricultural prosperity to the fertility gods of the Canaanites. Now they will learn its true source (cf. Hos. 2:8, 21-23). The clear implication is that they will be obedient as when they first entered the land (Deut. 7:12-14). The total situation will be transformed. Mourning, a salient feature of God's judgment in Jeremiah (9:10-22; 14:1-10; 15:5-9; 22:10-23), will be replaced by dancing (cf. Ps. 30:11). Pilgrimage had ceased in exile (Lam. 1:4), but now everyone will acknowledge God's overflowing provision (Jer. 31:14). The word used for "bounty" here, *tob,* connotes both physical satisfaction and the spiritual fulfillment which (as in Exod. 33:19) comes from seeing God for what he is.

Some are disturbed that a passage so powerful as Jeremiah 31:7-14 should end with a reference to abundant sacrifices, especially in view of Jeremiah's condemnation of sacrifice in chapter 7. If we take the passage as postexilic, then the problem partially goes away. Alternatively, the term "fatness" can be understood to be the "fat of the land" rather than the fat of the sacrifices reserved for the priests (so the New English Bible and the Revised English Bible). That Jeremiah criticized both priest and sacrifice, however, need not preclude the hope of restored sacrifice. The church often betrays a prejudice simply against sacrifice when it sees this as the one aspect of worship rejected by the prophets. That they also reject, on God's behalf, hymn singing, prayer, festivals, and "solemn assemblies" should alert us to the fact that the essence of what is rejected lies elsewhere than sacrifice. Rather than be dismayed at the use to which Jeremiah's own message is put in the concluding verse of this poem, we might do better to reflect on his passionate concern for the integrity of the temple in Jerusalem. It is hard to gainsay the view that the key message of Jeremiah (as also of the eighth-century prophets: Amos, Hosea, Isaiah, and Micah) revolves around God's implacable demand for justice in human life, without which worship — at whatever time, in whatever place, and in whatever form — becomes a nauseating sham.

The crucial questions are: What constitutes God's costly redemption and what is the human response to it? What does it mean for God to be both our shepherd and our father? Prophetic figures then and now have to spell this out in ways which give scope for the whole range of human desire and fulfillment. Get rid of the mention of "priests" from this passage and get rid of the historical Jeremiah, either as its author or, as some scholars prefer, generally, and we are still left with an address to God's people which makes it well-nigh impossible for us to discount ritual as a legitimate expression of spirituality. How it is integrated into the big idea of the messianic banquet, whether in Old Testament terms or also in New, surely needs exploring. Of vital importance must be the communal nature of both Old and New Testament religion. Absolutely never and nowhere does one hold a party just for oneself. A banquet for one is a contradiction in terms.

Christine E. Pilkington

Twenty-second Sunday after Pentecost, Year C

First Lesson: Jeremiah 31:27-34
(Psalm 119:97-104)
Second Lesson: 2 Timothy 3:14–4:5
Gospel Lesson: Luke 18:1-8

In the case of Isaiah, we can deduce that the book named after this prophet includes actual prophecies by Isaiah, stories about the prophet, and also prophecies and sermons by later prophets that were in part inspired by his. It may be that the same applies to the book called Jeremiah. If it does, then these may then break up in a similar way to the material in the book called Isaiah. Broadly speaking, Jeremiah's own prophecies will be the ones in poetry, while other people will have contributed the stories about him and the prose prophecies such as 31:27-34. But to be truthful, no one knows whether this is actually so; the evidence is much less clear than is the case with Isaiah. So we do not actually know whether this particular passage is a prophecy by Jeremiah or one by a later prophet. Fortunately this need make no difference to its interpretation. Its place in the book invites us to read it in the context of the fact that Judah and the city of Jerusalem were to fall to Babylon in 587.

The northern kingdom of Israel had fallen to Assyria, Babylon's predecessor as the great power in the Middle East, 150 years previously. Admittedly Jeremiah himself was living proof that God had not wholly cast off northern Israel, for he came from the clan of Benjamin. It lived just north of Jerusalem, but technically it belonged to northern Israel. Perhaps the continuing existence of the rump of Israel had thus encouraged people to believe that God had not abandoned it. If so, God is about to take away even that sign of hope. Judah and what is left of Israel will both fall. As the land of Israel once had its population taken away by Assyria, so Judah will have its population taken away by Babylon. God had thus appointed Jeremiah over nations and kingdoms in connection with plucking up and pulling down, destroying and overthrowing, and God's word was coming true (1:10).

But there had been more to God's appointment of Jeremiah. Perhaps surprisingly, God had gone on to speak about building and planting (1:10). Now God takes up those words from the beginning of Jeremiah's ministry (see 31:28). Most of God's words back then, and during Jeremiah's ministry, concerned plucking up and breaking down, overthrowing and destroying. In other words, they concerned bringing "evil" (v. 28). "Evil" denotes calamity or disaster. As in Isaiah 45:7, the implication is not that God does moral evil. Like English, Hebrew has a word that means moral evil (resha') and also a word that means "bad" (ra'), which can denote moral evil but can also refer to things that are calamitous or disastrous. It is the second word that appears here.

The words about calamity have been fulfilled. The prophecy presupposes the actual fall of the city and the taking away of its people. The upside to that fulfillment is that it opens up the possibility of believing that the words about restoration will be fulfilled. It does that in more than one way. The words about renewal could not be fulfilled until the words about destruction had been. But in addition, the fulfillment of Jeremiah's words about destruction was also grounds for trusting in the words about restoration. Jeremiah has been shown to be a true prophet, and his God had been shown to be really sovereign in events.

One outworking of that sovereignty will be the sowing of the land with new seed (v. 27). Jeremiah refers not to literal seed but to the metaphorical seed constituted by a new human and animal population. The prophecy presupposes that many of the people will indeed have been transported to Babylon, and many of the animals will die in war or in the chaos and neglect that follows Babylonian victory. It is noteworthy that the household to be rebuilt is the household of Israel and of Judah. It transpires that the continuing existence of a rump of the house of northern Israel was indeed a sign that God had not finished with it. How could this not be so? How could God abandon Israel?

There will be another feature of God's restoration of the people. They will then no longer complain that the children have a bad taste in their mouth as a result of their parents having eaten something unpleasant.

At present, they are asking, "Why do bad things happen to good people?" There is no one answer to this question, in Jeremiah's day or ours, though there are several different answers that may apply to different people. Jeremiah affirms that on the other side of this coming calamity, people will no longer have reason to make this complaint.

His declaration that we all stand individually before God, responsible for our own destiny, is congenial in the modern age, and people have been inclined to assume that of course this is the truth. The Old Testament is here getting beyond the view expressed elsewhere that children pay for their parents' sins. The people were simply misguided in suggesting that they were paying the penalty for their ancestors' wrongdoing. Because that is the unbalanced prejudice of our culture, we need to face the truth in what they were saying. Early in Jeremiah's ministry, King Josiah had tried to bring about a wide-ranging reform of religious and social life in Judah and the rump of Israel (see, e.g., 22:15-16; 2 Kings 22–23). This had included eliminating the Assyrian and Canaanite religious customs that prevailed in Jerusalem. But he had failed, and his successors had gone back on his work. And that was the cause of the calamity coming on the city. With hindsight one might say that matters had gone too far. It was already too late. The parents had eaten things that were bad, and the children were left with the bad taste.

It is a fact that the lives of parents affect children. That is part of the way God made humanity. We are bound up in the bundle of life together and not able to subsist on our own from the beginning of our lives, like some animals. That gives us great blessing, but in other contexts we pay a price. It does not mean that we are not responsible for making our own response to God and to life; we cannot blame our parents. It does mean that some people may have a harder time than others in making the right response.

In different contexts there may be a need to stress the importance of the

439

corporate relationships of family and community, or to stress the reality of individual responsibility. Jeremiah lived in a time when people were paralyzed by their awareness of the cost they were paying for their ancestors' actions, and they needed to be reminded that they could make their own response to God. Modern Western culture needs the reminder of the way our decisions affect our contemporaries and the people who come after us, who may not be able to avoid paying a price for what we do or fail to do.

Fifty years after the fall of Jerusalem, God began the process of sowing and building and planting and changing people. As Assyria had given way to Babylon, so Babylon gave way to Persia. The new Persian government commissioned Judeans living in Babylon to return to Judah to begin the renewing of city and community there, "in order that the word of Yahweh by the mouth of Jeremiah might be accomplished" (Ezra 1:1). The Christian church can thus read this prophecy in at least two ways.

One is that we see it as an instance of God's commitment to the Jewish people, not least when it is overcome by calamity. God ever says anew to the Jewish people, "I will watch over them to build and to plant." In our own lifetime we have seen a number of ways in which God has once more fulfilled this promise, not least against the terrible background of calamity in the Holocaust.

The second is that insofar as we as Christians have been admitted in Christ into membership of the people of God, the promises that God made to Israel apply to us — not in place of Israel, but through our association with Israel. In the West the church has also been plucked up, broken down, overthrown, and destroyed, and has gone through calamity. It is hard for us to acknowledge that this is so. It is harder in the USA than in Europe, because secularization has not proceeded as far in the USA and Christian faith still has considerable respect. But only when we acknowledge that it is so can we begin to claim the promise that God also watches over us "to build and to plant."

On verses 31-34, see also the comment that follows.

John Goldingay

Fifth Sunday in Lent, Year B

First Lesson: Jeremiah 31:31-34
(Psalm 51:1-12)
Second Lesson: Hebrews 5:5-10
Gospel Lesson: John 12:20-33

Jerusalem is about to fall to Babylon; many more of its people will be transported to Babylon; Davidic rule will be terminated; and the temple in Jerusalem will be destroyed. All this is a sign that the covenant relationship between Yahweh and Israel had broken down. In that context there is something that Yahweh has definitively said about the future (v. 31). A situation that seems hopeless therefore ceases to be so.

Yahweh's promise envisages more than a mere renewing of the Mosaic covenant. It had been renewed before, after the rebellion at Sinai (Exod. 34) and after the wandering through the wilderness (Deut. 29:1). Jeremiah 31 speaks rather of the making of a new covenant. The situation is thus more like that when the Sinai covenant itself succeeded the covenant with Israel's ancestors (see Gen. 17), when new acts of God and new forms of responsive human acts succeeded the preceding ones. On each occasion the new covenant was, of course, in continuity with the preceding covenant, yet it also involved substantial newness.

Like the Sinai covenant, this new covenant will involve the whole people, Israel and Judah (v. 31). In this context "Israel" refers to the northern tribes. On the eve of the fall of Jerusalem, it could have seemed that Judah was finished. It would have seemed even more certain that northern Israel had been finished long ago, for example, when Assyria brought its political life to an end, transported its people, and replaced them with other peoples from Mesopotamia. The promise about Israel and Judah results from the knowledge that when Yahweh has made a commitment to a people, that commitment never collapses.

But the promise recognizes that the situation requires a really new covenant, one with provisions that are different from the provisions of the Sinai covenant in any of its forms. Arguably that covenant had always been broken-backed. The Noah covenant and the Abraham covenant had been based entirely on Yahweh's gracious promise. They required no human response in order to "work," except for men's acceptance of the Abrahamic sign of circumcision. Indeed, Yahweh's commitment in the time of Noah explicitly recognized that this commitment needed to allow for inveterate human sinfulness. It was useless to make a covenant conditional on human response.

The Moses covenant shows the same recognition. At Sinai Israel had broken it, and it had needed renewing only minutes after it was made (Exod. 32–34). In the plains of Moab Moses keeps emphasizing the stubbornness of the people and envisages the relationship with Yahweh breaking down. It is not surprising, then, that the covenant has now broken down terminally. Its entire basis was inadequate.

In what way had it broken down? The essence of the covenant relationship lies in the expression "I am your God, and you are my people" (v. 33). A covenant is essentially a relationship, though a relationship that has been formalized and entered into solemnly. Admittedly, this particular covenant is not an equal relationship. Yahweh refers to the fact that the people had broken the covenant "though I was their husband" (v. 32). The term presupposes a relationship, but it is a hierarchical relationship. The ordinary Hebrew expression for "their husband" literally means "their man," and is thus open to an egalitarian interpretation. But this passage uses an expression that suggests "your master." It is a patriarchal marriage that is presupposed here. But arguably that providentially provides a more suitable model for understanding the relationship between God and the people. That is an unequal relationship, but a real one. It was supposed to involve a real mutual commitment.

The trouble is that Israel had always found it impossible to be faithful to Yahweh as husband. Archaeological discoveries give clear testimony to the worship of many gods and goddesses in Israel and Judah, supporting the picture that appears in the Old Testament. This archaeological work also shows that as well as worshiping other deities, they attempted to worship Yahweh by means of images. So they ignored the very basic requirements of the Torah expressed in the first two of the Ten Words, on acknowledging other gods and on worshiping Yahweh by means of images.

There is another aspect of the breaking of the covenant that incenses prophets such as Jeremiah. As well as failing to be faithful to Yahweh in these two ways, people fail to be faithful to one another. There is no faithfulness or compassion or mutual commitment in the land. People fail to behave rightly in their relationships with one another. To put it in terms of Jesus' summary of the Torah, they fail in their love for God and they fail in their love for one another.

It is such failure that has led to the collapse of the old covenant. Yahweh therefore promises a covenant with a different basis. Yahweh intends to make a covenant based on the inscribing of the Torah within people, in their minds. Anatomically the location of this inscription is their hearts, but in Old Testament–speak the heart is the center of the person. It is not so much the location of emotions as the location of thinking and the formation of attitude. So the heart stands for something closer to what we call the mind (cf. NIV).

So whereas Christians may assume that the point of this inscribing of the Torah in people's minds is to cause them to live lives characterized by a detailed obedience to all the individual requirements of the Torah, the context suggests that we thereby miss the point. What Yahweh is seeking is the success of that one-to-one exclusive relationship. The promise is designed to make it possible for the people to "know" Yahweh. In such contexts "knowledge" implies neither mere awareness of facts nor an inner personal relationship. It implies recognition, acknowledgment, and commitment (see, e.g., 1:5; 2:8; 5:4-5; 9:3). Yahweh intends to do something to the people's inner beings that will make them give Yahweh the response that the Torah looks for. Yahweh will then be their God, and they will be Yahweh's people. They will not need to be urged by people such as prophets to be loyal to Yahweh rather than following other gods or worshiping by means of images, and to be committed to one another. They will do it.

The Abrahamic covenant was based on a promise, which is something. The Mosaic covenant was based on an act of deliverance, which is more. The new covenant will be based on an extraordinary act of forgiveness. That is the most powerful, healing, and winsome act that any person can ever do for another. Of course, Israel's life had been based on forgiveness before — since Sinai, in fact (see Exod. 32–34). But the act of forgiveness that Yahweh will now undertake in restoring the people after the collapse of the covenant will break into their spirits in a wholly new way. They will know themselves as an extraordinarily loved and forgiven people. That will change them inside and make them respond to Yahweh in a way they never have before.

Like the promise in verses 27-30, this promise about a new covenant received its first fulfillment in the life of Judah after the exile. Whereas Josiah had failed in his reform project, since the return from exile the Jewish people have indeed acknowledged Yahweh alone, and they have done so in a way that gave up images of God. They thus fulfilled the fundamental expectations of the covenant relationship. Further, from the later prophets we get nothing like the social critique we got from the earlier prophets. The community is much nearer a mutual covenant commitment.

The idea of a new covenant was then one of many Old Testament ideas that Jesus and the New Testament writers used to illumine what Jesus did. It is for this reason that it appears in the lectionary for Lent 5. We do not have to claim that this is the first or only fulfillment of this promise of God's, and thereby downplay the significance of God's work in the Jewish people. Indeed, it is characteristic of New Testament use of such prophecies that they are reapplications of the Old Testament words, and this is another example. The death of Christ and the pouring out of the Spirit set relationships with God on a new basis. It was a new covenant.

Nor is that the end of the story. When Paul quotes verse 34 in Romans 11:27, he does so to reaffirm that the promise is still to be fulfilled. This, too, is not to deny that it has been fulfilled, but it does shut us off from the one-to-one prediction-fulfillment model that we often work with. Indeed, we only need to consider briefly the life of the Christian church to know that verses 31-34 still need some fulfillment. A reading of them now gives us grounds for gratitude for what God has done, confidence for what God will yet do, and prayer for God to do it now.

John Goldingay

Nineteenth Sunday after Pentecost, Year C

First Lesson: Jeremiah 32:1-3a, 6-15
(Psalm 91:1-6, 14-16)
Second Lesson: 1 Timothy 6:6-19
Gospel Lesson: Luke 16:19-31

Jeremiah's prophetic ministry took place from 626 to 586 B.C. This particular passage comes to us from the latter part of his ministry and is to be dated in 588, when Jeremiah is a prisoner of the last Judean king, Zedekiah. He is housed in the court of the palace guard while the armies of Nebuchadnezzar of Babylonia (605-562) are besieging Jerusalem. To understand this setting, we must therefore know something of its historical background.

In 593 Psammetichus II assumed the throne of Egypt, and both he and his son Hophra (Apries; 588-569) resumed the policy of interfering in the affairs of Asia and Palestine. Such a resurgence of Egyptian power fanned the

444

fires of rebellion that had smoldered in Judah since 597, and by 589 that country was in open revolt against its Babylonian masters. Nebuchadnezzar, however, was completely in control. He established his headquarters in Riblah in Syria, and in January 588 his troops placed Jerusalem under blockade. His strategy was simple, as can be seen in Jeremiah 34:7. He simply took, one by one, the outlying fortifications surrounding Jerusalem, finally taking even the last two remaining at Lachish and Azekah. In 588 Nebuchadnezzar's troops then laid siege to Jerusalem.

In the middle of that desperate military situation, Jeremiah played the traitor. As can be read in chapter 21, he preached to both king and people that whoever stayed in Jerusalem would die but whoever went out and surrendered to the Babylonians would save his or her life. The prophet was convinced by the Word of God that Babylonia was an instrument in the hands of God and that it was futile to fight against the Lord's will.

In a desperate move of religiosity, Zedekiah and the Judeans therefore entered into a covenant renewal ceremony based upon the covenant commands of Deuteronomy, but when news arrived of an approaching Egyptian force and the Babylonians lifted their siege, Judah forgot all about any covenant obedience. Jeremiah replied that the Babylonians would soon return. During the temporary lifting of the siege, however, Jeremiah tried to leave Jerusalem to redeem a piece of family property that had fallen to him by right of inheritance (37:11-21). At the gate of the city, he was arrested and charged with deserting to the Babylonians. The city leaders beat him and threw him into a dungeon cell to die, but a fearful Zedekiah, who still relied on the prophet's connection with God, transferred Jeremiah to the court of the palace guard. There Jeremiah at least had food, he could walk about, and he could continue to shout out to passersby to surrender to the Babylonians, who had indeed quickly resumed their siege of the capital city.

Other passages in Jeremiah (19:9), Ezekiel (5:10), and Lamentations (2:12, 19-20; 4:4, 7-10) all tell us that conditions were appalling in the besieged city. There was very little food and water, and toward the end of the siege parents were even driven to eating the flesh of their children. Epidemics and disease swept through the weakened and crowded population. Material property of course was of no value. Silver and gold were worthless, because there was nothing to buy. All commercial enterprises collapsed, because there was nothing to sell. Property values plummeted, as they always do in war, because everyone was trying to sell property and to flee the city. Who wanted any land when the Babylonians were knocking at the gates?

It is in this situation that the Lord tells Jeremiah ahead of time that his cousin Hanamel will come to his prison with the offer, "Buy my field which is at Anathoth, for the right of redemption by purchase is yours" — an offer in accord with the law of Leviticus 25:25. When Hanamel does indeed show up, Jeremiah knows it is the Lord who is prompting the transaction (v. 8). The prophet therefore goes through all the necessary legalities in order to purchase the field for seventeen shekels of silver. He signs and seals the deed, calls witnesses to observe the weighing and transfer of the silver, and then entrusts the deed of purchase and the deed to the land to his scribe, Baruch, in the presence of Hanamel and the witnesses and the other prisoners in the courtyard. At the word of God, Jeremiah also bids Baruch to put the deeds in an earthenware vessel so they will last for a long time.

It all seems like pure foolishness in the light of the situation of both the prophet and Jerusalem, and Jeremiah, despite his obedience to the directions of the Lord, recognizes how foolish it is. After the prophet gives the deed to Baruch, he hears a further word from God that promises, "Houses and fields and vineyards shall again be bought in this land" (v. 15). But is that possible?

In his prayer that follows our passage, Jeremiah recounts all that the Lord has done for Israel in the past — his mighty deeds in the exodus and in giving the Israelites the land and the Torah. But now! "But now," Jeremiah prays, "siege mounds have come up to the city to take it, and because of sword and famine and pestilence the city is given into the hands of the Chaldeans [Babylonians]. . . . Yet thou, O Lord GOD, hast said to me, 'Buy the field for money and get witnesses' — though the city is given into the hands of the Chaldeans" (vv. 24-25). And you say, Lord, that houses and field and vineyards shall again be bought in Judah! Is that possible?

The Lord answers his prophet: "Behold, I am the LORD, the God of all flesh; is anything too hard for me?" (v. 27). The Lord does not take back his word to destroy Jerusalem and Judah, however. Throughout its entire history, Judah and Jerusalem "have done nothing but evil" in the Lord's sight, and they will fall to the Babylonians and be carried into exile. "The wages of sin is death" (Rom. 6:23). Sin against God brings its awful consequences.

But that is never God's last word. In the history of the ancient Near East, of which we read in the Old Testament, it seemed as if the fate of Palestine and of Israel was determined by the perennial power struggles and clashes between the empires of Mesopotamia and Egypt, with Israel in the middle as their pawn, as it so often seems today that the fate of all countries is determined by the powers of this world and their political principalities. But the Bible knows that is not so. God is the Ruler over all the powers of this world, "and though the wrong seems oft so strong, / God is the Ruler yet." We saw that forever made true when a cross on a hill called Golgotha conquered the empire of Rome.

At the end of his prayer with the Lord, Jeremiah is therefore given a promise. God will bring his covenant people back to their land after their exile; he will make a new covenant with them (cf. Jer. 31:31-34); he will write his law on their hearts so that they want to be faithful. And, the Lord says, "I will rejoice in doing them good, and I will plant them in this land in faithfulness, with all my heart and all my soul" (v. 41). God wills good for his people and for us "with all my heart and all my soul," like a lover telling his beloved that she is loved "heart and soul."

Moreover, God makes those promises because he has a plan for his beloved people, as he has a plan for his world and for us. The future is never closed in the Bible, because God is never through moving toward his goal. He works with nations and societies and individuals to bring them all at last to his kingdom come on earth, even as it is in heaven. And the special people through whom he works out that plan are his covenant people Israel and his covenant church of Jesus Christ.

When it seems that we are at the end of our rope and desperate even in our troubled life as individuals, we must remember that purposeful plan of God. For when we stand beside the grave of a loved one and think that life is over, God has a plan, doesn't he? When we are fearful that the evil in our society is overwhelming our world and our lives, God has a plan. When the strong seem to crush the weak and the tongues of the proud and mighty strut through the earth, God has a plan. And when there seems to lie ahead of us nothing but a looming Golgotha, and we would rather do anything except obediently drink the cup given to us, God has a plan. It is a plan for good and for eternal life and for earth made fair again. And, you see, nothing is too hard for the loving "God of all flesh."

Elizabeth Achtemeier

First Sunday of Advent, Year C

First Lesson: Jeremiah 33:14-16
(Psalm 25:1-10)
Second Lesson: 1 Thessalonians 3:9-13
Gospel Lesson: Luke 21:25-36

One of the most striking features of this short unit is the opening phrase of each verse. It has the quality of certainty and yet at the same time a vagueness. "The days are surely coming" (v. 14) and "in those days" (vv. 15 and 16) refer to the same time, but when that time is remains anyone's guess. This is the nature of eschatology, words about the eschaton or "end" of time. The focus is not on the "when" but on the "what." What matters is not the timing but the content of what is coming. The first verse makes plain that what is coming is the fulfillment of God's promise, and the next two verses specify this in terms of justice and security for God's people.

Articulating the promises of God is popularly regarded as the main function of prophecy. The corrective to this overemphasis on the future lies in the indisputable fact that most of what the Old Testament prophets say is concerned with the present. The forward look of what they say is only significant insofar as it relates to the immediate life of the people addressed. This equally applies to the backward look of the prophets, as they seek to remind their hearers of how things were, either in times when loyalty to God was more in evidence and God's activity was clear or in times when disobedience explains why they are in such dire straits now. For all this, promise and its fulfillment are a recurrent feature of prophecy and are at the heart of this passage.

The promise is made "to the house of Israel and the house of Judah" (v. 14). That both the northern kingdom of Israel and the southern kingdom of Judah are named may be taken to suggest that the promise entails a united kingdom, as before the division which took place in the reign of Solomon's son Rehoboam, around 922 B.C. In any event, we are thrown back to ancient promises, and the emphasis right from the start is on the God who keeps his word. Whoever is the author of verses 14-16, he is only a messenger, who therefore prefaces the message with the formula, characteristic of the prophetic literature: "says the LORD."

Solomon's father, David, is viewed generally in the Old Testament as the ideal king. Therefore God's promise is that the Davidic line will continue, as in 1 Kings 8:25 and 9:5, for example. In the latter, "I will establish your royal throne over Israel forever, as I promised your father David, saying, 'There shall not fail you a successor on the throne of Israel'" is, however, prefaced by an important condition laid on his son: "if you will walk before me, as David your father walked" (v. 4). This "walking" with God (cf. Mic. 6:8) is characterized by "integrity of heart and uprightness" (1 Kings 9:4), keeping all that can possibly be kept of the human side of the agreement. Then and only then will God keep his side of the agreement (v. 5).

To "execute justice and righteousness in the land" is then no new requirement as expressed in Jeremiah 33:15. It is the mandate of the king (e.g., 1 Kings 10:9). The observation is often made that Judah, in the time of Jeremiah particularly, needed a king who would exemplify this, since a whole string of kings had failed. The point is further made that the last king known to Jeremiah was Zedekiah, whose very name means "Yahweh is my righteousness," but who seems to be too weak a monarch to be worthy of the name. (See also the exegesis of Jer. 23:1-6 above.) The promise is, however, not so particular or time-bound. By its very nature it is a constant wish of the subjects that their king will create the conditions for human flourishing. In the theological framework of ancient Israel, this means ruling according to Yahweh's demands.

In our passage, this hope is expressed in the phrase "a righteous Branch." Ancient Near Eastern usage shows that this can mean simply a legitimate ruler. The adjective from the Hebrew root ṣdq is more usually rendered "righteous," but it could equally well carry the meaning "rightful." It seems more than likely, however, that for our writer it includes the connotation of morality. Double meanings in Jeremiah are common and deliberate ways of expressing a richness of truth. Righteous or rightful are not alternative meanings. Rather, the king requires the one in order to be the other. The promise of a Davidic ruler is by definition the promise of a righteous ruler. In this lies the security not only of the dynasty but also of the nation (v. 16; cf. 2 Sam. 7:10, 16).

The criterion of what constitutes a "righteous Branch" is the same as in Jeremiah 22:15. The king must "do" righteousness, and the clearest manifestation of this lies in his ensuring fairness for the most vulnerable in society. Josiah "judged the cause of the poor and needy," in stark contrast to his son Jehoiakim, who fancied himself powerful because of his ostentatious (22:15) and brutally oppressive reign (22:17). Securing justice for those least able to achieve it for themselves is, in turn, equated with knowing God (22:16). Perhaps the most eloquent statement of what it is to be an Israelite king comes in Psalm 72, where we have the same preoccupation with the oppressed (vv. 2, 4, and 12-14).

The second word of the phrase in English, "branch," has been taken by some to mean another branch of the royal tree, namely, a continuance of the Davidic line, different from that which was coming to such a disastrous end, or had already done so, by the time of our writer. While not impossible, the greater likelihood is that it connotes an "offshoot," that is, a new shoot; hence the "springing" up from David.

The resulting safety of 33:16 is similarly a recurrent promise in the Old Testament (e.g., Ezek. 34:25; Lev. 26:5). Judah will be "saved," a word that usually carries a very practical sense, especially in the Psalms. Jeremiah himself appeals for God to save and heal him (17:14). What he needs is rescuing from those who oppose his prophetic ministry. When the whole nation enjoys this restoration, then its capital, Jerusalem, can be renamed "The LORD is our righteousness" (33:16). A name in Hebrew, whether of a person or a place, expresses the essential nature of the one named. The closing words of the book of Ezekiel rename Jerusalem "The LORD is There" (48:35). For a prophet so concerned with the presence of God in the Holy City, departing and then returning, this is highly appropriate. For Jeremiah, who has so much to say about the injustices of people and king, the hope that the heart of the nation will recognize God and his right dealings as crucial is similarly appropriate. The whole community will have confident faith in God.

Nonetheless, some deny the whole passage to Jeremiah. They point to the fact that the passage is absent from the Septuagint, the oldest Greek version of the Old Testament. They also draw attention to the close resemblance between 33:15-16 and 23:5-6. There are those who argue that there is no point of contact with what precedes it in 33:1-13, lending further suspicion to the authenticity of the passage, especially in its context of a promise of never-ending priests and sacrifices (vv. 17-18). Kings, priests, and an inviolable Jerusalem they dismiss as plain contradiction of Jeremiah's sharp criticism of irresponsible king and prophets and a self-righteous capital city. Maybe the passage represents later theological reflection on what should be or even an appeal to God to make it so, as in Psalm 132:9-18.

What is vital for us, however, is not establishing the precise origin and purpose of the words of Jeremiah 33:14-16. Though these do have a bearing on the details of interpretation, the essential thrust is clear. The key word is "righteousness," which has to be unpacked in very real terms to mean anything in communal life. The leaders of the nation, be they kings or priests, play a vital role in this. Priests are criticized not only by Jeremiah (e.g., 2:8) but also by other prophets, notably Hosea (e.g., 4:6). Remembering that their function was not only to offer sacrifice but also to teach covenant requirements, the Torah, we can see why priests who neglected this duty could do such damage.

The passage alerts us to the enormous power of leaders, especially those who purport to represent religion and to carry moral or spiritual authority. While some people prefer to "live dangerously," most of us crave a sense of stability, be it in local, national, or international terms. The revival of the common life of the people, as signaled by the resumption of normal transactions such as marriage and the worship of God (vv. 10-11), may offer a context for Jeremiah's message, after all.

The reading of this passage on the First Sunday of Advent indicates that it is commonly taken as messianic. As later Judaism and then Christianity interpreted messianism, this is not accurate and could be positively misleading. Its central concern is not with who is going to bring about God's just rule nor with when. This passage does not encourage "crystal-ball gazing," even if this is euphemistically called "theological reflection." It asks us to consider human responsibility and variously to support or challenge those who particularly serve as visible and tangible expressions of God's presence. It renders us particularly answerable to those who themselves lack power and influence. Its stance is clearly hopeful, but it sits alongside Jeremiah's general realism insofar as it cannot put a time on when it will all happen. We must surely beware, even on Advent Sunday, of overestimating its link with one messianic figure. On what does lasting security depend? Not on wishful thinking about either the future or the past, that's for sure.

Christine E. Pilkington

Twentieth Sunday after Pentecost, Year C

First Lesson: Lamentations 1:1-6
(Psalm 137)
Second Lesson: 2 Timothy 1:1-14
Gospel Lesson: Luke 17:5-10

Within the three-year Sunday lectionary, this is the only assigned reading from Lamentations. Furthermore, it comes as one episode in the midst of a series of Old Testament lections touching upon the course of Jer-

451

emiah's prophecies and life. In the present lectionary, then, the passage's purpose is to illustrate a historical moment determined by the contextual unfolding of the prophet's writings. But while it is important to read this text in such a light, it is also imperative that it be placed within the larger framework of the church's reading of Lamentations as a whole, since only within the latter context can its full meaning as Christian Scripture be maintained and explored.

The long-standing traditional ascription of the book to Jeremiah, which dates back to before the Septuagint, justifies this reading's placement in the lectionary at this point; in any case, its origin as a collection of dirges over the destruction of Jerusalem by the Babylonians is historically apt to the events the lectionary rehearses during this season. Following the previous week's Old Testament reading that recounts the hope for Jerusalem's future embedded even in its destruction (cf. Jer. 32:1-15), we now hear of the actual fulfillment of the prophecies of judgment Jeremiah had been long enunciating to his unmoved people (cf. Jer. 4:22-28 on Pentecost 17). These six short verses from the first chapter of Lamentations trenchantly present, in a nutshell, the historical fact that the entire book seems designed to hold up for unswerving scrutiny: God's judgment against his people's sin is sure and complete; God's word, repeatedly given through the prophet, is certain and powerful (cf. v. 5 esp.).

Read as an expression of Jeremiah's own reaction to this accomplished word, however, the poem's opening (as well as the remaining book as a whole) describes the deeply unsettled sorrow of the prophet, long since articulated on many occasions as he faced both the promised fate of his people and his own role in explaining its inescapable unfolding. On Pentecost 18 we heard him cry out — perhaps even in union with God's own heart-torn distress over Judah's self-destruction — at the sight and experience of the nation's sin and self-abandonment:

> My grief is beyond healing,
>> my heart is sick within me. . . .
>> I mourn, and dismay has taken hold on me.   (Jer. 8:18, 21)

Now he watches as the city of Jerusalem itself, having been reduced to the most wretched of conditions and horrors (cf. esp. Lam. 4), takes up the grief he was forced to bear alone with God for so many years. "She weeps bitterly" (1:2), he writes, pointing to a sorrow and suffering that has even rooted itself in the land and the stones ("the roads to Zion mourn . . . all her gates are desolate" [v. 4]). Physically destroyed, humanly decimated, politically annihilated, Jerusalem now embodies materially the spiritual alienation from God she had long enacted:

> How lonely sits the city
>> that once was full of people! (v. 1)

Though much of the collection of poems that constitute Lamentations aims at affirming the truths spoken by the prophet over the years, it does so by explicating a theology of judgment moored to the affections of divine holiness whose faithfulness to covenant remains unshaken. In chapter 3, especially, God's judgment is read in terms of "chastisement" for the sake of future redemption (cf. 3:25ff.), rather than as simple destruction. The sorrow of chapter 1, which opens the book, then, is the sorrow of *love,* and the mourning of "lamentation" here fulfills that side of suffering which is fueled by ongoing charity.

Jeremiah is often viewed as the prophet of "anguish," in the sense that his relation to his vocation is one of at least partial, and often profound, identification with the object of his divine reproaches. He is not merely an instrument of severe revelation, but he is placed symbolically into the midst of this revelation's experiential outcome. It is this unique prophetic role that has encouraged both Jewish and Christian traditions to read not only Jeremiah's own life, but also the history entwined with his life and words, as "typically" unveiling — in the theological sense of "typology" — the shape of God's own life in relation to creation. In this hermeneutical context, Lamentations describes not just a moment, dreadful and moving as it may be, in Israel's history, but embodies in its very words and referents the "form" of God's purposes for the world. This brings us to traditional meanings of the book for the Christian reader.

From the time of the exile, perhaps, Lamentations was used liturgically in festivals commemorating Jerusalem's (and later, the temple's) destruction. (Its acrostic poetic form was perhaps originally organized for such regular liturgical and corporate use.) The elevation of this tragic event into a religiously identity-defining reality derived from the episode's ability to manifest an aspect of the ongoing relation of God and Israel — in promise, judgment, and faithfulness. Its liturgical repetition — along with even more frequent reiterations in the use of a Psalter containing, for example, Psalms 79, 80, 102 — unveiled a continuing historical and divine reality that Jerusalem's fall was seen as exemplifying.

Taken over for the use of the Christian church's study and worship, this aspect of the meaning of Lamentations found its ultimate explication in the reality of the passion of the Christ. Jeremiah's sorrow, and Jerusalem's fall, stood as a figure of Jesus' own sorrow, *as well as* of his participation in the fate of the object of his grief (cf. Luke 13:34; 23:26ff.). The Gospels quite explicitly link the history of Jeremiah and his city with the path of Jesus' own death for the sake of his blind brethren (cf. especially Matthew's use of Jeremiah in his passion account). In this sense Lamentations — including the verses in our passage, which speak of desolation, judgment, humiliation, and mourning — becomes not a piece of descriptive history or emotional outpouring, but a prophecy fulfilled in the person of Jesus himself, the One who "suffers" for the "multitude of" the nation's "transgressions" (v. 5), much like Isaiah's "suffering servant." Jeremiah's prophetic identification with his people is literally perfected in the incarnate God's assumption of humanity's sins and brokenness, enacted in the relation of Messiah and nation.

These opening lines from Lamentations, along with other select passages from the book, became liturgically fixed in Christian usage during Holy Week, especially in what evolved into the Tenebrae service of Holy Wednesday. In this prayerful context, Jeremiah's lament becomes the lament of the whole people of God, of the church itself, both as subject and object, joined to Jesus, as fallen Jerusalem and as suffering body of Christ. Much like the Pauline call to be "crucified with" Christ but now enlarged explicitly to include the corporate life of the church, the "lonely city" of Zion was understood to be a description of the church's own destiny in sin and redemption, through God's grace.

On this reading, Lamentations 1 moves out from the historical referent of Jeremiah's mourning to embrace the vocation of the church's discipleship as a justified sinner, whose life is given only in conjunction with her Lord's passion. The passage prods us to a reflection upon the character of the church's common life, its self-understanding as an "earthen vessel," as it were, and its evaluation of the historical meaning of its mission. The contrast Luther drew between a "theology of glory" and a "theology of the cross" or of "humiliation" is rooted in this traditional interpretation and the topics it lays out for meditation.

More than most texts of the Old Testament lectionary, this reading constrains the Christian interpreter of Scripture to allow Israel to act as the proper delimitation for the church's self-understanding, through its mooring in the life of Israel's antitype, Jesus. There is no escape from the Old Testament — only a fulfillment of its meaning in the form of Christ as it embraces his followers. A homiletic exposition of the text, then, must attempt somehow to hold together these three elements of the traditional network of historical revelation: Israel, Jesus, and the church. Isolating the meaning of the text from any of these three mutually referring agents risks evacuating the text's meaning of its full descriptive range in referring to God's character of judgment in mercy, whose form is given in the death of Christ.

Ephraim Radner

Christk the King, Year A

First Lesson: Ezekiel 34:11-16, 20-24
(Psalm 100)
Second Lesson: Ephesians 1:15-23
Gospel Lesson: Matthew 25:31-46

At first glance, it might seem odd to have a reading about shepherds on Christ the King Sunday. It's an obvious choice for Good Shepherd Sunday, but on Christ the King Sunday one would expect a reading about, well, kings. However, upon closer inspection, one soon discovers that the selection of this text from Ezekiel 34 makes perfect sense and is most appropriate. For under the guise of shepherds, the text is actually talking about kings. In fact, the leaders of Israel, especially kings and other officials, were commonly referred to as shepherds (Ps. 78:70-71; Isa. 44:28; Mic. 5:4-5; Zech. 11:4-17; Jer. 23:1-3), and throughout the ancient Near East it was common to call the king "shepherd."

The connection between shepherd and king is a natural one. In Israel the king was responsible for protecting and caring for his people as a shepherd cares for his flock. He was to lead the people and defend them from their enemies (1 Sam. 8:20). David rose to fame behind the motto "Saul has slain his thousands, / and David his tens of thousands" (1 Sam. 18:7). The king, like the shepherd, was to rule his flock with gentleness and compassion. In describing the ideal king, the psalmist sings:

> He will defend the afflicted among the people
>   and save the children of the needy;
>   he will crush the oppressor. . . .

He will be like rain falling on a mown field,
    like showers watering the earth.
In his days the righteous will flourish;
    prosperity will abound till the moon is no more.   (Ps. 72:4-7)

The flock depended on their king to bring justice to their lives. Without him they were vulnerable prey to any attacker from within and without. The king was not to accumulate wealth for himself (Deut. 17:16-17), but, like the shepherd, his life was to be marked by humility and humble obedience to God's word. For this reason, upon his coronation each king was to write a copy of the Torah of Moses. According to Moses, "It is to be with him, and he is to read it all the days of his life so that he may learn to revere the Lord his God . . . and not consider himself better than his brothers . . ." (Deut. 17:19-20). The king was to be the spiritual leader and example for the people as well. If he was faithful, the people would remain faithful to Yahweh. If he went astray, the people would go astray too.

Unfortunately, that is what happened to the shepherd/king and his flock. The text is part of a prophecy that Yahweh commanded Ezekiel to speak against the shepherds of Israel for their failure to care for their flock as Yahweh had commanded. Our text (34:11, 16, 20-24) must be read in connection with the immediate context in which Yahweh condemns the shepherds for their apostasy. The prophecy is a vivid description of Israel's leaders and their crimes against Yahweh's flock. Rather than shepherds of Israel, these kings functioned as "antishepherds." Their behavior toward their sheep was closer to what an enemy of the flock would do, not a shepherd. Against Moses' words in Deuteronomy 17, the shepherds were accumulating the wealth of the land for themselves and exalting themselves above their brothers (vv. 2-3). Rather than nurturing the weak and showing compassion to the afflicted, as good shepherds do, their rule over the flock was harsh and brutal (v. 4).

As a result, the flock was scattered (in exile). Without the protection and defense of the king, the people had become easy prey for their enemies (vv. 5-6). The former prophets detail the slide of Israel's shepherds into apostasy. They did not remain faithful to Yahweh. The shepherds, with a few notable exceptions, were not the spiritual leaders they were supposed to be. And so they led the people into idolatry as well. Here Yahweh blames the shepherds for scattering the flock. The desolation and destruction of Jerusalem and the tragic exile into Babylon happened because the shepherds forgot that the flock was not theirs. The flock belongs to Yahweh.

But Yahweh, of course, would not forget his flock. Though the text is part of a rebuke against Israel's shepherds, the sheep hear it as comfort and promise. Yahweh would deliver the sheep from the hand of the unfaithful shepherds (v. 10), and he personally would gather his scattered sheep: "Look, I, I will seek my flock," Yahweh says. Verses 11-12 maintain the metaphor of the shepherd in describing Yahweh's activity toward his sheep. The end of verse 12 ("in a day of clouds and deep darkness") makes use of language used elsewhere to describe the Day of the Lord as a day of judgment (Ps. 97:2; Joel 2:2; Zeph. 1:15). Ezekiel's language suggests that the day the flock was scattered was the "Day of the Lord" for Israel.

Verse 13 briefly shifts into more literal language ("I will bring them out from the people, and I will gather them from the lands, and I will bring them to their land") before shifting back to the metaphor again. Thus, on the historical level it is clear that here Yahweh is promising the return of Israel from their Babylonian exile. "The Day of the Lord" came for Israel when Babylon destroyed Jerusalem. But beyond that day, Yahweh promises that his flock will return home.

Verse 16 further promises Yahweh's continuing care for the flock. Not only will he bring them to good pasture and plentiful water, but, like a faithful shepherd, he will continue to help the helpless: "The lost I will seek, and the stray I will return, and the broken I will bind, and the sick I will strengthen. . . ." In fact, he will do what the evil shepherds did not do. Verse 4 is almost a mirror image of verse 16: "The weak you did not strengthen, and the sick you did not heal, and the broken you did not bind, and the stray you did not return, and the lost you did not seek. . . ," Yahweh says in condemning the shepherds.

After rebuking Israel's leaders again in verses 17-21 (this time referring to them as "rams" and "goats" and "the fat" [cf. vv. 1-3]), Yahweh promises that another shepherd will rule his people, but this time he constructs his promise with the covenant language of 2 Samuel 7, the promise to David of a descendant who would rule forever: "I will raise over you one shepherd, and he will shepherd you, [namely] my servant David. He will shepherd them, and he will be their shepherd, and I Yahweh will be their God, and my servant David will be prince in their midst." Yahweh isn't somehow promising that David himself would rise again, but he is using a metonymy in saying that David is the source (the descendant) from whom this one shepherd would come.

Thus, in the text Yahweh promises Israel a great future. First, as Israel's shepherd he will bring his flock out of exile and continue to care for them. Second, he promises to raise another shepherd, a faithful king, like David and from David, in whom the promises Yahweh made with David would be fulfilled.

The first promise God fulfilled through his shepherd Cyrus (Isa. 45), who allowed Israel to return from exile. Through much hardship, Yahweh continued to care for his sheep and did not let the flock die. The New Testament makes that point abundantly clear. In John 8, for example, Jesus identifies not only his mission but also his person with that of his heavenly Father (8:54), and in John 10, which has Ezekiel 34 as background, Jesus calls himself the Good Shepherd who lays down his life for the sheep (cf. also Matt. 18:12-13; 25:32-33).

Ultimately, then, Christ is the one who "fills up" this prophecy, and it is in him that this text has relevance for God's people today. He is the "seed of David," Yahweh's servant, who will feed the flock. During his earthly ministry he "sought the lost, returned the stray, bound up the broken, strengthened the weak, and healed the sick." That ministry pointed to him as the one who would finally do that for all of his people. For we who are lost and dead in sin, he finds us and brings us to life. He is the one who has brought justice and righteousness into our lives, and it is he who "crushes the oppressor" and delivers his people from the mouth of the enemy. And his kingdom is an eternal kingdom. He is the one who protects the vulnerable sheep and keeps them from harm, and he promises that he will never hurt the sheep, "fleece them," or scatter them, as others have done. Indeed, no enemy will be able to overcome him.

And yet, there is a twist to this story which can be seen when it is looked at from the NT perspective. It is very easy for us to identify with the sheep. The poor sheep are victims of bad shepherding. They have been scattered, lost, hurt. In the same way, we like to think that we are nothing but poor, helpless sheep who are vulnerable to every evil from without. Thank heaven, Yahweh sent the shepherd to save us. You see, in the text it is the shepherds who are rebuked, not the sheep. We escape, as it were, unscathed. It is almost as if we are innocent.

But of course, that overlooks one thing. The seed of David, who came to save us, the shepherd whom God raised up to shepherd us — Yahweh's servant — we killed him (Acts 2:22-36; 3:13-16; Rom. 4:25; 2 Cor. 5:21). We are not just innocent victims. We are also evil sheep who put to death the promised Savior, the very Son of God. Ironically, in this scenario the Good Shepherd becomes the innocent lamb slain by our hand, and we take on the behavior of the evil shepherds. He was the one despised and rejected by men, a man of sorrows and familiar with suffering. "He was despised, and we esteemed him not," as Isaiah says. "We all, like sheep, have gone astray, each of us has turned to his own way, and the LORD has laid on him the iniquity of us all. . . . He was led like a lamb to the slaughter, and as a sheep before her shearers is silent, so he did not open his mouth." The day of Israel's judgment, a day of cloud and deep darkness, came not only when Babylon destroyed Israel, but when the enemy crucified Christ (Israel "reduced to one"). No wonder there was darkness over the face of the land when Christ died (Matt. 27:45; Mark 15:33).

We are not innocent people who happen to have stumbled into a little trouble. We have the blood of the Lamb of God on our hands, and we are without excuse. We can only repent and throw ourselves on the mercy of our God. But it is at precisely this point, when we realize the depth of our guilt, that the promises of the text become relevant to us. Remember, God promised that he would take care of his lambs. And isn't that exactly what he did for his Son, the Lamb? In the text Yahweh promises to return the flock from exile. That happened when Israel returned from Babylon. But that return only foreshadows the "return" of the faithful Israel, Christ, in the resurrection from the dead. There the Father vindicated the innocent lamb. In the resurrection the Lamb triumphed over every enemy, just as Yahweh had promised.

The great news is that he was not crucified for his offenses but for our offenses, and also was raised not for his justification but for our justification (Rom. 4:25). At the end of verse 16, when Yahweh says he will shepherd the flock with *mishpaṭ*, it is usually translated "with justice." But Christians should think in terms of "justification." The Lamb has brought justice/justification to the world through his death and resurrection, and that is how he heals us and strengthens us, and it is around this news that we gather. In him, we too look forward to our own resurrection on the last day. We have God's promise that he will not forsake his sheep, and those of us who belong to him certainly bear that name. Therefore, we need fear nothing. No foe can hurt us because the ultimate shepherd — the one who became a lamb for us — is protecting us. We do not fear the judgment of Yahweh. Christ took it for us, and he has been vindicated. Judgment is reserved for those who think they are strong enough to do without it (v. 16).

The seed of David, through his death and resurrection, ironically enough, does indeed now reign even over death and hell. His kingdom is presently invisible, hidden in the hearts of his sheep, spreading and growing through the preaching of the word and baptism (Matt. 28:19-20). It is a kingdom that no enemy can overcome, no shepherd will destroy. Again, we look forward to that final day when all eyes will see what great things Yahweh has done for his people. Not one of us will be lost. Not one of Yahweh's promises will fail.

Timothy E. Saleska

Fifth Sunday in Lent, Year A

First Lesson: Ezekiel 37:1-14
(Psalm 130)
Second Lesson: Romans 8:6-11
Gospel Lesson: John 11:1-45

E zekiel was both a priest and a prophet. He spoke his prophetic oracles
to his fellow exiles in Babylon over a period of about thirty years (approximately 593-563 B.C.E.). Recall that the Babylonians exiled the people of Judah in two waves, the leaders in 597 and much of the rest of the population in 587. The oracles in the book of Ezekiel may be divided roughly into three large clusters: (1) chapters 1–24 — oracles of warning dating from before the fall of Jerusalem in 587; (2) chapters 25–32 — oracles against the foreign nations belonging to the middle period of Ezekiel's ministry; and (3) chapters 33–48 — oracles of hope which come after the fall of Jerusalem.

We need to consider one important piece of background information as we examine this text about a valley full of dry human skeleton bones in Ezekiel 37. According to the biblical laws of ritual purity, anything which is dead, including a skeleton, conveys the severest impurity or uncleanness. There were elaborate rituals to cleanse those who had been contaminated by contact with the dead (Num. 19:16-18). Human bones were used to contaminate illegal altars and high places so that they could never be used again during the reforms of King Josiah in 2 Kings 23:14-16. In particular, priests had strict prohibitions imposed upon them which prevented them from attending funerals or being close to anyone who had died except for their immediate family (Lev. 21:1-9). Indeed, the high priest could not defile himself by going near a human corpse, even if it was the funeral of his mother or father (Lev. 21:10-11). Remember that Ezekiel is a priest. Thus the vision of chapter 37, which puts Ezekiel down in a valley "full of dry bones," is not only a matter of queasiness about being in an open human graveyard but also a matter of the severest condition of ritual impurity and contamination. There is a level of repulsion in this vision, and we moderns may need some help to sense the extent to which this repulsion was experienced by Ezekiel and his audience.

The scene in Ezekiel 37:1-14 breaks down into two clear parts: the vision (vv. 1-10) and its explanation (vv. 11-14). This basic pairing of a vision and its explanation is a frequent device used throughout the book of Ezekiel.

460

The vision (vv. 1-10). The Lord sets the prophet down in the valley full of dry bones, human skeletons lying down, "very many" and "very dry." No flesh remained on any bone. The word "bone-dry" could well apply here. It was the "spirit" *(ruaḥ)* of the Lord that brought the prophet here, and it will be the *ruaḥ* (the Hebrew word meaning "spirit," "breath," and "wind") that will figure prominently throughout this vision.

The critical question is raised by God to the prophet in verse 3: "Mortal, can these bones live?" The Old Testament contains some isolated instances of bodily resurrections of individuals who had recently died. The miracles of the prophets Elijah and Elisha (1 Kings 17:17-24; 2 Kings 4:32-37) include the resurrection of a child who had just died. But nowhere in the Old Testament do we have a precedent for bringing to life a long-dead skeleton of dry human bones without any skin or flesh. Ezekiel sees bones that are dead, really dead. And so the question, "Can these bones live?" would be difficult for Ezekiel to answer in the affirmative. So Ezekiel responds diplomatically, "O Lord God, you know." If there is any rising to life, only God knows how it will come to pass.

The how of this amazing skeletal resurrection will be through the "breath" *(ruaḥ* — spirit, wind, breath) of the Lord which will enter these bones and give them life. And that breath of God will come through a human priest/prophet speaking the word of the Lord in ordinary human language. That language is couched in the form of a divine promise spoken directly in the second person to these skeletons: "I will cause breath to enter you, and you shall live." Sinews will hook the bones together, and skin will reappear, and then "you shall know that I am the Lord" (v. 6). This last statement is the central theme throughout Ezekiel — this amazing resurrection will happen so that God's people may know that the Lord is God and there is no other.

Verses 7-10 record the prophet's implementation of the Lord's instructions. True to the promise, God causes a great "noise" and "rattling" as skeletal bones come together with sinews and flesh. But the bodies remain lifeless; "there was no breath in them" (v. 8). The crucial ingredient, the one thing that makes life happen, is the divine *ruaḥ,* the breath that comes from the four winds of the cosmos (north, south, east, and west). With the rush of wind, "the breath came into them, and they lived, and stood on their feet, a vast multitude" (v. 10). Ezekiel sees here a new creation so foundational as to be compared with the first creation in Genesis 1 and 2. In Genesis 1 God creates through the divine "spirit/wind" which hovers over the primeval chaos and brings order and life out of chaos through the divine word: "Let there be light," and there was light (Gen. 1:2-3). This motif is now joined in

461

Ezekiel's vision with the story of the creation of the human in Genesis 2:7 when God breathes the divine *ruaḥ* (breath, wind) into the human form made of dust, and only then does the human become "a living being."

The explanation (vv. 11-14). Now, what does all of this mean? The Lord tells the prophet that these dried-up bones of death are "the whole house of Israel," who say they are lifeless and without hope: "we are cut off completely" (v. 11). Thus the Lord instructs the prophet about the more direct meaning of the earlier vision. God promises, "I am going to open your graves, and bring you up . . . and . . . bring you back to the land of Israel" (v. 12). The prophet does not exhort or command the skeletons to get up; they have no power whatsoever to bring themselves back to life. That's the point. What lifts them up is God's word spoken through a prophet chosen by God to speak this powerful divine promise. God delivers these awesome words and promises in the form of common human language spoken by a human prophet named Ezekiel in a particular time and place in Israel's history. Although embodied in human language, the connection between the divine promise spoken and its result is assured: "I, the LORD, have spoken and will act" (v. 14). Israel will return. Israel will live again.

Theological reflections that may flow out of the text are the following:

1. Ezekiel's vision is not about a literal resurrection of dead individuals. Rather, it is a vision of a communal resurrection of a people frozen dead in hopelessness, feeling totally cut off. This is a community that sees no way forward. They are without resources, without energy, without motivation, without a plan, and without hope. The Christian hope of the resurrection is rightly proclaimed in the face of the death of individuals. But a full biblical understanding of resurrection should speak also about the death and resurrection of communities where life and vitality are gone, completely gone, and then somehow reappear as a miracle without any visible means of support or hope. The vision applies most vividly to communities of faith, communities of God's people and their death and resurrection. Here, just before we begin the final week of Lent and the walk toward the cross of Good Friday, individuals and communities are reminded that "neither death, nor life . . . nor anything else in all creation, will be able to separate us from the love of God in Christ Jesus our Lord" (Rom. 8:38-39).

2. Perhaps the clearest biblical reapplication of Ezekiel's vision comes in Acts 2 and Pentecost when God's *ruaḥ* (spirit/wind) blows through the community of God's people in a new and powerful way, creating out of Jesus' death and resurrection the resurrection of "the body of Christ" in the world to proclaim the good news of forgiveness, life, and salvation in the name of Jesus. As with Ezekiel, so there the word of God proclaimed in common hu-

man language that each listener could hear in his or her own language became the means for creating something entirely new, so new its nearest analogue was God's creation of the universe at the beginning of time or God's mighty return of Israel back through the wilderness from Babylon to Jerusalem, which was also described as God's "new creation."

Dennis T. Olson

Tenth Sunday after Pentecost, Year C

First Lesson: Hosea 1:2-10
(Psalm 85)
Second Lesson: Colossians 2:6-15, (16-19)
Gospel Lesson: Luke 11:1-13

T his reading from Hosea marks the first of two from the prophet done in succession in Year C, both of which are unrelated to the New Testament readings appointed with them. Further, the second week's selection from Hosea (11:1-11) stakes out a different thematic focus from the present text's concerns. The preacher, therefore, will both be free and will want to explore the general thrust of this text as it functions in its particular thematic context within the first three chapters of the book.

These first three chapters describe a single symbolic action, whose elements taken together represent a prophetic word about Israel and her narrative of historical relation to God. The action, in brief, is the divinely commanded marriage of the prophet with a prostitute named Gomer and the conception between them of three children, each of whom is given a symbolic name representing God's judgment on Israel. The malleability of these names, however, points to God's ability to turn that judgment into mercy, an act that is fulfilled in the later renaming of the children at the end of chapter 2 — already given in prelude at the end of chapter 1 — with appellations that bespeak God's forgiveness and gift of new life. It appears that this marriage, naming, and renaming were concretely realized enactments by Hosea of a divine command (though this has been disputed). If nothing else, chapter 3 contains a description of the strikingly physical process of the prophet "purchasing" Gomer to bring her (back?) into the marriage relationship with him, one degrading element within a series of literal dramatizations Hosea was asked to perform as a means of embodying God's message to Israel.

The key to this symbolic action is the character of "adulterousness" or "harlotry" on the part of Gomer — symbolizing Israel's infidelity with respect to God — and the ultimate fruitfulness that derives, through divine grace, from the fidelity of God in maintaining the partnership with her. There has been, to be sure, a variety of interpretations regarding the historical particulars behind the images. Not all scholars, particularly in the earlier stages of both Jewish and Christian traditions, have been willing to grant the historical realization of the actions on Hosea's part, and they have preferred to see the entire drama as a literary allegory. And even among those who have insisted on Hosea's actual enactment of the described details, there has been disagreement as to the exact status of Gomer's own relationship to her husband: Was she once a prostitute but no longer? Did she engage in adulterous affairs while married to Hosea, or only before their marriage? Was her "adultery" tied to ritual pagan acts, or was it the paid prostitution of the marketplace? Were her children Hosea's or the progeny of her extramarital engagements? Did Hosea repudiate her once, only to return to her later?

These kinds of disagreements only point to the way the symbolic action, in its distasteful details, still works as a stumbling block to hearing, and it seems to indicate the need — whatever the chronological details or the exact historicity of the referents — to hold up the offensive and challenging character of the relationship embodied: repulsive human infidelity, judgment, and the redemptive power of divine fidelity through it. Literarily, chapter 1 can be read as an overall description of the symbol, chapter 2 as its theological explication, and chapter 3 as a kind of summary, combining the offense and God's redemptive response within a single image.

Chapter 1 in particular, then, outlines the course of the drama, with Hosea being asked to bear the burden, in human analogy, of God's love for Israel. First, God asks him to marry a harlot. Gomer, whom he marries, is meant to stand for Israel's own religious "harlotry," which describes the people's "abandonment" of God, both in disobedience and in apostasy toward other gods. It is important to note that the initiative to the drama here is made in "taking" Gomer as Hosea's wife, not in repudiating her harlotry as such. The drama begins with a movement *toward* Israel's sinfulness, not away from it. The purpose of the act, however, lies in its fruit, that is, in the

464

bearing of "children of harlotry." Hosea is asked to marry a prostitute not simply as a means of engaging such a relationship in the abstract, but because this relationship will bring forth children whose own beings will reflect the purposes of God.

Initially, this purpose is one of designating the scope of divine judgment. The three children are given names, according to God's directive, that describe the experienced fate of Israel under punishment. The first child is named Jezreel, which, we are told, refers backward to the sins of the rebel "Jehu's house" in assassinating the royal households of both Judah and Israel on the plain of Jezreel, while ultimately reverting to apostasy as well (cf. 1 Kings 18:41ff. and 2 Kings 9–10). Deriving from the root "to sow," the name Jezreel points to the consequences "sown" by Israel's own sins. These consequences are then named in the next two children, each identified, respectively, as "Not Pitied" (*Lo'-ruhamah*) and "Not My People" (*Lo'-'ammi*), attitudes God now adopts toward Israel. Within these two appellations are contained the whole narrative of the people's subsequent suffering and destruction at the hands of foreign enemies.

Yet the divine "naming" of Israel in this manner is also an indicator of the possibility of transformation from the same creative source: the One who names can rename; the One who punishes can forgive and restore. And the final verses of chapter 1 — taken up again in 2:21-23 and 3:4-5 — point to the hope of having God as "father." Just as Hosea weds Gomer and fathers children of "harlotry," granting them a public character of divine reproach in their names, so too the father has the power to grant new names to his children. (The patriarchal dynamics, however foreign to our contemporary culture and values, are essential to the drama and to underlining, through its legal force, the initiatives of grace and fidelity in the story.) For those who were once repudiated in the world's forum as "Not My People" can and will one day be displayed as "Sons of the Living God," the seemingly disinherited now made legally enfranchised. The name Jezreel, furthermore, is recast from its role as the territory of Judah and Israel's common punishment to being the place wherein the two separated peoples are reunited in a common polity of redemption (1:11), wherein division and infidelity are transformed into a unified life of mutual commitment.

The context of these details reveals that the symbolic action is not to be taken in purely generalized terms. It is worth noting that Hosea himself seems to have lived through one of the most violent and turbulent periods of the northern kingdom's history. If we are to take the chronology of 1:1 seriously, it is likely that he witnessed events analogous in their viciousness and chaos to those he himself refers to in Jehu's time, and ones that only a short time later would result in Samaria's destruction by the Assyrians (721 B.C.). The symbolic judgments and prophesied redemption, then, are located in particular experiences that touch upon the actual life of a crumbling Israelite society, on the verge of virtual annihilation. The question of infidelity as religious and social apostasy and division, and fidelity as the experience of moving through and beyond this into a renewed unity of heart and life, cannot be answered in any way other than in the concrete actions by which such a movement takes place. On this basis, the symbolic character of marriage and child rearing is rightly seen as embodying the actual acts of God's relation with Israel — and vice versa.

The entire drama, in its distasteful details (perhaps heightened in our era of concern over the justice or injustice of sexual roles such as those enacted here), points to the pain of divine fidelity maintained through human sin that can only be grasped through the embodied character of the marriage relationship that Hosea initiates with Gomer. (This is particularly developed in chapter 2.) It is the connection between painful fidelity through sin and the character of its enactment, primarily through the image of marriage, that ought to be the prime focus of the Christian preacher.

For not only is this relationship reiterated in several key places in the prophetic literature (cf. esp. Ezek. 16 but also, e.g., Isa. 62:3-5), but it is taken up with extraordinary focus in the New Testament as one of the pre-eminent figures of the gospel concerning Jesus. On the one hand, there are the explicit descriptions of the shape of divine "husbandhood" that reflect Hosea's dramatized message, for example, Ephesians 5:21-33; on the other, there are the actual citations of Hosea 1:6, 10 and 2:23 in, for example, 1 Peter 2:10 and Romans 9:25ff., that speak to God's salvation shared now with the Gentiles (those once "not my people" or "not beloved" are so now). In each case, however, the referent, implied or explicit, is the work of God in Christ Jesus, suffering in fidelity the punishments of human infidelity. And it is this referent that is seen as both fulfilling and establishing, in a sacramental fashion, the marriage symbol of Hosea's life with Gomer.

Few Old Testament acts, therefore, so pointedly expose as this, in a prophetic way, the "scandal" and joy of the cross and its Christianly enacted signs (like marriage). This text, therefore, offers the preacher a startling entry into the shape of the central gospel message, its consistent enunciation through the Testaments, and its sacramental enactment through the daily lives of peoples and families.

Ephraim Radner

Eighth Sunday after the Epiphany, Year B

First Lesson: Hosea 2:14-20
(Psalm 103:1-13, 22)
Second Lesson: 2 Corinthians 3:1-6
Gospel Lesson: Mark 2:13-22

Hosea's ministry took place in the northern kingdom of Israel during the reign of Jeroboam II (786-746 B.C.). It was a relatively stable time, with economic prosperity, although, as Hosea's contemporary Amos shows, there was a great gap between the rich and the poor. Royalty and law court were corrupt, and a general breakdown of morality characterized Israel's society. Worst of all, as Hosea emphasizes, there was widespread syncretistic worship of the fertility gods of Baal. The people believed that by worshiping the Baals at various cult sites throughout the land, and by entering into sacred prostitution, the fertility gods were magically coerced into giving abundant crops and offspring. It is such idolatry with which our passage for the morning is most concerned.

Our text actually encompasses parts of two separate oracles, 2:2-15 and 2:16-23 (vv. 16-20 are also poetry, contra the RSV). As we can read earlier in 2:2-13, the relation between Israel and God is framed in terms of a marriage. The Lord is Israel's divine "husband," and Israel is the Lord's "bride" (cf. the metaphors of Jesus Christ as the "bridegroom" of the church or of the new Jerusalem in the New Testament). The Lord wooed his bride Israel in the wilderness, after he delivered her from slavery in Egypt, speaking to her heart (2:14 in the Hebrew) and making her his own beloved. As in Jeremiah (Jer. 2:1-3), the wilderness time was the time of their "honeymoon," a time of faithfulness, when there were no other gods to come between God and his beloved people.

Such is the characterization of the covenant relationship between God and Israel in the book of Hosea. In another figure, Hosea pictures that relationship in terms of a father's love for his son (11:1-4). In short, the covenant between God and his people is not a legalistic binding, but an intimate relation of deepest love and loyalty; not a relation between a stern Authority and a subject people, but one of tenderness and knowledge. God "knows" Israel, as a faithful husband knows his beloved wife. And Israel is to "know" her divine husband, because she lives in intimate communion with him day by day, delighting in his presence and gratefully walking in his way (cf. 13:4-5). Love is to be at the heart of the relation between the Lord and his folk. It is the primary requirement of the covenant (cf. Deut. 6:4-5). God loves Israel, and Israel is to love him in return.

As we can read in 2:8, however, Israel in the time of Hosea does not "know" the Lord. She has forgotten him (2:13) and gone after other lovers, namely, the fertility gods of Baal. As chapters 4–13 make clear, Israel will therefore suffer the results of her unfaithfulness, and finally, in 721, she will be overrun by the troops of the Assyrian Empire, be carried into exile, and disappear from history.

The love of God for his covenant people is never at an end, however (cf. 11:8-9; chap. 14), and his heart of faithfulness never allows him to give them up forever. In our stated text, therefore, we find this God of love planning a future for his idolatrous folk. The verses are eschatological, and in them the Lord tells what he will do in that final time. Once more God will lead his bride into the wilderness and (literally) "speak to her heart," as he did at the first, wooing her in his love. He will change her entrance into the Promised Land through the Valley of Achor ("the Valley of Trouble") that leads from the Jordan Valley southwest of Jericho up to the hill country of Palestine, into a door of hope for the future. And Israel will answer the Lord's love with her love, as she did in the time of her youth.

When Israel enters into the land, however, she will no longer turn to the worship of the fertility gods of the land, nor will she ever call on the Lord by the name of Baal. She will no longer confuse the Lord with any other god or goddess. Instead, the name of Baal will be eliminated from her vocabulary, and the worship of the fertility gods of nature will be gone forever.

More than that, the Lord will guarantee Israel's safe habitation in the land. He will still the enmity between beasts and human beings in a covenant of peace. Unlike us moderns, the Old Testament writers have always been aware of the fact that sin has disrupted the relation of human beings not only with one another but also with the animal kingdom (cf. Gen. 3:15, 17-18; 9:2; Deut. 7:22; Ps. 91:13), and animals can therefore be instruments of judgment (Jer. 5:6; 8:17; 15:3; Ezek. 5:17; etc.). But here Hosea begins the prophetic tradition of a future restoration of peace with the animal kingdom in the kingdom of God (Isa. 11:6-9; 35:9; Ezek. 34:25, 28).

Not only will God guarantee Israel's safe habitation by peace in the animal world. He will also give peace among Israel's neighbors by banishing all weapons of war from the land. As has often been noted, "land" here refers only to the land of Canaan, however, and does not encompass the universal peace that is typical of later prophetic promises (Isa. 2:4; Mic. 4:3; Ezek. 39:9; Zech. 9:10). The emphasis in our passage is on security for Israel that will come from the hand of God, when heretofore Israel has faithlessly looked for security only from Baal. The Lord is the only God who can make Israel "lie down in safety."

There then follows in verses 19-20 God's promise of a new betrothal with his beloved people. In 2:2 God divorced his faithless people (cf. 1:8). Now in God's eschatological future, he will take them to himself once more. A betrothal in Israel was tantamount to marriage (cf. Exod. 22:16; Deut. 20:7; 2 Sam. 3:14; Matt. 1:18-20) and was arranged by the payment of a bride-price to the father of the future bride, usually in the amount of fifty shekels or one and one-quarter pounds of silver (Deut. 22:29). The father's acceptance of the gift signified his acceptance of the marriage. The bride-price that the Lord will pay is not silver, however, but righteousness, justice, steadfast love, and mercy. Obviously, in the Lord's betrothal to Israel there is no father to whom payment is to be made, and some have thought that these are the qualities that the Lord will have in himself. But no. These are the gifts the Lord will bestow upon his bride, Israel. She will be transformed, so that she is "righteous," which means that she will fulfill the demands of the covenant relation. She will become "just," establishing God's order in her society, not her own. She will have steadfast, covenant love toward the Lord that will never fail. And she will be merciful toward the poor and the helpless in her society. Summing it all up, God will give Israel "faithfulness" toward him, so that she will worship and serve only him, loving him as he loves her and acting toward her Lord and toward her neighbors with justice and mercy, righteousness and peace.

The whole passage is a summary of what our Lord expects from us, isn't it? For we too are his covenant people, like Israel, wedded to God through the new covenant given us by Jesus Christ. And goodness knows, we are still worshiping our Baals — all those other things and persons to whom we look for security rather than to our Lord alone. But Hosea is here telling us that God can transform us too, in his new age of the future.

That's the stumbling block in the book of Hosea, however. It promises an eschatological future to Israel that never came for those people of the northern kingdom. They went into exile and disappeared from history. Did God not keep his promises to them then?

What we have here in 2:14-15 is the promise of God that he will start all over again in Israel's history to make for himself a new people "in that day," in that eschatological, indeterminate future when he leads them once more out into the wilderness after their redemption from slavery. And the Gospel according to Matthew picks up that promise. It quotes Hosea in Matthew 2:15, and it tells us that when our Lord Christ came up out of Egypt, after his family fled from Herod, that was the fulfillment of Hosea 11:1. In Jesus

Christ, God began all over again. He began to make the new people promised by the prophet — you and me and all the church, branches from the root of Israel — who can indeed be transformed by the Spirit of Christ to be God's faithful people — righteous, just, steadfast, merciful — in a loving, intimate, and eternal covenant with our Lord.

Elizabeth Achtemeier

Eleventh Sunday after Pentecost, Year C

First Lesson: Hosea 11:1-11
(Psalm 107:1-9, 43)
Second Lesson: Colossians 3:1-11
Gospel Lesson: Luke 12:13-21

The book named after Hosea is (almost) bracketed by two passages that reflect on the implications of Hosea's personal experience for his understanding of God and God's relationship with Israel.

Chapters 1–3 speak of Hosea's relationship with his wife, Gomer. That relationship becomes a prism through which the book invites people to look at Yahweh's relationship with Israel. And/or, Yahweh's relationship with Israel becomes a prism through which the book looks at the relationship between Hosea and Gomer. It is therefore, of course, Israel in its unfaithfulness to Yahweh that provides the lens through which the book looks at womanhood, as embodied in Gomer. This means that some harsh things get said about Gomer that can easily flow over into an attitude toward womanhood in general, reinforcing patriarchal attitudes that often prevail in the church. It also means that some tough statements are made about Yahweh as resembling a cuckolded husband incensed with violent fury, statements that may bolster perverted images of God and encourage marital abuse and violence.

In chapter 11, the other side of the main body of the book's prophecies, Hosea again presents us with the fruits of his reflection on his marital experience. It is a nice fact that this further reflection implies some rather different perspectives on God and on marriage and family. It suggests new insights on their interrelationship and on the way they help us understand each other. (The NRSV's marginal notes draw attention to some problems about details of the text and translation, but these do not affect the main drift of the passage. The preacher will be advised to concentrate on aspects of the text unaffected by these difficulties, and we will do that here. We can then safeguard ourselves from making a point on the basis of some detail that is uncertain.)

Yahweh gives us a testimony to a long history of parental experience. In the picture Yahweh paints, Israel starts off as an orphan in Egypt. There in Egypt was this lonely child, and Yahweh fell in love with it, the way a couple who cannot have children fall in love with a child in an orphanage. There is a huge reservoir of love in their hearts, and it longs to find an object. Yahweh *is* love, and this love in Yahweh finds its object.

So Yahweh summoned Israel out of Egypt as a son. Israel was adopted into Yahweh's family. The really weird thing is that Israel has not related to Yahweh as one might then have expected. Instead of calling responsively on Yahweh, they have made a habit of making offerings to the gods of Canaan (v. 2b).

Like a mother or a father, Yahweh taught Ephraim to walk (v. 3a; "Ephraim" means the northern kingdom as a whole). Yahweh picked this child up when it fell over, and tended its grazed knees. But it did not acknowledge that Yahweh was the one who healed it. The NRSV has "did not know," but the verb *yada'* covers the range of "acknowledge, recognize" as well as "know," and Hosea is fond of this usage. It is not that the child has received a present from an anonymous benefactor. It is that the child has refused to recognize where its benefactions came from.

Like a mother or father with a child that has just learned to walk, Yahweh has led Ephraim along and kept it on reins to make sure it did not wander too far and get into trouble. These are thus humane and loving reins. The love that set the adoption going continues as the parents bring up their child. Keeping control of children by means of "reins," of course, is an image from animal husbandry, and by the time of verse 4b Hosea is more explicitly picturing Yahweh as like a farmer caring for animals. The wise and caring farmer or parent does not pull on the reins in such a way as to hurt the animal or child, and makes sure it gets its food.

But the "child" has failed to "return" to Yahweh (v. 5). The verb is often translated "repent." "Return" helps to make clear the nature of repentance. It is an act of the will: we turn from walking in one direction to walking in another. The verb reappears in verse 7. Strictly it means "turn" rather than "return," and there the NRSV assumes it refers to the fact that the people are turning (away) and not turning (back). The usage further clarifies the Old Testament's understanding of the people's relationship with God. It should involve walking in the way Yahweh points and not turning from this way, but if we do turn away, our business is to turn back.

So far God's words have constituted a radical indictment of the people and a threat to bring a radical calamity upon them, and much of their power issues from Hosea's use of the parenthood metaphor. It is in keeping with Hosea's account of his parental experience in chapter 1, and his use of this image there to bring home the terrifying nature of what God will do to Israel. The parent owed this child nothing, but decided to love it, adopted it, delivered it from the place where it was being abused, taught it to walk, tended its hurts, protected it, nourished it, and so forth. But it has made no response. It has treated other people as its providers and not recognized who its parent was. It has been invited and challenged to come back, but has declined to do so. Therefore it will be thrown out.

But how could a parent do this (v. 8)? How can a parent divorce a child? Admah and Zeboiim are towns that shared the fate of Sodom and Gomorrah (Deut. 29:23), but they are obscure places, and that makes the point that Yahweh could hardly treat Ephraim as if it were somewhere that was hard to locate on the map. Yahweh recoils from the idea. Yahweh's tenderness makes it impossible to act in anger. Yahweh does not go back on the feeling of anger or abandon it. Rather, Yahweh determines to contain it, not to execute it (v. 9a). The Bible assumes that there is nothing wrong with anger in itself; it is part of the emotional repertoire that belongs to human beings through their being made in God's image. It is an appropriate emotional response to the way people sometimes treat each other. The question is what we do with our anger. Are we in control of the occasions when we may properly express it and the moments when we should absorb its force within ourselves? There is more obligation on the stronger of two parties to absorb its anger. That applies to parents in general, and thus to Yahweh in particular.

The reason is that Yahweh is God and not a man (v. 9b). The NRSV has "I am God and no mortal." It is natural for human beings to be overwhelmed by wrath and to have to express it, but God is different. God is "the holy one." The distinctive nature of God as the holy one, not a human being, is to restrain and absorb anger, and to let tenderness win out over the instinct to lash out.

All that is true, though Hosea may also make a more subtle point. The Hebrew word for human being as opposed to God or animal is 'adam. That is the word we would expect to find if Hosea is contrasting God and human beings. But the word that comes here is not *'adam* but *'ish*. That word means man as opposed to woman.

That would imply the assumption that there is something different between the relationship that men and women have with their children. No doubt cultural factors operate here, yet physiological ones also operate. Hosea's statements about his children in chapters 1-3 are perhaps ones that a woman could never make. But God's relationship with Israel is more like a mother's relationship with her children than a father's. A father is more likely to express anger; a mother is more likely to absorb it. In this respect God is more like a mother than a father. Motherhood involves your whole being in a way that fatherhood does not. Some such awareness lies behind verses 8-9. Perhaps Hosea learned it from Gomer. Whether that is so or not, Hosea seems to be reflecting the nature of a woman's experience and letting that contribute to an understanding of God's relationship with Israel. That provides a positive counterpart to the more negative tone of chapters 1-3.

Actually exile would come upon Israel. But that tenderness of Yahweh's would mean that exile was not the last word. Israel will be able to come back (vv. 10-11). The children will find that the parents throw them out of the house for a while, but the door is not closed and barred forever.

John Goldingay

Twenty-third Sunday after Pentecost, Year C

First Lesson: Joel 2:23-32
(Psalm 65)
Second Lesson: 2 Timothy 4:6-8, 16-18
Gospel Lesson: Luke 18:9-14

Uniquely among the prophetic books, Joel gives no concrete clue of its date. In the premodern era, Joel was assumed to be one of the earliest prophets — hence its position among the Twelve Prophets. In the modern era, he was assumed to be one of the last prophets: he refers to the Greeks in

473

3:6. In the postmodern era, we do not know when Joel lived, but that ceases to trouble us. The important thing is that the book arose out of a specific crisis, a locust plague (or conceivably an invasion pictured as a locust plague); see 2:25. The earlier part of the book thus offers guidance on how to understand and how to respond to a crisis of that kind, while here Joel looks to the other side of the disaster.

In Joel's vision God has begun the process of restoring the land. The first key to that is rain. While Israel can always be sure that the sun will shine to ripen the grain, it cannot be sure that at earlier stages in the agricultural year the rain will fall at the times when it is needed. The first of these comes in the fall, when people need the "early rain" to soften the ground so that it can be plowed and the seed then sown. The second comes in the spring, when people need the "later rain" to help the young plants grow to full size. Joel speaks as if both rains have fallen (v. 23). The vision is thus implicitly located in early summer. The rains have not only fallen, but fallen abundantly. Yet people have recently been reminded that rain is only the first key to a harvest. While the sun to ripen produce can be taken for granted, protection from pestilence cannot. The fulfillment of the "natural" cycle depends upon there being no further locust plague.

We cannot tell whether the rains have in reality yet fallen or whether so far this has only happened in Joel's vision. In verse 22 the verbs are also past tense ("the wilderness pastures have become green, / the tree has borne its fruit, / the fig tree and the vine have given their full yield"), but the NRSV rightly assumes that it is only within Joel's vision that the harvest has actually happened. It might make better sense of chapter 2 as a whole to assume that the rains, too, have actually arrived only within the vision. The vision as a whole would then belong to the period of the plague and its aftermath. Restoration is still entirely promise.

But either in vision or in history, the people stand between the gift of rain and the growth to harvest. Recent experience has reminded people that harvest is not guaranteed until it has happened. What if another plague comes? Either in life or in imagination, they stand at the moment when hope might die again. Joel promises that they will indeed see an abundant harvest (v. 24). The loss of the preceding years will thus be made up (v. 25).

It is a bold promise. Prophecy is difficult, the Chinese proverb says, especially regarding the future. We know how easy it is for weather forecasters to be embarrassingly wrong about what may happen tomorrow. But Joel has been given the conviction that this particular plague did not result from chance, from the vagaries of nature. It had a moral significance. That cannot be universalized; not every plague is an act of divine chastisement (cf.

the story of Job). But this one was. If the people have responded aright, or if they do respond aright, then they can be restored.

The way Joel makes the point is to speak of the gift of rain as an act of "righteousness" (v. 23). The Hebrew word, ṣedaqah, does not have an equivalent in English. Different translations use the words "vindication," "justice," "in due measure," or "kindness." Ṣedaqah is a relationship word, and it suggests doing what is right by people with whom one is in relationship. So when God acts faithfully toward Israel, and specifically when God restores Israel after some disaster, this is an act of ṣedaqah, an act of righteousness or justice. This is so not because Israel deserves this treatment, but because God is acting faithfully in the context of that relationship.

So far we might have read this promise as signifying the reversal of a single, isolated calamity. Verses 26-27 make clear that it is more than this.

Actually the calamity itself was more than a single calamity. It was a very realization of the Day of Yahweh (1:15; 2:1). Old Testament thinking typically understands matters in this way. When we experience God's judgment or God's blessing, it is an experience of God's final judgment and God's ultimate purpose finding realization within our own experience. So the calamity was the Day of Yahweh's wrath arriving, and the restoration will be the Day of Yahweh's love being consummated.

That day will have three aspects. First, it is a day when people will eat in plenty. It is easy for Western people to take food for granted and to see it as not very spiritual, but the Old Testament knew that food could not be taken for granted and that God was very concerned with it, as part of God's concern with the body. The body and food are spiritual realities.

Second, it is by means of these that people will know that God is in their midst. They will know once more that Yahweh is indeed God. Often prophets see God's acts in history as the proof that Yahweh is God. Joel promises that events in nature will do that. In each case the evidence is not merely that an event takes place, whether a political one or a natural one. It is that this event takes place in fulfillment of God's word. It is the ability to say what you are going to do and then do it that shows that Yahweh is God. This day will demonstrate that this is so, and thus make the day a day of worship.

Third, it is a day of glory. The calamity that the people have experienced has made the past year a time of shame (see v. 17). Like a political defeat such as the fall of Jerusalem, the locust plague indicates that either they are experiencing God's judgment or have been committed to an incompetent God. Either way, they look stupid. God's abundant blessing will prove that neither of these ideas is true. This calamity was the Day of Yahweh happening; therefore, Yahweh can also promise that they will never again be shamed. They have gone through the Day of Yahweh, and will not have to go through it again. The promise reminds us of God's promise after the flood, when God swore, "Never again."

There is another aspect of the people's need. From the beginning of their experience, God's spirit had been alive in their midst (see, e.g., Isa. 63:10, 11, 14; Hag. 2:5). A person's "spirit" is the person's personal dynamic, expressing itself in powerful actions that fulfill the person's will. So God's spirit is God's personal dynamic, expressing itself in powerful actions that fulfill God's will. Although Israel knew that God's spirit had come to dwell in their midst, at the same time they knew it was possible to grieve God's spirit and for God's spirit to be withdrawn (see Isa. 63:10; Ps. 51:11). The failure that had led to the locust plague would be bound also to involve the withdrawing of that spirit.

Merely renewing nature would therefore not resolve the problems that the locust plague exposed. Something else was needed. Verses 28-29 promise that further gift. In the past, women and men prophesied, had revelatory dreams, and saw visions. In Joel's day, that perhaps seemed to belong to the distant past. God promises that it will again become present reality. Indeed, God may promise to do something more spectacular than the people have previously known. Prophecy, dreams, and visions will be more prevalent than they have been before. Whether this is something new or not, age, sex, or class will not constrain the pouring out of God's spirit.

Acts 2 sees this promise fulfilled at the first Pentecost, but it is not now fulfilled in the life of the church. The promise therefore provides a basis for praying, expecting, and acting so that it may be so. Acts 2 also sees verses 30-32a as fulfilled at Pentecost. To us it probably looks more like a description of cataclysmic events at the End, of the kind that are also described in a passage such as Luke 21. That reflects the fact that Pentecost is itself indeed a partial realization of the End. Joel promises that when cataclysms like the flood threaten the world, it is an invitation to us to turn to God for protection.

John Goldingay

Eighth Sunday after Pentecost, Year C

First Lesson: Amos 7:7-17
(Psalm 82)
Second Lesson: Colossians 1:1-14
Gospel Lesson: Luke 10:25-37

The first lesson consists of two parts: the third (7:7-9) of four vision reports (see also 7:1-3; 7:4-6; 8:1-3) and a narrative about the prophet Amos that culminates with a divine oracle (7:10-17). The arrangement is not simply haphazard nor coincidental. Rather, the narrative and oracle explain the marked shift that has taken place between the first two visions and the third vision — namely, Israel and its royal house will be destroyed (7:8-9) rather than spared (7:3, 6).

Amos prophesied in Israel, the northern kingdom, toward the middle of the eighth century B.C. during the long and prosperous reign of Jeroboam II (usually dated 787-747). But he detected decay within Israel, evidenced by pervasive injustice that victimized the poor and was supported by empty worship (see 2:6-8; 4:1-3; 5:10-13, 18-24; 6:1-7; 8:4-6). As a result, the whole nation would be destroyed. The book of Amos was probably edited after the fall of the northern kingdom in 722, and was probably used to call Judah, the southern kingdom, to repentance. After the fall of Judah in 587, it was probably further edited to reflect the message that punishment is not God's final word (see 9:11-15). In any case, the book of Amos and, indeed, all the prophetic books in their final forms both indict God's people for faithlessness and injustice and look toward restoration beyond judgment and destruction.

This tension between mercy and judgment is reflected in the movement of Amos's vision reports. In the first two God "relented" concerning Israel's destruction (7:3, 6), but in the final two God "will never again pass them by" (7:8; 8:2) and destruction will occur. The tension suggests that judgment and destruction are not God's will, in the positive sense. Rather, God wills justice, righteousness, and peace (see 5:24). But when Israel (or any people) persistently fails to enact and embody God's justice, they will eventually experience the inevitably violent and disastrous consequences that injustice brings. In theological terms this is the wrath or punishment of God. God has standards, and while God does not positively wish to punish, the violation of God's standards of justice and righteousness will be destructive and eventually disastrous.

477

The third vision is difficult to interpret, because the meaning of its key word, which occurs four times, is unclear. It is traditionally translated "plumb line," and if this is correct, the primary intent of the vision is to portray Israel as an unsound, decaying structure and thus to articulate the rationale for Israel's impending destruction. This interpretation makes sense, and it seems to be supported by the inclusion of references to structures in verse 9 — "high places," "sanctuaries," "house." Several recent commentators have pointed out, however, that the Hebrew word in question probably means "tin," and since tin was used in the production of weapons, they suggest that the word is a metaphor for military action. For God to be "setting tin in the midst of my people Israel" (7:8) would then express not so much the rationale for destruction as the certain reality of Israel's destruction by God's action against it. This interpretation also makes sense; and the violent content of 7:9, 17 suggests military defeat.

In either case — whether the primary thrust of the vision is to articulate the reasons for Israel's destruction or the certainty of Israel's destruction (or perhaps both) — the following narrative and oracle further explain to the ancient hearers and to contemporary readers why this radical action was inevitable. Israel, after all, thought God was on its side (as do all peoples and nations), and in the third and fourth visions God claims Israel as "my people" (7:8; 8:2; see also 7:15). What 7:10-17 reveals is not that God has renounced Israel, but rather that Israel has renounced God. The choice to abandon God and God's will is what inevitably proves destructive.

Although Amaziah is "the priest of Bethel" (7:10), the site of one of the major shrines of the northern kingdom (see 1 Kings 12:29; Amos 4:4; 5:5-6), it is clear to whom Amaziah looks as his primary authority — namely, to King Jeroboam rather than to God. Even though Amaziah apparently recognizes Amos as a "seer" (7:12) and a prophet, he orders Amos not to "prophesy at Bethel" (7:13). In short, Amaziah's concern is not for the truth of God's word but rather for the security of his boss, King Jeroboam. Not surprisingly, Amaziah identifies Bethel, which literally means "the house of God," as "the king's sanctuary, and . . . a temple of the kingdom" (7:13). What rightfully belonged to God has been appropriated by Amaziah on behalf of Jeroboam.

In a word, this is idolatry — putting ourselves and our claims in place of God and God's claims. In contemporary terms, we might say Amaziah is worshiping the god of "national security." It is no wonder that Amaziah's report to King Jeroboam in 7:10 focuses not on the truth or falsehood of Amos's words, but rather on their potentially destabilizing effect on "the land" or the nation. For powerful people like Amaziah and Jeroboam, the temptation is to reduce truth to power: "might makes right." Amos and the other prophets dared to stand with the poor and the powerless and to declare precisely the opposite in God's name: "right makes might." In other words, an enduring future depends first on recognizing God's authority and God's will for justice and righteousness (see Ps. 82, the psalm for the day).

The conflict between Jeroboam's authority, articulated by Amaziah, and God's authority, articulated by Amos, comes to a head in 7:14-17. Amaziah had told Amos to "go" (7:12), meaning to "get lost." But, as Amos points out, God has also told him to "go" (7:15), meaning to prophesy; and it is clear which authority Amos obeys. In response to Amaziah, Amos can repeat clearly what "you say" (7:16), but his prophetic announcement consists of "thus says the LORD" (7:17). It is revealing that the Hebrew word for "say(s)" occurs six times in 7:10-17, suggesting that in a real sense the conflict between Amos and Amaziah, or God and Jeroboam, is a battle of words. Which word or message is true? Does "might make right"? Or does "right make might"?

Amos's answer to Amaziah in 7:14 is one of the most debated issues in Old Testament interpretation. Does Amos mean "I am no prophet, nor a prophet's son," thus distinguishing his mission and message from professional prophets who apparently served as yes-men for King Jeroboam, as Amaziah did in his priestly role? Or does Amos mean "I was no prophet, nor a prophet's son," with the implication that now he is a prophet, having been taken and commissioned by God? The Hebrew syntax permits either meaning, and both make a good deal of sense. In either case, the fundamental issue is the word and its authority. Amos's claim — over against other so-called prophets or over against his former vocation — is the compulsion to speak the word of God, which he does at the risk of being accused of treason (7:10) and perhaps of being deprived of his former livelihood (7:14-15).

The verbless clause in 7:14 features the Hebrew pronoun "I," which is quite similar to the rare word translated "plumb line" in 7:7-8. This raises the interesting possibility that the juxtaposition of 7:7-9 and 7:10-17 may at least hint at the possibility that Amos himself is the measuring device (plumb line) or weapon (tin) that God has placed "in the midst" (7:8) of the people. Amaziah's location of Amos "in the very center of the house of Israel" (7:10) may reinforce this possibility, since "midst" (7:8) and "center" (7:10) are the same Hebrew word. This hint would serve to reinforce the centrality of the word (see the exegesis of Amos 8:1-12). The prophetic word, here and elsewhere, is central in informing the people of God how they may not be measuring up, as well as warning them of the inevitably de-

479

structive and eventually disastrous consequences of persisting in idolatry and injustice.

The disastrous consequences for Amaziah are clearly in view in 7:17. That a priest, the guardian of purity and cleanness, should "die in an unclean land" is particularly ignominious. Thus 7:17 serves to highlight a concept which is especially pertinent in interpreting Amos and the other prophets, and which may be especially helpful in appropriating this message for today — irony (see also the exegesis of Amos 8:1-12). Amaziah's attempts to secure his future, the future of King Jeroboam, and Israel's future had precisely the opposite effect. Thus 7:7-17 prompts us to confront some disturbing and complex questions: How may our own efforts to secure our futures actually be undermining our futures? For Christians, who are citizens of both God's reign and a secular state, how may these realms of allegiance cohere or conflict? How shall we tell the difference?

Especially in view of these questions, 7:7-17 is a reminder of how easy it is to claim God's support for our own agendas, as opposed to submitting ourselves to God's claim. Idolatry and injustice are persistent temptations, and they have proven to be enduring realities. This discouraging recognition makes it all the more important for people of faith to attend to the witness of the prophets, who bring a divine word that not only unsettles, indicts, and warns, but also promises a better and more enduring future founded on a divine justice that is ultimately pursued by showing mercy to all. Ultimately, therefore, the prophet Amos calls for transformation grounded in the recognition of God's claim on our lives and the life of the world, thus anticipating Jesus' preaching — "The kingdom of God is at hand; repent, and believe in the good news" (Mark 1:15, NRSV note) — and Jesus' ministry of mercy for all (see Luke 10:25-37, the Gospel lesson for the day).

J. Clinton McCann

Ninth Sunday after Pentecost, Year C

First Lesson: Amos 8:1-12
(Psalm 52)
Second Lesson: Colossians 1:15-28
Gospel Lesson: Luke 10:38-42

The first lesson follows immediately upon the first lesson (Amos 7:7-17) for the Eighth Sunday after Pentecost, Year C. It begins with the fourth and final of Amos's vision reports (8:1-3). As in 7:7-17, the vision report is followed by material (8:4-12) that explains the grim message of the vision — that is, why God "will never again" spare Israel (8:2; see 7:8).

What Amos is shown in this vision is "a basket of summer fruit" (8:1-2). God's interpretation of the meaning of this object — "the end has come upon my people Israel" (8:2) — takes the form of a pun. The Hebrew word for "summer fruit" is *qayiṣ* while the word for "end" is *qeṣ*. What would normally suggest the end of the harvest season now points to the end of everything. The joyful songs that would normally accompany the celebration of the harvest will become funeral dirges (see 5:1-3). For the few who might happen to survive the coming calamity, the best policy will be to try to hide from the terrifying presence of God — that is, "Be silent!" (see 6:9-10).

As suggested in the exegesis of 7:7-17, there is a progression in the vision reports from God's relenting concerning destruction (see 7:3, 6) to the horror of 7:8-9 and 8:2-3. This movement indicates that punishment is not, in a positive sense, the will of God. Rather, God wills justice, righteousness, and peace (see 5:24). The terrifying culmination to the series of visions reveals not that God has abandoned those whom God still calls "my people" (8:2; see 7:8, 15), but rather that the people have abandoned God. Thus they will experience the inevitably destructive and violent results of their own injustice. The details of the people's injustice are documented in 8:4-6, while 8:7-10 elaborates upon the destructive results (see also 8:13-14). Verses 11-12 summarize the situation in terms of "the word" or "words" of God, thus linking the expansion of the fourth vision to the expansion of the third vision (see 7:16, as well as the sixfold repetition in 7:10-17 of the Hebrew verb "to say").

The opening "hear" of verse 4 recalls the material in Amos that precedes the vision reports and that also documents the people's injustice (see 3:1; 4:1; 5:1). Furthermore, the content of verse 4 recalls the very first indictment of Israel in 2:6-7, the culmination of a series of oracles against the nations. Just as other nations have set themselves over against God and will experience the results of their own injustice, so will Israel. God shows no partiality, except to "the needy" (vv. 4, 6; see 2:6; 4:1; 5:12) and "the poor" (the Hebrew words translated "poor" differ in vv. 4 and 6; for the first, see NRSV "afflicted" in 2:7, and for the second, see NRSV "poor" in 2:7; 4:1).

It was the special responsibility of the king to protect and deliver the poor and needy from oppression (see Ps. 72:1-4, 12-14), but the third vision report and its expansion have already indicted King Jeroboam (see 7:9, 11). Kings were also supposed to be models of obedience to God, including refraining from excessive wealth (see Deut. 17:14-20); however, while King Jeroboam may have been leading the way, he was apparently leading people in the wrong direction. Instead of being protected and delivered, the poor and needy are being trampled and exterminated, which is the sense of the Hebrew word the NRSV translates "bring to ruin" (v. 4).

Verses 5-6 suggest that King Jeroboam and Israel's domestic policy consists not of justice and righteousness but rather of greed and deceit. Merchants cannot wait until religious observances are over so they can go back to making more money. And apparently it was "good business" then, just as it is now, to get away with as much as possible. Then and now, the bottom line is making money, not caring for people. The God of the prophets has been replaced by the god of profit.

In her incisive assessment of contemporary North American culture, Mary Pipher concludes: "Our most organized religion is capitalism. . . . capitalism favors what's called the survival of the fittest, but really it's survival of the greediest, most driven and most ruthless. We have cared more about selling things to our neighbors than we've cared for our neighbors. The deck is stacked all wrong and ultimately we will all lose" (*The Shelter of Each Other: Rebuilding Our Families* [New York: Putnam, 1996], p. 94). Much the same could be said of the Israelite society that Amos addressed. King Jeroboam and the privileged cared more about selling things to people than about people. When this happens, everyone stands to lose.

How Israel will lose is portrayed in 8:7-10. The seriousness of Israel's sin of idolatry and injustice is indicated by the divine oath that begins verse 7. Ordinarily God swears by God's own self or name, as in 6:8, which also mentions "the pride of Jacob." But there God "abhor[s] the pride of Jacob," so it is unusual in 8:7 that God swears "by the pride of Jacob." Perhaps the phrase is used to name God, but if so it does so rather obliquely. Elsewhere "the pride of Jacob" describes Israel's land, which is a gift that results from God's sovereignty over all peoples and nations (see Ps. 47:4; Nah. 2:2). So, God may be swearing by God's own sovereignty (see Jorg Jeremias, *The Book of Amos* [Atlanta: Westminster/John Knox, 1998], pp. 148-49). The divine oath would have an ironic ring in view of Amos 6:8. God's gift of the land, bespeaking God's sovereign claim, is being abused by a self-centered, greedy people. A legitimate "pride" has become deadly arrogance, and the people can only stand to lose.

Not surprisingly, 8:8 suggests that "the land [will] tremble" because of the people's "deeds" (8:7; also see the imagery of an earthquake and its effects in 1:1; 9:1). The current stability is an illusion; because it is founded on injustice, it will falter and collapse. Human injustice will have an impact on the environment — "the land." "Everyone" will "mourn" because they are affected for the worse (see 9:5). In short, greed and injustice mean that everything and everybody will lose (see Ps. 52:1-7, the psalm for today; Ps. 82:5; Hos. 4:1-3).

Any bright future that the people might expect as a result of their greedy self-assertion will turn out to be darkness (8:9; see 5:18-20). Picking up the imagery of the fourth vision (8:3), 8:10 proclaims that anything that currently seems worth celebrating is simply the prelude to a funeral song. As in 8:7 and elsewhere in Amos (see esp. 3:1-2, 9-12; 5:18-20; and the exegesis of 7:7-17), the operative concept is irony. What the people think they are doing to insure future prosperity is actually killing them.

Not surprisingly, Mary Pipher accompanies her conclusion concerning the greediness of contemporary North American culture with the assertion that "ironies abound" (p. 81). Her assessment is not grounded theologically, but the book of Amos is ample evidence that irony is a biblical-theological category. So is the work of Reinhold Niebuhr, who argues that the Christian "interpretation of the nature of evil in human history is consistently ironic" (*The Irony of American History* [New York: Scribner, 1952], p. 155). Niebuhr's warning echoes Amos's prophecy, and it is perpetually timely: "We . . . are never safe against the temptation of claiming God too simply as the sanctifier of whatever we most fervently desire. Even the most 'Christian' civilization and the most pious church must be reminded that the true God can be known only where there is some awareness of a contradiction between divine and human purposes, even on the highest level of human aspirations" (p. 173). According to Amos, this "awareness" comes from "hearing the words of the LORD" (8:11).

Although Mary Pipher's analysis of the contemporary crisis is essentially secular, it is interesting that it parallels the imagery of 8:11-12. Quoting Peter Rowan, Pipher asserts that we are "thirsty in the rain" and that "we hunger for values, community and something greater than ourselves to dedicate our lives to" (p. 81). The communal and self-transcendent dimensions that we are missing are what "the word of the LORD" (v. 12) calls

483

justice and righteousness — the recognition of God's sovereign claim upon our lives that leads to the fulfillment of God's purposes of caring for each other rather than simply selling stuff to each other.

Recognizing God's sovereignty — what Jesus called entering the reign of God — is as simple but elusive as loving God with all our beings and loving our neighbors as ourselves (see Matt. 22:34-40). At this point, of course, Jesus' teaching is echoing the Torah, God's "teaching" or word (see Deut. 6:4; Lev. 19:18). Or, as Jesus put it when he was tempted to assert himself over against God's purposes:

> One does not live by bread alone,
>   but by every word that comes from the mouth of God.
>
> (Matt. 4:4)

Here again, Jesus echoes the Torah, God's word (see Deut. 8:3), and he also reinforces the message of Amos that the hope of Israel and the hope of the world rests ultimately on renouncing self-assertion and greed in conformity with "the word(s) of the LORD" (8:11-12). According to Niebuhr, "if we should perish," the fault will not be God's nor some external foe's, but rather our own "hatred and vainglory" (p. 124).

J. Clinton McCann

Third Sunday after the Epiphany, Year B

First Lesson: Jonah 3:1-5, 10
(Psalm 62:5-12)
Second Lesson: 1 Corinthians 7:29-31
Gospel Lesson: Mark 1:14-20

Anyone who still holds the old stereotypical opinion that the God of the Old Testament is wrathful and judgmental, in contrast to the God of the New, who is loving and merciful, should carefully study the book of Jonah. Above all else, Jonah is about the mercy and love of God.

While the book is included among the prophetic literature in the Old Testament, it is not made up of prophetic oracles but of a story about a man named Jonah who is never called a prophet in the book. There is only one verse in which it is said that "the word of the LORD came to Jonah" (v. 1), and only one verse in which he utters a prophetic word (3:4). Instead of preaching to Israel, he addresses Nineveh, the capital of the Assyrian Empire. With the exception of 2:2-9, the book is entirely a third-person prose narrative.

To be sure, the name "Jonah, the son of Amittai," is taken from 2 Kings 14:25, where we find a prophet by that name who preached during the reign of Jeroboam II (786-746 B.C.) in the northern kingdom of Israel. Thus we are to understand that the book is to be read against that eighth-century-B.C. background. But in 1:2 Nineveh is called a "great city," and in 3:3 it is so large that it would take three days to cross it. While Nineveh was one of the oldest cities in Mesopotamia, it was neither large nor important during the reign of Jeroboam II, and it did not reach the proportions ascribed to it in Jonah until the reign of Sennacherib (705-681). It was destroyed by the Medes and Babylonians in 612 and was never rebuilt.

Certainly, however, from the time of the resurgence of the Assyrian Empire in 745 until 612, Nineveh was the symbol of overwhelming and ruthless power of empire. Its pride in its power is set forth in Isaiah 10:2-4, and Nahum depicts it as a "city of blood" (Nah. 3:1) and of "endless cruelty (3:19). It became the symbol of the systematic Assyrian policy of deporting captive people and replacing them with alien populations, a fate that befell the northern tribes of Israel in 721. Thus Nineveh was hated throughout the ancient Near East. But it is Nineveh to which Jonah is sent by the Lord to preach (1:2).

By way of background to our text, it has often been held too that the book of Jonah is a protest against the exclusivism that characterized Judaism in the last half of the fifth century B.C., as that is set forth in Nehemiah and Ezra. But Jonah says nothing about the problems dealt with in those two books. And indeed, the theology of the book fits much better in the first half of the fifth century B.C., in the time of Malachi, when the attitude of the people of Israel was characterized by their belief that "it is futile to serve God" (Mal. 3:14). That is precisely the view of Jonah in Jonah 4:3.

Jonah, however, is not an unbeliever. His confession of faith in 1:9 is standard Hebrew orthodoxy, as is the creedal statement he employs in 4:2 (cf. Exod. 34:6-7; Pss. 86:15; 103:8; 111:4; 145:8; etc.). The psalm in 2:2-9 is a typical psalm of thanksgiving, like those found often in the Psalter (Pss. 30; 32; 34; 92; etc.). Many scholars have pointed out that 2:2-9 is not essential to the story, and it could well be a later addition to the book.

Jonah belongs in the ranks of orthodox believers. But he is an unwilling believer; that is, he does not want to obey the Lord's command to preach to the wicked city of Nineveh. Nineveh deserves nothing — no opportunity to hear the word of God, no chance for repentance. Nineveh should be destroyed! The difficulty is that Jonah knows that God is "gracious and merciful, slow to anger and abounding in steadfast love," repenting of any judgment he might decree for Nineveh (4:2), and Jonah does not want God to be merciful! He wants God to judge!

Clearly the problem posed by the book is not that of the "great fish" (1:17), which we erroneously call a "whale," nor should we engage in fanciful speculations about how Jonah could live for three days in the fish's belly. That totally misses the point of the story. Rather, the problem is the unbounded mercy of God in the face of overwhelming wickedness. We too want the wicked to "get what is coming to them," don't we? We can identify with Jonah. But the narrator of this story reveals to us something of the nature of our God with which we should reckon instead.

In order to bring the congregation to the point at which the morning text begins, it is necessary for the preacher briefly to recount the story that precedes our text. Jonah is commanded by the Lord to "arise, go to Nineveh . . . and cry against it" (1:2). Instead, Jonah takes a ship and goes in exactly the opposite direction toward Tarshish, whose location is unknown but is often identified with Tartessus on the southwest coast of Spain. The Lord pursues his unfaithful prophet, however, and causes a "mighty tempest," so that the ship is in danger of sinking. When the terrified sailors learn that their passenger Jonah is a worshiper of the Lord of heaven and sea and earth, they hurl him overboard. The storm is stilled, and the pagan sailors are converted to the worship of the Lord. Jonah does not drown, however. The Lord, the Creator and Master of all things, commands a great fish to swallow Jonah. But after three days of undigested prophet, the fish vomits Jonah out upon the land. Here our text begins.

Once more the Lord gives the same command to Jonah. "Arise, go to Nineveh . . . and proclaim to it the message that I tell you" (3:2). This time Jonah goes, and as soon as he has entered the city he proclaims, "Yet forty days, and Nineveh shall be destroyed!" So powerful is the Word of God that the Ninevites immediately believe the message and begin a fast of repentance, donning sackcloth and spreading the word. When the news reaches the king of Nineveh (although Nineveh had no king in the eighth century B.C.), he too repents and joins the fast, following the usual practices of wearing sackcloth and sitting in ashes. Indeed, he decrees that the fast is to be universal for both human beings and beasts, and even the beasts are covered in the cloth of repentance, a subtle Old Testament notice that nature too is fallen. It may be, declares the king, that the Lord will have compassion and turn from his judgment, so that we do not perish. When the Lord sees the repentance of the Ninevites and their mending of their evil ways, he does in fact change his mind and forgive the inhabitants of the city.

Several important facts should be noted from the text. First is God's forgiveness of unfaithful Jonah. Jonah has blatantly disobeyed his God, but God has saved Jonah's life. Moreover, there is no reason why God should not be angry with Jonah. Yet he utters no word of admonishment to the prophet. Instead, he simply commands him once more to go to Nineveh. And in fact, in chapter 4, which follows our text, the Lord never blasts out in wrath at Jonah. Instead, he simply teaches his prophet, gently and persuasively, causing him just a little discomfort, in order to impress on Jonah what suffering can mean. This is indeed a "God slow to anger."

We should also mark well that it is not the repentance and turning from their evil that coerces God to forgive the Ninevites. The pagan king of the city knows that no one coerces God. He says, "God may yet . . . turn from his fierce anger" (3:9). The Lord is free, always, to be gracious to whom he will be gracious and to show mercy to whom he will show mercy (Exod. 33:19). The incredible fact is that he so often and finally shows mercy, even to the extent of taking our sin upon himself in his Son. This God of the Old Testament is also the God of the New.

Most important, this God, who is gracious and merciful, slow to anger, and abounding in steadfast love, is the Lord who forgives the Ninevites of our world. Like Jonah, we are quite sure that we know upon whom God should wreak his wrath — not upon us, of course; Jonah didn't think God should judge him! But the Lord of heaven and earth and sea forgives and saves the most unlikely people — the Ninevites, a thief beside him on a cross, a bunch of deserting disciples, a Saul who had persecuted Christians, and yes, incredibly, even you and me. "Love so amazing, so divine, demands my soul, my life, my all."

Elizabeth Achtemeier

Fourth Sunday of Advent, Year C

First Lesson: Micah 5:2-5a
(Psalm 80:1-7)
Second Lesson: Hebrews 10:5-10
Gospel Lesson: Luke 1:39-45, (46-55)

The political world in which the ancient Israelite kingdoms lived was coming apart, but the prophet Micah took little note of it. He began preaching just a few years before the Assyrian Empire swallowed up the kingdom of Israel piece by piece until there was nothing left. The prophet must have been aware of the political intrigue and compromise that allowed the kingdom of Judah to preserve a semblance of independence while being totally subservient to the Assyrians. Still, Micah makes only allusions to the international scene, preferring to speak about the social and economic evils that were ruining the lives of ordinary folk in Judah.

In the name of Yahweh, the prophet condemned the injustices that were endemic to Judahite society in the eighth century. Yet the book of Micah does not present the prophet's words of judgment as the final word that God speaks to Judah. Today's pericope offers a vision of Judah's future that, given the circumstances of the prophet's day, could only come to reality through a new act of salvation. The prophet describes a future in which a new ruler will bring peace to both Judah and the world. Micah had no use for the political leaders of his day (3:1-2, 9-12). Instead of maintaining a just society, they were responsible for creating and sustaining a society that perverted equity and hated justice. To counter this the new David will bring an end to the injustice that the prophet condemned.

While today's lesson does not mention David by name, it clearly reflects the belief of some Judahites that the Davidic dynasty will have a central place in the future that God will create for them. Bethlehem was home to David and the scene of his anointing as king by Samuel (see 1 Sam. 16:1-13). The city was located in the region of Ephrathah in the north of Judah. Because David chose Jerusalem as his capital, Bethlehem's significance waned, though this text shows that it had not disappeared completely. Evidently there were people who saw Judah's future in terms of its past. This text reflects an idealization of David that hoped for a restoration presided over by another David who would rule over Judah in the name of God (v. 4). All peoples would recognize that ruler's greatness because he will bring peace to the world (v. 5a).

With the restoration that came with the rise of the Persian Empire in the sixth century B.C., there were some who hoped for the return of the Davidic dynasty and the Judahite state. These hopes were not fulfilled. The Deuteronomic movement, however, saw Judah's future as dependent on the people's obedience to the written authoritative Law. Deuteronomy purposely limits the role of the king in Judahite society (17:14-20) to show that his principal duty is to study the Law. Despite the growing popularity of Deuteronomic perspectives, there were still some who hoped for the restoration of the monarchy. They believed Judah's future was tied to the Davidic dynasty. They looked for the coming of an ideal Davidic king: the Messiah.

The first Christians believed that Jesus was this Messiah. Jesus, however, did not claim to be the new David, nor did his life follow the patterns of messianic expectations in early Judaism. Why, then, did the early church insist that Jesus was the Messiah? This belief was likely a response to Jesus' execution as "king of the Jews" — something all the Gospels attest (Matt. 27:37; Mark 15:26; Luke 23:38; John 19:19). Though the Romans crucified Jesus as a pretender to royal status, Jesus' followers came to understand the resurrection as God's affirmation that Jesus was indeed the Messiah. The resurrection showed that the human judgment about Jesus was mistaken. This Christian belief that Jesus was the Messiah led the Evangelists to search the Old Testament for texts that could be used to support this theological conclusion. Today's reading from Micah fit this purpose very well. Matthew's explicit citation of verse 2 in his Gospel (see Matt. 2:6) has led some interpreters to propose that the location of Jesus' birthplace in Bethlehem is a theological assertion without a historical basis, though there is no decisive argument for rejecting Bethlehem as the place of Jesus' birth.

Matthew's reinterpretation of the passage from Micah, like all New Testament readings of Old Testament texts, pushes Micah far beyond the place where the prophet wanted to lead his readers. The prophet had a much more immediate goal. He used very harsh and direct language in condemning the social and economic situation of his day. He did not bother much with subtle literary technique but preferred to speak bluntly about what he saw. He described the actions of Judah's leaders as cannibalism perpetrated against their own people (3:1-2). He accused Judah's priests, prophets, and rulers of being money-grubbers (3:11), and its people of being ingrates (6:3-5). The prophet announced that severe judgment awaited Judah. The Temple Mount would revert to a forest (3:12). Judah would suffer military defeat (5:10-15) and agricultural disaster (6:13-15). Family and friends would turn against each other (7:5-6). God would take away the inheritance that once was Israel's (2:4) and lead the people into exile (4:9-10)

As brutally honest as Micah was in describing the injustices that permeated Judah's economic system, and as unrelenting as he was announcing divine judgment on that system and the society that spawned it, he did not believe that God would abandon Judah forever. The book alternates between angry and anguished words of judgment and touching and assuring words of salvation. The prophet speaks of Judah as "daughter Zion" or "daughter Jerusalem" (e.g., 4:8), clearly implying a special bond between the people and their God. He foresees an end to war and a procession of the nations to Jerusalem to learn the Law from the people of Jerusalem (4:1-4). Micah states that God will cast the people's sins into the sea and fulfill the promises made to their ancestors (7:19-20).

The prophet's vision of a great ruler arising from Bethlehem in order to lead Judah to peace should be seen as one element in Micah's hopes for Judah's future. As convinced as he was about the inevitability of divine judgment upon Judah, the prophet did not and could not believe that judgment was God's last word to the people. As it happened with David, God's salvation will emerge from the most unlikely place: Bethlehem, the city that gave Judah its greatest king. Bethlehem will come out of the shadow cast on it by Jerusalem to provide Judah with another David who will rule in God's name and bring about peace.

Micah has few equals in the intensity of his condemnation of Judah — its leaders and people — for creating a society built on oppression and injustice. He also has few peers in the hope that he offered his people. Preachers can find a superb role model in the prophet. His words of comfort are not "cheap grace." Micah is certain that Judah will have to pay a very steep price for its infidelity. Those who proclaim the gospel must do so with the prophet's conviction about God's hatred for a society that feeds on itself. God is looking for a just society — one in which all people have the opportunity to live in dignity, sharing the fruits of the bounty that God has given the world. God expects those in positions of leadership within society to preserve justice — not be the principal perpetrators of injustice. A society without justice awaits the judgment of God.

God's justice, however, is not retributive. The preacher needs to balance prophetic denunciation of injustice with the type of optimism about the future that Micah displayed. It is this prophetic vision of the future that should energize believers as they work to create and maintain a just society. The words of the prophet ought to help Christians believe in the inevitability of a just social order according to the divine will. No sacrifice for the sake of justice then will ever be in vain. When Jesus returns, the triumph of justice will be complete. The church anticipates Christ's final victory and hastens the day of his return by working now for the transformation of this world. The church reads this Micah passage, then, not simply to remember an ancient prophet's words nor to assert its belief in their fulfillment in Christ. The church reads Micah's words today to proclaim its faith in a fulfillment that is yet to come.

The book of Micah speaks about an ideal ruler to come from Bethlehem in order to bring about the triumph of justice. Matthew wanted to demonstrate the relevance of the Old Testament for the Christian faith by showing that Micah's prophecy found its fulfillment in Christ. Believers today read the prophet's words as an incitement to join Jesus in the transformation of our world according to God's will. The prophet's vision still awaits its fulfillment. Jesus, the Messiah, the son of David born in Bethlehem, calls his followers today to join him in bringing peace to the ends of the earth.

Leslie J. Hoppe

Fourth Sunday after the Epiphany, Year A

First Lesson: Micah 6:1-8
(Psalm 15)
Second Lesson: 1 Corinthians 1:18-31
Gospel Lesson: Matthew 5:1-12

It is not all that often that we are struck with absolute clarity about our relationship with God; clarity of such a sort that we are overwhelmed with how far we have slipped away; crystal-clear realization of our forgetfulness of the things God has done for us, to us, through us, in us, and mostly, in spite of us. And though it is at first a word of judgment when God chooses to remind us of our ignorance, our deafness, or our obtuseness, we know that this reminder is ultimately a great gift. For without it we would only sink deeper in our amnesia.

Micah, that Old Testament prophet who lived at the same time as Isaiah, was graced and cursed with the clarity of which I speak. And he heard the Lord's outrage at Israel. First we hear the prophet's words:

Hear what the LORD says:
 Rise, plead your case before the mountains,
 and let the hills hear your voice.
Hear, you mountains, the controversy of the LORD,
 and you enduring foundations of the earth;
for the LORD has a controversy with his people,
 and he will contend with Israel.

Then we hear the Lord himself:

O my people, what have I done to you?
 In what have I wearied you? Answer me!
For I brought you up from the land of Egypt,
 and redeemed you from the house of slavery;
and I sent before you Moses,
 Aaron, and Miriam.
O my people, remember now what King Balak of Moab devised,
 what Balaam son of Beor answered him,
and what happened from Shittim to Gilgal,
 that you may know the saving acts of the LORD.

Micah is humbled. Standing in for the people of whom he is a part, he utters the sounds of one who wants to return to his father like the prodigal but realizes that a distance now exists that he cannot traverse. A gulf, a chasm, an insurmountable, unbridgeable space exists between the dismally forgetful, unclean prophet/people and the spurned and holy God. And so the prophet questions, perhaps rhetorically, perhaps in all honesty, how the abyss might be bridged. And he turns naturally to sacrifices — appropriate, costly offerings of life and sustenance that might be laid out between himself as sinner and God as Holy Other, sacrifices that might cover the offense, that might appease God's wrath.

But even as Micah ascends the mountain of sacrifice — to offer one after another, each more violent, extravagant, and more costly than the last — we detect a heightening sense of futility that any sacrifice will prove sufficient:

With what shall I come before the LORD,
 and bow myself before God on high?
Shall I come before him with burnt offerings,
 with calves a year old?
Will the LORD be pleased with thousands of rams,

with ten thousands of rivers of oil?
Shall I give my firstborn for my transgression,
   the fruit of my body for the sin of my soul?

It is possible to call this hyperbole. It is also possible to call it conviction bordering on despair, if one chooses theological language to describe it. The picture the prophet paints moves the hearer from the sacrifice of the reasonable — "calves a year old" — to the absurd, to the unthinkable: the offering of one's own child, human sacrifice. From a biblical perspective, the prophet has hit the high point of grief. For the offering of the firstborn was considered the greatest sacrifice possible, one that was banned in the Torah. The offering of the firstborn was what God had asked of Abraham to test his faith, making Abraham the father of the faithful, the ultimate paradigm of faithfulness — though God did not ultimately require Isaac's life to be given. The sacrifice of the firstborn was what God required of the Egyptians as the final of ten plagues. The slaughter of the firstborn was the one event that finally sprung the lock on four hundred years of growing oppression. The offering of the firstborn was what God required of Israel when they were finally free from Pharaoh and in the wilderness. Though this time they were to be a living sacrifice, not offered up in smoke to God but set apart as a constant reminder that it was at the price of the firstborn that God had given them their freedom, had remembered the covenant, and now led them toward the Promised Land (Exod. 13:1-2, 11-16). The offering of the firstborn is that pinnacle sacrifice that God made in sending Jesus to the cross to buy back all people everywhere, once for all. One last firstborn offered, one last lamb sacrificed. One last doorpost smeared with blood, so that the death angel would pass over all, forevermore, who live within the cruciform house smeared by this lamb's blood.

Micah's desperate muse puts him in a place where he realizes that there is absolutely nothing he can do to throw down a connector from his side of the rift to where God is. No bridge is possible.

Do you see the scene? The prophet/people on knees with head bowed low, minute grains of sand pressing into the forehead, and a priest — a living sacrament, with hand gently touching the back of the bowed head — saying quietly but reassuringly:

He has told you, O mortal, what is good;
   and what does the LORD require of you
but to do justice, and to love mercy,
   and to walk humbly with your God?

What kind of response is this? It doesn't even seem to answer the question. The question *was:* "With what shall I come before the LORD? With what shall I bow myself before God on high?" If that's the question, how is doing justice, loving mercy, and walking humbly with God the answer? And how, precisely, do these three things go together? For although the sheer economy of their expression (I feel a cross-stitch coming on) is delightful and even freeing, on closer inspection I detect a fundamental tension among this terse triad that is not immediately decipherable, especially with the first two.

Doing justice and loving mercy are strained partners. For if one sets about to do right by other human beings and make sure that the just thing is done in all relational situations, that means that injustice must be exposed, named, and rectified. And if we are truly committed to carrying out justice, wouldn't it be fudging to temper this quest with mercy?

The call for justice was a distinctive and persistent sound from the Hebrew prophets. For when God could no longer stand those in power who used their power not to serve but to manipulate, he would call a prophet. And the prophet wasn't simply to tell the future, as so many often think. Rather, the prophet was first of all a seer in the sense that he was forced by God to see what God saw and then tell the truth about that spectacle in all its heinousness and with the implications of injustice spelled out. The prophet told of the future primarily in terms of what God would make sure would come about for the people if they did not clean up their act in the present.

God sent a prophet to see injustice, to denounce it, and to remind the abusers that there still was a God and that God saw their atrocities and would vindicate those harmed by injustice. God's appointed eyes and voice announced that if they did not make their situations right by choice, he would insure the right by force. It is a striking fact in this regard that when one does a search to see what Scripture says "God loves," the most frequent object that comes up is "justice" and "righteousness." It grieves and angers God to see misuses of power in discrimination, prejudice, and the violation of the powerless, especially those who are the least of these, that is, the widow, the fatherless, the poor, and the sojourner (Zech. 7:9-10). God sees and God promises vindication.

Our path of action would be marked quite clearly if the answer Micah had received had been only to "do justice." But the call to do justice is set in tension with the call to "love mercy." A woman once said to me that mercy was a two-edged sword for her. She loved to receive mercy, but she hated to be the one who had to show it. I asked her why. She said, "Because to be in a position to show mercy means that you have been wronged, and thus to be in a position of power: you actually have 'the right' to exact a price. To give mercy means that I have to relinquish my advantage, even my control, over a situation and a person who has wronged me. Sometimes I hate to have to give mercy!"

Is it right, or just, to be merciful to someone who is in the wrong? Shouldn't there be appropriate penalties and prices for wrongdoing? I think that's my problem with the odd "answer" that has been given to Micah's question. If there were a sacrifice or a penance that I could do, then I could pay something appropriate for my sin. The greater the sin, the greater the sacrifice. The deeper the wound, the more difficult the penance. To work as hard for my atonement as I did to create the need for it would surely be beneficial for my psyche and soul. At least it would make sure that I took it seriously. To lose the family herd and flock, the family olive grove, and the family itself in a bloody, oily, yelping bath of sacrifice would certainly leave a lasting impression on me and all who saw it. Wouldn't that be worthwhile for this and future generations to experience? Talk about an effective children's sermon!

Here is where that third member of the triad comes in. "Walking with God" is a metaphor for one who is right with God. One who walks with God has been graced by God's presence and partnership in life and death. That walk is a humble walk when one realizes that it is due purely to the unearned grace, mercy, and call of God. The prophet, and by extension all of Israel, are subtly reminded here to get on with the walk to which God has given them privilege, but not proudly as if they had earned his presence by anything they have done — even some "appropriate sacrifice."

This is why the series of sacrifices are rejected. For even if one were to multiply by ten each of the sacrificial means of reunion with God that Micah suggests, they could be seen by the offerer as a way that he mended the fence. The prophet/people are reminded here that no sacrifice on their part is possible to renew the relationship. In the humility that this realization is designed to prompt, they are to proceed.

Moreover, this is why justice is not the only matter to which the people are called. For that would lead to a very cold and eventually litigious existence. Diogenes Allen once told a class in which I sat as a student that though humans often clamor for justice, in reality they would not like it very much. For if we were dealt with as we ought, we would all of us suffer much penalty and none of us be able to find enough bridge to lay down between ourselves and God to restore relationship.

We are therefore called to love mercy because that is what we have in fact been shown by God. It is only God's mercy that allows our walk. It is the realization of God's vast mercy poured out for us which makes our walk humble. And it is out of the experience of receiving God's unmerited mercy that we realize how we ought to "do justice" in the world among those who have wronged us and have no right to expect us to forgive them.

But why does the text say we ought to "*do* justice" but only to "*love* mercy"? That seems to take us off the hook from actually doing mercy. Perhaps we can just love the concept of mercy, even as we measure out justice. This is a natural, and good, question for one who is reading the text closely. On closer examination of the "mercy" here, one sees that the Hebrew word underneath is *ḥesed*. In Old Testament usage, *ḥesed* has to do with the kindness that one shows toward another. This is the case within human-to-human relations, as well as divine-to-human relations. More often than not, acts of *ḥesed* beget other acts of *ḥesed*. Moreover, *ḥesed* is clearly a relational concept. The book of Ruth illustrates this well as Ruth shows *ḥesed* to Naomi and Boaz. Boaz in return interprets Ruth's actions within the larger framework of God's covenant care for Ruth and Naomi. Hans-Joachim Zobel has noted that "there are three elements constitutive of the *ḥesed* concept: it is active, social, and enduring" ("Ḥesed," *TDOT,* 5:51). "Loving mercy" in this instance, then, in Micah 6:8, is not a call to love a concept but a call to love an action which is relational and social in its essence. "Mercy" here is not to be understood as an abstract concept. It is an action — an action of setting free those who don't "deserve" it by those who have experienced their own undeserved amnesty and have not forgotten the experience. God's people are those who give mercy freely as a gift because they have learned that this is the way God is.

It just could be that the priest has given us more than we realized. He has answered not only our immediate and burning question of how we are to be reconciled with God, but how God's merciful way of reconciling with us gives us a way of "doing justice in mercy" in the world. The apprehension of our mercifully given walk with God gives us a perspective out of which to be those who do justice. Our experience of receiving mercy from God becomes the frame of reference within which our acts of justice flourish. As Wendell Berry points out, justice that is not framed by love creates a downwardly spiraling society of anger, hate, and brutality. Relationships — family, neighborhood, and community — simply will not work without a framework of justice that is massaged and conditioned by mercy. Micah reminds us that, for the people of God, this springs from the memory of and participation in God's covenant love and forgiveness. This is the power that can free "the practice of mercy" from a mere feeling or concept to a power and praxis (see *Sex, Economy, Freedom, and Community* [New York: Pantheon Books, 1992, 1993], pp. 139-40).

André Resner, Jr.

Twenty-fourth Sunday after Pentecost, Year C

First Lesson: Habakkuk 1:1-4; 2:1-4
(Psalm 119:137-44)
Second Lesson: 2 Thessalonians 1:1-4, 11-12
Gospel Lesson: Luke 19:1-10

Though Habakkuk is a short book, consisting of only three chapters, it is a giant in the history of the church. Its teaching laid the foundation for the apostle Paul's understanding of justification by faith (Rom. 1:17; Gal. 3:11), and thus helped shaped the Protestant Reformation. Still today it is expressive of the trust of every faithful follower of Jesus Christ.

The historical setting of the book is 609-598 B.C., when Jehoiakim ruled as king in Judah. At first a vassal of the Egyptian empire, Jehoiakim was a tyrant who subjected his people to forced labor, who persecuted the prophets, among them Jeremiah, and who sanctioned widespread injustice, syncretism, and idolatry in his realm (cf. Jeremiah's oracle against him in Jer. 23:13-17). When Nebuchadnezzar of Babylonia defeated Egypt, however, in 605, Jehoiakim transferred his allegiance to that nation. The first chapter of Habakkuk mirrors the reign of Jehoiakim and the incursion of Babylonian forces.

Habakkuk differs from the other prophetic books in that it is made up not of the prophet's preaching to his compatriots, but of an extended dialogue between the prophet and God (chap. 1) which reaches its climax in 2:1-4. Then follow an extended illustration of 2:4 in 2:6-20 and a vision of the future granted to the prophet in 3:1-16, followed by a soaring expression of faith in 3:17-19.

Our text, 1:1-4, begins with a lament by Habakkuk marked by the typical "How long, O LORD?" The key word in the passage is *mishpat,* "justice," which is repeated twice in verse 4 and has the comprehensive meaning of God's or-der for Judean society. That order was to be established by the application of God's Torah. But the meaning of Torah is not confined to law. Rather, it sig-nifies the whole of Israel's religious tradition — her laws, her cultic practices, her narratives of God's past acts, the guidance given by priests and prophets. But life in the light of God's words and deeds has been abandoned, and the result is chaos in Judah's society. On every side, Habakkuk hears and sees the violent breach of God's just order — oppression of the weak, endless litiga-tions, quarrels and deceitful dealings, strife, destruction, in short, the total perversion of God's intention for Judah's life. When the righteous, that is, those who cling to God's will for life, try to set things right, they are over-whelmed by the magnitude of the evil around them, and any reformation that they accomplish is immediately distorted by the wicked.

The prophet has not been a passive observer of such perversions of God's will, however. Repeatedly he has prayed to God to intervene and to re-store his order to Judah. But it has seemed to him that God has not heard and that God will therefore not save. His cry, therefore, is "How long, O LORD?" How long will you let this evil situation continue?

In this initial lament Habakkuk is one with every faithful soul who has prayed for surcease from trouble and evil. He typifies every churchgoer who prays for peace in the world and finds only war; who prays for an end to crime and violence on city streets and reads only of assault and murder; who prays for healing beside a sickbed and is confronted with death; who prays for love in a home and finds it dissolved by anger and hatred; or who prays for emendation in a child's life and is greeted only with rebellion. Habakkuk is like every person confronted by the question of unanswered prayer, when God has seemed to do nothing. Equally, he is like every one of us who has grown so weary with the fight against wrong in our society and world and lives. Nothing seems to do any good anymore. "The wicked surround the righteous."

Before skipping immediately to 2:1-4, however, the preacher needs to let the congregation know that God does answer this initial complaint by the prophet. But the answer given in 1:5-11 is unsettling and astounding. God assures his prophet that he is at work, as God is always at work. As Jesus said, "My Father is working, and I am working still" (John 5:17). But God's answer is that he will destroy the evil in Judean society by bringing the troops of Babylonia to overwhelm it. Judah has rejected God's *mishpat;* Babylonia's will replace it (v. 7). Judah has opted for violence; Babylonia's vi-olence will be its punishment (v. 9). Judah has rejected the order and ways of its God; it will therefore serve Babylonia's god (v. 11).

In 1:12-17 Habakkuk accepts that answer given him by the Lord. He knows that God is using Babylonia as the instrument of his judgment (v. 12). But in his responding prayer, the prophet points out that the Babylonians are worse even than Judah (v. 13). Is that pagan empire, then, simply to keep on "mercilessly slaying nations forever" (v. 17)?

At this point our text in 2:1-4 begins, and it is a marvel of persistent faith. Habakkuk does not abandon his pleas to the Lord, nor does he turn to some worldly substitute to seek help. Instead he stations himself to see what the Lord will say to him. He knows that God is at work. He also knows that God has a further answer. So he waits, symbolically likening his waiting to a man climbing a watchtower to look into the distance.

We are not told how long Habakkuk waits, but he gives us that resounding testimony: "And the LORD answered me" (2:2). "Ask, and it will be given you; seek, and you will find; knock, and it will be opened to you" (Matt. 7:7). Persistent, patient prayer is given its answer. Moreover, that answer is not just for the prophet himself but for all his people to whom he will convey his words, for all the faithful down through the ages, and yes, for all of us who are the heirs of that word. Habakkuk is to write down the words in large letters — so large that anyone running by can read them.

"The vision awaits its time," says the Lord. We could call it the vision of the kingdom of God come on earth, that time when God brings to fruition his purpose for this world of ours — when he fulfills his promise to bring blessing on all the families of the earth; when he restores his creation to the goodness that he intended for it in the beginning; when men and women live by God's order in their societies and not by their chaotic ways; when the earth is made fair again, and steadfast love and faithfulness meet, and righteousness and peace are the ways of all (cf. Ps. 85:10). The kingdom comes, Habakkuk is told, "it will surely come" (v. 3).

But, runs the answer given to our prophet, "the vision awaits its time" (v. 3). That is, the vision awaits God's time and not ours. God holds our times in his hand, and he determines when his purpose will be fulfilled. In the fullness of time, when the hour has come, at the *kairos* when all is fully ripe, then God will bring in his new age of goodness. The New Testament tells us that that new age began in the person of Jesus Christ (cf. Mark 1:15; Matt. 12:28; Luke 11:20), and you and I have little foretastes of it sometimes in our worship and at the Lord's Supper. But when the fullness of the kingdom will come, no one knows, "not the angels in heaven, nor the Son, but only the Father" (Mark 13:32). "It will not delay" (v. 3). And our task is to work and wait for it, in the persistence of faith and prayer, as Habakkuk waited.

499

We are waiting, are we not, as persons like Habakkuk who are living in the "meantime," in the interim time between our redemption and God's final salvation of all? Verse 4 of our text therefore tells us how to live in this "meantime." It says that those, literally, who are "puffed up" shall not live. That is, persons who rely on themselves or human devices can have no life of good. In the English translation, their lives are not "upright," bent out of shape, distorted. But those who are "righteous," that is, those who trust God (for that is the central demand of righteousness), will have a life of good if they are steadfastly faithful: such is the meaning of "the righteous shall live by his/her faith." The word for "faith" in the Hebrew is 'emunah, which has the same stem as our word "amen." It signifies steadfastness, day-by-day commitment, through prayer and worship, Bible study and obedience, to the Lord. Steadfastness is putting one foot in front of the other and walking, ever surely, in God's ways and not in our own. And that way, testifies our prophet, is the way to life. Indeed, the New Testament tells us that is the way to abundant life and eternal life, by steady trust in our Lord Jesus Christ.

Elizabeth Achtemeier

Third Sunday of Advent, Year C

First Lesson: Zephaniah 3:14-20
(Isaiah 12:2-6)
Second Lesson: Philippians 4:4-7
Gospel Lesson: Luke 3:7-18

In our culture (and perhaps it has always been this way) there seems to be a persistent effort to disenfranchise or marginalize God from our lives, an effort "to water God down," as one theologian puts it. God has been successfully reduced to human dimensions so that he is compatible to humanity. He shares humanity's wants and aspirations, and he even thinks like a human does. And so, in the movies God is a gentle old man, or a cartoon character, or maybe just an "impersonal force" whose power can be harnessed with the proper training. What he is *not* is someone to be feared.

In contrast, the prophet Zephaniah has a surprisingly different picture of God. His prophecy may shock the modern ear, which doesn't often hear such language from its religious leaders. But that is just the point. Zephaniah's prophecy shakes people up and provides a much needed corrective to modern ideas about God.

The text, Zephaniah 3:(9-13), 14-20, has its counterpart in Zephaniah 1 and should be read in the context that the first part of the prophecy provides. Careful readers will feel the tension between the first part of the book and the text. Both chapters 1 and 3 talk about the coming Day of Yahweh. However, chapter 1 pictures that day as a dreadful day of wrath and judgment against the whole world and especially against God's own people, Israel. The prophet's vision, so to speak, moves from the universal Judgment Day against the whole world to the particular Judgment Day against Judah and Jerusalem, and then also to judgment against Israel's enemies (chap. 2).

Thus, in 1:1-3 Yahweh proclaims that he will "sweep everything from the face of the earth." That includes humans, animals, birds, fish. He makes a special point of emphasizing that he will cut off humanity from the face of the earth (v. 3). It is clear that God will spare nothing on that day. In 1:14-18 that day is described as one of wrath, distress, anguish, ruin, devastation, darkness, gloom, clouds, and thick darkness. Compare the language used to describe the theophany on Sinai. At Sinai, remember, the people were so terrified of God that they asked Moses to intervene for them (Exod. 20:18-21; Deut. 4:10-12). The description of the distress Yahweh will bring upon people on that day is especially vivid:

> Their blood shall be poured out like dust,
> and their flesh like dung. . . .
> the whole earth will be consumed;
> for a full, a terrible end
> he will make of all the inhabitants of the earth.   (1:17-18)

In between the proclamations of universal judgment, the prophet turns his eyes to the particular judgment of Judah and Jerusalem (1:4-13). Because of their idolatry and because they turned back from the Lord and did not seek him, Yahweh was going to stretch out his hand against all the inhabitants of Jerusalem. Yahweh had prepared a sacrifice, and his people were it (1:7). On that day, says Yahweh, loud crying will be heard throughout the city. No one will escape. Yahweh will "search Jerusalem with lamps" and punish the people for their sin.

On one level the "Day of Yahweh" as a day of judgment for the nation of

Israel was fulfilled in the Babylonian exile. This historical "Day of Yahweh" points to and warns of the coming day which brings judgment and destruction — the full wrath of God — on all the world. As God's judgment on Judah surely came to pass and meant the death of the nation, so will God's judgment on all the world most certainly come to pass as well.

In these texts God scares me. According to Zephaniah, God is not a kind and gentle old man who "puts up" with the many faults of his people. He is not a God who winks at our misbehavior like an adoring grandparent. Nor is God either impotent or apathetic when it comes to this world. The Creator is well able to do what he pleases with his creation. Zephaniah portrays God's anger toward the human race as growing . . . growing . . . until one day it will explode in full fury.

These aren't healing words. They are killing words. They function to kill our flesh of the misconceptions we may harbor about God and our relationship to him. They kill our sense of security and confidence in our own abilities. They ought to frighten us and shake us from our lethargy, and they need to be preached that way.

But surprise! They are not the last word, either. Appropriately, God's last word is reserved for the end of the prophecy, which includes our text. As many commentators have noted, there is almost a logical contradiction between the first chapter of Zephaniah and the last. If that day brings cosmic destruction as Yahweh says, how can there be a fresh start for humanity, as Yahweh also says? How can both complete destruction and hope be true, both the death of everyone and yet the salvation of his people?

First, it can be noted that the text (3:14-20) focuses particularly on the salvation of God's people, Israel. Emphasis on the day as a day of salvation is enhanced by the chiastic arrangement of verses 14-17:

> A Sing aloud, O daughter Zion; shout, O Israel. Rejoice and
> exult with all your heart. . . .
> B The LORD has taken away the judgments against you,
> he has turned away your enemies.
> C The king of Israel, the LORD, is in your midst;
> D You shall fear disaster no more.
> E On that Day it will be said to Jerusalem:
> D′ Do not fear, O Zion; do not let your hands grow weak.
> C′ The LORD, your God, is in your midst,
> B′ a warrior who gives victory.
> A′ He will rejoice over you with gladness, he will be silent
> in his love. . . .

Zephaniah announces some amazing news to God's people. He asks Israel to exult because beyond her death there is life! He announces forgiveness, victory over their enemies, and God's presence among them — their true king and their God (vv. 15, 17). As the day of destruction is described in terms of Sinai (1:15), so the day of salvation is described in terms of the covenant made to Abraham and David. In spite of all appearances to the contrary, the true king of Israel will not abandon them. He will not break his promises. This warrior will give them victory over every enemy. He promises his salvation to those who are afflicted, and he will gather the scattered (v. 19). He will give them a great name among all the people of the earth (cf. Gen. 12:2; 2 Sam. 7:9).

Again, on one level this prophecy was fulfilled when Israel returned from the Babylonian exile (see esp. 3:20). On that day the nation of Israel, for all intents and purposes dead, was brought to life. Beyond the exile, which meant death for the nation, Israel found new life in the return. And in fact, Ezekiel 37:11-14 pictures the exile/return in just these terms, as a death and a resurrection. By assuming a resurrection, we can resolve the tension between the two parts of Zephaniah. Death and judgment do not have the final word if God raises the dead. The return from exile, a dead nation coming to life again, points to that possibility.

Indeed, as Zephaniah's vision moves from the universal to the particular in chapter 1, so it does in chapter 3. The verses preceding the text (which really should be part of the assigned reading!) speak in just these terms. Salvation is depicted in universal terms. Thus, Yahweh says that at that time he will change the speech of people to pure speech so that all of them might call on the name of the Lord and serve him. And he says that from beyond Ethiopia his worshipers, his scattered ones, will bring him an offering (vv. 9-10). The world is included in Yahweh's salvation. And in fact, he even appears to identify these people as "the remnant of Israel" (v. 13), that is, his chosen people. Just as the exile foreshadows universal judgment, so the return of the captives from Babylon foreshadows salvation for all people — life beyond judgment and death — resurrection and hope.

The crucial question for the preacher/reader of this text, then, is: Where do I fit into all of this? When the Day of Yahweh comes, will it be for me a day of salvation or of judgment? How do I know that the glorious message of this text is for me?

The answer, finally, can be found in Christ. It is important to remember that from the perspective of the New Testament, Christ is "Israel reduced to one" (cf. Matt. 2:15; Luke 9:31). He is the one in whom the Father is well pleased. On the one hand, that means that the judgment proclaimed for the world and foreshadowed in the Babylonian exile has already fallen on Christ as he hung on the cross. On that day the wrath of God against our sin exploded on his only begotten Son. His own Father forsook him, and as Paul says, "God made him to be sin for us, who knew no sin" (2 Cor. 5:21). The darkness described at Christ's crucifixion (Matt. 27:45) testifies to the fulfillment of the prophetic word of Zephaniah 1:15, which tells of "a day of darkness and gloom, / a day of clouds and thick darkness."

But of course, death didn't have the last word when it came to Christ, either. For Christ there was life beyond the judgment of the cross. "The mighty one will save" (3:17). There was nothing less than a resurrection. And in Christ's resurrection there is vindication (Rom. 8:31-34). In the resurrection of Christ, the Day of Yahweh as a day of salvation for all people has already burst upon us. In the words of the text,

> The LORD has taken away the judgments against you,
>   he has turned away your enemies.

The Father rejoices over this faithful Israel with gladness. He exults over Christ with loud singing.

The great news for us is that we are heirs of this great salvation. The apostle Paul says some very important words to us: "Therefore we have been buried with him by baptism into death, so that, just as Christ was raised from the dead by the glory of the Father, so we too might walk in newness of life. For if we have been united with him in a death like his, we will certainly be united with him in a resurrection like his" (Rom. 6:4-5). Paul says that in baptism we have already died with Christ. We don't have to worry about Judgment Day anymore because Christ has been judged ahead of us. For we who have been buried and raised with Christ, there is a great victory even over death itself. Now "God rejoices over [us] with gladness . . . he exults over [us] with loud singing."

In Christ the day of salvation pictured by Zephaniah is ours. In him our judgments have been removed and the enemy has been turned away. He is the true King who rules over everything, and we who are the heirs of his kingdom need fear disaster no more. He has given us a name that will never end (3:20). "In him there is no longer Jew or Greek, there is no longer slave or free, there is no longer male and female. For all of you are one in Christ Jesus. And if you belong to Christ, then you are Abraham's offspring, heirs according to the promise" (Gal. 3:28).

After the killing words of Zephaniah 1–2, the text brings us back to life. It works joy and hope in our hearts and should be preached that way. People killed by the word of law are then brought to life by the word of the gospel. And so, we who live in the last days (Heb. 1:1-2) find great comfort in the words of the text. Though the "reality" remains hidden, though we too suffer our share of pain and sorrow, though the world laughs at our God and our faith, we know that victory is ours. Now our sin has been judged. Now we live not under law but under grace. We know that Christ is coming again, and we long for his return. We look forward to Christ's return when he will reveal his salvation for all to see because he will gather us to himself, and he will "exult over us with loud singing forever."

Timothy E. Saleska

Twenty-fifth Sunday after Pentecost, Year C

First Lesson: Haggai 1:15b-2:9
(Psalm 145:1-5, 17-21)
Second Lesson: 2 Thessalonians 2:1-5, 13-17
Gospel Lesson: Luke 20:27-38

I have included some additional verses to help place the passage for this week in context. The book of Haggai begins with a superscription, a prefixed statement that provides added historical or social context. Numerous books of prophecy, as well as the book of Psalms, contain superscriptions. The superscription at the beginning of Haggai provides detailed dating information — down to the year, month, and day: August 29, 520 B.C.E.; it also indicates an editorial structure that connects the books of Haggai and Zechariah.

The formula "the word of the LORD came to . . ." occurs frequently in both the Deuteronomistic History (Joshua, Judges, 1 and 2 Samuel, 1 and 2 Kings) and prophetic material (Zeph. 1:1; Mic. 1:1; Joel 1:1; Hos. 1:1; Ezek. 1:3; Jer. 1:2). Those occurrences consistently describe the prophet as the recipient of "the word of the LORD," as well as the one who reports that word to others. However, in Haggai 1:1 the word comes to the governor and the high priest, Zerubbabel and Joshua respectively. This superscription exhibits a different tone: the prophet reports the message that came to others.

505

The word of God comes "by the hand of Haggai." The Hebrew term can be translated "comes through," and the point here is to accent the instrumentality of the prophet. At the same time, we should note that the governor and high priest have prominence here in a different way than we have come to think typical in prophetic literature. Here the writer depicts the royal and priestly hierarchy in an altogether positive light.

"The word of the LORD" was delivered to Zerubbabel and Joshua by Haggai. The writer views the word of the Lord as an active and transformational communication from God. We should not confuse it with the "can we just talk" experience we have in modern culture.

Introduction to the call to repentance and preliminary indictment.

"Thus says the LORD . . ." (v. 2a). The prophetic speech formula "Thus says the LORD . . ." occurs often in the Old Testament. Here the formula occurs in an enlarged form. The writer uses a particular divine epithet, the Lord of Hosts, attached to the end of the formula, which has its roots in the "holy war" depiction of God. Over one-third of the Old Testament occurrences of this term are in Haggai, Zechariah, and Malachi.

God quotes the people (v. 2b). Typically the prophetic speech formula introduces divine speech. In this passage, however, the divine speech begins with a quotation of the people. While it is unusual to begin a divine speech with a quotation, the use of quotations of the people in the process of a prophetic indictment is quite common. The people argue among themselves that the appropriate time to build the house of the Lord has not yet come.

Transition formula (v. 3). The point of action changes as we move into the call to repentance that plays off this first preliminary indictment from the words of the people.

Call to repentance (vv. 4-7). The call to repentance is a well-constructed interaction with important parallelism. It sets up the final pronouncement (1:9-11). The introduction to the section, which consists of rhetorical questions (1:4), picks up on the tone set in the quotation of the people earlier. In fact, it seems to question the position of the people as quoted in verse 2. It furthers the dramatic tension by introducing the contrast between the houses of the people (which were paneled) and the house of the Lord. The writer contrasts the *ḥareb* of the Lord's house with the *sepunim* of the houses of the people. *Sepunim* occurs with reference to the temple of David and Solomon (1 Kings 6:15 refers to the roof, and 1 Kings 7:7 refers to interior paneling of cedar). The rhetorical question God asks, "Is it yet time?" functions as an implicit indictment and a call for repentance simultaneously.

The contrast between the two houses has been depicted in two ways. Some argue for the term "paneled," thereby making the contrast one of luxury to plainness. Others use the term "finished" for the house of the audience, in contrast to the unfinished and unusable one of the Lord. For most readers there is no reason to see these translations as mutually exclusive. On the contrary, the contrast is the plainness and inhabitability of a completed shelter as opposed to a building in process.

The contrast between *sepunim* (finished) and *hareb* (desolate) has also sparked a debate about the actual condition of the temple. The adjective *hareb* was used to describe the desolation of the temple in 587 (see Jer. 33:10-17; Ezek. 36:35, 38; Neh. 2:3, 17). But we have no reason from the text to propose that worship ceased from 587 until 520, leading some scholars to claim that the temple did exist, but in a plainer, postsack condition.

The prophetic speech formula "Thus says the LORD . . ." (v. 5a) introduces the rhetorical question "put to your hearts concerning your ways" (v. 5b). This leads into a description of folly in verse 6. Five actions that should have productive outcomes are recounted, but each redounds to frustration. The verbs do not seem to present any particular pattern of agrarian life other than the simple point of the commonality of self-maintenance. This section is enclosed in bookends forming an *inclusio*. The prophetic speech formula "Thus says the LORD . . ." (v. 7a) and the rhetorical question "put to your hearts concerning your ways" (v. 7b) parallel verse 5.

The audience is now prepared for the instructions and challenges presented, namely, to go and build. Verse 8 concludes with a traditional prophetic formula: ". . . says the LORD." But the recriminations are not over. The people looked in the wrong places for trust. So the writer again rehearses the folly of the audience (v. 9), but then describes the rationale for their disastrous consequences (v. 9). The writer next uses a result clause to connect the cosmic circumstances with the behavior of the people. Verses 10-11 further describe the disaster.

"Put it to your hearts concerning your ways." The tightly drawn set of contrasts functions almost as futility curses. The issue in this text drives the reader to the interface of stewardship and investment.

Resulting disaster (vv. 10-11). The temple piety of Haggai understands the restoration of the temple to be tantamount to the restoration of the nation. The link with the Davidic household is now broadened to a link between the temple and economic prosperity. The metaphor for this prosperity in an agrarian culture is the list of goods withheld pending the restoration of the temple (1:10-11).

The list is important. There is drought due to the withholding of dew, which parallels the creation story (see Gen. 2:5) and makes the point of the cosmological results of human activity. The land resources, the earth and

507

hills, and major food groups of crops (grain, new wine, and oil) are all stricken. In addition to what comes out of the soil, the vehicles of production — human labor and animal labor — are stricken. The result is a chiasm-like structure, a source-product-source (a-b-a) pattern. This pattern functions to underscore the totality of the catastrophe.

Narrative description of the prophetic word (vv. 12-15).

Description of the addressee's response. Now Zerubbabel and Joshua are joined by the remnant of the people in the act of obeying the word of God. The word order of the English translations (NIV and NRSV) mutes the force of the verse. This syntax of the typical Hebrew verbal clause begins with the verb, and then proceeds with the nouns, the first of which is usually the subject of the clause. This verse follows that pattern. English clauses, on the other hand, generally begin with the subject. The more effective translation follows the Hebrew pattern here. If we follow this, then we read: "Heard Zerubbabel. . . ." This not only maintains the typical Hebrew word order, but also accents the key verb of the sentence. Furthermore, the word "hear/obey" introduces a new section. The Hebrew term "hear/obey" accents the way the word evokes action. One might say that the people "really heard" the message of the prophet.

One should notice the language here: *hearing* and *obeying* are transitive verbs, that is, they require an object, in this case the voice of God. This is important because "hearing/obeying" is neutral: if what you listen to is right, then you come out right. On the other hand, if what you listen to is wrong, you come out wrong. Those addressed listen to the voice of God. The phrase "the voice of God" is in synonymous parallelism with the words of Haggai. The writer underscores Haggai's authority by stating for the record that God sent him; thus Haggai brings the "right word."

What makes the phrase "all the remnant/rest of the people" such a puzzle is the way the term "remnant/rest" in postexilic literature often indicates differentiation in the Jewish community. The phrase "all the remnant of the people" (Hag. 1:12, 14) also occurs in Jeremiah (41:10, 16), where it refers to the remaining hostages of the assassination of Gedaliah in Mizpah, part of the abortive revolt against the Babylonians. The phrase "the rest of the people" appears in Nehemiah 7:71 (Eng. 7:72) and in Haggai 2:22, but the latter instance seems to be a transition and connection to 1:12-15, and the former seems not to be speaking of a theologically distinct group. (The only place this phrase is used to refer to a religious party is possibly Zechariah 8:6, 12.)

"The people were afraid in the presence of the LORD." The issue of presence is an important element in this text, prefiguring the statement of assurance in the next verse. In this verse we are introduced to a new group, the remnant of

508

the people. This term generates much debate, for it goes to the heart of the conflict within the Jewish community of Jerusalem at the time. The problem is that the remnant of the people is a way of talking about everyone.

Stephen Breck Reid

Second Sunday of Advent, Year C

First Lesson: Malachi 3:1-4
(Luke 1:68-79)
Second Lesson: Philippians 1:3-11
Gospel: Luke 3:1-6

Malachi 3:1-4 is the text for the presentation and for the Second Sunday of Advent in Year C. Two themes dominate the season of Advent: a spirit of thanksgiving for the gift of Christ and an anticipation of the second coming. The accompanying Gospel passage (Luke 3:7-18) describes the ministry of John the Baptist; the Psalter reading, if replaced with the Benedictus, is Luke 1:68-79. The presentation in the temple (the story is recounted in Luke 2:22-40) is a special day that is celebrated forty days after the birth of Jesus, which would be February 2. The pattern of Hebrew observance was to dedicate the child in the manner dictated by the Holiness Code (Lev. 21:1-8).

It is wise to place Malachi in canonical context. In both the Hebrew Bible and the Old Testament, it is the final installment of the Book of the Twelve. As such, it is often bundled together with Haggai and Zechariah. These three have structural connections so strong that together they seem to constitute a series of oracles. Therefore the preacher is advised not to try to excavate an historical person named Malachi; rather, one should attend to the name of the book — Malachi, "my messenger." Several years ago, when I was directing a master's thesis on the "suffering servant" passages, the student, after poring over all the different suggestions regarding the identity of the suffering servant, concluded, "Maybe it is not a matter of who was the servant as much as it is who is a servant." Likewise, here in

Malachi the question is not "who was Malachi?" but "who is a *malachi?*" So we should ask about the office.

When the Old Testament was edited, the arrangement was shaped by the location of the book of Malachi, which concludes the Old Testament. The canonical location, just before the opening of the New Testament with the book of Matthew, whose early emphasis on the Elijah type we recognize as John the Baptist, shapes the interpretation of the passage. The root of the word *malachi* goes back to the Hebrew, which can be rendered either as "angel" or "messenger," an emissary from the divine council. Or one could note that in Isaiah 6 we see an example of a human who has temporary access to the divine council and then is charged to share that information with the believing public. One angle into the issue of the messenger can be found in Karl Barth's discussion of Christian life as rooted in the work of a witness.

The structure of this passage is obscured in the NRSV, which renders it as prose. The reader will bear in mind that most of the prophetic literature is rendered in poetic form. The editor of the Hebrew text thinks verses 1-2 are in poetic — that is, rhythmic — form, and that verses 3 and 4 move to a prose style. One finds a parallelism that organizes verse 1: the verse begins with the verb "send" and closes with the verb "come." That first element of verse 1 begins with the announcement about the sending of the divine messenger. The language of 3:1a ("I am sending . . .") also occurs in Joel, but especially in Jeremiah (Jer. 16:16; 25:9; 43:10; Joel 2:19).

The sending is not without a purpose, and its description is set forth in the second element of verse 1 ("in order to open a path before me"). One should note that the use of the first-person singular gives the verse a certain assonance that amounts to a rhyme in the Hebrew. This device accents that the messenger and the path are both related to the presence of the divine speaker. One should note another wordplay that does not come through in the English: the verb *panah* (prepare) and the preposition *lipnay* share the same root, *pnh,* and both have a sense of direction. The term has a semantics range as a noun ("face"). What is at stake in this passage is the presence of God; whether we focus on the messenger as human or divine, we must not lose track of the real stakes. This is somewhat reminiscent of Isaiah 40:3 ("prepare the way of the LORD . . ."), which is repeated in the Gospels (Matt. 3:3; Luke 3:4-6; Mark 1:3; John 1:23).

The NRSV has altered the order of the third element of the first verse for clarity, but this change also alters the emphasis. For the text opens up an irony that is paralleled in the earlier prophetic tradition. The text begins with the adverb "suddenly." Here the reader notes the shift to the third person; nonetheless, the actor is divine because the possessive form of "temple"

510

makes that clear. Here the verb of the third element of verse 1 contrasts with the verb of the fourth part of the verse: the coming of the divine agent is set over against the seeking of the prophet's audience. This reminds us of Amos 5:18-20: "Alas for you who desire the day of the LORD. . . ." The confidence of Amos is parallel to the confidence of Malachi's audience. The context of the divine coming must include a recollection of the divine evacuation of the temple recounted in the book of Ezekiel (10:1-22 and 11:22-25).

The parallelism also occurs in the final elements of verse 1: "The Lord whom you . . ." parallels the phrase "the messenger whom you. . . ." They use parallel positive verbs, "seeking" in the first case and "delighting" in the second. Now we merely wait for the other — the ironic — shoe to drop. The verse that began with the "sending," the assured vindication, ends with a scary surprise — the "coming" that brings an ominous tone — followed by the prophetic formula "says the LORD of Hosts" (Mal. 3:1b).

It is best to think of verses 2-4 as an interpretation of verse 1. The transition occurs in the double question: "Who can endure the day of his coming? And who can stand in the midst of his appearance?" (Mal. 3:2a). The "day of his coming" appears to be a reference to the Day of the Lord tradition. This impression is bolstered when one sees the identity of the messenger and the identity of the divine as fused. Therefore the day of the coming of the messenger is coterminous with God. Hence the association of the Day of the Lord and the phrase here in Malachi, "the day of his coming" (Joel 1:15; Zeph. 1:14-18). The "coming" and the "appearance" are in synonymous parallelism, and here we note the overlap of theophany and judgment inherent in the Day of the Lord motif.

The questions function literarily as a hinge. On the one hand, they connect the introduction of the messenger in verse 1 to the material following, but they also connect to the second half of the verse by describing the nature of the one who comes. The judgment themes of verse 2a are now given further expression: the Hebrew *ki* clause that marks the reason for the previous statement, in this case the previous questions, is usually translated "for." The causal *ki* introduces the description of the divine messenger through similes (with the use of "like"): the first simile compares the divine messenger with the burning fire; the second simile is more troublesome. The NRSV reads "like fullers' soap," while the NIV reads "like a launderer's soap." Both are technically correct, but they lack the powerful imagery that the preacher is after here. He wants a kind of soap made with lye, alkali, and potash, a soap popular on the North American frontier. It was known for its power but not its subtlety; it was not a gentle soap. One should think about this as a redemption but not a gentle redemption.

511

Verse 3 continues the metaphors of verse 2: the writer uses catchwords to connect the pieces. The participle "refining" is the same as the one used in the first simile of verse 2b. The role of refiner is now connected to that of purifier. This noun is then turned into a verb in the next section of the verse, creating a sense of emphasis. However, instead of precious metals that are being purified, it is the Levites, the priestly class in Judea. In verse 3b the language shifts back to the second person. This time we have a new word for "refine" and "purify." The simile of silver and gold is preserved, and now the Levites are at the center of the passage. They are like silver and gold, and at that point they have reached the status of being able to bring a "sacrifice of righteousness" to the Lord. One should note that it is the character of the supplicant that determines the appropriateness of the sacrifice.

After this process of rough redemption, the offering of Judah and Jerusalem will be pleasing to the Lord, a return to the days of old. Through this process of rough redemption the people can regain their place in the sacrificial world of Judaism. This passage makes the point that, first of all, this is a matter of God's initiative (thus the initial "sending" language of v. 1); second, the redemption will not be easy; third, the redemption restores the people to their rightful place in the universe of praise.

Stephen Breck Reid

Ascension of the Lord, Years A, B, C

First Lesson: Acts 1:1-11
(Psalm 47)
Second Lesson: Ephesians 1:15-23
Gospel Lesson: Luke 24:44-53

Luke provides us with two different ascension scenes in Luke 24 and Acts 1. The most important thing *not* to do with either passage is to engage in explanations about how they do or do not fit together. If we agree with prevailing scholarly opinion that the Acts of the Apostles was written by the writer of the Third Gospel, we must understand that Luke's two presentations of Jesus' ascension have different functions. This exegesis is based on that understanding.

Acts 1:1-11 begins with an introduction that ties Acts to Luke's Gospel. In verses 1-6 there is a review and highlighting of Gospel events and themes. We are reminded, along with Theophilus (see Luke 1:3), that we have already heard about everything that Jesus began to do and teach. We are also reminded of the presence of the Holy Spirit, who played such an important role in Jesus' life in the Gospel. The Spirit will now move and shape the experiences of the apostles in Acts. The apostles, whom Jesus himself chose (Luke 5), are brought into the picture in verse 2 and take on a central role immediately in verse 3. We hear again of the forty days (v. 3), here denoting the time of the apostles' instruction before taking up their calling. Once before it was the time of Jesus' own period in the wilderness before taking up his call (Luke 4:1-13). These forty-day periods of preparation show continuity with messengers of God's kingdom who were active throughout the entire history of the Jews. In this passage it is for the announcement of that very kingdom that the apostles, like Jesus before them, are being prepared (v. 3).

The kingdom of God is the link between the past events of Luke's Gospel and the future that Acts begins to reveal. As hope and confidence in the coming of God's kingdom lured — or drove — Jesus on his mission of healing and preaching, so now Jesus' resurrection is a sign of that kingdom as it begins to be revealed with yet more clarity and existential reality. It is no accident that the apostles must await a baptism before beginning their ministry, but a baptism for a new age, a baptism of fire. It is also no accident that John predicted this, in the company of the prophets of Scripture. Luke offers us a picture of profound continuity in the work of God based on promises made millennia before through promises made only thirty years before. Each promise points toward the future. Every experience of fulfillment creates confidence in the God who promises justice and freedom to worship without fear (Luke 1:74). In Acts 1:4, 5 there is a message of waiting for something to happen. The resurrection of Jesus is a turning point, but there is a whole future out there, a kingdom yet to come; it is toward that future (as will be emphasized in v. 11) that apostles and disciples are to look.

Before moving on to look carefully at verses 6-11, where the central focus of this passage lies, a word needs to be said about the phrase "through the Holy Spirit" in verse 2. Jesus teaches or gives commandments through the Holy Spirit. What does this mean? Was Jesus' teaching more inspired because it came through the Spirit? This would be a strange claim given Jesus' own resurrection life. Was the Holy Spirit present to the hearers to make Jesus' meaning intelligible, as the Spirit made intelligible the languages spoken at Pentecost (at which each foreigner in Jerusalem *heard* in his own tongue, Acts 2:6)? If so, it is difficult to account for the confusion in verses 6-8, where the hearers seem to have missed Jesus' meaning by the proverbial mile. It seems to me that the presence of the Holy Spirit as a teaching instrument in verse 2 suggests at least that unmediated contact with the risen Lord is not available even here.

That the apostles themselves in verse 6 are shown still not to understand what Jesus is up to and how the kingdom of God will differ from their own best, scripturally based understandings, should encourage in hearers today a humility about what it is they truly know. Theological truth seems always too much for women and men to comprehend fully. Even in the presence of Jesus, we, no less than the apostles, need the Spirit to make meaning incarnate. And even then, we may miss it. At the same time, we are called to trust that there is meaning and a promised kingdom and the presence of God in our sphere. It is this tension that creates an openness to God's future and an unwillingness to move quickly to harsh judgments of one another. Think of this as the mostly delightful tension of a family waiting and preparing together for the Christmas holiday. The element of surprise is part of the excitement and joy because of the confidence family members have in each other's goodwill and love.

The tension is always one that surprises us. Expectations are confounded, and, although mystified, we are encouraged or lured or driven by a new horizon. In verse 6 Jesus' disciples, who are living right in that tension on the threshold of the future, raise the wrong question. Jesus has opportunity to provide the right answer for them and for hearers down through the ages, not least Luke's own audience. Expectations are confounded! Having heard all that their Lord and teacher had said, the "ones who had come together" asked him about the timing of the restoration of the kingdom. "Will you restore the kingdom to Israel at this time?" Of course they wonder. The risen Messiah, preaching that the kingdom of God is at hand, spoke to those faithful enough to believe that he would still usher it in. Their question was consistent with hopes of what God would do, hopes that had been stored up by the people of God for millennia, hopes that had been echoed with joy by Mary and Zechariah and given voice by Jesus. (Mary — the Magnificat [Luke 1:46-55]; Zechariah [Luke 1:68-79]; and Jesus — the Sermon on the Plain [Luke 6:20-49] and the return of the seventy-two [Luke 10:17-20]. These are examples, not a definitive list.) For just a few examples of the hopes that those first-century Jews echoed, read Isaiah 60:1-7; Zechariah 8:20-23; Zephaniah 3:14-20. At the center of God's kingdom would surely be worship of God. Jerusalem was preeminently the place where such worship took place. The question is important, hopeful, exciting. "Then, will it be then, at the baptism of fire that God will take up the role only God can take up — king of God's own creation?" Then will such justice as Jesus had promised (Luke 6) be done? Then will the minions of Satan ultimately be overthrown?

We see how right the disciples were to be thinking of restoration in Acts 3:21. Here Peter, after his baptism by fire, is able to preach correctly about the "restoration of all," as prophesied by God's holy prophets. The "therefore" in verse 6 (oun) is not to be simply glossed over. It is the "therefore" of faithful, believing, Bible students filled with hope for a new day. Yet it is not the restoration of the kingdom to Israel or in Israel that Peter speaks of in 3:21. Jesus' response in 1:7-8 has changed Peter's perceptions, at least. First the question of time is dismissed; no one can know the times or seasons in which God the Father will act, for God acts on his own sovereign authority. But, even more important, Jesus also turns the expectations both about the center of the kingdom and the manner in which folks will enter it in a new direction.

People will not come to Jerusalem, as Isaiah for one had so beautifully depicted. Instead, those who trust that the kingdom will come, a trust now founded on the resurrection of Jesus and on his promises, will leave Jerusalem to go as far as the end of the earth to witness to what they believe. The future is not one of patiently waiting for God's glory to burst in. It is one of active witness in Jerusalem, yes, but also farther out. It is one of witness among those who might be expected to understand about God and God's Messiah to those who are a great distance geographically and conceptually from such hope. It is, in a word, a task still before those who believe that the future is God's. It will be clear in verse 11 that active earthly witness is the agenda for the Galileans who follow their Lord. Looking up is not the point. Standing around is not the point. Jesus will be back, as promised; therefore the other promises and commands of Jesus must be taken seriously as well. There is life to be lived while we wait together.

Jesus' most important promise in these verses is that his followers will receive the power of the Holy Spirit (v. 8). It is this power that will create witnesses and will drive the witnesses into the farthest reaches of human habitations. Similar to the beginning of Jesus' own ministry when the Spirit filled him and he went first into the wilderness and then on to his ministry, so these women and men (1:13-14) will receive the Spirit and go. This promise is the premise of all that follows in the story of the church from then until now.

Sarah Henrich

515

Seventh Sunday of Easter, Year A

First Lesson: Acts 1:6-14
(Psalm 68:1-10, 32-35)
Second Lesson: 1 Peter 4:12-14; 5:6-11
Gospel Lesson: John 17:1-11

I n Acts 1:1-5 Luke's hearers were brought up to date, so to speak, on the story thus far. These verses both remind us of the years of Jesus' earthly ministry and also tell us what has been happening during the forty days between his resurrection and ascension. One can imagine a narrator speaking these verses as a camera moves from a wide-angled view of the Galilean countryside to close in on Jerusalem. Finally the camera begins to focus on a small group of women and men seated somewhere in the city, caught up in intense discussion. What could be so important? As the camera draws close enough to pick up their words, our passage begins.

Imagine now Luke's post-Easter drama in three distinct scenes (vv. 6-8, 9-11, and 12-14). The first scene begins with a critical question from "those who had been gathered together" with Jesus. This question and response mark a turning point of the narrative (this passage for the Easter season includes five verses from the Ascension Day lection [Acts 1:1-11], which see). The second scene centers on heavenly instructions to the disciples at the time of Jesus' ascension. The third provides a glimpse of the messianic community engaged in activities that will be its hallmark and strength throughout the narrative. We'll look at each scene and note the way in which one builds on another. After the sheer power of resurrection and ascension events where God's hand is so clearly displayed, almost any event might seem anticlimactic. Yet in each scene the "ante" continues to be raised. It is Luke's gift to show us that our ordinary life is continually being transformed into vocation by God's power. The central rubric of Acts, it seems to me, comes in 1:8 and is underlined by the question in verse 11. I refer not to Jesus' prophecy that the disciples "will be his witnesses" at ever-lengthening geographic distances. After all, not everyone in Acts itself, in the Christian assemblies of Luke's time, or in ours has ranged far and wide in witness. Rather, Jesus' promise that all the disciples will receive power for witness is central. That promise, that reality, shapes the lives of all believers, whether they go "to the end of the earth" or not.

Let's move in for a closer look at verses 6-8. The crucial question concerns the timing of the restoration of God's kingdom to Israel. It was this divine action, for which the resurrection of Jesus had been a prologue, that the disciples eagerly awaited. It is tempting to make fun of Jesus' followers here, as if they "just don't get it." We are better served when we hear their question as a faithful one, one based on Scripture. For Jesus, his followers, and for the people of Luke's day, Scripture means what we call the Old Testament. Long, faithful, and hopeful reading of Scripture encouraged many Jews to hope for just the kinds of changes that we hear in the mouth of Zechariah in Luke 1:67-89 and Mary in Luke 1:46-55. God's kingdom of justice and peace, promised over and over again in Scripture, seems to have been inaugurated. When would that kingdom be fully known? These are questions we ourselves may ask.

Jesus' followers understood that God's kingdom involved restoration in or for Israel, as was promised in Scripture. Most Christians no longer think to ask the question the disciples asked about Israel, in part because believers for nearly two millennia have trusted the answer that Jesus gives here. We should not let familiarity with this answer mislead us; Jesus' response was shockingly different from most of the scriptural promises that his faithful followers would have trusted. Jesus did not answer the question of timing. Never mind the times, he said, there is no way we can know that. His answer reminds us that God's sovereign freedom will not be held to a timetable.

Having said this, he went on to challenge the assumptions about how God's kingdom would come about. Indeed, he reversed those expectations. It is not a matter of waiting for the kingdom to come "home," he said. It's all about going out to testify to what they know, what they have experienced. Everywhere they go, and they will go everywhere, they will be empowered by the Spirit to be witnesses to Jesus, whom they have known throughout his ministry, crucifixion, and in these postresurrection days. A community of witnesses is promised and envisioned here. God's plan looks to be active (literally "dynamic," from the Greek word *dynamis* or "power"). It will engage folks at every level of their lives, now transformed by the Jesus they have known and the Spirit whose power had led Jesus himself into the wilderness and onward into ministry.

The second scene (vv. 9-11) begins with a brief description of Jesus' ascension. In just fourteen words (out of a total of fifty-three), Jesus is gone and his followers are left on the ground staring up at where he has gone. The verb in verse 10 (a present participle with an imperfect indicative) emphasizes a long, continuous staring. "Their eyes stayed glued" to heaven. They couldn't move, couldn't walk away from this climactic moment in Jesus' life (cf. Peter, James, and John at the transfiguration scene, where they were also reluctant to depart from such an awesome scene). But this was not to be the climactic moment in the life of the community. Here is a sure sign that the calling of the church is not to look back to any past glories, no matter how marvelous.

In no uncertain terms the followers are addressed by two mysterious men in white garments, a sure sign of heavenly origin. Such speakers have jump-started followers before when they were overwhelmed by a glimpse of God's power in human events, for example, at the tomb (Luke 24:4). It will happen again in Acts, for example, when Peter is left confused and uncertain after his vision and hesitates to respond to the visitors who have come from Cornelius (Acts 10). At times when we would prefer to stand in contemplation of spiritual events or when we fear that our action will compromise God's good news, the word comes to us, "Why do you stand looking up into heaven?" Followers do not need to stand looking up, as if their attention will hasten Jesus' return. The assurance from the white-clad messengers is that Jesus will come again, indeed, "in the same way in which he departed." How we might long for the clarity of angelic messengers. Our challenge is to identify positively those messengers who call our attention to everyday matters. They may indeed be speaking to us on behalf of God's mission. "Why are you standing there looking up to heaven?" is akin to verse 7 where Jesus said that no one can know the times when the Father will act. Accepting our human limits is at the same time a challenge to accept our human calling. What we cannot do or know or control should not command our attention nor distract us from the gifts given precisely to us as God's people.

The third scene offers a glimpse of the life of God's people together (vv. 12-14). It is a partial glimpse, but not a misleading one. After the Spirit comes in Acts 2:1-4, there are numerous, more developed descriptions of the messianic community (2:42-47; 4:32-35) and many narrative examples of that community. Since these verses appear in the lectionary only on this day, they provide a wonderful opportunity to point to how Jesus' followers are called to and blessed in their waiting together. In Luke's skillfully presented narrative of life with Jesus and life as part of a community of followers, different words and different actions take center stage at different times and for different people. It is a great joy for Christians and, not least, preachers to see how change of circumstances requires changed behaviors, different interpretations, new ways of serving. This is a joy for two reasons. First, it corresponds to the way we experience real life, especially in these decades of rapid change. Secondly, it continues to call for our own best creative efforts and skills in all we do and say.

Verses 12-14 put several different points before us. After being addressed by two men in white clothing, the group did return to Jerusalem.

They were obedient to a very mysterious set of command and promise, returning to their ancient holy city, having shared very new and life-changing events. In these circumstances of uncertainty the group stuck together. Women and men, they needed each other. It was important for them to remember together, to imagine together, to counsel patience, and certainly to pray. Perhaps there is no better set of descriptions for the tasks and circumstances of contemporary congregations. Verse 14 emphasizes the community. "These all were continuing to devote themselves all together to prayer." The verbs again imply ongoing action. The combination of "all" and "as one *(homothymadon)*" paints a picture of inclusive community with a focus on continued relationship with their God. It is a period of preparation for the changed life that is to come. Such preparation suggests that the future will be anything but anticlimactic for believers whose future was laid out in verse 8.

Sarah Henrich

Seventh Sunday of Easter, Year B

First Lesson: Acts 1:15-17, 21-26
(Psalm 1)
Second Lesson: 1 John 5:9-13
Gospel Lesson: John 17:6-19

At first glance, the fact that this text is little preached on seems right on. The text, Acts 1:15-26, covers the election of Matthias to take the place of Judas the betrayer. Many of the themes of the text are somewhat perplexing to contemporary persons. Part of it, the description of Judas's gruesome death (vv. 18-20), is handily left out. Is it unedifying or simply unattractive? Taking potentially offensive verses out of the reading does a disservice to those who will hear it, not least because of the "therefore" in verse 21. Better that teachers and preachers at least deal with the whole passage as a piece and make decisions about whether and how to address the story of Matthias in the context of their particular congregations.

The passage seems distant from many contemporary hearers, esoteric even, because its dynamic depends on principles that may seem unfamiliar and antique. The principles include the role and understanding of biblical prophecy in this passage, the need to fill out the number twelve for the twelve tribes of Israel, and the choice of Matthias by lot, with the understanding that God's will can be truly revealed in this method. Each of these questions will get some treatment in the following short essay. Several additional points are also worth attending to, points that do not jump out at the hearer quite so readily. These points will get the bulk of our attention.

The text is set at some indefinite time between the ascension of Jesus and Pentecost. Jesus' followers, numbered here at about 120, are gathered in Jerusalem where they are all together, praying with one mind (1:14) for the Spirit that will empower them to be the witnesses Jesus has called them to be (1:8). Luke does not tell us why Peter initiated the process of calling a person to take Judas's place in ministry. Peter's motivation is not important. What is important is Peter's insistence on the truthfulness and reliability of Scripture. Scripture which has spoken beforehand must be fulfilled. This turn to Scripture is consistent with the way he will speak after Pentecost (2:16-36) and with Luke's description of how Jesus taught his followers to understand Scripture (Luke 24:27, 44-47; see also Acts 1:3). Such a turn would also make great sense to Luke's own audience, whose scripture was what we call the Old Testament and whose struggle was to understand it in light of Jesus.

The hermeneutic at work is that the Holy Spirit "spoke through the mouth of David." The Holy Spirit had been an active participant in the life of the people of God long before Jesus appeared on the scene. It becomes clear in Acts 2:33-34 that the ascended Jesus is the one who pours out the Holy Spirit in "these days." But the Holy Spirit had been a trustworthy prophet and had spoken beforehand of many things in Scripture. (This dynamic is familiar to us also from Paul. See as an interesting example Galatians 3:8, where Scripture personified saw beforehand and preached the good news beforehand. To have seen beforehand occurs in Acts 2:31, where it sets the conditions of David's speech.) The Psalms, therefore, are a source for considering who must take up the oversight (both *diakonia,* v. 17, and *episkopē,* v. 20, quoting Ps. 109:8, are used to describe this ministry) or ministry of Judas, whose death in Acts 1:20 was also in accord with Scripture (Ps. 69:25). (Note Luke's familiarity with and extensive use of the Psalms as truly of the Spirit for believers in later times as well. In Acts 4:24-28 he uses Psalm 2:1-2 to interpret directly the events happening to the Christian community.) Both the Gospel and Acts are full of references to psalms; these Scriptures are one way the Spirit acted on our behalf, by speaking them at an earlier time.

A second theme is the election of another disciple to replace Judas and so fill out the number of the Twelve. Notice the language of allotment in verse 17. The verbs are passive: he "was numbered" and "was allotted" his share. These cautious verbs with an unnamed subject are signs that God was the primary agent in the creation of the Twelve, even as God was in the formation and history of the twelve tribes of Israel. In Luke 22:28-30 it is Jesus who assigns, even as has been assigned to him, thrones for the Twelve in his kingdom. The exact relationship between the Twelve and Israel is not clear. It may include completion of God's originally called people at last in God's kingdom. To explore these possibilities, one should take note of the way God's kingdom is proclaimed — over and over — to be different from human kingdoms. The activity of judging has everything to do with service, even for Jesus himself (see Luke 22:24-27). It is to that service that another is being called in Acts 1:17, 20.

Thanks to work done by J. N. Collins (*Diakonia: Re-Interpreting the Ancient Sources* [Oxford University Press, 1977]), we know that the service referred to here is likely to have been a kind of ambassadorial activity. These twelve were called to deliver the message from their lord to others on that lord's behalf. In Luke and in Acts the message is a reminder of judgment (cf. Luke 16:28 in the context of judgment after death). A symbolically complete Israel now will fully take up her task as described by Isaiah and echoed by Simeon (see Luke 2:29-32 and 34, quoting Isa. 52:10; 42:6; 49:6). The witness to the nations is service, and it is about service. This witness to the nations is the subject of Acts.

Finally, there is the understanding of lots as yet another way in which God (or the Holy Spirit) acts to choose Matthias on behalf of disciples and the mission. Two important points are made in verses 23-26. First, the seemingly random choice of Matthias is by lot only from a contemporary human point of view. We will come back to this one. Secondly, God's work and God's presence continue among the gathered believers as the choice is made for their future life together. The process of Scripture interpretation, prayer, and drawing of lots reveals Luke's conviction of the continuity of God's presence and purpose in the past, present, and future.

There is no doubt that in Luke-Acts, God's plan and activity are coherent and continuous. They also transcend human discernment, which is always limited. In this passage God is addressed in prayer as God who knows the hearts of all (v. 24). (There is no reason whatsoever on the basis of the Greek text to translate "know the hearts of all men," as the RSV has done.

521

The word "all" is in a case which is not gender-specific. It is a substantive and therefore modifies no noun.) This characteristic of God and of Jesus in Luke's Gospel is worth our attention. A major Lukan theme, it strongly contrasts the human point of view with God's knowledge in such a way that humankind must be humble in any and all attempts to judge. The compound word "know the heart" occurs only here and in Acts 15:8 in the New Testament. In 15:8 God is remembered by Peter as having done the very surprising thing of pouring out the Holy Spirit on the Gentiles, because God is a knower of hearts. That is, what we might choose to do is limited by our discernment and all the structures we have erected, good and less so, to enable that discernment. What God chooses is based on no such limitations. Notice that in 15:8, as also here, God knows the hearts of people we haven't even met yet ("all" in 1:24 and Gentiles in 15:8).

Throughout Luke's Gospel, the word "heart" works in very interesting and distinctly nonsentimental ways. While a full discussion is impossible here, some passages are especially revealing. In Luke 2:35, it is said prophetically that what emerges from many hearts will be revealed. Jesus will be able to reveal what is in hearts in ways that will surprise. Two of the most interesting enactments of Jesus' ability to reveal come in Luke 7 where a Roman centurion is responded to by Jesus and then revealed as one with an amazing amount of faith. Then Jesus reveals the limitations of a Pharisee whose thought/heart Jesus perceives/knows. The same kind of insight has already been shown in 5:22, where Jesus addresses unasked questions (the word for questions is the same as that translated as "thoughts" in 2:35) and addresses them. Likewise, in 9:47 Jesus knows the "questions of their hearts" and answers them in a way that they still cannot comprehend. Luke is clear that the disciples were too frightened to ask questions, but Jesus knew what they were pondering. After all this, in 16:15 Jesus points out that God knows their hearts. This confirms for Luke's audience that Jesus shares this more-than-human quality of God and can be trusted in his prophetic statements. A last illustration: in Luke 24:38 Jesus addressed the women at the tomb who had questions in their hearts, questions quite unexpressed. His conversation with them presumes that he knows the questions (see also 1:51, 66; 2:19, 51; 3:15). It is a most profound characteristic of God and of Jesus that they can know the heart and respond in ways that bring comfort, judgment, and even a promise of right leadership as in Acts 1. That this knowing belongs to God and not humans is of no small significance for those who want to find litmus tests of "true belief."

One could understand this passage as a tale of just deserts. Judas got his, as God always knew he would, and Matthias, who had been there from the beginning, got his. This would be an unfortunate simplification of the rich themes that Luke raises for us at the beginning of Acts. These include:

Interest in ministry and witness. How are folk appointed to leadership? Who is part of the community called to witness? What does it mean to be enrolled? (The word translated "enrolled" is found in only one other place. Here it is most literally translated "chosen together by vote." *Psēphos* is the word for pebble, used in voting in juries and other assemblies.)

Interest in the continuity of God's care and God's will for the people witnessed to in Scripture and in the mysterious work of the Spirit within the community.

Interest in the reality of Jesus. The witnesses are important because they can all testify that this was really a man who was really baptized, really lived among them, was really killed and raised. These witnesses will be the foundation for the church's conviction two millennia later that these things were so. "Oversight" or "service" are connected backward to those who were there "during all the time that the Lord Jesus went in and out among us."

Interest in a large number of unknown believers gathered together, who knew Jesus and would receive the Spirit. Luke often expands the circle of faithful participants to those we cannot know and count. Who are the 120 in the community in verse 15, and where does their witness happen over the years?

Sarah Henrich

Day of Pentecost, Years A, B, C

First Lesson: Acts 2:1-21
(Psalm 104:24-34, 35b)
Second Lesson (Year A): 1 Corinthians 12:3b-13
Second Lesson (Year B): Romans 8:22-27
Second Lesson (Year C): Romans 8:14-17
Gospel Lesson (Year A): John 20:19-23
Gospel Lesson (Year B): John 15:26-27; 16:4b-15
Gospel Lesson (Year C): John 14:8-17, (25-27)

On Pentecost we celebrate the coming of the Holy Spirit to empower the church in ways not previously available for the whole people of God. Often God's people do not consider the immensity of the power God has provided for the task: our lives can betray spiritual mediocrity only when we underestimate the reality of the third person of the Trinity living and working in us.

We should understand Luke's portrayal of Pentecost in its fuller context in Luke-Acts. As Jesus' public ministry begins with his announcement of his Spirit empowerment in Luke 4:18-19 (quoting Isaiah), so the church's service to the Lord begins with the announcement of our Spirit empowerment in Acts 2:17-21 (quoting Joel). The Gospel of Luke moves from the temple to Galilee and back to Jerusalem, but Acts will move from Jerusalem to the ends of the earth (1:8).

Jesus prepared his disciples for the coming of the Spirit with the promise of Pentecost (1:4-8). He promised that his followers would be "baptized in the Holy Spirit." Different church traditions interpret this promise in different ways, in part because the Spirit accomplishes many things in believers' lives, and different passages focus on different aspects of his ministry. Such aspects include re-creating us spiritually when we become Jesus' followers and subsequently renewing us further into Christ's image. But Luke-Acts emphasizes especially one aspect of the Spirit's work, namely, inspiring believers to speak God's message (2:17-18). This "prophetic" activity of the Spirit is mentioned frequently in the Old Testament, early Judaism, and the New Testament, but Luke focuses on it almost exclusively.

Thus it is not surprising that the thesis statement of Acts appears to be the claim that Christ empowers his first followers to be his "witnesses" (1:8). As the Gospel of Luke emphasized Jesus' ministry to the marginalized, Acts

524

emphasizes the ministry of the first Jewish Christians to the Gentiles, hence the crossing of cultural and geographical boundaries (1:8).

For the first disciples, this promise of empowerment would have appeared extraordinary. The prophets had linked this final outpouring of the Spirit with the end time (Isa. 44:3; Ezek. 36:26-27; Joel 2:28–3:1), so the disciples respond to Jesus' promise with the obvious question: Since this is the end time, when will you restore the kingdom to Israel (1:6)? Jesus declares that they need not know when this era will end, but in the meantime they will be witnesses for him, as Isaiah declared Israel's remnant would be for God in the end time (Isa. 43:10, 12; 44:8). In a sense the disciples would experience the end time breaking into history — a dramatic and unexpected event!

If Acts notes the promise of Pentecost (1:4-8), it also recounts the disciples' preparation for Pentecost (1:12–2:1). The disciples prayed and remained in unity together (1:12-14; 2:1); trusting Jesus' promise of the coming Spirit, they also reorganized to get their leadership in order (1:15-26). Luke probably wished such prayer, unity, and preparation for God's calling to characterize the church in his day, and would undoubtedly desire it in our own as well. Although the Day of Pentecost is a finished event in history, God continues to pour out his Spirit subsequently (4:31; 8:17), sometimes in ways similar to the first Pentecost (4:32-35; 10:44-45; 19:6) and sometimes in answer to prayer (4:30; 8:15; cf. Luke 11:13). This may have implications for those of us today who take seriously the need for the Spirit's active empowerment in our churches and our lives.

Following its account of the preparation for Pentecost, Acts recounts the proofs of Pentecost: the sound of a powerful wind (2:2), the appearance of flames (2:3), and climactically, the experience of tongues-speaking (2:4). A quieter, subtler wind might have recalled God breathing life into humanity (Gen. 2:7; cf. John 20:22) or God's gentle voice (1 Kings 19:12), but this is not a quiet or subtle wind. While this wind might evoke such gentler associations in a secondary way, the strongest allusion is probably to the life-giving, end-time wind of Ezekiel 37:5-10.

Biblical writers used fire to symbolize a variety of things, but most often for judgment, sometimes end-time judgment. This is probably how John the Baptist meant his prophecy about the end-time Messiah baptizing in the Holy Spirit and fire: the fire would be God's judgment on the wicked (Luke 3:9, 16-17), as the Spirit was his gift for the righteous. Others associate the fire here with the appearance of fire at Mount Sinai when God gave his law; later Jewish tradition connects Pentecost with God giving the law at Sinai. In either case, its appearance on the Day of Pentecost may symbolize the promise of the future, again as a reminder that the future had invaded history.

The speaking in tongues in some way is the least demonstrative of the three signs, but no less dramatic. Indeed, because of contemporary movements that emphasize speaking in tongues, some modern readers are all the more uncomfortable with this aspect of the narrative. Their discomfort, however, provides the expositor a special opportunity to offer helpful clarification. Given the subsequent turn of events in this narrative, tongues here is not simply highly emotional ecstatic speech unintelligible in any language; it represents genuine languages (2:5-12). Although the matter is more debated, the same might be the case for Paul's discussion of speaking in tongues and may be the case with some of the genuine experiences of prayer in tongues today. The key, however, is that the languages were unknown to the speakers, explaining why the activity demonstrated that a miracle had occurred (2:4, 8, 17).

Speaking in other tongues recurs with outpourings of the Spirit in 10:46 and 19:6; why does Luke choose to emphasize it by recording it in three instances? Jesus announced that the Spirit would empower his disciples to be cross-cultural witnesses (1:8). God was prophetically empowering the disciples to speak the divine message of the gospel, and demonstrating this empowerment through their inspired praise in other languages. What greater sign of empowerment for cross-cultural ministry could he have provided than inspiring them to worship in others' languages? And if disciples can worship God in languages they do not know, as the Spirit enables them, how much more can they prove sensitive to his direction in their continuing witness? That Luke does not report speaking in other tongues in every instance of Spirit empowerment in Acts allows that we need not expect it in every case today. But neither need we rule it out, as one gift among many Christ gives to his church (1 Cor. 12:10, 30).

Peter soon explains the tongues by means of Joel's prophecy pertaining to the end time (2:17-18). The wind, flames, and tongues-speaking may all evoke the arrival of the future era. Thus, as Jesus' very promise of the Spirit's coming implied, the future kingdom was breaking into history. This suggests that the world around should be able to look at the church and tell what the future kingdom will be like!

After recounting the proofs of Pentecost, Acts focuses on the peoples of Pentecost: Jewish people from many nations serve as the first representatives of the gospel crossing all cultural barriers (2:5-11). Some have compared the list of hearers here with the table of nations in Genesis 10, updated into the language of Luke's day. If so, this passage may reverse the judgment on the tower of Babel in Genesis 11: as God once scattered the nations by dividing their languages, he now empowers his church to transcend those divisions. One of the activities of the Spirit in the rest of Acts is guiding the church to cross cultural barriers beyond its comfort zones (8:27-29; 10:17-20; 11:12; 13:2, 4). An expositor could easily apply this example to racial reconciliation, cultural sensitivity, cross-cultural ministry, and church unity today (Rom. 15:16; 1 Cor. 12:13; Eph. 2:18-22).

Luke then turns to the prophecy of Pentecost (Acts 2:16-21). The crowd responds to the speaking in various languages in two ways: some conclude that the glossolalists are drunk, whereas others ask what this phenomenon indicates. Peter quickly dismisses the accusation of drunkenness (2:15), then addresses the question about the significance of the tongues: This fulfills Joel's prophecy about God empowering his people to speak as the Spirit would inspire them (2:17-18). This empowerment would cross gender and age barriers (2:17-18; Joel's text also specifies class barriers); to emphasize the prophetic nature of the empowerment, Peter even adds a few explanatory words to Joel's text ("they shall prophesy," 2:18). From the standpoint of Luke-Acts, some of the heavenly signs mentioned in 2:19-20 may have been fulfilled in Luke 23:44-45, but the passage again adapts the wording to emphasize the signs on earth (2:19) fulfilled in Jesus' ministry (2:22). Whatever may remain future — and Luke does not deny the future (1:7, 11; 17:31) — the power of the future has erupted into history. The tongues indicate that God is pouring out his Spirit (2:17-18), which indicates that the final era has been inaugurated in some sense (2:20) — and thus that the era of salvation has also come (2:21).

Luke follows this with the preaching of Pentecost (2:22-40). Here Peter argues that his hearers should call on the Lord's name (2:21; in Joel's Hebrew, the divine name) by being baptized in Jesus' name (2:38), because Jesus is the Lord (2:25-36). The aftermath of Pentecost may in a sense supply the purpose of Pentecost: God's people live in unity, sacrificing for one another's needs and living in such a faithful way that the world around gets a foretaste of the future kingdom (2:41-47).

Although the "witnesses" to whom Jesus initially spoke were the eyewitnesses of his ministry (1:8, 22; 2:32; 10:41; 13:31), they provide a model in many respects for our witness for Jesus today (witness is not limited to the first group of eyewitnesses — 2:33; 22:20; 23:11; 26:16). If we feel that we lack the requisite power to carry out Christ's commission in our generation, we should remember that the promise of the Spirit is for God's people in all generations (2:38-39), and the Spirit continues to bear witness (5:32). The first disciples Jesus recruited in Luke were hardly the models of power we would expect when they began following him (e.g., Luke 5:8). The entire point of Pentecost is that God will accomplish his purposes through us, not because we are powerful in ourselves, but because he will show his power through us.

Craig S. Keener

Second Sunday of Easter, Year A

First Lesson: Acts 2:14a, 22-32
(Psalm 16)
Second Lesson: 1 Peter 1:3-9
Gospel Lesson: John 20:19-31

When he lifts up his voice in Acts 2:14, Peter becomes the first "Christian" preacher, surmises Gerhard Schneider, the highly regarded German interpreter of Acts. But is he really? An answer hangs closely on the function of Peter's speech to explain something that has already happened. What has happened is so bizarre that witnesses are at a loss to make sense of it.

We readers, modern ones though we are, are a leg up on those witnesses in Jerusalem. The narrator has built anticipations for readers by reiterating a pledge from Jesus. At the end of Luke Jesus assures the Eleven and those with them: "I am sending upon you what my Father promised; so stay here in the city until you have been clothed with power from on high" (Luke 24:49). This power from on high is not entirely mysterious because Jesus had already declared that what the Father has promised is to give the Holy Spirit to those who ask (Luke 11:13). But for readers shifting from volume 1 (Luke) to volume 2 (Acts), one pledge may not be enough to keep the kettle steaming. So the narrator gives it again at the beginning of Acts to readers who are caught up in waiting along with the apostles: "He ordered them not to leave Jerusalem, but to wait there for the promise of the Father. '. . . you will be baptized with the Holy Spirit not many days from now'" (Acts 1:4-5).

With anticipation running high, the wait is not long — not many days, and not many verses. The narrator tells us about the coming of the Spirit, with sound and sign and speech — strange sound, explained by a near analogy of rushing wind; strange sign, explained by a near analogy of tongues as of fire; and strange speech, explained not by a near analogy but directly as "other tongues." The Spirit drives people who are inside outside, and these folk filled with the Spirit create enough of a spectacle to draw a crowd. That is when the first postresurrection preaching occurs.

This preaching has an attractive curiosity to it, because foreigners from wide and far understand when Galileans speak. Highbrow people of antiquity took Galilean speech as inferior, like East End Londoners speaking cockney. But the foreigners understand the Galileans with inferior speech in their own language. They hear them speaking about God's deeds of power, and this is the first "Christian" preaching. But the entire event leaves the foreigners perplexed. What has happened is so bizarre that they do not understand.

So the first Christian proclamation is not on the lips of Peter. But precisely on whose lips is it? Acts 1:13 begins to give a brief description of the followers of Jesus who are left after the crucifixion and resurrection. There are apostles and certain women; those with them altogether number about 120. On Pentecost they "all" were together in one place. Initially, we are uncertain who is included in "all." It could be the apostles from 1:26, or it could be the 120 from 1:13-15. For an answer, we have to wait on Peter's speech that explains what has happened for the foreigners, who witness the first Christian preaching, who are perplexed, and who do not understand.

In the meantime, some of the witnesses of the bizarre events make a stab at explaining for themselves. The narrator has given analogies so that readers could understand the noise in the upper room and the appearance of tongues as if of fire. Now the foreigners scan their experiences for an analogy to enable them to understand the first Christian Pentecost, and the Pentecost events are bizarre enough for them to infer that the first Christian preachers are drunk. The Galileans, who speak in other tongues that are intelligible to foreigners, must be intoxicated. And readers get an opportunity to test out this explanation along with the foreigners.

On the other hand, Peter's speech offers a competing explanation. And readers get an opportunity to test out his explanation along with him. Pentecost is an event that is without analogy. No analogy from human experience matches the bizarre phenomena, and so Peter explains Pentecost by Scripture. It is an audacious citation of Scripture. Peter does not say that something has occurred that is similar to Joel or fulfills Joel, but "this *is* what was spoken through the prophet Joel" (Acts 2:16). For Peter, Joel is incomplete without Pentecost, Pentecost is incomprehensible without Joel.

But now readers have enough information in the story to enable them to deduce who the original preachers were. The direct equation between Pentecost and what was spoken through Joel clarifies that the original preachers were those who numbered about 120, including certain women.

> I will pour out my Spirit upon all flesh,
>   and your *sons and your daughters* shall prophesy. . . .
> Even upon my slaves, both *men and women*,
>   in those days I will pour out my Spirit;
>   and they shall prophesy.   (2:17-18)

In fact, Acts reinforces the identity of both men and women by a slight change in the citation from Joel. Joel indicates that God's Spirit will be poured out on "the male and female slaves" (Joel 2:29). When Acts slips in the little word "my," it is all the more clear that these men and women are *God's* servants. For a church that throughout its history has debated the place of women in ministry, it is significant that women were among the first Christian preachers in the story of Pentecost in Acts.

Acts understands this as a new era of history ("the last days"). But the direct equation with Joel also means that the new era does not break away from the history of Israel. Pentecost is equated with a prophecy of Israel, and even though many interpreters argue (erroneously, I think) that Acts breaks Christianity off from Judaism, Pentecost links Christianity to Israel.

On the other hand, Peter anticipates a new kind of Israel that he himself does not yet envision. He says the right words: "Everyone who calls on the name of the Lord shall be saved" (Acts 2:21). But to anticipate the development of plot in Acts, not until Acts 10–11 does he clearly know that "everyone" includes Gentiles. Israel with Gentiles who call on the name of the Lord added on, is a new kind of Israel. It is Israel of the period of time that Acts calls "the last days."

But the events of Pentecost also have a christological explanation. God pours out the Spirit about which Joel spoke through Jesus. This claim is a problem because Jesus was a problem. He was executed as a criminal. This means that he was subjected to a ritual of degradation that proved for citizens of antiquity that he was beyond the pale of the social order. Peter relies on three ways to rehabilitate Jesus. (1) God attested the earthly Jesus by working deeds of power, wonders, and signs through him. (2) Those who subjected him to the ritual of degradation did so unlawfully. (3) God reversed the ritual of degradation by raising Jesus from the dead. The resurrection functions here primarily as a divine attestation of Jesus.

This divine reversal of an unlawful human declaration of social deviance is also without analogy, and it also is explained by Scripture. First, Peter cites the Greek form of Psalm 16:10 from the Septuagint, and takes the psalmist's (the psalm is attributed to David) claim that God's "holy one would not see corruption" as naming beforehand the resurrection of Jesus. That is, God acted in raising Jesus so that his body did not decay. Not only does the psalmist make a prophetic prediction, but the words of the psalm are now on the lips of Jesus. For Peter, Jesus is the one who addresses the words of the psalm to God, "You will not . . . let your Holy One experience corruption" (Acts 2:27). Mixed in with Psalm 16 is an allusion to 2 Samuel 7:12 — God's promise to David that his "seed" would sit on the throne of Israel forever. In 2 Samuel 7:12 "seed" is a collective noun that means "descendants." Understood on one level, God's promise to David is the promise of a dynasty. But on Peter's level, "seed" is understood as a literal singular, and the one seed is Jesus, whom God establishes on the throne of David forever. Gabriel had announced to Mary at the beginning of Luke that God would give her son the throne of his ancestor David forever (Luke 1:32-33). Not until this point in Peter's speech, however, do readers learn about Jesus' enthronement, and along with that readers learn that David's throne is at the right hand of God. On the one hand, a political kingdom has been denationalized. On the other, the kingdom has been universalized.

The passage is highly christological. God has been at work through Jesus. But it remains theocentric; that is, Pentecost is the proclamation of God's mighty deeds. God attested the earthly Jesus by performing deeds of power through him. God raised Jesus from the dead. God swore an oath to put a descendant of David on the throne of David. God acts through Jesus to pour out the Spirit. But this God remains the God who in Joel says, "I will pour out my Spirit upon all flesh."

Robert L. Brawley

Third Sunday of Easter, Year A

First Lesson: Acts 2:14a, 36-41
(Psalm 116:1-4, 12-19)
Second Lesson: 1 Peter 1:17-23
Gospel Lesson: Luke 24:13-35

Until Acts 2:33, Peter's speech is ostensibly an explanation of the wild phenomena of speech and the comprehension of speech on the Day of Pentecost. This explanation centers on the Spirit. The pouring out of the Spirit is an act of God that is correlated with God's promise in Joel to pour out the Spirit on all flesh. But it is also correlated with Jesus' claim in Luke 11:13, as mediated through Luke 24:49 and Acts 1:4, that God will give the Holy Spirit to those who appeal to God like children to a parent. But the focus on the Spirit quickly bleeds over into Christology. Peter's citation of Joel portrays the pouring out of the Spirit first as God's act, but then as God's act through an agent, namely, the risen Jesus.

On the one hand, Jesus the agent is a criminal subjected to execution. His execution is a ritual of degradation that characterizes him as totally beyond the pale of the social order. But God has acted in direct contrast to the ritual of degradation to rehabilitate Jesus by raising him from the dead. This rehabilitated Jesus is God's agent who pours out the Spirit.

On the other hand, the agent who pours out the Spirit is also a character in Joel. The last words that Peter quotes from Joel are "Then everyone who calls on the name of the Lord shall be saved" (Acts 2:21). In the last chapter of Luke, the risen Jesus provides for a revisionary understanding of Scripture (Luke 24:27, 45). When Peter interprets Scripture with this revisionary understanding, the Lord on whose name those who will be saved call, is Jesus. The confirmation of Jesus of Nazareth (Acts 2:22) as the Lord at the end of the quote from Joel runs on a path through two other biblical texts that takes close attention to follow. Peter first recalls Psalm 16:8-11 (Acts 2:25-28), but then blends Psalm 110:1 with it (Acts 2:34). Peter interprets Psalm 16 as an affirmation of Jesus' resurrection, but also as a characterization of him as Lord. There are two Lords in Psalm 110:1. The first is God. The second is the risen Jesus who is at the right hand of the first Lord. In Peter's reading of the two psalms, God as the first Lord commands the enthronement of the second Lord, who is the risen Jesus. This melding of the two psalms means, however, that the risen Jesus is also the one who is at the right hand of God in Psalm 16.

With this move, Peter's sermon also points to the fulfillment of another promise. In Luke 1:32-33 Gabriel announces to Mary with respect to Jesus: "The Lord God will give to him the throne of his ancestor David. He will reign over the house of Jacob forever, and of his kingdom there will be no end." Significantly, Gabriel's announcement is in interplay with 2 Samuel 7:12-13, where Nathan declares God's covenant to put one of his "seed" on the throne of David forever. "Seed" is singular both in the Hebrew and in the Greek Septuagint. It can, however, be taken as a collective noun to mean "descendants." But in his announcement in Luke 1, Gabriel takes it as a literal singular. Mary's son Jesus is the one seed of David who will reign over the house of Jacob forever. In his Pentecost speech, Peter testifies that the enthronement Gabriel anticipated has taken place. To be sure, this is the stuff of the Davidic covenant, but with a revisionary perspective that universalizes it just as certainly as the God of Luke-Acts is universal.

Peter uses Joel, Psalm 16, and Psalm 110 to explain Pentecost. But he then reverses his line of persuasion. Pentecost testifies to Jesus as Lord and Messiah. "Therefore let the entire house of Israel know with certainty that God has made him both Lord and Messiah, this Jesus whom you crucified" (Acts 2:36). One could claim a logical fallacy of circular reasoning. The risen Jesus makes Pentecost significant; Pentecost makes the risen Jesus significant. Or one could claim a reciprocal relationship and say the same thing — the risen Jesus makes Pentecost significant; Pentecost makes the risen Jesus significant.

The reality that we live after the Holocaust should make us sensitive interpreters of the kinds of claims that Luke-Acts makes. One could take Peter's revisionary perspective on the Davidic covenant as a devaluation of the Judaism of that time (not to be connected in an uncritical way directly with the Judaism of our time). Or one could take his perspective as a revaluation that drives the Judaism of that time toward universal significance. Most assuredly Peter does not leave Israel behind. Rather, he proclaims that the risen Jesus is Lord and Messiah for all Israel (Acts 2:36). Some interpreters take Peter's reference to the participation of Jerusalemites in the crucifixion of Jesus as the seed of anti-Judaism, if not outright anti-Semitism. In addition to being anachronistic, such interpretations contradict the context. In the context Peter is not characterizing Judaism. Rather, he is contrasting the crucifixion of Jesus as a ritual of social degradation with the resurrection as God's rehabilitating affirmation of Jesus.

The audience accepts Peter's interpretation of Pentecost as an indication of God's affirmation of the risen Jesus as Lord and Messiah. Further, they perceive that God's enthronement of Jesus as Lord implies consequences for them. So they associate themselves with the apostles by addressing them as "brothers," and ask a deliberative question: "What should we do?" (Acts 2:37). The essentials of Peter's answer are repeated enough in Luke-Acts to be thematic — repentance, baptism, and reception of the gift of the Holy Spirit. But these themes should not be separated from the earlier proclamation that "everyone who calls on the name of the Lord will be saved." Three thousand apparently do call on the name of the Lord, repent, receive baptism, and presumably receive the gift of the Holy Spirit. As such, they too become part of the people in the period of history called "the last days" announced by Joel — God's servants upon whom the risen Jesus pours out the Spirit.

But Peter bases the promise of the Spirit not only on Joel but also on another promise that is for the Israelites, their children, and all those who are far away. What is this promise? The conventional wisdom is that Peter is making a reference back to a claim he has already made, namely, that those who call on the name of the Lord will be saved. An allusion to Joel is in fact hardly in doubt, because "everyone whom the Lord our God calls to him" in Acts 2:39 continues the words of Joel 2:32 just where Peter's original quotation of Joel broke off in Acts 2:21.

That is not all, however, because though the promise in Joel has much to do with the salvation of those who call on the name of the Lord, it has nothing to do with a promise for the descendants of the Jews ("your children") or for "all who are far away." To discern what Peter means by the promise "for you, for your children, and for all who are far away" (Acts 2:39) requires jumping forward to Acts 3:25, where in another speech Peter clearly spells out that the people of Israel are Abraham's descendants (corresponding to "your children" in Acts 2:39) through whom all the families of the earth are to be blessed (corresponding to "all who are far way" in Acts 2:39). The earlier interplay between Jesus' Lordship and the Davidic covenant fits into this picture of the Abrahamic covenant. The Davidic covenant, as fulfilled in Acts 2, is a specific way God blesses all the families of the earth. Salvation, the gift of the Spirit, and the integration of believers into a fellowship of teaching, breaking of bread, and prayer are parts of the way God's promise to Abraham to bless all the families of the earth is coming to its fulfillment. Pentecost is, therefore, full of the Spirit and very christological. But as the fulfillment of God's promise, it is theocentric.

For Luke-Acts, Pentecost has a special character as the initiation of a new period of time — the last days announced by Joel. As the initiation of a new period of history, it cannot be repeated. But the aspects of Pentecost — calling on the name of the Lord, repentance, baptism, salvation, fellowship, and prayer — are replicated precisely in the three thousand persons who were added to the nascent community (see Acts 2:38). For Luke-Acts, these aspects are replicated again and again through proclamation of the gospel.

The Abrahamic covenant, as understood in Luke-Acts, has a major influence on the good news of Peter's speech. The primary point of this covenant promise from God in Luke-Acts is the blessing of all the families of the earth. The pouring out of the Spirit on Pentecost is not only the confirmation of Jesus as Lord and Messiah, not only the basis for a Christian mission, not only the foundation of the Christian church, but also an event on the way toward the fulfillment of God's blessing of all the families of the earth. Any preaching that is not aimed at the replication of Pentecost for the blessing of all shortchanges the good news of Acts 2.

Robert L. Brawley

Fourth Sunday of Easter, Year A

First Lesson: Acts 2:42-47
(Psalm 23)
Second Lesson: 1 Peter 2:19-25
Gospel Lesson: John 10:1-10

In quick narrative, this remarkable passage tells us what "church" means. When you find "telling," "doing," "being," and "celebrating" in Christ, there it is. For the first Christians these marks of kerygma, *diakonia, koinōnia*, and *leitourgia* took form in foundational ways. We look at them in that context and ask what their counterparts today might be. But to get the full picture, these verses have to be situated in the sweep of chapters 1 to 4.

The initial chapters of Acts can be read with the imagery of light and fire in mind. They presuppose the Easter dawn ending of Luke's other book (his Gospel). The Acts drama begins in chapter 1 with the ascension of the Son of God to the heavenly realm. Acts 2, the Day of Pentecost, is marked by "tongues of fire" that descend from the ascended Easter Sun — manifestations of the Holy Spirit poured out from the reigning Son. This Pentecostal power gathers a new people with the four signs of the Spirit described in chapter 3. So constituted by this nurturing Person, the church then moves in mission, a drama that continues in the following chapter. We turn, initially, to the inreach of chapter 3, then to the outreach of chapter 4.

Telling/Kerygma. Acts 2:14-36, Peter's sermon, is the first kerygma of the newborn church. Reference to this telling of the Christian story in our lection is in the form of its "teaching," *didachē* (2:42), but its content is the same kerygmatic declaration of the reconciling deeds of God. The Reformation tradition cites this proclaiming of the Word as an essential mark of the church. In another description based on the Nicene Creed, the church is "apostolic" and thus authentic where the apostles' teaching and preaching are found.

What is the tale so told? In this chapter it is the story "writ large" directed to a special audience, taking the hearers from the originating "plan" of God, through the covenant with Israel, to its center point in the life, death, and resurrection of Christ, and from there to its chapters on the birth of the church and the coming of salvation. The Christian community later summarized this drama of God's deeds in its baptismal "rule of faith," one we have now in developed form as the Apostles' Creed with its sequel, the Nicene Creed, refined in the fires of the early christological controversies. Today the narrative that makes the church the church is kept alive in confessional lore, catechisms, contemporary statements of faith, church-year lections, eucharistic prayers, the loci of courses in systematic theology, and faithful preaching and teaching.

Now, as then, is a ripe time for telling this story. With spiritual hungers everywhere, and a generation asking ultimate questions, there is a readiness to "welcome" a "message" that speaks joyfully of the journey of the triune God from creation and fall to the covenants with Noah and Israel, and then to the defining "last days" of the coming of Christ, the pouring out of his saving Spirit on sons and daughters, and the final Great Day when God is "all in all."

Doing/Diakonia. This account of the Spirit's descent is in a book called the "Acts" of the apostles, not their "talks." As the Word of God is enfleshed, so the words of his followers are inseparable from their deeds. The sign of a Spirit-filled church is the doing of *diakonia* as well as the telling of kerygma, the care of the body as well as the soul: "They would sell their possessions and goods and distribute the proceeds to all, as any had need" (2:45).

The description of the radical sharing in which the early Christians engaged has spawned a host of interpretations and launched a thousand experiments. Revolutionaries have declared, "There it is in the Bible: 'from each according to ability, to each according to need.' See, the church was practicing communism, our mandate to overturn a corrupt society!" But another says, "No, this was communitarianism, not communism, a radical model for Christians, showing them how to live outside a corrupt society!" And another, "No, it's only meant for the first century, a symbol not to be taken literally!" And on and on.

Some clarifications: "communism" is a theory that demands the collectivization of the means of production. Not so the early Christians who worked at their own trades, as Jesus did. Yet they "had all things in common" (2:44), pooling the fruits of their labor and parceling out the "proceeds" according to human need. Does this mean that being the church demands that we do the same?

Ironically, among those who reject the application today of this early church practice are many hard-line inerrantists. When it comes to this account, the "fundamentalist" becomes a "modernist," denying the literal reading of Scripture. For that matter, few congregations in Christian history would qualify as "biblical" if the first-century absolute sharing of possessions served as the standard of *diakonia*. Yet, do we just dismiss the point of the practice because it may have been related to early Christian expectation of an imminent end of time and therefore a matter of getting ready for the soon-coming perfect kingdom?

One continuity between the early church and subsequent practice is the presence of the "deacon" in church order. However reconceived, this office is charged with the care of those in need, a recognition that *diakonia* is a sign of the Spirit and mark of a faithful church. But deaconing is more than the responsibility of a designated office; it is the commission to the whole church to carry out acts of mercy. In this passage the economic welfare of fellow Christians is to the fore, *diakonia* as "inreach." We'll see in a subsequent passage how this mark is related to "outreach" as well. Thus, whatever the historical contextuality of its communitarian expression, the claim on us all to practice the care of bodies as well as souls continues, and the radicality of the primitive church stands over us as both lure and judge of our lesser approximations.

Being/Koinōnia. "They devoted themselves to the apostles' . . . fellowship . . ." (2:42). While the word "fellowship" has been much weakened in popular parlance, and language inclusivists worry about its masculine import, we do get a hint of its apostolic intention in the "fellowship hall" of many a congregation. Sociability, yes, in a world where we're often too busy to sit down for a meal with friends or gather in a group to discuss deep issues. But the early Christians were about something much more than an after-worship coffee hour, as welcome as that kind of fellowship is.

537

Dietrich Bonhoeffer captured something of the import of Acts 2:42 in his *Life Together*, the deep sharing of burdens and joys in a Christian community under the cross. We are no church in exile in a Nazi land, as was the underground seminary that was background to his book, but we are aliens in a culture with very different premises. "Being together," *koinōnia* in the profound New Testament sense, is as much a gift and claim today as it was in first-century Jerusalem and Germany of the 1930s.

Koinōnia is the deepest kind of "support system" there is. It gives back every John and Jane Doe their face and their name. In New Testament times, it meant that all those rejected and marginalized by ancient cultures — slaves, women, widows, orphans, the weak, the old, the sick, the dying, the unwanted infant — were welcomed into the circle of Christian inclusion. We have our counterparts today.

Koinōnia as this loving life together is grounded, as are the other marks of the church, in the stigmata of Christ's own ministry. He was catalyst of the same life together, within his band of disciples and beyond that in all his relations with others. And driving it deeper, the shared life in Christ and the church has its ultimate source in the very *koinōnia* that God is. The triune God *is* love, the loving unity of Father, Son, and Holy Spirit. Here is a fellowship so together that the three Persons are really One. Thus the trinitarian life-together is a model for the church, with import, as in its other marks, for the world.

The early church's *koinōnia* did not escape the notice of the general public. So the remark of some has been preserved in our lore: "See how those Christians love one another!" Surely this witness cannot be separated from the fact that "day by day the Lord added to their number" (2:47).

Celebrating/Leitourgia. Spending "much time together in the temple" and breaking bread "at home" — what was that all about (2:46)? We're told it had to do with "prayers" and "praising God" (2:42, 47). Praise and prayer over bread point to a very special communion with God as well as with one another, a "holy communion," the heart of Christian worship. We speak of it today as a sacrament: the "celebrating" of the Eucharist, or the Lord's Supper, or Holy Communion, or the Mass, or the Divine Liturgy — many names for the innermost sanctuary of Christian prayer and praise. This celebration, the "work of the people," the central liturgy of the church (with its circumference comprised of other prayer and praise), is another mark of the church, *leitourgia*. An ecumenical consensus has developed that describes this center of Christian worship in trinitarian terms as "thanksgiving to the Father," "memorial of [the real presence of] Christ," and "invocation of the Spirit," with its fruits an intimate "communion of the faithful" sharing a "meal of the Kingdom" that calls them to be servants in the word. (See *Baptism, Eucharist, and Ministry* [Geneva: World Council of Churches, 1982].)

The Reformers focused on two marks of the church, the preaching of the Word and the celebration of the sacraments. Why? They are "objective," done by sinners, and open to sinners. They do not depend on our "subjective" merits, our good works, and thus are a "means of grace" through which an unconditional *agapē* is poured out on us. In this sense the kerygmatic and liturgical/sacramental signs of the Spirit bring the church to be even among sinners, indeed especially for sinners. Yet for the church to be what it was in its New Testament origins, its telling and celebrating will issue in doing and being. Such a church is sanctified by love as well as justified by faith, graced by all the signs of the Holy Spirit, giving evidence of *diakonia* and *koinōnia*, as well as being grounded in kerygma and *leitourgia*.

Gabriel Fackre

Third Sunday of Easter, Year B

First Lesson: Acts 3:12-19
(Psalm 4)
Second Lesson: 1 John 3:1-7
Gospel Lesson: Luke 24:36b-48

Acts 2 describes the marks of the living church in its inner life, and now chapter 3 moves us from that *nurture* of the faithful to their *mission* outside "the gate of the temple" (3:2). The *inreach* of the church issues in *outreach* to the world, both by the power of the Holy Spirit.

The first evidence of the Spirit's work in mission is the care for those in human need, the healing of the lame, a *diakonia* without that is counterpart to the previous chapter's *diakonia* within. Like its Lord who healed the sick on the highways and byways, the Acts church, then and now, does deeds of mercy toward broken bodies outside the temple gate. This claim upon it, and gift to it, come even when the church has "no silver or gold." God works miracles when we are resourceless.

What of the times when we *have* resources? The mandate is no less pressing, and the power no less available. With our silver we can build a hospital in war-torn Laos or send a rescue team to flood-ridden Mozambique, for the Spirit blows where the Spirit will blow. Acts 3 says Christians in mission are recognizable by diaconal acts of mercy however executed, empowered as they are by the Holy Spirit.

But what about a miracle of healing like this one, without benefit of silver and gold? Does it still happen? Of course. Even the skeptic must acknowledge the evidence, whether from medical testimony to the mind-body interface or academic studies of the mysterious correlation of prayer and physical recovery. But Christian faith does not rest its case on the latest secular data or psychosomatic theory. It has its own grounds for hope in the possibilities of wholeness — of body as well as soul — where all human hope fails or in the absence of scientific warrants.

These other grounds have to do with the God who established and honors the world's natural laws but is not bound by them. The freedom and love of the Creator that chose the "new" by bringing creation to be, continues free and loving to do a new thing in the midst of nature's open, not closed, system. Intercessory and petitionary prayer assume just that. The apostles' act here manifests their faith that Jesus risen from the dead defeated the enemy powers, and they are on the run. God gives us, now as then, a glimpse of that defeat in a miracle of the arriving kingdom with its signs of wholeness. Of course, it is the Almighty who chose to leave such signs. Healing is not based on our control of the free God, not even by our most fervent prayers. Nor is that divine freedom enchained to the magic touch of some purported "faith healer," often too ready to take from the gullible their "silver and gold."

Care for broken bodies is the context of our passage, but the primary content takes us to a second sign of the Spirit and mark of the church, now also aimed outward: kerygma. As astonished people gathered to see the deed done, Peter flings the faith joyfully in the air: "The God of Abraham, the God of Isaac, and the God of Jacob, the God of our ancestors has glorified his servant Jesus . . . !" (3:13). So unfolds a second telling of the story in these initial chapters of Acts, this time to those outside the gate. As befits a missionary situation, the telling is done in the idiom of the hearers, the cross set in the midst of Israel's history, "Abraham . . . Isaac . . . ancestors."

After the story is told comes the altar call: "Repent therefore, and turn to God so that your sins may be wiped out" (3:19). Here is the classical call to conversion, the "turn" — the about-face — that happens when the gospel hits home. Scholars commenting on New Testament descriptions of this turnabout distinguish between the *turn away* from old allegiances, *metanoia* as repentance, and the *turn to* God in faith, *epistrophē*. That new posture of turning includes as well a *turn into* the church by baptism and a *turn toward* the neighbor in need. Conversion is a fourfold turning: repent, believe, be baptized, serve.

The conjunction of the Word spoken and the deed done in this Acts evangelism — *action* evangelism — is a lesson in full-orbed mission. While different members of the body of Christ have different gifts (1 Cor. 12), some tellers and others doers, the wholeness of Christian witness beyond the doors of the church requires the partnership of deed and word. In recent times the church has been plagued by the polarization of the doers and the tellers, the advocates of social action or social service as the true mission and the proponents of evangelization by word as the only meaning of outreach. In Jesus' own ministry, and in this Acts model of mission, they are never separated. And in Acts 3 it is the witness of the deed done that opens those present to the Word spoken.

One other current question is raised by some of the words in this lection. Peter says to his audience: "You rejected the holy and Righteous One . . . you killed the Author of life . . ." (3:14-15). Language like this sounds like words heard from the mouths of pogrom makers: "You Jews are Christ-killers!" What about the history of Christian complicity in anti-Semitism and anti-Judaism? And passages that seem to accredit it? And just what is the place of Israel in Christian faith?

Inflammatory rhetoric is no new problem. The Hebrew Bible has its own troubling texts. Injunctions and accounts in Joshua and Deuteronomy speak of a God who calls for the slaughter of the residents of the land to be occupied by the chosen people. Here is the much discussed *ḥerem,* the divine charge to the occupying Israelite army to "kill everything that breathes" (see, e.g., Deut. 13:12-17 or Zech. 14:12). Can these words of Scripture be the Word of God?

An edited Scripture is one way to go. Scissor out these "texts of terror" in both Testaments. Or select only lections which offend no one's sensibilities. Acts 3:14-15 was not excised from the New Revised Standard Version, nor was this lesson removed from the church calendar. Its presence forces us to deal with the issue of genocide, anti-Judaism, and the larger question of the place of Israel in the narrative of redemption.

For the biblical story to be authentic, no chapter can be left out. Censorship of events is disallowed. Historical-critical study helps us see contextual factors that prompt fierce polemics in tense intergroup relations. Literary-critical methods open our eyes to the standard use in ancient times of Oriental hyperbole. Both also press us to learn something from "texts of terror," as Phyllis Trible has argued. Theological exegesis will take us further by searching for a canonical purpose behind the time-bound settings. In this passage, and in larger New Testament teaching, what might be the basic theological points regarding the role of Israel in the Christian scheme of things?

Point one is that the Christian story cannot be told without the Good Friday and Easter that Peter here recounts. *Point two* is that Israel, with whom God has a special relationship, is not the last stop along the way. *Point three* is that in this unfolding drama the Jewish people of God have a permanent place.

Much discussed today is the "antisupersessionist" point three. (See the World Council of Churches, *The Theology of the Churches and the Jewish People: Statements by the World Council of Churches and Its Member Churches* [Geneva: WCC, 1988].) It requires us to read texts like this one by the "analogy of faith," the interpretation of difficult passages in the light of clearer ones, or better, to read every text "canonically," against the background of the whole of Scripture and its regnant refrains. The analogy of faith vis-à-vis Peter's sermon takes us to Paul's struggle with the place and destiny of Israel in Romans 9-11, and in larger sweep to the canonical story itself.

The pain that attended the birth pangs of the early church, the infant's cry as it leaves the womb, is echoed in these verses. Their focus is on the immediacies of a severed umbilical cord, the church's separation from its Jewish mother. To come later was Paul's sober reflection on the unities of mother and child, as well as the difference between them. So his judgment that, in God's mysterious ways, it is for the very sake of the Gentiles that Jews reject Jesus, albeit only for a time (Rom. 11:1-36). This interim alienation did not preclude the finale when "all Israel will be saved" (Rom. 11:26). And in the midst of this already–not yet, the covenant with Israel is not abrogated but continues, for as "regards election they are beloved, for the sake of their ancestors; for the gifts and the calling of God are irrevocable" (Rom. 11:28-29). Paul was able to hold together the confidence in the irrevocability of the covenant with Jewish people and the affirmation that "if you confess with your lips that Jesus is Lord and believe in your heart that God raised him from the dead, you will be saved" (Rom. 10:9), a paradox that led to his conclusion and ours: "O the depth of the riches and wisdom and knowledge of God! How unsearchable are his judgments and how inscrutable his ways!" (Rom. 11:33).

Acts 3:12-19 is a rich passage bringing up a cluster of central themes. It reminds us again of the story we have to tell, and how it can turn people right around. It counsels us to leave out no chapter, but forces us to look into our hearts and use our heads about how we speak about the covenant with Israel and in Christ. And it does not let us forget that there is a world outside that awaits its message, and will look up and listen when that Word of truth is conjoined to the deed of mercy.

Gabriel Fackre

Fourth Sunday of Easter, Year B

First Lesson: Acts 4:5-12
(Psalm 23)
Second Lesson: 1 John 3:16-24
Gospel Lesson: John 10:11-18

Peter and John are in trouble with the power structure, the "rulers of the people and elders" (4:8, 5). The reason given in this passage is a good *deed* done (4:10). Earlier, the provocation that led to arrest is described as the apostles' *word*, "proclaiming that in Jesus there is the resurrection of the dead" (4:2). If the Word is boldly declared in the context of a deed boldly done, the church gets into hot water.

When was the last time we tangled with the principalities and powers of this fallen world? This passage is a reminder that a mark of faithfulness is persecution by establishments that brook no challenge to their hegemony. Where they suspect that another "power" (4:7) is challenging their own entrenched power, or another "name" (4:7) claims to transcend their own, we find a church under the cross. Testify by word or deed that there is "no other name under heaven given among mortals" (4:12), and watch out! But why should we be surprised when such opposition comes? Christ told us to love our enemies. First, we have to make some.

What about this claim that "there is no other name . . . by which we must be saved" (4:12) made in our pluralist twenty-first century? How dare we declare this "scandal of particularity" when we need to get along with the variety of religions on our doorstep? When there is so much good in people of other faiths or even no faith?

The pressures of religious pluralism have evoked a range of theological responses to the foregoing questions. They are reviewed in the exegesis of a parallel text, John 14:6, where the scandal is seen as threefold: Christ as the singular *way* God makes into the world; Christ as the defining *truth* about God; Christ as the giver to the world of a unique saving *life*. Here we explore and evaluate representative explanations of 4:12 that take either an unqualified pluralist position that accommodates to the current culture or an unqualified particularist one unaffected by pluralist questions. And we do so in the light of a "canonical hermeneutic," a theological interpretation of this text in the light of the whole of Scripture.

The offensive particularity of 4:12 is explained by some pluralists as the predictable rhetoric of a new underdog religion, an expression of "survival theology" calculated to shore up the self-confidence of the early Christian believers who were surrounded by other dominant faiths. How else to empower Christians at that time to stand fast in an alien culture and even to encourage them to penetrate it with zeal? To have a saving secret unknown to these multitudes enables Christians to smile on their follies, and to go among them with evangelistic fervor. Today, however, the language of 4:12 must be read as *metaphorical* rather than *metaphysical*, words used as a symbol of ultimate commitment, not as a straightforward assertion that salvation really comes only through Christ.

This pluralist view holds that Christians can believe that Christ is true *for them* in making sense of *their* world. But other religions, it is argued, have the same right to say that their adherents have found their faith meaningful *for them* and for their world. "Different strokes for different folks." While we understand that our religious forebears in survival situations used exclusive language to define themselves, their metaphors are inappropriate for our pluralist world. They have to be replaced by theologies and practices that make no universal truth claims for our own religious particularities.

At the other end of the spectrum of theological response to modern religious pluralism is an unqualified particularism. Not rhetoric but reality is what goes on here in Peter's stark words. They are to be understood and asserted literally, not figuratively, both yesterday and today. That means every person before he or she dies must confess Christ as his or her personal Lord and Savior in order to be saved from the wrath of God. Peter wanted to rescue sinners from hellfire and damnation. They had not heard of the one way out, and he was telling them what it was. That passion for souls sent missionaries and evangelists on their way throughout Christian history, growing the church in every land. And it is this same unvarnished truth that must be told today. So a sharp particularism is here juxtaposed to an accommodating pluralism.

These two interpretations part ways on whether we try to fit Christianity into the ongoing human situation, on the one hand, or flatly assert a divine truth regardless of questions posed by the current culture, on the other. The polarization between the two is reminiscent of fierce debates in the early centuries about the status of Jesus. One side, taking its signals from its surrounding culture, insisted that while the brightest and best, he was just a human being like us. And the other, convinced of his unworldliness, declared him to be only divine. So the earliest partisanships — humanizing Ebionites pitted against divinizing Docetics, followed by comparable disputants with increasingly subtle Christologies in the succeeding centuries, adoptionism versus modalism, Arianism versus Apollinarianisn, Nestorianism versus Monophysitism. Finally came the call for a defining colloquy, the Council of Chalcedon in 451, which rejected the history of half-truths and asserted a formula shared now by the church ecumenical: Christ is one undivided Person in two distinct natures, human and divine.

Is there a counterpart to the Chalcedonian formula in the christological controversies of our own time? Can we relate the scandalous particularity of Acts 4:12 to our culture's questions but not capitulate to its pluralist ideologies?

Acts 4:12 is not a foreign body in the New Testament, for it states in terse terms the teaching found throughout concerning the singular saving deed of God in Jesus Christ. The early Christians declared, "Something new has happened, and we must get this Word out!" Their passion and excitement about the good news rises from this particularity. The scandal is twofold: (1) Christ is the very hinge of history; the grand narrative turns on this chapter. The rebel creation is finally reconciled with its Creator in the life, death, and resurrection of Jesus Christ. There is "no other name under heaven" by which the world is saved from sin, evil, and death. (2) This affirmation of "objective soteriology" is inseparable from its companion, "subjective soteriology," the reception by faith alone through grace alone of Christ alone (the Reformation *solas*). A hundred New Testament passages echo John 3:16, which puts the objective and subjective together: "God so loved the world that he gave his only Son, so that everyone who believes in him may not perish but may have eternal life."

Does this scandal mean that the billions who have not even heard the Name will perish eternally? Does it preclude any grace being found in other religions? These are the questions of our pluralist times. A hermeneutic that reads Acts 4:12 in the setting of the whole of Scripture can no more settle for an imperial exclusivism than for a postmodern relativism. An interpretation of the verse against this canonical background will affirm these things:

1. In Acts, and throughout Scripture, a thread of teaching appears which declares that God "has not left himself without a witness" (Acts 14:17) among those who have not heard the name of Jesus. The witness is given to others "so that they would search for God and perhaps grope for him and find him" (Acts 17:27). A "common grace" is at work in human history, grounded in the universal rainbow covenant with the world, one that both Christians and Jews call "the Noachic covenant" (Gen. 9:12-16). While not saving the rebel world from sin — for Christians, Christ is the only name under heaven for that deed and deliverance — this divine generosity gives a light "which enlightens everyone" (John 1:9), enough illumination of the good, the holy, and the true, and enough power to pursue them, to sustain creation on its journey toward both the Center and the End. The great religions of the world can be instruments of this grace. Christians discern where and when the signs of the holy, good, and true are to be found through the lens of Christ. And because all such gifts have their origin in the triune God, this universal grace itself is christic as well as common, traceable to Christ's reconciling Person and Work.

2. If our salvation is by the three great *solas* — a grace alone that brings Christ alone to faith alone — then a gracious God will deny to no one the offer of that gift. If so, can the pursuit of the last and the least who have not heard this Word by the Hound of Heaven be confined to earth's options or closed off by death's door? Evidence of a no to this question is found in the later writings of the New Testament, faced as they were by the first indications of multitudes never to be reached by the gospel. The proclamation of the gospel "even to the dead" (1 Pet. 4:6 and 3:18-20), echoed in the Apostles' Creed in Christ's "descent to the dead," is a way early Christians sought to hold together both the divine particularity and God's universal generosity.

Acts 4:5-12 is a teaching moment in tough love. Are we up to going against the stream? In resisting the regnant powers and principalities by loyalty to the Name that is above every name, and taking the consequences? In affirming the scandals of his particularity and universality in the face of the conventional wisdoms of the day?

Gabriel Fackre

Second Sunday of Easter, Year B

First Lesson: Acts 4:32-35
(Psalm 133)
Second Lesson: 1 John 1:1–2:2
Gospel Lesson: John 20:19-31

This little snapshot of the early church looks for all the world more like something from fictional Lake Wobegon than anything anywhere in the real world. At least at first glance, Luke's summary descriptions here and at the end of chapter 2 seem so ideal, so fanciful, that some have suggested that he must have made them up.

Luke pictures those early followers of Jesus living in what might seem like their own perfect little world. They meet together regularly like one big happy family. You can see them greeting each other as they gather to listen to the apostles' teaching. Big smiles, warm embraces, and cheery hellos characterize the daily meetings. As they gather, you'd almost think they were best friends who hadn't seen each other in months. In Luke's picture they are "one in heart and mind."

The crowd quiets down as one of the apostles begins to speak. He talks about Jesus, about the day Jesus died and how, as far as he was concerned, hope died along with him, and then how the risen Lord appeared to them on that first Easter. And then he goes on to teach them the things he and the others had learned from Jesus: "He's not just some dead rabbi," he tells them, eyes gleaming. "He's definitely alive." And as he talks, he seems to hold them in the palm of his hand as they hang on his every word. The apostles continued to witness to the resurrection of the Lord Jesus with great power, the power of the Holy Spirit.

After the teaching session there's a potluck supper. People seem to have outdone themselves in bringing things to please and delight the others. Laughter fills the room and eyes dance as people luxuriate in each other's company and in animated conversation: "Did you hear about how God healed that blind man?" somebody says. "My neighbor was practically raised from her deathbed when James prayed for her," reports another, "and now the whole family has begun to follow the Lord." And the potluck ends with a joyful celebration using bread and wine to commemorate how Jesus died on the cross to save them and rose from the dead to bring them to heaven. And as people eat the bread and drink the wine, you can tell they believed that the risen Jesus is actually there as they eat and drink. Luke calls them believers, people who had faith in the risen Jesus.

Yes, in Luke's picture those early Christians are like one big happy family. If somebody needs something, they fall all over each other to be the first to give. Nobody claims that the things they own are reserved for their own personal use. None of them is in dire need because they share like family. This does not mean that there were no differences in income or social standing, but that people with disposable property did not hesitate to sell various items among their holdings and to bring the money to the apostles for distribution. By the sound of it, it is almost too good to be true. A community pulsing with the love of God and percolating with the power of the Holy Spirit.

If Luke chooses to emphasize the more praiseworthy features of the early Christian community, it is not because he is in denial about the problems. In the very next chapter of his report to Theophilus, Ananias and Sapphira, two members of the community just described, conspire to lie and cheat to bolster their reputations and end up dying as they fraudulently lay the proceeds of a property sale at the feet of the apostles. Perhaps Luke chooses to paint the picture of the early community he does here both to describe it and, inasmuch as he pictures it at its best, to recommend it. Here is the way the church works when things are going as they should. And who in the church today has not experienced a similar shifting of perspective when one day the church seems to conform so well to Luke's picture and only days later seems almost unrecognizable to it. In recommending his airbrushed picture, Luke means to affirm the church as a community in which the love of Jesus mediated by the Spirit made life-changing difference in the lives of the people associated with it.

Some have pointed to the communitarian economic arrangements here and at the end of chapter 2 as biblical endorsement of a communist approach to economics: "from each according to his (or her) ability, to each according to his (or her) need." Voices to the contrary have pointed to the economic hardship signaled in Paul's letters as evidence of the wrongheadedness of this communitarian approach. "No wonder," they say, "the Gentile churches had to take collections for the church in Jerusalem. It only stands to reason." But the offering of those who sell part of what they have and lay it at the apostles' feet for the sake of others who are more needy is not a complete renunciation of individual ownership of property. Rather, these activities find their roots in the Torah, in which God is the ultimate owner and people are entrusted with his gifts (e.g., Ps. 24). The activity of the early church also has roots in the Torah commands to remember the needy (Deut. 15:4) and to bring tithes (Lev. 27:30).

Perhaps one of the reasons Luke's picture of the early Christian community seems overly ideal is that the church, at least in North America, has fallen sway to a kind of cool individualism with loose associations and weaker commitments. And even when the church rises above such superficial individualism, people would often be inclined to characterize too many churches as groups of genuinely nice people who do not seem to make much of a difference in the outside world one way or another. The church at its best may be a warm, caring group of people, but violence, sadness, and pain grip the world outside it.

Henri Nouwen points to the novel *Less Than Zero* by Bret Easton Ellis as one poignant picture of modern life outside the church. The novel offers a portrait of sex, drugs, and violence among the teenage children of superrich Los Angeles entertainers. Nouwen says that "the cry that arises from behind all of this decadence is clearly: 'Is there anybody who loves me; is there anybody who really cares? Is there anyone who wants to stay home for me? Is there anyone who wants to be with me when I am not in control, when I feel like crying? Is there anybody who can hold me and give me a sense of belonging?'" (*In the Name of Jesus* [New York: Crossroad, 1989], pp. 21-22). Luke portrays the early church as a first-century Christian community living out a strong affirmative answer to these questions. One wonders if the community that characterizes the contemporary church is less strongly affirmative in its answer to them. Sometimes it seems that the Holy Spirit that pulsated in and animated those early Christians has slowly seeped out of the church over the intervening centuries.

And yet even today there are lively pockets of the church that look every bit the spitting image of its ancestor pictured in Acts 4. God is still using those who follow his Son Jesus to save the world. God uses the love, joy, and peace of those who follow his Son Jesus to extend the good news of the gospel. God uses people whom he fills with the grace of Jesus Christ to pour out his love upon his world. God uses those who follow Jesus to answer Nouwen's questions raised so poignantly in the turmoil of today's world and by so many. Those of us gripped by the power and love of Jesus answer yes to those questions. God loves you more deeply than you will ever know; God cares. And we will show you the love of God and the love of his Son Jesus as God's love spills out from our lives into yours.

You see, the work that God is doing through the church is not just a pipe dream; it's a dream coming true. God uses the church to draw people into the world of his love. As the church invites hurting people into its community, God continues to pour out his grace and to witness to the resurrection of his Son.

John M. Rottman

Second Sunday of Easter, Year C

First Lesson: Acts 5:27-32
(Psalm 118:14-29)
Second Lesson: Revelation 1:4-8
Gospel Lesson: John 20:19-31

The most familiar verse in this passage, verse 29, "We must obey God rather than men," is not necessarily the most important, and may indeed be the one most fraught with danger for the preacher. Much has been made in recent decades of Bonhoeffer's concern that the preacher beware of cheap grace; here we meet the similar threat of cheap obedience. It is too easy to justify some posture, political or ecclesial, as "prophetic" simply because it appears to fly in the face of established authorities of some kind. We must, however, remember that prophets are rarely so designated by themselves and, more important, what the nature of the obedience is to which the Christian is called. Crucial therefore is the wider context of the passage.

Noteworthy is the atmosphere of fear which appears to pervade both the world of the apostles and that of the authorities. The apostles and those who have been convinced by the apostolic preaching are now clearly divided from the mass of the people. The latter have high regard for those who are walking the new way — still, we must be careful to note, a way within rather than outside the Jewish faith — but do not dare to join them (vv. 12f. above). Our part of the narrative follows a double arrest of the apostles, who have been taken into custody for the second time after a miraculous release from prison (v. 19). As later events were to show, those arrested were in danger of execution. Politically, the situation is tense and threatening.

On the other hand, the Jewish authorities also are manifestly fearful. For fear of the people, they have been careful not to use force in arresting

550

the apostles (v. 27). They are particularly anxious about the effect of the preaching upon their standing. "You have filled Jerusalem with your teaching and are determined to make us guilty of this man's blood." Here, great care must be exercised in speaking of this passage. We are emerging from a period of Christian history when we are aware that the charges of bloodguilt upon the Jews for their part in the crucifixion of Jesus have been both politically disastrous and theologically wrong. We have in this passage an encounter between two forms of Jewishness. The arresting authorities are Sadducees: those who, according to Matthew 22:23, deny the resurrection. Their accused are Jews who base their teaching on the resurrection of the one put to death by those same authorities.

It is at this place that we can see clearly in what the determination of the apostles to obey God consists: not in a political protest or moral stand but in preaching the resurrection of Jesus. It is the proclamation of Jesus which is at the heart of their obedience and of the offense it caused — and indeed, causes still, sometimes as much within the church as without. The cause of their arrest is no more and no less than this: they attest God's action in raising Jesus from the dead. And that brings us to the heart of the theological importance of this passage, about whose historical place something must first be said. It is sometimes claimed that the speeches in Acts represent an early and perhaps "low" Christology. Jesus is not being presented as the divine Son of God, but as a human figure. That, of course, is evidence for the integrity of the things recorded here, but has no bearing on the rightness of later developments which went on to draw the conclusion that this is not just an exalted man, but also and at the same time the one come from the Father to be the Savior of the world.

What the passage, with its concentration on the human career of Jesus, enables the preacher to do is to say something about the theological significance of the human Jesus. The writer of Acts is, however, blessedly far from the view of Jesus' humanity held by the priest-scholars in the academy who think the solution of the riddle of the New Testament Jesus can be solved by historical investigation and democratic votes. His human and historical importance consists for this writer in what *happened to* him. The authorities killed him; God raised and exalted him. One of the burdens of this second volume of Luke's work is that what happened in and with the church is part of the gospel. It is God who is responsible for what happens with Jesus and with the proclamation of his death and exaltation, God who sees to it that the message is embodied in a people as it spreads outward beyond the place of Jesus' death and resurrection.

Full attention must be paid to both of those words "raised" and "exalted," which are not synonyms. The resurrection is that divine act in which God refuses to allow death to determine the outcome of Jesus' ministry, but rather shows it to be the heart of his saving action. The description of the cross as a tree is repeated in 10:39 and 13:29, and alludes to the degrading of the corpse associated with judicial execution (see Deut. 21:22-23). The resurrection is therefore the giving of life out of the depths of a death of utter rejection, and connects with Luke's view of the gospel as the gift of life (see v. 20: "the full message of this new life"). The new life given to Jesus is the basis of that proclaimed by the apostles. The resurrection is succeeded by the ascension — which is clearly important for Luke, as for other New Testament authors (Luke 24:51-53; Acts 1:9-11). It is this that assures the church of the continuing significance of the human Jesus, a significance spelled out in detail in the Letter to the Hebrews. At the center here, as there, is the priesthood of Jesus, and Peter's speech gives clear expression to its meaning: this is the Ruler and Savior whose meaning is to "give repentance and forgiveness of sins to Israel."

It is again surely another measure of the historical integrity of this text that it does not anticipate the discovery, enabled according to later chapters by the Holy Spirit, that the new life is also for those beyond the people of Israel. The preacher may make something of the later development, but must surely make very clear — as Paul does in Romans — that the gospel is first for Israel, and only then for Gentiles. The Gentile church is chosen to be God's people alongside and after Israel. The notion, however, that we are here at the heart of a debate within Israel is here reinforced. The dispute is over the way Israel is truly to be God's holy people. It is noteworthy that in the passage following ours it is the Pharisee Gamaliel who implicitly supports the apostles, recommending that they leave the outcome to God's judgment. Luke's message in this book is that in the spread of the gospel message to Rome, the center of empire, God's vindication of Jesus is demonstrated.

It is the heart of Luke's message that what happened in the first decades of the church was the result of the work of the Holy Spirit. That is why, while studying this passage, we can wait patiently for the later outcome. And, as the final verse of our passage indicates, Luke's theology of the Spirit is somewhat more sophisticated than is sometimes noticed. The use in chapter 2 of the cosmic imagery of fire in expressing the giving of the Spirit can be misleading if we fail to notice that Luke tells us it is *imagery* — "what seemed to be tongues of fire," literally "tongues as of fire" (Acts 2:3). The Holy Spirit is here most definitely personal, as the *witness* to what the apostles are saying. (See also Acts 10:19; 11:12 for references to the Spirit speaking.) Acts is written by one who is confident that the Spirit guides the fledgling church in what she does.

For us, things are rather different, for our guidance is mediated by the written text in a way that makes direct appeal to the Spirit more complicated, possibly more dangerous, and our preaching must take that into account. This passage shows us that the integrity of the church's teaching derives from the attention it pays to Jesus, the risen and ascended way to life with God the Father. It is that which must shape our preaching, and we must leave the Spirit to contribute his witness as and when God wills.

Colin E. Gunton

Fifth Sunday of Easter, Year A

First Lesson: Acts 7:55-60
(Psalm 31:1-5, 15-16)
Second Lesson: 1 Peter 2:2-10
Gospel Lesson: John 14:1-14

One of Luke's chief purposes in writing Acts is to show that the Holy Spirit is the main agent of what takes place in the years after Jesus' death and resurrection. Stephen, the first martyr, has been among the first truly to act in the light of the promise of Luke 12:11, that "When you are brought before synagogues, rulers and authorities, do not worry about how you will defend yourselves . . . for the Holy Spirit will teach you. . . ." In the previous chapter, Stephen was the first named of those deacons chosen to free the apostles from other tasks for the ministry of the word of God. Yet — and this is characteristic New Testament evidence that there need be no fixed roles in ministry — it is the ministry of the word to which events call him, and for whose proclamation he is, as our passage begins, about to die.

Having inspired his long speech — whose theology has been noted to bear similarities to that of the Epistle to the Hebrews — the Spirit now prepares Stephen for the ultimate test. He sees a vision of the "Son of Man," Jesus' self-description which is rarely used outside the Gospels, and uniquely here in Acts. The reason for its use here seems to be that Luke is, as the later verses show, drawing a parallel between the death of Stephen and that of Jesus. The point for us is that it is a trinitarian vision: in and through the Spirit, Stephen sees the ascended Son at the right hand of God the Father. (When the New Testament uses God *simpliciter*, it is usually with reference to God the Father.)

The allusion to the ascension, which is clearly important to Luke, as to other New Testament authors (Luke 24:51-53; Acts 1:9-11), brings out another parallel to the interests of the Letter to the Hebrews, which is oriented to the ascension as the basis of Jesus' continuing priesthood. The hearers know what Stephen is claiming, and that is the reason for their precipitate and murderous action. The vision of the Son of Man is a symbol — one meant to be taken seriously and realistically — for Jesus' joint rule with God the Father. In that, it clearly ascribes to him an equality of status with God. The charge against Stephen, as against Jesus before him, was in the first place of blasphemy, but we have been told that it was *false* witnesses who accused him of "speaking against this holy place and against the law" (Acts 6:11ff.). In fact, in his speech he does not speak against the temple and the law, but rather reminds his people of their disobedience and false worship. Where previously they were merely furious at him (v. 54), they now truly believe that he has blasphemed, and his death follows as night follows day. By effectively making Jesus equal with God, Stephen has far overstepped the mark.

And it was not only this particular mob who were to believe that. The confession of Jesus as the sole vehicle of divine rule is what seems to have been at the heart of the persecution of Christians in the New Testament period and beyond. The writer of Revelation attributes the persecution he describes and prophesies about to the church's faithful witness to Jesus, while later refusal to sacrifice to the Roman emperor is thought to have been the cause at once of persecution and of the growth of the church. There is only one Lord, and anything impugning his Lordship threatens the very integrity of the gospel. The confession of Jesus' divine being is one of the articles of faith by which the church stands or falls, because without it the way lies open to worshiping gods other than the Lord made known in Scripture. It can be ventured that it is the modern Western church's weak Christology which founds the weakness of her worship and witness, and that will only be repaired by a return to the centrality of the confession of Jesus' eternal Lordship.

As a matter of fact, it appears to be a general truth that those who are faithful in times of persecution attract both admiration and converts.

Tertullian famously said that the blood of the martyrs is the seed of the church, and our passage shows wherein the specifically Christian truth of the observation consists. Stephen does two things which define the kind of martyr he is. First, he prays to the Lord he has glimpsed and asks him to receive his spirit. And then he shows that he still is imbued with the Spirit of Jesus, for, like his Lord, he asks forgiveness for those who have stoned him.

The problem of the imitation of Christ is a difficult one, for it can lead to all kinds of anxious straining to be like him that encourages an unhealthy self-preoccupation — that very turning in upon ourselves from which the gospel frees us. The heart of the matter, it is often argued, is not in imitating Christ, which may appear to lean too much on our own efforts, but in being so conformed to him in the Spirit that a Christlike pattern of life follows. We cannot, however, escape the fact that Christians are called to imitate Christ, for in Stephen we meet a prime example of faithful witness which is also an imitation. In 1 Corinthians 4:12, 16 Paul makes a related point when he tells the church to imitate Christ in answering curse with blessing, while Ephesians 5:1 urges imitation of God in a life of love. That is precisely what Stephen does here in following his Lord in asking forgiveness for those who have killed him.

It may be that it is the combination of witness to Christ and imitation of him that provides the key: only by witnessing — rather than anxiously attempting to be like him — are we able to reproduce the pattern of his life in our relations with others. At any rate, the story of Stephen gives the preacher a prime opportunity to explore what following Christ might involve. But this should never be attempted without due attention to the part played by God the Spirit. The story ends with a verse that is not included in our lection, that the young Saul was there approving, though not apparently participating in, the stoning. Luke says nothing else at this stage, but Stephen's death appears to have been one of the things preparing the way for Saul's conversion. Thus does the Spirit work, redemptively turning evil into ultimate blessing, as he did in raising the crucified Jesus from the dead.

Colin E. Gunton

Fifth Sunday of Easter, Year B

First Lesson: Acts 8:26-40
(Psalm 22:25-31)
Second Lesson: 1 John 4:7-21
Gospel Lesson: John 15:1-8

N o one is coming to hear us preach a lesson in geography, so we do well to get location out of the way quickly. The key figure in this story is identified as being from Ethiopia. From ancient clues we deduce that he was serving in what today is the Sudan. His partner in the plot — we hear nothing of the ox-driver — is the disciple named Philip. An angel stirs Philip to go southward to the road from Jerusalem to Gaza. Think of Gaza as one thinks of gas stations at the edge of deserts: "Last chance for 150 miles...." After Gaza: desert.

The geography lesson ends with Philip being "snatched away" and finding himself at Azotus or Ashdod, north of Gaza, a convenient location for him to keep on spreading good news, which he did.

Nor do people come to hear an anthropological speculation: Was the Ethiopian a Jew? He had been observing a Jewish festival. Was he black? People positioned to serve as treasurer to Candace, the queen — queens ran things in Ethiopia — should likely have been black, as Ethiopians tended to be. That means he would have been a "God-fearing Gentile," at the margins of Judaism.

While we are ruling out items that inspire curiosity but not the engagement of the heart, it is time to bring up anatomy and physiology. While no one likely came for a lecture on this, it cannot fail to inspire curiosity. Was the eunuch a eunuch? Most courtiers in Ethiopia would have been castrated and possibly dismembered. That would rule him out from ever being fulfilled in Judaism, thanks to scriptural rulings-out of such from any place closer than the Court of the Gentiles in Jerusalem. But eunuch was often also a title for people who served in the court. Luke, the author of Acts, is not interested in all that.

After dismissing geography, ethnography, and anatomy, the wise preacher will revisit the scene and tease out some meanings associated with each. Here is where hearers come in.

Thus geography: clearly, this story is here to help us realize how we got to be part of this story. Gaza is not Jerusalem and Ethiopia is far from Jerusalem, yet the lead character gets reached, thanks to an angel, "the Spirit," and their ambassador, Philip. Where would we be were it not for their reach toward us. And however far away we start, as the baptism of the eunuch shows, we get to be fully accepted, central to the plot, no longer on the margins.

Anthropology, race, and more: this text, like another story involving Peter and the Gentile Cornelius in Acts, says boldly if not colloquially, "Y'all come." And here we are, in front of a scroll or book and a preacher, a kind of hitchhiker on our wagons, wherever we are going. The good news we hear today is for everyone; hop aboard.

Anatomy and physiology: it is not likely that people in range of our voices have been mutilated or hold courtly position. It is likely that everyone out there knows of something or other about themselves — their jobs, status, calling, physical condition, being shunned — that has them on the margins. We are all marginal, and eager to be let in.

The people in range of these words will clearly identify at a key point in the story. Here is where the word "happened" begins to be of help. Conveniently for Luke, who wants to show that the good news of Christ is universal, the character "happens to be" different. From his angle, Philip just happened to have come along. And, think of this, the seeker in that chariot just happened to be reading aloud, so Philip could overhear him. Most people then and there read aloud, so that is not too remarkable, but it helps the story along. Because the man just happened to be reading a text from Isaiah that was becoming central to the Jesus story, the Christ plot, the good news. And, here we identify, he happened to need help.

Proverbially, men ("guys") don't ask for directions when lost, but upon being prompted, this man welcomes help. We hear echoes here of the story about disciples on the way to Emmaus. There a stranger converses with them and finds they have not made much success of connecting the weekend event, the death of Jesus, with the Scriptures that foresee it. They get help.

Call what "just happens" luck, providence, coincidence, a stylistic reworking of complex events by simplifier Luke, or anything else: we hearers of the word can now identify with what is going on.

There is no way, no way, that an Ethiopian could be reading about a sheep led to the slaughter and a lamb being silent as having anything to do with what has made Jerusalem become astir. "Do you understand what you are reading?" "How can I, unless someone guides me." Luke and the earliest Christians, by seeing Jesus as the sheep being slaughtered and the lamb being silent, help us make connections with a story of loving sacrifice. The preacher who has studied the texts can serve as a guide to help the more ca-

557

sual, the less learned, or those not called to preach find their way into plots that come from long ago but are as fresh as tomorrow. For that matter, if an hour of worship does no more than quicken curiosity so that a congregation develops background to a text, readiness to probe its meanings, it has helped hearers along their way.

They may not get as far as fast as did Philip's one-person congregation. In fact, so compelling were the text and its interpreter that the eunuch sees everything, as if at once. And at once, in his newfound faith, he knows something: he wants to be part of the story, an initiate. Telling such a story might undercut the effort of early Christians to prepare people strenuously for the anything-but-casual act of baptism. And here it all seems too easy.

Congregants who have contemporary Bible translations with them might look at a footnote whose small print will say after the man asks for baptism, "Other ancient authorities add . . . *And Philip said, 'If you believe with all your heart, you may [be baptized]. And he replied, 'I believe that Jesus Christ is the Son of God.'*" That probable intrusion was designed to keep rigorous-minded leaders happy; it tidies up the process.

Luke, however, does not concern himself with such details. He takes the story of a foreign official heading home and a disciple who is guided into being a hitchhiker and speaks to us today. It just "happens" — isn't the lectionary a kind of set of happenings to those who will preach and hear the texts? — that we are where the eunuch was. By that I don't mean needing guidance, though we do. Meaning instead: positioned to hear the heart of the story.

The question about the slaughtered sheep, the silent lamb comes out: "About whom, may I ask you, does the prophet say this, about himself or about someone else?" Philip, aware that the pace in the ox wagon will be slow, the road bumpy, and the desert dreary, takes his time by speaking, and "starting with this scripture," proclaiming to him "the good news about Jesus."

That's it. At last we find what this text is about and what we are to do with it and to let it do to us and the congregation. At last we move from the margins to the center, from being curious to being passionately involved. This is what we came to hear.

The text is quoted from the Greek translation of the Hebrew in Isaiah 53:7-8. Not often does the New Testament cite it directly, but it is clear that the early believers who would be reading Luke were making a clear identification between Jesus and the sheep, the lamb, the slaughter. Isaiah says interesting things just before and just after these words, and almost certainly they would help guide the conversation. But Luke has enough here to advance his story and our engagement with it.

What it comes to is that Christ's suffering did not occur so that disciples could ride in wagons next to a higher-up being jostled by speed bumps. What is clear is that Christ's suffering, and belief in the value of that self-giving instead, is the means whereby the burdens of sin and error and lack of guidance get lifted and their bonds broken, so that we are free. Justice did not win the day the lamb was silent, and the sheep was humiliated and then killed. The main point this day is not the *where, what, when, how,* and *why* of it all, but the *who.* Connect the sheep with the promises of God and the life and gift of Christ, and you will have met needs of soul and spirit that long outlast issues of geography in the ancient world.

The eunuch, after baptism and learning, "went on his way rejoicing." We will have missed the point of this story and this day if we are not participants in helping send people "on their way rejoicing."

Martin E. Marty

Third Sunday of Easter, Year C

First Lesson: Acts 9:1-6, (7-20)
(Psalm 30)
Second Lesson: Revelation 5:11-14
Gospel Lesson: John 21:1-19

In the lectionary, parentheses can be dangerous. They suggest that the verses contained within them are optional for the preacher. On this particular Sunday, however, nothing could be further from the truth. The theological richness of this story requires the inclusion of verses 7-20 (and even 21-22). When these verses are included, the story embodies the movement of the season of Easter toward its climax at Pentecost. Just as Jesus' resurrection moves to the outpouring of the Holy Spirit and the mission of the church, so Saul's encounter with the risen Christ leads him to the community of faith, the gift of the Spirit, and his mission in the world.

If the preacher were to conclude with verse 6, these important theological realities would be short-circuited. The text might simply become the source of a sermon about dramatic, individual conversion. Saul's "mountaintop" encounter with the risen Christ, as critical and transformative as that is, could become an end in itself, apart from the mission to which Saul is called through his experience and apart from the community which interprets that mission to Saul and ordains him to his work.

The text itself makes this reality abundantly clear. At the end of verse 6, following his "mountaintop experience," Saul is stuck. He's blind; he's helpless; he's dependent not only on the living Christ but also on other people to help him take the next step. Rather than entering Damascus in power, he must be led into the city by others, and there he must wait for someone to come and tell him what to do. Indeed, the last word of verse 6 in the NRSV is "do." The living Christ is calling Paul to *do* something — to carry out the mission to the Gentiles, as we learn later in the story. The key theological focus here is not conversion, but calling (see Krister Stendahl's important essay, "Paul among Jews and Gentiles," in *Paul among Jews and Gentiles and Other Essays* [Philadelphia: Fortress, 1976], esp. pp. 7-23).

Undoubtedly, Paul's experience on the Damascus road was transformative. He moves from being a persecutor of those on the Way to becoming one of them, who will himself suffer persecution (see v. 16; also vv. 23 and 29, where both Jews and Hellenists almost immediately seek his death). He changes from being a person opposed to the Way of Jesus to one who serves Jesus as Lord (though we should *not* view this as a conversion from Judaism to Christianity; Stendahl, pp. 7-23). He turns from violence to preaching as the means for furthering his convictions. (Paul himself highlights this transformation in Galatians 1:13-16.) Paul is transformed by his experience on the Damascus road; such is the power of an encounter with the living Christ.

The purpose of this encounter, however, is the mission to the Gentiles. At its deepest level Acts 9:1-20 is Saul's call story. The text — indeed, the living Christ — is not primarily concerned about Saul's "inner life" in any psychological sense. The focus is not on the "introspective conscience" that characterizes our individualistic Western culture (Stendahl, pp. 7-23). The emphasis, rather, is on Paul's calling to be the apostle to the Gentiles — a calling and a mission that come not from human wisdom or efforts, but from the initiative of God in the resurrected Christ. The living Christ has something for Paul to *do,* and Paul is dependent on the community of faith to interpret his "mountaintop experience" and clarify his calling.

Consequently, the bulk of the text (vv. 7-19) focuses on, as Calvin puts it, "the ministry of the church" (*The Acts of the Apostles, 1–13,* trans. John W. Fraser and W. J. G. McDonald, ed. David W. Torrance and Thomas F.

Torrance, Calvin's Commentaries [Edinburgh: Oliver & Boyd, 1965], p. 261). Paul has encountered the living Christ, but now he waits, blind and helpless, dependent on the community of faith — the very community he had persecuted — to tell him the next step to take. This community is represented by the amazing figure of Ananias. The Lord appears to Ananias and tells him to go to Saul. Ananias, knowing Saul has the authority to bind him and put him in prison, is understandably hesitant. But the Lord persists, telling Ananias that Paul is a chosen instrument to "bring my name before Gentiles and kings and before the people of Israel" (v. 15). Demonstrating extraordinary courage and faithfulness, Ananias, an "ordinary" Christian, goes to Saul to tell him his mission and "ordain" him to that work through the laying on of hands and the gift of the Holy Spirit.

This development is extraordinary. Saul's mountaintop encounter with the living Lord finds its completion only through the ministry of an "ordinary" member of the Christian community who helps him discern the shape of his calling. God uses not just the dramatic experiences of faith, but the ongoing life of the Christian community, to shape our calling and mission. In fact, the text suggests that "mountaintop experiences" by themselves are inadequate. They require the interpretation of a community grounded in the life of faith. A "call" is not simply a matter between "me and Jesus," but something that requires the discernment, confirmation, and direction of the community of faith.

From day one Saul learns that the Christian life is not an individualistic or isolated undertaking. He learns that as a believer he is part of a community larger than himself and a mission greater than his own vision. He learns that he is dependent on the wisdom, discernment, and faithfulness of other members of that community as he pursues his ministry. It is thus not surprising that Paul's lifework would involve building up churches rather than simply "converting" individuals. And it is not surprising that Paul would later write so eloquently about the community of faith as a body with many parts, each part dependent on the others for its full flourishing (see 1 Cor. 12:14-31; Rom. 12:3-8). Such was Paul's experience from the first day of his calling.

The final verses of the text provide a remarkable description of the life of this community. The description begins with Ananias's first words to Saul. Going beyond anything the Lord had told him to do in his vision, Ananias enters the house, lays hands on Saul, and calls him "Brother." There are few more dramatic pictures of the reconciling power of the risen Christ. The persecuted Ananias, in the power of the risen Christ, calls his former persecutor "Brother." In Jesus, that is the kind of reconciled commu-

561

nity that is possible. And for the rest of his ministry Paul will emphasize this reconciliation between "Jew and Greek, slave and free, male and female." Not only Paul's life is changed by his encounter with the risen Christ, but the very character of the community itself begins to undergo a transformation.

What follows is nothing less than an "ordination" service, complete with baptism and, possibly, the Lord's Supper. Ananias lays hands on Saul, and Saul regains his sight and receives the gift of the Holy Spirit. Thanks to Ananias, Saul not only sees the next step to take, but he receives the power to pursue the mission to which God has called him. The intimate connection between the risen Christ, the community of faith, and the work of the Holy Spirit is highlighted, reminding believers of the movement of the season of Easter to its climax at Pentecost, when the Spirit is poured out on the disciples and the church begins its mission to the world.

Next, Saul is baptized; he is formally initiated and welcomed into the community of faith. He dies to his old life and is raised to "walk in newness of life" (Rom. 6:4). Following his baptism, Saul shares food — possibly the Eucharist — with the community, embodying the intimacy of shared life in the body of Christ. In the deep soil of the community — ordination, baptism, meals, worship, fellowship — Saul regains his strength and receives the nurture that prepares him to pursue the mission to which he has been called. Finally, the text concludes with the beginning of Saul's mission, toward which the entire call story has been moving: "and immediately he began to proclaim Jesus in the synagogues, saying, 'He is the Son of God'" (v. 20).

The living Christ is "loose" in the world, encountering people and shaping the community of faith, often in surprising ways, for our mission in the world. In the presence of the living Christ persecutors become allies who share the suffering of the persecuted. "Ordinary" believers provide the gift of discernment. Enemies become brothers and sisters. Violence is replaced by witness. Ordination, baptism, and Eucharist become vehicles for the transforming and empowering work of the Spirit. And the Word is lived and proclaimed "in Jerusalem, in all Judea and Samaria, and to the ends of the earth" (Acts 1:8).

Charles L. Campbell

Fourth Sunday of Easter, Year C

First Lesson: Acts 9:36-43
(Psalm 23)
Second Lesson: Revelation 7:9-17
Gospel Lesson: John 10:22-30

"Tabitha, get up."
So Tabitha got up.

Luke, the master storyteller, makes it sound so simple and direct. The woman named "Gazelle" died. She was really dead. Peter prayed and commanded her to get up. So she sat up. "He showed her to be alive."

What is preachable — or able to be listened to — and what is less likely to be so, in this story? What will advance faith in the good news and what will run the risk of being turned into an exercise of preacherly dexterity, evasion, verbal sleight of hand or time wasting in respect to a story of an incident different from the incidents we know.

We begin by having to make some sort of guess as to what is on the minds of hearers when this story comes up and gets proclaimed. No one authorized us, at least no one authorized me, to read the minds of members of the modern congregation. Few of us would have qualifications to engage in psychological studies of the ways people grasp the uncanny, the wondrous, the miraculous. Few of us have resources or ambitions to engage in opinion research, to ask people in range of pulpits exactly what they think goes on in stories like this one of Tabitha, who was alive and then who was dead and then who was alive.

Since we haven't taken the surveys and can't read minds, we generalize, perhaps on the basis of generalizations. "Modern man/woman," we will read, cannot believe stories in which the central theme is a miracle, especially a resurrection story. So we often read. Or: "Even in the modern world, there are many gullible, naive, credulous people who don't think deeply enough to have any doubts about 'sittings up' by the once-dead." Or: "Research today tells us so much about near-death experiences, and leaves us wondering about so many things surrounding death, that there are all kinds of ways to tell and receive stories like this."

Take your choice.

If we cannot read minds, we can look out over congregations and ponder presences, postures, and faces. Worshipers have all kinds of questions for their doctors and lawyers and pastors. Many of them do cross fingers

563

and furl brows and scrunch noses over the stories of Noah and the ark and Jonah and the whale ("It Ain't Necessarily So," they sing or hear sung without a flinch). Yet these same people hear stories about risings from the dead and are less ready to ask questions or bother to express skepticism.

What has happened? What makes it possible for hearers so regularly to glide over such miracle stories, not raising questions. There are a couple of such accounts in the Old Testament, like that of the widow at Zarephath, or its New Testament counterpart, of the widow at Nain, both of whom have sons restored thanks to a prophet and to Jesus.

For a parallel, there is the story of the daughter of Jairus. Remember the Aramaic words that survive in our translations? *Talitha, qumi,* "maiden, rise," to match *"Tabitha, qumi"* here. The replication after the model of Jesus cannot be accidental. And of course, there was Lazarus, "who stinketh" — a sign that he was really dead. Read to congregations those stories and others about raisings from the dead, the really dead, and eyes do not get batted or backs turned from the sanctuary. Modern, sensible, skeptical, thoughtful people *somehow* have found a way to interpret and incorporate such testimony into their lives.

What this means for the preacher:

In many a homily we hear efforts to prove the possibility of resurrections or to explain the biblical stories as accounts of swoons or altered styles of consciousness. But it is futile to try to "prove" the resurrection, and nothing is gained by de-miracleizing the stories. It is not to the point to pose issues of the literal and the figurative and then make the test of how one grasps these stories the test of faith itself.

The people who hear us in the twenty-first century know that when today someone in a Pentecostal revival gets declared as "resurrected," no one outside that revival circle believes it or cares. Certainly it does not make page one of the newspapers or the church papers. If we witnessed something that bore some marks of the Tabitha-like "sitting up," the risen one would be on the late-night TV shows, a momentary sensation — and then forgotten. Harvard Medical School experts might analyze the presence of the person in the light of ESP and quantum physics and mindfulness and other physical and clinical tests. But the world would be the same whether or not we believed.

Not so with the death-and-life issues connected with Christ's resurrection and the apostles' preaching. Certainly, awareness of people like Lazarus and Tabitha in events like these did not solve everything for everyone. Luke, who wrote this, was a person of faith who knew he would die and not be called to "sit up" on earth. So did Paul. Church rolls were never swelled because people sat up after having been dead. They swelled and endure because people who have faced in faith what Karl Rahner called death, "the abyss of mystery," are content to leave the details and reportings in the realm of mystery. They want something else.

Through and in it all they have seen and known and experienced Jesus Christ's rising as something that breaks the mold and ushers in a new age in history, including in our personal histories. Half-believers do not need "proof" — what would convince? *They do need testimony* to lives changed as a result of identification with Christ's death and resurrection.

Here I am, supposed to being doing exegesis to see what congregations might be ready to hear, and I've spent half the time telling what is unnecessary, overkill, beside the point for preachers. So, to the point:

The Acts 9 story leads us, as so many Scriptures do, to the value of testimony, to its context and eruptions and effects. Maybe the key lines that throw light on this subject in Acts have to do with Barnabas. He was sent to Antioch, where people were first called Christian. He "came and saw the grace of God, he rejoiced, and he exhorted them all to remain faithful to the Lord with steadfast devotion." And now: "for he was a good man, full of the Holy Spirit and of faith. And a great many people were brought to the Lord." Read that: "And so," or "And there," or "because of him. . . ."

Barnabas did not wave the Shroud of Turin and say, "This proves it, he is risen." He did not give a lecture on historical method and evidence, to show what tests we make to discern what an empty tomb is saying about the risen Christ. Barnabas instead testified to the reality of the risen Christ and witnessed by his own character shaped by that reality.

Which brings us back to Tabitha and the context of this event, told so matter-of-factly, in such everyday and ordinary tones. Tabitha is not raised *because* she is good. Many good people lay dead. But it helps to know that she filled her days with kindness and charity. There are some clues that she was a person of means, an important figure in the community, a pillar of that church-in-the-making. She was surrounded by women who washed bodies to purify them for burial, by body-washers, disciples, ambassadors, and widows in tears who showed off shirts and coats that good Tabitha, a.k.a. Dorcas, had made.

Two messengers come for Peter. We are not told what they told him or what he told bystanders. No "Ooh!" or "Aah!" by Peter followed word of her good ways. Peter simply sent them all outside and prayed and commanded. One translation has it, "Then he called the members of the congregation and the widows and showed her to them alive."

People who "believed in the Lord" thereafter did so not because they had seen life and death and life. They heard no lectures on near-death experiences. They were beneficiaries of witness by credible people. The God of the living still lets the faith thus spread.

Martin E. Marty

Resurrection of the Lord, Years A, B, C

First Lesson: Acts 10:34-43
(Psalm 118:1-2, 14-24)
Second Lesson (Year A): Colossians 3:1-4
Second Lesson (Year B): 1 Corinthians 15:1-11
Second Lesson (Year C): 1 Corinthians 15:19-26
Gospel Lesson: John 20:1-18

Peter's speech in Acts 10:34-43 is embedded within the story of the conversion of Cornelius, a Roman centurion, and his household. This story anticipates a key decision church leaders will make. As described in Acts 15, they will decide that Gentile converts need not follow Jewish law when they become Christians. Why is this decision so important? Because it completes the promise given in Acts 1:8 that early Christians will "receive power when the Holy Spirit has come upon you" and become Jesus' witnesses "in Jerusalem, in all Judea and Samaria, and to the ends of the earth." Specifically, it signals that the location of the Spirit's activity in the church has shifted from Jerusalem (3:1–5:41) — and Judea and Samaria (6:1–9:30) — to the broader Gentile world (starting in 9:32). Luke gives Peter a central role in this movement outward into the Gentile world. Indeed, the sermon Peter gives in Cornelius's household anticipates his later statement in Acts 15:7 that "in the early days God made a choice among you, that I should be the one through whom the Gentiles would hear the message of the good news and become believers."

Cornelius's conversion story is a long one, spanning 10:1–11:18. But it is not only Cornelius who undergoes a conversion in this story. If he is converted to Christianity, then Peter undergoes a conversion as well, a conversion in his understanding of the church. This double conversion is described by way of a double vision or dream, a literary device found elsewhere in Greek literature. Cornelius's vision, in which an angel tells him to invite Peter to his house (10:1-8), is immediately followed by Peter's vision, in which a voice tells him to eat ritually unclean food. Cornelius is prepared by a vision for his encounter with Peter; likewise, Peter is prepared by a vision for his encounter with Cornelius. The command Peter, as a Jew, hears to eat "unclean" or "profane" food is a symbolic command that he visit Cornelius, who, as a Gentile, is "unclean" or "profane" to Jews (10:28). This double vision is followed by the sending of messengers from Cornelius's household to Peter (10:17-23a), Peter's visit to Cornelius's household — where he gives this speech (10:23b-48) — and his later justification of this visit to the Christians in Jerusalem (11:1-18).

The speech Peter gives in Cornelius's household is his last great speech in Acts. Like the other missionary speeches he gives (in chaps. 2–4), it depicts the key facts about Jesus' life, death, and resurrection and their relevance for its hearers. What is unique about this speech is that it addresses in a very explicit way how God views Gentile God-fearers who want to become Christians. Hence, it plays an important role in Acts in inaugurating the church's ministry to Gentiles.

The sermon itself can be divided into three parts. The first part (vv. 34-36) states that the "impartial" God has sent Jesus to be "Lord of all." Peter begins by literally "opening his mouth," which is a way of indicating that he will say something important (cf. 8:35 and 18:14). What he has to say is this: God "shows no partiality." In other words, God is "no respecter of persons" but judges all people by the same standards. Developed elsewhere in the New Testament (e.g., Rom. 2:10-11), this theme draws on the Old Testament sense of God's justice and compassion for all people (Deut. 10:17; cf. Lev. 19:15). Peter develops this point in verse 35, where he states that anyone who fears God, which essentially means anyone who "practices righteousness," is "acceptable" to God — regardless of nationality. Again, this point echoes Old Testament sources, especially Proverbs 15:8, which states that "the prayers of the righteous are acceptable to him" (see also Prov. 12:22). Peter goes on to link this Jewish insight into God's impartiality to the Christian task of bringing Jesus' message of peace from those to whom it was first given — the people of Israel — to all people. Thus he declares: Jesus Christ is "Lord of all" (v. 36), an assertion reinforced at the end of the speech in verse 42 with a reference to his being judge over the living and dead. Jesus brings a message of "peace," a theme Luke explicitly identifies with his messianic ministry (see, e.g., Luke 2:14). This "peace" is anticipated by the Old Testament notion of shalom — which, in turn, is defined as bounty, concord, harmony, security, order, and prosperity (see, among others, Isa. 48:18; 54:10; Ezek. 34:25-29).

The second part of the speech delineates what this message of peace is about; it presents a comprehensive summary of Jesus' career (vv. 37-41). (But note that two different Greek words are used for the word "message" in verses 36 and 37, an indication perhaps — in addition to the awkward syntax of these verses — that Luke is drawing on another source in this speech even as he is using it to develop his theological purposes.) In this summary Jesus' public ministry begins after John's baptism, a point Luke makes elsewhere (Luke 3:23). As in other parts of Luke-Acts, the Holy Spirit plays an important role in Jesus' ministry (e.g., at his baptism, Luke 3:22; his entry into the wilderness, Luke 4:1; his return to Galilee at the beginning of his ministry, Luke 4:14; and so on). Indeed, Luke highlights the link between "the Holy Spirit and power" (see also Luke 1:17; 4:14; 24:49; and Acts 1:8). God charismatically "anoints" Jesus — recalling the way God called prophets in the Old Testament (see also Luke 3:22; 4:14). Thus, Jesus' ministry of healing and exorcism is Spirit-empowered. Jesus goes about "doing good" in verse 38, healing those "oppressed" by the devil, a term usually only used in the New Testament to describe how the rich "oppress" the poor (e.g., in James 2:6). This verse recalls Jesus' quoting of Isaiah, that the "Spirit of the Lord" was upon him to proclaim good news to the poor, release the captives, recover sight to the blind, and set free those who are oppressed (in Luke 4:18-19; cf. Isa. 61:1, 2 and 58:6). It is fitting that Jesus' ministry should be summarized with the phrase "God was with him" (v. 38c; see Luke 5:17 among others). In verse 39 Peter stresses his own and the other disciples' role as witnesses to all this, a point he will make again in 41a, where he makes clear that not everyone was chosen to be a witness (see also Luke 24:48; Acts 1:18, 21-22). Peter's description of Jesus' death echoes Deuteronomy 21:23 — "cursed be everyone who hangs on a tree" — perhaps to highlight how it fulfills God's plan. Here, as in previous speeches, Peter describes Jesus' death as that of a righteous martyr killed for and by the people (cf. 2:36 and 3:14-15; 4:10; cf. Isa. 53). But again, as God does in Peter's previous speeches, God intervenes, raising Jesus on the third day (v. 40). Jesus then appears to those chosen in a very tangible way (v. 41), as he did when he ate and drank with friends (note the importance of eating and drinking for Luke; see, e.g., Luke 24:30-31, 36-43; Acts 1:3-6).

The last part of the speech (vv. 42-43) concludes with a summary of the message these "witnesses" have to "preach": Jesus has the power to forgive precisely because he is ordained by God to judge "the living and the dead"

(v. 42b), a motif repeated in a speech to pagans in 17:31 (cf. Luke 24:44-47). It is the risen Christ, precisely as "Lord of all," who exercises the role of judge (cf. Rom. 14:9; 2 Tim. 4:1; 1 Pet. 4:5). What this risen Christ gives is "forgiveness of sins through his name" to all who believe in him (v. 43b).

We misread this speech if we think its point is only for the early Jewish-Christian community. Rather, its point is one we need to continually hear, whenever we establish our own criteria for delimiting who God finds acceptable. The forgiveness of sins in Jesus' name is for all people, even those our prejudices — whatever form they take — compel us to ignore or reject. But, although this message has a universal scope, its content is concrete and specific. Echoing the Old Testament notion of shalom, its message of peace enacts in concrete ways the good Jesus does for us — the ways he heals us from our sicknesses of body and soul and liberates us from the many forms of demonic oppression we as individuals and communities suffer from. This concrete message about Jesus is what we, like Peter, have to give. Like the witnesses described in his speech, we too have been given the Holy Spirit and power to carry Jesus' message to all people, even those we consider unclean. And all of us — both those who witness and those who are witnessed to — need to hear again and again how the risen Christ not only judges but heals and forgives, and enacts among us — with the Holy Spirit and power — God's peaceful reign of justice and compassion.

Lois Malcolm

Sixth Sunday of Easter, Year B

First Lesson: Acts 10:44-48
(Psalm 98)
Second Lesson: 1 John 5:1-6
Gospel Lesson: John 15:9-17

This lection tells about how the Holy Spirit "fell upon" the Gentile household of Cornelius, a Roman cohort. The theological point of the story is best understood within the broader context of the story of

Cornelius's conversion (depicted in 10:1–11:18) and how Luke uses this story within the book of Acts to describe how the Holy Spirit works. This story, which describes the Spirit's fourth outpouring in Acts, anticipates the fact that the message about Jesus of Nazareth is to be proclaimed to Gentiles and not only circumcised Jews (11:20). The "apostles and believers" in Jerusalem will have to decide publicly how to respond to this new development in the church (see the discussion of this in Acts 15). This development, however, is anticipated in the beginning of Acts, where Jesus promises his followers that they will be baptized with the Holy Spirit (1:5), a baptism that will lead them to be his witnesses "in Jerusalem, in all Judea and Samaria, and to the ends of the earth" (1:8). If Acts 1:8 is programmatic for the structure of the book as a whole, it is not insignificant that Luke describes at least one outpouring of the Spirit for each major location described in that verse: with two outpourings set in Jerusalem (2:1-4 and 4:31), another one set in Samaria (8:17), and now this scene in a Gentile household, which anticipates the Spirit's work "to the ends of the earth." What will this fourth outpouring depict for us? That our notions of who or what is unclean must not — and indeed cannot — hinder the Spirit's activity even as it is being "poured out" on those we consider unclean.

Luke makes this point in four different ways in his story of Cornelius's conversion: by way of (1) a narrative of a double vision, a common story pattern in ancient Greek literature, in which Cornelius and Peter each receive visions that tell them to meet the other (10:1-33); (2) a speech Peter gives in Cornelius's household, where he makes an argument for God's impartiality and Jesus Christ's Lordship over all people (10:34-43); (3) this scene in which the Spirit falls upon Cornelius's household even before they are baptized (10:44-48); and (4) Peter's later justification of his actions to the "apostles and believers" in Jerusalem (11:1-18). What is distinct about the outpouring of the Spirit in Cornelius's household — in contrast to the three previous ones — is that it deals specifically with the outpouring of the Spirit among uncircumcised Gentiles. As Peter describes the occasion later in 11:15, "The Holy Spirit fell upon them just as it had upon us at the beginning," referring to Pentecost (in Acts 2). Hence, he reasons: "If then God gave them the same gift that he gave us when we believed in the Lord Jesus Christ, who was I that I could hinder God?" (11:17).

The scene begins with the Holy Spirit interrupting Peter while he is still speaking (v. 44; cf. 11:15). This interruption makes clear that it is the Spirit, and not Peter, who is the chief agent of this event. But Peter's hearers have already heard his message. Thus, at this point, the Holy Spirit "falls upon" them (v. 44) and the "gift of the Holy Spirit" is "poured out" upon them

(v. 45). The language Luke uses here is reminiscent of his description of the first outpouring of the Spirit at Pentecost, where he describes how the Spirit descends with the sound of "the rush of a violent wind" (2:2) and believers are "filled with the Holy Spirit" (2:4), a phrase Luke will use again when he describes how the Spirit was given to embolden the new believers in Jerusalem (4:31). And, as in that first event, the bystanders to the event in Cornelius's household are "astounded" (v. 45a) in the same way the devout Jews at Pentecost were "amazed and astonished" (2:7) — and even "perplexed" (2:12) — about what was happening around them. But there is a difference between these two events. At the first Pentecost, the bystanders — Jews from all over the world — are perplexed because the Galilean believers were speaking in languages they, as Galileans, could not speak, but which the bystanders could understand. In Cornelius's household, by contrast, the bystanders — who are Jewish Christians — are perplexed because it is uncircumcised Gentiles who have received the gift of the Holy Spirit (10:46). And there is another difference between the two events. Although in both cases the proof of the Spirit's presence is something the bystanders can see and hear — the gift of tongues (v. 46; cf. 2:1-4) — the nature of this gift is very different in the two events. At Pentecost the believers actually spoke in languages that were intelligible to their native speakers; what they said served as a witness to the Spirit's power. By contrast, the gift of tongues given at Cornelius's household is more like that described in 1 Corinthians 14:2, where the gift is given for praising God (14:2) and building up the one praying (14:4), and not for witnessing to unbelievers (14:22).

After this visible outpouring of the Spirit's presence, Peter asks the circumcised Christians around him: Can we withhold baptism from these people when they have received the Holy Spirit "just as we have" (v. 47)? Peter appeals to the fact that these Gentiles have received the same Spirit the circumcised believers have received, and asks: What hinders us from baptizing them? — a question that recalls the Ethiopian eunuch's question to Philip after he had heard the good news: "Look, here is water! What is to prevent me from being baptized?" (8:36). In his retelling of the Cornelius event to the Jerusalem Christians, Peter appeals to Jesus' statement that "John baptized with water, but you will be baptized with the Holy Spirit" (11:16). This appeal is also found at the very beginning of Acts (1:5), where Jesus promises the baptism of the Holy Spirit to the new believers before he is taken up to heaven (although we should note, to be wholly accurate, that in the Gospels it is John who makes this prediction, not Jesus; see Mark 1:8; Matt. 3:11; Luke 3:16; John 1:33). If this promise of the Spirit's power anticipates what will occur in the rest of the book of Acts, especially as the Spirit's activity

571

moves from Jerusalem to Samaria to the "ends of the earth" (1:8), then it makes sense that this story of the Spirit's outpouring — which occurs after descriptions of the Spirit's outpouring in Jerusalem and Samaria — should revolve around a Gentile household's experience of the Spirit. Indeed, Cornelius's story is poised just before reference begins to be made to the way the message of Jesus Christ is being proclaimed to Gentiles (11:20).

So Peter orders that the members of Cornelius's household be baptized in the name of Jesus. Now baptized but still uncircumcised, these new Christians invite Peter to "stay" with them, a verb that in Greek can also mean "eat" (cf. 1:4). He does for several days, causing his fellow Christians in Jerusalem to later question how he could "go to uncircumcised men and eat with them" (11:3)? In Luke's earthy perspective on things, it is fitting that Jesus' followers eat and drink with one another, especially if Jesus himself ate and drank with them before and after his death (see 10:41 in Peter's speech; cf. Luke 24:30-31, 36-43; Acts 1:3-6). The fact that Peter stays and eats with members of this household after their baptism is not insignificant. Indeed, as noted above, the early descriptions of the Spirit's outpouring are all followed by some form of sharing — from the "breaking of bread" (2:46) to the holding of all things "in common," which is mentioned soon after the first two events of the Spirit's outpouring in Jerusalem (2:44-46 and 4:32).

This lection depicts the crowning scene in the Cornelius story, reinforcing the point made in the double vision and in Peter's speech: that the Holy Spirit's work cannot be hindered by our preconceived notions of who or what is unclean. Luke has the bystanders to this event express the same kind of perplexity expressed at Pentecost, perhaps suggesting that we too — as the future readers of this text — will be amazed by how the Spirit continues to work among us, in spite of our prejudices. And this text also tells us something about the Spirit's tremendous power, a power that makes visible the Spirit's presence among us with tangible "signs and wonders," to use Luke's language. The Spirit Jesus promised the early church was one who would come with "power" and enable Jesus' followers to carry on his "good" work — of healing and exorcism, and of bringing his message of peace and forgiveness in his name to all people (10:34-43; cf. 4:29-31). But as this event in Cornelius's household reminds us, this power is not to be kept to ourselves, or for those who are just like us. Rather, this power is one that will, in the name of Jesus, continually lead us to stay and eat with all kinds of people — wherever the Spirit is at work fulfilling Joel's prophecy that God's Spirit is to be poured out "upon all flesh" (Acts 2:17-21; cf. Joel 2:28-32).

Lois Malcolm

Fifth Sunday of Easter, Year C

First Lesson: Acts 11:1-18
(Psalm 148)
Second Lesson: Revelation 21:1-6
Gospel Lesson: John 13:31-35

Many preachers belong to circles of fellow preachers with whom they study lectionary texts. Others have friends with whom they compare notes and check signals.

Here's an exercise to be used any week, but maybe especially with Acts 11:1-18 in view. Read the text and then ask each other: "What is the most obvious thing that comes to mind for preaching this text?" Usually there'll be a good match. The obvious is obvious. Then, think: If it's all that obvious, what's the point of gathering a congregation to expound this? Let them read it at home. If it's so patent, their eyes will glaze over.

Looking beyond the obvious does not mean heading for the arcane, the cryptic, the tangential, the oblique, or, worst of all, the cute. It means probing deeply to discern why the text was preserved, and to look for meanings that connect it with the larger message of God.

To the point of this text: the obvious thing is to see it as a good prompt or primer for a Brotherhood Week sermon. Obviously, it has something to say about all kinds of people being God's common creation, and we should treat them thus. Be nice.

What a waste! You do not have to be a Christian to promote brotherhood or tolerance. Conferences and councils of Christians and Jews and now Muslims and more do that well. Agnostics and atheists can be reasoned with and convinced that they should accept everyone. Thank God for all such efforts; the world can use them. But that is not the point of the church or this text.

That Luke, the author of Acts, thought he had something important to say in telling this story is obvious because he retells it. First it shows up in the story in Acts 10, and now it reappears when Peter gives a *Reader's Digest* version of it, skipping many details, holding to the essentials, and adding a little twist here and there. (We all, don't we, tell our stories a bit differently for different audiences?) Within the story there are also some repetitions, after the manner of speakers and storytellers of the time when Acts was written. And it is clear that the setting in chapter 11 is solemn. A congregation needs to know that this is a story to be leaned-forward for; it tokens a basic shift in the way the early church was getting conceived and the way we now should receive the gift.

Commentators and critics in general often have some trouble with this story, a trouble we cannot and do not need to overcome for the point. From the letters of Paul, which antedate Acts, we learn much about how the good news was taken "to all the world" and to the Gentiles especially. And we learn of the resistance of the Jerusalem church. Now Luke tells this in such a way that we get the impression that the home folks in Jerusalem were to get the impression that Peter was the pioneer, the breakthrough person. And from the end of this text, with its witness to the Holy Spirit's activity, it was God who caused the breakthrough and endorsed it.

Whatever attitude we take to Doctor Luke's possible doctoring of Peter's role, there is good news for hearers today in the role as described. Today? Look out at a congregation with its cliques and parties and factions; with its tendency to represent a fairly homogeneous social set; with the enduring problems that follow lines of race and ethnicity; with the shunning of the unattractive and the homeless that most congregations engage in by instinct and sometimes by policy.

There is no need to overdraw the point. The place to check is at the table. In these two tellings of the story, Peter was on the spot with the headquarters church made up of Jews turned "Christian" in Jerusalem. Why? For baptizing Gentiles? That was not yet a settled issue, but it is not the one Luke stresses. No, the controversy had to do with commensality.

Commensality. So that seldom used and hardly known word is supposed to get people to lean forward, open their ears, and be ready to change their hearts? Yes. The sociologist of religion Max Weber and others have made much of this word that says you share the *mensa*, the table, with someone else. That is often hard to do. The homeless are not clean. People above us in class and status are snooty. Below us are rednecks and ill-mannered clods.

A moment of history: after the Civil War the question rose whether free blacks and whites of the same denomination and creed would make up congregations. Oh yes, said most white congregations: you can keep coming with us to the Lord's house, as you did in slave days. Yes, we'll reserve choice seats for you in the balcony. But commune with us at the Lord's Table? And stay to eat with us at the tables in the church annex or on the church lawn, for a picnic? Never. Historians report that some of the segregation of Christian congregations in America resulted from African Americans' "self-exclusion." They knew where they weren't wanted; it was at the communion table, where believers are intimate with their Lord, close to each other; or at the festive table, where they share their secrets and bare their souls as they feed their bodies.

If we think commensality is an issue in our churches today or was after 1865, we learn it was a much bigger issue when Luke wrote Luke-Acts. The disciples had come to faith in Christ, but they kept to rites like circumcision and to rules ingrained in them as Jews. And one was more than a tradition or a taboo: there was a strict rule against Jews sitting at table with the uncircumcised. We recall that Jesus was often in trouble for his commensality with tax collectors, prostitutes, and the unwashed. But let us assume that they were Jews. Peter violates custom and law by eating with the uncircumcised.

So he must defend himself. Luke is a bit careful not to overidentify the rigorous Jerusalemites. But we know the names of many of them: James, John, Andrew, Philip, and more. Disciples. How can they jump out of their skins and their exclusive benches and adapt to sharing benches with Gentiles? There is no way for this to happen if Peter only argues. He is on trial. And he must show how commensality and with it the spread of the good news is God's idea.

That is why he receives this vision. "Now the apostles and the believers who were in Judea heard that the Gentiles had also accepted the word of God." Picture them leaping; picture us leaping when the good news gets accepted. Did you ever report to a committee or employers expecting to get congratulated, only to find out that something you did offended them? Picture Peter "going up" to Jerusalem and then getting a comedown: "the circumcised believers criticized him"; "Why did you go to uncircumcised and eat with them?" Baptize them? Well, maybe. Yes, fine. But *eat with them?*

There may be little need to use homily time to retell the twice-told story of the vision itself. It is so graphic that it will stick in the minds of those alert to it when it was read. We can move to the climax. Poor pure Peter: "Nothing profane or unclean has ever entered my mouth." He is a veteran by now. He might have looked ahead and figured that he could go through life with that mouth unviolated. And God in the vision challenges him. A voice: "What God has made clean, you must not call profane" ("pro" + "fane": that which stands outside the temple, the *fanum,* the sacred sphere).

Repetition: this happened three times. Then come three men, plus the Spirit, who "told me to go with them and not to make a distinction between them and us." "Them" and "us": few issues trouble humans, including Christian humans, more than knowing who are "we" and how we are to relate to "the others."

How could Peter resist? The man he was to approach told how an angel had reached him to say that a man called Peter "will give you a message by which you and your entire household will be saved." Which is exactly what a preacher today is announced and supposed to be doing. And Peter did. And the rest is history: out of such incidents the good news came to be universalized, so that the many of us who are not Jews "will be saved."

Every preacher who has to justify herself or himself for following up the implications of commensality and the radical breakthroughs of the good news — and each had better be prayerfully sure that that is what she or he is doing — can identify with plaintive and self-justifying Peter here: "Who was I that I could hinder God?" Staying out of God's way when our ways get in the path is the main element in the preacherly vocation.

Back to the disciples and their fellow Jewish-Christian communicants at the table in Jerusalem: Who were they that they could hinder God? "When they heard this, they were silenced." But not silent. "They praised God, saying, 'Then God has given even to the Gentiles the repentance that leads to life.'" As we leave them, they seem to be catching on. Now it's someone else's turn to deal with "them" and "us" and share the intimacy of the Table and the tables with "the other," "the different."

Martin E. Marty

Sixth Sunday of Easter, Year C

First Lesson: Acts 16:9-15
(Psalm 67)
Second Lesson: Revelation 21:10, 22–22:5
Gospel Lesson: John 14:23-29

The incidents in this lectionary reading find background in the three verses immediately preceding it. Sometimes it is helpful or necessary to adjust the reading to include a verse or two. The incidents in this reading happen on what has come to be called Paul's second missionary journey. Paul and a man named Silas, a prophet in the Antioch church, set out to visit the churches that Paul and Barnabas had planted on the first missionary journey. After visiting the churches, their plans thinned a bit; they would go wherever and all over preaching the gospel of Jesus.

The second trip started out exactly as they had planned it. They had visited the young churches, but then just as the second phase of the journey was about to begin, things seem to just plain stall out. The immediate background to the lectionary verses is the big stall that begins in Acts 16:6. The Holy Spirit tells the missionaries not to preach the gospel in the province of Asia. Can you believe it — orders from God to ignore a whole province? "Keep your lips zipped, Paul. Don't talk about Jesus in Asia." How odd of God to tell the missionaries not to preach, to keep quiet.

And then when they came to the region of Mysia and tried to enter Bithynia, the Spirit of Jesus, the Holy Spirit, would not give them a visa. A barrier stood in their way. Not the local politicians or the Jewish opposition or the forces of evil, but God seems to have blocked their way. It was as if God had slipped some blank pages into the itinerary of the second missionary journey and left them baffled about where he wanted them to go. How can a person understand the ways of God? Prior to these roadblocks, Paul seems in part to be finding out where God wants them to go by trying out some possibilities. Perhaps this is how Paul ends up in Troas. But with all the roadblocks and now stalled out in Troas, Paul needs some direction. And in verse 10, where Luke describes what happened in Troas, he begins to employ the first-person plural, probably indicating that he joined Paul and the others there.

Far from Troas a woman in our passage named Lydia must have been asking similar questions about the ways of God. She lived a fair distance from Troas in the ancient city of Philippi. A successful businesswoman, she made her money dealing in purple fabric from her native city of Thyatira. She was likely single, probably widowed.

Despite her obvious prosperity, Lydia, it seems, sensed a certain emptiness in her life. She was not Jewish by birth, but in her search for God she had begun to join with a tiny group of Jewish women each Saturday outside the city by the Gangites River for prayer. The Romans, it seems, barely tolerated religions like Judaism, and made adherents meet outside the city limits. So each Saturday a few women met to offer prayer and worship to the God of faraway Israel. But did the God of distant Israel whom they worshiped on the outskirts of this large pagan city care about or even notice this handful of foreign women by the bank of the Gangites River?

The answer to that question comes from the apostle Paul and his entourage stalled out in Troas. Paul might very well have started to second-guess himself. Just before this second missionary journey, Acts says he had a

577

disagreement and falling out with his old partner, Barnabas. And Acts 13 says Barnabas was one of the prophets in the church at Antioch. Prophets, of course, are people with a special gift for hearing what God is saying, and no doubt Barnabas had been a great help on that first journey as the two missionaries tried to discover where God wanted them to go and what God wanted them to say. But Paul and Barnabas had argued, and Paul had teamed up with another prophet, a man named Silas. And Silas seemed to have a knack for hearing only what God didn't want them to do. Don't preach in Asia. Stay out of Mysia. Don't preach, don't go. Well, what did God want them to do? Where was reliable old Barnabas when they needed to hear positive direction from the Lord? Did God have further plans for them, or had he left them to cool their heels for no good reason in Troas?

The big stall ends during their first night in Troas when Paul has a vision. In his dream he sees a man from Macedonia, standing and begging. "Please," the man begs, "come over to Macedonia and help us." Paul takes this dream/vision as an indication that God just might want them to go to Macedonia. So the next morning they pack their bags and book passage for Macedonia. And as subsequent events will suggest, it looks for all the world that God has diverted Paul and Silas to meet with Lydia and her obscure little group of women in Philippi. Notice the trouble to which God goes to initiate this personal meeting between the missionaries and the women's prayer group that Saturday down by the river. God seems to have diverted the apostle Paul hundreds of miles, to have stopped him from preaching in Asia and from entering Mysia, all so he would be right on time to preach that day to that handful of women down by the river in Philippi.

As Paul preaches, God works a miracle for Lydia. As Paul tells the women's prayer meeting about Jesus, the Holy Spirit opens Lydia's heart to respond to Paul's message. That means Lydia said she wanted God's forgiveness for herself, that she accepted Jesus as her Lord and Savior. Once committed, she is baptized along with her whole household, which would have included servants and children, if she had any. And that day was the real start for her of a deep, close, and intimate relationship with God. God poured out his Holy Spirit upon Lydia, and Lydia recognized herself as God's own child.

Many Christians probably have times when their lives may not seem to be going anywhere. It may seem like God has left the next episode unwritten or is only experimenting with the next chapter. But God reveals that he directs not only the whole story of the universe, but each of the particular parts that he gives his people to play, and he directs them to a fruitful end.

Of course, in all of this there are times when God calls people to be patient, to wait. And for many people this is really hard, to wait for God's timing, to wait for his direction. God is the director, after all. He is in charge of the lives of his people. He's the one calling the shots. And he's always calling the shots in ways that serve our best interest in the end, even as he works through us to minister to others. As someone once said, "God may not act exactly when we want him to, but he is always right on time."

Like a prompter in a play, God invites his people to listen for directions within the ongoing drama. He uses a variety of ways to prompt us in the direction that he wishes for us to go. Frequently he directs through the words of the Bible or through the advice of others, friends or family members. Sometimes God speaks through circumstances, a job offer, a so-called chance meeting. God shuts some doors and opens others, as people sometimes say. And Christians ought to be open to the possibility that God still directs his people through dreams, as he did the apostle Paul.

God not only directs the story of his saving relationship with the world, but he reveals that the heart of its plot is a love story. People may have some difficulty believing it, but the Creator of the universe wants a personal, Holy Spirit-mediated relationship with each one of his creatures. As in the case of Lydia, God moves the action and opens the hearts of those who respond to him. This opening up to God is not only of personal significance, but has a social impact that spills over into the lives of others.

Some would try to buttress the doctrine of infant baptism through Luke's description of Lydia's baptism. Since it included her household, children would have been included. Those who object to the practice point out that children are not specifically mentioned, and they are not. Equally worthy of reflection is the baptism of those in the household without any mention of God's opening their hearts as he had that of Lydia. A more corporate idea of family and the people of God seems to be underlying what happens on this score.

John M. Rottman

Seventh Sunday of Easter, Year C

First Lesson: Acts 16:16-34
(Psalm 97)
Second Lesson: Revelation 22:12-14, 16-17, 20-21
Gospel Lesson: John 17:20-26

After crossing into Europe from Asia on his second missionary journey, Paul began his work in Philippi, "a leading city of the district of Macedonia and a Roman colony" (Acts 16:13). With him were Silas and Timothy as well as Luke, as suggested by this text being one of the "we" passages of Acts written in the first rather than the third person (see also 20:5ff.; 27:1ff.). The narrative unfolds in three scenes: Paul casts out a spirit from a female slave (vv. 16-18); Paul and Silas are publicly "tried" before city magistrates (vv. 19-22); Paul and Silas are imprisoned and subsequently convert their jailer (vv. 23-34).

Paul and company are on their way to "the place of prayer," a daily occurrence while in Philippi. The riverside destination is the place where they had previously baptized Lydia (16:15). As they go, a female slave who is possessed by a "spirit of divination" confronts them. This woman stands in marked contrast to Lydia, who was free and apparently had her own business interests (16:14). The slave's owners use the girl to tell fortunes for their financial benefit. But each day when Paul and Silas pass by she goes after them, naming them also as slaves, of "the Most High God" (see Gen. 14:19 and Ps. 46:4 as other examples of this divine name), and as proclaimers "of a way of salvation." Day after day this occurs, at no charge, but much to Paul's annoyance. Why he is irritated is not specified. Certainly the girl is not bearing false witness. Perhaps Paul desires to be in charge of how his teaching and identity are presented and conveyed in the city. He does not seem to be annoyed at her enslavement, but does cast the spirit out of her.

Their source of easy revenue ruined by Paul's action, the girl's owners seize Paul and Silas, hauling them to the marketplace at the city center in order to bring charges against them before the authorities. This action draws a crowd, as might well be expected. Paul and Silas are not accused of interfering with presumably legal, though despicable, commerce, but rather of disturbing the peace. They are identified as Jews (presumably the distinction of Jews and Christians is not yet known nor understood) and as advocates of customs illegal for Romans, although what these might be are never specified. It may be that the owners' complaint against the two involves not only their personal loss but also awareness of what Paul and Silas have been teaching down by the riverside. In short, Paul and Silas are fully credentialed outside agitators: Jewish foreigners bringing in new and disruptive practices. Confirming the abuse the crowd is already heaping upon Paul and Silas, the magistrates find them guilty in short order and have them stripped, severely beaten, and securely imprisoned. No word of defense from Paul is recorded.

In the "innermost cell," their feet in stocks, Paul and Silas pray and sing, using the occasion to witness to the other prisoners. A miraculous midnight earthquake shakes the foundations of the jail, knocking the doors from their hinges and the shackles from bolts in the walls. The jailer, equally sure the prisoners will have fled and of what happens to jailers who fail in their duty, decides to put himself to the sword, when Paul intervenes, assuring him no one has left. When the situation has calmed a bit, the jailer asks Paul what he must do to be saved. Does he mean from the consequences of his job failure? Does he mean from his sins, whatever they may be? Paul assumes the later, and after offering the formula for belief implied by the slave girl, baptizes the jailer and his entire household (as he had done with Lydia). The tending to wounds, bringing of food, and rejoicing ensue.

Clearly the possessed girl of this narrative is enslaved, doubly so in fact, to both her owners and to the spirit speaking through her. But many other characters in this story are enslaved as well. The slave girl's owners are enslaved to their greed, which is supported by an economic system that condones their exploitation of the girl. The magistrates seem influenced to the point of being in bondage to the crowd's expectations, and their "court" is of the kangaroo variety (compare Pilate's relationship to the crowd in Mark 15:15). The jailer is enslaved by a judicial system that offers only death for failure; his life is centered in, defined, and bound by nothing larger than the legal system he is to enforce.

And in a certain way, Paul and Silas are also enslaved. Certainly the girl is right that they are "slaves of the Most High God," the only acceptable form of servitude. But some blindness to the breadth of Christ's invitation to discipleship prevents them from extending the offer made to Lydia to the slave girl. They free her from the possessing spirit (and thereby show that the spirit itself is subject to the power of God), but do not invite her into the freedom of faith offered to Lydia earlier or the jailer later. Not only does she continue in bondage to her owners, but also to her separation from the very God she names. Paul does not yet seem to have added "no longer slave or free" to "no longer Jew or Greek" and "no longer male and female" (Gal. 3:28).

Paul and Silas bring the jailer and his whole household to faith, but the story is haunted by the question: But what about the slave girl? She, unlike the jailer, doesn't ask what she must do to be saved; but in her possession, she may not be able to seek the path of freedom. Why do Paul and Silas not reach out to her? What social prejudice enslaves them so they do not perceive her as one for whom Christ died and rose?

Certainly they are not afraid or unwilling to challenge implicitly the economic system of the day, for surely it is this, rather than the trumped-up charges of being antiestablishment, that lands them in jail. Indeed, Paul and Silas are to be commended for their courage in challenging a corrupt and exploitative business practice. Would that they would go even further and challenge the institution of slavery itself! Nevertheless, the Christian community of today would do well to emulate them by having the courage to challenge unjust economic practices that are cruelly exploitative of human beings and the creation.

Everyone in this story, not just the jailer, stands in need of salvation. The girl needs not only to be saved from possession and slavery, but also to be brought into communion with the Most High God whose emissaries she can somehow recognize. The slave owners need to be saved from their exploitation of human beings and from their idolatry of financial gain. The magistrates need to be saved from meting out popular justice (Paul· does even the score with them in vv. 35-40). The jailer needs to be saved from a life bound by an unjust legal system. And Paul and Silas need to be saved from a too narrow view of the gospel's invitation. The broad appeal of the gospel with which Luke began the book of Acts in his account of the Day of Pentecost is not easy to hold on to and must ever be renewed, particularly if Luke's understanding of Christ as a messiah for all people is to be honored.

Like Paul and Silas, all Christians struggle with the unconverted aspects of themselves, the parts yet resistant to the fullness of Christ's desire for the whole person, as they make the journey of growth in faith. "Being saved" surely begins in baptism, as it does here for the jailer and his household, but it continues in the process of sanctification wherein the believer comes ever more fully to comprehend, live, and extend to all others, regardless of social station or circumstance, the gracious acceptance known in Christ as Lord and Savior. This text's unspoken question, But what about the girl? leads to each hearer asking, "But what about me? What is yet to be saved in my perception and behavior?" Answers abound in this story — from financial idolatry to classism to fear of public opinion to xenophobia to anti-Semitism to legalism — and in every human life, time, and place.

Lawrence W. Farris

Sixth Sunday of Easter, Year A

First Lesson: Acts 17:22-31
(Psalm 66:8-20)
Second Lesson: 1 Peter 3:13-22
Gospel Lesson: John 14:15-21

A prominent word in homiletics today is "contextualization." This text is one of the best examples in the entire Bible and, for that reason, a wonderful text for preaching, both to show the audience how Paul proclaims the gospel to an unfamiliar audience and then for the preacher to preach in the same manner to his/her own audience.

In Paul's first sermon recorded in Acts, he preaches to the Jews in the synagogue at Antioch of Pisidia (13:26-41). There he is on familiar ground, speaking to people who know the Old Testament. Beginning with the exodus, he summarizes Israelite history through David, then speaks of Jesus and the resurrection as the fulfillment of God's promises. The sermon speaks directly to the context of the listeners.

In Athens he finds himself facing an altogether different crowd. He knows that the Greeks pay homage to a whole panoply of gods and goddesses. They believe these deities flit in and out of human affairs, meddling in people's lives, sometimes helpfully, other times harmfully. Furthermore, these divine beings operated with no sense of morality. They could be as mean and petty as any human being. Shrines were built in cities all across the Greco-Roman world, paying tribute to these Olympic beings in the hopes that they would be benevolent.

Paul also knows that belief in this traditional pantheon of divine beings was waning. Many regarded it more as mythology than religion. Skepticism was rife, particularly among learned people, for whom sophistication and skepticism were the primary intellectual virtues.

What makes the best missionary preaching? Paul could have stood in the marketplace and denounced this whole religious tradition. After all, the capricious and chaotic behavior of the gods and goddesses was abhorrent to anyone who believed in the God of the Old Testament.

But denunciation seldom persuades. Paul needed an entry point into the thinking of his audience. He needed a foothold into their belief from which he could begin sympathetically, then open new horizons for his listeners.

He found it. Some artisan had erected a shrine "to an unknown god" to ensure that there wouldn't be some god angry at being neglected. With all the mischief the gods could bring about, one couldn't take risks. This was the entry Paul needed. Note (1) how he moved into their thinking and (2) how he gave it a new twist.

He acknowledges their shrine. There is indeed a god unknown to them. Now he has caught their attention, and we follow each phrase as he moves masterfully from this unknown god to the God of the Bible and finally to the resurrection.

First, this God "made the world and everything in it." The Greek creation myths were the most complicated and bizarre aspect of their religion. With adherence to their mythology waning, the idea that there was one creator behind all this might be appealing to reflective Greeks. Second, gods do not "live in shrines made by human hands." To an already skeptical mind, this would make sense. Third, this unknown god is not served by human hands but "gives to all mortals life and breath and all things."

Step-by-step Paul builds a case for a God who is the Sovereign of all things, even the nations. Finally, lest they think this God is unattainable, Paul affirms that though we might search and grope for him, "indeed, he is not far from each one of us."

Paul then quotes two lines of poetry from their own literature, which many of the listeners undoubtedly knew. (Verse 28a is attributed to Epimenides, 28b is from *Phaenomena*, a poem by the Greek poet Aratus.) It was a masterful move, because these would have been familiar to knowledgeable listeners.

With that foundation Paul moves to his conclusion: such a God would know human ignorance, so we stand in judgment and need to repent. Then Paul jars his listeners with an abrupt closing statement that sparks their intense curiosity: we will be judged, but the judgment will be done in righteousness by one whom God has raised from the dead!

This was new! Some scoffed, others were determined to hear more. Even though the lectionary passage ends with verse 32, a preacher should note the concluding two verses, reporting the effect of the sermon. The conversion results were moderate: "[some men] including Dionysius the Areopagite and a woman named Damaris." Faithful preaching effects results, though preachers may never know what they are.

Rather than simply summarize Paul's adaptation of the gospel to the thinking of the Greeks, a good preacher of this text needs to *do* what Paul does with his audience — adapt the message to the listeners.

How do we "contextualize" the gospel to our people? What are their "unknown gods," those things we pay homage to, maybe even without realizing it? Our society is similar to that of first-century Athens, which thought itself to be religious but in which the actual content of faith seemed to be losing its hold.

How more modern could Paul become, then, when he writes that people "would search for God and perhaps grope for him" (v. 27)? After a century shattered by two world wars, the Holocaust, the A-bomb, and millions of refugees living in exile, it is no wonder that so many people today "grope" for a God they have difficulty perceiving behind all this suffering! An equally large number of people have become disenchanted with the institutional church. How can one find God where there is such skepticism about the community of God's people?

What are our "unknown gods," those things we have deified? A half-century ago Will Herberg said the unknown God of Americans seems to be faith itself (*Protestant, Catholic, Jew* [New York: Doubleday, 1955]). Sincerity of faith is of paramount value, not its content. Not knowing the true God, we have substituted faith itself as the object of religion.

A similar example of an unknown god is spirituality itself. Spirituality has become like a mantra in our society. Many people declare themselves to be spiritual, with no content or object in their spiritual life. Meditation is valued more for its relaxing and therapeutic value, not for what one meditates *in* or *about*. Being rootless of content, such "spirituality" is usually not deeply engaged in society. There is little sense that because this world is God's creation, we are deeply involved in its pathos.

An "unknown god" today might also be the kind of sentimental notion one has about God. The idea of a "man upstairs who likes me" is a far cry from the awesome God of the Bible or the Suffering Servant on the cross. But it is a starting point for proclamation.

What the preacher needs for this text is a clear-eyed insight into the hearts of the audience. The sermon will be shaped by the "context" of the congregation. We can affirm that which the audience holds dear — whether it be faith, spirituality, a rather benign God, or whatever — then probe those ideas for their inadequacies and need of content.

Another preaching approach to this text would be a theme like "What do we know about God and how do we know it?" "American Civil Religion" is a vague Unitarianism or Deism. This view of God grows out of an unreflective natural theology, now heavily influenced by New Age sentimentalism; that is, we see God in the beauty of nature and feel his presence when we see the daisies in the field, etc.

Paul's approach would be to appropriate the truth of that — "yes, God did create it all . . ." — then steer the listener's thinking to the biblical view of

God, with all the richness of God's activity among humans through the broad sweep of human history.

Paul's sermon to the Jews in Acts 13 sets out from a totally different place than this sermon to the Greeks in Acts 17, but both sermons end with the resurrection of Jesus. *All* of Paul's sermons end with the resurrection. *This* is finally how we know God, by knowing Jesus of Nazareth who was crucified and raised for us. *This* is God's revelation. Of course we glimpse the power of God in creation, but we *know* God fully through the cross and empty tomb.

In preaching this text, there is an obvious link to this Sunday's Gospel lesson, John 14:15-21. Just as Paul speaks about an unknown god to the Greeks, so here Jesus speaks to his disciples, who will soon face an unknown and frightening future without him. Both texts are written for assurance in the time of doubt and uncertainty. The assurance of both texts is God's presence with us and the hope of eternity through Jesus' resurrection.

The connection with the Epistle lesson (1 Pet. 3:13-22) is that Peter exhorts his readers to speak the gospel with courage, even though they are maligned and suffer. Paul knew very well he would be ridiculed in Athens, because the whole notion of one sovereign creator God sending a "son" to earth to suffer, die, and be raised would strike the Gentile Athenians as total foolishness (1 Cor. 1:18-25). What a fitting message for our day, when so many people think the whole idea of religion is foolish!

Michael Rogness

Preaching as Worship

HUGHES OLIPHANT OLD

The value of preaching seems to have come under question recently. One wonders whether it is as indispensable to the church as we have traditionally thought. Preaching has lost much of its popularity in our day. One is a bit hard-pressed to name outstanding preachers in our generation who have carried on the preaching traditions of the great preachers of a generation ago. Where have all the Buttricks, the Truetts, the Fosdicks, and the McCartneys gone? Why are so many pulpits vacant and so many churches empty?

We could discuss the value of preaching from a number of different angles. Is it really so vital in inspiring the religious spirit of the age? Does preaching really help us get along with life? Does it kindle faith, does it nourish our hope, does it strengthen the bond of love? One could speak of a time when indeed preaching did all this, but does it still do it today? Maybe on the threshold of the third millennium preaching has lost its power to do this and should therefore be de-emphasized.

This is certainly a problem worthy of discussion, but it is not the basic problem. As I see it, the fundamental question which needs to be discussed is how preaching serves God's glory. How do we serve God in preaching? In the end we have been called to serve God, and we preach because God has called us to serve him in this special ministry. What we need to be clear about is how our preaching serves God's glory.

Right here in America there must be hundreds of thousands of ministers who spend a good portion of their time preparing and preaching sermons. Does all this effort, all this busyness and intellectual exertion, all this homiletical lather, have any point? Is it somehow misdirected? Are we really doing what God has called us to do?

I. The Preaching of Moses

Preaching seems to go back to Moses, at least preaching as both the church and the synagogue know it. Moses had never thought of himself as an orator. When God spoke to him out of the burning bush, he hesitated to go to the court of Pharaoh and deliver the word God gave him because he was not gifted as a public speaker. And yet, as the story develops, we learn again and again that God entrusted his word to Moses, and Moses faithfully delivered that word both to the court of Pharaoh and to the children of Israel. To Pharaoh Moses preached judgment. That was the word God had given him. To the children of Israel Moses preached deliverance. That was the word God gave for that unlikely bunch of slaves whom God had called out of Egypt to be his people. There must have been a lot of preaching on the way to Sinai. How often the people wanted to turn back. Their murmuring constantly bogged things down. When Israel reached the shores of the Red Sea, fear fell upon them and Moses preached God's faithfulness, "Fear not, stand firm, and see the salvation of the LORD, which he will work for you today; for the Egyptians whom you see today, you shall never see again. The LORD will fight for you, and you have only to be still" (Exod. 14:13-14; this and all biblical quotes in this article are from the RSV).

Israel received God's word and passed through the sea dry-shod. The people knew God had been faithful to them, at least for a time. Out in the wilderness, however, the food began to give out and the people began to murmur. They remembered the fleshpots of Egypt and how they had bread to the full. Their hearts sank, and again Moses had to preach the faithfulness of God to them (Exod. 16:12). All this preaching took place before the Law was revealed at Mount Sinai. Sometimes preaching can only prepare us to hear the Word of God. Sometimes it does no more than lead us to Scripture. This was what was happening on the way to Sinai. The people were being prepared to receive the Law.

When Moses had brought his people to the foot of Sinai, he preached his great eagles'-wings sermon in which he opened up Israel's destiny to be a holy people and a royal priesthood to serve God's glory. There it was that God gave his people the Law, and again Moses preached, interpreting it and explaining it to the people so that it became the foundation of the covenant community. Right from the days of Moses, preaching involved the proclamation and interpretation of the Book of the Covenant (Exod. 24). Scripture became the basis of preaching.

The Book of the Covenant opened up the Decalogue. Right there at Sinai the interpretation of the Law became a sacred ministry. As the tradition of the synagogue has it, Moses and Aaron, Nadab and Abihu, and the seventy elders of Israel were called up into the mountain and entrusted with the interpreting of the Law. It was the sacred task of the elders of Israel. They studied the Law, memorized it, meditated upon it, and taught it to the next generation. Passing on the Law through teaching and preaching became a sacred vocation (Deut. 5).

In Deuteronomy the picture of Moses as a preacher broadens considerably. There we find him urging his people to be faithful to the Law, to guard it and live by it. But another thing about the sermons in Deuteronomy which interests us is that the preaching there suggests a high preaching culture. There are clear indications of a cultivated use of rhetoric. Moses may at first have lacked training in the arts of oratory, but in the providence of God he had learned these arts. Perhaps as a boy growing up as the son of Pharaoh's daughter he had studied the arts of oratory in the palace school, but they had never caught fire until the burning bush ignited those gifts God had long before hidden in his heart.

In time the Law was set in the Torah, the five books of Moses. Much of the meaning of the Law could only be understood in the context of salvation history. The Torah provided that historical context. It recounted the traditions of the patriarchs. It showed how God, generation after generation, calls out people to serve him. It tells us how God leads the people he calls into an ever newer and richer life. God's people are on a pilgrimage, and on that pilgrimage there are trials and temptations, but God brings his people through. All these experiences teach us; they impart to us sacred wisdom. All this is found in the Torah to help us understand the Law. For centuries it has been preached in order to open up to us the manifold wisdom of God.

Moses served God by proclaiming his word. This was the service to which he had been called. Moses taught the Word, and this glorified God. There is something so magnificent about the Torah — its wonder for God's creation of the world and all things living, its pure awe before God's mighty acts of providence, its ardent devotion before the mystery of God's love in his mighty works of redemption. There is something dazzling about the moral majesty of the Law, something fresh and clean about the righteousness of God's commandments. The Torah glorified God because it is the very Word of God. It is the perfect praise he himself has ordained.

II. The Preaching of the Prophets

The preaching of the prophets was worship as well. In many ways it continued in the tradition of Moses in that it remembered the Law of the Lord, it proclaimed that Law, and it interpreted that Law. That is what we find Jeremiah doing in the sermon God sent him to deliver before the temple gates one year at the celebration of the great feast. God gave Jeremiah a specific Word for a particular time and a distinct place. He reminded the people of the Ten Commandments. Worship has a way of involving remembering. That is made clear by the fourth commandment, Remember the Sabbath day to keep it holy. Jesus made the same point when he instituted the Lord's Supper. He told his disciples, "Do this in remembrance of me." Jeremiah in his preaching made a specific point of reminding God's people of the Word he had given them. That was the basis of his exhorting them to be faithful to God's Word: "Will you steal, murder, commit adultery, swear falsely, burn incense to Baal, and go after other gods that you have not known, and then come and stand before me in this house . . . ?" (Jer. 7:9-10). Jeremiah glorified God by insisting on purity of devotion. God is glorified by his holiness, and when we reflect that holiness he is truly worshiped.

That was the mystery that was revealed to Isaiah in the temple in that year when King Uzziah died (Isa. 6:1-13). His ears and his eyes were opened so that he was confronted with the heavenly worship, and it all had to do with holiness:

> Holy, holy, holy is the LORD of hosts;
> the whole earth is full of his glory. (Isa. 6:3)

The glory of God fills the earth, even if we fail to see it, but when we do see it we are transformed by it. Then when we are transformed by the glory of God, we reflect God's glory and God's glory is magnified. This is worship!

For the prophets the preaching of righteousness was essential to the serving of God's glory. We find this with particular eloquence in the preaching of the prophet Micah:

> "With what shall I come before the LORD,
>   and bow myself before God on high?
> Shall I come before him with burnt offerings,
>   with calves a year old?
> Will the LORD be pleased with thousands of rams,
>   with ten thousands of rivers of oil?

Shall I give my first-born for my transgression,
    the fruit of my body for the sin of my soul?"
He has showed you, O man, what is good:
    and what does the LORD require of you
but to do justice, and to love kindness,
    and to walk humbly with your God?   (Mic. 6:6-8)

The justice of a Christian society, its mercy toward the suffering, the alienated, the impoverished, and the excluded reflect the very being of God. God is of his essence merciful and gracious. That had been made clear at Sinai (Exod. 34:6). But there is something else of great importance here. When God's people walk humbly and with modesty, the glory that belongs to God and God alone is intimated. A humble walk is the most effective witness of God's glory. This is worship. The glory of God implies for his people simplicity and sincerity. To enter into a true pilgrimage is to be humble toward God as well as the neighbor. Surely, when a concern for such matters is preached in the course of a service of worship, God is honored in a consequential and substantial way.

The prophets could be very critical of the worship of God's people. Idols compromised the uniqueness of God. The Sabbath was abused, the covenant was forgotten, the Law was transgressed, the poor were taken advantage of, the needy were sold into slavery, the sacred bonds of the family were violated, and the property rights of neighbors were ignored. God sent the prophets to preach against all this. The preaching of Amos denounced the fake worship of the sanctuary at Bethel:

I hate, I despise your feasts,
    and I take no delight in your solemn assemblies.
Even though you offer me your burnt offerings and cereal offerings,
    I will not accept them,
and the peace offerings of your fatted beasts
    I will not look upon.
Take away from me the noise of your songs;
    to the melody of your harps I will not listen.
But let justice roll down like waters,
    and righteousness like an everflowing stream.   (Amos 5:21-24)

The trouble was that the worship of a sinful people beclouded the glory of God. Dishonest business practices, confiscatory taxation, bribery in the courts, fornication, prostitution, and marital infidelity on the part of those who claimed to be God's people confused the witness of those who worshiped.

The preaching of the prophets glorified God because it made clear the righteousness of God. It stressed the implications of God's holiness. We, his people, must be holy because we are his people (Matt. 5:48).

III. Preaching in the Temple

In the temple an important part of worship was the recounting of the history of salvation. The Levites in particular were responsible for passing on the sacred stories of the patriarchs. Much of preaching was simply a matter of recounting salvation history, retelling the story. We get a good picture of this in Psalm 105:

> O give thanks to the LORD, call on his name,
>   make known his deeds among the peoples!
> Sing to him, sing praises to him,
>   tell of all his wonderful works!
> Glory in his holy name;
>   let the hearts of those who seek the LORD rejoice!
> Seek the LORD and his strength,
>   seek his presence continually!
> Remember the wonderful works that he has done,
>   his miracles, and the judgments he uttered,
> O offspring of Abraham his servant,
>   sons of Jacob, his chosen ones! (vv. 1-6)

The psalm continues with a long hymnic recounting of the story of the patriarchs, the descent into Egypt, the years of slavery, then deliverance from Pharaoh and his armies at the Red Sea. Finally, the psalm tells of the entry into the Promised Land. All this is done in hymnic form, as we find it in this psalm, but the same thing was done in the preaching of the Levites as well. The hymns were but a recapitulation of what was preached in the pulpit. What is interesting about the psalm is that it suggests the theology that was behind the recounting of this story. Telling this story glorified God. It was a sacred memorial of God's mighty acts of redemption.

The passing on of the story of God's mighty acts of creation and redemption was worship at its most profound. It stands in awe before the mystery of salvation and bears witness to the saving love of God. Again this is made very clear in the opening lines of Psalm 78, another one of the historical psalms:

> Give ear, O my people, to my teaching;
>> incline your ears to the words of my mouth!
> I will open my mouth in a parable;
>> I will utter dark sayings from of old,
> things that we have heard and known,
>> that our fathers have told us.
> We will not hide them from their children,
>> but tell to the coming generation
> the glorious deeds of the Lord, and his might,
>> and the wonders which he has wrought.   (vv. 1-4)

Many things might be treated in preaching, but it never got too far from recounting the holy history of how God had revealed himself to his people. It is clear all through Scripture that the recounting of holy history is worship. God presents himself to us when we hear, "I am the Lord your God, who brought you out of the land of Egypt" (Exod. 20:2). It is in God's mighty acts of redemption that he meets us, and it is on the basis of these mighty acts that we worship him.

IV. Preaching in the Synagogue

Another picture we get of preaching as worship is in the story of Ezra's reconstituting the worship of Israel after the return of the Jews from their exile in Babylon (Neh. 8:1-8). There we read of how all the people were gathered together in a sacred assembly and how the scroll of the Law was brought and read publicly before the men, the women, and even the children. This solemn, public reading of the Law was obviously understood as worship. It was a cultic act which constituted the community of God's people and made of it a sacred communion. The reading was introduced with prayer, and after the reading the text was explained by the Levites. All this was done in a definite liturgical order, an order of worship which is maintained in the synagogue down to this day. In the synagogue, of course, there was never any question but that the reading and preaching of the Law belonged to the essence of worship, and the church quite obviously followed along in the same tradition.

This story of Ezra's public reading of the Law has always been regarded as the prototype of the worship of the synagogue. It was hardly an innovation, of course. The great reverence with which the Scriptures were opened, read, and preached must have gone far back in the history of God's people. One can well imagine that it went back to the story of Moses reading the Book of the Covenant before the solemn assembly at the foot of Mount Sinai (Exod. 24:1-11).

The cultivation of sacred wisdom was an act of devotion among the Jews of antiquity. Rabbis devoted their whole lives to the study of Scripture. They committed extensive passages of Scripture to memory. The copying of the scrolls was a time-consuming but sacred task. In those days it all had to be done by hand. The rabbis were meticulous in their concern for accuracy. The writing out of the manuscripts was a sacred service, and so was the interpreting of those sacred texts. There was a long, carefully guarded tradition of this interpretation. It, too, was carefully memorized. All this devotion to God's Word found its culmination in the preaching and teaching of Scripture.

Study and prayer went hand in hand. We find as a sort of introduction to the Psalms a description of the spirituality of the rabbi:

> But his delight is in the law of the LORD,
>   and on his law he meditates day and night.　　　　(Ps. 1:2)

Meditation on Scripture was at the center of the devout life.

Prayer and Scripture were never very far apart. In the best tradition of the synagogue, prayer and the study of Scripture were in a constant dialogue. One approached Scripture with prayer, and one approached prayer with the study of Scripture. The worship of the synagogue began with prayer. Only after prayer were the scrolls opened up. After the Scriptures had been read and preached, again the faithful offered prayer. Preaching led to prayer; one might even say it demanded prayer or, even more, came to flower in prayer. Worship for the synagogue was simply made up of prayers, psalms, and hymns on one hand, and the reading and preaching of Scripture on the other.

V. The Preaching of Jesus

Preaching was a major part of the ministry of Jesus. As all four Gospels present him, Jesus was a preacher. One gathers from the Gospels that Jesus preached often, not just once a week on Sabbath mornings. Like George

594

Whitefield or John Wesley, he seems to have preached whenever he had a chance. We read that when he was in Jerusalem he preached daily (Matt. 26:55 and par.). One gets the impression he did the same thing as he went from town to town in Galilee. Jesus often preached in the synagogue. All the evidence suggests that he followed the usual traditions of synagogue preaching. The Gospel of Luke tells us about a sermon he preached in his hometown synagogue (Luke 4:16-30). There he took as his text several verses from the prophet Isaiah:

> The Spirit of the Lord God is upon me,
>   because the Lord has anointed me
> to bring good tidings to the afflicted;
>   he has sent me to bind up the brokenhearted,
> to proclaim liberty to the captives,
>   and the opening of the prison to those who are bound;
> To proclaim the year of the Lord's favor. . . .   (Isa. 61:1-2)

In this sermon Jesus proclaimed God's faithfulness to his covenant promises. God had for centuries promised a Savior through the prophets. That covenant promise had been renewed generation after generation. Now in this sermon God is praised for its fulfillment. This is even today at the core of Christian preaching: God is faithful; he has in the gift of his Son fulfilled his promises. This proclamation glorifies God.

This proclamation of release to the captives, sight to the blind, and liberty to the oppressed is good news, news so good we cannot but praise God, receive the gospel, and live by it. True worship is a heartfelt response to the proclamation of the gospel. So it is that the preaching of the gospel engenders worship. Not only is preaching itself worship, it leads to worship as well. It inspires the worship of those who listen.

The proclamation that the kingdom of God had come was the recurring theme of Jesus' preaching. He proclaimed that finally the poor in spirit would enter into their rightful inheritance. At last those who mourn shall be comforted and the meek shall inherit the earth. Finally the hungry would be satisfied and the pure in heart would see God (Matt. 5:1-12). In proclaiming the kingdom, Jesus announced the immanence of God. The presence of God's kingdom was the manifestation of the presence of God himself. To enter the kingdom and take part in the life of the kingdom was to draw near to God. It was to have communion with God. When Jesus proclaimed the kingdom, he opened up the very presence of God. He preached the gospel not only in the synagogues but in the marketplaces, in the fields and on the beaches. Wherever the kingdom was proclaimed, God was worshiped. The people heard the gospel and rejoiced.

Jesus preached faith. He urged his hearers to believe in him, to follow him, and to walk in the ways of God. "I am the way, and the truth, and the life," said Jesus (John 14:6). He invited Nicodemus to believe in him that he might have eternal life (3:1-16). Alluding to the story of the brazen serpent in the wilderness, Jesus promised this prominent Jewish theologian, "As Moses lifted up the serpent in the wilderness, so must the Son of man be lifted up, that whoever believes in him may have eternal life" (3:14-15). Having healed the paralytic at the pool of Bethesda, Jesus preached the healing power of faith. "Truly, truly, I say to you, he who hears my word and believes him who sent me has eternal life; he does not come into judgment, but has passed from death to life" (5:24). Preaching faith makes clear the healing power of God. It is a witness to his power and so to his glory. After feeding the multitude on the mountain, he preached faith to them and promised them, "Truly, truly, . . . he who believes has eternal life" (6:47). In preaching faith he revealed himself to be the bread of life. In him there is a sustaining and nurturing power. His power is a power that gives us power. He was the bread of life, and whoever ate that bread would live forever. He preached faith in revealing himself to be the Good Shepherd. "I am the good shepherd. The good shepherd lays down his life for the sheep" (10:11). To preach faith is to witness to the wisdom of God. It is to confess that the ways of God are good and true. It is to devote oneself to following those ways, and when we follow those ways God is glorified.

Jesus preached the way, the truth, and the life. Such a message is very practical for this life, but it also makes clear that in Christ God has opened up a way to eternal life. After the raising of Lazarus Jesus proclaimed, "I am the resurrection and the life; he who believes in me, though he die, yet shall he live, and whoever lives and believes in me shall never die" (11:25-26). In preaching eternal life we give witness to the transcendent, heavenly glory of God.

Preaching faith glorifies God because it confesses him to be worthy of our faith. It witnesses to God's worth. That, after all, is the root meaning of our English word "worship." To worship God is to tell of his worth. God is the one in whom we can be confident. Ultimately he is the only one in whom we can put our trust. When we as preachers bear witness to this truth, then God is worshiped.

Jesus preached in the synagogues, in the fields, and in the marketplaces, but he also preached in the temple at Jerusalem (Mark 11; 12 and par.). In fact, his preaching in the temple in the week before his passion was something of a climax to his preaching ministry. In this he fulfilled the preaching ministry of Israel. Of particular importance in this preaching is his exposition of a number of key passages of Scripture. The interpretation of Scripture was always the basis of Jesus' preaching. That had been the case in the synagogue, and that was the course Jesus set for the church. We hear of his interpretation of Isaiah 56:7,

> My house shall be called a house of prayer
> for all peoples. (cf. Mark 11:17)

With this text Jesus taught that God had called not only the Jews to worship him, but the Gentiles as well. Then we hear his interpretation of Psalm 118:22,

> The stone which the builders rejected
> has become the head of the corner.

With this text Jesus taught that although the rulers of the Jews might reject him, yet he would fulfill the role God had appointed for him. A bit further on we read of how Jesus interpreted the story of the burning bush (Mark 12:26). It was there that God revealed his name. He is the God of Abraham, the God of Isaac, and the God of Jacob. Jesus then explained that God is not the God of the dead but of the living. As Jesus interpreted this passage, it clearly indicates the resurrection and life eternal.

Another key passage of Scripture which Jesus explained in his preaching in the temple was the Shema (cf. Deut. 6:4): "Hear, O Israel: The Lord our God, the Lord is one; and you shall love the Lord your God with all you heart, and with all your soul, and with all your mind, and with all your strength" (Mark 12:29-30). This passage, Jesus taught, is the first and greatest commandment. Here, in the preaching of Jesus, we learn that love for God is our ultimate worship. Preaching is worship because it is both the revelation of God's love for us and an expression of our love for God. So it was for Jesus, and so it should be for us.

Finally we are told of how Jesus understood Psalm 110:1:

> The Lord says to my lord:
> "Sit at my right hand,
> till I make your enemies your footstool."

Here Jesus taught that not only was he the son of David but also the Son of God (Mark 12:35-37). As we find throughout the New Testament, these passages were key to the interpretation of Scripture which Jesus taught in his preaching. They were for Jesus the messianic promises, and their interpretation was fundamental to the preaching of Jesus. It was on the basis of a number of such passages of Scripture that Jesus interpreted and then fulfilled the role of the Messiah.

In Luke's account of the appearance of the risen Jesus to two disciples on the road to Emmaus (Luke 24:27, 44-47), we get yet another glimpse of this. This was not the first time Jesus had opened the Scriptures to his disciples. He had been doing just that throughout his whole ministry. Only after the resurrection did it finally make sense. The preaching of the gospel was based on Jesus' interpretation of Scripture.

To understand the preaching of Jesus at its most profound, we need to hear it in a trinitarian dynamic. Jesus as the Word bore witness to the Word. In the end it is the very Word of God which glorifies the Father. It is in the outpouring of his glory that he is glorified.

VI. The Preaching of the Apostles

Jesus, as we have said, continued the homiletical traditions of the synagogue, but it is also true that he recast that tradition and gave it a completely new direction. With Jesus preaching became the proclamation of the gospel. The preaching of the apostles followed Jesus very closely in that the apostles preached the gospel.

We find this very clearly in Peter's sermon at Pentecost. The story of what God had done in the death and resurrection of Christ was recounted. "Men of Israel, hear these words: Jesus of Nazareth, a man attested to you by God with mighty works and wonders and signs which God did through him in your midst, as you yourselves know — this Jesus, delivered up according to the definite plan and foreknowledge of God, you crucified and killed by the hands of lawless men. But God raised him up, having loosed the pangs of death, because it was not possible for him to be held by it" (Acts 2:22-24). This proclamation of God's mighty acts of salvation in Christ demanded an affirmation of faith on the part of those who heard that proclamation. The hearing of the gospel is as much an act of worship as its preaching. It is in hearing our Master that we manifest our discipleship. We read that those who heard Peter's preaching of the gospel received it and became disciples. "So those who received his word were baptized, and there were added that day about three thousand souls. And they devoted themselves to the apostles' teaching and fellowship, to the breaking of bread and the prayers"

(2:41-42). When God's Word is received, God is worshiped. Quite naturally from this receiving of the Word the devotion to the fellowship of the community and the life of prayer develop. Yet the very receiving of the Word itself is of the essence of worship. The celebration of baptism and the Lord's Supper seals the receiving of the Word and is therefore worship.

Ultimately worship is a matter of our entering into a covenant relationship with God. To worship is to become the children of God in spirit and in truth. It is for God to manifest himself as our God, and for us to experience him as our God. It is for us to discover ourselves as his children in receiving his Fatherly blessing. Worship claims God as he has revealed himself in Jesus Christ; it is to embrace him. It is to recognize Christ as present in both Word and sacrament. It is to experience the fraternal bond we have in God's Son. It is to live in the fellowship of the household of faith. It is to know truth welling up in us by the enlightening of the Holy Spirit.

Just before the ascension, Jesus commissioned his disciples to go out to all nations and preach repentance and the forgiveness of sins in his name (Luke 24:47). In their preaching the disciples were to teach everything Jesus had commanded them (Matt. 28:20). They were to do this in the name of Jesus. That is, they were to continue the preaching ministry of Jesus. They were to teach what he had taught, and they were to teach it as he had taught it. We find Peter and John doing just this. In fact, they were even so bold as to do it in the temple at Jerusalem. This was a scandal for the religious authorities of the day, especially "because they were teaching the people and proclaiming in Jesus the resurrection from the dead" (Acts 4:2). The authorities forbade the apostles "to speak or teach at all in the name of Jesus" (4:18). But the apostles could not give up preaching the gospel Christ had preached. That was one thing they could not do. They knew that they were bound to obey God rather than man. It was their divine commission to preach in the name of Jesus, to continue his preaching ministry. Christian preaching was preaching in the name of Jesus. It was continuing the ministry of the Word as Jesus had exercised it.

Further on in the Acts of the Apostles we read of the conversion of the apostle Paul. He was scarcely converted when he took up a preaching ministry. Having already had a very thorough theological education, he was especially suited for this calling. The text is very clear that right from the beginning, he "preached boldly in the name of Jesus" (Acts 9:27-29). He was able to present Jesus as the Messiah in the synagogues of the Diaspora and as risen Lord and Savior in the Areopagus of Athens. For Paul preaching Jesus was, to be sure, a matter of preaching what Jesus had preached. That was fundamental, but there was something else. It was also a matter of bearing witness to the risen and ascended glory of his Lord. His conversion came about because the risen, glorified Christ had confronted him on the Damascus road. This experience made him a witness to the resurrection (1 Cor. 15:8). His preaching passed on that witness. Passing on the witness is one of the basic dimensions of Christian worship. In the worship of the temple, witnessing to God's saving acts was an important part of worship. Thanksgiving was offered to God for his saving grace as a witness to these saving acts, whether they were to the nation as a whole or to one individual in particular. Whether in the ancient temple or in the church today, the thankful witness of those who have experienced God's saving grace is fundamental to the serving of God's glory. As Jesus himself put it, "You shall be my witnesses in Jerusalem and in Judea and Samaria and to the end of the earth" (Acts 1:8). The apostolic witness is at the center of Christian worship.

Paul was a witness throughout the world. The worldwide extent of his preaching ministry was one of its characteristics. He preached to Jews and Greeks; he preached in Syria, in Asia, in Macedonia, and even in Rome itself. God was glorified in the universality of his preaching ministry. For Paul there was a spiritual beauty in the proclamation of the gospel. It was so perfectly expressed in the prophecy of Isaiah which the apostle quotes in Romans 10:15, "How beautiful are the feet of those who preach good news" (cf. Isa. 52:7). In God's sight preaching is beautiful and well pleasing to God because it is through preaching that faith is spread among all peoples. As the old King James Version put it, "Faith cometh by hearing, and hearing by the Word of God." The RSV translates it, "So faith comes from what is heard, and what is heard comes by the preaching of Christ" (Rom. 10:17). For the apostle Paul the preaching of the gospel through all the world served God's glory and was therefore worship.

In his first epistle to the Corinthians, Paul tells us that in Christian preaching "we preach Christ crucified" (1:23). This may be a stumbling block to the Jews and folly to the Gentiles, "but to those who are called, both Jews and Greeks, Christ [is] the power of God and the wisdom of God" (1:24). Here again we find a sort of preaching which recounts the mighty acts of God for our salvation. Simply telling the story of redemption has a magnificent and mysterious power in it that transforms lives, and when this takes place the wondrous glory of God is made manifest. We are confronted by the saving power of God, and we can do nothing but praise God.

In 1 Timothy we have the beginnings of a church order. It is very clear from this epistle that the reading and preaching of Scripture is a major component of the worship of the early church. Paul instructs Timothy, "Attend to the public reading of scripture, to preaching, to teaching" (4:13). We notice here that the apostle is quite explicit that the good order of the church has both the reading of Scripture and the preaching of Scripture. The public reading should not be swallowed up by the sermon. There is a sort of dialectic between the reading and the preaching. We noticed this with Ezra. With reading, the timeless, unchanging Word of God is set forth, but with preaching the continual, ongoing interpretation of that Word is expressed. Every generation must appropriate the Word for itself. In every land and every age it must be heard and understood anew. And yet the eternal Word of God abides forever.

But also we see from this epistle that preaching and teaching are both underlined. They are synonymous. True Christian preaching has a strong element of teaching in it, and true Christian teaching has a sermonic intention. It is to the end of admonition, edification, and spiritual nourishment that we teach the Scriptures.

The apostle Paul had many insights on the subject of preaching as worship, but one of the most significant is found in his epistle to the Ephesians. The whole epistle seems set in a context of worship. It opens with a prayer uttered in terms of the most profound adoration.

> Blessed be the God and Father of our Lord Jesus Christ, who has blessed us in Christ with every spiritual blessing in the heavenly places, even as he chose us in him before the foundation of the world, that we should be holy and blameless before him. He destined us in love to be his sons through Jesus Christ, according to the purpose of his will, to the praise of his glorious grace which he freely bestowed on us in the Beloved. In him we have redemption through his blood, the forgiveness of our trespasses, according to the riches of his grace which he lavished upon us. For he has made known to us in all wisdom and insight the mystery of his will, according to his purpose which he set forth in Christ as a plan for the fulness of time, to unite all things in him, things in heaven and things on earth. (1:3-10)

For Paul the preaching of the gospel is the revelation of the mystery of God's eternal purposes. This unveiling of God's purposes shows forth his glory. It makes known "the unsearchable riches of Christ" (3.0). It opens up "the manifold wisdom of God" (3:10).

In the biblical tradition the wisdom of God is a very rich concept. It has to do with the creation and the establishing of the earth and stretching out of the heavens with its myriad of stars. It has to do with the providential governing of history. The wisdom of God is particularly revealed in the law and the moral order of life. Above all is the wondrous wisdom of God in providing for our redemption in the passion of Christ and his triumphant victory over sin and death in the resurrection. The wisdom of God's grace is beyond our understanding, and yet in preaching it is opened up to our understanding. In preaching the mystery is unveiled so that we might not only fall down before it but embrace it and make it our own.

Wisdom and knowledge and understanding are closely related. In the biblical tradition there was no greater delight than the study of Scripture because there one drew close to the divine wisdom.

The wisdom of God is glorious, just as the power of God is glorious, just as the love and mercy of God are glorious. When preaching opens up the wisdom of God, then we are enlightened and inspired. We are filled with wonder. We are so enthralled with the divine wisdom, what else is this but worship?

Conclusion

Much could be said about preaching as worship, but perhaps the word with which we should conclude is a word of Jesus. I have in mind that word of promise with which he closed his earthly ministry. He sent the apostles out to preach. They were to preach the gospel throughout the whole world. They were to teach everything Jesus had taught them, and they were given the promise, "And lo, I am with you always" (Matt. 28:20). The commission to preach bore the promise of presence. Preaching is worship because it is the means of the divine presence. Just as there is a eucharistic presence in our worship, so there is a kerygmatic presence. In the reading and preaching of Scripture we experience the covenantal bond between God and his people. Worship is a *koinōnia*, a sacred communion, and one way we experience that communion is in the reading and preaching of God's Word.

Contributors

William J. Abraham
Perkins School of Theology
Dallas, Texas

Elizabeth Achtemeier
Union Theological Seminary
Richmond, Virginia

Ronald J. Allen
Christian Theological Seminary
Indianapolis, Indiana

Dale C. Allison
Pittsburgh Theological Seminary
Pittsburgh, Pennsylvania

Gary A. Anderson
Harvard Divinity School
Cambridge, Massachusetts

Martyn D. Atkins
Cliff College
North Sheffield, England

Raymond Bailey, Pastor
Seventh and James Baptist Church
Waco, Texas

Andrew Bandstra
Calvin Theological Seminary
Grand Rapids, Michigan

Andrew H. Bartelt
Concordia Seminary
St. Louis, Missouri

Charles L. Bartow
Princeton Theological Seminary
Princeton, New Jersey

Richard Bauckham
University of St. Andrews
St. Andrews, Scotland

C. Clifton Black
Princeton Theological Seminary
Princeton, New Jersey

Robert L. Brawley
McCormick Theological Seminary
Chicago, Illinois

Annette G. Brownlee
Ascension Episcopal Church
Pueblo, Colorado

CONTRIBUTORS

John P. Burgess
Pittsburgh Theological Seminary
Pittsburgh, Pennsylvania

Richard A. Burridge, Dean
King's College
London, England

Charles L. Campbell
Columbia Theological Seminary
Decatur, Georgia

Lewis R. Donelson
Austin Presbyterian Theological Seminary
Austin, Texas

Patricia Dutcher-Walls
Knox College
Toronto, Ontario

Craig A. Evans
Trinity Western University
Langley, British Columbia

Gabriel Fackre
Andover Newton Theological School
Boston, Massachusetts

Lawrence W. Farris, Pastor
Presbyterian Church (USA)
Three Rivers, Michigan

Stephen Farris
Knox College
Toronto, Ontario

Robert A. J. Gagnon
Pittsburgh Theological Seminary
Pittsburgh, Pennsylvania

Thomas W. Gillespie, President
Princeton Theological Seminary
Princeton, New Jersey

John Goldingay
Fuller Theological Seminary
Pasadena, California

Colin J. D. Greene
British and Foreign Bible Society
Swindon, England

Sidney Greidanus
Calvin Theological Seminary
Grand Rapids, Michigan

Colin E. Gunton
King's College
London, England

Sarah Henrich
Luther Seminary
St. Paul, Minnesota

Scott Hoezee, Pastor
Calvin Christian Reformed Church
Grand Rapids, Michigan

John C. Holbert
Perkins School of Theology
Dallas, Texas

David E. Holwerda
Calvin Theological Seminary
Grand Rapids, Michigan

Leslie J. Hoppe
Catholic Theological Union
Chicago, Illinois

Arland J. Hultgren
Luther Seminary
St. Paul, Minnesota

George Hunsinger
Princeton Theological Seminary
Princeton, New Jersey

Robert W. Jenson
Center of Theological Inquiry
Princeton, New Jersey

Robert Jewett
Garrett-Evangelical Theological Seminary
Evanston, Illinois

Karen Jobes
Westmont College
Santa Barbara, California

Scott Black Johnston
Austin Presbyterian Theological Seminary
Austin, Texas

Donald Juel
Princeton Theological Seminary
Princeton, New Jersey

James F. Kay
Princeton Theological Seminary
Princeton, New Jersey

Craig S. Keener
Eastern Seminary
St. David's, Pennsylvania

Leonard R. Klein, Pastor
Christ Lutheran Church
York, Pennsylvania

Joel E. Kok, Pastor
Trinity Christian Reformed Church
Broomall, Pennsylvania

James Limburg
Luther Seminary
St. Paul, Minnesota

Tremper Longman III
Westmont College
Santa Barbara, California

F. Dean Lueking, Pastor
Grace Lutheran Church
River Forest, Illinois

Lois Malcolm
Luther Seminary
St. Paul, Minnesota

Martin E. Marty
The Fairfax M. Cone Distinguished
  Service Professor
The University of Chicago
Chicago, Illinois

Peter W. Marty, Pastor
St. Paul Lutheran Church
Davenport, Iowa

J. Clinton McCann, Jr.
Eden Theological Seminary
St. Louis, Missouri

Douglas Moo
Wheaton Graduate School
Wheaton, Illinois

Thorsten Moritz
Cheltenham and Gloucester College
  of Higher Education
Cheltenham, England

Roland E. Murphy, O. Carm.
George Washington University
Washington, D.C.

Hughes Oliphant Old
Research Theologian
Trenton, New Jersey

Dennis T. Olson
Princeton Theological Seminary
Princeton, New Jersey

Earl F. Palmer, Pastor
University Presbyterian Church
Seattle, Washington

Steven D. Paulson
Luther Seminary
St. Paul, Minnesota

Mary Margaret Pazdan, O.P.
Aquinas Institute of Theology
St. Louis, Missouri

CONTRIBUTORS

Christine E. Pilkington
Christ Church University College
Canterbury, England

Daniel J. Price, Pastor
First Presbyterian Church
Eureka, California

Paul R. Raabe
Concordia Seminary
St. Louis, Missouri

Ephraim Radner, Rector
Ascension Episcopal Church
Pueblo, Colorado

Stephen W. Ramp, Pastor
First Trinity Presbyterian Church
Laurel, Mississippi

Barbara E. Reid
Catholic Theological Union
Chicago, Illinois

Stephen Breck Reid
Austin Presbyterian Theological Seminary
Austin, Texas

André Resner, Jr., Pastor
Lamington Presbyterian Church
Bedminster, New Jersey

Michael Rogness
Luther Seminary
St. Paul, Minnesota

John M. Rottman
Emmanuel College
Toronto, Ontario

The Reverend Fleming Rutledge
Priest of the Episcopal Church
Diocese of New York

Timothy E. Saleska
Concordia Seminary
St. Louis, Missouri

Marguerite Shuster
Fuller Theological Seminary
Pasadena, California

Graydon F. Snyder
Chicago Theological Seminary
Chicago, Illinois

Frank Anthony Spina
Seattle Pacific University
Seattle, Washington

Brent A. Strawn
Candler School of Theology
Atlanta, Georgia

Roger E. Van Harn, Pastor
Christian Reformed Church
Grand Rapids, Michigan

Robert W. Wall
Seattle Pacific University
Seattle, Washington

William H. Willimon, Dean of the Chapel
Duke University
Durham, North Carolina

Paul Scott Wilson
Emmanuel College
Toronto, Ontario

Stephen I. Wright, Director
College of Preachers
London, England

Index of Authors

Abraham, William J., II:468, II:472,
II:475, II:478, II:481, III:162, III:165,
III:168, III:172, III:175

Achtemeier, Elizabeth, I:4, I:23, I:27,
I:69, I:120, I:243, I:310, I:327, I:343,
I:407, I:444, I:467, I:484, I:497

Allen, Ronald J., III:26, III:30, III:33,
III:37, III:41, III:45

Allison, Dale C., III:101, III:118,
III:129, III:133, III:136, III:140,
III:154

Anderson, Gary A., I:85, I:88, I:95, I:99,
I:102

Atkins, Martyn D., II:3, III:365, III:465,
III:592

Bailey, Raymond, III:237, III:376,
III:400, III:429, III:432, III:436

Bandstra, Andrew, II:488, II:492,
II:499, II:502, II:510, II:514

Bartelt, Andrew H., I:314, I:320, I:324,
I:336, I:350, I:384

Bartow, Charles L., II:66, II:71, II:76,
II:81, II:86, II:94

Bauckham, Richard, III:147, III:220,
III:380, III:489, III:530

Black, C. Clifton, III:603

Brawley, Robert L., I:528, I:532, II:21,
II:25, III:415

Brownlee, Annette G., II:420, II:423,
II:426, II:583, II:596

Burgess, John P., II:214, II:225, II:589,
II:593, III:505

Burridge, Richard A., III:472, III:498,
III:537, III:540, III:544, III:552,
III:555, III:559, III:566, III:569

Campbell, Charles L., I:559, III:209,
III:282, III:318, III:482

Donelson, Lewis R., II:485, II:496,
II:518, II:550, II:570

Dutcher-Walls, Patricia, I:189, I:192,
I:196, I:203, I:214

Evans, Craig A., II:410, III:240, III:265,
III:269, III:322, III:325, III:328,
III:348, III:476

Fackre, Gabriel, I:535, I:539, I:543,
II:562, III:547

Farris, Lawrence W., I:32, I:160, I:163,
I:236, I:580, II:340, III:8, III:52,
III:115

Farris, Stephen, II:173, II:197, II:200,
II:207, II:211, III:290, III:294,
III:301, III:354, III:358, III:383

607

Gagnon, Robert A. J., II:17, II:28, II:36, II:100, II:104, II:137, II:463, II:506

Gillespie, Thomas W., II:276, II:280, II:283, II:287, II:291, II:295, II:299

Goldingay, John, I:36, I:108, I:111, I:437, I:441, I:470, I:473

Greene, Colin J. D., II:395, II:398, II:402, II:406, II:416

Greidanus, Sidney, I:11, I:43, I:52, I:56, I:64

Gunton, Colin E., I:550, I:553, II:228, II:621

Henrich, Sarah, I:512, I:516, I:519, III:443, III:447

Hoezee, Scott, I:1, I:39, I:76, I:92, I:172, II:150, II:310, II:378, II:413, II:574, III:5, III:206, III:403, III:521, III:599

Holbert, John C., I:72, I:166, I:176, I:179, I:206, I:210, I:339, I:415

Holwerda, David E., III:56, III:60, III:64, III:68, III:331, III:336, III:340, III:344

Hoppe, Leslie J., I:347, I:353, I:360, I:367, I:422, I:488

Hultgren, Arland J., II:375, III:75, III:79, III:144, III:150, III:595

Hunsinger, George, II:41, II:45, II:51, II:56, II:61, II:131

Jenson, Robert W., I:124, I:128, I:132, I:135, I:139, I:143

Jewett, Robert, II:10, II:14, II:109, II:120, II:124, II:128, II:142

Jobes, Karen, I:257

Johnston, Scott Black, III:492, III:495, III:524, III:527, III:573, III:585

Juel, Donald, III:250, III:276, III:479, III:509, III:512, III:515, III:518

Kay, James F., II:243, II:247, II:250, II:253, II:257, II:261

Keener, Craig S., I:524, III:1, III:12, III:158, III:216, III:297

Klein, Leonard R., II:385, II:392, II:593, III:126, III:279, III:308, III:485

Kok, Joel E., II:314, II:318, II:322, II:325, II:329, II:336

Limburg, James, I:291, I:295, I:298, I:302, I:316

Longman, Tremper, III, I:146, I:150, I:153, I:222, I:225, I:230, I:233, I:239, I:246

Lueking, F. Dean, III:16, III:19, III:23, III:48, III:72, III:94, III:98

Malcolm, Lois, I:566, I:569, III:575, III:578, III:582

Marty, Martin E., I:556, I:563, I:573, II:1

Marty, Peter W., III:122, III:213, III:243, III:305, III:361, III:425, III:468

McCann, J. Clinton, Jr., I:156, I:371, I:388, I:477, I:481

Moo, Douglas, II:33, II:91, II:347, II:372, II:382, II:389, II:522, II:529, II:539

Moritz, Thorsten, II:525, II:532, II:535, II:542, II:547, II:554, II:558, II:566

Murphy, Roland E., I:260, I:265, I:267, I:271, I:278

Old, Hughes Oliphant, I:587

Olson, Dennis T., I:61, I:194, I:356, I:378, I:396, I:460

Palmer, Earl F., II:344, II:350, II:355, II:358, II:362, II:365, II:369, II:450, II:453

Paulson, Steven D., II:232, II:236, II:264, II:271

Pazdan, Mary Margaret, II:333, III:351, III:501, III:533, III:562, III:588

Pilkington, Christine E., I:411, I:426, I:430, I:434, I:448

Price, Daniel J., II:117, II:218, II:221, II:599, II:603, II:606, II:610, II:613, II:616

Raabe, Paul R., I:402, I:419

Radner, Ephraim, I:451, I:463, II:113, II:240, II:268

Ramp, Stephen W., III:178, III:189, III:223, III:247

Reid, Barbara E., III:91, III:202, III:372, III:393

Reid, Stephen Breck, I:375, I:381, I:392, I:400, I:505, I:509

Resner, André, Jr., I:491, II:146, II:154, II:162, II:166, II:170, II:176, III:193, III:230, III:254, III:258, III:262, III:272

Rogness, Michael, I:583, II:180, II:184, II:187, II:194, II:303, II:307

Rottman, John M., I:547, I:576, II:7, III:199, III:227

Saleska, Timothy E., I:169, I:217, I:253, I:363, I:455, I:500

Shuster, Marguerite, III:105, III:108, III:112, III:390, III:418

Snyder, Graydon F., II:158, II:191, II:204, III:182, III:185

Spina, Frank Anthony, I:20, I:48, I:105, I:182, I:185, I:249

Strawn, Brent A., I:79, I:115, I:305, I:330, II:577, III:286

Van Harn, Roger E., III:82, III:86, III:368, III:407, III:411

Wall, Robert W., II:429, II:433, II:438, II:441, II:445, II:456, III:460

Willimon, William H., I:7, I:17, I:30, I:274, I:281, I:285, I:288

Wilson, Paul Scott, III:312, III:451, III:459, III:462

Wright, Stephen I., III:315, III:386, III:397, III:422, III:440, III:455

Index of Readings for Years A, B, and C

YEAR A

First Sunday of Advent
Isaiah 2:1-5   I:295
(Psalm 122)
Romans 13:11-14   II:128
Matthew 24:36-44   III:140

Second Sunday of Advent
Isaiah 11:1-10   I:320
(Psalm 72:1-7, 18-19)
Romans 15:4-13   II:137
Matthew 3:1-12   III:12

Third Sunday of Advent
Isaiah 35:1-10   I:324
(Psalm 146:5-10 or Luke 1:47-55)
James 5:7-10   II:535
Matthew 11:2-11   III:64

Fourth Sunday of Advent
Isaiah 7:10-16   I:310
(Psalm 80:1-7, 17-19)
Romans 1:1-7   II:10
Matthew 1:18-25   III:1

Nativity of the Lord (Christmas Day)
Isaiah 9:2-7   I:316
(Psalm 96)
Titus 2:11-14   III:456
Luke 2:1-14 (15-20)   III:294

OR

Isaiah 62:6-12   I:388
(Psalm 97)
Titus 3:4-7   II:460
Luke 2:(1-7), 8-20   III:297

OR

Isaiah 52:7-10   I:360
(Psalm 98)
Hebrews 1:1-4, (5-12)   II:468
John 1:1-14   III:476

First Sunday after Christmas Day
Isaiah 63:7-9   I:392
(Psalm 148)
Hebrews 2:10-18   II:475
Matthew 2:13-23   III:8

Second Sunday after Christmas Day
Jeremiah 31:7-14 I:434
(Psalm 147:12-20)
Ephesians 1:3-14 II:303
John 1:(1-9), 10-18 III:472

Epiphany of the Lord
Isaiah 60:1-6 I:375
(Psalm 72:1-7, 10-14)
Ephesians 3:1-12 II:318
Matthew 2:1-12 III:5

**First Sunday after the Epiphany
(Baptism of the Lord)**
Isaiah 42:1-9 I:336
(Psalm 29)
Acts 10:34-43 II:3
Matthew 3:13-17 III:16

Second Sunday after the Epiphany
Isaiah 49:1-7 I:350
(Psalm 40:1-11)
1 Corinthians 1:1-9 II:146
John 1:29-42 III:482

Third Sunday after the Epiphany
Isaiah 9:1-4 I:314
(Psalm 27:1, 4-9)
1 Corinthians 1:10-18 II:154
Matthew 4:12-23 III:23

Fourth Sunday after the Epiphany
Micah 6:1-8 I:491
(Psalm 15)
1 Corinthians 1:18-31 II:162
Matthew 5:1-12 III:26

Fifth Sunday after the Epiphany
Isaiah 58:1-9a, (9b-12) I:371
(Psalm 112:1-9 (10))
1 Corinthians 2:1-12, (13-16) II:166
Matthew 5:13-20 III:30

Sixth Sunday after the Epiphany
Deuteronomy 30:15-20 I:139
(Psalm 119:1-8)
1 Corinthians 3:1-9 II:170
Matthew 5:21-37 III:33

Seventh Sunday after the Epiphany
Leviticus 19:1-2, 9-18 I:115
(Psalm 119:33-40)
1 Corinthians 3:10-11, 16-23 II:173
Matthew 5:38-48 III:37

Eighth Sunday after the Epiphany
Isaiah 49:8-16a I:353
(Psalm 131)
1 Corinthians 4:1-5 II:176
Matthew 6:24-34 III:41

Ninth Sunday after the Epiphany
Deuteronomy 11:18-21, 26-28 I:128
(Psalm 31:1-5, 19-24)
Romans 1:16-17; 3:22b-28, (29-31) II:14
Matthew 7:21-29 III:45

**Last Sunday after the Epiphany
(Transfiguration Sunday)**
Exodus 24:12-18 I:102
(Psalm 2 or Psalm 99)
2 Peter 1:16-21 II:570
Matthew 17:1-9 III:101

First Sunday in Lent
Genesis 2:15-17; 3:1-7 I:7
(Psalm 32)
Romans 5:12-19 II:45
Matthew 4:1-11 III:19

Second Sunday in Lent
Genesis 12:1-4a I:20
(Psalm 121)
Romans 4:1-5, 13-17 II:21
John 3:1-17 III:495

611

Third Sunday in Lent
Exodus 17:1-7 I:95
(Psalm 95)
Romans 5:1-11 II:41
John 4:5-42 III:501

Fourth Sunday in Lent
1 Samuel 16:1-13 I:182
(Psalm 23)
Ephesians 5:8-14 II:333
John 9:1-41 III:521

Fifth Sunday in Lent
Ezekiel 37:1-14 I:460
(Psalm 130)
Romans 8:6-11 II:71
John 11:1-45 III:521

Palm/Passion Sunday
Isaiah 50:4-9a I:566
(Psalm 118:1-2, 19-29 or Psalm 31:9-16)
Philippians 2:5-11 II:355
Matthew 21:1-11 III:115

Easter Day (Resurrection of the Lord)
Acts 10:34-43 I:566
(Psalm 118:1-2, 14-24)
Colossians 3:1-4 II:385
Matthew 28:1-10/John 20:1-18 III:154/588

Second Sunday of Easter
Acts 2:14a, 22-32 I:528
(Psalm 16)
1 Peter 1:3-9 II:542
John 20:19-31 III:595

Third Sunday of Easter
Acts 2:14a, 36-41 I:532
(Psalm 116:1-4, 12-19)
1 Peter 1:17-23 II:547
Luke 24:13-35 III:462

Fourth Sunday of Easter
Acts 2:42-47 I:535
(Psalm 23)
1 Peter 2:19-25 II:554
John 10:1-10 III:524

Fifth Sunday of Easter
Acts 7:55-60 I:553
(Psalm 31:1-5, 15-16)
1 Peter 2:2-10 II:550
John 14:1-14 III:547

Sixth Sunday of Easter
Acts 17:22-31 I:583
(Psalm 66:8-20)
1 Peter 3:13-22 II:558
John 14:15-21 III:555

Ascension of the Lord
Acts 1:1-11 I:512
(Psalm 47 or Psalm 93)
Ephesians 1:15-23 II:307
Luke 24:44-53 III:468

Seventh Sunday of Easter
Acts 1:6-14 I:516
(Psalm 68:1-10, 32-35)
1 Peter 4:12-14; 5:6-11 II:566
John 17:1-11 III:575

Day of Pentecost
Acts 2:1-21 I:524
(Psalm 104:24-34, 35b)
1 Corinthians 12:3b-13 II:204
John 20:19-23 III:592

Trinity Sunday
(First Sunday after Pentecost)
Genesis 1:1–2:4a I:1
(Psalm 8)
2 Corinthians 13:11-13 II:271
Matthew 28:16-20 III:158

Second Sunday after Pentecost
Genesis 6:9-22; 7:24; 8:14-19 I:11
(Psalm 46)
Romans 1:16-17; 3:22b-28, (29-31) II:17
Matthew 7:21-29 III:45

Third Sunday after Pentecost
Genesis 12:1-9 I:23
(Psalm 33:1-12)
Romans 4:13-25 II:25
Matthew 9:9-13, 18-26 III:48

Fourth Sunday after Pentecost
Genesis 18:1-15; (21:1-7) I:32
(Psalm 116:1-2, 12-19)
Romans 5:1-8 II:36
Matthew 9:35–10:8, (9-23) III:52

Fifth Sunday after Pentecost
Genesis 21:8-21 I:36
(Psalm 86:1-10, 16-17)
Romans 6:1b-11 II:51
Matthew 10:24-39 III:56

Sixth Sunday after Pentecost
Genesis 22:1-14 I:39
(Psalm 13)
Romans 6:12-23 II:56
Matthew 10:40-42 III:60

Seventh Sunday after Pentecost
Genesis 24:34-38, 42-49, 58-67 I:43
(Psalm 45:10-17)
Romans 7:15-25a II:61
Matthew 11:16-19, 25-30 III:68

Eighth Sunday after Pentecost
Genesis 25:19-34 I:52
(Psalm 119:105-12)
Romans 8:1-11 II:66
Matthew 13:1-9, 18-23 III:72

Ninth Sunday after Pentecost
Genesis 28:10-19a I:52
(Psalm 139:1-12, 23-24)
Romans 8:12-25 II:81
Matthew 13:24-30, 36-43 III:75

Tenth Sunday after Pentecost
Genesis 29:15-28 I:56
(Psalm 105:1-11, 45b or Psalm 128)
Romans 8:26-39 II:94
Matthew 13:31-33, 44-52 III:79

Eleventh Sunday after Pentecost
Genesis 32:22-31 I:61
(Psalm 17:1-7, 15)
Romans 9:1-5 II:100
Matthew 14:13-21 III:82

Twelfth Sunday after Pentecost
Genesis 37:1-4, 12-28 I:64
(Psalm 105:1-6, 16-22, 45b)
Romans 10:5-15 II:104
Matthew 14:22-33 III:86

Thirteenth Sunday after Pentecost
Genesis 45:1-15 I:69
(Psalm 133)
Romans 11:1-2a, 29-32 II:113
Matthew 15:(10-20), 21-28 III:91

Fourteenth Sunday after Pentecost
Exodus 1:8–2:10 I:76
(Psalm 124)
Romans 12:1-8 II:117
Matthew 16:13-20 III:94

Fifteenth Sunday after Pentecost
Exodus 3:1-15 I:79
(Psalm 105:1-6, 23-26, 45c)
Romans 12:9-21 II:120
Matthew 16:21-28 III:98

Sixteenth Sunday after Pentecost
Exodus 12:1-14 I:85
(Psalm 149)
Romans 13:8-14 II:124
Matthew 18:15-20 III:105

Seventeenth Sunday after Pentecost
Exodus 14:19-31 I:88
(Psalm 114 or Exodus 15:1b-11, 20-21)
Romans 14:1-12 II:131
Matthew 18:21-35 III:108

Eighteenth Sunday after Pentecost
Exodus 16:2-15 I:92
(Psalm 105:1-6, 37-45)
Philippians 1:21-30 II:347
Matthew 20:1-16 III:112

Ninteenth Sunday after Pentecost
Exodus 17:1-7 I:95
(Psalm 78:1-4, 12-16)
Philippians 2:1-13 II:350
Matthew 21:23-32 III:118

Twentieth Sunday after Pentecost
Exodus 20:1-4, 7-9, 12-20 I:99
(Psalm 19)
Philippians 3:4b-14 II:358
Matthew 21:33-46 III:122

Twenty-first Sunday after Pentecost
Exodus 32:1-14 I:105
(Psalm 106:1-6, 19-23)
Philippians 4:1-9 II:365
Matthew 22:1-14 III:126

Twenty-second Sunday after Pentecost
Exodus 33:12-23 I:108
(Psalm 99)
1 Thessalonians 1:1-10 II:395
Matthew 22:15-22 III:129

Twenth-third Sunday after Pentecost
Deuteronomy 34:1-12 I:143
(Psalm 90:1-6, 13-17)
1 Thessalonians 2:1-8 II:398
Matthew 22:34-46 III:133

Twenty-fourth Sunday after Pentecost
Joshua 3:7-17 I:146
(Psalm 107:1-7, 33-37)
1 Thessalonians 2:9-13 II:402
Matthew 23:1-12 III:136

Twenty-fifth Sunday after Pentecost
Joshua 24:1-3a, 14-25 I:153
(Psalm 78:1-7)
1 Thessalonians 4:13-18 II:410
Matthew 25:1-13 III:144

Twenty-sixth Sunday after Pentecost
Judges 4:1-7 I:156
(Psalm 123)
1 Thessalonians 5:1-11 II:413
Matthew 25:14-30 III:147

Christ the King
Ezekiel 34:11-16, 20-24 I:455
(Psalm 100)
Ephesians 1:15-23 II:307
Matthew 25:31-46 III:150

YEAR B

First Sunday of Advent
Isaiah 64:1-9 I:396
(Psalm 80:1-7, 17-19)
1 Corinthians 1:3-9 II:150
Mark 13:24-37 III:279

Second Sunday of Advent
Isaiah 40:1-11 I:327
(Psalm 85:1-2, 8-13)
2 Peter 3:8-15a II:547
Mark 1:1-8 III:162

Third Sunday of Advent
Isaiah 61:1-4, 8-11 I:378
(Psalm 126)
1 Thessalonians 5:16-24 II:416
John 1:6-8, 19-28 III:479

Fourth Sunday of Advent
2 Samuel 7:1-11, 16 I:199
(Luke 1:47-55)
Romans 16:25-27 II:142
Luke 1:26-38 III:286

Nativity of the Lord (Christmas Day)
Isaiah 9:2-7 I:316
(Psalm 96)
Titus 2:11-14 II:456
Luke 2:1-14, (15-20) III:294

OR

Isaiah 62:6-12 I:388
(Psalm 97)
Titus 3:4-7 II:460
Luke 2:(1-7), 8-20 III:297

OR

Isaiah 52:7-10 I:360
(Psalm 98)
Hebrews 1:1-4, (5-12) II:468
John 1:1-14 III:476

First Sunday after Christmas Day
Isaiah 61:10–62:3 I:381
(Psalm 148)
Galatians 4:4-7 II:291
Luke 2:22-40 III:301

Second Sunday after Christmas Day
Jeremiah 31:7-14 I:434
(Psalm 147:12-20)
Ephesians 1:3-14 II:303
John 1:(1-9), 10-18 III:472

Epiphany of the Lord
Isaiah 60:1-6 I:375
(Psalm 72:1-7, 10-14)
Ephesians 3:1-12 II:318
Matthew 2:1-12 III:5

**First Sunday after the Epiphany
(Baptism of the Lord)**
Genesis 1:1-5 I:4
(Psalm 29)
Acts 19:1-7 II:7
Mark 1:4-11 III:165

Second Sunday after the Epiphany
1 Samuel 3:1-10, (11-20) I:272
(Psalm 139:1-6, 13-18)
1 Corinthians 6:12-20 II:180
John 1:43-51 III:485

Third Sunday after the Epiphany
Jonah 3:1-5, 10 I:484
(Psalm 62:5-12)
1 Corinthians 7:29-31 II:184
Mark 1:14-20 III:172

Fourth Sunday after the Epiphany
Deuteronomy 18:15-20 I:132
(Psalm 111)
1 Corinthians 8:1-13 II:187
Mark 1:21-28 III:175

Fifth Sunday after the Epiphany
Isaiah 40:21-31 I:330
(Psalm 147:1-11, 20c)
1 Corinthians 9:16-23 II:191
Mark 1:29-39 III:178

Sixth Sunday after the Epiphany
2 Kings 5:1-14 I:249
(Psalm 30)
1 Corinthians 9:24-27 II:194
Mark 1:40-45 III:182

Seventh Sunday after the Epiphany
Isaiah 43:18-25 I:347
(Psalm 41)
2 Corinthians 1:18-22 II:232
Mark 2:1-12 III:185

Eighth Sunday after the Epiphany
Hosea 2:14-20 I:467
(Psalm 103:1-13, 22)
2 Corinthians 3:1-6 II:236
Mark 2:13-22 III:189

Ninth Sunday after the Epiphany
Deuteronomy 5:12-15 I:124
(Psalm 81:1-10)
2 Corinthians 4:5-12 II:247
Mark 2:23–3:6 III:193

615

Last Sunday after the Epiphany (Transfiguration Sunday)
2 Kings 2:1-12   I:243
(Psalm 50:1-6)
2 Corinthians 4:3-6   II:243
Mark 9:2-9   III:240

First Sunday in Lent
Genesis 9:8-17   I:17
(Psalm 25:1-10)
1 Peter 3:18-22   II:562
Mark 1:9-15   III:168

Second Sunday in Lent
Genesis 17:1-7, 15-16   I:30
(Psalm 22:23-31)
Romans 4:13-25   II:28
Mark 8:31-38   III:237

Third Sunday in Lent
Exodus 20:1-17   I:99
(Psalm 19)
1 Corinthians 1:18-25   II:158
John 2:13-22   III:492

Fourth Sunday in Lent
Numbers 21:4-9   I:120
(Psalm 107:1-3, 17-22)
Ephesians 2:1-10   II:310
John 3:14-21   III:498

Fifth Sunday in Lent
Jeremiah 31:31-34   I:441
(Psalm 51:1-12 or Psalm 119:9-16)
Hebrews 5:5-10   II:485
John 12:20-33   III:540

Palm/Passion Sunday
Isaiah 50:4-9a   I:356
(Psalm 118:1-2, 19-29 or Psalm 31:9-16)
Philippians 2:5-11   II:355
Mark 11:1-11   III:265

Easter Day (Resurrection of the Lord)
Acts 10:34-43   I:566
(Psalm 118:1-2, 14-24)
1 Corinthians 15:1-11   II:214
Mark 16:1-8/John 20:1-18   III:282/588

Second Sunday of Easter
Acts 4:32-35   I:547
(Psalm 133)
1 John 1:1–2:2   II:577
John 20:19-31   III:595

Third Sunday of Easter
Acts 3:12-19   I:539
(Psalm 4)
1 John 3:1-7   II:583
Luke 24:36b-48   III:465

Fourth Sunday of Easter
Acts 4:5-12   I:543
(Psalm 23)
1 John 3:16-24   II:586
John 10:11-18   III:527

Fifth Sunday of Easter
Acts 8:26-40   I:556
(Psalm 22:25-31)
1 John 4:7-21   II:590
John 15:1-8   III:562

Sixth Sunday of Easter
Acts 10:44-48   I:569
(Psalm 98)
1 John 5:1-6   II:593
John 15:9-17   III:566

Ascension of the Lord
Acts 1:1-11   I:512
(Psalm 47 or Psalm 93)
Ephesians 1:15-23   II:307
Luke 24:44-53   III:468

Seventh Sunday of Easter
Acts 1:15-17, 21-26   I:519
(Psalm 1)
1 John 5:9-13   II:597
John 17:6-19   III:578

Day of Pentecost
Acts 2:1-21 I:524
(Psalm 104:24-34, 35b)
Romans 8:22-27 II:91
John 15:26-27; 16:4b-15 III:569

Trinity Sunday
(First Sunday after Pentecost)
Isaiah 6:1-8 I:302
(Psalm 29)
Romans 8:12-17 II:76
John 3:1-17 III:495

Second Sunday after Pentecost
1 Samuel 3:1-10, (11-20) I:172
(Psalm 139:1-6, 13-18)
2 Corinthians 4:5-12 II:247
Mark 2:23–3:6 III:193

Third Sunday after Pentecost
1 Samuel 8:4-11, (12-15), 16-20
   (11:14-15) I:176
(Psalm 138)
2 Corinthians 4:13–5:1 II:250
Mark 3:20-35 III:199

Fourth Sunday after Pentecost
1 Samuel 15:34–16:13 I:179
(Psalm 20)
2 Corinthians 5:6-10, (11-13), 14-17 II:253
Mark 4:26-34 III:202

Fifth Sunday after Pentecost
1 Samuel 17:(1a, 4-11, 19-23), 32-49 I:185
(Psalm 9:9-20)
2 Corinthians 6:1-13 II:261
Mark 4:35-41 III:206

Sixth Sunday after Pentecost
2 Samuel 1:1, 17-27 I:189
(Psalm 130)
2 Corinthians 8:7-15 II:264
Mark 5:21-43 III:209

Seventh Sunday after Pentecost
2 Samuel 5:1-5, 9-10 I:192
(Psalm 48)
2 Corinthians 12:2-10 II:268
Mark 6:1-13 III:213

Eighth Sunday after Pentecost
2 Samuel 6:1-5, 12b-19 I:196
(Psalm 24)
Ephesians 1:3-14 II:303
Mark 6:14-29 III:216

Ninth Sunday after Pentecost
2 Samuel 7:1-14a I:203
(Psalm 89:20-37)
Ephesians 2:11-22 II:314
Mark 6:30-34, 53-56 III:220

Tenth Sunday after Pentecost
2 Samuel 11:1-15 I:206
(Psalm 14)
Ephesians 3:14-21 II:322
John 6:1-21 III:509

Eleventh Sunday after Pentecost
2 Samuel 11:26–12:13a I:210
(Psalm 51:1-12)
Ephesians 4:1-16 II:325
John 6:24-35 III:505

Twelfth Sunday after Pentecost
2 Samuel 18:5-9, 15, 31-33 I:214
(Psalm 130)
Ephesians 4:25–5:2 II:329
John 6:35, 41-51 III:515

Thirteenth Sunday after Pentecost
1 Kings 2:10-12; 3:3-14 I:222
(Psalm 111)
Ephesians 5:15-20 II:336
John 6:51-58 III:515

Fourteenth Sunday after Pentecost
1 Kings 8:(1, 6, 10-11), 22-30, 41-43 I:225
(Psalm 84)
Ephesians 6:10-20 II:340
John 6:56-69 III:518

Fifteenth Sunday after Pentecost
Song of Solomon 2:8-13 I:288
(Psalm 45:1-2, 6-9)
James 1:17-27 II:522
Mark 7:1-8, 14-15, 21-23 III:223

Sixteenth Sunday after Pentecost
Proverbs 22:1-2, 8-9, 22-23 I:281
(Psalm 125)
James 2:1-10, (11-13), 14-17 II:525
Mark 7:24-37 III:227

Seventeenth Sunday after Pentecost
Proverbs 1:20-33 I:274
(Psalm 19)
James 3:1-12 II:259
Mark 8:27-38 III:230

Eighteenth Sunday after Pentecost
Proverbs 31:10-31 I:285
(Psalm 1)
James 3:13–4:3, 7-8a II:532
Mark 9:30-37 III:243

Nineteenth Sunday after Pentecost
Esther 7:1-6, 9-10; 9:20-22 I:257
(Psalm 124)
James 5:13-20 II:539
Mark 9:38-50 III:247

Twentieth Sunday after Pentecost
Job 1:1; 2:1-10 I:260
(Psalm 26)
Hebrews 1:1-4; 2:5-12 II:472
Mark 10:2-16 III:250

Twenty-first Sunday after Pentecost
Job 23:1-9, 16-17 I:265
(Psalm 22:1-15)
Hebrews 4:12-16 II:478
Mark 10:17-31 III:254

Twenty-second Sunday after Pentecost
Job 38:1-7, (34-41) I:267
(Psalm 104:1-9, 24, 35c)
Hebrews 5:1-10 II:481
Mark 10:35-45 III:258

Twenty-third Sunday after Pentecost
Job 42:1-6, 10-17 I:271
(Psalm 34:1-8, (19-22))
Hebrews 7:23-28 II:488
Mark 10:46-52 III:262

Twenty-fourth Sunday after Pentecost
Ruth 1:1-18 I:160
(Psalm 146)
Hebrews 9:11-14 II:492
Mark 12:28-34 III:269

Twenty-fifth Sunday after Pentecost
Ruth 3:1-5; 4:13-17 I:163
(Psalm 127)
Hebrews 9:24-28 II:496
Mark 12:38-44 III:272

Twenty-sixth Sunday after Pentecost
1 Samuel 1:4-20 I:166
(1 Samuel 2:1-10)
Hebrews 10:11-14, (15-18), 19-25 II:502
Mark 13:1-8 III: 276

Christ the King
2 Samuel 23:1-7 I:217
(Psalm 132:1-12, (13-18))
Revelation 1:4b-8 II:599
John 18:33-37 III:585

YEAR C

First Sunday of Advent
Jeremiah 33:14-16   I:449
(Psalm 25:1-10)
1 Thessalonians 3:9-13   II:406
Luke 21:25-36   III:451

Second Sunday of Advent
Malachi 3:1-4   I:509
(Luke 1:68-79)
Philippians 1:3-11   II:344
Luke 3:1-6   III:308

Third Sunday of Advent
Zephaniah 3:14-20   I:500
(Isaiah 12:2-6)
Philippians 4:4-7   II:369
Luke 3:7-18   III:312

Fourth Sunday of Advent
Micah 5:2-5a   I:488
(Luke 1:47-55 or Psalm 80:1-7)
Hebrews 10:5-10   II:499
Luke 1:39-45, (46-55)   III:290

Nativity of the Lord (Christmas Day)
Isaiah 9:2-7   I:316
(Psalm 96)
Titus 2:11-14   II:456
Luke 2:1-14, (15-20)   III:294

OR

Isaiah 62:6-12   I:388
(Psalm 97)
Titus 3:4-7   II:460
Luke 2:(1-7), 8-20   III:297

OR

Isaiah 52:7-10   I:360
(Psalm 98)
Hebrews 1:1-4, (5-12)   II:468
John 1:1-14   III:476

First Sunday after Christmas Day
1 Samuel 2:18-20, 26   I:169
(Psalm 148)
Colossians 3:12-17   II:392
Luke 2:41-52   III:305

Second Sunday after Christmas Day
Jeremiah 31:7-14   I:434
(Psalm 147:12-20)
Ephesians 1:3-14   II:303
John 1:(1-9), 10-18   III:472

Epiphany of the Lord
Isaiah 60:1-6   I:375
(Psalm 72:1-7, 10-14)
Ephesians 3:1-12   II:318
Matthew 2:1-12   III:5

**First Sunday after the Epiphany
(Baptism of the Lord)**
Isaiah 43:1-7   I:339
(Psalm 29)
Acts 8:14-17   II:1
Luke 3:15-17, 21-22   III:315

Second Sunday after the Epiphany
Isaiah 62:1-5   I:384
(Psalm 36:5-10)
1 Corinthians 12:1-11   II:200
John 2:1-11   III:489

Third Sunday after the Epiphany
Nehemiah 8:1-3, 5-6, 8-10   I:253
(Psalm 19)
1 Corinthians 12:12-31a   II:207
Luke 4:14-21   III:322

Fourth Sunday after the Epiphany
Jeremiah 1:4-10   I:402
(Psalm 71:1-6)
1 Corinthians 13:1-13   II:211
Luke 4:21-30   III:325

Fifth Sunday after the Epiphany
Isaiah 6:1-8, (9-13) I:305
(Psalm 138)
1 Corinthians 15:1-11 II:214
Luke 5:1-11 III:328

Sixth Sunday after the Epiphany
Jeremiah 17:5-10 I:419
(Psalm 1)
1 Corinthians 15:12-20 II:218
Luke 6:17-26 III:331

Seventh Sunday after the Epiphany
Genesis 45:3-11, 15 I:72
(Psalm 37:1-11, 39-40)
1 Corinthians 15:35-38, 42-50 II:225
Luke 6:27-38 III:336

Eighth Sunday after the Epiphany
Isaiah 55:10-13 I:367
(Psalm 92:1-4, 12-15)
1 Corinthians 15:51-58 II:228
Luke 6:39-49 III:340

Ninth Sunday after the Epiphany
1 Kings 8:22-23, 41-43 I:225
(Psalm 96:1-9)
Galatians 1:1-12 II:276
Luke 7:1-10 III:344

**Last Sunday after the Epiphany
(Transfiguration Sunday)**
Exodus 34:29-35 I:111
(Psalm 99)
2 Corinthians 3:12–4:2 II:240
Luke 9:28-36, (37-43) III:358

First Sunday in Lent
Deuteronomy 26:1-11 I:135
(Psalm 91:1-2, 9-16)
Romans 10:8b-13 II:109
Luke 4:1-13 III:318

Second Sunday in Lent
Genesis 15:1-12, 17-18 I:27
(Psalm 27)
Philippians 3:17–4:1 II:362
Luke 13:31-35 III:397

Third Sunday in Lent
Isaiah 55:1-9 I:363
(Psalm 63:1-8)
1 Corinthians 10:1-13 II:197
Luke 13:1-9 III:390

Fourth Sunday in Lent
Joshua 5:9-12 I:150
(Psalm 32)
2 Corinthians 5:16-21 II:257
Luke 15:1-3, 11b-32 III:407

Fifth Sunday in Lent
Isaiah 43:16-21 I:343
(Psalm 126)
Philippians 3:4b-14 II:358
John 12:1-8 III:537

Palm/Passion Sunday
Isaiah 50:4-9a I:356
(Psalm 118:1-2, 19-29 or Psalm 31:9-16)
Philippians 2:5-11 II:355
Luke 19:28-40 III:440

Easter Day (Resurrection of the Lord)
Acts 10:34-43 I:566
(Psalm 118:1-2, 14-24)
1 Corinthians 15:19-26 II:221
Luke 24:1-12/John 20:1-18 III:459/588

Second Sunday of Easter
Acts 5:27-32 I:550
(Psalm 118:14-29 or Psalm 150)
Revelation 1:4-8 II:599
John 20:19-31 III:595

Third Sunday of Easter
Acts 9:1-6, (7-20) I:559
(Psalm 30)
Revelation 5:11-14 II:603
John 21:1-19 III:599

Fourth Sunday of Easter
Acts 9:36-43 I:563
(Psalm 23)
Revelation 7:9-17 II:606
John 10:22-30 III:530

Fifth Sunday of Easter
Acts 11:1-18 I:573
(Psalm 148)
Revelation 21:1-6 II:610
John 13:31-35 III:544

Sixth Sunday of Easter
Acts 16:9-15 I:576
(Psalm 67)
Revelation 21:10, 22–22:5 II:613
John 14:23-29 III:559

Ascension of the Lord
Acts 1:1-11 I:512
(Psalm 47 or Psalm 110)
Ephesians 1:15-23 II:307
Luke 24:44-53 III:468

Seventh Sunday of Easter
Acts 16:16-34 I:580
(Psalm 97)
Revelation 22:12-14, 16-17, 20-21 II:616
John 17:20-26 III:582

Day of Pentecost
Acts 2:1-21 I:524
(Psalm 104:24-34, 35b)
Romans 8:14-17 II:86
John 14:8-17, (25-27) III:552

Trinity Sunday
(First Sunday after Pentecost)
Proverbs 8:1-4, 22-31 I:278
(Psalm 8)
Romans 5:1-5 II:33
John 16:12-15 III:573

Second Sunday after Pentecost
1 Kings 18:20-21, (22-29), 30-39 I:233
(Psalm 96)
Galatians 1:1-12 II:276
Luke 7:1-10 III:344

Third Sunday after Pentecost
1 Kings 17:8-16, (17-24) I:230
(Psalm 146)
Galatians 1:11-24 II:280
Luke 7:11-17 III:348

Fourth Sunday after Pentecost
1 Kings 21:1-10, (11-14), 15-21a I:239
(Psalm 5:1-8)
Galatians 2:15-21 II:283
Luke 7:36–8:3 III:351

Fifth Sunday after Pentecost
1 Kings 19:1-4, (5-7), 8-15a I:236
(Psalms 42 and 43)
Galatians 3:23-29 II:287
Luke 8:26-39 III:354

Sixth Sunday after Pentecost
2 Kings 2:1-2, 6-14 I:246
(Psalm 77:1-2, 11-20)
Galatians 5:1, 13-25 II:295
Luke 9:51-62 III:361

Seventh Sunday after Pentecost
2 Kings 5:1-14 I:249
(Psalm 30)
Galatians 6:(1-6), 7-16 II:299
Luke 10:1-11, 16-20 III:365

Eighth Sunday after Pentecost
Amos 7:7-17 I:477
(Psalm 82)
Colossians 1:1-14 II:372
Luke 10:25-37 III:368

Ninth Sunday after Pentecost
Amos 8:1-12 I:481
(Psalm 52)
Colossians 1:15-28 II:378
Luke 10:38-42 III:372

Tenth Sunday after Pentecost
Hosea 1:2-10   I:463
(Psalm 85)
Colossians 2:6-15, (16-19)   II:382
Luke 11:1-13   III:376

Eleventh Sunday after Pentecost
Hosea 11:1-11   I:470
(Psalm 107:1-9, 43)
Colossians 3:1-11   II:389
Luke 12:13-21   III:380

Twelfth Sunday after Pentecost
Isaiah 1:1, 10-20   I:291
(Psalm 50:1-8, 22-23)
Hebrews 11:1-3, 8-16   II:506
Luke 12:32-40   III:383

Thirteenth Sunday after Pentecost
Isaiah 5:1-7   I:298
(Psalm 80:1-2, 8-19)
Hebrews 11:29–12:2   II:510
Luke 12:49-56   III:386

Fourteenth Sunday after Pentecost
Jeremiah 1:4-10   I:402
(Psalm 71:1-6)
Hebrews 12:18-29   II:514
Luke 13:10-17   III:393

Fifteenth Sunday after Pentecost
Jeremiah 2:4-13   I:407
(Psalm 81:1, 10-16)
Hebrews 13:1-8, 15-16   II:518
Luke 14:1, 7-14   III:400

Sixteenth Sunday after Pentecost
Jeremiah 18:1-11   I:422
(Psalm 139:1-6, 13-18)
Philemon 1-21   II:463
Luke 14:25-33   III:403

Seventeenth Sunday after Pentecost
Jeremiah 4:11-12, 22-28   I:411
(Psalm 14)
1 Timothy 1:12-17   II:429
Luke 15:1-10   III:411

Eighteenth Sunday after Pentecost
Jeremiah 8:18–9:1   I:415
(Psalm 79:1-9)
1 Timothy 2:1-7   II:433
Luke 16:1-13   III:415

Nineteenth Sunday after Pentecost
Jeremiah 32:1-3a, 6-15   I:444
(Psalm 91:1-6, 14-16)
1 Timothy 6:6-19   II:438
Luke 16:19-31   III:418

Twentieth Sunday after Pentecost
Lamentations 1:1-6   I:451
(Lamentations 3:19-26 or Psalm 137)
2 Timothy 1:1-14   II:441
Luke 17:5-10   III:422

Twenty-first Sunday after Pentecost
Jeremiah 29:1, 4-7   I:430
(Psalm 66:1-12)
2 Timothy 2:8-15   II:445
Luke 17:11-19   III:425

Twenty-second Sunday after Pentecost
Jeremiah 31:27-34   I:437
(Psalm 119:97-104)
2 Timothy 3:14–4:5   II:450
Luke 18:1-8   III:429

Twenty-third Sunday after Pentecost
Joel 2:23-32   I:473
(Psalm 65)
2 Timothy 4:6-8, 16-18   II:453
Luke 18:9-14   III:432

Twenty-fourth Sunday after Pentecost
Habakkuk 1:1-4; 2:1-4   I:497
(Psalm 119:137-144)
2 Thessalonians 1:1-4, 11-12   II:420
Luke 19:1-10   III:436

Twenty-fifth Sunday after Pentecost
Haggai 1:15b–2:9   I:505
(Psalm 145:1-5, 17-21 or Psalm 98)
2 Thessalonians 2:1-5, 13-17   II:423
Luke 20:27-38   III:443

Twenty-sixth Sunday after Pentecost
Isaiah 65:17-25 I:400
(Isaiah 12)
2 Thessalonians 3:6-13 II:426
Luke 21:5-19 III:447

Christ the King
Jeremiah 23:1-6 I:426
(Luke 1:68-79)
Colossians 1:11-20 II:375
Luke 23:33-43 III:455